LEARNING ABOUT LEARNING DISABILITIES

SECOND EDITION

LEARNING ABOUT LEARNING DISABILITIES

SECOND EDITION

Edited by
Bernice Y. L. Wong
Faculty of Education
Simon Fraser University
Burnaby, British Columbia, Canada

Academic Press

San Diego   London   Boston
New York   Sydney   Tokyo   Toronto

Photo cover credit: Images © 1995 Photo Disc, Inc.

This book is printed on acid-free paper. ∞

Academic Press
a division of Harcourt Brace & Company
525 B Street, Suite 1900, San Diego, California 92101-4495, USA
http://www.apnet.com

Academic Press Limited
24-28 Oval Road, London NW1 7DX, UK
http://www.hbuk.co.uk/ap/

Library of Congress Card Catalog Number: 97–80822

International Standard Book Number: 0–12–762532–1

PRINTED IN THE UNITED STATES OF AMERICA
98 99 00 01 02 03 MM 9 8 7 6 5 4 3 2 1

This book is dedicated to Barbara Keogh and my family (hubby, Rod, and daughter, Kristi).

Contents

SECTION I

Conceptual, Historical, and Research Aspects of Learning Disabilities

1. Learning Disabilities: An Historical and Conceptual Overview
Joseph K. Torgesen

2. Assessment in Learning Disabilities with a Focus on Curriculum-Based Measurement
Gerald Tindal

3. Attention Disorders
Richard Conte

4. Learning Disabilities and Memory
H. Lee Swanson, John B. Cooney, and Tam E. O'Shaughnessy

5. Language Problems: A Key to Early Reading Problems
Virginia Mann

6. Visual Processes in Learning Disabilities
Dale M. Willows

7. Social Competence of Students with Learning Disabilities
Tanis Bryan

SECTION II

Assessment and Instructional Aspects of Learning Disabilities

12. Writing Instruction
Steve Graham, Karen R. Harris, Charles MacArthur, and Shirley Schwartz

13. Instructional Interventions for Students with Mathematics Learning Disabilities
Margo Mastropieri, Thomas E. Scruggs, and SuHsiang Chung

14. Social Competence of Students with Learning Disabilities: Interventions and Issues
Sharon Vaughn and Jane Sinagub

SECTION III

A Life Span Approach to Understanding Learning Disabilities

19. Adults with Learning Disabilities
Pamela B. Adelman and Susan A. Vogel

Contributors

Numbers in parentheses indicate the pages on which the authors' contributions begin.

Pamela B. Adelman (657)
Department of Education
Barat College
Lake Forest, Illinois 60045

Patricia A. Alexander (343)
Department of Human Development
University of Maryland
College Park, Maryland 20742

Virginia W. Berninger (529)
Department of Educational Psychology
University of Washington
Seattle, Washington 98195

Tanis Bryan (237)
Department of Curriculum and Instruction
College of Education
Arizona State University
Tempe, Arizona 85287-1011

Deborah L. Butler (277)
Department of Educational Psychology
and Special Education
Faculty of Education
University of British Columbia
Vancouver, British Columbia
Canada V6T 1Z4

Victoria Chou (343)
Department of Education
University of Illinois at Chicago
Chicago, Illinois 60680

SuHsiang Chung (425)
Department of Educational Studies
Purdue University
West Lafayette, Indiana 47907

Richard Conte (67)
Department of Psychology
University of Calgary
Calgary, Alberta
Canada T2N 4N9

John B. Cooney (107)
Department of Educational Psychology
Division of Research Evaluation and
Development
University of Northern Colorado
Greeley, Colorado 80639

Jean Crockett[1] (489)
Department of Special Education
University of Virginia
Charlottesville, Virginia 22903

Edwin S. Ellis (557, 585)
Department of Special Education
College of Education
University of Alabama
Tuscaloosa, Alabama 35487

Ruth Garner (343)
Department of Education
University of Illinois at Chicago
Chicago, Illinois 60680

[1]Current address: Virginia Polytechnic Institute and State University, Blacksburg, Virginia 24061.

Lynn M. Gelzheiser (311)
Department of Educational Psychology
  and Statistics
State University of New York at Albany
Albany, New York 12222

Steve Graham (391)
Department of Special Education
University of Maryland
College Park, Maryland 20740

Victoria Chou Hare (343)
Department of Education
University of Illinois at Chicago
Chicago, Illinois 60680

Karen R. Harris (391)
Department of Special Education
University of Maryland
College Park, Maryland 20740

James M. Kaufmann (489)
Department of Special Education
University of Virginia
Charlottesville, Virginia 22903

Martha Larkin (557, 585)
School of Education
The College of William and Mary
Williamsburg, Virginia 23187

Charles MacArthur (391)
Department of Special Education
University of Delaware
Newark, Delaware 19711

Virginia Mann (163)
Department of Cognitive Sciences
University of California, Irvine
Irvine, California 92651

Margo A. Mastropieri (425)
Department of Educational Studies
Purdue University
West Lafayette, Indiana 47907

Louisa C. Moats[2] (367)
Sacramento County Office of Education
Center for the Improvement of Reading
  Instruction
Sacramento, California 94823

Tam O'Shaughnessy (107)
Department of Psychology
University of California, Riverside
Riverside, California 92521

Shirley Schwartz (391)
Department of Special Education
University of Maryland
College Park, Maryland 20740

Thomas E. Scruggs (425)
Department of Educational Studies
Purdue University
West Lafayette, Indiana 47907

Jane M. Sinagub (453)
School of Education
University of Miami
Coral Gables, Florida 33124

Christopher T. Sperl (343)
Department of Human Development
University of Maryland
College Park, Maryland 20742

H. Lee Swanson (107)
Department of Psychology
University of California, Riverside
Riverside, California 92521

Gerald Tindal (35)
Behavioral Research and Teaching
College of Education
University of Oregon
Eugene, Oregon 97403

[2]Current address: 4545 Connecticut Avenue NW, Washington, DC 20008.

Joseph K. Torgesen (3)
Psychology Department
Florida State University
Tallahassee, Florida 32306

Sharon Vaughn (453)
Department of Special Education
University of Texas at Austin
Austin, Texas 78712

Susan Vogel (657)
Department of Psychology, Counseling,
    and Education
Northern Illinois University
De Kalb, Illinois 60015

Dale M. Willows (203)
Department of Human Development and
    Applied Psychology
Ontario Institute for Studies in Education
University of Toronto
Toronto, Ontario
Canada M5S 1V6

Diane M. Wood (311)
Department of Educational Psychology
    and Statistics
State University of New York at Albany
Albany, New York 12222

Preface

From a pedagogic viewpoint, I want students to learn about the contemporary issues in learning disabilities, to understand their origins and impact on the field. I want to rouse their interests about these issues, provoke them to deep reflections about the impact, and help them to anticipate future issues and trends in research. Clearly I have given myself a tall order. But I can fulfill it with the help of the friends who wrote quality chapters on these important, contemporary issues. Herein I am richly blessed.

In this revised edition of *Learning about Learning Disabilities,* my esteemed colleagues and good friends have been most generous to me. They have all written chapters that have both depth and breadth. I could not have assembled a better group of colleagues whose standards and commitment to scholarship are self-evident in their respective chapters. Not only do they impart knowledge to readers, they also model scholarship in the way they approach and treat their respective topics. Students of learning disabilities will assuredly make impressive gains when they read these chapters. I am very much indebted to all my good friends and colleagues who contributed chapters.

The range of topics in the book ensures a comprehensive and balanced coverage of important areas in learning disabilities. They include conceptual issues, basic research in memory processes and social aspects of learning disabilities intervention research in academic areas and a nonacademic area (social skills intervention), issues in service delivery, and a life span perspective of learning disabilities that focuses on the child, adolescent, and adult with learning disabilities.

Learning about Learning Disabilities (second edition) is targeted for the advanced student. Readers interested in a more basic introduction to the field are advised to read *The ABCs of Learning Disabilities.*

Bernice Wong

Acknowledgments

I thank Nikki Levy, executive editor, for her patient understanding and guidance throughout the process and completion of the revisions of the present book. Moreover, I appreciate her openness and receptiveness to ideas.

I also thank Barbara Makinster (née Curtis). Without her ceaseless tracking of necessary details and keeping me on schedule, the revised manuscripts would never have appeared in print! Additionally, I enjoy her sense of humor!

For all those who are responsible for the production end of this revised edition of my book, including Eileen Favorite, I say thank you. Last but not least, I thank Jean Pehrsson for her valiant efforts to publicize this book and *The ABCs of Learning Disabilities.*

To the Student[1]

As you embark on your studies in learning disabilities, you will find much to learn. You may be surprised by some of the topics and contents in courses that you are asked to take.

A glance at the table of contents of the present edited and revised book will show what you should learn about learning disabilities. It is natural and perfectly understandable that you would find some chapters more appealing than others. Your preference reflects individual interests and background experiences. Nevertheless, you must read and study those chapters in which you initially harbor less interest if you are to be well trained in the field of learning disabilities.

The chapters all have depth and breadth. If you expend effort and activate your cerebrum in reading and rereading carefully and thoughtfully, you will have a thorough grasp of the issues raised by the authors in their respective chapters. With a firm grasp of relevant issues, you will find that you automatically begin to draw conclusions about the impact of those issues. Thence, your stimulated mind will be in a whirlwind of further questions! When that happens, congratulate yourself because students who are eager to learn, gluttons for work, and keen to hone their critical thinking are prized by all of us, your profs.

When you find that you are buoyed with enthusiasm for a particular chapter that you have read in this book and impatient for answers to questions you have regarding it, seize the moment and storm the office of your course instructor. Go boldly forth to justly demand his or her attention and time. For you deserve all of it! You've worked hard, read with thoroughness, and thought hard!

I hope very much that you enjoy learning about all the topics in learning disabilities contained in this book. More important, I hope that you obtain the knowledge base here to guide your future studies in learning disabilities.

Cheers!

Bernice Wong

---

[1]This letter is addressed to students in an advanced undergraduate course or graduate course in learning disabilities.

Conceptual, Historical, and Research Aspects of Learning Disabilities

CHAPTER 1

Learning Disabilities: An Historical and Conceptual Overview

Joseph K. Torgesen

I. CURRENT STATUS OF THE FIELD

The current strength and extent of the field of learning disabilities (LD) can be appreciated by considering its achievements in four areas. First, more children are currently being served in LD programs than in any other area of special education. According to the data currently available from the United States Department of Education, Office of Special Education Programs, 51% of all children identified for special services in the schools are classified as LD. During the 1994–1995 school year, approximately 2.5 million students were identified as LD in the United States, while about 571,000 were identified as mentally retarded, and 428,000 as emotionally handicapped.

In addition to being the largest field of special education, LD also continues to grow at a rapid rate. Although it has not continued to grow as fast as it did during its very early years, recent data suggest that there has been a slight upswing in growth rate in the recent past. The most rapid period of growth in the numbers of students identified as LD occurred in the 6 years following the passage of legislation requiring schools to provide services to students with LD. From 1976 to 1982, the number of LD children served by schools in the United States grew by 130%!

In contrast, during the period between 1983 and 1988, the growth rate slowed to 11%. The most recent figures indicate that the growth rate between 1990 and 1995 was 17%, which continues to be significantly higher than other major fields of special education.

Overall, approximately 5% of all children in public schools in the United States are being served in programs for the learning disabled. However, a continuing problem is that prevalence rates do vary considerably from state to state, with a range from about 3% to close to 10%. Of course, the differing criteria used by various states can create problems for children and their families when they move across state boundaries. Although these figures from the United States amply document the importance of LD as a field within special education, formal programs for LD children are not restricted to the United States. Canada has an extensive system of services for LD children, as do most of the countries of Western Europe.

A. Legal Status within the Law

The extensive services to children and youth with LD in the United States are the result of the field's firm status within the law. Beginning with P.L. 94-142 (The Education of the Handicapped Act of 1975), all school districts are required to provide free and appropriate education to children identified as LD. The law, and federal regulations developed to implement it, specified a wide range of practices that were to be followed in delivering services to LD children. The essential provisions of P.L. 94-142 were reaffirmed in P.L. 98-199 (The Education of the Handicapped Act of 1983), which also contained some provision for expansion of services at preschool, secondary, and postsecondary levels. Finally, this legislation, now known as the Individuals with Disabilities Education Act (IDEA) was reauthorized in 1997, with provisions to assist with discipline, assessment and accountability, and development of individualized educational programs for children with disabilities.

B. Professional Associations

A third indication of the current status of the LD field is found in the number of associations that have been formed to advocate on behalf of LD children, support professional development, and provide a forum for discussion of research. There are currently seven major organizations that focus exclusively on the interests of LD children and professionals. The largest of these organizations is the Learning Disabilities Association of America (LDA), formerly known as the Association for Children and Adults with Learning Disabilities. Formed in 1964, this organization has over 50,000 members, with local chapters in 50 states, Washington, D.C., and Puerto Rico. It has been concerned primarily with advocacy for LD children at the state and federal level, parental issues, and the communication of information about educational programs and practices. The Learning Disabilities Association of Canada was incorporated in 1971, has an additional 10,000 members, and has very similar goals to its sister organization in the United States.

The Division for Learning Disabilities (DLD) within the Council for Exceptional Children has about 10,000 members and is focused on enhancement of professional practices in the field. The Council for Learning Disabilities (CLD) is an independent organization of 4,000 members that has goals similar to those of DLD. The oldest professional organization in the field is the Orton Dyslexia Society, which recently changed its name to the International Dyslexia Association. It was formed in 1949, currently numbers about 11,400 members, and contributes primarily to professional development and communication of research about children with specific reading disabilities.

Two smaller organizations focus primarily on discussion of issues and dissemination of information about LD. The National Joint Committee on Learning Disabilities (NJCLD) is a small organization composed of appointed representatives from the other major LD associations and other groups that have an interest in LD. The NJCLD's purpose is to provide a forum for communication among associations and interdisciplinary consideration of many issues confronting the field. This organization periodically makes position statements on many of these issues. The NJCLD is uniquely influential because its member organizations represent such a large portion of the entire LD community. Another relatively small organization whose mission is to disseminate information about LD is the National Center for Learning Disabilities (NCLD).

Finally, the only organization devoted exclusively to promoting and disseminating research about LD is the International Academy for Research in Learning Disabilities (IARLD). Membership in this group is by invitation and consists mainly of active researchers. Its purpose is to provide a means for international communication about research on LD.

These organizations play a very important role in contributing to the development and continuing visibility of the field. Most of them hold at least annual meetings at the national level, and several of them publish professional journals on a monthly or quarterly basis. Their large and growing membership attests to the high level of concern for children with LDs manifest by parents, educators, and researchers.

C. Active Area of Research

A final indicator of the current status of the LD field is the level of interest in the topic among researchers. It is a very active area of research. Research on LD within the United States received a major impetus with the passage of the Health Research Extension Act of 1985, which mandated the formation of an Interagency Committee on Learning Disabilities. This committee was charged to examine the current state of knowledge in the field of LD and then make a report to congress with recommendations for a research initiative in the area. This report was submitted in 1987, and a year later, its major contents were published as the Proceedings of the National Conference on Learning Disabilities (Kavanagh & Truss, 1988). The report recommended that the National Institute of Child Health and Human Development, within the National Institutes of Health, take the lead in establishing a comprehensive, multidisciplinary program of research on LD. In the words of the report,

> A major goal of this research should be the development of a classification system that more clearly defines and diagnoses LD, conduct disorders, and attention deficit disorders, and their interrelationships. Such information is prerequisite to the delineation of homogeneous subgroups and the delineation of more precise and reliable strategies for treatment, remediation, and prevention that will increase the effectiveness of both research and therapy. (Interagency Committee on Learning Disabilities, 1987, p. 224)

On the basis of these recommendations, the NICHD has made available a number of large research grants to support programmatic research on LD. This research is already beginning to bear significant fruit (Lyon, in press) and promises to have a continuing impact for the foreseeable future. The effect of the additional support for research in LD has been to attract professionals from fields other than those traditionally associated with LD (i.e., special education) to research in this area. In particular, well-trained researchers from the fields of psychology, medicine, and linguistics promise to make important new contributions to knowledge about LD.

Communication about research and professional issues in LD is aided by the publication of six journals devoted exclusively to the topic. The most widely circulated of these is the *Journal of Learning Disabilities* (published by PRO-ED, Inc.). Others include *Learning Disabilities Quarterly* (published by CLD), *Learning Disabilities Research and Practice* (published by DLD), *Learning Disabilities: An Interdisciplinary Journal* (published by LDA), and *Annals of Dyslexia* (published by the International Dyslexia Association). IARLD also publishes two or three monographs a year on topics related to LD, and a periodical called *Thalamus*. In addition to these outlets devoted exclusively to topics on LD, research related to LD is also frequently published in journals such as *Journal of Educational Psychology, Reading Research Quarterly, Brain and Behavior, Developmental Medicine and Child Neurology, Scientific Studies of Reading,* and the *Journal of Applied Behavior Analysis,* which accept articles on a variety of topics.

II. AN HISTORICAL PERSPECTIVE

When considering the history of the field of LD, it is helpful from the outset to make a distinction between LD as an applied field of special education, and LD as an area of research on individual differences in learning and performance. In the former sense, the field shares many attributes with other political/social movements, while in the latter sense it is a loosely jointed, interdisciplinary area of scientific inquiry. It will be a central point of this chapter that confusion and occasional conflict between these two aspects of the field has created many problems over the course of its history, and continues to be a source of many difficulties for the field. It is also true that although both aspects have some elements of history in common, the primary impetus for LD as a social/political movement has a narrower historical base than the field as a whole. In this discussion, I will outline the broad history of ideas about individuals with specific learning difficulty, but will also point out the special historical antecedents of the field as a movement. This discussion will be brief, but more detailed information about many historical points is available in other sources (Coles, 1987; Doris, 1986; Hallahan & Cruickshank, 1973; Hallahan, Kauffman, & Lloyd, 1985; Kavale & Forness, 1985; Myers & Hammill, 1990; Wiederholt, 1974).

A. Early Developments

Interest in the possible causes and consequences of individual differences in mental functioning extends back at least as far as early Greek civilization (Mann, 1979). However, the beginning of scientific work of immediate relevance to LD was probably that of Joseph Gall at the beginning of the nineteenth century (Wiederholt, 1974). Gall described a number of cases in which specific loss of mental function in adults occurred as a result of brain damage. His description of one of his patients is interesting because it shows his concern with establishing that the patient's loss of functioning was isolated to one particular ability:

> In consequence of an attack of apoplexy a soldier found it impossible to express in spoken language his feelings and ideas. His face bore no signs of a deranged intellect. His mind (espirit) found the answer to questions addressed to him and he carried out all he was told to do; shown an armchair and asked if he knew what it was, he answered by seating himself in it. He could not articulate on the spot a word pronounced for him to repeat; but a few moments later the word escaped from his lips as if involuntarily. . . . It was not his tongue which was embarrassed; for he moved it with great agility and could pronounce quite well a large number of isolated words. His memory was not at fault, for he signified his anger at being unable to express himself concerning many things which he wished to communicate. It was the faculty of speech alone which was abolished. (Head, 1926, p. 11)

Over the next century, many clinical studies of speech and language disorders were reported; among the best known being those of Bouillaud, Broca, Jackson,

Wernicke, and Head (Wiederholt, 1974). The major goals of this work were to document the specific loss of various speech and language functions in adults who had previously shown these abilities, and to identify the types of brain damage associated with the different kinds of functional disturbance. Of relevance to the study of LD, this work did establish the fact that very specific types of mental impairment can occur as a result of damage to isolated regions of the brain.

The first systematic clinical studies of specific reading disability were reported in 1917 by James Hinshelwood, a Scottish ophthalmologist. Hinshelwood had examined a number of cases in which adults suddenly lost the ability to read while other areas of mental functioning remained intact. As with cases of sudden loss of oral language facility, the loss of reading ability was attributed to damage to specific areas of the brain. Hinshelwood tried to support this hypothesis by citing evidence from the patient's history or postmortem examination.

In addition to his work on loss of function with adults, Hinshelwood also saw cases of children who had extreme difficulties acquiring reading skills. In his descriptions of these cases, Hinshelwood (1917) was careful to document that their reading difficulties occurred alongside quite normal abilities in other intellectual skills. For example, in his description of one 10-year-old boy with severe reading problems, he states:

> The boy had been at school three years, and had got on well with every subject except reading. He was apparently a bright, and in every respect an intelligent boy. He had been learning music for a year, and had made good progress in it. . . . In all departments of his studies where the instruction was oral he had made good progress, showing that his auditory memory was good. . . . He performs simple sums quite correctly, and his progress in arithmetic has been regarded as quite satisfactory. He has no difficulty in learning to write. His visual acuity is good. (pp. 46–47)

Hinshelwood attributed the boy's problems to a condition that he called "congenital word blindness" resulting from damage to a specific area of the brain that stored visual memories for words and letters. Given the similarities in symptoms between his cases of developmental reading problems and those of the adults he had observed, as well as his medical orientation, it is easy to see how Hinshelwood arrived at his explanation for specific reading disability in children. However, recent analysis of several of his cases suggests that he may have overlooked a number of environmental influences that could also have explained the reading problems of children he studied (Coles, 1987). Whatever the ultimate cause of the reading problems he studied, Hinshelwood clearly showed that severe reading problems could exist in children with average or superior intellectual abilities in other areas. He also believed that cases of true "word blindness" were very rare, with an incidence of less than one in a thousand.

Following Hinshelwood, the next major figure to report clinical studies of children with reading disabilities was Samual Orton, an American child neurologist. Based on his clinical examinations of children over a 10-year period, Orton (1937) developed an explanation for reading disability that was quite different from Hinshelwood's. Rather than proposing that children with specific reading disabilities had actual damage to a localized area of their brains, he proposed that the difficulty was caused by delay, or failure, in establishing dominance for language in the left hemisphere of the brain. He used the term *strephosymbolia,* or twisted symbols, to refer to the fact that reading-disabled children, as he observed them, frequently had special difficulties reading reversible words (saw–was, not–ton) or letters (b–d, p–q) correctly. His theory explained reversals as resulting from confusions between the visual images of these stimuli projected on the two different brain hemispheres. Since, according to his theory, these projections were mirror images of one another, and since neither hemispheric image was consistently dominant, sometimes the child saw the stimulus as "b," and sometimes as "d."

Neither Orton's particular neurological theories of dyslexia (reading disability), nor his ideas that reversals are especially symptomatic of the disorder have stood the test of subsequent research (Liberman, Shankweiler, Orlando, Harris, & Berti, 1971). However, his broad emphasis on dysfunction in the language-related areas of the brain as a cause of specific developmental dyslexia is consistent with important current theories in the field (Torgesen, in press,a; Shankweiler & Liberman, 1989).

Orton's work did have a broader contemporary impact than Hinshelwood's, principally in the stimulation of research and the founding of several special schools and clinics to serve children with reading disabilities. The special educational techniques he developed for helping reading-disabled children were particularly influential, and in 1949, the Orton Dyslexia Society was formed in partial recognition of his contributions. It is interesting that the educational programs developed by Orton and Hinshelwood were similar: they both recommended systematic instruction combined with intensive, skill-building practice in using letter–sound relationships (phonics) to recognize words. In their emphasis on direct instruction and practice in skills required for reading, these educational programs were quite different from the "process training" approaches that were advocated 30 years later by many educators, once the field of learning disabilities was officially established.

Although Orton's work did have an impact on the treatment of reading disorders in a number of isolated special schools and clinics, neither his nor Hinshelwood's theories about the neurological basis for reading disorders was widely assimilated in scientific and educational circles as an explanation for individual differences in reading ability (Doris, 1986). Educators and psychologists who dealt with the vast majority of reading disability cases in the public schools attributed reading problems to a variety of environmental, attitudinal, and educational problems. Texts on the diagnosis and remediation of reading problems published during the 1940s (Durrell, 1940) and 1950s (Vernon, 1957) generally discredited these theories, and suggested that, at best, inherent brain dysfunction accounted for only a very small proportion of reading failure.

B. Immediate Precursors to the Field of Learning Disabilities

The work described thus far is part of the overall history of ideas concerning specific LD in children. However, the research and clinical activity that led most directly to the initial establishment of a formally organized field of LD was conducted by Heinz Werner and Alfred Strauss at the Wayne County Training School in Northville, Michigan. In fact, the historical threads between the work of Hinshelwood and Orton, and the development of the LD movement in special education are quite tenuous. In retrospect, it seems that their work has assumed greater historical importance with the developing recognition that the vast majority of LD children have reading as their primary academic problem (Lyon, 1985), and as scientific interest in specific reading disabilities has increased over the last several years (Stanovich, 1990).

The work of Werner and Strauss was fundamentally different from that of Hinshelwood and Orton, in that they sought to describe deficient general learning processes rather than seeking to describe and explain failure on a specific academic task. Their work was interpreted as establishing the existence of a subgroup of children who, presumably because of mild brain damage, experienced specific limitations in ability to process certain kinds of information. Werner and Strauss's work placed much more emphasis on deficient learning processes themselves (which were presumed to powerfully affect learning in many different situations) than on the specific academic tasks that were affected.

What were these deficient learning processes? They centered mostly on what would be called today distractibility, hyperactivity, visual perceptual, and perceptual/motor problems. Werner and Strauss were influenced heavily by the work of Kurt Goldstein, who had studied the behavior of soldiers with head wounds during World War I. Goldstein observed that a number of behavioral characteristics were reliably found in many of his patients: inability to inhibit responding to certain external stimuli, figure–background confusions, hyperactivity, meticulosity, and extreme emotional lability.

Werner and Strauss sought to document the presence of similar behavioral/cognitive difficulties in a subgroup of children at their school. These children were presumed to have brain damage because of their medical histories and other aspects of their behavior. They compared the behavior of these "brain-damaged" children with that of other mentally retarded children who were presumed not to be brain damaged. Their general conclusions were that the brain-damaged children showed specific difficulties in attention (distractibility) and perception. These findings were coupled with other observations (Kephart & Strauss, 1940) that the subgroup identified as brain damaged did not profit from the educational curriculum at the Wayne County School as much as other children. Specifically, although the IQs of the non-brain-damaged children tended to increase over several years at the school, the IQs of the brain-damaged children declined.

From these observations, Werner and Strauss concluded that the brain-damaged children needed special educational interventions designed to overcome the weaknesses their research had identified (Strauss, 1943). In Strauss's words (Strauss & Lehtinen, 1947), "the erratic behavior of brain-injured children in perceptual tasks might be explained by a figure–ground deficiency, and an approach to remedy such deficiency should be directed toward strengthening the figure–ground perception" (p. 50). Strauss's educational orientation was toward interventions that focused on either remediation of deficient learning processes (primarily perceptual in nature) or educational adjustments (eliminating distracting stimuli in the classroom) that sought to minimize the impact of these deficient processes. In the classic volumes, *Psychopathology and Education of the Brain-Injured Child* (Strauss & Lehtinen, 1947) and *Psychopathology and Education of the Brain-Injured Child: Progress in Theory and Clinic* (Vol. 2) (Strauss & Kephart, 1955), Strauss and his colleagues developed an extensive set of educational recommendations that became very influential in the education of mentally retarded and brain-injured children.

As Hallahan and Cruickshank (1973) have pointed out, Werner and Strauss's influence on the future LD field was profound. Not only did they develop specific educational recommendations that focused on a special set of deficient learning abilities, but they provided a general orientation to the education of exceptional children that became very influential. The elements of this general orientation were that (1) individual differences in learning should be understood by examining the different ways that children approached learning tasks (the processes that aided or interfered with learning); (2) educational procedures should be tailored to patterns of processing strengths and weaknesses in the individual child; and (3) children with deficient learning processes might be helped to learn normally if those processes are strengthened, or if teaching methods which did not stress weak areas could be developed. As the LD movement began to gather strength after its initial inception in 1963, these three concepts were repeatedly used to provide a rationale for its development as a separate entity from other fields of education. They provided the core of what was "unique" about educational programming for LD children.

In retrospect, it is interesting to note that the scientific support for Werner and Strauss's ideas about unique processing disabilities in brain-damaged children was exceedingly weak. As far back as 1949, Sarason attacked their work because of the way they formed their groups of children with and without brain damage. Werner and Strauss sometimes assigned children to the brain-damaged group on the basis of behavior alone, even in the absence of direct evidence from neurological tests or medical history. Unfortunately, some of the behaviors that led to selection of children as brain damaged were very similar to those that were studied in the experiments. The circular reasoning involved in attributing experimental differences between groups to brain damage is obvious.

Apart from the problems of interpretation caused by weaknesses in their experimental design, it also turns out that the actual differences between groups in distractibility and perceptual/motor problems were not very large. For example, Kavale and Forness (1985) report a meta-analysis of 26 studies conducted by Werner, Strauss, and their colleagues comparing brain-damaged and non-brain-damaged children. When all measures are combined, the overall difference between groups was .104 standard deviations! When the results were examined for different dependent variables (perceptual-motor, cognition, language, behavior, and intelligence), none of the estimates of effect size were statistically significant. Kavale and Forness concluded that "this meta-analytic synthesis offered little empirical support for the alleged behavioral differences between exogenous (brain injured) and endogenous (non-brain injured) mentally retarded children" (p. 57).

Although the scientific work of Werner and Strauss on learning deficiencies resulting from brain damage does not stand up well to close scrutiny, their ideas strongly influenced a number of colleagues who carried their work forward. William Cruickshank, for example, showed that cerebral palsied children of normal intelligence exhibited some of the same intellectual characteristics as the "brain-damaged" retardates in earlier studies (Cruickshank, Bice, & Wallen, 1957). Cruickshank also extended the teaching methods advocated by Werner and Strauss to children of normal intelligence, and his extensive evaluation of these techniques is reported in *A Teaching Method for Brain Injured and Hyperactive Children* (Cruickshank, Bentzen, Ratzeburg, & Tannhauser, 1961).

About this same time, another former staff member at the Wayne County Training School, Newell Kephart, wrote *Slow Learner in the Classroom* (1960). In this work, he embellished a theory first proposed by Werner and Strauss, that perceptual-motor development is the basis for all higher mental development, such as conceptual learning. A suggestion derived from this theory was that training in perceptual-motor skills should be helpful to many children experiencing learning difficulties in school. In his book, which was to be very helpful in providing "unique" educational procedures for LD classrooms, he detailed a number of procedures that teachers could use to enhance the perceptual-motor development of their students.

It should be emphasized that all during the 1940s and 1950s, and into the early 1960s there was no field of LD per se. Rather, researchers and clinicians were observing a variety of problems in children of normal intelligence that seemed to interfere with learning. Children manifesting these difficulties went by a variety of labels, including minimally brain damaged, perceptually impaired, aphasic, or neurologically impaired. In addition to perceptual motor processing difficulties, a variety of disorders with auditory and language processes were also being studied.

Helmer Mykelbust, who had extensive experience working with the deaf, became interested in children who had more subtle problems in auditory and linguistic processing (Johnson & Mykelbust, 1967):

> Children who have auditory verbal comprehension disabilities resulting from central nervous system dysfunction hear but do not understand what is said. . . . Language disabilities of this type have been described in both children and adults and have been designated as receptive aphasia, sensory aphasia, auditory verbal agnosia, or word deafness. . . . These disabilities should be differentiated from the language deficits resulting from deafness or mental retardation. Frequently such a distinction is not easy to make in those who have serious impairments, but it is essential in planning an adequate educational program. (p. 74)

Language disabilities were also emphasized in the work of Samual Kirk, who had served for a brief time as a staff member at the Wayne County Training School with Werner and Strauss. In 1961, he published the experimental version of the *Illinois Test of Psycho-Linguistic Abilities* (McCarthy & Kirk, 1961). The purpose of this instrument was to allow an examination of a child's strengths and weaknesses in the area of language processing. It stimulated the development of a number of educational programs that specified unique interventions for children with different patterns of disabilities (Bush & Giles, 1969; Kirk & Kirk, 1971), and thus it was used in a way consistent with the original educational ideas of Werner and Strauss. Although there were many other important researchers and teachers concerned with specific learning disorders during this time, the major themes of the period are represented in the work already described. Concern was being focused on children who appeared normal in many intellectual skills, but who also displayed a variety of cognitive limitations that seemed to interfere with their ability to learn in the regular classroom. Not only were educational and mental health professionals concerned about these children, but also the concerns of parent's groups were becoming more focused and mobilized.

C. Formal Beginnings of the LD Movement

In 1963, at the Conference on Exploration into Problems of the Perceptually Handicapped Child, which was sponsored by the Fund for Perceptually Handicapped Children, Inc., Samual Kirk proposed the term *learning disabilities* as a descriptive title for the kind of children being generally discussed at the conference:

> I have used the term "learning disabilities" to describe a group of children who have disorders in development in language, speech, reading, and associated communication skills needed for social interaction. In this

group I do not include children who have sensory handicaps such as blindness or deafness, because we have methods of managing and training the deaf and the blind, I also exclude from this group children who have generalized mental retardation. (Kirk, 1963, pp. 2–3)

This speech served as a catalyst to focus the concern of many of those in attendance, and that evening they voted to form the Association for Children with Learning Disabilities (ACLD). The establishment of the ACLD represents the formal beginnings of the LD field as a social/political/educational movement. It was primarily an organization for parents. Its professional advisory board was formed from many of the leading professionals of the day (i.e., Kirk, Cruickshank, Kephart, Frostig, Lehtinen, Mykelbust), but its Board of Directors was composed of parents and leaders from other segments of society. As the leader of a movement, its goal was to mobilize social and political concern for the plight of LD children and to create public sector services for them. The material presented in the beginning of this chapter attests to the enormous influence that ACLD and associated organizations have had on education over the past 30 years.

At its inception, the movement faced three major challenges. First, it had to establish a clear sense of its identity as a field separate from special and remedial education areas that already existed. Second, it had to develop a broad base of support for publicly funded educational programs for LD children. Third, it had to encourage training efforts to prepare a large group of professionals for service in the field.

The LD movement approached the first challenge by selecting and promoting ideas about LD children that emphasized their differences from other children currently receiving services in the schools. The centerpiece of the distinction between LD and other children having trouble in school was that their learning problems were the result of inherent and specific difficulties in performing some of the psychological processes required for learning. This was a powerful idea, in that it implied these children were genuinely handicapped through no fault of their own, their parents, or their teachers. The idea was also appealing because it was optimistic; if the right remediation for deficient processes were prescribed, these children's achievement in school might become consistent with their generally "normal" abilities in other areas.

The research and theories of Werner and Strauss were instrumental in providing support for these foundational assumptions about LD. For example, the focus of the new field on remediation of disabilities in fundamental learning processes separated it from the fields of remedial reading and remedial math both by making it more general, and by giving the impression that it was attacking educational difficulties in a more basic and powerful way (Hartman & Hartman, 1973). Professional fields are characterized by the "special" knowledge and expertise they possess. Claims about special knowledge in the diagnosis and treatment of specific processing disorders were instrumental in helping the LD movement to establish an identity of its own.

It was also important for the young field to establish that its clients, and the services to be provided them, were distinct from the existing fields of mental retardation and emotional/behavior disorders. Here, an emphasis on the generally "normal" academic potential of LD children, and on the specific, and probably short-term interventions they would require, were helpful in distinguishing between LD and mentally retarded children. In differentiating LD from children with behavior disorders, the idea that LD children's learning problems are inherent (caused by brain dysfunction), and not the result of environmental influences, was also important.

As we shall see, some of the ideas the helped support the formation of the new field of LD were soon questioned by professionals within the field itself (Mann and Phillips, 1967; Hammill, 1972). Further, all of the basic assumptions about LD that were so strongly advocated in the early days have been seriously challenged in recent research (Coles, 1987; Fletcher et al., 1994; Francis, et al., 1995; Siegel, 1989; Stanovich, 1986; Torgesen, in press, a). Original support for these ideas had come primarily from the clinical experience of the field's founders with a broad variety of unusual children. These clinically unique children thus provided the basis for what became a very broad social movement. At least part of the power of this movement came from the strength and certainty with which it generalized its assumptions about LD to relatively larger groups of children in the public schools. As Gerald Senf (1986) has pointed out, the young field had strong motives to include as many children under the LD umbrella as possible.

Although one certainly cannot blame those who provided impetus for the original movement (they were attempting to develop public support for their clients and their children), their very success in publicizing the concept of LD has created problems for the science of LD. Research attempting to verify foundational assumptions about LD using samples of LD children being served in the public schools frequently obtains negative results (Ysseldyke, 1983). However, as Stanovich (1990) has shown in his model of reading disabilities, these negative results are the likely product of overgeneralization of the LD label in current practice. Thus, the political success of the LD movement, in generating funds for services to very large numbers of children, created inevitable ambiguities in the LD concept. The resolution of these ambiguities can only come through a more carefully disciplined use of the LD label in research and practice.

Historical developments with regard to public programs for LD children and training of LD professionals are closely entertwined and shall be reported together. Involvement of the U.S. government in activities that supported development of the field began as a series of Task Force reports between 1966 and 1969. These reports reviewed a variety of topics including characteristics of LD children, extent of current services, methods of treatment, and estimates of prevalence. The report of Task Force III (Chalfant & Sheffelin, 1969) described how little was actually known about assessing and remediating psychological processing disorders.

The first major legislative success came in 1969 with the passage of the Children with Learning Disabilities Act, which authorized the U.S. Office of Education to establish programs for LD students. The government also sponsored an institute in which plans for the training of LD professionals were discussed (Kass, 1970). In 1971, the Bureau of Education of the Handicapped initiated a program to fund Child Service Demonstration Projects to be conducted in the different states. These demonstration projects were to directly serve children with LD as well as provide a means for developing professional expertise in the area. Further support for professional development came through the Leadership Training Institute in Learning Disabilities at the University of Arizona that was funded for 2 years beginning in 1971. In 1975, the LD field achieved a firm basis in law with the passage of PL 94-142, which required all states to provide an appropriate public education for children with LD. It was this law that stimulated the enormous growth in the field that has occurred since the mid-1970s.

D. The Role of Psychological Processes in LD

As was mentioned earlier, at least part of the LD field's claims for a unique professional identity came from its focus on identifying and remediating the specific psychological processing difficulties of LD children. A number of tests to identify specific processing disorders were developed such as the *Developmental Test of Visual Perception* (Frostig, Lefever, & Whittlesey, 1964), and the *Illinois Test of Psycho-linguistic Abilities* (McCarthy & Kirk, 1961), and various programs to remediate specific deficits in these processes were published. Popular activities in many LD classrooms during the 1960s and 1970s included practice in various visual/motor, auditory sequencing, visual/perceptual, or crossmodality training exercises. The rationale for these exercises was that improvement in deficient underlying learning processes would allow children to achieve their full potential in learning academic skills such as reading and math. Since many of the leading professionals at the time placed an emphasis on visual/perceptual and visual/motor processing difficulties as a fundamental cause of LD, many of the training activities had a decided emphasis on visual perceptual processes (Hallahan & Cruickshank, 1973).

The first published attacks on this approach to the education of LD children came from Lester Mann (Mann & Phillips, 1967, Mann, 1971), who criticized the approach on theoretical and philosophical grounds. Shortly thereafter, a number of empirical investigations of the efficacy of perceptual/motor training began to appear, and many of these were summarized and commented on by Donald Hammill and his colleagues (Hammill, 1972; Hammill, Goodman & Wiederholt, 1974; Wiederholt & Hammill, 1971). Criticism of process training soon spread to psycholinguistic processes (Hammill & Larsen, 1974; Newcomer & Hammill, 1975), with the research reviews generally demonstrating that process training did not generalize to improvements in learning academic skills.

These initial reviews sparked a period of intense controversy within the LDs movement for almost a decade. The scientific questions at issue became politicized and polarized, with discussions sometimes containing more personal acrimony than reasoned debate (Hammill, 1990). This is not too surprising, for these criticisms were directed at one of the foundational pillars of the LD movement. It seems natural that the LD movement, with its political/social aims would strongly resist a weakening of any aspect of its raison d'être. When further evidence (Arter & Jenkins, 1979; Vellutino, Steger, Moyer, Harding, & Niles, 1977; Ysseldyke, 1973) effectively closed the case against process training as a means for treating LD, the field turned to direct instruction of academic skills as its dominant mode of intervention. In Hammill's (1990) words: "Learning disabilities needed an approach with a better data base for its foundation; at the time, the principles of direct instruction satisfied this purpose" (p. 11).

By 1977, dissatisfaction with the processing orientation to diagnosis and remediation of LD had become widespread. In fact, the federal regulations implementing PL 94-142 did not require assessment of psychological processes as part of procedures to identify LD children for public school programs. Although LD were still defined as resulting from deficiencies in the basic psychological processes required for learning, LD children were to be diagnosed primarily in terms of a discrepancy between general measures of intelligence and measures of achievement in specific areas of learning.

Both the lack of positive criteria for the identification of LD (it was identified as underachievement not explicable in terms of physical, cultural, or environmental handicap), and the adoption of direct instruction as the treatment of choice, undermine the rationale for LD as a distinct field within remedial and special education. Although direct instruction in academic skills may be effective with LD children, these procedures do not provide a foundation for LD as a distinct field of professional expertise in education. Rather, as Hallahan, Kauffman, and Lloyd (1985) suggest, the striking similarities in educational procedures across various remedial and special education programs seriously undermine the educational placement of LD children in programs separate from those of other children experiencing academic problems.

There are at least two possible explanations for the failure of the LD movement to document the utility of process-oriented approaches to identification and treatment of LD children. The first is to concede that the fundamental assumptions are simply wrong. Coles (1987), for example, maintains that there is insufficient evidence that LD children actually have inherent limitations in the ability to process specific kinds of information. Others (Hammill, 1990; Mann, 1979) suggest that there is no evidence to suggest training in "hypothetical processes" can be more effective than direct instruction in academic skills as an intervention for LD children.

In contrast to these views, Torgesen (1979, 1986, 1993) has suggested that the LD field's problems with psychological processes arose because it was an idea ahead of its time. That is, approaches to identifying and training deficient processes in LD children were pressed into service when our understanding of mental processing operations, and their relationships to learning academic tasks, were at only a rudimentary stage of development. Since the 1960s, we have learned an enormous amount about how to measure mental processing operations, and many of our fundamental conceptualizations about them have changed (Butterfield & Ferretti, 1987; Brown & Campione, 1986; Lyon, 1994). For example, we now recognize that processing operations are much more context sensitive than previously supposed, which makes the problem of generalization of training particularly important. Further, we have a much better understanding of how differences in background knowledge can influence performance on tasks supposedly measuring processing differences (Ceci & Baker, 1990). Finally, we have come to appreciate the enormous influence that differences in cognitive strategies can play on many different kinds of tasks (Meltzer, 1993). All of these improvements in understanding suggest that future developments in cognitively oriented training of psychological processes as an aid to academic improvement will look very different from that used in the past. In fact there are some strong indications that cognitively oriented training programs in reading comprehension strategies (Brown & Palincsar, 1987; Palincsar et al., 1993), writing strategies (Graham & Harris, 1993), phonological awareness (Blachman, 1997), and general study strategies (Ellis, Lenz, & Sabornie, 1987) can be quite effective in raising academic achievement in school. However, whether any of these interventions will prove uniquely useful to LD children, as opposed to other types of poor learners, remains to be demonstrated.

III. CURRENT AND FUTURE ISSUES

This section contains very brief discussions of several issues that are of current importance to the field of LD. Some of these issues, such as those of definition, have the potential to alter drastically the identity of the field, while others have more to do with practical issues of identification and service delivery. Because each of the issues to be discussed is very complex, I cannot hope to represent them fully in the brief space allotted. Rather, I will state the essential questions in each area, suggest why they are important to the field, and provide a very limited exposure to current work in the area.

A. The Problem of Definition

Definitions, such as those proposed for LD, are offered to specify a particular type of condition or individual. They are valid as long as there is at least one individual to whom they apply. Definitions of LD are frequently critiqued because they almost universally state that neurological impairment is the presumed cause of the problem. However, even the most severe critics of the LD concept (cf. Coles, 1987) agree that at least a few children may have specific neurological impairment that interferes with school learning. The important question for these critics is how many of the 5% of school children currently identified as LD are adequately described by current definitions. Answers to this question may affect the numbers of children legitimately served under current law, but they do not threaten the validity of the concept.

The definition of LD accepted by the majority of persons in the field has changed in subtle ways since it was first formalized in 1967 by the National Advisory Committee on Handicapped Children (the definition later incorporated in PL 94-142). Most of the changes reflect additions to our knowledge about LD derived from research and practice. That first formal definition stated:

> Specific learning disability means a disorder in one or more of the basic psychological processes involved in understanding or in using language, spoken or written, which may manifest itself in an imperfect ability to listen, think, speak, read, write, spell, or to do mathematical calculations. The term includes such conditions as perceptual handicaps, brain injury, minimal brain dysfunction, dyslexia, and developmental aphasia. The term does not include children who have learning problems which are primarily the result of visual, hearing, or motor handicaps, of mental retardation, of emotional disturbance, or of environmental, cultural, or economic disadvantage. (p. 220)

The inter-agency report to the U.S. Congress (1987) identified at least four problems with this definition: (1) it does not indicate clearly enough that LD are a heterogeneous group of disorders; (2) it fails to recognize that LD frequently persist and are manifest in adults as well as children; (3) it does not clearly specify that, whatever the cause of LD, the "final common path" is inherent alterations in the way information is processed; and (4) it does not adequately recognize that persons with other handicapping or environmental limitations may have an LD concurrently with these conditions. Newer definitions, such as those proposed by the NJCLD in 1981 and revised in 1988, or that proposed by ACLD in 1986, attempted to incorporate this new information in their definitions.

An interesting controversy was stimulated by the definition proposed in the interagency committee's report to Congress (1987). Recognizing research findings on the problems LD children show in many social interactions, this definition added deficits in social skills as a type of LD. This proposal was explicitly rejected by the U.S. Department of Education. NJCLD's new definition, given below, also specifically excludes problems in social interaction as a defining characteristic of children with LD:

Learning disabilities is a general term that refers to a heterogeneous group of disorders manifested by significant difficulties in the acquisition and use of listening, speaking, reading, writing, reasoning, or mathematical abilities. These disorders are intrinsic to the individual, presumed to be due to central nervous system dysfunction, and may occur across the life span. Problems in self-regulatory behaviors, social perception, and social interaction may exist with learning disabilities but do not by themselves constitute a learning disability. Although learning disabilities may occur concomitantly with other handicapping conditions (for example, sensory impairment, mental retardation, serious emotional disturbance) or with extrinsic influences (such as cultural differences, insufficient or inappropriate instruction), they are not the result of those conditions or influences. (NJCLD Memorandum, 1988, p. 1)

In an article in the *Journal of Learning Disabilities,* Hammill (1990) argued strongly that the NJCLD definition represents the broadest current consensus in the field.

It is important for LDs as an educational/political movement to obtain relatively wide acceptance of a single broad definition of LD. However, this type of definition also has some serious drawbacks. The most important of these limitations may be that such definitions are not helpful in guiding research because they allow study of too great a variety of children under the same definition (Wong, 1986). When researchers attempt to compare findings across studies that have used broad definitions as a guide to sample selection, they often find, not surprisingly, that they have obtained different results. Many scholars now feel that it may be time for a moratorium on the development of such broad definitions. For example, Stanovich (1993) argues

Scientific investigations of some generically defined entity called "learning disability" simply make little sense given what we already know about heterogeneity across various learning domains. Research investigations must define groups specifically in terms of the domain of deficit (reading disability, arithmetic disability). (p. 273)

An example of such a domain-specific definition of a type of LD is found in the definition of reading disabilities that was recently proposed by the research committee of the Orton Dyslexia Society in collaboration with the National Center for Learning Disabilities and scientists from the National Institute of Child Health and Human Development (Lyon, 1995). This definition incorporates what has been learned about reading disabilities as a result of recent research initiatives in this area:

Dyslexia is one of several distinct learning disabilities. It is a specific language-based disorder of constitutional origin characterized by difficulties in single word decoding, usually reflecting insufficient phonological processing. These difficulties in single word decoding are often unexpected in relation to age and other cognitive and academic abilities; they are not the result of generalized developmental disability or sensory impairment. Dyslexia is manifest by variable difficulty with different forms of language, often including, in addition to problems with reading, a conspicuous problem with acquiring proficiency in writing and spelling. (p. 9)

It is beyond the scope of this chapter to detail the enormous amount of research knowledge about reading disabilities that is reflected in this definition (cf. Brady & Shankweiler, 1991; Share & Stanovich, 1995; Torgesen, in press, a). It is important to recognize that this definition does not cover all possible forms of reading disability, only the most common one (Fletcher & Francis, 1997). Although the definition will undoubtedly change as more knowledge about reading disabilities is acquired, it may serve as a model for the development of other domain-specific definitions of LD as we acquire more understanding of the specific factors that are responsible for difficulties learning in other academic areas.

B. Etiology

As I mentioned earlier, the concept of LD is not threatened by our inability to show that every school-identified LD child has a processing disability resulting from neurological impairment. However, if only a minuscule percentage of children being served as LD actually fit the definition, this would clearly create problems for the LD movement. The fundamental assumption about LD at present is that they result from neurological impairment affecting specific brain functions. This is why they are given special status as a handicapping condition.

The LD movement has not been strongly concerned with questions about etiology (preferring to focus instead on problem description and intervention). However, its ultimate integrity as a separate field of education depends upon finding answers to questions about the extent of brain pathology in the population it serves.

At present, the best evidence that LD are a genuinely handicapping condition arising from differences in brain function come from studies of the genetic transmission of reading disabilities. These studies (Olson, 1997; Olson, Forsberg, & Wise, 1994) indicate that approximately 50% of all variability in the phonological processes that cause specific reading disability can be attributed to genetic factors. Furthermore, very recent work (Wood, 1997) has replicated earlier evidence that at least one type of reading disability can be linked to a specific region on chromosome 6.

These genetic studies are being supplemented by very active research programs to identify the specific locus of brain dysfunction responsible for difficulties learning to read. At present, most of the evidence points to either structural (Galaburda, 1988) or functional (Flowers, Wood, & Naylor, 1991; Shaywitz, 1996) anomalies of development in the posterior region of the left hemisphere. Fortunately for current theories of reading disability, this is just the region of the brain most closely associated with the phonological processing skills that are commonly found to be deficient in reading-disabled children (Damasio & Geschwind, 1984).

Although these findings do provide strong support for the concept of constitutionally based reading disabilities, they do not answer questions about the proportion of students identified as LD that actually have these kinds of disabilities. The findings from the genetic studies suggest that biologically based reading disabilities may be relatively common among school-identified samples of LD children. Certainly, studies of the cognitive abilities of reading-disabled children indicate that difficulties processing phonological information are the most common cause of this disorder (Fletcher, et al., 1994). However, at least half of the variability in phonological processing "talent" is the result of environmental influences, and phonological abilities themselves are influenced by how well children acquire reading skills (Wagner, Torgesen, & Rashotte, 1994). Thus, it would be difficult to defend the proposition that all, or even most, children currently being served as reading disabled in public schools have reading disabilities of constitutional origin. One of the very interesting questions now being pursued by researchers (Vellutino, et al., 1996) is how to differentiate, or whether it is important to differentiate, between children with constitutionally based or experientially based reading disabilities.

Compared to our knowledge about reading disabilities, we have very little information about potential biological bases for other types of LD. Byron Rourke (1989) has proposed a theory of nonverbal LD that identifies a clear biological basis for difficulties acquiring certain types of skills in mathematics. However, by Rourke's own estimate, this type of disability is very rare, and it thus may not provide an adequate description of the factors that are most commonly responsible for academic disabilities in the area of math.

C. Differentiation of LD from Other Conditions

The issue of etiology is important to the field of LD because it provides a basis for establishing that the learning problems of LD children are fundamentally different from those experienced by other types of poor learners. Another way to address the question of differences between LD and other poor learners is in terms of their cognitive or behavioral characteristics. Differences at this level are important to our ability to differentiate reliably between LD and other poor learners during the assessment/diagnostic process.

This issue was forcibly raised relatively early in the history of LD as a formal discipline through the research of James Ysseldyke and his colleagues at the Minnesota Institute for the Study of Learning Disabilities. For example, Ysseldyke summarized over 5 years of research on assessment issues by stating that it was not possible, using current procedures, to reliably differentiate LD from other low achievers (Ysseldyke, 1983). In support of this contention, his group reported data in several studies showing a large degree of overlap in test scores, and test score patterns, between groups of school-identified LD children and nonidentified slow learners (Ysseldyke, Algozzine, Shinn, & McGue, 1982; Shinn, Ysseldyke, Deno, & Tindal, 1982). Further, they also showed that a sample of school psychologists and resource room teachers could not reliably classify children as LD or slow learners using clinical judgment applied to test data (Epps, Ysseldyke & McGue, 1981). Other investigators have found similarly high degrees of commonality on cognitive, affective, and demographic variables between samples of LD, educable mentally retarded, and behaviorally disturbed children in the public schools (Gajar, 1980; Webster & Schenck, 1978).

Although these findings are potentially troublesome to the LD movement because they suggest that public moneys are being selectively channeled to support a group of children (LD) who are not being reliably differentiated from other poor learners, they are irrelevant to basic scientific and conceptual issues. They say more about the socio/political process of identification in the public schools than they do about the scientific validity of the concept of LD (Senf, 1986). Although these findings may suggest that the concept has been overextended in practice, or that factors other than data about the child's psychological characteristics are important to placement decisions (Ysseldyke, 1983), they do not address basic scientific questions about the uniqueness of LD children.

However, recent work on reading disabilities has addressed this question directly. The preponderance of this work directly challenges the validity of traditional operational definitions of reading disability that have utilized a discrepancy between general intelligence and reading ability as part of the diagnostic process. Traditional diagnostic practices have assumed that specific reading disability (reading ability discrepant from intelligence) was fundamentally different from reading problems in children whose level of general ability was consistent with their poor reading skills. There are now four major kinds of evidence against this assumption.

First, early reports (Rutter & Yule, 1975) that reading disabilities were distributed bimodally (implying that there were two different underlying populations of poor readers) have not been replicated in more recent, well-designed epidemiological studies (Shaywitz, Escobar, Shaywitz, Fletcher, & Makuch, 1992; Silva, McGee, & Williams, 1985; Stevenson, 1988). Second, careful investigations of the cognitive profiles of discrepant and nondiscrepant poor readers indicate that they do not differ in the cognitive abilities most related to word-level reading difficulties (Fletcher, et al., 1994; Stanovich & Siegel, 1994). Third, discrepant and nondiscrepant groups show a similar rate of growth in word-level reading skills, both during early elementary school (Foorman, Francis, & Fletcher, 1995) and into early adolescence (Francis, Shaywitz, Stuebing, Shaywitz, & Fletcher, 1995). Finally, studies of the genetics of reading disabilities have shown that discrepant and nondiscrepant word level reading disabilities are equally heritable (Pennington, Gilger, Olson, & DeFries, 1992). Stanovich and Siegel (1994) summed up the evidence against the use of discrepancy-based formulae in identifying reading disabled children this way:

> Neither the phenotypic or the genotypic indicators of poor reading are correlated in a reliable way with IQ discrepancy. If there is a special group of children with reading disabilities who are behaviorally, cognitively, genetically, or neurologically different, it is becoming increasingly unlikely that they can be easily identified by using IQ discrepancy as a proxy for the genetic and neurological differences themselves. Thus, the basic assumption that underlies decades of classification in research and educational practice regarding reading disabilities is becoming increasingly untenable. (p. 48)

Although movement away from discrepancy-based definitions of reading disability toward more inclusive definitions will create many difficult issues in practice (i.e., how to serve the expanded numbers of children with genuine disabilities in reading), it will assist in the early identification of children at risk for reading failure. At present, identification must wait for a discrepancy between IQ and reading ability to develop. However, a more valid approach would be to identify children who show the specific linguistic/phonological characteristics of reading-disabled children (without regard to general ability level) and provide special services to them.

D. Issues in Identification and Service Delivery

As was mentioned earlier, there is currently no convincing evidence that children with LD require qualitatively different kinds of instructional interventions than other types of poor learners. What we do know is that they must be provided with a different kind of instruction than is typically available in the regular classroom. After all, it is their inability to profit from regular classroom instruction that usually leads to a diagnosis of LD! In the case of reading disability, which is the most common form of learning disability and the one we know the most about, it appears that these children require instruction that is more explicit, more intensive, and more supportive than is typically provided in the classroom (Torgesen, in press, b).

Instruction must be more explicit in the sense that it makes fewer assumptions about preexisting skills or children's abilities to make inferences about language regularities that are useful in reading. In other words, children with reading disabilities must be directly taught almost everything they need to know in order to be good readers (Gaskins et al., 1996; Iverson & Tunmer, 1993).

In addition to being more explicit, reading instruction for children with disabilities in this area must be more intense. Greater intensity can be achieved either by lengthening instruction time or by reducing teacher–pupil ratios. Greater intensity of instruction is required not only because reading-disabled children learn skills in this area more slowly, but also because increased explicitness of instruction requires that more things be taught directly by the teacher. Unless beginning reading instruction for children with reading disabilities is more intensive (or lasts significantly longer) than normal instruction, these children will necessarily lag significantly behind their peers in reading growth. Substantially increased intensity of instruction seems especially critical in remedial settings, where children *begin* the instruction already significantly behind their peers.

A third way in which instruction for children with reading disabilities must be modified in order to be successful involves the quality of support that is provided. At least two kinds of special support are required. First, because acquiring reading skills is more difficult for children with reading disabilities than others, they will require more *emotional* support in the form of encouragement, positive feedback, and enthusiasm from the teacher in order to maintain their motivation to learn. Second, instructional interactions must be more supportive in the sense that they involve carefully scaffolded interactions with the child. In a recent investigation of the characteristics of effective reading tutors, Juel (1996) identified the number of *scaffolded* interactions during each teaching session as one of the critical variables predicting differences in effectiveness across tutors. A scaffolded interaction is one in which the teacher enables the student to complete a task (i.e., read a word) by directing the student's attention to a key piece of information or by breaking the task up into smaller, easier to manage ones. The goal of these interactions is to provide just enough support so the child can go through the processing steps necessary to find the right answer. With enough practice, the child becomes able to go through the steps independently. Juel's finding about the importance of carefully scaffolded instructional interactions is consistent with the emphasis on these types of interactions in the teacher's manuals that accompany two instructional programs shown to be effective with children who have severe reading disabilities (Lindamood & Lindamood, 1984; Wilson, 1988).

Although these instructional needs seem well established from research and theory, there is, at present, little consensus about how they can be met within typical school settings. The traditional approach to educating LD children has been in pull-out programs in which one teacher works with relatively small groups (5–15) of children in a special classroom setting. This approach has been criticized both because it does not lead to normal academic growth for many LD children, and because it may negatively affect their emotional/social growth (Osborne, Schulte, & McKinney, 1991). However, the model that has emerged as its replacement, variously labeled the regular education initiative, mainstreaming, or the inclusion movement, is also problematic. For example, Vaughn and her colleagues (Vaughn & Schumm, 1996), after extensive studies of regular classroom teachers' responses to LD students indicate, "general education teachers find many more accommodations desirable than feasible, and are unlikely to make extensive, time consuming adaptations to meet the individual needs of students" (p. 109). Further, "practices that require an inordinate amount of teacher effort for an individual child or subgroup of children are not likely to be adopted" (p. 122). In a series of studies of academic outcomes for LD children being educated with inclusionary practices, Zigmond (1996) reported very discouraging outcomes for the majority of LD students in these settings.

Can LDs be prevented? One obvious consequence of moving toward more inclusive definitions of LDs (that do not require aptitude–achievement discrepancies) is that children at-risk for LDs may be identified very early in their school experience. If special preventive instruction could be provided at the appropriate time, will this eliminate the need for further special instruction of LD children? At present, there are two different ways to answer this question, and both indicate that we do not yet have viable preventive solutions for reading disabilities. First, several early intervention studies have been conducted using a range of service delivery methods from one-on-one instruction, to small group instruction, to whole class instruction (Brown & Felton, 1990; Foorman et al., in press; Torgesen et al., in press; Vellutino et al., 1996). After total instructional times varying from 88 to 340 hr, these interventions proved to be ineffective with from 2 to 4% of the total population. That is, these interventions failed to produce normal reading growth in a significant number of children during the period of intervention. It is not yet known whether the children in these studies who had reading skills in the average range at the conclusion of the intervention will be able to maintain that rate of growth after the special intervention is concluded.

Where long-term follow-up data are available, it also indicates that we do not yet understand all the conditions that need to be in place to prevent reading disabilities in children. For example, follow-up studies of children who successfully complete the popular Reading Recovery program as first graders indicate that a very substantial portion of them either fall behind in reading development or require special reading interventions at some point later in elementary school (Shanahan & Barr, 1995). Another problem with Reading Recovery, from the present point of view, is that many children with the most severe reading disabilities do not complete the program or do not qualify for it.

One promising intervention technique, which is not presently regarded as feasible within most school settings, is to provide very intensive instruction over relatively brief periods of time to children with severe LDs. For example, in an intervention study we are currently conducting, we provide 80 hours of one-on-one instruction in reading over an 8-week period (Torgesen, et al., in press) to third-through fifth-grade children with very serious reading disabilities. In that period, the children make significant gains in reading ability that have been stable, or slightly improved, 1 year postintervention. One clear advantage of this intensive approach is that the students can easily feel themselves improving in reading skill and it requires them to leave their normal classroom for a relatively brief period of time.

In summary, the most critical issue for service delivery is one that has been with the field since its inception. How can we deliver high-quality, effective instruction to all children with LDs? At present, the Zeitgeist suggests that the regular classroom is the place where all LD children should be educated. However, LD children who need instruction that is more explicit, more intensive, and more supportive than normal are going to be very difficult to teach in most regular classroom settings. In addition to the time constraints involved, in the case of reading, added explicitness of instruction implies that teachers need much more knowledge about language and reading processes than they currently possess (Moats, 1995). Much of our current research on reading disabilities (Olson, Wise, Johnson, & Ring, in press) suggests that we have seriously underestimated the amount and quality of instruction these children require in order to acquire useful reading skills. One of the great challenges for our field in the next decade will be to learn the conditions that need to be in place, and then to accomplish the political work to put them in place, for all children with LDs to acquire a full range of useful academic skills.

IV. CONCLUDING COMMENTS

When I wrote an earlier version of this introductory chapter 7 years ago, I predicted that the coming decade would be a time of great change for the field of LDs. I was right in one sense and wrong in another. I was wrong because there has been little change in the status of the field as a social/political/educational movement over the past 7 years. Learning disabilities continues to be a strong and vital force within the larger special and regular education communities. Its services, which are mandated by recently reaffirmed law, are offered to vast numbers of children with a variety of very difficult and unusual educational problems. Professionals in the field continue to organize themselves into strong associations that provide adequate means for communication about research and professional issues. Additionally, the interests of LD children and adults are served by a number of strong associations that have as a primary aim the protection of their rights to a free and appropriate education as well as appropriate accommodations in the workplace. Finally, research in the area is growing and becoming more diverse, and many new research initiatives are supported by governmental agencies.

I was right that there would be substantial improvements in our knowledge about LDs, particularly for the most common disability that affects acquisition of reading skills. We know, for example, that reading disability most frequently involves difficulties in learning to identify words rapidly and accurately, and that the primary cause of this problem is deficiencies in the ability to process the phonological features of language. Furthermore, we know that a substantial proportion of individual differences in phonological abilities is transmitted genetically, and we are beginning to form relatively clear ideas of the specific locations in the brain that are affected. All these facts support traditional definitions of LDs that suggest they arise from intrinsic processing disabilities that are constitutionally based. However, the consistent finding that reading problems arise from essentially the same handicapping conditions in children whose reading levels are discrepant and nondiscrepant from their IQ invalidates commonly used aptitude-achievement discrepancy formulae to identify LD children. In order to bring practice in line with the best scientific information currently available, the field should adopt a more inclusive definition of reading disabilities. Children should not be denied LD services because their aptitude–achievement discrepancy is not large enough; rather, all children who show the primary symptoms of phonologically based reading disabilities should receive appropriate instructional interventions.

At this point in time, the field of LD is on an exciting path. It is solidly supported in law, it has an enormous number of well-informed advocates and professionals working on its behalf, and it is the subject of challenging and programmatic research. Let us hope that the next decade brings continued new knowledge and appropriate expansion of services to all children and adults with LD.

References

Arter, J. A., & Jenkins, J. R. (1979). Differential diagnostic prescriptive teaching: A critical appraisal. *Review of Educational Research, 49,* 517–555.

Blachman, B. (1997). Early intervention and phonological awareness: A cautionary tale. In B. Blachman (Ed.), *Foundations of reading acquisition and dyslexia: Implications for early intervention* (pp. 409–430). Mahwah, NJ: Lawrence Erlbaum Associates.

Brady, S., & Shankweiler, D. (1991). *Phonological processes in literacy: A tribute to Isabelle Y. Liberman.* Hillsdale, NJ: Lawrence Erlbaum Assoc.

Brown, A. L., & Campione, J. C. (1986). Psychological theory and the study of learning disabilities. *American Psychologist, 14,* 1059–1068.

Brown, A. L., & Palincsar, A. S. (1987). Reciprocal teaching of comprehension strategies: A natural history of one program for enhancing learning. In L. Borkowski & L. D. Day (Eds.), *Intelligence and Exceptionality: New directions for theory, assessment, and instructional practices* (pp. 81–132) New York: Ablex.

Brown, I. S., & Felton, R. H. (1990). Effects of instruction on beginning reading skills in children at risk for reading disability. *Reading and Writing: An Interdisciplinary Journal, 2,* 223–241.

Bush, W. J., & Giles, M. T. (1969). *Aids to psycholinguistics teaching*. Columbus, OH: Merrill.

Butterfield, E. D., & Ferretti, R. P. (1987). Toward a theoretical integration of cognitive hypotheses about intellectual differences among children. In L. Borkowski & L. D. Day (Eds.), *Cognition in special children: Comparative approaches to retardation, learning disabilities, and giftedness* (pp. 195–234). New York: Ablex.

Ceci, S. J., & Baker, J. G. (1990). On learning . . . more or less: A knowledge × process × context view of learning disabilities. In J. K. Torgesen (Ed.), *Cognitive and behavioral characteristics of children with learning disabilities* (pp. 159–178). Austin, TX: PRO-ED.

Chalfant, J. C., & Scheffelin, M. A. (1969). *Central processing dysfunction in children: A review of research*. NINDS Monographs, Bethesda, MD, U.S. Department of Health, Education, and Welfare.

Coles, G. S. (1987). *The learning mystique: A critical look at "learning disabilities."* New York: Pantheon.

Cruickshank, W. M., Bentzen, F. A., Ratzeburg, F. H., & Tannhauser, M. T. (1961). *A teaching method for brain-injured and hyperactive children*. Syracuse: Syracuse University Press.

Cruickshank, W. M., Bice, H. V., & Wallen, N. E. (1957). *Perception and cerebral palsy*. Syracuse: Syracuse University Press.

Damasio, A. R., & Geschwind, N. (1984). The neural basis of language. *Annual Review of Neurosciences, 7,* 127–147.

Doris, J. (1986). Learning disabilities. In S. J. Ceci (Ed.), *Handbook of cognitive, social and neuropsychological aspects of learning disabilities* (pp. 3–53). Hillsdale, NJ: Erlbaum Assoc.

Durrell, D. D. (1940). *Improvement of basic reading abilities*. New York, NY: World Book Company.

Ellis, E. S., Lenz, B. K., & Sabornie, E. J. (1987). Generalization and adaptation of learning strategies to natural environments: Part 2: Research into Practice. *Remedial and Special Education, 8,* 6–23.

Epps, S., Ysseldyke, J. E., & McGue, M. (1981). *Differentiating LD and non-LD students: "I know one when I see one."* Minneapolis, MN: Institute for Research on Learning Disabilities.

Fletcher, J. M., Shaywitz, S. E., Shankweiler, D. P., Katz, L., Liberman, I. Y., Stuebing, K. K., Francis, D. J., Fowler, A. E., & Shaywitz, B. A. (1994). Cognitive profiles of reading disability: Comparisons of discrepancy and low achievement definitions. *Journal of Educational Psychology, 86,* 6–23.

Fletcher, J. M., & Francis, D. J. (1997, May). *Classification of LD: What have we learned?* Address presented at conference on Progress and Promise in Research and Education for Individuals with Learning Disabilities. Washington, DC.

Flowers, L., Wood, F. B., & Naylor, C. E. (1989). *Regional cerebral blood flow in adults diagnosed as reading disabled in childhood.* Unpublished manuscript, Bowman-Gray School of Medicine.

Foorman, B. R., Francis, D. J., & Fletcher, J. M. (1995, March). *Growth of phonological processing skills in beginning reading: The lag versus deficit model revisited.* Paper presented at the Society for Research on Child Development, Indianapolis, IN.

Foorman, B. R., Francis, D. J., Beeler, T., Winikates, D., & Fletcher, J. M. (in press). Early interventions for children with reading problems: Study designs and preliminary findings. *Learning Disabilities: A Multi-Disciplinary Journal.*

Francis, D. J., Shaywitz, S. E., Stuebing, K. K., Shaywitz, B. A., & Fletcher, J. M. (1995, March). *Developmental lag versus deficit models of reading disability: A longitudinal, individual growth curves analysis.* Paper presented at the Society for Research in Child Development, Indianapolis, IN.

Frostig, M., Lefever, D. W., & Whittlesey, J. R. B. (1964). *The Marianne Frostig developmental test of visual perception.* Palo Alto: Consulting Psychology Press.

Gajar, A. H. (1980). Characteristics across exceptional categories: EMR, LD, and ED. *Journal of Special Education, 14,* 165–173.

Galaburda, A. M. (1988). The pathogenesis of childhood dyslexia. In F. Plum (Ed.), *Language, communication, and the brain* (pp. 127–137). New York: Raven Press.

Gaskins, I. W., Ehri, L. C., Cress, C., O'Hara, C., & Donnelly, K. (1996). Procedures for word learning: Making discoveries about words. *The Reading Teacher, 50,* 312–327.

Graham, S., & Harris, K. R. (1993). Teaching writing strategies to students with learning disabilities: Issues and recommendations, In L. J. Meltzer (Ed.) *Strategy assessment and instruction for students with learning disabilities* (pp. 271–292). Austin, TX: PRO-ED.

Hallahan, D. P. & Cruickshank, W. M. (1973). *Psycho-educational foundations of learning disabilities.* Englewood Cliffs, NJ: Prentice-Hall.

Hallahan, D. P., Kauffman, J. M., & Lloyd, J. W. (1985). *Introduction to learning disabilities.* Englewood Cliffs, NJ: Prentice-Hall.

Hammill, D. D. (1972). Training visual perpetual processes. *Journal of Learning Disabilities, 5,* 552–559.

Hammill, D. D. (1990). On defining learning disabilities: An emerging consensus. *Journal of Learning Disabilities, 23,* 74–84.

Hammill, D. D., Goodman, L., & Wiederholt, J. L. (1974). Visual motor processes: What success have we had in training them? *The Reading Teacher, 27,* 469–478.

Hammill, D. D., & Larson, S. C. (1974). The efficacy of psycholinguistic training. *Exceptional Children, 41,* 5–14.

Hartman, N. C., & Hartman, R. K. (1973). Perceptual handicap or reading disability? *The Reading Teacher, 26,* 684–695.

Head, H. (1926). *Aphasia and kindred disorders of speech.* Vol. I. London: Cambridge University Press.

Hinshelwood, J. (1917). *Congenital word blindness.* London: H. K. Lewis.

Interagency Committee on Learning Disabilities (1987). *Learning disabilities: A Report to the U.S. Congress.* Bethesda, MD: National Institutes of Health.

Iversen, S., & Tunmer, W. E. (1993). Phonological processing skills and the reading recovery program. *Journal of Educational Psychology, 85,* 112–126.

Johnson, D. J., & Mykelbust, H. R. (1967). *Learning disabilities: Educational principles and practices.* New York: Grune & Stratton.

Juel, C. (1996). What makes literacy tutoring effective? *Reading Research Quarterly, 31,* 268–289.

Kass, C. E. (1970). *Final report: Advanced institute for leadership personnel in learning disabilities.* Contract No. OEG-09-121013-3021-031, U.S. Office of Education, Department of Special Education, University of Arizona, Tucson, Arizona.

Kavale, K., & Forness, S. R. (1985). *The science of learning disabilities.* San Diego, CA: College Hill Press.

Kavanagh, J. F., & Truss, T. J. (1988). *Learning disabilities: Proceedings of the national conference.* Parkton, MD: York Press.

Kephart, N. C. (1960). *The slow learner in the classroom.* Columbus, OH: Charles E. Merrill.

Kephart, N. C., & Strauss, A. A. (1940). A clinical factor influencing variations in IQ. *American Journal of Orthopsychiatry, 10,* 345–350.

Kirk, S. A. (1963). *Behavioral diagnosis and remediation of learning disabilities.* Proceedings of the Annual Meeting of the Conference on Exploration into the Problems of the Perceptually handicapped Child. Vol. 1.

Krik, S. A., & Jirk, W. D. (1971). *Psycholiguistic learning disabilities: Diagnosis and remediation.* Chicago, IL: University of Illinois Press.

Liberman, I. Y., Shankweiler, D., Orlando, C., Harris, K. S., & Berti, F. B. (1971). Letter confusions and reversals of sequence in the beginning reader: Implications for Orton's Theory of Developmental Dyslexia. *Cortex, 7,* 127–142.

Lindamood, C. H., & Lindamood, P. C. (1984). *Auditory discrimination in depth.* Austin, TX: PRO-ED, Inc.

Lyon, G. R. (1985). Identification and remediation of learning disability subtypes: Preliminary findings. *Learning Disabilities Focus, 1,* 21–35.

Lyon, G. R. (1994). *Frames of reference for the assessment of learning disabilities: New views on measurement issues.* Baltimore, MD: Brooks Publishing.

Lyon, G. R. (1995). Toward a definition of dyslexia. *Annals of Dyslexia, 45,* 3–27.

Lyon, G. R. (in press). Research initiatives and discoveries in learning disabilities: Contributions from scientists supported by the National Institute of Child Health and Human Development. *Journal of Child Neurology.*

Mann, L. (1971). Psychometric phenology and the new faculty psychology: The case against ability assessment and training. *Journal of Special Education, 5,* 3–14.

Mann, L. (1979). *On the trail of process.* New York: Grune & Stratton.

Mann, L., & Phillips, W. A. (1967). Fractional practices in special education: a critique. *Exceptional Children, 33,* 311–317.

McCarthy, J. J., & Kirk, S. A. (1961). *Illinois Test of Psycholinguistic Abilities: Experimental Version.* Urbana: University of Illinois Press.

Meltzer, L. J. (1993). Strategy assessment and instruction for students with learning disabilities. Austin, TX: PRO-ED, Inc.

Moats, L. C. (1995). The missing foundation in teacher education. *American Educator, 19,* 9–51.

Myers, P., & Hammill, D. D. (1990). *Learning disabilities: Basic concepts, assessment practices, and instructional strategies.* Austin, TX: PRO-ED.

Newcomer, P. L., & Hammill, D. D. (1975). ITPA and academic achievement. *The Reading Teacher, 28,* 731–741.

National Joint Committee on Learning Disabilities. (1988). (Letter to NJCLD organizations).

Olsen, R., Forsberg, H., & Wise, B. (1994). Genes, environment, and the development of orthographic skills. In V. W. Berninger (Ed.), *The varieties of orthographic knowledge I: Theoretical and developmental issues* (pp. 27–71). Dordrecht, The Netherlands: Kluwer Academic Publishers.

Olson, R. (1997, May). *The genetics of LD: Twin studies.* Address presented at conference on Progress and Promise in Research and Education for Individuals with Learning Disabilities. Washington, DC.

Olson, R. K., Wise, B., Johnson, M., & Ring, J. (1997). The etiology and remediation of phonologically based word recognition and spelling disabilities: Are phonological deficits the "hole" story? In B. Blachman (Ed.), *Foundations of reading acquisition* (pp. 305–326). Mahwah, NJ: Lawrence Erlbaum Associates, Inc.

Orton, S. T. (1937). *Reading, writing, and speech problems in children.* New York: Norton.

Osborne, S. S., Schulte, A. G., & McKinney, J. D. (1991). A longitudinal study of students with learning disabilities in mainstream and resource programs. *Exceptionality, 2,* 81–95.

Palincsar, A. S., Winn, J., David, Y., Snyder, B., & Stevens, D. (1993). Approaches to strategic reading instruction reflecting different assumptions regarding teaching and learning. In L. J. Meltzer (Ed.), *Strategy assessment and instruction for students with learning disabilities.* Austin, TX: PRO-ED, Inc.

Pennington, B. F., Gilger, J. W., Olson, R. K., & DeFries, J. C. (1992). The external validity of age-versus IQ-discrepancy definitions of reading disability: Lessons from a twin study. *Journal of Learning Disabilities, 25,* 562–573.

Rourke, B. P. (1989). *Nonverbal learning disabilities: The syndrome and the model.* Guilford Publications, Inc: New York.

Rutter, M., & Yule, W. (1975). The concept of specific reading retardation. *Journal of Child Psychology and Psychiatry, 16,* 181–197.

Sarason, S. B. (1949). *Psychological problems in mental deficiency.* New York: Harper.

Senf, G. M. (1986). LD research in sociological and scientific perspective. In J. K. Torgesen & B. Y. L. Wong (Eds.), *Psychological and educational perspectives on learning disabilities* (pp. 27–54). New York: Academic Press.

Shanahan, T., & Barr, R. (1995). Reading recovery: An independent evaluation of the effects of an early instructional intervention for at-risk learners. *Reading Research Quarterly, 30,* 958–996.

Shankweiler, D., & Liberman, I. Y. (1989). *Phonology and reading disability.* Ann Arbor: University of Michigan Press.

Share, D. L., & Stanovich, K. E. (1995). Cognitive processes in early reading development: A model of acquisition and individual differences. *Issues in Education: Contributions from Educational Psychology, 1,* 1–35.

Shaywitz, S. E. (1996). Dyslexia. *Scientific American, 97,* 98–104.

Shaywitz, S. E., Escobar, M. D., Shaywitz, B. A., Fletcher, J. M., & Makuch, R. (1992). Evidence that dyslexia may represent the lower tail of a normal distribution of reading ability. *The New England Journal of Medicine, 326,* 145–150.

Shinn, M. R., Ysseldyke, J., Deno, S., & Tindal, G. (1982). *Comparison of psychometric and functional differences between students labeled learning disabled and low achieving.* Research report no. 71, Institute for Research on Learning Disabilities, University of Minnesota.

Siegel, L. S. (1989). IQ is irrelevant to the definition of learning disabilities. *Journal of Learning Disabilities, 22,* 469–479.

Silva, P. A., McGee, R., & Williams, S. (1985). Some characteristics of 9-year-old boys with general reading backwardness or specific reading retardation. *Journal of Child Psychology and Psychiatry, 26,* 407–421.

Stanovich, K. E. (1986). Cognitive processes and the reading problems of learning-disabled children: Evaluating the assumption of specificity. In J. K. Torgesen & B. Y. L. Wong (Eds.), *Psychological and educational perspectives on learning disabilities.* New York: Academic Press.

Stanovich, K. E. (1990). Explaining the differences between the dyslexic and the garden-variety poor reader: The phonological-core variable-difference model. In J. Torgesen (Ed.), *Cognitive and behavioral characteristics of children with learning disabilities* (pp. 87–122). Austin, TX: PRO-ED.

Stanovich, K. E. (1993). The construct validity of discrepancy definitions of reading disability. In G. R. Lyon, D. Gray, J. Kavanagh, & N. Drasnegor (Eds.), *Better understanding learning disabilities: New views on research and their implications for public policies.* Baltimore: Paul H. Brookes Publishing.

Stanovich, K. E., & Siegel, L. S. (1994). The phenotypic performance profile of reading-disabled children: A regression-based test of the phonological-core variable-difference model. *Journal of Educational Psychology, 86,* 24–53.

Stevenson, J. (1988). Which aspects of reading disability show a "hump" in their distribution? *Applied Cognitive Psychology, 2,* 77–85.

Strauss, A. A. (1943). Diagnosis and education of the cripplebrained, deficient child. *Journal of Exceptional Children, 9,* 163–168.

Strauss, A. A., & Kephart, N. C. (1955). *Psychopathology and education of the brain-injured child: Progress in theory and clinic* (Vol. 2). New York: Grune and Stratton.

Strauss, A. A., & Lehtinen, L. E. (1947). *Psychopathology and education of the brain injured child.* New York: Grune & Stratton.

Torgesen, J. K. (1979). What shall we do with psychological processes? *Journal of Learning Disabilities, 12,* 514–521.

Torgesen, J. K. (1986). Learning disabilities theory: Its current state and future prospects. *Journal of Learning Disabilities, 19,* 399–407.

Torgesen, J. K. (1993). Variations on theory in learning disabilities. In R. Lyon, D. Gray, N. Krasnegor, & J. Kavenagh (Eds.), *Better understanding learning disabilities: Perspectives on classification, identification, and assessment and their implications for education and policy.* Baltimore: Brookes Publishing.

Torgesen, J. K. (in press, a). Phonologically based reading disabilities: Toward a coherent theory of one kind of learning disability. In R. J. Sternberg & L. Spear-Swerling (Eds.), *Perspectives on learning disabilities.* Hillsdale, NJ: Lawrence Erlbaum Assoc.

Torgesen, J. K. (in press, b). Instruction interventions for children with reading disabilities. In S. Shapiro, D. Accardo, & C. Capute (Eds.), *Dyslexia: Its conceptualization, diagnosis, and treatment.* Parkton, MD: York Press.

Torgesen, J. K., Wagner, R. K., Rashotte, C. A., Alexander, A. W., & Conway, T. (in press). Preventive and remedial interventions for children with severe reading disabilities. *Learning Disabilities: An Interdisciplinary Journal.*

Vaughn, S., & Schumm, J. S. (1996). Classroom ecologies: Classroom interactions and implications for inclusion of students with learning disabilities. In D. L. Speece & B. K. Keogh (Eds.), *Research on classroom ecologies* (pp. 107–124). Mahwah, NJ: Lawrence Erlbaum Associates.

Vellutino, F. R., Scanlon, D. M., Sipay, E. R., Small, S. G., Pratt, A., Chen, R., & Denckla, M. B. (1996). Cognitive profiles of difficult-to-remediate and readily remediated poor readers: Early intervention as a vehicle for distinguishing between cognitive and experiential deficits as basic causes of specific reading disability. *Journal of Educational Psychology, 88,* 601–638.

Vellutino, F. R., Steger, B. M., Moyer, S. C., Hardin, C. J., & Niles, J. A. (1977). Has the perceptual deficit hypothesis led us astray? *Journal of Learning Disabilities, 10,* 375–385.

Vernon, M. D. (1957). *Backwardness in reading.* London: Cambridge University Press.

Wagner, R. K., Torgesen, J. K., & Rashotte, C. A. (1994). The development of reading-related phonological processing abilities: New evidence of bi-directional causality from a latent variable longitudinal study. *Developmental Psychology, 30,* 73–87.

Webster, R. E., & Schenck, S. J. (1978). Diagnostic test pattern differences among LD, ED, EMH, and multi-handicapped students. *Journal of Educational Research, 72,* 75–80.

Wiederholt, J. L. (1974). Historical perspectives on the education of the learning disabled. In L. Mann & D. A. Sabatino (Eds.), *The second review of special education* (pp. 103–152). Austin, TX: PRO-ED.

Wiederholt, J. L., & Hammill, D. D. (1971). Use of the FrostigHorne Visual Perceptual Program in the urban school. *Psychology in the Schools, 8,* 268–274.

Wilson, B. A. (1988). *Instructor manual.* Millbury, MA: Wilson Language Training.

Wong, B. Y. L. (1986). Problems and issues in the definition of learning disabilities. In J. K. Torgesen & B. Y. L. Wong (Eds.), *Psychological and educational perspectives on learning disabilities* (pp. 1–25). San Diego: Academic Press.

Wood, F. (1997, May). Electrophysiological and metabolic linkages to the genetics of learning disabilities. Address presented at conference on Progress and Promise in Research and Education for Individuals with Learning Disabilities. Washington, DC.

Ysseldyke, J. E. (1973). Diagnostic-prescriptive teaching: The search for aptitude-treatment interactions. In L. Mann & D. Sabatino (Eds.), *The first review of special education.* Austin, TX: PRO-ED.

Ysseldyke, J. E. (1983). Current practices in making psychoeducational decisions about learning disabled students. *Journal of Learning Disabilities, 16,* 209–219.

Ysseldyke, J. E., Algozzine, B., Shinn, M., & McGue, M. (1982). Similarities and differences between students labeled underachievers and learning disabled. *Journal of Special Education, 16,* 73–85.

Zigmond, N. (1996). Organization and management of general education classrooms. In D. L. Speece & B. K. Keogh (Eds.), *Research on classroom ecologies* (pp. 163–190). Mahwah, NJ: Lawrence Erlbaum Associates.

CHAPTER 2

Assessment in Learning Disabilities with a Focus on Curriculum-Based Measurement

Gerald Tindal

I. ASSESSMENT IN LEARNING DISABILITIES

The purpose of this chapter is to address assessment issues and options in learning disabilities (LD). This is an update of the original chapter in an earlier edition of this book with a primary focus of coverage on curriculum-based measurement (CBM). This form of assessment continues to be a critical area in which teachers and psychologists need to be skilled for two reasons. First, in special education, the most significant direction to emerge in the past decade is the inclusion of students with disabilities in general education settings. Second, in the field of measurement, the most significant area of research and development to appear is the use of performance tasks. CBM is applicable in both general and special education and can be considered a good example of performance assessment. Therefore, these two developments increase the likelihood that CBM is a significant assessment strategy in the classroom.

Another obvious reason for the emphasis on CBM includes the extensive research and development on this subject that has occurred over the past two

Learning about Learning Disabilities, Second Edition

decades, which reflects the need to use a measurement system capable of covering a range of educational decisions in which considerable technical adequacy has been documented. For example, CBM has been used in investigations that focus on the utility of basic measurement systems, teacher planning, computer-based measurement, peer tutoring, program evaluation, and instructional evaluation. In all of these applications, data have been collected and empirical outcomes generated. In many different studies, the purpose has been to establish reliable measures that allow valid conclusions to be made. Basically, from the initial identification of students who are at risk of academic failure and/or with LDs to the formative evaluation of instructional outcomes and the summative evaluation of programs, CBM has been used to tie many different educational decisions together.

The literature reviewed here begins with 1984, the last year of the Institute for Research on Learning Disabilities (IRLD), where much of the early technical research on CBM was conducted and the year in which these studies began to appear in the professional literature. The chapter begins with a definition of CBM that entails an important perspective on assessment. Next, three contexts are considered within which all assessment in special education needs to be viewed. Then, the chapter is organized around a series of decisions that reflect the various areas within which CBM has been studied and practiced: (a) screening and identification of students with disabilities; (b) grouping students; (c) setting goals on Individualized Educational Plans (IEPs); (d) measuring the individual progress of students; (e) formatively monitoring the success of instructional programs; and (f) monitoring student progress with computers. Finally, two applications of CBM in secondary content areas are presented: one identifies general outcome indicators and the other focuses on a conceptual understanding of teaching and learning.

Because most of the technical research that was originally conducted in the development of the reading, spelling, and writing measures has been reviewed extensively (see Marston, 1989), this chapter focuses on the application of CBM as classroom assessments for students with LDs; only in the extension of CBM into secondary programs is the more basic technical research emphasized dealing with reliability and criterion validity.

II. CURRICULUM-BASED MEASUREMENT: A DEFINITION AND A PERSPECTIVE

Various definitions of CBM have been used over the years (cf. Tindal, 1988). Throughout the history of CBM, a number of published papers have defined it as a general outcome indicator. In an early description of CBM, Deno (1987) describes two distinctive features that characterize CBM: (a) presentation of reliability and validity data, and (b) use of constant task measurement. Although the former attribute is generally assumed to be important and hopefully present in most assessments for students with LDs, the latter attribute is rarely seen or considered with most assessment programs in special education. Ironically, it may be the fundamental premise upon which all assessments need to be based within special education.

This view of CBM distinguishes it from other forms of curriculum-based assessment (CBM). For example, Tucker (1985), Gickling (cf. Gickling & Thompson, 1985) and Howell's (cf. Fox, Howell, Morehead, & Zucker, 1993) models of assessment reflect specific subskill mastery measurement (Fuchs & Deno, 1991b) and fail to depict the three critical features noted in this chapter (time series measurement, systematic decision making, and empirical basis used to validate instruction). In the definitions by Tucker and Gickling, little development of either application in classrooms or a program of research has ever been conducted, leaving its utility to speculation. In the definition by Howell, application has tended to focus primarily on curriculum design and instruction with less emphasis on measurement over time and across various decisions. As a consequence, less emphasis has been placed on empirically validating CBM as a measurement system (Deno & Fuchs, 1987).

As Deno (1990) notes, the essential focus in special education is on both individual differences and individual difference. This seeming paradox arises from a history of assessment in which two models have been used to frame tests and measures. Individual differences are established through a nomothetic approach in which individuals are measured within groups, and programs are evaluated in terms of group differences (a norm-referenced approach). In contrast, an individual difference assessment is based on an idiographic approach (individual-referenced) in which each student is measured as a single subject, and change over time is the major outcome in evaluating the effectiveness of programs. This latter aspect requires comparability in measures over time, which in turn requires constant task measurement.

A major issue, however, is that assessment practices in special education historically have been premised on the nomothetic approach, emphasizing placement of individuals within programs on the shaky proposition that an aptitude-by-treatment interaction is both extant and operational. Yet as Deno (1990) notes, this interaction has not proven to be helpful in 20 years of research in the social sciences:

> What seems clear from reading current research on aptitude-treatment interactions (ATIs) is that general laws are difficult to obtain and that the traditional diagnostic-prescriptive teaching approach upon which P.L. 94-142 (now I.D.E.A.) rests is technically infeasible. Indeed, although we talk a great deal about diagnostic procedures in special education, the use of those procedures very likely rests on superstitious tradition. (p. 163)

The fundamental problem with all nomothetic measurement is that any (and all) outcomes, while providing guidance in making predictions to groups of individuals, fail to be equally clear or accurate in making predictions to individual members within that group or similar groups. In reporting outcomes from this approach, a significant effect simply means that most individuals in a group performed at a specific level (usually referenced as the average). This average, however, depicts the group *in general* and always is accompanied by a measure of variance (usually referenced as the standard deviation). In the end, in any group, many students are present for whom the average is not representative (i.e., they are above or below the average). And, in traditional statistical analyses, for these students, the more they are deviant, the less reliable is the mean for reflecting their score. For students with LDs, who frequently are quite below the average, this approach is insensitive to making decisions about program effects.

The alternative to this paradigm is an idiographic approach in which predictions are treated as hypotheses and student performance data are used to adjust the programs in an effort to continuously optimize individual effectiveness. This view of assessment, though seemingly simple and straightforward, contains a number of assumptions that need to be articulated. First, it requires time-series measures, which allow for continuous collection of student performance, which in turn requires adequate alternate forms of the stimulus materials used to generate student performance. Second, this system requires a decision-making model for ascertaining the degree to which programs are working, which in turn implies easy replication across diverse settings and different decisions. Third, the psychometric adequacy of the entire data collection and decision-making process needs to be validated using Messick's (1989) conception of validity as a singular construct, necessitating a line of research that provides empirical justification. Importantly, it is not the measurement system that is validated but the decision made from the measures. In this sense, then, the evidential and the consequential bases are considered in the use and interpretation of tests and measures.

The last caveat to be addressed in demarcating CBM is the term *curriculum,* which originally was considered by Deno (1992) as a framework and process that could be applied by teachers to any curriculum. Indeed, because the purpose of CBM is to formatively evaluate instructional programs, the measurement of success often uses materials that are not curriculum bound (Fuchs & Deno, 1991a) in order to avoid confusing the independent variable with the dependent measure. Therefore, as Fuchs and Deno (1994) have argued, sampling measurement materials within instructional programs "is not essential for ensuring measurement validity of decisions about student achievement or the instructional utility of the measurement" (p. 19). Rather, they posit that better assessment systems would (a) provide for repeated testing on material of comparable difficulty; (b) yield valid outcome indicators by addressing an important question about the degree to which instruction is effective and the skills being learned are part of improvement in generalized outcomes; and (c) make student work available for judgment to help determine what types of instructional adjustments are needed.

III. THE CONTEXT OF ASSESSMENT
AND LEARNING DISABILITIES

Three important contexts need to be considered in understanding the range of assessment options for students with LDs. The first is the prevalence of large-scale assessments in most districts, often mandated by state education agencies (SEAs). In the latest authorization of Individuals with Disabilities Education Act (IDEA) (1997), students with disabilities need to be considered for participation in these tests. The second is the need to develop IEPs that are procedurally correct as well as technically adequate and functional. In assessing students with LDs, a connection needs to exist between these two measurement systems; large-scale, statewide tests and the IEPs. The third context is the focus on experimentally developing instructional programs: Student outcomes need to be used for vindicating programs. In summary, special education teachers must develop educational programs that prepare students to take part in and succeed on high-stakes tests and as well, ensure that the IEP is appropriate and effective. This outcome can be achieved only with effective measurement systems.

A. Ensuring the Success of Students with LDs on High-Stakes Tests

In many current educational programs, a large gap exists between the measures of the classroom and the measures of the larger system (local educational agencies [LEAs] and SEAs, the latter of which are increasingly used to judge the effectiveness of programs for both individuals and groups). Most large-scale tests look like other norm-referenced measurement systems, yet also continue to take on many features of criterion-referenced measurement procedures. Yet, several distinctions appear that have led some to use the term "standards-based" measures in describing them (cf. Taylor, 1994). The reason is that assessment in education, whether special or general, is focused on passing high and challenging benchmarks and standards.

As of 1994, 45 states had initiated these types of large-scale assessment programs. Students were tested in math, language arts, writing, science, and social science. These assessments were composed primarily of writing samples as well as norm- or criterion-referenced multiple-choice tests. The primary purpose for statewide assessment has been to improve instruction of the curriculum, evaluate programs, report on school performance, and diagnose students in order to place them in programs or matriculate them from school. Yet, in many states the stakes have been high, with several possible consequences including placement of schools on probation, loss of accreditation or funding, takeover, or dissolution of schools (Bond, Breskamp, & Roeber, 1996).

An even more pervasive issue with many of the new forms of assessment used in large-scale testing programs is the confluence of skills needed to be successful. No longer are the skills demarcated as reading, math, or writing. Rather, success depends on being proficient in many of these areas concurrently. Math problems are being used that, in reflecting the NCME standards, require students not only to solve the problem but explain why they have solved the problem as they have. Many multiple-choice tests require extensive reading skills. Scoring guides are used that reflect complex constructs of reading and writing with multitrait scoring. Therefore, teachers increasingly need to plan their assessments to reflect these complex constructs, and they also must consider teaching from a different perspective.

Finally, in most states, accommodations are being implemented to allow increased participation of students with disabilities in these testing programs. Generally, they are organized into either of two groups (Thurlow, Scott, & Ysseldyke, 1995): (a) acceptable for use because they make no changes in score meaning, thereby allowing scores to be aggregated; or (b) not acceptable for use because they are thought to change the construct measured with results that are either dissaggregated or unreported. Although these accommodations are critical in assessment of students with LDs and may legitimately and significantly help students perform better (see, Tindal, Heath, Hollenbeck, Almond, & Harniss, in press, for a description of the effects from reading a math test during administration), many teachers are not aware of what is and what is not allowed (Hollenbeck, Almond, & Tindal, 1997). As a consequence, either (a) the performance for students receiving special education services is lowered needlessly because of the influence of the disability and the lack of an accepted accommodation, or (b) accommodations are made in the test in an inappropriate manner that therefore disqualifies the performance. Importantly, as states begin to establish clearer policy on implementation of large-scale tests, documentation of accommodations on the IEP is required for them to be applied during the testing.

B. Technically Adequate and Functional IEPs

IEPs can, therefore, be based either on these large-scale assessments or on some type of classroom measurement system. In making this decision, teachers need to consider two issues of a measurement system: (a) it must be predictive of performance on the large-scale tests, and (b) it must be sensitive to individual student (educational) programs. Generally, these large-scale tests are not sensitive to instructional programs over a short period of time. Rather, they are constructed to reflect the effects of instruction over long periods of time. Furthermore, these tests often are limited to benchmark standards in key grade levels rather than all grade levels. Therefore, they are of limited utility in application within an IEP.

In contrast, the perspective promulgated in this chapter fosters development of IEPs using initial assessment data that (a) are technically adequate, (b) relate to other general outcomes established for groups of students, and (c) are based on general outcome indicators sensitive for individual students. In this process, then, all parts of the IEP—the present level of performance, long-range goals, and short-term objectives—need to be systematically developed and used to make an individual difference. In this process, we distinguish between informal and formal assessment. Although some educators view teacher-made tests and measures as informal, CBM is generally viewed as a formal measurement system to avoid the problems noted by Fuchs and Fuchs (1984b) when teacher assessment is unsystematically conducted.

In this particular study (Fuchs & Fuchs, 1984b), conducted with 20 teacher trainees, 17 relied upon unsystematic observations for determining student success on behavioral objectives *they had written.* Although they and their cooperating teachers were "very sure" of the success of their lesson, frequently they were inaccurate: "When pupils achieved the instructional objectives, trainees' and cooperating teachers' judgments were always accurate; when objectives were not met, evaluation tended to be inaccurate" (p. 31). In a later study on this issue, Bentz and Fuchs (1993) asked nine teachers to make judgments about mastery in math for students they had taught. Concurrently, students' progress was tracked with a computer analysis that placed each student on a continuum of mastery scale for several different skills. Even with this information, however, teachers identified most skills as mastered, even though the actual percentage of students identified as mastered by the CBM probes never exceeded 75% for any skill; only 3 of 41 judgments corresponded to actual student mastery greater than 70%.

As a consequence, an emphasis is placed on the formal collection of student performance indicators and the explicit use of decision rules to evaluate the effects of program outcomes. Furthermore, the IEP is viewed as the key document to include both of these components by reference to a present level of performance in generating goals and objectives, all of which are sensitive for individual students. The data used in the IEP, therefore, need to be related to placement in programs, the content of these programs, and a summative review of outcomes from these programs.

C. Experimentally Monitoring the Effects of Instruction

The last context to be addressed within CBM is analyzing instructional programs. Not only must measurement systems be crafted that are predictive of large-scale tests and sensitive to change as part of the IEP, they must be used to evaluate instruction. For example, using the form listed in Figure 2.1, which reflects an early taxonomy for organizing instruction, Wesson and Deno (1989) analyzed teachers' instructional plans in reading to determine the (a) general features; (b) prevalence of various activities, arrangements, and motivational strategies; (c) percentage of instructional time devoted to the various categories; and (d) overlap of plans across students. They found a relatively consistent picture of instruction (similar to that found in general education) that changed little over the year.

IEP GOAL AREA ——————————————— INSTRUCTION: ———————— STUDENT NAME	INSTRUCTIONAL PLAN		TIME AVAILABLE LOCATION —————	
Instructional Procedures	Arrangement	Time	Materials	Motivational Strategies

Figure 2.1   Taxonomy of instruction for formative evaluation.

An example of this approach has been described for evaluating whole-language programs in a study by Tindal and Marston (1996). In this study, both a nomothetic analysis was conducted on a large normative sample of students in grades 2 through 6 *and* an idiographic analysis was applied to a case study student who had been monitored throughout the year with instruction systematically evaluated. On a variety of curriculum-based reading measures, student performance was highly correlated with published test performance, levels of performance were distinguished by grade, and growth over time was apparent. Importantly, change over time was evident on the case student with a measure of reading fluency and story understanding.

IV. DECISION AREAS WITHIN CURRICULUM-BASED MEASUREMENT

Six decision areas are considered in this section of the chapter: (a) screening and identification of students with LDs, (b) grouping students, (c) setting goals on IEPs, (d) measuring individual progress of students, (e) formatively evaluating the success of instructional programs, and (f) monitoring student progress with computers. Generally, these decision areas represent both a chronology of research, with the first topics having been addressed earlier in the history of CBM, as well as a continuum of sophistication with the later topics representing advanced areas of research in which student performance data are rendered in a complex integration of feedback and instructional design.

A. Screening and Identification of Students with LDs

Although initially researched as a measurement system to formatively evaluate the effects of instruction, a number of studies were conducted in the early 1970s in which CBM was used to identify students at risk of failure or with LDs. A few more studies have been conducted since then, with three areas of research completed: (a) further identification (eligibility) research, (b) reintegration (into general education settings) research, and (c) alternative placement paradigms research.

Following a slew of studies reported by Shinn (1989) with a typical focus from a school psychologist, three studies have been done in the last 12 years. Shinn and Marston (1985) noted significant differences between students with LDs, those from Title 1 programs, and students considered low achieving; as one might expect, those with LDs performed the lowest. Shinn, Tindal, and Spira (1987) examined the reading performance of students who had been referred by teachers for placement in special education programs and compared them to a normative sample of students who had not been referred; they found significantly lower performance in the referred students, suggesting that teachers actually serve as the test in making the initial referral decision. Finally, Merrill and Shinn (1990) reported that "the most critical variables in the decision to classify students as learning disabled (LD) in the study appear to be low academic achievement levels, particularly in reading and written language" (p. 78). The results of Marston, Mirkin, and Deno (1984) confirmed these findings in that referrals for special education appeared to be based primarily on academic achievement, and when CBM data were used to initiate the referral process, similar rates of identification occur and similar students seemed to be identified as the students referred with a more traditional criterion of discrepancy between ability and achievement (that is, CBM-referred students had the same discrepancy).

In the second area of research, which appears to be old wine in new bottles, Rodden-Nord and Shinn (1991) and Shinn, Habedank, Rodden-Nord, and Knutson (1993) have used oral reading fluency to study the range of skills in special and general education students. In particular, they recommended the use of such data to help teachers determine when to reintegrate special education students into general education environments.

Finally, in a novel application of CBM in making decisions about placement, students have been frequently measured in reading during a 30-day assessment period (Marston, 1987–1988). For students who have been found eligible for special education, their rate of progress has been compared to that achieved while they were in general education with significantly different (reading) rates obtained, essentially validating the placement process. Finally, Marston (1987) questioned the placement of students with LDs into programs taught only by teachers with a license in that (disability) category versus the noncategorical placement of students into special education programs taught by cross-categorical specialists. He reported that

> over the course of an academic year, LD students taught by LD [certified] teachers do not improve more than LD students taught by EMR [educa-

ble mental retardation] teachers. Likewise, EMR pupils taught by EMR licensed teachers do not improve more than EMR students taught by teachers with LD certification. Rather, both LD and EMR pupils make similar gains when taught by teachers with varying certification. (p. 427)

B. Grouping Students

In a few studies, CBM has been used to group students. For example, Wesson (1990, 1992) and Wesson, Vierthaler, and Haubrich (1989a, 1989b) described the steps for establishing reading groups using CBM data as an alternative to the more traditional strategies based on student files or informal reading inventories. Likewise Fuchs (1992) described how the Vanderbilt research team has used computerized administration and scoring of CBM probes in math to form peer groups. With this system, student pairs have been matched with tutors who are skilled in a particular deficit area of the tutee.

C. Setting Goals on IEPs

Setting goals has been an important component of CBM. A general outcome approach has been used to structure measurement goals as long-range targets. Often these goals have been used in the CBM research to study a number of implementation issues. For example, in a study in which four different forms of consultation were employed with teachers, Wesson (1991) compared four systems for developing goals and employing follow-up consultation: (a) teacher-developed goals versus CBM goals and monitoring systems and (b) individual consultation versus group follow-up consultation. She reported that CBM helped teachers develop goals and resulted in greater progress over that achieved when teachers developed goals on their own in an unsystematic manner. No differences were found, however, between the individual versus group form of consultation.

Not only is the process important in setting goals, but the ambitiousness and modification of the goals also may be important components. For example, after reviewing different goal-setting strategies, Fuchs, Fuchs, and Hamlett (1990) report on their previous studies:

1. When teachers use "dynamic goals" (in math) they increase the goals for 60% of the students, whereas when teachers did not use dynamic goals, they raised the goal for only 1 in 20 students (Fuchs, Fuchs, & Hamlett, 1989d).
2. When students participate in selecting goals in math, performance is significantly greater than when they are assigned goals (Fuchs, Bahr, & Reith, 1985).
3. Achievement (in reading) is greater for students when they receive instruction by teachers who set highly ambitious or moderately ambitious goals over that attained by teachers who set low goals (Fuchs, Fuchs, & Deno, 1985).

4. Fuchs, Butterworth, and Fuchs (1989) report students using CBM performance are more clear and specific in their knowledge of goals (in spelling) and perceptions of goal attainment than students without such performance information.

D. Measuring Individual Progress of Students

In keeping with the fundamental premise upon which CBM is based, the bulk of research has been oriented toward formatively evaluating student performance to maximize instructional effectiveness. Two different strategies have been explicated for graphing student performance and evaluating instruction. Tindal (1987) used the term performance *monitoring* to describe procedures in which assessment materials are sampled from a large domain reflecting many skill areas within the entire instructional program to be delivered over the course of the year (long range goal). In contrast, *mastery monitoring* refers to a sampling plan in which materials are drawn from a much more narrow skill range representing the immediate instructional plan to be delivered over a few days or weeks.

Irrespective of sampling plans for developing the measures, the other issue to emerge involves the scaling of behavior on the graph, whether it is on an equal interval scale or a ratio scale. Few differences have been reported, however, when comparing these types of scales. For example, Fuchs and Fuchs (1987) computed the average effect size and found equal interval graphs to be .46 and ratio graphs to be .53; both values were significantly different from zero but not different from each other. In this study, the average slope of improvement was about one word per week in oral reading fluency, less than one-half of a replacement word on a maze task, between one half and one letter sequence per week in spelling (whether the words were sampled from a graded list or a common list), and nearly one digit per week in math. Marston (1988) compared the two systems in reading and writing and found only one measure (the number of words written incorrectly) to result in significant differences, favoring the equal interval model.

E. Formatively Monitoring the Success of Instructional Programs

Probably the most significant area within which CBM has had an impact on assessment in LD is developing instructional programs that provide both a reasonable basis for diagnosis to begin teaching and an extended data basis for evaluating the effects of that teaching. In a typical CBM study, students have been assessed in long-range goal materials (using a performance assessment system rather than mastery progress monitoring system). With each measure, performance has been analyzed for specific correct and incorrect performance, and instructional strategies have been designed for remediating those areas within which many or consistent errors have been made. "Children whose teachers employed the ongoing measurement and evaluation . . . achieved better than students whose teachers used conventional monitoring methods, such as periodic teacher-made tests, informal observation, and workbook samples" (Fuchs, Deno, & Mirkin, 1984, p. 456). These findings occurred on all measures of reading, even those not similar in format to the progress-monitoring measures. In a comparison of gain scores (in reading) for "high" versus "low" implementation (of CBM), teachers from the high-implementation group revealed greater improvement in reading than those in the low-implementation group (Wesson, Skiba, Sevcik, King, & Deno, 1984).

F. Monitoring Student Progress with Computers

A number of studies have been conducted in which students' performance is monitored with formative evaluation systems to identify not only which skills are being mastered and which ones are still deficient, but also what types of instructional changes to make. Most of these studies have been done by the Fuchs and Fuchs team from Vanderbilt University. In this system, teachers are presented output that charts the student's progress over time using a line graph and also provides an analysis of specific skills on a continuum of mastery. Figure 2.2 is a math example in which the skills are labeled. *A1* refers to a particular addition skill, *S* refers to subtraction, *M* refers to multiplication, and *D* refers to division.

1. Skills Analysis

For example, in a study of spelling, Fuchs and Fuchs (1991) compared the outcomes from a group of teachers as they tracked student performance over 15 weeks. These teachers had been randomly assigned to (a) use CBM with skills analysis, (b) use CBM without skills analysis, and (c) use their own performance indicators without CBM or skills analysis. They found that when teachers had available a skills analysis with the CBM data, students significantly outperformed

Mastery Status	Skill Areas:	Format
☐ Not Attempted	A1	Dates for Individual Students-->
▥ Nonmastered	S1	MEASURES LISTED VERTICALLY
▦ Partially Mastered	M1	
▪ Probably Mastered	M2	Measures for Groups Students-->
■ Mastered	D1	SINGLE DATE FOR GROUP
	F1	

Figure 2.2   Skill output on the computer-generated report from the Vanderbilt University team.

those in either of the other two conditions. In a similar study done by Fuchs, Fuchs, Hamlett, and Stecker (1990) in math using the same three conditions, teachers using CBM with skills analysis made more instructional changes and increased student achievement significantly more than teachers in the other groups. Finally, in a study of reading, Fuchs, Fuchs, and Hamlett (1989b) found that when monitoring student performance with diagnostic information, teachers identified greater numbers of story grammar elements for instruction, used more instructional packets, and attained greater levels of achievement than teachers who had no such diagnostic information available concurrent with the student performance data. Likewise, in another study of reading, the same team of researchers found that both student recall of passages and their slope of improvement in oral reading proficiency were better when teachers received evaluation information with student performance outcomes rather than the performance outcomes alone (Fuchs, Fuchs, & Hamlett, 1989c).

It is important to note, however, that the type of skills analysis researched with CBM is not the typical diagnostic assessment that occurs typically prior to instruction. Rather, in keeping with the emphasis on formative evaluation, skill analyses are done concurrently with instruction and ongoing measurement. As discussed later in this chapter, instructional programs are either vindicated or modified based on the analysis of skills and outcomes. In this system, the skills analysis is an important indicator of *what* to change and the outcome data are critical in highlighting *when* to make a change in an instructional program.

2. Investigations of Instructional Planning, Feedback, and Achievement

This system of computer-based assessment has been used to study a range of other issues: (a) the efficiency of a measurement system, (b) the use of different kinds of feedback to teachers and students, (c) the use of measurement information to help set goals, and finally (d) teachers' use of information on instructional effects and recommend changes when programs are not working well. The following are some of the studies conducted by Fuchs and Fuchs and other colleagues.

1. In an early study on efficiency of CBM systems that use a computer data collection system, Fuchs, Fuchs, Hamlett, and Hasselbring (1987) found no improvements in efficiency, though teachers reported greater satisfaction. Teachers actually spent more time charting progress using computers than they did with paper and pencil. In a later study in reading, spelling, and math, Fuchs, Hamlett, Fuchs, Stecker, and Ferguson (1988) reported improvements in efficiency in measurement and evaluation with the use of computer data collection. In fact, they noted that with about 5 min saved across these three academic areas, a teacher with a case load of 20 students would save 5 hr per week. In an early study reported by Wesson, Fuchs, Tindal, Mirkin, and Deno (1986), a series of strategies were implemented to in-

crease the efficiency of measurement. They reported significant time reductions when teachers were more planful in the preparation of materials and sequence of measurement.

2. In an area of research that blends the components of CBM, skill analysis, goal setting, and performance monitoring, Fuchs (1988) worked in all basic skill areas of reading (with a maze task), spelling, and math. For example, in this particular study in spelling, teachers were assigned to four groups that were crossed with each other: (a) with and without computers, and (b) with goal- versus experimental-oriented monitoring of performance. She found that students achieved significantly more when taught using computers under the goal-based data utilization system rather than the experimental analysis system; no differences, however, were found between the computer- versus hand-managed data analysis systems.

3. One year later, Fuchs, Fuchs, and Stecker (1989) investigated the effects of CBM on teachers' instructional planning and decision making in reading and concluded that "the CBM process structures and improves the process" (p. 57). Although no differences were found between teachers who used a computer system to analyze student performance and progress and those who had no such system, the use of CBM helped teachers write better goals, judge pupil progress better, and introduce more interventions than teachers who used unsystematic instruction.

4. Fuchs, Fuchs, Hamlett, and Allinder (1991a) found that student achievement was significantly greater when teachers used CBM than that attained in a control group in which no CBM was used. Furthermore, teachers using CBM in spelling increased goals for an average of 90% of their students and introduced changes to instruction an average of three times during the 18-week study. In the end, however, the amount of achievement gains was similar for both groups of students participating in the CBM condition—those with and without the use of an expert system detailing the types of instructional changes to make.

5. Fuchs, Fuchs, Hamlett, and Stecker (1991) studied teacher planning in math instruction with CBM; 33 teachers in grades 2–8 set goals, analyzed first the baseline and then weekly progress, and made changes to instruction when prompted by graphed decision rules. With a treatment that focused on structure (establishing goals), measurement (frequent testing), and evaluation (using data to change instruction), they found a significant effect size for student achievement over that obtained by teachers in a control condition. This outcome, however, was not due to simply a greater number of instructional changes made: Only with an expert system for prompting changes were student achievement gains substantial. Teachers who used CBM with and without expert systems for prompting instructional changes made about two to three modifications over the 20 weeks of the study.

6. Ferguson and Fuchs (1991) found significant differences in spelling when

teachers used a computer to score student performance as opposed to scoring performance themselves; an increase in accuracy occurred with a concurrent increase in consistency from score to score.

7. Fuchs, Fuchs, Hamlett, and Ferguson (1992) investigated the use of a computer-based expert system of consultation in reading that utilized a maze task. For 17 weeks, 33 special education teachers tracked student progress with the computer used to display goal level, expected rate of progress, actual trend of progress, a prompt to make instructional changes when expected and actual progress was discrepant, and a summary of the changes made. The two groups differed only in that one group devised their own changes while the other group was provided recommended changes based on each student's profile. Although both groups made changes to instruction equally as often (about 2.3 times over 17 weeks) and had comparable levels of ambitiousness, the nature of the changes made by the groups differed considerably. On several outcome measures, teachers using the expert system made greater student achievement gains than those without this system. Nevertheless, both groups significantly outperformed teachers in a control condition.

8. Fuchs and Fuchs (1993) used two strategies to monitor student progress in reading, one of which involved the use of a computer and another which utilized paper and pencil; they found no significant differences between the data utilization conditions but reported a large effect size for accurate implementation of CBM (es = 1.14).

9. In another study of expert planning in spelling in which computers were used to provide teachers a menu of instructional options, Fuchs, Fuchs, and Hamlett (1994) described four features considered with their system: (a) student performance and rate of progress, (b) general instructional context, (c) survey of student's daily work habits and motivation, and (d) instructional suggestions including directions on implementation. When teachers were provided these expert systems in reading and math, along with CBM data on student progress (both quantitative and qualitative analyses), they made two to three instructional changes over 17 weeks and showed greater growth than teachers with no CBM data or expert system; in spelling no such differences were found (either in the instructional changes or the student growth).

10. In a related study, Fuchs, Fuchs, Hamlett, Phillips, and Bentz (1994) compared two groups of teachers who conducted weekly measurement with student feedback; only one of them received teacher feedback (twice-monthly printouts of student progress and skill profile and instructional recommendations). They found that, within a general education classroom, teachers who received this additional information produced better student achievement growth than the contrast teachers; with this additional information, these teachers reported greater use of classwide peer tutoring and computer-assisted instruction as well instruction on a greater variety of math skills.

11. In a study of teachers' adaptations of instruction in math for students with

LDs, Fuchs, Fuchs, Hamlett, Phillips, and Karns (1995) reported implementation of six specialized and just less than three unique adaptations over a 6- to 12-week period. During the study, these 20 teachers of grades 2–4 used peer-mediated instruction with CBM, which consisted of weekly measures that provided teachers and students with quantitative and qualitative feedback. They also found that teachers who implemented the intervention package also reported modifications in the goals and teaching strategies, and that the skills they taught were less similar than those taught to other low performers. Finally, these teachers used the CBM information more than the criterion-referenced information traditionally available to them.

12. Allinder (1996) has studied differential implementation of CBM using three critical components: (a) measurement frequency, (b) compliance with decision rules to modify instruction, and (c) ambitiousness of goals. She found that only when CBM is implemented with high fidelity are the achievement gains made. In contrast, when it is implemented with low fidelity, the gains are no better than a control group in which CBM is not implemented at all. Importantly, these differences are not related to teacher efficacy, though in an earlier study (Allinder, 1995), she had reported that teachers who were higher in personal efficacy made a greater number of goal changes, and those who were higher in teaching efficacy made more ambitious goals and changed their goals more frequently.

In summary, the use of CBM for screening students, grouping students, planning instruction, measuring progress, and evaluating instructional programs reflects a host of issues. First, the research indicates that a classroom focus on achievement is not only feasible but imperative for developing an integrated assessment system for students with LDs. Assuming that a formal assessment system is constructed in which critical behaviors are sampled (oral reading fluency, maze performance, digits computed, words and letter sequences spelled correctly, and words written) and performance tasks are developed and administered, teachers have access to the most critical information needed or possible. Second, the research indicates that teachers need to have a wide range of achievement outcomes, both quantitative and qualitative. However, outcomes alone may not be adequate; rather, a menu of instructional options also may be needed to affect achievement. Even with this much assessment support, it appears that teachers may be able to make instructional changes only a few times during the greater part of the school year. Third, as teachers prepare for instruction and assessment in the 21st century, they need to consider using computers as part of the information management systems. No longer are grade books adequate for storing students' progress information. Not only is the metric of grades a poor substitute for a technically adequate performance indicator, but the manner in which it is stored, filed, and manipulated is simply not vindicated. Teachers need systems that prompt adjustments in teaching at the right time and with a modicum of structure.

V. EXTENSION OF CURRICULUM-BASED MEASUREMENT INTO SECONDARY PROGRAMS

Before addressing the research in middle and high schools, it is critical to consider the context of any assessment system in secondary programs and the role of special education teachers in these settings. The most critical feature to consider in secondary programs is the focus on context. No longer are single teachers providing instruction in all subject areas. Although some subject areas are blocked together in the middle school (typically social studies with language arts and science with math), in high schools, teachers begin to take on subject-specific, discipline-based responsibilities. Furthermore, the textbook becomes more prominent with information used as both a way of framing teaching and as an information reference for students. In addition, schedules becomes more complicated, if for no other reason than the sheer number of different options (courses) and teachers to consider in completing a quarter or semester program plan. Finally, the role of students in both planning and managing their academic program becomes more active with teachers serving as mentors or guides in the process. These issues converge to change the role of special education teachers in secondary programs.

McKenzie (1991b) describes a dual tension that arises from secondary special educators' job responsibilities. On the one hand, teachers may use a *skills approach,* defined as "instruction to students with learning disabilities to improve their basic reading, writing, computational, and social skills for the purpose of enhancing their performance in mainstream content classes" (p. 467). In contrast, they may use a *content area approach,* in which they "provide instruction in core areas such as English, language, social studies, science, etc. to those students with learning disabilities who are judged to be unable to profit from inclusion in one or more mainstream content area courses" (p. 467). Interestingly, the vast majority of special education coordinators (79%) cited use of the content approach; only 19% characterized their high schools as skills based. Although this finding was limited to Kentucky teachers only, McKenzie's (1991a) earlier surveys with all state departments of education in the United States reflected the same pattern, with almost half of the schools in the U.S. using the content model to teach at least half the content from special educators. Twenty percent of the students with LDs received *all* content instruction from special education teachers (McKenzie, 1991a). These findings are significant considering only 19% of students age 12–17 are being served in regular classes and that resource rooms serve 35% of these students while 32% are served in separate classes (U.S. Department of Education, 1995).

If a skills approach is used, it generally focuses on critical basic skills that reflect access to the content; it rarely includes instruction on the content directly. However, if a content approach is used, students in special education may not be receiving the best instruction possible: Few special education teachers have backgrounds comparable to content area teachers in multiple fields such as English, earth science, geography, and health. Although this model may function at the practical level of coordinating schedules and programs, serious questions arise when considering the impact on teaching and learning. With these issues inherent in secondary programs, assessment systems must be developed that reflect responsibilities appropriate to both general and special educators as well as the outcomes needed for success.

In the first assessment system to be described, the special educator remains focused on basic skills and uses a measurement system to monitor progress of critical access skills. Hence the term "general outcome indicator" is used to reflect this emphasis. Espin has been the prime researcher in identifying general outcome measures. In the second assessment system, the special educator works with general education to remove the need for access to the content through basic skills by focusing on a conceptual basis to structure information and reduce to that which is most explanatory. Therefore, it is described with a "conceptual" frame of reference. Tindal is the lead researcher in developing this assessment system that is implemented only with systemic restructuring of the relationship between general and special educators.

A. General Outcome Indicators in Content Areas

There are four major studies in which CBM systems have been used as general outcome indicators. In this line of research, the focus is on basic skills as access to content areas. In fact, many students with learning disabilities have problems reading; because content is organized in secondary programs with a heavy emphasis on reading, it is likely that they can not succeed without also developing a range of accommodations. In the early work reported by Espin and Deno (1993a, 1993b), these general outcome indicators are used to identify areas in which students need assistance and accommodations to succeed in the general education setting.

In the first study noted above, Espin and Deno (1993a) examined the use of reading aloud to predict performance in content areas. After reading aloud for one minute from three English and science textbooks, then silently reading a longer passage and answering 25 multiple-choice questions from that text, students again read aloud for 1 min. Oral reading fluency (number of words read correctly) was compared to performance on the classroom task and to a standardized reading test as well as grade point averages. They concluded that reading aloud was a valid predictor of student academic success in secondary content classrooms. The measures were especially useful for "identifying students who are likely to experience difficulties in content areas" (Espin & Deno, 1993a, p. 56).

In the second study, Espin and Deno (1993b) used reading aloud to separate students with general reading disabilities from students with reading difficulties caused by lack of knowledge in the content areas. After completing a background knowledge vocabulary test in English and science, students read the text in the same manner as earlier (aloud for 1 min, then silently with 25 questions to complete, and finally, aloud again for 1 min). They reported that the oral reading fluency measure was a useful index for teachers to identify "educationally relevant subtypes of students with learning difficulties in the content areas" (Espin & Deno, 1993b, p. 321).

Espin and Deno (1994) also have studied reading aloud from text and completion of a vocabulary meaning task as performance indicators. In this study, students matched content vocabulary words, read aloud from the text for 1 min, completed a content area assignment, and read a loud again from the text. They found that the vocabulary measure was the strongest predictor of student success in content areas, although oral reading proficiency also predicted student success.

Finally, Espin and Foegen (1996) used oral reading fluency, maze, and vocabulary matching to predict performance on a content task. In this study, students completed a knowledge pretest and each of these other measures before completing three content tasks. They reported moderately high correlations for all three measures as valid predictors of student performance on the content tasks. Again, they found that vocabulary correlated more highly with the content-based tasks than either the maze or oral readings.

In summary, technically adequate general outcome indicators can be developed by teachers in secondary special education programs. In this system, progress monitoring focuses on those basic skills that are predictive of performance on content tasks. When students show high levels of proficiency in these skill areas (orally reading from the text and like matching vocabulary), they also should show higher levels of performance in the content area. Because of the generic nature of the measures (English and science), teachers in special education programs can remain relatively focused on support systems that teach students basic access skills like reading and writing.

B. Developing a Concept-Based Assessment System in Content Areas

In this version of assessment and LDs in secondary programs, a more systemic restructuring is required of both special and general education. The general approach of this line of CBM research and development is to reframe subject matter content so that concepts and principles are emphasized over facts. The goal is fourfold: (a) reduce the amount of text that needs to be read and mastered; (b) increase the redundancy of information so that, through multiple chapters of different content, the same concepts appear in similar contexts; (c) allow problem-solving tasks to be developed with alternate forms so that students can be taught directly yet receive near-transfer tasks as part of the assessment; and (d) develop a common language so that general education teachers can structure the content and allow special education teachers to play a role in both instruction and assessment.

The process typically has begun with teachers, from both general and special

| Date: |
| Teacher: |
| Class: |
| Textbook: |
| Other Curriculum Materials: |

Approximate Schedule of Content to be Delivered

Week	Dates		Textbook Unit	Chapters	Quiz Dates	Test Dates
1	From:	To:				
2	From:	To:				
3	From:	To:				
4	From:	To:				

KEY CONCEPTS

1. _____   6. _____
2. _____   7. _____
3. _____   8. _____
4. _____   9. _____
5. _____   10. _____

IMPORTANT IDEAS

1. _____

2. _____

3. _____

Figure 2.3   Content planning form.

education environments, working together to reframe the content using a concept planning form as depicted in Figure 2.3. This form has three parts in which (a) basic schedule information is listed on top, followed by (b) a list of key concepts, attributes, and examples or nonexamples, and finally, (c) a description of three principles or big ideas that use the concepts.

Although a series of studies has been conducted, many of them reflect preliminary data because they have employed a naturalistic design rather than an experimental design which generally has been used by the Vanderbilt group. Furthermore, because the system is based on systemic restructuring of roles and responsibilities among general and special education, the model needs to be implemented with care. For not only has assessment of students with LDs changed substantially, but instruction for all students has been subjected to equally significant changes.

In an early study by Tindal, Rebar, Nolet, and McCollum (1995), a variety of different outcomes were analyzed after the curriculum had been reframed to allow students with LDs a conceptual rendering of the content. Although no differences were found between general and special education students on social studies multiple-choice fact tests or short-answer problem-solving tasks, students in special education performed significantly worse on extended-answer problem-solving tasks. This finding for eighth graders was somewhat different to that found for a group of sixth graders who were taught a unit on law. In this second study, Hollenbeck and Tindal (1996) reported significant differences between students in special versus general education on a facts test but no such differences on short-answer problem-solving tasks. Finally, Hall, Tindal, and Wininger (1997) studied a group of fifth graders who had been taught with a comparable curriculum rendering that emphasized a conceptual basis for problem solving: For many students with disabilities, performance was comparable to a nonequivalent control group on short-answer problem-solving tasks, though significant differences had been found between the two groups on their reading proficiencies. Finally, in a study reported by Tindal and Nolet (1996), a science unit was reframed, and both the curriculum and instruction were analyzed according to frequency of concept presence, which was, in turn, compared to student perception of importance and correctness on an end-of-unit test. The outcomes indicated no uniform pattern of usage, correctness, or correlation, reflecting the complexities inherent in teaching and learning that exist in most general education classrooms.

Although empirical studies are just beginning in this latter system, which is based on a conceptual organization of content subject matter, several issues already are apparent. The most important issues involve the need to consider assessment with three main components: (a) framing the curriculum and actively teaching problem solving; (b) developing comparable tasks so that student performance can be tracked over time; and (c) graphically depicting change over time to formatively evaluate instructional programs.

First, all teachers (both general and special education) need to be adequately prepared for this model. Inservice staff development is needed so that teachers can learn important principles of assessment and its relation to teaching and learning. For example, in a recent study (McCleery, Heath, Helwig, & Tindal, 1997), five concepts were identified around the general principle that *human actions modify the physical environment while the physical environment, in turn, affects human actions* (reflecting a paraphrasing of language of the National Geographic Society's Standards for Life, 1995, Standards 14 and 15). These concepts and their attributes (in parentheses below) require knowledge of the professional standards and a firm grounding in the content, clearly quite difficult for special educators and frequently difficult even for general educators. In this particular study, the concepts were *regions* (cultural, geographic, economic, political), *culture* (language, beliefs, ethnicity, SES, age), *economic systems* (exchange, natural resources, labor, manufacturing), *political systems* (laws, public service, decision making, systems of influence), and *geography* (landforms, area, map, climate). These concepts were highlighted in the curriculum and integrated within instruction using explicit modeling of problem solving across a range of contexts.

Second, the performance tasks used to generate the short and extended essays need to be carefully crafted and made comparable so that change over time can be measured and plotted. In this same study by McCleery et al. (1997), a series of tasks were developed in conjunction with geographic maps so that students could become proficient in solving similar problems. For example, the task in Figure 2.4 was constructed as one of 16 eventually administered over 7 weeks. All tasks were constructed with a similar architecture that established a context, identified relevant information, and framed a problem centered around key concepts and required specific intellectual operations (i.e., thinking skills like making predictions, explaining outcomes, or evaluating decisions with certain criteria).

Finally, scoring systems need to be established that provide reliable and systemically valid (Frederiksen & Collins, 1989) indicators of learning. For example, in an early study in which teachers were trained to score student performance, Tindal, Nolet, and Blake (1993) used a flow chart to help judges evaluate student responses. The flow chart simply helped the judges make more objective decisions during the scoring process than was likely to occur without such guidelines or with only a scoring rubric. An example of a flow chart is depicted in Figure 2.5. In this scoring chart, the two main criteria involve (a) student argumentation for several points of view in which justification is provided both *for* a choice and *against* any alternative reasons that were not selected as a choice and (b) an emphasis on multiple reasons over singular reasons. As can be seen in this example with the Servpac factory problem, several potential sites are likely to exist in solving the problem. In scoring the answer, however, the best choice is not the actual site but the reasons for it and against alternatives; and the best answer would include multiple reasons on both of these sides.

With comparability of tasks and a potentially reliable scoring system, then, it is

---

Attached is a map of the north-central region of Colorado. Look very closely at the key and the map itself so that you can identify the following: cities, agricultural (farming) areas, roads and highways, and mountain regions. Recently a large company called Servpac made the decision to locate a new factory in this Colorado Region. The Servpac factory would can vegetables grown by the local farmers and then ship the goods to other regions. Think about what Servpac will need to run the factory and how important it is for them to choose the right location. In addition, think about how Servpac will influence the cultural, economic, and political systems of the region. *First*, draw an X on the map showing the spot you believe to be the best location to put the Servpac factory. *Second*, explain why you chose that location AND how you think Servpac will influence the cultural, economic, and political systems of the region. Remember to use specific ideas about geography and cultural, economic, and political systems when writing your answer.

Figure 2.4   Example of a problem-solving task.

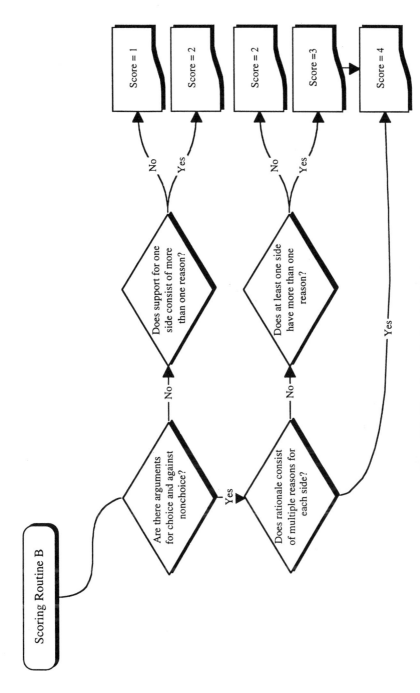

Figure 2.5 Flow chart evaluating student performance.

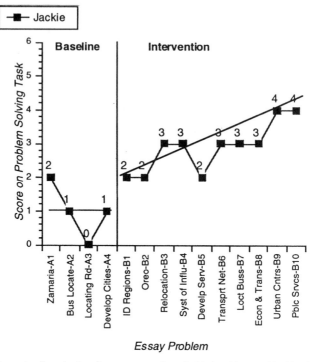

Figure 2.6 Example of graph of performance over time. Jackie is a 12-year-old white female in sixth grade. In the social studies passage words correct per minute (WCM) were 40 and prosody (Pros) was 2. For the science passage, WCM was 46, Pros was 2. For the narrative passage, WCM was 74, Pros was 2.

possible to graphically display performance over time. In the graph in Figure 2.6, one student's performance was plotted in two phases. The student is described below the figure in terms of demographics and then reading performance (words correct per minute (WCM) and prosody or expressiveness in reading (Pros) on three passages (social studies, science, and narrative). The first phase reflects measurement without systematic instruction in the conceptual basis of the geography content, whereas the second phase reflects outcomes when the five concepts noted above were taught with explicit models and examples. These results reflect an idiographic emphasis on assessment as described earlier in the chapter.

Although research is continuing on this system, on the practical side, this model of assessment provides an integrated view in which teaching and learning are considered together and in which the emphasis of validation is on the consequential basis for decision making (Messick, 1989). In this view, identifying consequences implies that instruction is evaluated to determine not only if it was effective, but also to define the potential reasons why or why not any effects were found. In this view, some sense of cause and effect is implied: The assessment information can be both diagnostic and formative. Finally, with an emphasis on change over time, each student's performance is compared to previous levels rather than another student's performance.

VI. SUMMARY

Although the title of the chapter is "Assessment in Learning Disabilities," the focus reflected a more singular purpose: to implement empirically based assessments in making educational decisions for children with LDs. Rather than address all types of assessment, which would have been far too encompassing, a particular perspective was used to narrow the topic to a manageable scope. One important perspective included an idiographic approach to assessment, in which the individual was viewed as the most important unit for analysis. Another critical perspective, however, was that the approach to assessment be empirically based. In many of the studies summarized in the chapter, nevertheless, a nomothetic approach was used. The third important perspective that helped delimit the content of the chapter was an in-depth review of CBM research dating back to 1984. Because the assessment field is proliferating with all kinds of CBAs that can include anything from authentic assessment to the use of portfolios, a fairly demarcated definition of CBM was used. Basically, the term referred to any standardized measure with supporting technical adequacy, capable of measuring student performance over time, sensitive to program effects, and useful in making a variety of decisions.

Three important contexts were highlighted within which assessments for students with LDs are likely to occur. First, in the current standards-based model of assessment, which is predominant in the field, large-scale testing has become common and the *coin of the realm*—the language used to exchange meaning—has become passing or mastery on some high-stakes standard. In this context and for students with LDs, measures used by special education teachers and school psychologists would be linked to these standards, predictive of passing them, and capable of showing performance changes over time in a more sensitive manner. Included within this context was a view of assessment in which skills were integrated (e.g., reading and math or writing and math). Performance indicators, therefore, reflected such constellations of skills. Furthermore, assessments were considered within the instructional program, often in the presence of both the opportunity to learn and any accommodations used to maximally reflect performance unhindered by a disability.

The IEP was considered a critical document for operationalizing this assessment system. By including CBM within IEPs, three benefits were listed: (a) a forum was established for teacher-developed measures in relation to both large-scale assessments and student performance over time, (b) a context was identified that has increasingly been required for accommodations to be used, and (c) instructional programs were empirically derived in an efficient manner providing an outcomes criterion of accountability.

In reviewing the CBM research in six decision areas, the literature reflected many positive outcomes. In making screening and eligibility decisions, CBM has continued to be useful and efficient. An obvious benefit noted from using this system over a single-event published test was that the information can be translated into meaningful classroom practices for subsequently defining what and how to teach. Another decision in which CBM has been used is grouping students, often representing simply a more refined version of a placement decision. As teachers plan their schedule, CBM has provided quickly accessible and useful information for organizing classrooms so that teaching and learning begins in an efficient manner. Of course, the next decision on where to target instruction also has been made from various forms of CBM information. Indeed, a considerable amount of literature has been generated to help teachers select appropriate goals for their students. These goals often have become important also as a proxy for expectations, which in turn have been found to be quite important in the eventual achievement of students. With students placed, grouped, and oriented toward a goal, the next decision addressed monitoring of student performance. This area actually reflected a major thrust for a considerable amount of CBM research, which eventually encompassed yet another decision area: the formative evaluation of instructional programs. Two strategies for monitoring performance were offered along with a summary of several studies on instructional evaluation. Suffice it to say that two critical issues were listed when using student performance information to evaluate instruction: fidelity of data collection and use of data. In addressing the generally difficult issue of getting teachers to actually use student performance information in a thoughtful and reflective manner, computers have begun to be used. Led by the pioneering work of the Fuches at Vanderbilt University, a number of studies were summarized that pointed to many specific issues in how data were collected, stored, displayed, and eventually used to plan instruction, provide feedback, and increase achievement by targeting key skill areas.

In the early years in which CBM was initially researched and developed, the focus had been on basic skills in the elementary grades, primarily reading, writing, and computing. In the last section of the chapter, however, an extension of CBM into secondary programs was described. In particular, two approaches were presented.

In the first approach, CBM was considered from a general outcomes orientation in which performance on basic skills tasks was used to predict performance on content tasks. Clearly, this application of CBM has provided all teachers, both those in special but also those in general education, useful information about the requisite teaching and learning that needs to occur as part of access to the subject matter.

In a second approach, CBM was included within subject discipline areas from a concept development perspective. In organizing secondary content into concepts and principles, with attributes and a range of examples and nonexamples, this system provided the technical bridge for creating comparable measures to monitor student progress over time. After summarizing a few of the early studies in this area, three key issues were identified: (a) creating problems for students to solve that indeed are comparable, (b) providing explicit instruction on alternate forms of the tasks to ensure adequate opportunity to learn, and (c) scoring performance in a manner that is maximally reliable. In summarizing this approach to CBM in secondary programs, a graphic display (Figure 2.6) was presented that was designed to emphasize formative evaluation of instruction.

In summary, CBM as a specific assessment alternative has a long tradition of research and application. In managing educational programs for students with LD, this form of measurement is both technically adequate and practically viable. Indeed, it is only with widespread application in the field that further validation is likely to occur. In this validation, however, the focus is and needs to be on consequential validity: Are programs working and why? Assuming that consequences imply cause and effect, CBM provides educators with an assessment system focused on this question.

References

Allinder, R. M. (1996). When some is not better than none: Effects of differential implementation of curriculum-based measurement. *Exceptional Children, 62*(6), 525–535.

Allinder, R. M. (1995). An examination of the relationship between teacher efficacy and curriculum-based measurement and student achievement. *Remedial and Special Education, 16*(4), 247–254.

Bentz, J. L., & Fuchs, L. S. (1993). Teacher judgment of student mastery of math skills. *Diagnostique, 18*(3), 219–232.

Bond, L. A., Breskamp, D., & Roeber, E. (1996). *The status report of the assessment programs in the United States: State Students Assessment Programs Database School Year 1994–1995.* Oak Brook, IL: North Central Regional Educational Laboratory.

Deno, S. L. (1992). The nature and development of curriculum-based measurement. *Preventing School Failures, 36*(2), 5–10.

Deno, S. L. (1990). Individual differences and individual difference: The essential difference of special education. *Journal of Special Education, 24*(2), 160–173

Deno, S. L. (1987). Curriculum-based measurement. *Teaching Exceptional Children,* Fall, 41–47.

Deno, S. L., & Fuchs, L. S. (1987). Developing curriculum-based measurement systems for data-based special education problem solving. *Focus on Exceptional Children, 19*(8), 1–16.

Espin, C. A., & Deno, S. L. (1994). Curriculum-based measures for secondary students: utility and task specificity of text-based reading and vocabulary measures for predicting performance on content-area tasks. *Diagnostique, 20*(1–4), 121–142.

Espin, C. A., & Deno, S. L. (1993a). Content-specific and general reading disabilities of secondary-level students: identification and educational relevance. *Journal of Special Education, 27*(3), 321–337.

Espin, C. A., & Deno, S. L. (1993b). Performance in reading from content area text as an indicator of achievement. *Remedial and Special Education, 14*(6), 47–59.

Espin, C. A., & Foegen, A. (1996). Validity of general outcome measures for predicting secondary students' performance on content-area tasks. *Exceptional Children, 62*(6), 497–514.

Ferguson, C. L., Jr., & Fuchs, L. S. (1991). Scoring accuracy within curriculum-based measurement: A comparison of teachers and microcomputer applications. *Journal of Special Education Technology, 11*(1), 26–32.

Fox, S. L., Howell, K. W., Morehead, M. K., & Zucker, S. H. (1993). *Curriculum-based evaluation: Teaching and decision-making.* Pacific Grove, CA: Brooks Cole Publishing.

Fredericksen, J. R., & Collins, A. (1989). A systems approach to educational testing. *Educational Researcher, 18*(9), 27–32.

Fuchs, L. S. (1992). Classwide decision-making with computerized curriculum-based measurement. *Preventing School Failure, 36*(2), 30–33.

Fuchs, L. S. (1988). Effects of computer-managed instruction on teachers' implementation of systematic monitoring programs and student achievement. *Journal of Educational Research, 81*(5), 294–304.

Fuchs, L. S., Bahr, C. M., & Reith, H. J. (1985). Effects of goal structures and performance contingencies on the math performance of adolescents with learning disabilities. *Journal of Learning Disabilities, 22*(9), 554–560.

Fuchs, L. S., Butterworth, J. R., & Fuchs, D. (1989). Effects of ongoing curriculum-based measurement on student awareness of goals and progress. *Education and Treatment of Children, 12*(1), 63–72.

Fuchs, L. S., & Deno, S. L. (1994). Must instructionally useful performance assessment be based in the curriculum? *Exceptional Children, 61*(1), 15–24.

Fuchs, L. S., & Deno, S. L. (1991b). Paradigmatic distinctions between instructionally relevant measurement models. *Exceptional Children, 57*(6), 448–499.

Fuchs, L. S., & Deno, S. L. (1991a). Effects of curriculum within curriculum-based measurement. *Exceptional Children, 58*(3), 232–243.

Fuchs, L. S., Deno, S. L., & Mirkin, P. K. (1984). The effects of frequent curriculum-based measurement and evaluation on pedagogy, student achievement, and student awareness of learning. *American Educational Research Journal, 21*(2), 499–460.

Fuchs, L. S., & Fuchs, D. (1993). Effects of systematic observation and feedback on teachers' implementation of curriculum-based measurement. *Teacher Education and Special Education, 16*(2), 178–187.

Fuchs, L. S., & Fuchs, D. (1991). Curriculum-based measurements: Current applications and future directions. *Preventing School Failure, 35*(3), 6–11.

Fuchs, L. S., & Fuchs, D. (1987). The relation between methods of graphing student performance data and achievement: A meta-analysis. *Journal of Special Education Technology, 8*(3), 5–13.

Fuchs, L. S., & Fuchs, D. (1984a). Teaching beginning reading skills: A unique approach. *Teaching Exceptional Children, 17*(1), 48–53.

Fuchs, L. S., & Fuchs, D. (1984b). Criterion-referenced assessment without measurement: How accurate for special education? *Remedial and Special Education, 5*(4), 29–33.

Fuchs, L. S. Fuchs, D., & Deno, S. (1985). Importance of goal ambitiousness and goal mastery to student achievement. *Exceptional Children, 52*(1), 63–71.

Fuchs, L. S., Fuchs, D., & Hamlett, C. L. (1994). Strengthening the connection between assessment and instructional planning with expert systems. *Exceptional Children, 61*(2), 138–146.

Fuchs, L. S., Fuchs, D. & Hamlett, C. L. (1990). Curriculum-based measurement: A standardized, long-term goal approach to monitoring student progress. *Academic Therapy, 25*(5), 615–632.

Fuchs, L. S., Fuchs, D., & Hamlett, C. L. (1989a). Effects of instrumental use of curriculum-based measurement to enhance instructional programs. *Remedial and Special Education, 10*(2), 43–52.

Fuchs, L. S., Fuchs, D., & Hamlett, C. L. (1989b). Monitoring reading growth using student recalls: Effects of two teacher feedback systems. *Journal of Educational Research, 83*(2), 103–110.

Fuchs, L. S., Fuchs, D., & Hamlett, C. L. (1989c). Computers and curriculum-based measurement: Effects of teacher feedback systems. *School Psychology Review, 18*(1), 112–125.

Fuchs, L. S., Fuchs, D., & Hamlett, C. L. (1984d). Effects of alternative goal structures within curriculum-based measurement. *Exceptional Children, 55*(5), 429–438.

Fuchs, L. S., Fuchs, D., Hamlett, C. L., & Allinder, R. M. (1991a). Effects of expert system advice within curriculum-based measurement in teacher planning and student achievement in spelling. *School Psychology Review, 20*(1), 49–66.

Fuchs, L. S., Fuchs, D., Hamlett, C. L., & Allinder, R. M. (1991b). The contribution of skills analysis to curriculum-based measurement in spelling. *Exceptional Children, 57*(5), 443–452.

Fuchs, L. S., Fuchs, D., Hamlett, C. L., & Ferguson, C. (1992). Effects of expert system consultation within curriculum-based measurement, using a reading maze task. *Exceptional Children, 58*(5), 436–450.

Fuchs, L. S., Fuchs, D., Hamlett, C. L., & Hasselbring, T. S. (1987). Using computers with curriculum-based monitoring: effects on teacher efficiency and satisfaction. *Journal of Special Education Technology, 8*(4), 14–27.

Fuchs, L. S., Fuchs, D., Hamlett, C. L., Phillips, N. B., & Karns, K. (1995). General educators' specialized adaptation for students with learning disabilities. *Exceptional Children, 61*(5), 440–459.

Fuchs, L. S., Fuchs, D., Hamlett, C. L., Phillips, N. B., & Bentz, J. (1994). Classwide curriculum-based measurement: Helping general educators meet the challenge of student diversity. *Exceptional Children, 60*(6), 518–537.

Fuchs, L. S., Fuchs, D., Hamlett, C. L., & Stecker, P. M. (1990). The role of skills analysis in curriculum-based measurement in math. *School Psychology Review, 19*(1), 6–22.

Fuchs, L. S., Fuchs, D., Hamlett, C. L., & Stecker, P. M. (1991). Effects of curriculum-based measurement and consultation on teacher planning and student achievement in mathematics operations. *American Educational Research Journal, 28*(3), 617–641.

Fuchs, L. S., Fuchs, D., & Stecker, P. M. (1989). Effects of curriculum-based measurement on teachers' instructional planning. *Journal of Learning Disabilities, 22*(1), 51–59.

Fuchs, L. S., Hamlett, C. L., Fuchs, D., Stecker, P. M. & Ferguson, C. (1988). Conducting curriculum-based measurement with computerized data collection: Effects on efficiency and teacher satisfaction. *Journal of Special Education Technology, 9*(2), 73–86.

Gickling, E. E., & Thompson, V. P. (1985). A personal view of curriculum-based assessment. *Exceptional Children, 52*(3), 205–218.

Hall, T. E., Tindal, G., & Wininger, J. (1997). Content area modification and instruction: A model of inclusion and coordination of special needs students. Paper submitted for publication.

Hollenbeck, K., & Tindal, G. (1996). Teaching law concepts within mainstreamed middle school social studies settings. *Diagnostique, 21*(4), 37–58.

Hollenbeck, K., Almond, P., & Tindal, G. (1997). *Teachers perceptions on accommodations on high stakes testing.* Manuscript submitted for publication.

Individuals with Disabilities Education Act Amendments of 1997, P.L. 105–17, 105th Congress, 1st session.

Marston, D. (1989). A curriculum-based measurement approach to assessing academic performance: What is it and why do it? In M. Shinn (Ed.), *Curriculum-based measurement: Assessing special children* (pp. 18–78). New York: The Gilford Press.

Marston, D. (1988). Measuring progress on IEPs: A comparison of graphing approaches. *Exceptional Children, 55*(1), 38–44.

Marston, D. (1987–1988). The effectiveness of special education: A time series analysis of reading performance in regular and special education settings. *The Journal of Special Education, 21*(4), 13–26.

Marston, D. (1987). The effectiveness of special education: A time series analysis of reading performance in regular and special education settings. *Journal of Special Education, 21*(4), 13–26.

Marston, D., Mirkin, P. K., & Deno, S. L. (1984). Curriculum-based measurement: An alternative to traditional screening, referral, and identification. *The Journal of Special Education, 18*(2), 109–117.

McCleery, J., Heath, B., Helwig, B., & Tindal, G. (1997). *Promoting geographic knowledge through content specification and explicit instruction.* Paper submitted for publication.

McKenzie, R. G. (1991a). Content area instruction delivered by secondary learning disabilities teachers: A national survey. *Learning Disabilities Quarterly, 14,* 115–122.

McKenzie, R. G. (1991b). The form and substance of secondary resource models: Content area versus skill instruction. *Journal of Learning Disabilities, 24*(8), 467–470.

Merrill, K. W., & Shinn, M. R. (1990). Critical variables in the learning disabilities identification process. *School Psychology Review, 19*(1), 74–82.

Messick, S. (1989). Validity. In R. Linn (Ed.). *Educational measurement (3rd ed.)* (pp. 13–104). New York: Macmillan.

National Geographic Society (1995). *Standards for Life.* Washington, DC: Author.

Rodden-Nord, K., & Shinn, M. R. (1991). The range of reading skills within and across general education classrooms: Contributions to understanding special education for students with mild handicaps. *Journal of Special Education, 24*(4), 441–453.

Shinn, M. (1989). *Curriculum-based measurement: Assessing special children.* New York: The Gilford Press.

Shinn, M. R., Habedank, L., Rodden-Nord, K., & Knutson, N. (1993). Using curriculum-based measurement to identify potential candidates for reintegration into general education. *Journal of Special Education, 27*(2), 202–221.

Shinn, M., & Marston, D. (1985). Differentiating mildly handicapped, low-achieving, and regular education students: A curriculum-based approach. *Remedial and Special Education, 6*(2), 31–38.

Shinn, M. R., Tindal, G. A., & Spira, D. A. (1987). Special education referrals as an index of teacher tolerance: Are teachers imperfect tests? *Exceptional Children, 54*(1), 32–40.

Taylor, C. (1994). Assessment for measurement or standards: The peril and promise of large scale assessment reform. *American Educational Research Journal, 31*(2), 231–262.

Thurlow, M. L., Scott, D. L., & Ysseldyke, J. E. (1995). *A compilation of states' guidelines for accommodations in assessments for students with disabilities,* [Synthesis Report No. 18]. Minneapolis, MN: University of Minnesota National Center on Educational Outcomes.

Tindal, G. (1988). Curriculum-based measurement. In J. L. Graden, J. E. Zins, M. C. Curtis (Eds.), *Alternative educational delivery systems: Enhancing instructional options for all students* (pp. 111–136). Washington, DC: National Association of School Psychologists.

Tindal, G. (1987). Graphing performance. *Teaching Exceptional Children, 20*(1), 44–46.

Tindal, G., Heath, B., Hollenbeck, K., Almond, P., & Harniss, M. (in press). Accommodating students with disabilities on large-scale tests: An empirical study of student response and test administration demands. *Exceptional Children.*

Tindal, G., & Marston, D. (1996). Technical adequacy of alternative reading measures as performance assessments. *Exceptionality, 6*(4), 201–230.

Tindal, G., & Nolet, V. (1996). Serving students in middle school content classes: A heuristic study of critical variables linking instruction and assessment. *The Journal of Special Education, 29*(4), 414–432.

Tindal, G., Nolet, V., & Blake, G. (1993). *Teaching and assessment in content areas.* Research Consultation and Teaching Program Training Module No. 4. Eugene, OR: University of Oregon.

Tindal, G., Rebar, M., Nolet, V., & McCollum, S. (1995). Understanding instructional outcome options for students with special needs in content classes. *Learning Disabilities: Research and Practice, 10*(2), 72–84.

Tucker, J. (1985). Curriculum-based assessment: An introduction. *Exceptional Children, 52*(3), 199–204.

U.S. Department of Education. (1995). *Seventeenth Annual Report to Congress.* Washington, DC: Author.

Wesson, C. L. (1992). Using curriculum-based measurement to create instructional groups. *Preventing School Failure, 36*(2), 17–20.

Wesson, C. L. (1991). Curriculum-based measurement and two models of follow-up consultation. *Exceptional Children, 57*(3), 246–256.

Wesson, C. L., & Deno, S. L. (1989). An analysis of long-term instructional plans in reading for elementary resource room students. *Remedial and Special Education, 10*(1), 21–28.

Wesson, C., Fuchs, L., Tindal, G., Mirkin, P., & Deno, S. L. (1986). Facilitating the efficiency of on-going curriculum-based measurement. *Teacher Education and Special Education, 9*(4), 166–172.

Wesson, C. L., Vierthaler, J. M., & Haubrich, P. A. (1989a). An efficient technique for establishing reading groups. *Reading Teacher, 42*(7), 466–469.

Wesson, C. L., Vierthaler, J., & Haubrich, P. (1989b). The discriminative validity of curriculum-based measures for establishing reading groups. *Reading Research and Instruction, 29*(1), 23–32.

Wesson, C., Skiba, R., Sevcik, B., King, R. P., & Deno, S. (1984). The effects of technically adequate instructional data on achievement. *Remedial and Special Education, 5*(5), 17–22.

CHAPTER 3

Attention Disorders

Richard Conte

I. THE DOMAIN OF ATTENTION

Explaining the role of attention as an aspect of learning disabilities (LDs) is problematic because the term *attention* has taken on a variety of meanings across different disciplines. For instance, attention has come to mean one thing in psychology and quite another in the study of LDs. Even within the LD field, the term attention has been used differently at different times. As we shall see, in the early years of LD research, some investigators believed that attention was the central factor in explaining LDs. More recently, attention deficits have become a field of study in their own right, and they are generally viewed to be quite different from LDs.

A. The Psychological Study of Attention

Within the field of psychology, the investigation of attention has centered around the variation in one's ability to attend to external events. Everyone experiences lapses of attention at least some of the time. Every student has been frustrated by an inability to attend, even in situations where unpleasant consequences have ensued. For example, even though it may mean the difference between a good grade and a poor one, students sometimes cannot resist dwelling on the pleasant events in the after-school hours at the expense of understanding the math lesson at hand. At classical music concerts, one may become lost in extraneous thoughts despite

Learning about Learning Disabilities, Second Edition

the fact that ticket prices are exorbitant. Suddenly, when the music tempo changes, and one refocuses on the music, wondering where the mind has been for the past few minutes. Every parent has wondered why their child can attend to video games for hours but cannot stand math homework for more than a few minutes.

Although attention is a prerequisite to almost everything, it is a difficult and complicated concept. Consider the number of terms that have been used to describe attention. Moray (1969) identified seven components of attention: mental concentration, vigilance, selective attention, search, activation, set, and analysis by synthesis. Somewhat more simply, Posner (1975) suggested three components to attention: alertness, selection, and effort. In the field of special education, Keogh and Margolis (1976) described coming to attention, decision-making, and sustaining attention.

Some attempts to understand attention make intuitive sense and are apparent in our everyday lives. Taking Posner's three-component model (alertness, selection, and effort), *alertness* or receptivity to external signals varies considerably over the course of a single day. Thus, after a hard day at work or study, one is often less able to focus on a task than when one is fresh in the morning. If a meal is skipped and blood sugar drops to a critically low level, one may find it difficult to attend to even very simple events. In addition to these internal factors, alertness can vary as a function of external circumstances (i.e., certain types of situations [a TV program] are inherently easier to attend to than others [a teacher's explanation of a math lesson]. As the name implies, *selection* refers to the ability to choose certain features of the environment for special processing. Selective attention occurs whenever one concentrates on some aspect of the environment in the face of distracters. For example, workers in a factory utilize selective attention to stay focused on their assigned tasks against a background of loud machine noise. Also, members of the audience at a play or concert likely use their selective attention to help keep focused on the event at hand when someone in the audience crinkles the wrapping paper on a piece of hard candy. Last, it has been discovered that expending *effort* in attending to one source of information compromises the ability to attend to other sources. For example, at a noisy party one usually can attend to only one conversation at a time. In the laboratory, if a subject is asked to monitor a message in one ear, he or she seems to have little conscious awareness of the content of messages delivered to the other ear.

B. The Study of Attention within the LD Field

In early LD research of the 1970s, a number of investigators explored the hypothesis that LDs were caused by deficits in attention. Specifically, the role of selective and sustained attention deficits in LDs was investigated. There is some evidence that attention does play a role in LDs.

C. Attention Deficits

The inability to pay attention has been studied as a medical condition (attention deficit hyperactivity disorder, or ADHD) that has little overlap with attention as it has been studied in psychology. In this field, diagnostic criteria have been developed, and these have focused on three primary characteristics: inattention, impulsivity, and overactivity. This area of study is important for the LD field because many of the children who have LDs also meet the diagnostic criteria for ADHD. In addition, evidence also suggests that there may be certain types of learning deficits associated with ADHD.

II. SCOPE AND SEQUENCE

In this chapter, LDs and attention disorders are assumed to be different entities. Whereas LDs are characterized by the specificity of dysfunction (e.g., a deficit in reading or spelling), attention disorders tend to be relatively diffuse and affect functioning in a wide range of contexts. Not everyone agrees with the position that attention disorders and LDs are essentially different (indeed some have thought that LDs are caused by attention disorder), but this view is consistent with that put forward at the most recent National Conference on Learning Disabilities (Kavanagh & Truss, 1988). As will be evident in this chapter, although LDs and attention disorders are different, they often occur together.

In the LD field, attention has been studied in two different ways, and in each of these the term attention has been defined somewhat differently. One line of research has been concerned with the possibility that LDs are caused by deficiencies in one or more of the components of attention that are described in the preceding section. So, for example, a large number of studies have been conducted in which the performance of LD children and non-LD children are compared on various measures of selective attention. The second line of research has focused on children with ADHD. However, in this area of study, attention is not defined in terms of the components of attention; instead, diagnostic criteria have been developed for use by experienced clinicians. These diagnostic criteria (to be described in a subsequent section) consist of descriptions of behaviors that are thought to be characteristic of children with ADHD: inattention, impulsivity, and hyperactivity. With respect to attention deficit disorder (ADD), it is important to note that a variety of labels have been used for this condition. To some extent these labels reflect changes in understanding of this condition over time. For example, in early research, the terms *hyperkinesis* or *hyperactivity* were used, consistent with the prevailing view of the times that abnormal activity level was a central feature. More recently, researchers have placed more emphasis on the attentional components of the disorder and thus the term ADD has emerged, and then ADD with and without hyperactivity and most recently ADHD. For the sake of simplicity, we will employ the term in current use, ADHD, as the general term to describe this population.

Over the years, as the conception of ADHD has changed, there have been changes in the procedures used to assess this condition. As might be expected, earlier methods focused on activity level, whereas more recently, assessment procedures have become more elaborate to take in other components of attention disorder such as inattention and impulsivity.

In addition, there has been debate focused on whether attention disorder is a single entity or several entities. Again, as we shall see, these changes have had implications for assessment procedures.

As more and more children with ADHD have been identified, there has been much interest in finding ways to help these patients overcome their difficulties. Stimulant drugs have been the most widely used treatment. Recently, other nonstimulant drugs such as tricyclic antidepressants have been used with some success. Moreover, there have been a wide range of behavioral and psychological treatments that have had varying degrees of success.

Lastly, as has been the case in the LD field, the definition of ADHD has been broadened to include adults. There has been an increasing realization that ADHD is not restricted to childhood, but that a substantial number of children with this condition continue to show symptoms in adulthood. As a result, many of the assessment methods that were designed for children have been modified to suit adults. And as might be expected, many of the same treatment methods have been adapted for use with adults. The present chapter will deal primarily with ADHD as it occurs in children. The lack of attention to adults by no means suggests that adult ADHD is an unimportant issue, but rather it cannot be covered here because of space limitations. For those interested in obtaining more information about ADHD in adults, please see Hallowell and Ratey (1994).

Of the two approaches to attention that have been described above, the major portion of this chapter is concerned with ADHD. This is justifiable because far more research has been conducted on issues related to ADHD than on deficiencies in attentional components in LDs.

It is important to note that the terms ADHD and LD stem from different classification systems. ADHD is found in the *Diagnostic and Statistical Manual of Mental Disorders,* 4th ed., (*DSM-IV;* American Psychiatric Association, 1994), whereas the term LD may be found (in the United States, at least) in P.L. 94-142. ADHD does not appear in P.L. 94-142; however, LDs are referred to in the *DSM-IV* as specific developmental disorders such as developmental arithmetic disorder and developmental reading disorder, among others.

From this chapter readers should understand the following:

1. The role of attention in LDs
2. The characteristics of ADHD
3. Methods of diagnosing ADHD
4. Theories of the causes of ADHD
5. Methods of treating ADHD

III. WHY IT IS IMPORTANT TO STUDY ATTENTION DEFICITS

In this section, the two approaches to the study of attention that are described above are elaborated upon.

A. Role of Attention Deficits in LDs

The exploration of attention deficits in LDs was motivated by the belief that LD was caused by deficiencies in attention (Dykman, Ackerman, Clements, & Peters, 1971; Ross, 1976). This issue was investigated primarily in terms of performance on two types of attention tasks: selective attention tasks and sustained attention tasks.

1. Selective Attention

As was discussed previously, selective attention is usually defined as the ability to maintain attention to target stimuli when distractors are present. Hagan's (1967) incidental learning task will be used to exemplify a selective attention task. In this methodology, a central stimulus (e.g., a picture of an animal) is presented together with an incidental or background stimulus (e.g., a picture of a household object). A subject in such an experiment is told to pay attention to the central stimulus; usually nothing is said about the incidental stimulus. Presumably, a child with good selective attention skills will focus only on the central item, whereas a child with more diffuse attention will attend to both the central and incidental items. These different patterns are revealed by asking subjects what they remember after exposure to a list of items, each of which contains a central and incidental stimulus. In a large number of studies (see Hallihan & Reeve, 1980) it has been found that non-LD children retain more central items than do LD children, but LD children retain more incidental items than do non-LD children. On the basis of such findings, it was concluded that LD children were deficient in selective attention.

One of the difficulties in evaluating the role of selective attention in LDs is that the studies described by Hallihan and Reeve (1980) used mixed samples of subjects. Specifically, as many as 30–40% of LD children are known to have ADHD, and if such a large proportion of ADHD subjects were included in samples of LD children, then it is possible that the deficit in selective attention was due to the presence of ADHD rather than LD.

A few studies have segregated subjects into homogeneous groups of LD subjects with and without ADHD, and the findings from these studies are consistent with the hypothesis that there is a selective attention deficit in children with LD. On an incidental learning task, LD children performed more poorly relative to normal controls, whereas children with ADHD and no LDs performed similarly to controls (Tarnowski, Prince & Nay, 1986). Richards et al. (1990) obtained a similar result with a letter distraction task. Although these studies indicate a selective attention deficit in LD children, they do not tell us whether a selective attention deficit is responsible for the learning problems experienced by LD children. To do this, they would have to establish that a relationship exists between performance on selective attention tests and measures of either the type or severity of LDs.

2. Sustained Attention

As the name implies, sustained attention means that one must attend for an extended period of time. There does not appear to be a precise definition for what is meant by sustained. For the most part it seems to refer to a set of conditions that require a subject to maintain relatively constant attention to a task for a period of at least 10 min. Sustained attention will be illustrated by the continuous performance task. In a commonly used version of this task, subjects are instructed to monitor a series of either visually or auditorily presented individual letters or numbers, and are required to respond when a certain target stimulus is present. For example, they might be asked to press a button whenever the letter "x" is preceded by the letter "a." This method provides an index of sustained attention because items are presented at a relatively brisk rate so that subjects have to maintain nearly constant attention in order to perform at a high level. There is an inconsistent pattern of findings across the studies that have used the continuous performance test (CPT) and that have segregated subjects into LD and ADHD groups. On the one hand, Chee, Logan, Schachar, Lindsay, and Wachsmuth (1989) Richards, Samuels, Turnure, and Ysseldyke (1990), and Tarnowski et al. (1986) found that LD children did not differ from controls. In contrast, children with ADHD tended to make more errors of commission (i.e., make responses to nontarget stimuli) (Chee et al., 1989; Richards et al., 1990). This pattern of behavior is usually interpreted as a reflection of impulsive behavior (acting without thinking), which is one of the defining characteristics of ADHD. On the other hand there are three studies that found that both LD and ADHD children performed more poorly than controls on the CPT. Robins (1992), August and Garfinkel (1990), and Kupietz (1990) have found that CPT performance did not differ when ADHD and LD children were compared. Both of these groups performed more poorly than children without either disability. The implication of these studies is that if CPT is a measure of sustained attention, then both LD and ADHD children are deficient in this process. It is not clear why the literature is inconsistent with regard to CPT performance in LD and ADHD. It may mean that the procedures used in defining these populations are still inadequate.

Clearly, there are unresolved issues with regard to the role of attention in LDs, and on the basis of the present analysis a number of recommendations can be made for future research. First, more research is needed in which a variety of measures of both selective and sustained attention is used with groups of subjects identified as having LDs without ADHD, LDs with ADHD, and ADHD without LDs. Second, these studies should also attempt to demonstrate that the deficit in attention is related to the problems that subjects experience outside the testing situation. For LDs, are deficiencies in selective attention related to the type of LDs? In ADHD, is the deficit in sustained attention related to symptoms that are expressed at school and home?

B. Many Children Have Both LDs and ADHD

Individuals who are responsible for providing service to LD children must be aware of the characteristics of and treatment procedures used for children with ADHD, because they will undoubtedly encounter many of these children in their practice. Recent estimates indicate that a substantial number of children have both LD and ADHD, although estimates of the degree of overlap vary considerably. For instance, Halperin, Gittelman, Klein, and Ruddell (1984) found that 9% of children with ADHD also had LD, whereas Silver (1980) found the degree of overlap to be 92%. Also, a range of studies (see Barkley, 1996, for review) has indicated that between 19 and 26% of children with ADHD have at least one type of LD. The considerable variation in these estimates is probably due to a range of factors including sampling error and difference in subject selection criteria across studies.

Given the large degree of overlap, does this mean that ADHD and LD are causally related? There are four lines of evidence against this hypothesis. First, attention measures do not seem to be strongly related to measures of ability in core academic areas. For instance, Shaywitz, Fletcher, and Shaywitz (1994) found relatively strong relationships between language measures and reading measures but very little association between attention measures and measures of reading ability, suggesting that attention deficit is not causally related to reading ability. Second, neurological measures have indicated that different areas of the brain are involved in reading and attention problems. Reading functions appear to be subserved by the areas in the left hemisphere of the brain that are related to language processing; specifically those areas of the brain near the perisylvian association cortex in the left hemisphere (Ojemann, Ojemann, Lettich, & Berger, 1989). In contrast, ADHD is associated with quite different brain areas. Zametkin et al. (1990) found that in adults who had a childhood history of ADHD, there was reduced glucose metabolism throughout the brain, with the largest reductions in the premotor and superior prefrontal cortex. Third, a number of performance differences have been observed when children with LD and ADHD are compared. For example, Felton and Wood (1989) have shown that rote memory tends to pose problems for ADHD children but not for LD children. In contrast, one segment of the LD population (children with reading disabilities) tends to show deficits on rapid automatized naming (RAN) tasks (Denkla & Rudel, 1976; Felton & Wood, 1989; but for an exception, see Dykman et al., 1985), whereas children with ADHD do as well as controls. In RAN tasks, the speed at which pictures of objects, colors, or symbols can be named is measured. Fourth, Tant and Douglas (1982) found that on a 20-questions task, ADHD children asked less efficient questions and used less efficient strategies than either normal or reading-disabled children. The latter two groups did not differ from each other.

These differences in cognitive processing skills may have important implications for the assessment and treatment of children with LDs and ADHD. The lack of efficient learning strategies in children with ADHD suggests that learning strategies should be examined during assessment, particularly in children suspected of having ADHD. It seems reasonable that training in the use of more efficient strategies could be of benefit in overcoming the difficulties in rote memory that were described by Felton and Wood (1989). The picture for LD children is more complicated: they appear to have deficiencies in selective attention as well as in RAN tasks. Is it possible that these two areas of learning are related? It may be relevant that selective attention tasks and RAN require relatively rapid responses. Perhaps LD children have difficulty with situations that require such quick responses. To confirm this, one would have to examine the performance of LD children in different situations that require speeded responses. Comparisons should be made between tasks that involve selective attention and those that do not, so that the relative importance of both processes could be assessed.

Groups that have had the responsibility of developing definitions of LDs have generally taken the position that LDs and attention disorders are different. The reformulation of the definition of LDs by the National Joint Conference on Learning Disabilities (Kavanagh & Truss, 1988) does not specifically comment on the relationship between attention disorders and LDs. The only statement relevant to disorders like ADHD is that problems in "self-regulatory behaviors, social perception and social interaction may exist with learning disabilities but do not by themselves constitute a learning disability" (Kavanagh & Truss, 1988). In the definition proposed by the Interagency Committee on Learning Disabilities, there is an explicit statement that while attention disorders may cause learning problems, they do not cause LDs. This statement makes the important point that a learning problem is not necessarily an LD.

Regardless of whether ADHD is an LD or a learning problem, it has been documented that children with ADHD perform more poorly in school than children without ADHD. They are more likely to be behind in reading and arithmetic

(Cantwell, 1978). Holborow and Berry (1986) found that children with ADHD were much more likely to be rated by their teachers as having very much difficulty in academic areas as compared to their classmates without ADHD. Consequently, it is important for LD professionals to be very familiar with the type of learning problems presented by children with ADHD.

To summarize, there appears to be clear evidence that ADHD and LDs are different both in terms of behavioral manifestations and neurological underpinnings. On the other hand, it is the case that children with ADHD are more likely to experience academic difficulties than children without ADHD, and teachers and other LD professionals must be prepared to deal with the problems presented by children with ADHD in academic settings. There is evidence that the types of problems presented by children with LDs and ADHD are different. Existing evidence suggests that children with ADHD have poorer rote memory and problem-solving skills as compared to reading-disabled children. It should also be noted that more research is needed in this area to explore similarities and differences between children with LD and ADHD.

IV. HOW IS AN ATTENTION DISORDER DEFINED?

A. *DSM* Criteria

As we have seen in this chapter, the term attention has been used in several different ways. In one sense, attention can signify the various processes (alertness, selection, effort) that are described in attention theories. Thus, there is a body of literature that selective attention deficits are quite prevalent in the population of LD children. However, as used in describing children with ADHD, the concept of attention is considerably more complicated, and in fact, attention is just one aspect of the symptomatology of ADHD. Current conceptions of ADHD have been heavily influenced by the DSMs of the American Psychiatric Association. These manuals are developed to provide assistance to practitioners in establishing diagnoses for a wide range of mental disorders, including ADHD. Every few years the *DSM* is revised, and with each revision there are usually modifications in the diagnostic criteria for the various disorders. This is clearly evident in the most recent three revisions which are summarized in Table 3.1. It is important to review these changes in the diagnostic criteria because it provides insight into many of the basic issues in this area of research. Across the three versions of the *DSM,* there are three classes of symptoms considered: inattention, impulsivity, and hyperactivity. An example of an inattention symptom is that the individual has difficulty completing tasks or doesn't seem to listen. Impulsivity symptoms describe instances of acting without thinking (blurting out answers or having difficulty taking turns). As might be expected, the hyperactivity symptoms contain descriptions of restless or fidgety behaviors such as squirming while seated in a chair, or re-

Table 3.1

The Evolution of the Defining Characteristics of Attention Deficit Disorder[a]

DSM-III	DSM-III-R	DSM-IV
ADD without hyperactivity (ADDWO) defining symptoms:	ADHD defining symptoms:	ADHD (primarily inattentive type) defining symptoms:
Three symptoms of inattention	Eight symptoms from a list of fourteen indicators of inattention, impulsivity, and hyperactivity	Six symptoms of inattention from a list of nine symptoms
Three symptoms of impulsivity		
ADDH defining symptoms: Two symptoms of hyperactivity		ADHD (primarily hyperactive-impulsive type) defining symptoms: Six symptoms from a list of nine items (six hyperactivity items and three impulsivity items)
		ADHD (combined type) defining symptoms: Meets the criteria for inattention, impulsivity, and hyperactivity as noted above

[a]ADD, attention-deficit disorder; ADHD, attention-deficit hyperactivity disorder; *DSM, Diagnostic and Statistical Manual of Mental Disorders.*

peatedly getting up from a chair for no apparent reason. According to the *DSM-III* (American Psychiatric Association, 1980) there were two types of attention disorder: ADD with hyperactivity (ADDH), and ADD without hyperactivity (ADDWO). In order to meet the criteria for ADDWO, one must have three symptoms of inattention and three symptoms of impulsivity. To meet the criteria for ADDH, one must have two symptoms of hyperactivity in addition to the symptoms for inattention and impulsivity. In the *DSM-III-R* (American Psychiatric Association, 1987), the system was revised so that the distinctions between the different types of ADHD were eliminated. In this system, there was a list of 14 symptoms that were a mix of inattention, impulsivity, and hyperactivity. To meet the criteria for ADHD, it was necessary to have at least 8 of the 14 defining symptoms. Most recently, in the *DSM-IV* (American Psychiatric Association, 1994) there has been a return to a system that is reminiscent of the *DSM-III*. In the *DSM-IV* there are three types of ADHD: primarily inattentive type, primarily hyperactive-impulsive type, and a combined type. To meet the criteria for ADHD inattentive type, one must have at least six symptoms of inattention. To meet the criteria for ADHD hyperactive-impulsive type one must have at least six symptoms from a list of nine items (six hyperactivity items and three impulsivity items). To meet the criteria for ADHD combined type, all the symptoms for inattention, hyperactivity, and impulsivity must be present.

To some extent the revisions specified in the *DSM-IV* were prompted by evidence that the attentional and hyperactivity components are not highly correlated (Lahey, Pelham et al., 1988). In addition, Lahey, Pelham et al. (1988) also showed that the impulsivity components cannot be clearly segregated from those of hyperactivity.

In summary, it is important to keep in mind that the definition of ADHD is in a state of flux. Undoubtedly, the definition will be revised again before long, and with each of these revisions, there will be a shift in our understanding of the characteristics of ADHD.

B. Situational versus Pervasive ADHD

The diagnostic criteria specified in the *DSM-III* and *DSM-IIIR* indicated that a diagnosis of ADHD could be made when the symptoms were situational (occurred in a limited number of situations; e.g., at home but not at school, or vice-versa) or pervasive (occurred in many situations; e.g., at both home and school). According to the *DSM-III,* information from both school and home should be considered in diagnosing ADHD. In case of disagreement between these two sources, the school report should be given the most weight. In the *DSM-III-R,* the definition was broadened with the statement that the symptoms of ADHD may be confined to one situation. Thus, in this system the findings from both school and home were given equal weight.

There is reason to question the legitimacy of situational ADHD. For instance, Goodman and Stevenson (1989a) found that only pervasive, but not situational, ADHD subjects could be distinguished from non-ADHD antisocial subjects on the basis of measures of inattention and specific learning problems. In response to these data and others, the *DSM-IV* criteria have been made more stringent in that it is specified that some impairment from the symptoms should be present in *two or more* settings (at school [or work] and at home).

C. ADHD and Psychiatric Disorders

Diagnosing ADHD is made even more complex by the fact that other disorders often co-occur with it. The large number of LD children with ADHD has been discussed previously. In addition, ADHD often co-occurs with a number of other psychiatric conditions. As discussed in Barkley (1996), between 35 and 60% of children with ADHD meet the criteria for oppositional defiant disorder (ODD) by age 7 or later and 30 to 50% meet the criteria for conduct disorder (CD). In addition, 15 to 25% eventually qualify for a diagnosis of antisocial personality disorder.

It is not clear if there are causal relationships among ADHD, CD, and ODD. Some studies suggest that CD and ADHD are independent. For example, Szatmari, Offord, and Boyle (1989) found that family dysfunction is more likely when ADHD and CD are both present, but not with ADHD alone. Also, Lahey, Piacentini, et al. (1988) observed that a relationship exists between familial psychiatric dysfunction and CD, but not ADHD. Both of these studies would lead one to conclude that there are different causal factors involved in CD and ADHD. On the other hand Biederman, Faraone, and Lapey (1992) have data which suggest familial associations among these disorders.

V. WHAT HAS BEEN DONE IN THIS RESEARCH AREA?

A. Characteristics and Developmental Course of ADHD

The characteristics and developmental course of ADHD have to be discussed at the same time because as a developmental problem, the symptoms of ADHD have to be examined in light of the naturally occurring changes in developmental expectations and norms. For example, while activity level is a very prominent symptom of ADHD, it is also the case that in the normal population there are striking changes in activity level with increasing age. It is more acceptable to be highly active as a young child, but constant fidgeting in an adolescent or adult strikes most of us as peculiar. Similarly, although difficulties in social functioning are apparent in ADHD, the nature and importance of social functioning undergo dramatic changes during development. It should also be kept in mind that the determination of the characteristics and developmental course of ADHD are made more complicated by the fact that large numbers of these children also show signs of the comorbid disorders of ODD and CD. Many of the studies that have provided information on the developmental course of ADHD do not always examine children for the presence of comorbid psychiatric disorders. Recent estimates suggest that ADHD affects between 4 and 6% of the school-age population and that it is about three times more common in males than females. Developmentally, attention disorders are more common in the age range of 6–8 years, perhaps because the assessment criteria for ADHD include activity level and, even in normal functioning children, this is a developmental period characterized by high activity level. Some parents indicate that they identified their child as showing difficult behavior soon after birth; however, the deviant behaviors such as noncompliance with parental requests and perhaps also aggressive conduct may emerge when the child is 3 or 4. By the time these children enter school, problems of inattention and lack of task completion start to become apparent. Very likely, these symptoms appear because the attentional requirements within the school environment are much more taxing than those the child is likely to encounter at home.

As the child approaches the teen years, the nature of the problems may undergo change. As is the case in normally developing children, activity level tends to decrease with increasing age. However, other aspects of ADHD assume greater importance. As homework assignments become more demanding, difficulties with assignment completion become increasingly apparent. The increasing importance of social relationships is likely to be problematic for children with ADHD. Indeed, it has been documented that children with ADHD tend to be the least popular in a school classroom. With little reflection one can appreciate the fact that a child who tends to impulsively blurt out the first thing that occurs to him or her is likely to offend others.

In adulthood, as many as 60% continue to show signs of ADHD, although interpersonal problems continue to trouble as many as 75% (Barkley, 1989). Other findings indicate that the long-term prognosis is worsened considerably when CD occurs in combination with ADHD. For instance, Mannuzza et al. (1989) found that there is increased risk of criminal behavior only in ADHD children with an associated CD.

B. Causes of ADHD

1. Biological versus Environmental Factors

We approach the study of the causes of ADHD by first considering the relatively broad issue of biological versus environmental causes. More specific factors are considered in subsequent sections. The investigation of biological factors has included research on the genetics of ADHD and also investigations of physical maladies (delay in developmental milestones, chronic diseases), which appear to be commonly associated with ADHD. Research on environmental factors has considered the importance of psychosocial factors, perinatal influences, and dietary sensitivities.

a. Epidemiological Data   The Ontario Child Health Study (OCHS) (Szatmari et al., 1989) set out to examine the relative contribution of biological versus psychosocial factors in attention disorders by analyzing the characteristics of children with and without ADHD. It should be noted that in this study subjects were randomly selected from the general population (rather than clinic samples) and, therefore, the findings are more likely to reflect characteristics of the general population. It found that developmental problems (difficulty with speech, clumsiness, slowness to talk, slowness to walk, and low birthweight) were 1.8 times as common in children with ADHD as in those without ADHD. Also, children with ADHD were 1.9 times as likely to have a chronic health problem as children without ADHD. There were few indications of the relevance of psychosocial variables; however, ADHD children were more likely to live in cities than in rural areas. Also, there was an increased likelihood that children with ADHD would come from a family on welfare, but this relationship was restricted to females. A female with

ADHD was 3.2 times as likely to be on welfare as females without ADHD; no relationship existed between welfare and ADHD in males. This may mean that ADHD in females is of a different character than that observed in males. In another study, Kaplan, McNicol, Conte, and Moghadam (1987) found a high incidence of physical signs and symptoms such as rhinitis, bad breath, skin rash, red cheeks, and dry skin that are common indicators of allergies. In this sample, approximately 70% of the children with ADHD were affected as compared with 8–13% of controls.

In summary, the epidemiological data reviewed here suggest that children with ADHD are distinguished primarily by the presence of a number of developmental abnormalities. These data lend credence to theories of the biological causation of ADHD.

b. Twin Studies   Information regarding the causes of ADHD has also been obtained from twin studies. One approach taken in these studies has been to compare the co-occurrence of ADHD in monozygotic (identical) and dyzygotic (fraternal twins). Because only monozygotic twins are genetically identical, if ADHD is inherited, one would expect to find that ADHD would co-occur more commonly in monozygotic twins. On the other hand, if ADHD were due to environmental factors, then it would co-occur in monozygotic and dyzygotic twins at the same rate. Gilger, Pennington, and Defries (1992) and Goodman and Stevenson (1989b) both found that ADHD was more likely to occur in both members of a twin pair when they were monozygotic. In the Gilger et al. (1992) study the rate of concordance was 81% in monozygotic twins, and only 29% in dyzygotic twins. Both of these studies and others are consistent with the view that there are substantial genetic influences underlying the development of ADHD.

c. Adoption Studies   Several studies have reported a much higher incidence of adoption in ADHD children than in non-ADHD children. Deutsch et al. (1982) reported a 17% rate of nonrelative adoption in children with ADHD. In contrast, the rate of nonrelative adoption for controls (children referred to hospitals for other problems such as kidney transplant or allergies) was <2.5%. The samples of children in this study were drawn from clinic referrals in two different cities. In interpreting these data, Deutsch et al. (1982) pointed to the high incidence of psychopathology in unwed mothers, who are the source of most adoptions, and suggested that this may be indicative of genetic factors in the causation of ADHD. However, this line of reasoning is not supported by other data (Lahey, Piacentini, et al., 1988) that indicate no association between familial psychopathology and ADHD. Instead, Lahey, Piacentini, et al. (1988) found that familial psychopathology was only related to cases of CD or where both ADHD and CD were present in the same child.

Dalby, Fox, and Haslam (1982) obtained a similar rate of adoption (approximately 17%) for children with ADHD who were identified from hospital records; however, they suggested that perinatal factors such as poor nutrition, maternal alcohol consumption, or low birthweight may be the relevant factors in determining the high rate of ADHD among adoptees. However, there are several studies that would lead one to question this interpretation. For instance, Goodman and Stevenson (1989b), Nichols and Chen (1981), and Werner and Smith (1977) found no association between pre- and perinatal problems and ADHD. Indeed, the only known relationship that has been verified is that children with fetal alcohol syndrome appear to be at risk for ADHD (Streissguth, Hennan, & Smith, 1978).

One of the criticisms directed at adoption studies in which samples are drawn from clinics is that the overrepresentation of adoptees in samples of ADHD children may be an artifact of an inordinately high rate of utilization of health-care services by adoptive parents. This may be so because adoptive parents tend to be predominantly middle class and also because they may be more sensitive to problems than nonadoptive parents. One way to resolve this issue is to examine the data from studies that have sampled ADHD children from the general population and not from a hospital or clinic. In one study where this procedure was followed (Szatmari et al., 1989), no relationship was obtained between ADHD and separation from natural parents in the first 4 years of life. This suggests that there is no connection between adoptive status and ADHD. However, Deutsch (1989) sent out questionnaires to parents in the Ontario Adoption Registry and found an overrepresentation of ADHD children among adoptees as compared with biological children of the same parents. It may be significant that a much lower rate of ADHD was obtained in this study (approximately 10%) as compared with the 17% rate of adoption in the studies that sampled ADHD children from clinics. This lower rate may be due to the fact that a nonclinic sample was studied. Clearly, there are unresolved issues in the literature on the relationship between adoption and ADHD. One of the factors that may be complicating these data is that most studies of adoption (Dalby et al., 1982; Deutsch et al., 1982) have failed to distinguish ADHD children with and without CD. Because a high incidence of psychopathology appears in mothers who give up their children for adoption, and familial psychopathology tends to be related to CD and not ADHD (Lahey, Pelham, et al., 1988), there may be an overrepresentation of adoptees in the population of children with CDs. The relationship between adoption and ADHD that has been found in some studies may be due to the fact that many children with ADHD also have CD.

The implication of the studies on adoption is that there is probably substantial biological causation of ADHD, although the exact nature of the cause is not clear. There does not appear to be any uniform abnormality in the nervous system that can be tied to the symptoms. The causes may be nonspecific, and ADHD may stem from a number of different developmental abnormalities. The findings also suggest that faulty parenting or general environmental deprivation are probably not viable candidates as causes of ADHD.

2. Neurological Abnormalities

Given the evidence of biological causation of ADHD, one might expect to find specific abnormalities in the nervous system. For many years there have been suspicions that attention disorders stem from brain damage. This view was reflected in the use of the term minimal brain dysfunction of the 1950s and 1960s. Eventually, it became clear that there was a lack of compelling evidence of brain damage. It now appears that <5% of children with ADHD have documented brain damage (Rutter, 1977). It is also the case that most children with brain damage do not show symptoms of ADHD.

Instead of brain damage, the research in the past 10–15 years has focused on two issues: (a) the structural features of the brains of patients with ADHD and (b) the functional characteristics of the nervous systems of patients with ADHD. First, with respect to structural features of the brain, there is evidence that the brains of patients with ADHD do show some abnormality in the size of several brain structures. For instance, most human brains show a pattern of asymmetry in that some brain structures are larger in the left hemisphere than in the right hemisphere. In many instances this asymmetry is thought to be due to the presence of specialized mechanisms for language processing in the left hemisphere. Most people also show an asymmetry in handedness, and this may also account for larger brain areas in the left hemisphere. One structure, called the caudate nucleus, which plays an important role in regulating movements, is smaller in the left hemisphere than in the right in children with ADHD. In most normal brains the opposite pattern is observed (Hynd et al., 1993). It is conceivable that this abnormality in the motor system may be related to the characteristic high activity level of children with ADHD, although this connection has not yet been studied in detail.

In terms of brain function, a number of studies suggest that abnormal activity in the frontal lobes may be related to ADHD. First, damage to the frontal lobes of the brain results in performance that in some ways parallels the symptoms of ADHD. One of the hallmarks of frontal lobe lesions is a lack of ability to inhibit responses, which may be similar to the lack of inhibition that is a common symptom of ADHD. There is also some evidence that children with ADHD show deficits on the Wisconsin Card Sorting Task, which is a diagnostic test for frontal lobe dysfunction (Chelune, Ferguson, Koon, & Dickey, 1986). However, other data suggest that the utility of neuropsychological tests of frontal lobe functioning in detecting ADHD may be limited. In a review of nine neuropsychological tests, Barkley and Grodzinsky (1994) found that only two of them predicted ADHD. However, although scores on these two tests predicted the presence of ADHD, a normal score on the tests did not predict the absence of ADHD. Evidence supporting malfunctioning of the frontal lobes in ADHD has also been suggested by physiological studies. For instance, Lou, Henriksen, and Bruhn (1984) found that cerebral blood flow in that region is compromised in patients with ADHD. Also, as mentioned above, Zametkin et al. (1993) have observed a relationship between cerebral glucose metabolism in the left frontal lobe and the degree of severity ADHD symptoms.

Another line of research is concerned with responsivity of the nervous system. Some of this research was oriented toward the study of the physiologic arousal. Arousal can be thought of as a measure of the background activity of the nervous system. High arousal is associated with states of high alertness, whereas low arousal is associated with states of drowsiness. Arousal theory suggests that a moderate level of arousal is desirable for the performance of most tasks. A level of arousal that is too high would result in behavioral disorganization; one that is too low would lead to drowsiness. For the most part the studies of children with ADHD have indicated lower levels of arousal than normal functioning children, although the results across studies have been far from consistent.

An alternative approach to the study of responsivity has been to examine evoked responses of the brain to different types of stimuli. In such studies subjects are given a task to perform, such as a reaction time test, and the reactions of the brain to the presented stimuli are recorded from electrodes on the scalp. Most of these studies have shown that the brains of children with ADHD are less responsive to stimuli. It has also been found that smaller evoked responses are associated with lower levels of performance on the behavioral task being performed while the responses were being recorded from the scalp. The particular components of the evoked response that were diminished in children with ADHD likely reflect activity in the prefrontal regions of the brain, which is consistent with the other evidence cited above that suggests that there is deficient frontal lobe activity in ADHD. Low-arousal theories of ADHD attracted some interest because they suggested that the high activity levels and stimulus-seeking behaviors of children with ADHD might be attempts to increase arousal level. Low arousal also made sense because the most commonly used medications to treat ADHD (such as Ritalin) increase arousal levels.

In summary, there are several promising areas of research that are beginning to pinpoint the specific brain structures that are implicated in ADHD. There are three important points to remember about this information. First, there is evidence of abnormal asymmetries in the brains of patients with ADHD. Second, evidence from studies of cerebral blood flow, anatomy, and evoked potentials implicate the frontal lobes of the brain in ADHD. Third, the nervous system of children with ADHD seems to be characterized by lower levels of arousal.

C. The Clinical Management of ADHD

The primary purpose of the information presented in this section is to familiarize the reader with research concerned with the treatment of ADHD. The first section presents the standard diagnostic procedures used so that the reader will have some idea of the procedures used to help clinicians arrive at treatment decisions.

1. Diagnosis of ADHD

The diagnostic process for ADHD is similar in many ways to those used for other mental disorders for which there is no accepted diagnostic test. For the most part clinicians must rely on information provided by the patient or by someone who is very familiar with the patient's history, such as a parent or teacher. The starting point in the investigation of a patient is usually a statement of the presenting problem. In obtaining this information, it is important to obtain as objective a description as possible rather than an evaluation of the patient's behavior. This initial description is usually followed by a detailed history of the patient, including birth history, recollections of early diseases, and a family history, noting any incidences of developmental difficulties in immediate family members. In taking this history, the clinician will carefully record the age of onset of any problem behaviors and any external events (e.g., a death in the family) that may have precipitated these problems. As part of this history, the parent will also be asked to provide information on the child's history at school. In addition to the parent history, the clinician will usually obtain a separate history from the school. Ordinarily, this information will be obtained by sending a questionnaire form to the school. Third, the clinician will interview the parents with regard to family functioning. Fourth, the clinician will spend more time interacting with the child, perhaps asking the child to perform a few simple tasks. In addition to the detailed history obtained from the parents, the clinician will also have the parents and school personnel complete a standardized checklist so that the information about the patient can be compared with normative information. A number of such checklists have been developed, such as the Conners Parent and Teacher Rating Scales (Conners, 1990). These scales can discriminate between children with and without ADHD, and they are also sensitive to treatment effects. Further descriptions of many of the checklists that are used in the diagnosis of ADHD may be found in Barkley (1990). It can also be helpful for the clinician to visit the child's school and home to observe the problems firsthand. Although many clinicians do not have the resources to do home and school visits, they are invaluable sources of information in developing an intervention program for the child. The clinician may find that there is some factor in the home or school that is exacerbating the child's problems.

The decision regarding the diagnosis is arrived at by considering all the information that is gathered. A diagnosis of ADHD is made if the information obtained is consistent with the *DSM-IV* criteria: the onset of symptoms must be prior to age 7, some impairment from the symptoms must be evident in two or more settings such as school and home, and there must be evidence of clinically significant impairment in social, academic, or occupational functioning. Furthermore, the individual must satisfy the criteria regarding inattention, hyperactivity, and impulsivity. Last, there must be no compelling evidence that the symptoms are due to other factors, such as low intelligence or the presence of a psychiatric disorder such as schizophrenia or pervasive developmental disorder. The clinician may also use information from the standardized checklists to make sure that the child differs significantly from the population of normal children with regard to ADHD symptoms.

2. Treatment

Ideally, the treatment program that is developed should follow from the types of problems that are presented by the individual. Although most children with ADHD are treated with stimulant medication, most professionals recommend the use of a multimodal treatment approach that may include medication, behavior modification, and parent training. The importance of nonpharmacological treatments is also underscored by the fact that 20–30% of the children diagnosed with ADHD do not benefit from stimulant drug therapy, and a significant percentage of parents object to the use of stimulant drugs for their children.

a. Stimulant Medication The administration of stimulant medication is the most common treatment for children with ADHD. The term *stimulant drug* refers to activating effects of this class of drugs on the nervous system. For instance, it is well documented that stimulant drugs increase autonomic activity as indicated by increases in heart rate (Porges, Walter, Korb, & Sprague, 1975), blood pressure, and skin conductance (Cohen, Douglas, & Morgenstern, 1971). Evidence also indicates that stimulants potentiate the production of the neurotransmitters dopamine and norepinephrine in the central nervous system (Levy & Hobbes, 1988). Ritalin (which is the trade name for the genetic drug methylphenidate) is the one most widely used for ADHD. However, it is not the only drug used in the treatment of ADHD. Other stimulant drugs such as d'amphetamine, benzedrine, and pemoline have been used as well as a number of tricyclic antidepressants (e.g., anafranil and desipramine).

For the most part, stimulant drugs are relatively short acting. Ritalin, for example, usually has a period of efficacy of about 4 hr, so most school children take a dose at breakfast and another at noon. Some children take an additional dose at 4:00 to get them through the evening hours. This third dose is often used for children who have difficulty completing their homework assignments or who are otherwise difficult to manage in the evening hours at home. There is also a time-release form of Ritalin that has an active life of 6 or 7 hr, so that children taking this form of the medication need only one dosage to get through the school day. However, it has become evident that not all children who are positive responders to Ritalin also respond positively to time-release Ritalin. Pemoline also has an active life of around 6 hr. The tricyclic antidepressants are longer acting, although it takes longer to build up a sufficient blood level of the drug for it to be effective. In practice, most clinicians will try using Ritalin first, and if the child does not respond positively, then other medications will be tried.

The research literature on stimulant treatment of children with ADHD is extensive, and a number of generalizations can be made about this form of treatment.

First, one-half to two-thirds of the children diagnosed with ADHD appear to show at least some benefit from stimulants (Barkley, DuPaul, & McMurry, 1990; Spencer, et al., 1995). Furthermore, stimulants appear to exert their effects on a wide range of behaviors. They increase on-task behavior and reduce fidgeting and motoric activity (Douglas, Barr, Amin, O'Neill, & Britton, 1988). In addition, they improve the level of compliance with parental commands (Humphries, Kinsbourne, & Swanson, 1978). Last, they seem to have positive effects on peer interactions. Stimulants also improve performance on a number of laboratory tasks such as reaction time (Porges et al., 1975), vigilance (Sykes, Douglas, Weiss and Minde, 1971), and paired associate learning (Swanson & Kinsbourne, 1976). Recent studies have indicated that stimulants are about as effective in adults as they are in children. Spencer et al. (1995) found that about 78% of adult patients with ADHD responded positively to Ritalin, which is roughly comparable to the percentage of children who respond positively. It should also be noted that the nature of the response is somewhat unique to the individual. Douglas, Barr, O'Neill, and Britton (1986) found that if a wide range of outcome measures are used, nearly all patients show a positive response to stimulants on at least some of the tests. Douglas et al. (1986) pointed out that the 70–80% positive response rate obtained in most studies is due to the fact that most of them use only a single outcome measure.

There are a number of commonly occurring negative side effects of stimulants that should be monitored. The two most common are sleep loss and appetite suppression. The appetite suppression is usually restricted to the hours of the day when the drug is active. For most children taking Ritalin, appetite loss is restricted to the noon hour meal. Typically, children make up for the lack of food intake at noon by eating more in the evening.

There is some evidence that the different drugs used to treat ADHD do not all have identical therapeutic effects. Rapport, Carlson, Kelly, and Pataki (1993) found that although only methylphenidate improved vigilance performance, short-term memory performance and visual problem solving were enhanced equally by methylphenidate and the tricyclic antidepressant desipramine. However, only the combination of the two drugs enhanced the learning of higher order relationships.

The evidence is less clear with regard to the effects of stimulants on academic performance. Studies that have employed achievement tests as outcome measures suggest that there is no benefit from stimulant drugs (Aman, 1980; Gadow, 1983). Many of these studies have been criticized because achievement tests are not typically sensitive to short-term changes in behavior. Recent studies that have examined specific aspects of math performance suggest that stimulants may improve performance. For example, Douglas et al. (1986) demonstrated that stimulants increase the number of math problems attempted and the number correct, and they also enable students with ADHD to work more quickly. However, there has not yet been a demonstration that stimulants enable children with ADHD to acquire math concepts more readily.

Although there is general agreement on the short-term benefits of stimulants for the majority of children with ADHD, the long-term picture is less clear. What is meant by long-term has not been succinctly defined, but most long-term studies examine the effects of stimulant treatment over at least a 5-year period. Long-term studies are usually retrospective in nature, meaning that children are classified into groups a number of years after they began receiving treatment for ADHD. A group of children with ADHD who have been taking medication for a number of years is identified and contrasted with another group of children with ADHD who have not been taking stimulant medication. These two groups are then compared on a mix of cognitive and behavioral measures. Although virtually every study of this kind has failed to find evidence of long-term benefit of stimulant drugs, it is important to note that long-term drug studies are exceedingly difficult to undertake. As one might expect, it is extremely unlikely that one can come up with equivalent samples using this approach. It is possible that the children in the two groups differ in ways besides the use of stimulant medication. For instance, children not treated with stimulant drugs may not be as severely affected by ADHD as the children who are treated with stimulants. The consensus among researchers who have carefully reviewed the longitudinal studies (Douglas et al., 1988; Pelham, Murphy, 1986) is that existing long-term studies are fraught with so many methodological problems that it is not possible to base any firm conclusions on them.

Because stimulants seem to reduce so many of the symptoms of ADHD, one might be tempted to believe that the beneficial response to stimulants is unique to children with ADHD. If this were so, then one would be able to use a positive response to stimulants as a diagnostic indicator of ADHD. However, other research (Rappoport et al., 1980) has shown that children without ADHD show improved performance on memory tests and are less active and more attentive after taking stimulants. These findings suggest that the beneficial effects of stimulants are not unique to ADHD, and that a positive response to stimulants cannot be used as a diagnostic indicator.

To summarize, stimulant drugs appear to exert positive cognitive and behavioral effects on children with ADHD. They enhance the ability to concentrate, increase on-task behavior, and they also appear to have a positive impact on social behavior. The positive response to stimulants does not appear to be unique to children with ADHD, since similar benefits have been obtained in children without ADHD. Existing studies indicate that stimulants do not have long-term benefit on behavior, but methodological problems make it difficult to base firm conclusions on these studies.

b. Behavior Modification   Behavior modification (BM) is a treatment approach derived from the classical behaviorism of B. F. Skinner and other twentieth-century psychologists. In this approach, reward or punishment is made contingent (or depends) on the performance of certain behaviors. For instance, in using contingent rewards to increase on-task behaviors, a teacher may give verbal praise to a child who is engaged in an assigned academic task. The rationale underlying the use of BM is that the presentation of the reward will increase the likelihood that the on-task behavior will occur again. Alternatively, in a punishment paradigm, a teacher may deliver a verbal reprimand to a child who is out of her seat at a time when she is supposed to be completing an assignment at her desk. For the most part, a theoretical rationale for using BM for ADHD has not been well developed. In most applications, it is viewed as a set of simple procedures to obtain control over the behavior of a child who is out of control much of the time. The one exception to this largely atheoretical approach stems from Barkely's (1989) view of ADHD as a developmental delay in the regulation of behavior by its consequences. In terms of this theory, BM is a way of increasing the salience of the consequences such that they will exert control over the behavior of the child.

As applied to ADHD, BM is considerably more complex than the simple application of rewards and punishment. As detailed by Carlson, Pelham, Milich, and Dixon (1992), BM consists of a number of components including classroom structure (i.e., a set of consistent routines) and classroom rules, and involves the application of several techniques including time out (the temporary removal of the child from a desirable environment), response cost (removal of reinforcers such as tokens when an undesirable behavior is performed), daily home reports, and an honor-role system that enables students who consistently follow the rules to obtain special recognition. There is considerable evidence that reducing the levels of inappropriate behavior at home and school is possible with the procedures of BM. However, as detailed in Pelham and Murphy's (1986) review, a number of shortcomings of BM make it less than an ideal treatment for ADHD. One such shortcoming is that not all children respond to BM. Even for those who do respond, BM does not normalize the behavior of most children, and the effects that are observed usually fail to persist at 1-year follow-up assessment sessions. Compliance problems are also evident with some studies (e.g., Firestone, Kelly, Goodman, & Davey, 1981), suggesting that as many as 50% of the parents of ADHD children discontinue the treatment.

One alternative approach has been to combine BM with stimulant drug therapy. This approach is appealing because it is possible that the cognitive benefits associated with stimulant therapy will make it possible for children to derive greater benefit from BM. In one study, Carlson, Pelham, Milich, and Dixon (1992) examined the effects of BM and Ritalin (both individually and combined) on classroom behavior and on academic performance. They found that BM and Ritalin were both effective in reducing problem behaviors in the classroom and that these two therapies were more effective when combined than when used separately. The only difference in the efficacy of the two treatments was that only Ritalin improved academic performance (i.e., increased the number of problems attempted in reading and math and led to greater completion of seat work); there was no such effect with BM. The authors also noted that when used alone, a higher dose of Ritalin (.6

mg/kg) was more effective than a lower dose (.3 mg/kg) but when used in combination with BM the two doses were equally effective. This result suggests that it may be possible to reduce the drug dosage used when Ritalin is combined with BM.

In developing BM systems one has to decide which types of behaviors to target and which types of reinforcers to use. One finding that might shape one's approach is that several studies (Rosen, O'Leary, Joyce, Conway, & Pfiffner, 1984) have found that while positive reinforcement is effective in increasing the frequency of positive behaviors, only punishment methods (such as response cost) are effective in reducing the frequency of inappropriate behaviors.

In summary, it has been shown that BM can be an effective technique in helping reduce the disruptive behaviors of children with ADHD. It is also the case that the efficacy of BM is maximized when it is used in combination with stimulant drug therapy. There are a number of shortcomings of BM (lack of compliance, lack of persistence of effects) that should be kept in mind before undertaking this type of treatment.

c. Cognitive Behavior Modification   Of all the treatments used with ADHD, cognitive behavior modification (CBM) would appear to be the one that was specifically designed for this population. This is so because CBM attempts to train such behaviors as planning skills and self-regulation, which are deficient in children with ADHD.

The theoretical rationale for CBM stems from the work of Russian psychologists Luria and Vygotsky, who stressed the importance of verbal control over behavior in normal development. In earlier stages of development the verbalizations tend to be overt. With development, this control becomes more covert.

One can view the impulsivity of children with ADHD as the antithesis of self-talk. Impulsivity is often defined as acting without thinking, but it could be just as easily defined as acting without self-talking. The rationale for the use of CBM in ADHD is that self-talk is less likely to develop spontaneously in these children, and consequently, one must provide explicit training in its use. The use of self-talk is emphasized in applications of CBM with ADHD children.

So what is the content of the self-talk that one is taught in CBM? In most applications of CBM (Kendall & Braswell, 1984; Meichenbaum, 1977), students are taught skills that are thought to be essential to effective problem solving. These include problem definition, solution generation, solution monitoring, and self-reinforcement. In acquiring CBM skills, children are taught to verbalize these steps as they attempt to solve problems. For example, in the realm of math, a child might be presented with a problem in which two numbers were presented with a plus sign. The child would be taught to ask herself, "What's my problem here?" The appropriate response might be, "Well, the plus sign tells me that this is an addition problem." Next, the child would ask herself, "How can I solve this problem?" The answer here might be, "I have to remember to combine the top and bottom numbers and carry over numbers one column to the left if the value of the sum is 10 or more." Next, after the child has formulated a response, a self-checking routine would be performed: "Since this is an addition problem, I can check my answer using the subtraction method." Finally, when the child is satisfied that the answer is correct, she would say, "I did a good job." In some applications of CBM, external reinforcers are used to motivate the children to use the CBM strategies appropriately. In their procedure, Kendall and Braswell (1984) start the children out with a number of chips that can be exchanged for concrete rewards. Each time the child fails to follow the CBM steps appropriately, one of the chips is taken away. Over time, children are prompted to internalize their speech.

Research studies have shown that it is possible for children with ADHD to acquire the problem-solving steps that are taught in CBM, and that use of these steps improves performance on cognitive tasks. However, it has been difficult to show that the effects of CBM can generalize over time or across situations (Abikoff, 1991; Hinshaw & Erhardt, 1991). In other words, children tend to use CBM strategies in the situations in which they were trained. However, when removed from the training situation or when put back in the original training situation a few months after the training has been completed, most fail to use the CBM strategies.

It is not clear why CBM strategies do not generalize. It may be that the skills that are taught in CBM are so antithetical to the temperament of children with ADHD that they simply do not perceive the value of using the strategies. Another possibility is suggested by the findings from a recent study (Berk & Landau, 1993) in which it was observed that LD children and particularly children with both LD and ADHD were *more likely* to use task-relevant self-talk than normal functioning children. This study also showed that self-talk tended to be associated with more difficult tasks, suggesting that self-talk was a technique that children use to help with particularly challenging problems. Furthermore, the development of internalized speech may be delayed in children with LD and ADHD because the development of problem mastery is delayed. Consequently, contrary to the assumptions of CBM therapy, it may not be necessary to teach children with ADHD to use self-talk; it is a skill that comes to them naturally. Moreover, one problem with some CBM applications is that therapists may rush children to internalize speech before they are ready to do so. The implication here is that classroom teachers should be sensitive to the needs of children with ADHD to use self-talk while doing seat work. It may be warranted to organize the classroom with study carrels so that children would feel freer to use self-talk.

d. Parent Training   Difficulties in obtaining transfer of training when using behavioral interventions has led to the view that therapy for ADHD children must be ongoing over a substantial time period, and must be carried out in the environments in which the child's problems are most often expressed. Because it is far too expensive to enlist the services of a therapist for such long-term intervention, some investigators have begun exploring the efficacy of parent training programs. Parents are usually the only adults who have a continuing daily presence in the child's life, and if they can be taught to deal with problematic behaviors more effectively, then perhaps it might be possible to improve the child's long-term prognosis.

Relatively few studies have investigated parenting intervention programs specifically designed for children with ADHD. However, a much larger body of literature (Forehand & McMahon, 1981) pertains to parenting interventions with heterogeneous groups of aggressive and CD children. Because many children with ADHD are aggressive and meet the criteria for CD, it has prompted some investigators to adapt these programs to the ADHD population. For the most part these parenting programs have applied the principles of BM to parent training. Thus, parents are taught how to use such techniques as establishing a home token economy and using time out for noncompliance. In general, parents are taught to apply these techniques to a limited range of problem behaviors. If they are successful in managing this limited set of behaviors, they then attempt to expand the range of behaviors that they seek to manage.

In order to arrive at an adequate understanding of parenting programs, it is important to understand that many parents come into a program with a rather negative view of themselves as parents. Quite commonly, they feel angry and frustrated because one or more children in their family is out of control, and they feel helpless to do anything about it. A parent in this frame of mind has little chance of effectively coping with a child's difficult behavior. Before the parent can begin to effectively manage the child's behavior, it is first necessary to help get the parent's emotions under control and to place the relationship between parent and child on a more positive note. Most parenting programs (Barkley, 1987; Conte, Blakemore & Shindler, 1995; Pisterman et al., 1989) rely on three techniques to achieve these objectives. First, parenting programs provide parents with background knowledge about ADHD. This information serves the important purpose of conveying to parents that the sometimes irritating behavior of their children is not intentional. If parents perceive the behavior of their child as unintentional, they are less likely to be angered by it and also less likely to resort to punishment practices. Presumably, if they are less angry and less prone to punishment, they may be more likely to adopt the techniques that are being taught in the parenting program. Second, parents are taught ways to enhance the value of parental attention. Parents of difficult-to-manage children spend an inordinate amount of time attending to the child's inappropriate behavior and very little time attending to appropriate behavior. As a consequence, some children arrive at the conclusion that the only way to receive attention from the parent is to misbehave. Once the parent and child get into this pattern of action and reaction it can be very difficult to break out of it. To break this cycle, parents are prompted to look more carefully for instances of appropriate behavior and to verbally praise the child when it occurs. In other words, parents are instructed to spend relatively more time attending to behavior that they would like to see and less time attending to behavior that they don't want to see. Also, parents are asked to try to build a more positive relationship with their child by spending a few minutes each day engaging the child in an activity that the child finds especially pleasurable. In undertaking these activities, they are told to avoid "managing" the child's behavior. Presumably, these activities will serve to restore some of the trust that may be lacking in the parent–child relationship, which may increase the reinforcing value of parental attention. Third, parents are instructed in ways to improve communication skills. Parents often unintentionally confuse children because they do not clearly convey what they expect from the child. For example, a parent who wants their child to clean their room might say, "Would you like to clean up your room?" The child may take this to mean that he or she has a choice in the matter. In fact, the parent may be intending to say that the child has to clean up the room and there is no choice in the matter. In another situation a parent may be bothered because the child is making a lot of noise and will react by saying "Stop that!" An impulsive, distractible child may have no idea that he is making noise that is bothering someone else. In this case the parent would be instructed to say what they wanted more explicitly.

Using a 12-week program composed of many of the components described above, Pisterman et al. (1989) found that parent training was effective in improving compliance of preschool ADHD children with parental commands and in improving the management techniques of the parent. Temporal generalization did occur insofar as the changes in parent and child behaviors were maintained at a 3-month follow-up testing session. However, they did not obtain generalization to nontrained behaviors or to the school environment. The findings from this study are quite typical and suggest that parent training needs to be extended to all problem behaviors if it is to be effective. One cannot expect the program to spontaneously generalize to the school setting. This is a serious limitation because most children with ADHD experience their most serious difficulties at school. The lack of transfer to the school suggests that an intervention program (hopefully one that is similar to the one being implemented at home) needs to be implemented in the school as well.

It should be noted that there are approaches to parent training that differ from the BM approach described above. One criticism that has been made of BM programs is that they may diminish a child's intrinsic motivation. The term intrinsic motivation refers to the child's inherent interest in an activity. It can be measured in terms of the willingness to perform a task in the absence of external incentives. It has been found in studies with normal children that when parents adopt a controlling approach to their child's behavior, it can undermine intrinsic motivation. When mothers approach their child's behavior in a way that is supportive of the child's autonomy, it has been found that the child's intrinsic motivation is enhanced (Deci et al., 1993).

VI. CURRENT RESEARCH ISSUES

A. Issues in Diagnosis

It was noted in this chapter that there has been considerable uncertainty concerning the relationship among the components of ADHD. For instance, in the *DSM-III,* it was believed that inattention and impulsivity were linked in the inattentive subtype, and that there was another subtype that was characterized by hyperactivity. In the *DSM-IV,* there are three subtypes of ADHD: a primarily inattentive type (ADHD-PI), a primarily hyperactive-impulsive type (ADHD-HI), and a combined type (ADHD-C). In contrast to the *DSM-III,* in this system, impulsivity is linked with hyperactivity.

As Barkley (1996) has pointed out, it is not clear if these subtypes really exist or if they are just a manifestation of developmental change. He points out that in the field trials that were conducted for the *DSM-IV,* the ADHD-HI consisted of primarily preschool-age children, whereas most of those with the combined type were school age. This suggests that the inclusion of the inattention symptoms may not be necessary, since they may develop later in those children who were impulsive and hyperactive in the preschool years. The lack of importance of the inattention symptoms is also suggested by the fact that most of the impairments associated with ADHD are most highly related to the symptoms of impulsivity-hyperactivity and not to inattention (Barkley, 1996, and references therein). In longitudinal studies, inattention was found to be related to difficulties in homework completion, whereas hyperactivity-impulsivity predicted most of the other areas of impairment associated with ADHD (e.g., social difficulties and disruptive behavior). Moreover, as we have noted previously, the role of inattention may be downplayed because children with ADHD are not known to be deficient on the components of attention as they are defined in attention theories.

Consequently, it may be that the conceptualization of ADHD may change in the relatively near future such that it will include only impulsivity and hyperactivity. This change in the conception of ADHD will also require a name change, since it would be a misnomer to call it an attentional difficulty. Children with symptoms of inattention only may come to be identified as having a completely different condition. If these future developments result in greater homogeneity of the ADHD population, then it may lead to advances in the understanding of these disorders that have eluded researchers up to this point.

B. How Do ADHD and LDs Interact

The evidence reviewed in this chapter strongly suggests that although many children with ADHD also have LD, these two conditions are different in a number of important ways. Estimates of the degree of overlap between LD and ADHD must be tempered by the fact that there is still considerable diagnostic uncertainty regarding both of these conditions and that if and when the diagnostic procedures improve, the estimates of the degree of overlap may be revised. In any case, it should be the expectation of LDs professionals that they will have to deal with many children who have both LD and ADHD. It is important to be aware that children with either of these two conditions tend to have learning problems, although as we have seen in this chapter the characteristics of these learning problems are somewhat different.

What is the nature of the learning differences between individuals with LD and ADHD? Douglas and Peters (1979) argued that both LDs and ADHD can lead to learning problems but they do so for different reasons: Deficits in ADHD are related to short attention span and impulsivity, whereas deficits in LD are due to specific processing deficits. Examinations of the differences in the characteristics of learning problems in LD and ADHD have been relatively sparse, but those that have been conducted shed some light on the issue. Several lines of research underscore the difficulties that ADHD children have in the utilization of a number of higher level intellectual skills such as working memory, learning strategy utilization, and organizational skills. One line of research has suggested that the higher than expected number of ADHD children with spelling problems may be due to problems with working memory (Levy & Hobbes, 1989). In a study in which the skills of LD children with and without ADHD were compared (Conte, 1992), it was found that LD children with ADHD had more difficulties in the area of written language than children with LD alone. This may also be a manifestation of difficulties in working memory, given the heavy demands that written language assignments place on organizational ability. The Tant and Douglas (1982) finding that children with ADHD had poorer problem-solving performance than children with reading disabilities could also be indicative of a deficit in higher level skills.

C. Behavioral Intervention

Much of the research that has been carried out on children with ADHD has focused on behavioral interventions that rely heavily on the use of external rewards. As has been reviewed in this chapter, much of this research has shown that these types of behavioral interventions are successful in helping parents, teachers, and other caregivers in managing the behavior of children with ADHD. However, there has been relatively little success in obtaining transfer of training over time or across situations.

Behavioral intervention procedures have been criticized for taking the perspective of the caregiver rather than that of the child. As has been noted previously, for the most part the use of BM in ADHD does not stem from a theoretical explanation of ADHD. Rather, BM is viewed as a simple set of procedures that can assist caregivers in obtaining better control over a child's behavior. There is little sense that in using BM the child is learning self-management skills. In this regard, there is a body of research that has shown that an important consideration in behavior management is the child's intrinsic interest in the task. Some of the research conducted in this area (Deci & Chandler, 1986) has suggested that the excessive use of external rewards can diminish a child's intrinsic interest in a task. For instance, when a child is induced to perform a task with the use of rewards, there is a strong tendency to stop performing the task when the reward is no longer made contingent on task performance. The tendency of rewards to diminish intrinsic motivation may explain the lack of transfer obtained using BM procedures. Perhaps if ways could be found to enhance intrinsic motivation, transfer might be more readily obtained.

Other work has suggested that it may not be external rewards per se that cause intrinsic motivation to be diminished, but rather the context in which external incentives are used (Scott, Deci, Patrick, & Ryan, 1992). Koestner, Ryan, Bernieri, and Holt (1984) make the distinction between informational versus controlling limits that are placed on a child's behavior. A limit is controlling if it is communicated as a pressure towards a specified outcome. In contrast, informational outcomes are those that provide knowledge related to the outcome of an event or episode, but where the experience of autonomy or choice is preserved. Typically, in informational outcomes, the adult also makes some attempt to acknowledge the feelings the child may have in the situation. Koestner et al. (1984) demonstrated that there is greater intrinsic interest as measured by the amount of time children will spend working on a task during a free-choice period when informational rather than controlling limits are placed on their behavior. Similar findings were reported by Pittman, Davey, Alafat, Wetherill, and Kramer (1980) and Ryan (1982). One can surmise from this research that if a child's intrinsic interest in tasks is diminished, then it would tend to have a negative impact on self-control. Ideally, in designing a behavioral intervention program that focuses on the development of self-control, one would want to maximize the child's intrinsic motivation.

Blakemore, Shindler, and Conte (in press) and Conte et al. (1995) have developed a parenting program that attempts to give parents the skills needed to manage their child's behavior in a context that preserves the child's sense of autonomy. The rationale for this program is that the arbitrary nature of the reinforcers used in BM can diminish intrinsic motivation. The essential feature of this program is that it presents behavior-management situations as a choice that the child must make. If the child chooses to comply with the household rules, then positive consequences will ensue, whereas if the child chooses not to comply, a negative consequence will follow. Another critical feature of this program is that it relies on consequences that are logically related to the target behavior rather than on arbitrary extrinsic reinforcers that are used in BM. So, if the target behavior in the behavior-management situation is concerned with eating (e.g., if you choose to get up more than once from the dinner table), then the consequences will also be concerned with eating or at least with some behavior that is connected with the eating situation (e.g., "if you choose not to finish your dinner, you are choosing not to go out after dinner"). This feature of the program is important because the arbitrary rewards used in BM heighten the degree of parental control at the expense of the child's control.

Research on this program (Conte et al., 1995) has indicated that it has effects on both parenting stress and the child behavior at home that are comparable to the effects obtained using BM approaches.

In summary, there is evidence that approaches other than BM may have relevance to the treatment of ADHD. The thrust of some of these alternative approaches is to give children a greater sense of control in managing their behavior than has been the case in traditional BM. The challenge presented to these alternative therapies is to determine if they can be effective in managing ADHD, and if they can promote the transfer of skills to novel situations.

VII. PRACTICAL IMPLICATIONS OF THE RESEARCH ON ADHD

A. Diagnostic Criteria

The *DSM-IV* criteria represent an advance in the sense that the criteria were developed on a more empirical basis than previous *DSM* versions. For example, the linking of impulsivity and hyperactivity into ADHD/hyperactive-impulsive type was done after careful analysis of empirical studies, whereas in the *DSM-III*, the impulsivity and inattention had been linked together as a subtype largely on the basis of anecdotal evidence. However, there is still considerable diagnostic uncertainty in ADHD. At the present time, the ADHD primarily inattentive type is coming under scrutiny, and some researchers are questioning whether this subtype is really needed.

Diagnostic uncertainty is especially problematic in ADHD because of issues associated with the use of stimulant medication. This picture is made even more complicated because the response of ADHD children to stimulants is not unique: Rapoport et al. (1980) found that normal children benefited from stimulants in much the same way as children with ADHD (i.e., they showed improved performance on memory tasks, were less active, and demonstrated greater sustained attention to tasks). Without well-founded diagnostic criteria, there is an increased risk that stimulant medication will be used inappropriately. This uncertainty should prompt caution and a conservative approach to the use of medication. Prudence would seem to require that the conditions in which the attentional difficulty is expressed should be thoroughly investigated, and interventions other than medication should be attempted prior to the use of medication. Medication trials should be attempted only when the professionals who are overseeing the child's treatment are convinced that the attention problem is serious and is likely to persist into the future even if available behavioral treatments are implemented. One last caution-ary procedure would be to reserve the label of ADHD only to those cases where the symptoms are pervasive, as has been recommended in the *DSM-IV.*

B. What Schools Can Do

1. Providing Continuity in Treatment

Attentional difficulties require long-term intervention, which is often difficult to undertake in school settings. Children in most schools change teachers every year, and thus even if an adequate treatment program is established in one teacher's classroom, there is no assurance that the program will be carried over to the fol-lowing year. In addition, the distractibility of ADHD children very likely makes it very difficult for them to adapt to new situations. School districts that require stu-dents to change teachers with every subject, particularly in the junior high years, also place a special burden on the ADHD child.

It is undoubtedly the case that the move toward the integration of special needs children (Andrews & Lupart, 1993) into regular classes will have substantial im-pact on children with ADHD. It is hoped that as schools move toward integration they will place more special education consultants within the school to provide as-sistance to the classroom teachers in coping with special needs students. These consultants can provide the very important function of continuity in treatment from 1 year to the next. Given that most students change teachers each year, and in ju-nior and senior high they are exposed to a variety of teachers each school day, it is important to have such consultants at the school to provide consistency over time and across subject areas. The work of these consultants should be supplemented with in-house professional development programs that focus on ways of dealing with problem behaviors of children.

2. Supporting a Multimodal Approach to Treatment

The evidence reviewed in this chapter strongly suggests that a multimodal treat-ment program is called for in dealing with most children with ADHD. The multi-modal treatment regimen usually consists of stimulant drug therapy coupled with some form of behavioral treatment such as behavior management, parent training, or social skills training. It is likely that in children who show a particularly strong response to stimulants, caregivers may come to believe that nothing else needs to be done. Insofar as the results of longitudinal studies indicate no long-term bene-fit from the use of stimulants, one must assume that stimulant drugs provide only symptomatic treatment. Professionals who work with children with ADHD must very strongly advocate for the use of a multimodal treatment regimen even for those who are seemingly well controlled by medication.

VIII. SUMMARY

Early in this chapter, a distinction was drawn between the meaning of the term attention in (a) attention theories and (b) ADHD. The former refers to processes such as alertness, selection, and effort, which are measured by information-processing tasks. In contrast, in ADHD, inferences regarding attention are based largely on the perceptions of a child's behavior by parents, teachers, and professionals. There have been two trends evident in more recent work on attention. First, the role of attentional processes in LD has been minimized. Increasingly, the thrust in LD research has been to investigate the role of mechanisms that are specialized to process certain types of information. Thus, rather than investigating the role of attention, contemporary LD researchers are more likely to emphasize the role of phonemic awareness in the development of reading skills. Second, the role of attention in ADHD is beginning to be minimized. Evidence from longitudinal studies has indicated that inattention develops relatively late in children with ADHD. The predominant early symptoms tend to be impulsivity and hyperactivity. Thus, it is possible that in future revisions of the conceptions of ADHD, attention will be excluded or else there will be a sharp division created between attention disorders and hyperactivity-impulsivity.

Although it is quite common for LD and ADHD to co-occur in the same individual, there is considerable evidence that the two conditions are not causally related. The strongest evidence against a causal relationship between these two conditions stems from neurological evidence that different brain regions seem to be involved in each. Also, there are a number of performance measures that distinguish children with LD and ADHD, with the latter showing weakness on rote memory and problem-solving tasks.

The major focus of the chapter is to provide an overview of the various facets of ADHD. Generalizations about ADHD are tempered by the definitional confusion that still besets this area of study. Diagnostic criteria are still in a state of flux, as evidenced by the most recent *DSM* revisions. It is noteworthy that there is much stronger empirical support for the procedures specified in the *DSM-IV*. However, with these diagnostic considerations in mind, a number of conclusions about ADHD will be offered. First, the findings reviewed in the chapter from epidemiological and twin studies support the view that there is strong biological causation of attention disorder. Epidemiological studies indicate that ADHD is associated with a number of chronic health problems and developmental problems. These studies also indicate that relatively few environmental factors are associated with ADHD. Twin studies indicate that ADHD is much more likely to occur in monozygotic twin pairs than in dyzygotic twin pairs, again supporting a theory of biological causation. However, this does not mean that symptoms similar to those observed in ADHD could not occur because of environmental factors. Moreover, it is the case that environmental factors (e.g., a death in the family, divorce, or a new sibling) can exacerbate the symptoms of ADHD. One must carefully investigate the role of environmental factors in ADHD.

Although earlier theories focused on brain damage as a cause of ADHD, more recent work suggests there is brain damage in only a small minority of children with ADHD. Rather than brain damage, most evidence points to atypical functioning in particular areas of the brain, particularly the frontal lobes. Also, it has been found that children with ADHD lack some of the normal asymmetry that is found in parts of the brain that regulate movement: The caudate nucleus tends to be larger in the left hemisphere of individuals without ADHD, whereas the opposite pattern has been found in individuals with ADHD. In terms of the clinical management of ADHD, the diagnosis process tends to make use of clinical histories, behavior checklists, and observation in gathering evidence. There is no widely accepted diagnostic test. The diagnostic process is complicated by the high degree of comorbidity with other conditions.

Stimulant drug therapy is the most common form of treatment. It can produce quite striking changes in behavior in some children with ADHD, although about 20–30% do not benefit from this form of treatment. It has been documented that stimulants increase attention span, reduce impulsivity, increase compliance with requests from adult caregivers, and improve performance on academic tasks. Although there is no evidence that stimulant drugs produce any long-term benefit in terms of academic and social functioning, the existing longitudinal studies have been fraught with methodological problems. A number of other types of drugs besides stimulants (e.g., tricyclic antidepressants) have been used with some success. The advantage of some of the nonstimulant drugs is that they act over a much longer period of time.

A large number of studies have indicated that behavioral interventions such as BM and CBM can lead to short-term changes in behavior. Most investigations of these treatments have failed to obtain transfer of skills out of the training environment. It is also the case that there are considerable compliance problems in implementing such programs. One response to the lack of transfer has been the development of parenting programs. The rationale for such programs is that parents are potential therapeutic agents who are present throughout a child's formative years. As such, they can provide the continuity in treatment that is virtually impossible for professionals to provide. One thing to consider is the timing of interventions. It is possible that children must attain a certain level of maturity before CBM can be attempted. For young children it may be more advisable to use BM.

References

Abikoff, H. (1991). Cognitive training in ADHD children: Less to it than meets the eye. *Journal of Learning Disabilities, 24,* 205–209.

Aman, M. (1980). Psychotropic drugs and learning problems: A selective review. *Journal of Learning Disabilities, 13,* 87–97.

American Psychiatric Association. (1980). *Diagnostic and statistical manual of mental disorders, Third Edition.* Washington, DC: American Psychiatric Association.

American Psychiatric Association. (1987). *Diagnostic and statistical manual of mental disorders, Third Edition—Revised.* Washington, DC: American Psychiatric Association.

American Psychiatric Association. (1994). *Diagnostic and statistical manual of mental disorders, Fourth Edition.* Washington, DC: American Psychiatric Association.

Andrews, J., & Lupart, J. (1993). *The inclusive classroom: Educating exceptional children.* Scarborough, ON: Nelson, Canada.

August, G. J., & Garfinkel, B. D. (1990). Comorbidity of ADHD and reading disability among clinic-referred children. *Journal of Abnormal Child Psychology, 18,* 29–45.

Barkley, R. A. (1987). *Defiant children: A clinician's manual for parent training.* New York: Guilford.

Barkley, R. A. (1989). Attention deficit-hyperactivity disorder. In E. J. Mash & R. A. Barkley (Eds.), *Treatment of childhood disorders* (pp. 39–72). New York: Guilford.

Barkley, R. A. (1990). *Attention-deficit hyperactivity disorder: A handbook for diagnosis and treatment.* New York: Guilford.

Barkley, R. A. (1996). Attention-deficit/hyperactivity disorder. In E. Mash & R. Barkley (Eds.), *Child Psychopathology* (pp. 63–112). New York: Guilford.

Barkley, R. A., Dupaul, G. J., & McMurray, M. B. (1990). Comprehensive evaluation of attention deficit disorder with and without hyperactivity as defined by research criteria. *Journal of Consulting and Clinical Psychology, 58,* 775–789.

Barkley, R. A., & Grodzinsky, G. (1994). Are tests of frontal lobe functions useful in the diagnosis of attention deficit disorders? *Clinical Neuropsychologist, 8,* 121–139.

Berk, L., & Landau, S. (1993). Private speech of learning disabled and normally achieving children in classroom academic and laboratory contexts. *Child Development, 64,* 556–571.

Biederman, J., Faraone, S. V., & Lapey, K. (1992). Comorbidity of diagnosis in attention-deficit hyperactivity disorder. In G. Weiss (Ed.), *Child and adolescent psychiatric clinics of North America: Attention-deficit hyperactivity disorder* (pp. 335–360). Philadelphia: Saunders.

Blakemore, B., Shindler, S., & Conte, R. (in press). *A problem solving training program for parents of children with attention deficit disorder.* Calgary, AB: Acton House.

Cantwell, D. P. (1978). Hyperactivity and antisocial behavior. *American Academy of Child Psychiatry, 17,* 252–262.

Carlson, C., Pelham, W., Milich, R., & Dixon, J. (1992). Single and combined effects of methylphenidate and behavior therapy on the classroom performance of children with attention-deficit hyperactivity disorder. *Journal of Abnormal Child Psychology, 20,* 213–232.

Chee, P., Logan, G., Schachar, R., Lindsay, P., & Wachsmuth, R. (1989). Effects of event rate and display time on sustained attention in hyperactive, normal, and control children. *Journal of Abnormal Child Psychology, 17,* 371–391.

Chelune, G. J., Ferguson, W., Koon, R., & Dickey, T. (1986). Frontal lobe disinhibition in attention deficit disorder. *Child Psychology and Human Development, 16,* 221–234.

Cohen, N., Douglas, V. I., & Morgenstern, G. (1971). The effect of methylphenidate on attentive behavior and autonomic activity in hyperactivity. *Psychopharmacologia, 22*, 282–294.

Conners, C. K. (1990). *Manual for the Conners' Rating Scales*. Toronto: Multi-Health Systems.

Conte, R. (1992). *A comparison of academic and behavioral skills in learning disabled children with and without attention deficit hyperactivity disorder.* Unpublished manuscript.

Conte, R., Blakemore, B., & Shindler, S. (1995). A mediational approach to the training of parents of children with attention deficit hyperactivity. *Canadian Journal of Special Education, 9*, 33–68.

Dalby, J. T., Fox, S. L., & Haslam, R. (1982). Adoption and foster care rates in pediatric disorders. *Journal of Developmental and Behavioral Pediatrics, 3*, 61–64.

Deci, E., & Chandler, C. (1986). The importance of motivation for the future of the LD field. *Journal of Learning Disabilities, 19*, 587–594.

Deci, E., Driver, R. E., Hotchkiss, L., Robbins, R. J. et al. (1993). The relation of mothers' controlling vocalizations to children's intrinsic motivation. Special Issue: Social context, social behavior and socialization. *Journal of Experimental Child Psychology, 55*, 151–162.

Denkla, M. B., & Rudel, R. G. (1976). Naming of object drawings by dyslexic and other learning disabled children. *Brain and Language, 3*, 1–15.

Deutsch, C. K. (1989). Adoption and attention deficit disorder. *Journal of Child Psychology*, Suppl: Attention-deficit disorder, IV, 67–79.

Deutsch, C. K., Swanson, J. M., Bruell, J. H., Cantwell, D. P., Weinberg, F., & Baren, M. (1982). Overrepresentation of adoptees in children with the attention deficit disorder. *Behavior Genetics, 12*, 231–238.

Douglas, V. I., Barr, R., O'Neill, M., & Britton, B. G. (1986). Short term effects of methylphenidate on the cognitive, learning and academic performance of children with attention deficit disorder in the laboratory and the classroom. *Journal of Child Psychology and Psychiatry, 27*, 191–211.

Douglas, V. I., Barr, Amin, K., O'Neill, M., & Britton, B. (1988). Dosage effects and individual responsivity to methylphenidate in attention deficit disorder. *Journal of Child Psychology and Psychiatry, 29*, 453–475.

Douglas, V. I., & Peters, K. B. (1979). Toward a clearer definition of the attentional deficit of hyperactive children. In G. A. Hale & M. Lewis (Eds.), *Attention and the development of cognitive skills* (pp. 173–247). New York: Plenum Press.

Dykman, R., Ackerman, P., Clements, S., & Peters, J. (1971). Specific learning disabilities: An attentional deficit syndrome. In H. Myklebust (Ed.), *Progress in learning disabilities* (Vol II, pp. 56–93). New York: Grune and Stratton.

Felton, R. H., & Wood, F. B. (1989). Cognitive deficits in reading disability and attention deficit disorder. *Journal of Learning Disabilities, 22*, 3–13.

Firestone, P., Kelly, M. J., Goodman, J. T., & Davey, J. (1981). Differential effects of parent training and stimulant medication with hyperactives. *Journal of the American Academy of Child Psychiatry, 20*, 135–147.

Forehand, R., & McMahon, R. J. (1981). *Helping the non-compliant child: A clinician's guide to effective parent training.* New York: Guilford Press.

Gadow, K. (1983). Effects of stimulant drugs on academic performance in hyperactive and learning disabled children. *Journal of Learning Disabilities, 16,* 290–299.

Gilger, J. W., Pennington, B. F., & DeFries, J. (1992). A twin study of the etiology of comorbidity: Attention-deficit hyperactivity disorder and dyslexia. *Journal of the American Academy of Child and Adolescent Psychiatry, 31,* 343–348.

Goodman, R., & Stevenson, J. (1989a). A twin study of hyperactivity—I. An examination of hyperactivity scores and categories derived from Rutter Teacher and Parent Questionnaires. *Journal of Child Psychology and Psychiatry, 30,* 671–689.

Goodman, R., & Stevenson, J. (1989b). A twin study of hyperactivity—II. The aetiological role of genes, family relationships and perinatal adversity. *Journal of Child Psychology and Psychiatry, 30,* 691–709.

Hagan, J. (1967). The effect of distraction on selective attention. *Child Development, 38,* 685–694.

Hallihan, D., & Reeve, R. E. (1980). Selective attention and distractibility. In B. Keogh, (Ed.), *Advances in special education* (Vol. 1, pp. 141–181). Greenwich, CT: JAI Press.

Hallowell, E. M., & Ratey, J. J. (1994). *Driven to distraction.* New York: Simon & Shuster.

Halperin, J. M., Gittelman, R., Klein, D. F., & Ruddel, R. G. (1984). Reading disabled hyperactive children: A distinct subgroup of attention deficit disorder with hyperactivity? *Journal of Abnormal Child Psychology, 12,* 1–14.

Hinshaw, S., & Erhardt, D. (1991). Attention-deficit hyperactivity disorder. In P. C. Kendall (Ed.), *Child and adolescent therapy: Cognitive-behavioral procedures* (pp. 98–128). New York: Guilford.

Holborow, P., & Berry, P. (1986). A multinational, cross-cultural perspective on hyperactivity. *American Journal of Orthopsychiatry, 56,* 320–322.

Humphries, T., Kinsbourne, M., & Swanson, J. (1978). Stimulant effects on cooperation and social interaction between hyperactive children and their mothers. *Journal of Child Psychology and Psychiatry, 19,* 13–22.

Hynd, G. W., Hern, K. L., Novey, E. S., Eliopulos, D., Marshall, R., Gonzalez, J. J., & Voeller, K. K. (1993). Attention-deficit hyperactivity disorder and asymmetry of the caudate nucleus. *Journal of Child Neurology, 8,* 339–347.

Kaplan, B. J., McNicol, J., Conte, R., & Moghadam, H. (1987). Physical signs and symptoms in pre-school aged hyperactive and non-hyperactive children. *Journal of Developmental and Behavioral Pediatrics, 8,* 305–310.

Kavanagh, F., & Truss, T. J. (1988). *Learning disabilities: Proceedings of the National Conference.* Parkton, MD: York Press.

Kendall, P. C., & Braswell, L. (1984). *Cognitive behavioral therapy for impulsive children.* New York: Guilford Press.

Keogh, B., & Margolis, J. (1976). Learn to labor and wait: Attentional problems of children with learning disorders. *Journal of Learning Disabilities, 9,* 276–289.

Koestner, R., Ryan, R., Bernieri, F., & Holt, K. (1984). Setting limits on children's behavior: The differential effects of controlling vs. Informational styles on intrinsic motivation and creativity. *Journal of Personality, 52,* 248.

Kupietz, S. (1990). Sustained attention in normal and in reading-disabled youngsters with and without ADDH. *Journal of Abnormal Child Psychology, 18,* 357–372.

Lahey, B., Pelham, W., Schaughency, E., Atkins, M., Murphy, H., Hynd, G., Russo, M., Hartdagen, S., & Lorys-Vernon, A. (1988). Dimensions and types of attention deficit disorder. *Journal of the American Academy of Child and Adolescent Psychiatry, 27,* 330–335.

Lahey, B., Piacentini, J., McBurnett, K., Stone, P., Hartdagen, S., & Hynd, G. (1988). Psychopathology in the parents of children with conduct disorder and hyperactivity. *Journal of the American Academy of Child and Adolescent Psychiatry, 27,* 163–170.

Levy, F., & Hobbes, G. (1988). The action of stimulant medication in attention deficit disorder with hyperactivity: Dopaminergic, noradrenergic or both? *Journal of the American Academy of Child and Adolescent Psychiatry, 27,* 802–805.

Lou, H. C., Henriksen, L., & Bruhn, P. (1984). Focal cerebral hypoperfusion in children with dysphasia and/or attention deficit disorder. *Archives of Neurology, 41,* 825–829.

Mannuzza, S., Gittelman-Klein, R., Konig, P., & Giampino, T. (1989). Hyperactive boys almost grown up: IV. Criminality and its relationship to psychiatric status. *Archives of General Psychiatry, 46,* 1073–1079.

Meichenbaum, D. (1977). *Cognitive behavior modification.* New York: Plenum Press.

Moray, N. (1969). *Attention: Selective processes in vision and hearing.* London: Hutchinson.

Nichols, P., & Chen, T. C. (1981). *Minimal brain dysfunction: A prospective study.* Hillsdale, NJ: Lawrence Erlbaum.

Ojemann, G., Ojemann, J., Lettich, E., & Berger, M. (1989). Cortical language localization in the left, dominant hemisphere. *Journal of Neurosurgery, 71,* 316–326.

Pelham, W. E. (1986). The effects of psychostimulant drugs on learning and academic achievement in children with attention-deficit disorders and learning disabilities. In J. Torgesen & B. Wong (Eds.), *Psychological and educational perspectives on learning disabilities* (pp. 259–295). New York: Academic Press.

Pelham, W. E., & Murphy, H. A. (1986). Attention deficit and conduct disorders. In M. Hersen (Ed.), *Pharmacological and behavioral treatment: An integrative approach* (pp. 108–148), New York: John Wiley & Sons.

Pisterman, S., McGrath, P., Firestone, P., Goodman, J., Webster, I., & Mallory, R. (1989). Outcome of parent-mediated treatment of pre-schoolers with attention deficit disorder with hyperactivity. *Journal of Consulting & Clinical Psychology, 57,* 628–635.

Pittman, R. S., Davey, M. E., Alafat, K. A., Wetherill, K. V., & Kramer, N. A. (1980). Informational vs controlling verbal rewards. *Personality and Social Psychology Bulletin, 39,* 228–233.

Porges, S. W., Walter, G. F., Korb, R. J., & Sprague, R. L. (1975). The influence of methylphenidate on heart rate and behavioral measures of attention in hyperactive children. *Child Development, 46,* 727–733.

Posner, M. (1975). Psychobiology of attention. In M. Gazzaniga & C. Blakemore (Ed.), *Handbook of psychobiology* (pp. 441–479). New York: McGraw-Hill.

Rapoport, J. L., Buchsbaum, M., Weingartner, H., Zahn, T., Ludlow, C., & Mikkelson, E. J. (1980). Dextroamphetamine: Cognitive and behavior effects in normal and hyperactive boys and men. *Archives of General Psychiatry, 37,* 933–934.

Rapport, M. D., Carlson, G. A., Kelly, K. L., & Pataki, C. (1993). Methylphenidate and desiprimine in hospitalized children: Separate and combined effects on cognitive function. *Journal of the American Academy of Child & Adolescent Psychiatry, 32,* 333–342.

Richards, G. P., Samuels, S. J., Turnure, J., & Ysseldyke, J. (1990). Sustained and selective attention in children with learning disabilities. *Journal of Learning Disabilities, 23,* 129–136.

Robins, P. (1992). A comparison of behavioral and attentional functioning in children diagnosed as hyperactive or learning disabled. *Journal of Abnormal Child Psychology, 20,* 65–82.

Rosen, L. A., O'Leary, S., Joyce, S. A., Conway, G., & Pfiffner, L. (1984). The importance of prudent negative consequences for maintaining the appropriate behavior of hyperactive students. *Journal of Abnormal Child Psychology, 12,* 581–604.

Ross, A. O. (1976). Psychological aspects of learning disabilities and reading disorders. New York: McGraw-Hill.

Rutter, M. (1977). Brain damage syndromes in childhood: Concepts and findings. *Journal of Child Psychology and Psychiatry, 139,* 21–33.

Ryan, R. M. (1982). Control and information in the interpersonal sphere: An extension of cognitive evaluation theory. *Journal of Personality and Social Psychology, 43,* 450–461.

Scott, R., Deci, E., Patrick, B., & Ryan, R. (1992). Beyond the intrinsic-extrinsic dichotomy: Self-determination in motivation and learning. Special Issue: Perspectives on intrinsic motivation. *Motivation and Emotion, 16,* 165–185.

Shaywitz, B. A., Fletcher, J. M., & Shaywitz, S. (1994). Interrelationships between reading disability and attention deficit-hyperactivity disorder. In A. J. Capute, P. J. Accardo, & B. K. Shapiro (Eds.), *Learning disabilities spectrum* (pp. 107–120). Baltimore: York Press.

Silver, L. (1980). The relationship between learning disabilities, hyperactivity, distractibility, and behavioral problems. *Journal of the American Academy of Child Psychiatry, 20,* 385–397.

Spencer, T., Wilens, T., Biederman, J., Faraone, S., Ablon, J., & Lapey, K. (1995). A double-blind, crossover comparison of methylphenidate and placebo in adults with childhood onset attention-deficit hyperactivity disorder. *Archives of General Psychiatry, 52,* 434–443.

Streisguth, A. P., Herman, C. S., & Smith, D. W. (1978). Intelligence, behavior and dysmorphogenesis in the fetal alcohol syndrome: A report on 20 patients. *Journal of Pediatrics, 92,* 363–367.

Swanson, J. M., & Kinsbourne, M. (1976). Stimulant-related state dependent learning in hyperactive children. *Science, 192,* 1754–1757.

Sykes, D., Douglas, V., Weiss, G., & Minde, K. (1971). Attention in hyperactive children and the effect of methylphenidate (Ritalin). *Journal of Child Psychology and Psychiatry, 12,* 129–139.

Szatmari, P., Offord, D. R., & Boyle, M. H. (1989). Correlates, associated impairments and patterns of service utilization of children with attention deficit disorder: Findings from the Ontario Child Health Study. *Journal of Child Psychology and Psychiatry, 30,* 205–217.

Tant, J. L., & Douglas, V. I. (1982). Problem solving in hyperactive, normal and reading-disabled boys. *Journal of Abnormal Child Psychology, 10,* 285–306.

Tarnowski, K. J., Prinz, R. J., & Nay, S. M. (1986). Comparative analysis of attentional deficits in hyperactive and learning disabled children. *Journal of Abnormal Psychology, 95,* 341–345.

Werner, P. H., & Smith, R. S. (1977). *Kauai's children come of age.* Honolulu: University of Hawaii Press.

Zametkin, A. J., Nordahl, T. E., Gross, M., King, A. C., Semple, W. E., Rumsey, J., Hamburger, S., & Cohen, R. M. (1990). Cerebral glucose metabolism in adults with hyperactivity of childhood onset. *New England Journal of Medicine, 323,* 1361–1366.

Zametkin, A. J., Liebenauer, L. L., Fitzgerald, G. A., King, A. C., Minkunas, D. V., Herscovitch, P., Yamada, E. M., & Cohen, R. M. (1993). Brain metabolism in teenagers with attention-deficit hyperactivity disorder. *Archives of General Psychiatry, 50,* 333–340.

CHAPTER 4

Learning Disabilities and Memory

H. Lee Swanson, John B. Cooney, and Tam E. O'Shaughnessy

I. INTRODUCTION

Memory is the ability to encode, process, and retrieve information. As a skill, it is inseparable from intellectual functioning and learning. Individuals deficient in memory skills, such as children and adults with learning disabilities (LD), would be expected to have difficulty on a number of academic and cognitive tasks. Although memory is linked to performance in several academic (e.g., reading) and cognitive areas (e.g., problem solving), it is a critical area of focus in the LD field for three reasons. First, it reflects *applied* cognition; that is, memory functioning reflects all aspects of learning. Second, several studies suggest that the memory skills used by students with LD do not appear to exhaust, or even to tap, their ability, and therefore we need to discover instructional procedures that capitalize on their potential. Finally, several cognitive intervention programs that attempt to enhance the overall cognition of children and adults with LD rely on principles derived from memory research. This chapter characterizes and selectively reviews past and current research on memory skills, describes the components and stages of processing that influence memory performance, and discusses current trends and the implications of memory research for the instruction of children and adults with LD.

II. AN HISTORICAL PERSPECTIVE

The earliest link between LD and memory was established in the literature on reading disabilities by Kussmaul. In 1877, Kussmaul called attention to a disorder he labeled word blindness, which was characterized as an inability to read, although vision, intellect, and speech were normal. Following Kussmaul's contribution, several cases of reading difficulties acquired by adults due to cerebral lesions, mostly involving the angular gyri of the left hemisphere, were reported (see Hinshelwood, 1917, for a review). In one important case study, published by Morgan (1896), a 14-year-old boy of normal intelligence had difficulty recalling letters of the alphabet. He also had difficulty recalling written words, which seemed to convey "no impression to this mind." Interestingly, the child appeared to have good memory for oral information. This case study was important because word blindness did not appear to occur as a result of a cerebral lesion. After Morgan's description of this condition, designated as a specific reading disability, research on memory was expanded to include children of normal intelligence who exhibited difficulties reading. Hinshelwood's (1917) classic monograph presents a number of case studies describing reading disabilities in children of normal intelligence with memory problems. On the basis of these observations, Hinshelwood inferred that reading problems of these children were related to a "pathological condition of the visual memory center" (p. 21).

At the same time Hinshelwood's monograph appeared, a little known text by Bronner (1917) reviewed case studies linking memory difficulties to children of normal intelligence. For example, consider Case 21:

> "Henry J., 16 years old, was seen after he had been in court on several occasions. The mental examination showed that the boy was quite intelligent and in general capable, but had a very specialized defect. The striking feature of all the test work with this boy was the finding that he was far below his age in the matter of rote memory. When a series of numerals was presented to him auditorially, he could remember no more than four. His memory span for numerals presented visually was not much better. . . . he succeeded here with five. Memory span for syllables was likewise poor. . . . On the other hand when ideas were to be recalled, that is, where memory dealt with logical material, the results were good. (p. 120)

A majority of case studies reviewed in Bronner's text suggested that immediate (short-term) memory of children with reading disabilities was deficient and that remote (long-term) memory was intact. Bronner also noted that little about memory and its application to complex learning activities was known. For example, the author stated that very many practically important laws of memory have not yet been determined; those most firmly established concern themselves mainly with nonsense or other type of material quite unlike the activities of everyday life. In a common sense way we are aware that both immediate and remote memory are essential, that we need to remember what we see and hear. . . . that to remember an idea is probably more useful in general, than to have a good memory for rote material, but a defect for the latter may be of great significance in some kinds of school work. (p. 110)

Researchers from the 1920s to the 1950s generally viewed reading difficulties as being associated with structural damage to portions of the brain that support visual memory (e.g., see Geschwind, 1962, for a review; also see Monroe, 1932). A contrasting position was provided by Orton (1925, 1937), who suggested that reading disorders were reflective of a neurological maturational lag resulting from a delayed lateral cerebral dominance for language. Orton described the phenomenon of a selective loss or diminished capacity to remember words as strephosymbolia (twisted symbols). Orton (1937) noted that

although these children show many more errors of a wide variety of kinds it is clear that their difficulty is not in hearing and not in speech mechanism . . . but in recalling words previously heard again or used in speech, and that one of the outstanding obstacles to such recall is *remembering* [italics added] all of the sounds in their proper order. (p. 147)

In cases of visual memory, Orton stated that such children with reading disabilities have major difficulties in "recalling the printed word in terms of its spatial sequence of proper order in space." (p. 148) Thus, for Orton, reading-disabled children's memory difficulties were seen as reflecting spatial sequences in visual memory or temporal sequences in auditory memory. Although the conceptual foundation of much of Orton's research was challenged in the 1970s (see Vellutino, 1979, for a review), much of the evidence for linking LD and memory processes was established from the earlier clinical studies of Morgan, Hinshelwood, and Orton. Today, reading difficulties are viewed primarily as language problems (e.g., Siegel, 1993; Stanovich & Siegel, 1994), and memory difficulties are popularly conceptualized in terms of language processes.

It was not until the late 1960s and early 1970s that experimental (nonclinical) studies appeared comparing children with LD and nondisabled children's performance on memory tasks. The majority of these studies focused on modality-specific memory processes (i.e., auditory vs. visual memory) and cross-modality (e.g., visual recognition of auditorially presented information) instructional conditions, but they provided conflicting evidence. For example in the area of visual memory, Conners, Kramer, and Guerra (1969) compared children with LD and normally achieving children on their abilities to remember numbers presented to them on a dichotic listening task. The results of their study were that children with LD did not differ from their nondisabled peers to short-term recall. In contrast, Bryan (1972) compared LD and normally achieving children on a task that required them to recall a list of words presented by tape recorder and words presented by slide projector. Learning-disabled and comparison samples performed better with the visual than with the auditory stimuli, but children with LD performed more poorly than the nondisabled children under both conditions.

Conflicting results were also found among studies investigating visual memory information-processing abilities of children with reading disabilities. Goyen and Lyle (1971, 1973) investigated young reading-disabled student's (children under 8.5 years) recall of critical details of visual stimuli presented tachistoscopically for various exposure duration intervals. Their results showed that the students with reading disabilities did not recall as well as younger and older normal readers. In another study, Guthrie and Goldberg (1972) compared disabled and skilled readers on several tests designed to measure visual short-term memory. In contrast to Goyen and Lyle, they found that the performance of children on visual memory subtests did not clearly differentiate the ability groups.

Conflicts in findings also emerged in cross-modality research. For example, Senf and Feshbach (1970) found differences between good and poor readers' memory on cross-modality presentation conditions. That is, students were compared on their recall of digits presented auditorially, visually, and audiovisually and retrieval responses were verbal or written. Samples included culturally deprived, LD, and normal control readers of elementary and junior high school age. The sample with LD exhibited poor recall of stimuli organized into audiovisual pairs, which was attributed to problems of cross-modality matching. Older culturally deprived and normal children recalled the digits in paired order more accurately than their younger counterparts, whereas older children with LD recalled no better than younger children with LD. The sample with LD also exhibited a higher prevalence of visual memory errors. The implication of this research was that some prerequisite skills of pairing stimuli had not developed in the children with LD and the possession of these skills was essential for reading. In contrast to this study, Denckla and Rudel (1974) found that poor recall of children with LD was not related to visual encoding errors, but rather to temporal sequencing. Their results suggested that children who had difficulties in temporal sequencing would have difficulty recalling information from spatial tasks or tasks that required matching of serial and spatial stimuli (as in the Senf & Feshbach, 1970, study).

To summarize, the studies in the late 1960s and early 1970s, although contradictory, did establish a foundation for the study of LD in the context of memory. Children with LD experienced memory difficulties on laboratory tasks that required the sequencing of information presented visually and auditorily. Differences in results were most likely due to variations in how the ability groups were defined and selected. We now turn to a discussion of the more recent conceptualizations related to memory problems of children and adults with LD.

III. CONTEMPORARY RESEARCH

A. Overview

For the last 25 years, the study of memory in the area of LD has been strongly influenced by the hypothesis that variations in memory performance are rooted in the children's acquisition of mnemonic strategies. *Strategies* are deliberate, consciously applied procedures that aid in the storage and subsequent retrieval of information. Most strategy training studies that include children with LD can trace their research framework back to earlier research on *metacognition* (to be discussed); (Flavell, 1979) and/or research on *production deficiencies* (Flavell, Beach, & Chinsky, 1966). In this research, a distinction is made between the concepts of production and mediational deficiencies. Mediational deficiencies refer to the fact that children are unable to utilize a strategy efficiently. For example, young children may not spontaneously produce a potential mediator to process task requirements, but even if they did, they would fail to use it efficiently to direct their performance. On the other hand, production deficiencies suggest that children can be taught efficient strategies that they fail to produce spontaneously and that these taught strategies will direct and improve their performance. The assumption when applied to LD was that the more strategic information needed for effective memory performance, the more likely the task will be affected by the cognitive growth in the child.

The preeminence of this strategy hypothesis (various names have been used, e.g., *passive learner*) has been virtually synonymous with the study of memory in children with LD up to the late 1980s. Studies that focused on memory activities such as clustering, elaboration, and rehearsal were studies that were primarily motivated by this hypothesis. The emphasis in these studies was on teaching children with LD under various conditions or with different types of memory strategies how to remember presented material (e.g., Scruggs & Mastroperi, 1989). In general, these studies showed that children with LD can be taught through direct instructions (e.g., Gelzheiser, 1984), modeling (e.g., Dawson, Hallahan, Reaves, & Ball, 1980), and reinforcement (e.g., Bauer & Peller-Porth, 1990) to use some simple strategies that they do not produce spontaneously (e.g., Dallego & Moely, 1980). Further, the strategy hypothesis was generalized into other areas beside memory, such as reading comprehension (e.g., Borkowski, Wehying, & Carr, 1988; Wong & Jones, 1982), writing (e.g., Harris, Graham, & Pressley, 1992), mathematics (e.g., Geary & Brown, 1991; Montague, 1992), and problem solving (e.g., Borkowski, Estrada, Milstead, & Hale, 1989).

In the last few years memory research has been moving in a different direction, toward an analysis of nonstrategic processes that are not necessarily consciously applied. The major motivation behind this movement has been that important aspects of memory performance are often *disassociated* with changes in mnemonic strategies. The most striking evidence has come from research that is strategy oriented, which still shows differences between children with and without LD after using an optimal strategy (a strategy shown advantageous in the majority of studies). Prior to reviewing the current focus of memory research, however, an understanding of research conducted in the late 1970s to the early 1990s is necessary. This review will be divided into two parts: (a) studies that parallel normal child development in memory and (b) studies that identify memory components in which children or adults with learning disabilities are deficient.

IV. PARALLELS TO NORMAL MEMORY DEVELOPMENT

There is some agreement among researchers that what we know about the memory of children with LD is somewhat paralleled by what we know about the differences between older and younger children's memory (e.g., Siegel & Ryan, 1989). Such parallels in performance do not mean that LD children experience a lag in all memory processes or that faulty memory performance is primarily related to immature development. Rather, faulty memory performance reflects overt performance in some memory areas that is comparable to young children. Therefore, in most studies, memory performance of children with LD has been likened to that of younger non-LD children even though the mechanisms that underlie LD children's poor performance may not be the same as those that underlie younger children. The parallels between LD versus nondisabled chronologically age matched children and research on younger versus younger nondisabled children are apparent in that performance differences (a) emerge on tasks that require the use of cognitive strategies (e.g., rehearsal and organization); (b) emerge on effortful memory tasks, but not for tasks requiring automatic processing; (c) are influenced by the individual's knowledge base; and (d) are influenced by the individuals' awareness of their own memory processes (metacognition). We briefly review each of these parallels.

A large body of research suggests that remembering becomes easier with age because control processes become more automatic through repeated use (e.g., Pressley, 1994; for review). Control processes in memory reflect choices as to which information to scan as well as choices of what and how to rehearse and/or organize information. Rehearsal refers to the conscious repetition of information, either vocally or subvocally, to enhance recall at a later time. Learning a telephone number or a street address illustrates the primary purpose of rehearsal. Other control processes include organization, such as ordering, classifying, or tagging information to facilitate retrieval and mediation, such as comparing new items with information already in memory. Various organizational strategies studied (e.g., Baker, Ceci, & Hermann, 1987; Borkowski, et al., 1988; Dallego & Moely, 1980; Krupski, Gaultney, Malcolm, & Bjorklund, 1993; Lee & Obrzut, 1994) that have been linked to children with LD include the following:

1. Chunking: Grouping items so that each one brings to mind a complete series of items (e.g., grouping words into a sentence).
2. Clustering: Organizing items into categories (e.g., animals, furniture).
3. Mnemonics: Idiosyncratic methods for organizing information.
4. Coding: Varying the qualitative form of information (e.g., substituting pictures for words).

Studies (e.g., Scruggs & Mastropieri, 1989; Swanson, 1989) have also been directed to procedures to help children with LD mediate information:

1. Making use of preexisting associations, thereby eliminating the need for new ones.
2. Utilizing instructions: asking the student to mediate information verbally or through imagery, to aid in organization and retrieval.
3. Employing cuing: using verbal and imaginary cues to facilitate recall.

An excellent example of a study to enhance mediation of information in a LD student is provided by Mastropieri, Scruggs, Levin, Gaffney, and McLoone (1985). Mastroperi et al. conducted two experiments in which adolescents with LD recalled the definitions of 14 vocabulary words according to either a pictorial mnemonic strategy (the "keyword" method) or a traditional instructional approach. The keyword method involved constructing an interactive visual image of the to-be-associated items. For example, to remember that the English word *carlin* means *old woman* via the keyword method, the learner is directed to the fact that the first part of carlin sounds like the familiar word car. Then the learner constructs an interactive image that relates a car and an old woman, such as an elderly woman driving an old car. The results of the first experiment (experimenter-generated mnemonic illustrations) and the second experiment (student-generated mnemonic images) indicated that the keyword strategy was substantially more effective than the traditional approach.

Perhaps one of the most significant studies in terms of bringing research in memory with LD students into a developmental perspective was conducted by Tarver, Hallahan, Kauffman, and Ball (1976). In their first study, they compared LD children of approximately 8 years of age to normal achieving boys on a serial recall task of pictures that included central and incidental information. They found that the serial position curve of normals revealed the common primacy–recency effect (remembering the first and last presented items better than the middle items), whereas the performance of LD children revealed a recency effect only. In the second study, they compared LD boys of 10 and 13 years of age on the same tasks. They found that the 10- and 13-year-old LD children exhibited both a primacy and recency effect for nonrehearsal and rehearsal conditions. For both studies, an analysis of central recall (children attend to specific items based on experimenter instructions) in the three age groups revealed a constant age-related increase in overall recall and in primacy (recalling the first few items presented) performance. The normal achievers recalled more information that was central to the task when compared to LD children, whereas LD children recalled more incidental information than normal achievers. Thus, although LD children were deficient in selective attention, their selective attention improved with age. These results were interpreted as reflecting a *developmental lag*. Learning-disabled students were viewed as delayed in their utilization of the strategies for serial recall (verbal rehearsal) and selective attention.

Earlier studies that covered some of the same developmental themes as the Tarver et al. (1976) study were Torgesen and Goldman (1977), in which they investigated the role of rehearsal on serial and free recall performance, Swanson (1977), in which he investigated the role of primary performance on the nonverbal serial recall of visual information, Bauer (1977), in which he investigated the role of rehearsal and serial recall, and Wong (1978), in which she investigated the effect of cued recall and organization on children with LD. For example, in the Bauer (1977) study LD and non-LD children were required to free-recall as many words as possible from lists of monosyllabic nouns. Recall for each serial position showed that children with LD were deficient in the recall of items early in the list (primary), but not recency performance. Primacy performance at that time was associated with rehearsal (Ornstein & Naus, 1978), as well as elaborative encoding (e.g., Bauer & Emhert, 1984). In contrast to research on primary performance, studies that examined the recency effect have found that LD children are not unlike non-LD youngsters, and that younger and older children are comparable in performance (e.g., Bauer, 1977; Swanson, 1977; Tarver et al., 1976). It is assumed that recall of the most recently presented items represents the encoding of information in an automatic (noneffortful) fashion (i.e., without the benefit of using deliberate mnemonic strategies; Swanson, 1983a).

The trend found with free-recall tasks in the majority of studies published in the late 1970s and early 1980s was that ability-group and age-related differences tend to be limited to items that occur at the beginning and middle serial positions and thus reflect strategy deficits, such as rehearsal. For example, when Torgesen and Goldman (1977) studied lip movements of children during a memorization task, LD children were found to exhibit fewer lip movements than the NLD students. To the extent that these lip movements reflect the quantity of rehearsal, these data support a rehearsal-deficiency hypothesis. Haines and Torgesen (1979) and others (e.g., Dawson et al., 1980; Koorland & Wolking, 1982) also reported that incentives could be used to increase the amount of rehearsal. Bauer and Emhert (1984) found that the difference between LD and NLD students is in the quality of the rehearsal rather than the quantity of rehearsal, per se.

In addition to the ability-group and age-related differences in the use of rehearsal, differences in the use of organizational strategies were also investigated. Ability-group and age-related differences have suggested that LD and younger children are less likely to organize or take advantage of the organizational structure of items (Swanson & Rathgeber, 1986). Intervention strategies (i.e., directing children to sort or cluster items prior to recall) have in many cases lessened or eliminated ability-group differences (e.g., Dallego & Moely, 1980; however, see Gelzheiser, Cort, & Shephard, 1987; Krupski et al., 1993). Although LD and younger children tend to make less use of semantic relationships inherent in the free-recall material (Swanson, 1986; Swanson & Rathgeber, 1986), when organizational instructions are provided, both LD and younger children are capable of using a semantic organization strategy with some degree of effectiveness (e.g., Lee & Obrzut, 1994).

Difficulties in categorization that children with LD experience during their attempts to memorize difficult material were highlighted in an earlier study by Gelzheiser, Solar, Shepherd, and Wozniak (1983). These authors recorded a brief statement made by a student with LD following an attempt to retain a passage containing four paragraphs about diamonds. The student reported that she could identify major themes of the story, but could not categorize the various pieces of information under major topics. She was able to abstract the essence of the story, but was unable to use her knowledge as a framework to organize the retention of the specific passage. This research suggests that students with LD may be capable of abstracting categories of words from serially presented lists of words, but they may not be able to chunk (i.e., categorize together) these words for use at later retrieval.

Cermak (1983) presented evidence to support this thesis in a study in which LD and non-LD children were asked to learn a list of 20 common nouns in five trials. The children were told to rehearse the words aloud during each trial. At the conclusion of each trial, they were asked to recall as many of the words as they could. Three types of word lists were used: a random list of unrelated words, a list containing five words from each of four categories randomly distributed within the list, and a list containing five words from each of four categories with the words presented in category blocks. The students with LD recalled fewer words than nondisabled students following all types of presentation.

Swanson (1983b) arrived at a similar conclusion when he found that children with LD rarely reported the use of an organizational strategy when they were required to rehearse several items. He reasoned that, because these children were capable of rehearsal, the problem was not an inability to rehearse, but instead a failure to perform elaborative processing of each word. Elaborative processing was defined as the processing that goes beyond the initial level of analysis to include more sophisticated features of the words and ultimately the comparison of these features with others in the list.

The research of the early 1970s to the late 1980s also suggested that a distinction can be made between the development of memory processes that are dependent upon overt conscious "effort" and those that are not (e.g., Ceci, 1984; Swanson, 1984). Memory that results only after some conscious intent to remember is said to be effortful; that which occurs without intent or effort is considered to be automatic (e.g., Guttentag, 1984; Miller, Woody-Ramsey, & Aloise, 1991). Effortful memory is assumed to be dependent upon the development of an available store of "cognitive resources." Thus, differences in memory performance between ability groups (LD vs. nondisabled) and age groups are presumed to be dependent upon effortful memory, that is, memory that is due to individual differences in the amount of cognitive resources available (e.g., Howe, Brainerd, & Kingma, 1989; Swanson, Ashbaker, & Lee, 1996). In contrast, automatic memory is assumed to be comparable between ability groups (e.g., Ceci, 1984). The empirical evidence for this effortful–automatic distinction has emerged with respect to the presence or absence of individual differences across ages in measures of memory functioning (e.g., Harnishfeger & Bjorklund, 1994; Miller & Seier, 1994). The research on memory of children with LD directly parallels memory development in the area of effortful processing. For example, it has been shown that normally achieving children below the age of 9 years and children with LD perform quite poorly relative to older children or age-related counterparts, respectively, on tasks such as free recall (e.g., Guttentag, 1984). Older children and nondisabled age-related counterparts have been found to utilize deliberate mnemonic strategies to remember information (e.g., see Pressley, 1994; for a review). An example of studies that suggest high effort demands underlie ability-group differences can be found when comparing LD and non-LD children on verbal tasks (Swanson, 1984a). Swanson (1984a) conducted three experiments related to performance of students with LD on a word recall task, and found that recall is related to the amount of cognitive effort or the mental input that a limited capacity system expends to produce a response. He found that readers with LD were inferior to nondisabled readers in their recall of materials that made high-effort demands. Furthermore, skilled readers accessed more usable information from semantic memory for enhancing recall than LD readers. In a subsequent study, Swanson (1986) found that LD children were inferior in the quantity and internal coherence of information stored in semantic memory, as well as the means by which it is accessed. The implication of this finding is also tested in a study by Swanson (1989) that compares the use of elaborative encoding strategies by students with LD, mental retardation, giftedness, and average development. The results suggested that slow learners, average, and gifted children improved in performance using *elaborative* strategies (strategies that embellish information) when compared with nonelaborative strategies. In contrast,

LD children were less positively influenced by elaborative strategies, possibly due to excessive demands placed on central processing capacity.

Another important parallel between LD research and age-related normal memory development comes from studies that focus on children's knowledge about the world (see Bjorklund & Schneider, 1996; Bjorklund, Coyle, & Gaulty, 1992; Kee, 1994, for review). For example, familiarity with words, objects, and events permits people to integrate new information with what they already know (e.g., see Bjorklund, 1985, for a review). One way in which a knowledge base may affect memory performance is through its influence on the efficiency of mental operations performed upon the to-be-memorized items. Several authors (e.g., Bjorklund, Schneider, Cassel, & Ashley, 1994) have suggested that, in some situations, an individual's knowledge base may mediate strategy use; that is, organizational and rehearsal strategies may be executed more spontaneously and efficiently contingent upon an individual's knowledge base. Indirect support for this view as provided by Torgesen and Houck (1980). Learning-disabled students with severe short-term memory problems, LD youngsters with normal short-term memory, and normal children were compared for their recall of material scaled for familiarity. Their results indicate that children who learn normally and children with LD who have no short-term memory problems gained an advantage in recall as their familiarity with the items increased; that is, recall differences were reduced with less familiar material. This finding suggests that an individual's knowledge base (i.e., an individual's familiarity with material) influences the development or utilization of memory processes (also see Torgesen, Rashotte, Greenstein, & Portes, 1991; for an update on these findings).

Another important link between LD memory research and age-related research is the focus on children's *thinking* about cognitive strategies. Earlier, Brown (1975) summarized this development as "knowing how to know" and "knowing about knowing." Developmental improvement in remembering and the advantage accrued by non-LD children is associated with the use of rehearsal, organization, and elaboration strategies to facilitate encoding and retrieval. Recent research (e.g., see Borkowski, Carr, Rellinger, & Pressley, 1990; Borkowski & Muthukrishna, 1992; Hasselhorn, 1992) has focused on how and to what degree the effective use of effortful processes (e.g., cognitive strategies) relates to metacognition. *Metacognition* refers to knowledge of general cognitive strategies (e.g., rehearsal); awareness of one's own cognitive processes; the monitoring, evaluating, and regulating of those processes; and beliefs about factors that affect cognitive activities (e.g., see Pressley, 1994). Differences in metacognition have been proposed as one source of individual differences in intelligence and memory (Brown & Campione, 1981; Borkowski & Muthukrishna, 1992). Comparisons of various groups of children (e.g., normal, mentally retarded, disabled) have revealed substantial differences in metacognitive knowledge, at least about memory and the memorial processes (see Campione, Brown, & Ferrara, 1982; Male, 1996, for a review). At present, what we know from the literature is that children between 4 and 12 years of age become progressively more aware of the person, task, and strategy variables that influence remembering (e.g., Pressley, 1994). When applied to children with LD, Wong (1982) compared children with LD, normally achieving, and gifted children in their recall of prose. Her results indicated that when compared with the normal and gifted children, children with LD lacked self-checking skills and were less exhaustive in their selective search of retrieval cues. These results suggest that LD children were less aware of efficient strategies related to prose recall.

As reviewed, there are some parallels between the performance of younger children and those of older children with LD. The performance of LD children may reflect deficits and/or immature development. We will next turn our attention to the components and stages of processing that may underlie some of the memory problems of children with LD.

V. COMPONENTS AND STAGES OF INFORMATION PROCESSING

The majority of memory research, whether of developmental and/or instructional interest, draws from the information-processing literature, because this is the most influential model in cognitive psychology to date (see Anderson, 1990; Baddeley, 1986; 1992, for a review). The central assumptions of the information-processing model are (a) a number of operations and processing stages occur between a stimulus and a response, (b) the stimulus presentation initiates a sequence of stages, (c) each stage operates on the information available to it, (d) these operations transform the information in some manner, and (e) this new information is the input to the succeeding stage. In sum, the information-processing approach focuses on how input is transformed, reduced, elaborated, stored, retrieved, and used.

One popular means of explaining LD students' cognitive performance is by drawing upon fundamental constructs that are inherent in most models of information processing (e.g., see Hulme, 1992; Pressley, 1991). Three constructs are fundamental:

1. A constraint or *structural* component, akin to the hardware of a computer, which defines the parameters within which information can be processed at a particular stage (e.g., sensory storage, short-term memory, working memory, long-term memory)
2. A *strategy* component, akin to the software of a computer system, which describes the operations of the various stages
3. An *executive* component, by which learners' activities (e.g., strategies) are overseen and monitored.

These constructs are represented in Figure 4.1.

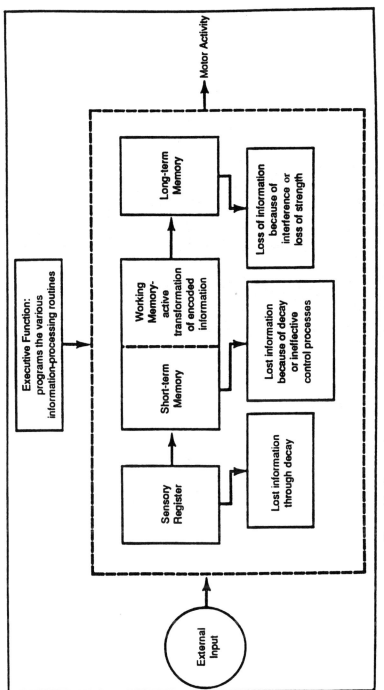

Figure 4.1 Stages and components of information processing. (From Swanson, 1987b.)

As shown in Figure 4.1, this multistore model views information as flowing through component stores in a well-regulated fashion, progressing from the sensory register, to short-term memory, and finally to long-term memory. These stores can be differentiated in children's functioning by realizing that (a) short-term memory has a limited capacity, and thus makes use of rehearsal and organizing mechanisms; (b) storage in long-term memory is mostly semantic; and (c) two critical determinants of forgetting in long-term memory are item displacement and interference, possibly as a result of a lack of retrieval strategy.

Briefly, the structural components are sensory, short-term, working, and long-term memory. Sensory memory refers to the initial representation of information that is available for processing for a maximum of 3–5 sec; short-term memory processes information between 3 and 7 sec and is primarily concerned with storage, via rehearsal processes. Working memory also focuses on the storage of information as well as the *active interpretation* of newly presented information plus information from long-term memory, whereas long-term memory is a permanent storage with unlimited capacity. The executive component monitors and coordinates the functioning of the entire system. Some of this monitoring may be automatic, with little awareness on the individual's part, whereas other types of monitoring require effortful and conscious processing. These components will become clearer when we later discuss current research findings (also see Pressley, 1994, for a review).

A. Sensory Register

As shown in Figure 4.1, basic structural environmental information (e.g., visual auditory) is assumed first to enter the appropriate sensory register. Information in this initial store is thought to be a relatively complete copy of the physical stimulus that is available for further processing for a maximum of 3–5 sec. An example of sensory registration for the visual modality is an image or icon. In a reading task, if an array of letters is presented on a computer screen and the child is then asked to press the appropriate key of the letters after a 30-sec delay between instructions, the child can correctly reproduce about six or seven letters. Incoming information from other modalities (auditory, kinesthetic) receives sensory registration, but less is known about their representation. For example, students who are presented a letter of the alphabet may produce a photographic trace that decays quickly, or they may physically scan the letter and transfer the information into an auditory (e.g., echo of sound)-visual-linguistic (meaning) representation. In other words, information presented visually may be recorded into other modalities (e.g., the transfer of a visual image to the auditory-visual-linguistic store). In the reading process, each letter or word is scanned against information in long-term memory and the verbal name. This representation will facilitate transfer of information from the sensory register to a higher level of information processing. A common paradigm used to assess the processing of sensory information is recognition. The participant is asked to determine whether information that was presented briefly (i.e., millisecond) had occurred. The task may be simply "yes" or "no" to individual items, or may require selecting among a set of items. Common dependent measures are correct detection and response time (RTs).

In general, research on the sensory register of LD children suggests it is somewhat intact (see Aaron, 1993; Eden, Stein, Wood, & Wood, 1995; Lorsbach, Sodoro, & Brown, 1992; Santiago & Matos, 1994 for review). For example, Elbert (1984) has provided evidence that LD and non-LD students are comparable at the encoding stage of word recognition, but that LD children require more time to conduct a memory search (also see Manis, 1985; Mazer, McIntyre, Murray, Till, & Blackwell, 1983). Additional evidence that LD and non-LD children are comparable at the recognition stage of information processing was provided by Lehman and Brady (1982). Using a release from proactive inhibition procedure (see Dempster & Cooney, 1982), Lehman and Brady found that reading-disabled and normal readers were comparable in their ability to encode word information (e.g., indicating whether a word was heard or seen and information concerning a word's category). However, reading-disabled children relied on smaller subword components in the decoding process than did normal readers.

Many accounts of poor recognition of quickly presented information by LD students has been attributed to attention deficits (e.g., see Hallahan & Reeve, 1980; for review), although this conclusion has been questioned (e.g., see Samuels, 1987). For example, using a psychological technique free of memory confounds, McIntyre, Murray, Coronin, and Blackwell (1978) reported a lower-than-normal span of attention in students identified as LD. Mazer et al. (1983) attributed the lower span of attention to a slower rate of information pickup from the sensory store. Despite the common assumption of differences between LD and non-LD children in attention to visual and auditory stimulus, an earlier study by Bauer (1979a) argued that the attentional resources of the LD children are adequate for performance on a variety of memory tasks. In other words, the residual differences are not great enough to account for the differences in memory performance. For example, LD and non-LD children are comparable in their ability to recall orally presented sets of three letters or three words within 4 sec after presentation (Bauer, 1979a). Similarly, LD and non-LD students are comparable in their ability to recognize letters and geometric shapes after a brief visual presentation when recognition is less than 300 msec after stimulus offset (Morrison, Giordani, & Nagy, 1977). In view of these findings, the retrieval of information from sensory storage is an important, although not a major, factor in the memory deficits exhibited in LD students (see Lorsbach, Sodoro, & Brown, 1992; Willows, Corcos, & Kershner, 1993, for a review).

B. Short-Term Memory

From the sensory register, information is transferred into the limited-capacity short-term memory. Short-term memories are retained as auditory-verbal linguistic representations (Atkinson & Shiffrin, 1968; Baddeley, 1986). Information lost in this memory is assumed to decay or disappear, but actual time of decay is longer than in the sensory register. Exact rate of decay of information cannot be estimated, because this component of memory is controlled by the subject. Using the example of a child recalling letters, the child may rehearse the letters by subvocally repeating them over and over. This is a control process that helps keep the letters in short-term memory until they are either transferred to long-term memory or the information decays.

The primary measures used to assess short-term memory are recall tasks that measure free recall or serial recall of items such as numbers, shapes, or words. Free recall tasks are those in which the subject recalls stimuli without regard to order immediately after auditory or visual presentation. In contrast, serial recall tasks require the subject to recall stimuli in the exact order in which they are presented. Variations of these tasks include probe recall and cued recall. In probe recall, the subject must recall particular elements within a sequence of stimuli, whereas in cued recall, the subject is given a portion of previously presented stimuli, and the subject is asked to reproduce the remainder of the items. This measure has been employed to determine the extent to which recall may be prompted by appropriate cues, thus highlighting the difference between item accessibility (i.e., processing efficiency) and item availability (i.e., storage).

One major source of difficulty related to short-term memory processing has been attributed to LD children's lack or inefficient use of a phonological code (sound representation within the child's mind). Hulme (1992) has reviewed several studies of subjects who performed in the retarded range of verbatim recall on sequences of verbal information. His analysis of the literature on LD students' memory performance deficits suggests that they represent the phonological feature of language (also see Mann, Cowin, & Schoenheimer, 1989). He suggests that LD children's memory problems relate to the acquisition of fluent word identification and word analysis skills.

Support for the notion of phonological coding errors comes from studies suggesting that good and poor readers differ in the extent to which they recall similar- and dissimilar-sounding names (Siegel, 1993; Stanovich & Siegel, 1994). Several researchers have found that good and poor readers differ in the way they access phonological information in memory (see Hulme, 1992, for a review). An earlier seminal study by Shankweiler, Liberman, Mark, Fowler, and Fischer (1979) compared the ability of superior, marginal, and poor second-grade readers to recall rhyming and nonrhyming letter strings. The superior readers were found to have a great deal of difficulty recalling the rhyming letter strings and the nonrhyming strings. Poor readers, however, appeared to perform comparably on rhyming and nonrhyming tasks. The authors suggested that the phonological confusability created by the rhyming letters interfered with good readers' recall because these readers relied on phonological information to a greater degree than poor readers.

Thus, an interaction is usually found in which poor readers perform better on "rhyming-word and similar letter-sounding tasks" because they have poor access to a phonological code (e.g., Shankweiler et al., 1979; Siegel & Linder, 1984). That is, good readers recall more information for words or letters that have distinct sounds (e.g., mat vs. book, A vs. F) than words or letters that sound alike (mat vs. cat, b vs. d). In contrast, poor readers are more comparable in their recall of similar and dissimilar words or sounds than skilled readers. This finding suggests that good readers are disrupted when words or sounds are alike because they process information in terms of sound (phonological) units. In contrast, poor readers are not efficient in processing information into sound units (phonological codes) and, therefore, are not disrupted in performance if words or letters sound alike.

In a study by Johnson, Rugg, and Scott (1987), 8- and 11-yr-old good and poor readers of average and below-average intelligence were compared on their ability to recall strings of similar- and dissimilar-sounding letters. When a control was made of differences in memory span between ability groups, high- and low-IQ poor readers were comparable with their chronological age (CA) and reading-level-matched controls in similarity effects (i.e., the study did not directly support the contention that difficulties in immediate memory are primarily due to difficulty with phonological coding). Some other contrasting studies (e.g., Sipe & Engle, 1986) have suggested that poor readers may be adequate in phonological coding, but show a fast decline in their ability to recall as the retention interval (time between item presentation and recall) is increased. Hall, Wilson, Humphreys, Tinzmann, and Bowyer (1983) also did not find consistent differences between good and poor readers on serial letter recall task. The author suggested that this task was more difficult for poor readers, which obscured phonological similarity effects, suggesting that the actual differences in access or use of phonological information in memory may be comparable between ability groups. Unfortunately, small sample sizes, differing degrees of task difficulty, and sampling differences make comparisons difficult across these studies.

Although information in short-term memory can be represented in sound (phonological) units, it can also be represented semantically (Shulman, 1971). Research in the area of semantic coding (attaching *meaning* to information) appears more mixed than in the area of phonological processing. Waller (1976) suggested that both reading-disabled and nondisabled children rely on semantic information for retention, but the disabled children appeared to rely on this type of memory to an even greater degree than nondisabled subjects (also see Siegel, 1993). However, other studies have found semantic coding deficits in LD children (e.g., Ceci, Ringstrom, & Lea, 1980; Swanson, 1984a; Vellutino, Scanlon, & Spearing, 1995).

Dallego and Moely (1980) found that poor readers performed similarly to their peers on a free recall task when items were semantically cued. Dallego and Moely concluded that reading-disabled subjects could use semantic cues in recalling information, but they had difficulty in the deliberate use of such strategies. In other words, LD children were able to make use of semantic information, but did not take advantage of the semantic properties of information initially.

Perhaps the issue regarding whether phonological and semantic coding underlies short-term memory deficits in LD children has to do with when and where the memory system occurs. Some researchers embraced the notion that there are dual storages of memory and they have suggested that storage differs with regard to type of information coded (Conrad, 1964; Baddeley, 1976), with the phonological code utilized in short-term memory and a semantic code in long-term memory. Evidence of a phonological code use in long-term memory (Gruneberg & Sykes, 1969) and semantic information use in short-term memory (Shulman, 1971), however, suggest that simplistic views of short-term memory are unlikely. Some researchers argued for a *connectionist* model of information processing, whereby learning and memory occur over repeated associations (i.e., strength of activations) rather than stages or storage compartments (Seidenberg, 1989). Such an activation model suggests that the focus on short-term memory or long-term memory storage is not as important as a memory system based on the strength of associations, whereby associations are built on phonetically, semantically, and/or visual-spatial information. Unfortunately, research on the interaction of phonological and semantic processes with the reading-disabled is scarce (Swanson, 1984b; Waterman & Lewandowski, 1993).

1. Meta-Analysis

Because short-term memory is clearly the most widely researched area related to the cognitive processing problems of students with LD, a meta-analysis was conducted to quantitatively summarize the literature (O'Shaughnessy & Swanson, in press; see Cooper & Hedges, 1994, for discussion of meta-analysis calculation procedures). Toward this end, a standard ERIC and PSYCHINFO computer search, covering the years 1974–1994, was conducted to identify experimental studies comparing the performance of LD and non-LD students on short-term memory tasks. To be included in the present analysis, each study was required to meet the following criteria: (a) directly compare LD readers with average readers, as identified on a standardized reading measure, on at least one short-term measure; (b) report standardized reading scores that indicate that LD students are at least 1 year below grade level; and (c) report intelligence scores for LD students that are in the average range (e.g., 85–115). Although the search resulted in approximately 155 articles on immediate memory and LD, only 38 studies met the criteria for inclusion (24.5%). Hedge's g was computed for each experiment; g was defined as the mean memory score of the LD group minus the mean memory score of the non-

LD group divided by the pooled standard deviation of both groups and then corrected for sample size. Negative values for g^* (effect size) represent poorer immediate memory performance in the LD group. The interpretation of effect size is similar to a z-score if one assumes the data are normally distributed. For comparisons, an effect size magnitude of 0.20, in absolute value, is considered small, 0.50 is moderate, and 0.90 is considered a large effect size (Cohen, 1969).

Based on a review of the studies included in this analysis, two broad categories were developed to organize the results: studies that use (a) verbal stimuli and/or (b) nonverbal stimuli. In addition, the following subcategories were developed to organize each of the broad categories: (a) free recall and serial recall memory tasks, (b) with and without instruction in mnemonic strategies, (c) auditory and visual presentation, and (d) age (7–8 years, 9–11 years, 12–13 years, 14–17 years, and 18 years and older). The analysis of each category or subcategory was performed separately, but in each case the same analytic method was used. An overall average estimate of immediate memory difference was obtained across all appropriate study outcomes as shown in Table 4.1. Although results of both the total averaged data and the data without outliers are reported, the focus of results will be on the findings obtained when outliers were removed (g score > 3.00).

2. Descriptive Analysis

The 38 studies included in the meta-analysis produced 186 effect sizes, for an average of 4.89 comparisons per study. The average year of publication was 1984. The most frequent journal publications were the *Journal of Learning Disabilities* (7 studies) and the *Journal of Educational Psychology* (5 studies). Thirty-four studies detailed the ratio of males to females in subject selection; however, no study separated results as a function of gender. In addition, only 11 of 38 studies reported information on the ethnicity of subjects. Thus, memory performance as a function of gender and/or ethnicity could not be compared across studies.

The average sample size per study was 36 (range 8 to 66; $n = 1354$) for students with LD, and 42 (range 8 to 88; $n = 1600$) for average students. Within the LD group of subjects, the average age was 11 years with 240 females and 894 males. Within the nondisabled group, the average age was 11 with 382 females and 949 males. The majority of studies, 23 out of 38, involved fourth-, fifth-, and sixth-grade students.

As shown in Table 1, the results of this synthesis support a large body of research demonstrating that as a group LD students exhibit deficits in immediate memory processes compared to normally achieving students of the same general intelligence. The overall mean effect size across all studies is -0.64 ($SD = 0.41$). Based on Cohen's criteria, this is a moderate effect size. In terms of percentiles, 74% of the average reading group exceeded the mean score of the LD group.

Also as shown in Table 1, the overall effect size was disaggregated as a function of the broad categories (i.e., verbal and nonverbal stimuli). In addition, fur-

Table 4.1
Overall Magnitude of Immediate Memory Differences[a]

Category	Effect sizes (ES) excluding outliers				All effect sizes (ES)			
	No. of studies	ES	g	SD	No. of studies	ES	g	SD
Overall	33	126	-0.64	0.41	38	158	-0.68	0.73
Verbal	35	115	-0.68	0.40	38	146	-0.72	0.73
Free Recall	16	54	-0.55	0.34	19	68	-0.52	0.55
Serial Recall	21	63	-0.80	0.48	23	78	-0.90	0.83
Auditory Presentation	15	41	-0.70	0.52	16	53	-0.77	0.92
Visual Presentation	24	73	-0.66	0.35	27	91	-0.69	0.62
With Mnemonic Instruction	7	13	-0.54	0.23	8	18	-0.52	0.32
Without Mnemonic Instruction	31	102	-0.71	0.44	35	128	-0.75	0.77
7–8 years old	6	10	-0.57	0.48	8	12	-0.76	0.62
9–11 years old	17	19	-0.89	0.29	23	25	-1.01	0.71
12–13 years old	7	8	-0.78	0.41	9	10	-0.76	0.49
14–17 years old	2	3	-0.34	0.49	2	3	-0.34	0.49
18 years old and older	2	3	-0.58	0.62	2	3	-0.58	0.62
Nonverbal (low verbal)	6	9	-0.15	0.15	7	12	-0.17	0.50
Free Recall	1	1	0.00	na	1	1	0.00	na
Serial Recall	6	8	-0.17	0.15	7	11	-0.19	0.52
Auditory Presentation	na				na			
Visual Presentation	6	9	-0.15	0.15	7	12	-0.17	0.50
With Mnemonic Instruction	0				0			
Without Mnemonic Instruction	6	9	-0.15	0.15	7	12	-0.17	0.50
7–8 years old	2	2	-0.27	0.03	2	2	-0.27	0.03
9–11 years old	2	3	0.35	0.60	2	2	-0.34	0.50
12–13 years old	3	5	-0.41	0.48	3	3	0.35	0.60
14–17 years old	2	3	-0.34	0.50	3	5	-0.34	0.50
18 years old and older	0				0			

[a] g indicates unbiased effect size; negative effect size indicates poorer performance in learning disabled group; NA indicates not applicable.

ther disaggregation occurred within verbal and nonverbal stimuli categories under the subcategories of free recall, serial recall, auditory presentation, visual presentation, with mnemonic instruction, without mnemonic instruction, and age. The important findings were as follows:

1. Consistent with numerous other research findings, the LD group performed poorly on tasks requiring memorization of *verbal information* in comparison to the non-LD group. More specifically, verbal memory tasks yielded an overall mean effect size of −0.68, which indicates that 75.17% of students in the average reading group performed above the mean of the reading-disabled group.
2. Memory tasks that employed stimuli that could not easily be named, such as abstract shapes, did not produce large differences between good and poor readers ($g^* = -0.15$). In this case, only 55.96% of the non-LD group performed above the mean of the LD group.
3. Memory tasks requiring LD readers to recall *exact sequences* of verbal stimuli, such as words or digits, immediately after a series was presented yielded a much greater overall mean effect size ($g^* = -0.80$) than nonverbal serial recall tasks ($g^* = -0.17$). Thus, reading-disabled students' serial recall performance with verbal material was over three-quarters of a standard deviation below that of average readers compared to their memory performance with nonverbal stimuli, which was less than one-quarter of a standard deviation below that of average readers.
4. The overall mean effect size for studies that provided instructions in mnemonic strategies (e.g., rehearsal and sorting items into groups) prior to recall and used verbal stimuli is −0.54; whereas the overall mean effect size for studies using verbal stimuli, but that did not provide instructions to students about how to use mnemonic strategies, is −0.71. This indicates that although the memory performance of students who are reading disabled improved with training in mnemonic strategies, the memory performance of 70.5% of average readers is still above the mean of the reading-disabled group.
5. Memory tasks that involved the auditory presentation of verbal stimuli resulted in an overall mean effect size of −0.70, whereas those that involved a visual presentation of verbal stimuli resulted in an overall mean effect size of −0.66. In terms of percentiles, 75.8% and 74.5% of normally achieving students scored above the mean of the reading-disabled group respectively. Thus, the inferior verbal memory performance of reading-disabled students appears *unrelated* to the modality in which a stimulus is received.
6. Memory tasks that involved the visual presentation of nonverbal stimuli, such as abstract shapes, resulted in an overall mean effect size of −0.15. This can be interpreted as a small difference between the average and LD reading groups.

Table 4.2 provides effect sizes by how LD students were categorized by their problems in reading. Thirteen different reading achievement tests were used to distinguish students who are LD in reading from normally achieving students. As shown in Table 4.2, 16 studies used word recognition alone, 16 studies used word recognition and reading comprehension, and 4 studies used reading comprehension alone as the reading analysis used to define LD. Two studies were listed as "other" because one study did not specify which reading achievement measure was used. As shown in Table 4.2, the largest overall effect size was exhibited by studies that used both word recognition and reading comprehension as a means of distinguishing LD subjects ($g^* = -0.68$). Studies that used either word recognition alone or reading comprehension alone resulted in similar effect sizes of $g^* = -0.59$ and $g^* = -0.56$, respectively. Thus, studies that used *both* word recognition and reading comprehension as the criteria for assessing reading skills resulted in a sample of LD subjects that demonstrate more severe immediate memory problems.

In summary, this quantitative analysis of the literature clearly indicates that children and adults with LD are inferior to their counterparts on measures of short-term memory. Most critically, students with LD are at a distinct disadvantage compared to their normal-achieving peers when they are required to memorize verbal information. Students with LD have difficulty remembering familiar items such as letters, words, and numbers, and unfamiliar items such as abstract shapes that can be used. A brief description of some of the individual studies supporting this conclusion follows.

Bauer and Peller-Porth (1990) investigated the effects of incentive on verbal free recall performance. Children with and without LD were matched on age, gender, IQ, and race. The mean age of participants was 9.87 years. Children were classified as LD based on a discrepancy between expected and actual academic achievement (i.e., in spite of normal IQs, children with LD were 2–3 years behind their expected reading grade level). The stimuli and procedure used were similar to those described above in Bauer (1979b); however, 4–5 days after participating in a first free recall session, the same children were tested again on immediate free recall with incentives. Although incentives improved the recall of both groups to a similar degree, overall recall was significantly higher by students without LD than by students with LD ($g^* = -1.01$). In addition, the LD group displayed lower recall of the first few words which, again, suggests deficient memorization strategies such as rehearsal. In contrast, recall of the last few words was similar between disabled and nondisabled children indicating that attention and immediate memory are comparable.

In a second set of similar experiments, children with and without LD 9–10 and 11–12 years of age were compared. Overall, recall was significantly higher by nondisabled children than by disabled children ($g^* = -1.23$), and recall was higher by older than by younger children. In addition, tokens increased recall more for

Table 4.2

Magnitude of Differences in Immediate Memory as a Function of Reading Analysis Used to Define Learning Disability[a]

Reading analysis category	Effect sizes (ES) excluding outliers				All effect sizes (ES)			
	No. of studies	ES	g	SD	No. of studies	ES	g	SD
Word Recognition								
Overall	16	65	-0.59	0.41	16	83	-0.60	0.68
Verbal	15	64	-0.60	0.41	16	82	-0.60	0.69
Nonverbal	1	1	-0.24	na				
Reading Comprehension								
Overall	4	8	-0.56	0.38	4	10	-0.50	0.71
Verbal	4	6	-0.74	0.20	4	8	-0.75	0.44
Nonverbal	1	2	0.52	0.73	1	2	0.52	0.73
Word Recognition and Reading Comprehension								
Overall	14	51	-0.68	0.47	16	60	-0.82	0.82
Verbal	13	42	-0.75	0.45	16	51	-0.91	0.85
Nonverbal	5	9	-0.32	0.37	5	9	-0.32	0.37
^Other[b]	2				2			

[a] g indicates unbiased effect size; negative effect size indicates poorer performance in learning disabled group; nonsignificant Q reflects homogeneity within category; *$p < .05$. **$p < .01$. ***$p < .001$.

[b] ^ Other indicates two studies were not included in table; one study did not specify reading achievement measure used and one study used the Illinois Test of Psycholinguistic Abilities (ITPA) which measures various aspects of language ability, but not word recognition or reading comprehension directly.

older children than for younger children. Similar to the first experiments, recall of the first three words was higher by the nondisabled children than by the disabled children, and there was little difference in recall between groups on the last three words. Lastly, receiving a reward did not significantly increase the primacy positions of younger disabled and nondisabled children, suggesting that rehearsal and other encoding processes are inefficient or underdeveloped in younger and disabled children.

Swanson (1978) obtained a very large negative effect size for a serial recall experiment using verbal stimuli ($g^* = -2.63$) and no difference between groups for an experiment using nonverbal stimuli ($g^* = 0.00$). In this investigation, a probe-type serial recall task was used in which a series of abstract shapes are laid down in a horizontal row in front of subjects and each item is exposed for a few seconds before it is turned face down. Then, a probe item is displayed and the subject is required to point to the card in the horizontal array that matches the probe. Normally achieving children and children who were LD in reading were matched on chronological age, IQ, and gender. The children who were LD in reading performed as well as average readers on the unnamed condition. In contrast, naming the abstract shapes prior to recall led to a significant improvement in recall for average readers, although not for LD readers. The author postulates that the reading difficulties of LD children may be attributable to deficiencies in verbal encoding. That is, labels may serve to integrate visual information and improve its retrieval for normal readers; whereas, naming for LD children does not facilitate these processes.

Siegel and Linder (1984) compared the short-term memory performance of 45 children with an LD in reading and 89 children who were normally achieving in school. The children, aged 7 to 13 years, were administered several verbal serial recall tasks involving visual or auditory presentation of rhyming and nonrhyming letters. In this study, reading disability was defined as a Wide Range Achievement Test reading score below the 21st percentile. The mean reading percentile for the normally achieving children was 74.9, which is in the average range. In addition, to be included in the study a child had to achieve a *Peabody Picture Vocabulary Test* (PPVT) score of at least 80. The results of this study indicated that the youngest children (7 to 8 years) with a reading disability did not show any difference between recall of nonrhyming letters (e.g., H, K. L, Q) and rhyming letters (e.g., B, C, D, G), whereas, the normally achieving children of the same age found the rhyming items more difficult to remember than the nonrhyming ones. It was postulated that the poorer performance by normally achieving children is due to their use of a speech-based coding system in short-term memory that presents greater difficulty with similar than nonsimilar sounds. In contrast, the older reading-disabled children (9 to 13 years), similar to their normally achieving peers, exhibited significantly poorer recall of rhyming than nonrhyming letters. The authors concluded that a deficiency in phonological coding may characterize younger children with LD; whereas, older children with LD appear to be using a speech-based coding system, but have a more general deficit in short-term memory. The effect sizes for this study were collapsed across age groups because data were not available to calculate separate effect sizes for each age group. The overall mean effect size for this study was −1.50 (range −1.22 to −1.84), indicating that overall the children with LD displayed inferior memory performances on verbal serial recall tasks compared to their normally achieving counterparts.

Finally, Wilhardt and Sandman (1988) examined immediate free recall of words in adults with LD. In this study, 21 adults with LD between 18 and 33 years of age were compared with 88 age- and education-matched controls. Adults with LD had a mean Wechsler Adult Intelligence Scale full-scale IQ of 80.5 and a mean Wide Range Achievement Test reading grade level of 7.5. The participants in this study were tested individually. Instructions were shown on a computer screen telling them to "memorize the following words." Words would then appear on the screen one at a time until 10 words had been presented followed by instructions to recall the words. A variation of this procedure involved cued recall in which after all 10 words are presented, a cue word related to one of the other memorized word sets, is presented to initiate each response. This study resulted in a moderate effect size ($g* = -0.51$) for the free recall task and a large effect size ($g* = -1.17$) for the cued recall task. This indicates that 69.5% (free recall) and 87.9% (cued recall) of the nondisabled adults exceeded the mean performance of the adults with LD. Thus, the overall memory performance of adults with LD is inferior to that of nondisabled adults. In addition, the use of mismatched prompts in the cued recall task interfered with the performance of the learning disabled group more than the nondisabled group.

3. Summary

The most important conclusion to be drawn from the literature review on short-term memory is that LD readers, as a group, are distinctly disadvantaged compared to their peers who are average readers when they are required to memorize verbal information. That is, students who are LD in reading have difficulty remembering familiar items such as letters, words, numbers, and unfamiliar items that can easily be named and stored phonetically in memory. Moreover, when a task demands that verbal information be recalled in sequential order, the memory performance of students with reading disabilities declines even farther. Because skillful reading involves processing ordered information (i.e., words are written from left to right and comprised of specific sequences of letters) it seems likely that memory deficits could play a role in reading disabilities. For example, beginning readers must obtain the sounds of words from their written representations. These print-to-sound codes must be stored in memory in order and then blended together, while stimultaneously searching long-term memory for a word that matches the string of sounds. Because low verbal materials do not produce large differences between skilled and LD readers in recall, the memory deficits of LD readers do not appear to involve general short-term memory ability.

C. Long-Term Memory

The amount of information as well as the form of information transferred to long-term memory is primarily a function of control processes (e.g., rehearsal). Long-term memory is a permanent storage of information of unlimited capacity. How information is stored is determined by the uses of links, associations, and general organizational plans. Information stored in long-term memory is primarily semantic. Forgetting occurs because of item decay (loss of information) or interference.

In comparison to the volume of research on short-term memory processes, research on LD children's long-term memory is meager; however, the available research provides considerable support for the assertion that storage and retrieval problems are primary sources of individual differences in long-term memory performance (e.g., Ceci, 1984; Swanson et al., 1996). Concerning retrieving information from long-term memory, LD children can use organized strategies for selecting retrieval cues (Wong, 1982) and different word attributes (e.g., graphophonic, syntactic, semantic) to guide retrieval (Blumenthal, 1980); however, they appear to select less efficient strategies, conduct a less exhaustive search for retrieval cues, and lack self-checking skills in the selection of retrieval cues (Wong, 1982). Swanson (1984b, 1987) also provided evidence suggesting that long-term memory deficits may arise from failure to integrate visual and verbal memory traces of visually presented stimuli at the time of storage or retrieval. His findings suggested that semantic memory limitations underlie LD children's failure to integrate verbal and visual codes. Ceci, Ringstrom, and Lea (1980) presented data that suggested separate pathways for auditory and visual inputs to the semantic memory system and that LD children may have an impairment in one or both of these pathways. For children with visual and auditory impairments, the recall deficit arises in both storage and retrieval. When only one modality is impaired, the long-term memory deficit is hypothesized to arise at the time of storage. Furthermore, semantic orienting tasks were found to ameliorate the recall deficits of the children with single modality impairments but not those with impairments in both visual and verbal modalities (Ceci et al., 1980; Experiment 2).

Some earlier reviews (e.g., see Worden, 1986) have suggested that LD children's long-term memory is intact, but the strategies necessary to gain access to this information are impaired. This notion has been challenged (Baker et al., 1987), and evidence suggests that LD children's long-term memory for tasks that require semantic processing is clearly deficient when compared with that of non-LD peers (Brainerd, Kingma, & Howe, 1986; Howe, Brainerd, & Kingma, 1989; Swanson et al., 1996). Moreover, some experimental evidence suggests that LD children may have problems in the structural component of information processing (e.g.,

Swanson et al., 1996). Noting the inconsistencies of the early research on the short-term memory processes of children with LD, Brainerd and his colleagues undertook a series of analyses to investigate the development of long-term memory processes in children with LD and normally achieving children (see Brainerd & Reyna, 1991 for a review). For example Howe, O'Sullivan, Brainerd, and Kingma (1989) reported that non-LD children exhibited better recall when the to-be-remembered items belonged to taxonomic categories than when the to-be-remembered items are unrelated. However, recall by children with LD was not greatly enhanced when the to-be-remembered items are taxonomically related. Both LD and non-LD children exhibit better cued recall relative to free recall. Although children with LD appear to derive some benefit from cued recall procedures, it is not nearly as great as that exhibited by non-LD children. Additional experiments reported in Brainerd, Reyna, Howe, and Kingma (1990) indicate that children with LD exhibit higher rates of storage failure than non-LD children, regardless of whether the to-be-learned information is taxonomically related or not.

In a review of several studies, Brainerd and Reyna (1991) suggest that children with LD (a) may have generalized cognitive difficulties and (b) that cognitive difficulties are larger on the acquisition side of the learning process than on the forgetting side. That is, children with LD have more difficulty establishing new memory traces relative to retaining memory traces once they have been acquired. An important implication of this work is that although much of the difference between children with LD and non-LD children in learning declarative information can be ameliorated, children with LD exhibit slightly higher rates of forgetting (via storage failure). Procedures for mitigating storage failure remain the subject of future research.

Taken as a whole, the results reviewed here suggest that the processes involved in entering a memory trace into the long-term store are important sources of ability-group differences in children's long-term recall. Research to discover methods for remediating these deficits is certainly warranted. More direct research linking deficits in memory performance to mechanism in long-term memory is provided below in research on working memory. Working memory is considered an active component of long-term memory (Cantor & Engle, 1993).

D. Working Memory

One of the new perspectives on the study of memory in LD samples is the focus on working memory. Before this research is reviewed a brief overview of the most popular model is in order. Baddeley and Hitch (1974) suggested that short-term store model should be replaced with the concept of working memory. This is because *working memory* is viewed as a more dynamic and active system because it simultaneously focuses on processing and storage demands, whereas short-term memory focuses primarily on the storage of information and is considered a more passive system. Baddeley (1986) describes working memory as a limited-capacity central executive that interacts with a set of two passive store systems used for temporary storage of different classes of information: the speech-based articulatory loop, and the visual sketch pad. The phonological or articulatory loop is responsible for the temporary storage of verbal information; items are held within a phonological store of limited duration, and the items are maintained within the store via the process of articulation. The sketch pad is responsible for the storage of visual spatial information over brief periods and also plays a key role in the generation and manipulation of mental images. Both storage systems are in direct contact with the central executive system. The central executive is considered to be primarily responsible for coordinating activity within the cognitive system, but it can also devote some of its limited capacity to increasing the amount of information that can be held in the two subsystems. An important assumption of this model is that two specific store systems and the central executive occupy separate but interrelated capacity pools. Provided that the storage demands of the specific store systems can be met, the central executive uses its capacity for separate activities. When storage demands exceed storage capacity in one of the specific store systems, however, some central executive capacity must be devoted to storage, with the result that fewer resources will be available for alternative activities.

How does this working memory formulation help us understand LD better than the concept of short-term memory? First, it suggests that strategies play a *smaller* role in learning and memory than previously thought. This is an important point because some studies do show that performance deficits of children with LD are not related rehearsal, per se (e.g., see Bauer, 1979a; Torgesen & Goldman, 1977; then see Swanson, 1983a, 1983b). Second, the idea of a working memory system is useful because it is viewed as an active memory system directed by a central executive. This is important because the central executive can become a focus of instruction and influence on academic performance. Finally, most importantly, working memory processes are highly related to achievement (e.g., Daneman & Carpenter, 1980; Engle, Cantor, & Carullo, 1992).

There have been several points of convergence that working memory plays a critical role in integrating information during comprehension (e.g., Just & Carpenter, 1992). Several models explicitly posit a dual role of working memory: (a) it holds recently processed text to make connections to the latest input, and (b) it maintains the gist of information for the construction of an overall model of passage comprehension (e.g., see Engle et al., 1992; Shah & Miyake, 1996, for a review). In terms of individual differences, if a reader has a large working memory capacity for language, then the execution of various fundamental comprehension processes (such as word encoding, lexical access, syntactic and semantic analysis, etc.) does not delete the limited resource pool as much as for a reader with a smaller capacity (e.g., Miyake, Carpenter, & Just, 1994). As a result, readers with a larger working memory capacity would have more resources available for storage while comprehending text. On the other hand, readers with smaller working memory capacity might have fewer resources available for the maintenance of information for comprehension. This view is supported by the findings showing that working memory correlates highly with comprehension (e.g., Engle et al., 1992), and this relationship holds (at least for adults) even after low-level decoding processes are factored in (Baddeley, Logie, Nimmo-Smith, & Brereton, 1985).

Several studies (Siegel & Ryan, 1989; Swanson, 1992; Swanson, Cochran, & Ewers, 1989; Swanson, et al., 1996) have shown that children with LD in reading suffer from working memory deficiencies. For example, in Swanson et al. (1989) used a sentence-span task (Daneman & Carpenter, 1980; also see Baddeley et al., 1985) to measure the efficiency of storage and processing operations combined. The task required children to recall the last word of several sentences, as well as to answer a comprehension question about a sentence. Materials for the sentence-span task were unrelated declarative sentences, 7 to 10 words in length. The sentences were randomly arranged into sets of two, three, four, or five. The following are three examples of sentences for which the child was to recall the last words:

1. We waited in line for a *ticket.*
2. Sally thinks we should give the bird its *food.*
3. My mother said she would write a *letter.*

To ensure that children comprehended the sentences (i.e., processed their meaning) and did not merely try to remember the target word (i.e., treat the task as one of short-term memory), they were required to answer a question after each group of sentences was presented. Questions were related to a randomly selected (but never the last) sentence in the set. For the above three-sentence set, for example, they were asked, "Where did we wait?" The results of this study suggest that working memory deficits of readers with LD were inferior to those of nondisabled readers.

An important issue is how short-term memory (discussed earlier) and working memory relate to one another and what each contributes to the understanding of the poor academic achievement of children and adults with LD. Answers to this question are beginning to emerge in the area of reading. There seems to be some evidence suggesting that short-term memory tasks, such as the traditional digit span task, reflect processes (e.g., phonological coding) relevant to reading recognition and working memory tasks drawn on processes (e.g., executive processing) relevant to reading comprehension. For example, Swanson (1994) compared 74 children and adults with LD (age range of 5.0–53.60 yrs.) and 180 normal-achieving children and adults (age range 5.2–58.0 yrs.) on short-term memory (digit, word span, visual-spatial sequential recall) tasks and working memory tasks. For both ability groups, the factor analyses indicated that short-term memory and working memory loaded on different factors and that these different factors accounted for separate variance in reading recognition and reading comprehension.

A second study (Swanson & Berninger, 1995) was more specific about the contributions of the two memory systems to reading. This study included two exper-

iments that directly tested the notion that individual differences in a general working memory system are primarily linked to reading comprehension, whereas individual differences in phonological short-term memory (articulatory coding) are
primarily linked to reading recognition (e.g., Bisiacchi, Cipolotti, & Denes, 1989).
The rationale behind the above two hypotheses is as follows. Working memory is
seen as drawing resources from long-term memory (e.g., Cantor & Engle, 1993),
whereas short-term memory is seen as a system that can operate independent of
long-term memory (e.g., Dempster, 1985; Klapp, Marshburn, & Lester, 1983).
Furthermore, the phonological processes that are directly associated with reading
recognition are seen as modular (Stanovich, 1990), and can operate independent
of an executive processing system. Therefore, the researchers predicted that
phonological short-term memory operations make independent contributions to
reading recognition beyond the contribution of a general system (Pennington, Van
Orden, Kirson, & Haith, 1991; Siegel & Ryan, 1988). The sample consisted of 115
skilled and LD readers who were fourth, fifth, and sixth graders. Based on standardized reading test scores the participants were divided into four ability groups:
High comprehension/High Word Recognition, Low comprehension/High Word
Recognition; High comprehension/Low Word Recognition, Low Comprehen-
sion/Low Word Recognition. The results were straightforward: Working memory
measures were related to reading comprehension, whereas phonological short-
term memory measures were related to reading recognition. Most critically, the
findings clarify two important issues. First, children who have difficulties in reading comprehension and working memory do not necessarily suffer from difficulties in accessing a small specialized pool of verbal resources (phonological coding). The results clearly show that working memory and phonological short-term
memory tasks reflect independent operations and that WM and STM tasks did *not*
interact with high/low comprehension and high/low reading recognition. Thus, the
results appear consistent with the hypothesis that deficits in reading comprehension by LD readers are partly attributable to inefficiencies in working memory due
to the central executive (as a nonspecialized resource system) failing to support
verbal processing. Second, because no significant interaction emerged, the results
suggest that the comorbid group (low comprehension and low word recognition)
has *combined* memory deficits (deficits reflective of the poor comprehension
group-only and deficits reflective of the poor recognition group-only). In general,
the results provide support for the assumption that reading comprehension and
word recognition deficits may draw resources from independent memory systems.

E. The "Executive" Component

As shown from the research in the 1970s and 1980s, many investigators argued
that LD readers' memory problems reflect difficulties with specific processes, such
as selective attention, organization, rehearsal, and phonological coding. Theoretically, one could argue, however, that many of these deficient verbal processing

mechanisms are under the control of an executive system (Baddeley, 1986). Learning-disabled readers' memory problems have only recently been explicitly related to executive processing, although several studies in the 1980s suggest some role of executive processing. For example, executive processing may underlie ability-group differences in verbal memory performance and/or set limits within which memory processes may vary. Further, it is important to discuss the role of executive processing in LD students' memory performance because several strategy intervention programs are directed toward those skills (e.g., Borkowski & Muthukrishna, 1992; Brown & Palincsar, 1988; Lucangeli, Galderisi, & Cornoldi, 1995).

Executive processes have been described by Neisser (1967) as those mechanisms that "orchestrate cognition." An analogy related to the functions of the executive processor can be made by comparing it to an industrial plant. A work space (available floor space) is provided in an industrial plant that is available for assembling components. The executive process is the manager, or overseer, that coordinates the manufacturing process, and information in memory is the warehouse facility. If there is too much incoming work for the operatives in the plant, the executive will have to make decisions about how to allocate work, particularly with respect to specialized equipment (e.g., verbal coding), and some of this load may accumulate in the general work space. Thus, the executive is seen as coordinating information that should occupy the work space, as well as that information that should be dealt with at a specialized level.

In its simplest form, executive processing is looked upon as a divided attention manipulation (Baddeley, 1992). That is, the majority of studies assessing executive processes involve situations in which subjects must successfully coordinate performance on multiple tasks (see Baddeley, 1986; Gathercole & Baddeley, 1993, for a review). It is assumed that performance on multiple tasks is high when demands on processing are minimal. However, under conditions that place high processing demands on multiple tasks, processing changes (such as modifying and reprioritizing processing behavior) must be made on operations by the executive system. In one study, Swanson (1993a) implemented three experiments to determine whether memory difficulties experienced by LD readers may be attributable, in part, to executive processing. In Study 1, LD readers, matched to skilled readers on chronological age and reading comprehension ability, were compared on the Concurrent Digit Span Measure presented under high (six-digit) and low (three-digit) memory load conditions as they concurrently sorted cards into verbal or nonverbal categories. Study 2 utilized the same task as the previous experiment, except that LD readers of low and average working memory capacity were compared with skilled readers of average and high working memory capacity. Both experiments clearly showed that LD readers' performance is depressed under high load memory conditions. Study 2 also indicated that overall performance of nondisabled readers was predictable from LD readers, suggesting that ability-group differences are related to global processing efficiency rather than to isolated verbal and nonverbal systems. In Study 3, LD and non-LD readers were compared on their ability to recall central and secondary information from base and elaborative sentence tasks under high and low effort encoding conditions. LD readers had significantly poorer secondary recall during high effort encoding conditions when compared to skilled readers. The difficulties that children with LD experienced on these multiple tasks were attributed to deficits in executive processing.

A more recent study by Swanson et al. (1996) investigated whether the limitations in LD children with working memory were related to an executive system. There were two experiments in which Swanson et al. compared LD children under *initial* working memory conditions (those conditions in which they did not receive help), gain conditions in which the researchers attempt to correct the errors and bring the children up to an asymptotic level (that is, provide cues and prompts that would help them retrieve the information until cues are no longer helpful), and then *maintenance* conditions (representing the conditions that were the best they could do (gain condition), but this time without help). The results tended to support the notion that working memory difficulties are related to a general storage or executive system in that (a) reading group differences are best predicted from situations (maintenance condition) that reflect increasing demands on working memory; (b) reading group differences remain on high-demand (maintenance) conditions when variables related to item accessibility (performance on the initial and gain conditions) are partialed out from the analysis; and (c) all reading groups benefited from cues, but there were still differences between ability groups on the gain conditions. Their results showed that although LD readers' working memory could be significantly modified, they still remain at a clear disadvantage when compared to their same-age normal-achieving counterparts. Under both verbal and visual-spatial conditions, the results indicated that there was a greater involvement of the central executive system in LD readers' performance than previously recognized in the literature.

1. Summary

Overall, current research suggests that LD children experience problems with a number of information-processing components related to memory. Most of the earlier research has focused on short-term memory, whereas more recent research focuses on working memory. As yet, research has only begun to identify the independent effects and contributions of various working memory components to LD students' overall memory functioning. Thus, it is best to view their memory difficulties as reflecting interactive problems between and among various memory-processing components.

F. Studies of Everyday Memory

Although a consistent finding in the literature is that LD children suffer deficiencies on verbal memory tasks, whereas their performance on nonverbal (low verbal) tasks appears to be comparable to nondisabled children, conclusions related to LD children's deficits in the processing of verbal information is open to question because most of the findings are related to laboratory tasks. Thus, we have little understanding of how the verbal memory of children and adults with LD operates in everyday life. Only two naturalistic experiments were identified in the memory literature. The most comprehensive was done by Swanson, Reffel, and Trahan (1990) in which thy assessed LD children's naturalistic memory in three studies. In Study 1, 10-year-old LD and non-LD readers were compared on their recall of common objects and events (recall name of kindergarten teacher, items on a telephone and a penny), as well as information related to the space shuttle disaster. (These children had watched the space shuttle disaster 2 years earlier on television in a classroom setting.) Also studied, via a questionnaire, was how the memory of these children may affect strategies for recalling activities of their daily life. Sample Items on Everyday Memory Questionnaire included the following:

1. You need to take something to school tomorrow. What do you do to make sure that you won't forget it?
2. There is a special show on television tonight that you want to be sure to see. How do you remember to watch it?
3. You look in your tote tray (locker) and see that you need new supplies. How do you remember what you need to tell your mom to buy for you?
4. You have a substitute teacher today. What do you do to remember his or her name?

There were three important findings when comparing the ability groups. First, recall differences on the coin task (recalling information on a penny) indicated that children with LD are poorer than skilled readers in their recall of common visual and verbal information. Second, children with LD are less likely to remember facts about a consequential event (e.g., date of the space shuttle disaster) or facts that include their earlier experiences in school (e.g., name of their kindergarten teacher). Finally, the results from the questionnaire suggest that LD readers are less likely to report using an external memory aid (e.g., write a note to themselves) so they will remember information than skilled readers.

Study 2 sought to better understand the relationship between everyday memory and reading ability with a group of adolescents (15 and 16 year olds). They substituted a number of tasks from Study 1. The space shuttle task was expanded to include a larger array of questions in order to better assess the scope of children's recall for consequential events. The children in Study 2 were asked to recall the presidents of the United States in their correct ordinal position according to their term of office. Some sample questions for the shuttle recall task, in order of presentation, were as follows:

1. What happened to the *Challenger?*
2. Where did the liftoff occur?
3. What do the initials NASA stand for?

4. What were the last instructions given to the *Challenger* crew?
5. How many women were on the *Challenger?*

In this study adolescents with LD were poorer in recall across the majority of tasks than non-LD readers. But what was unclear from Study 2 was whether poor recall performance in adolescents with LD was related to memory storage (item availability) or the fact that all ability groups have difficulty accessing certain types of information. This issue was addressed in Study 3. Cuing procedures were implemented for the coin, presidential, and space shuttle tasks. The results of Study 3 indicated that LD readers were comparable to CA controls in the recall of common objects (coins) and consequential events (shuttle task), and the serial recall of some long-term memory information (presidents). When the results of Experiment 3 are combined with Experiment 2, they indicate that *storage* of everyday information in adolescents with LD is comparable to CA-matched skill readers on some tasks. Taken together, the results suggest that memory deficits in children with LD are pervasive across naturalistic and laboratory measures at the younger age, but those deficits on naturalistic tasks diminish for adolescents.

VI. MEMORY RESEARCH IN PERSPECTIVE

As can be surmised from a cursory review of the historical and contemporary literature, there are a number of hypotheses that have occurred over the last 25 years in memory research linked to LD samples. Several hypothesized mediators of memory problems could be metacognitive ability, strategy effectiveness, strategy utilization, strategy awareness, knowledge (quantity or quality), efficacy of a specific component (encoding, retrieving, storage), working memory capacity (executive function, phonological system, visual spatial system), and attentional capacity, as well as other areas that were not discussed (e.g., self-efficacy beliefs, and motivation). We have attempted to capture some of the findings during early and contemporary time periods. We will now attempt to place the memory research in theoretical perspective by reviewing the major hypothesis that has directed research on LD, summarize the assumption, and point out a major limitation.

An early hypothesis, the perceptual (visual) and cross-modality hypothesis, suggested that memory difficulties in children with LD is related to their inability to perceive visual-spatial information and remember visual-spatial relationships and/or integrate information across modalities (visual to writing). This theory was popularized in the early development of the field as related to reading problems. This was disbanded in the early 1970s, primarily by research that showed that LD and non-LD children were statistically comparable in their recall of visual-spatial and nonverbal information, suggesting that memory problems primarily reside in the language domain.

A hypothesis that emerged during the 1970s and 1980s was the assumption that improvements in memory performance for children with LD were strongly related to the acquisition and automatization of increasing amounts of learning and recall strategies. Although recall strategies were found to play a primary role in improvements related to memory performance, the strategy hypothesis did not provide the whole picture about differences between children and adults with and without LD. Some studies indicated that when rehearsal was controlled, or organization was provided to the LD sample, ability-group differences still emerged. That is, rehearsal or organization did not account for enough of the significant variation in the groups to remain a viable hypothesis in isolation by itself.

Another hypothesis that was popular in the late 1980s was the assumption that the availability of memory strategies is not enough to determine performance. Instead, a critical factor was the accessibility of knowledge about appropriate and effective strategies in a particular situation. Thus, the development of metamemory was seen as an important variable in accounting for problems to be found in memories of the LD child. However, the mnemonic model or the metamemory model has not always been shown to find differences between children with and without LD (McBride-Chang, Manis, Seidenberg, Custodio, & Doi, 1993). In addition, some of the metacognitive questionnaires are imbedded in language, and therefore the evidence on actual metacognitive differences separate from language competence between children and adults with and without LD is equivocal.

Two additional hypotheses that are certainly popular in the developmental child literature, but have not been adequately tested in the LD literature was the notion of a knowledge hypothesis and a capacity hypothesis. The knowledge hypothesis is based upon an assumption that changes in memory performance depend upon the quality and quantity of domain-specific knowledge. As a consequence, memory development is determined by increased general world knowledge and the acquisition of content-specific knowledge in many domains. Although the knowledge hypothesis is important in child development, there are *no* studies that we came across that actually tested this hypothesis with LD samples. No published study manipulated relevant knowledge about a domain to see if in fact the LD sample's memory performance matches the nondisabled sample with comparable knowledge base. Indirectly, there have been studies that measure clustering that do not necessarily reflect a deliberate strategic expression of organizing information (Lee & Obrzut, 1994; Krupski et al., 1993). That is, clustering is a by-product of general learning ability and that differences you find between children with and without LD are probably related to this general knowledge.

Another hypothesis that has not been thoroughly tested in the LD research is the capacity hypothesis. The assumption of this model is that differences in memory are somehow related to the maturational growth of working memory capacity. Some researchers suggest that the relationship between LD and memory might be partially attributable to processing capacity or a limitation of resources (e.g.,

Swanson, 1984a). However, these speculations are controversial because a concept of capacity or resource is not usually defined explicitly. Explanations related to the inability of students with LD to hold, receive, store or accommodate information suggest that there is a sort of a basic processing inefficiency, whereas explanations about their inability to apply a strategy refers to something about their mental capability. The fundamental assumption, however, is that an LD is somehow reflective of a quantitative and/or qualitative restraint in processing. In addition to its restrictions on strategy application, capacity is associated with the quantity or quality of effective application of different types of knowledge. The relative importance of these structural or capacity factors will vary across task, but the basic assumption is that processing capacity is attributable to some of the variation we find between LD and non-LD children across various tasks.

In summary, there are a number of gaps on the research on memory that need to be tended to if researchers are to make progress in understanding the cognitive dimensions of memory dysfunctions in children and adults with LD. Although this chapter reviewed some of the empirical evidence regarding mechanisms that are different between children and adults with and without LD on many memory phenomenon, there are no descriptive models about the interrelationship between the acquisition, the availability, and the accessibility of content-specific knowledge, general strategies, and metacognitive skills on memory performance in samples with LD (e.g., Borkowski et al., 1989). There are discussions about the theoretical frameworks and processes that are suggested as accounting for the reason why we find memory deficits in LD samples; however, there has not been a comprehensive model linking low-order processing (e.g., phonological coding) and high-order processing (executive processing), strategy use, knowledge, metacognition, capacity constraints, and so on. Research in working memory may play a major role in helping this movement (Siegel, 1993). However, there seems to be some misapprehension in the use of the executive processing component of working memory and that some see working memory as a by-product of achievement outcomes (e.g., Bowey, Cain, & Ryan, 1992). That is, better readers have better working memory and the relationship is seen as not necessarily reciprocal but causal. Perhaps more theoretically motivated research does not see nonstrategic factors and strategic factors as competing models, but cooperative models (e.g., see Brown, Pressley, Van Meter, & Schuder, 1996). What needs to be established in the research, however, is what the relative contributions of strategies versus basic processes are considered in overall memory performance.

VII. MEMORY DEVELOPMENT

As previously reviewed, explanations of LD children's memory problems have been drawn from studies that focus on non-LD children's strategy development.

That is, poor memory performance across age in children with LD is seen as an increasing tendency to use or not use strategies. LD children's memory development has usually been described in terms of a major deficiency in production; that is, children with LD could improve their memory performance when shown a strategy but failed to do so spontaneously. The theoretical hegemony of memory development and strategy development as it applied to LD breaks down in that ability-group differences could not always be explained by variations in strategy performance, manipulations and performance as a function of rehearsal categorization, incentives, and so on.

An alternative model to consider for future research on strategies, drawing from Miller (1990), is related to strategy utilization. Miller has suggested that when children use an appropriate strategy—one similar or identical to that of older children—but, unlike the older children experience no enhancement of performance, as a utilization efficiency (e.g., Miller, Haynes, DeMarie-Dreblow, & Woody-Ramsey 1986). Miller describes the acquisition of the strategies reflecting four steps. First, children failed to produce a strategy; second, the strategy is used partially. In the third step, children use a strategy, but it provides them with no gains in task performance. This she coins as a *utilization deficiency*. Finally, there is a fourth step, in which children use a strategy and realize the benefits in task performance. From this perspective, the utilization deficiency reflects "a development lag between spontaneously producing the strategy and receiving any benefits from it" (p. 160). Bjorklund and his colleagues (e.g., Bjorklund et al. 1992; Bjorklund et al. 1994) have also reported such discrepancy between levels of organization and strategy performance and corresponding levels of memory performance. That is, in some of his studies, Bjorklund has found near perfect levels of clustering of information, but these levels of organization do not correspond adequately to level of recall.

It is clear from our previous descriptive analysis that LD children have been shown to benefit from mnemonic instruction when training is sufficiently rigorous. In the manipulations that we looked at, however, LD children do not use the strategies on their own, but in most conditions, they merely comply with explicit directions. Thus, they may be characterized as suffering from a utilization deficiency. Of course, the question is why should a technique, such as strategy instruction, not produce appreciable changes in memory performance by LD children when compared to their peers?

One explanation is that one cannot adequately separate in the literature a deficit in verbatim memory (verbatim representation of a verbal task, e.g., digits) from a memory that accesses "gist" representations (see Brainerd & Gordon, 1994; Brainerd & Reyna, 1990a, 1990b, for a comprehensive discussion of this contrast). Perhaps the constructs identified as being deficient in children with LD (e.g., verbal recall of verbatim information) do not map well on tasks that facilitate access to the "gist" of information.

Another explanation is that the mental effort that LD children must expend needs to be taken into consideration. We did find that tasks that include high and low processing demands in the full model were related to LD-non-LD effect sizes. Currently in the literature, there are several examples of working memory studies that have demonstrated that LD children exert greater mental effort to execute recall than those of chronological age-matched or even in some cases younger normal-achieving children (Siegel & Ryan, 1989; Swanson, 1994). Perhaps strategies are expensive in terms of how much effort has to be put into them, and the major advantages of strategy instruction are more likely to occur in non-LD children. This is because too much of the LD child's limited mental resources are used in executing the strategy, leaving probably too few resources to allocate to other sorts of tasks. It could also be through extended practice that other children are more strategic and much more automated in their performance.

Regardless of the above explanations, a strategy model is clearly not an adequate account for LD differences on memory tasks. This is because strategies are complicated kinds of activities, and their use and influence is reflected by a variety of factors. For example, noncognitive factors, such as motivation, self-attribution, and perceived self-efficacy, have been suggested as influencing non-LD children's strategic behavior and therefore, may be good candidates for understanding memory deficits. For example, research indicates that motivational factors are related to metacognitive and effective strategy use (see Pressley, Borkowski, & Schneider, 1987). Particularly important to understanding strategy development are the attributions of success and failure concerning performance on cognitive tasks (Borkowski, Weyhing, & Carr, 1988). Borkowski et al. (1988) report, for example, that children who believe that effort plays an important role in producing success on cognitive tasks demonstrate higher levels of strategy use on transfer tasks following memory training then do children who tend to attribute success to noncontrollable factors. Regardless, there has not been adequate investigation of the self-attributions of success and failure on memory tasks.

VIII. TRENDS IN MEMORY RESEARCH

Since 1992, memory research on LD samples has indicated more new cycles and activity than did research conducted in the 1980s. First, the main line of inquiry on memory in LD children no longer concentrates on just an empirical description of general changes of memory performance and memory processes, but rather how the memory performance does or does not change under certain situational conditions. For example, Swanson et al.'s (1996) study looked at working memory performance under initial conditions, under conditions in which memory can be influenced, and under conditions in which memory can be retained after help has been provided. Second, a general lesson seems to be that there is a great deal of variability in samples with LD, and only by attempting to explain this variability can we advance our understanding about the mystery of why LD children have memory difficulties. Studies that subtype LD children by achievement suggest that different components of memory may underlie performance. Different subgroups as a function of reading and mathematics problems reflect executive and/or phonological, and/or visual spatial memory deficits (Siegel & Ryan, 1989; Swanson, 1991; 1993b). A third trend is that there seems to be some fusion between memory performance and research on reading. The literature goes back and forth on whether reading influences memory performance or memory performance is independent of reading. For the time being, the research interests concentrate on both the interdependence of different cognitive processes, understanding memory, and on the development of the cognitive processes that are employed.

Fourth, another trend is that researchers in LD are seeking out and finding associations between cognitive hypotheses and neurological and genetic indices (e.g., Wadsworth, DeFries, Fulker, & Olson, 1995). This applies to research in reading, as well as working memory. Fifth, LD are no longer studied exclusively as a childhood phenomenon. Increasing numbers of investigations have looked at adults with LD (Bruck, 1992).

Finally, there are indications emerging for looking at memory under laboratory-based kinds of conditions and extending those findings to everyday conditions in an environmental context (Swanson, Reffel, & Trahan, 1990). This involves also looking at the motivational influences of memory performance. The question of how the results across research can be applied to memory instruction in schools or performance of the LD student in an everyday community context is only beginning to be investigated (however, see Scruggs & Mastropieri, 1989, for an earlier review).

IX. IMPLICATIONS FROM CONTEMPORARY MEMORY RESEARCH FOR INSTRUCTION

In general, memory researchers have converged on the notion that LD students' ability to access information remains inert, unless they are explicitly prompted to use certain cognitive strategies. The previous review has established that LD students may be taught to (a) organize lists of pictures and words in common categories, (b) rehearse the category names during learning, and (c) use the names and retrieval cues at the time of the test. The data suggest that when LD children are explicitly encouraged to use such strategies on some tasks, their performance improves and thus the discrepancy between their general intellectual ability and contextually related memory deficits is lessened. However, strategy training does not eliminate ability-group differences between LD students and their nonhandicapped peers in a multitude of situations. Some of the causes of strategy ineffectiveness or utilization deficiencies could be related to individual differences in information-processing capacity (i.e., children without an LD benefit more from the strategy than children with LD) and/or a particular level of strategy effectiveness may have different causes in different children. An LD child, for example, may be unable to benefit from a strategy because of his or her limited capacity, whereas another child may be constrained by her lack of knowledge relevant to the task. Thus, different children may follow different developmental routes to overcome their utilization deficiency.

Good memory performance as indicated by Pressley (1994) is a product of a number of factors: strategies, knowledge, metacognitive processing and understanding, motivation, and capacity. None of these factors operate in isolation, but rather, effective cognition is a product of these components and interactions. As indicated by Pressley (1994), sometimes strategic processing will be more prominent in cognition than other factors; sometimes relating content to prior knowledge will be the most salient mechanism, and on still other occasions there will be obvious reflections by a child on the task demands (on what he or she knows how to do in this particular situation, or situations similar to it that have been encountered in the past). On some occasions metacognition is more salient than other components in thinking in task performance, and there will be situations when the child's motivation will be especially apparent, so that many observers would report that the individual succeeded simply by trying hard. All of these processes depend heavily on consciousness, knowledge, working memory, attributions, and motivation.

Based on this extensive literature, some very practical concepts and principles from memory research can serve as guidelines for the instruction of students with LD. We can assume that effective instruction must entail information (a) about a number of strategies, (b) about how to control and implement those procedures, and (c) about how to gain recognition of the importance of effort and personal causality in producing successful performance. Furthermore, any of these components taught in isolation is likely to have a rather diminished value in the classroom context. The following section describes eight major principles that must be considered if strategy instruction is to be successful (also see Montague, 1993; for further application of these principles).

A. Memory Strategies Serve Different Purposes

One analysis of the memory strategy research suggests there is no single best strategy for LD students. Some of the memory strategies that have been used to enhance LD children's performance are shown in the Appendix. A number of studies, for example, have looked at enhancing LD children's performance by using advanced organizers, skimming, asking, questioning, taking notes, summarizing, and so on. But apart from the fact that LD students have been exposed to various types of strategies, the questions of which strategies are the most effective is now known. We know in some situations, such as when remembering facts, the key word approach appears to be more effective than direct instruction models (Scruggs & Mastropieri, 1989), but, of course, the rank ordering of different strategies changes in reference to the different types of learning outcomes expected. For example, certain strategies are better suited to enhancing students' understanding of what they previously read, whereas other strategies are better suited to enhancing students' memory of words or facts. The point is that different strategies can effect different cognitive outcomes in a number of ways.

B. Good Memory Strategies for Non-LD Students Are Not Necessarily Good Strategies for LD Students and Vice Versa

Strategies that enhance access to knowledge for normally developing students will not be well suited for all children with LD. For example, Wong and Jones (1982) trained LD and non-LD adolescents in a self-questioning strategy to monitor reading comprehension. Results indicated that although the strategy training benefited the adolescents with LD, it actually lowered the performance of non-LD adolescents. To illustrate this point further children with LD, Swanson (1989) presented students with LD, mental retardation, giftedness, and average development a series of tasks that involved base and elaborative sentences. Their task was to recall words embedded in a sentence. The results of the first experiment suggested that children with LD differ from the other groups in their ability to benefit from elaboration. It was assumed that the elaboration requirement placed excessive demands on the central processing strategies of children with LD when compared with the other ability groups. This finding was qualified in the next experiment and suggested that encoding difficulty must be taken into consideration when determining strategy effects, but the results suggested that children with LD may require additional strategies for their performance to become comparable to that of their cohorts. In another study (Swanson, Cooney, & Overholser, 1988) college students with LD were asked to recall words in a sentence under semantic and imagery instructional conditions. The results suggested, contrary to the extant literature, that readers with LD were better able to remember words in a sentence during instructional conditions that induced semantic processing. In contrast, non-LD readers favored imagery processing over semantic processing conditions. In sum, these results suggest that strategies that are effective for non-LD students may be less effective for students with LD.

C. Effective Memory Strategies Do Not Necessarily Eliminate Processing Differences

It appears logical that if children with LD use a strategy that allows them to process information efficiently, then improvement in performance is due to the strategies' affecting the same processes as they do in non-LD students. This assumption has emanated primarily from studies that have imposed organization on seemingly un-organized material. For example, considerable evidence indicates that readers with LD do not initially take advantage of the organizational features of material (e.g., Dallego & Moely, 1980; Lee & Obrzut, 1994). However, the notion that readers with disabilities process the organizational features of information in the same manner as non-LD students is questionable (Swanson, 1986). For example, Swanson and Rathgeber (1986) found in categorization tasks that readers with LD can retrieve information without interrelating superordinate, subordinate, and coordi-nate classes of information, as the non-LD children do. Thus, children with LD can learn to process information in an organizational sense without knowing the mean-ing of the material. The point is that simply because children with LD are sensi-tized to internal structure of material via some strategy (e.g., by cognitive strate-gies that require the sorting of material), it does not mean they will make use of the material in a manner consistent with what was intended from the instruction-al strategy.

D. The Strategies Taught Are Not Necessarily the Ones Used

The previous principle suggests that during intervention different processes may be activated that are not necessarily the intent of the instructional intervention. It is also likely that students with LD use different strategies on tasks in which they seem to have little difficulty, and these tasks will likely be overlooked by the teacher for possible intervention. It is commonly assumed that although students with LD may have isolated memory deficits (verbal domain) and require general learning strategies to compensate for these processing deficits, their processing of information is comparable with that of their normal counterparts on tasks with which they have little trouble. Several authors suggest, however, that there are a number of alternative ways for achieving successful performance (Pressley, 1994), and some indirect evidence indicates that the LD may use qualitatively different mental operations (Shankweiler, et al., 1979) and processing routes (e.g., Swan-son, 1988) from their non-LD counterparts.

E. Memory Strategies in Relation to a Student's Knowledge Base and Capacity

One important variable that has been overlooked in the LD intervention literature is the notion of processing constraints (Swanson et al., 1996). Memory capacity seems to increase with development with a number of factors potentially con-tributing to the overall effect. It appears that short-term memory capacity increases with age (Case, Kurland, & Goldberg, 1982). The number of component process-es increases the speed with development, with faster processes generally consum-ing less effort than slow processes and thus the same amount of capacity can seem greater (i.e., there is a functional increase of capacity with increasing efficiency of processing). The older children are likely to have more and more organized prior knowledge that can reduce total number of chunks of information that is processed and decrease the amount of effort to retrieve information from long-term memory. Because of these developmental relationships, as well as the constraints that provide the development, this could play a role in strategy effectiveness. To test this possibility, Pressley, Cariglia-Bull, and Schneider (1987) studied children's ability to execute a capacity-demanding imagery representation strategy for the learning of sentences. Children in the experimental condition of these experiments represented a series of highly concrete sentences (for example, the angry bird shouted at the white dog, the turkey pecked the coat). They were asked to imagine the meanings of these sentences. Control condition participants were given no instruction. Further, children benefited from imagery instruction (there was an imagery versus control difference on the memory posttest). However, performance depended on the child's functional short-term memory capacity, as reflected by individual differences in performance on classic memory span task. That is, the imagery versus control difference in performance was only detected when functional short-term memory was relatively high.

F. Comparable Memory Strategy May Not Eliminate Performance Differences

Several studies have indicated that residual differences remain between ability groups even when ability groups are instructed and/or prevented from strategy use (Gelzheiser et al., 1987). For example, in a study by Gelzheiser et al. (1987), LD and non-LD children were compared on their ability to use organizational strategies. After instruction in organizational strategies, the LD and non-LD children were compared on their abilities to recall information on a posttest. The results indicated that LD children were comparable in strategy use to non-LD children, but were deficient in overall performance. In another study, Swanson (1983b) found that the recall of a group with LD did not improve from baseline level when trained with rehearsal strategies. They recalled less than normally achieving peers, although the groups were comparable in the various types of strategy used. The results support the notion that groups of children with different learning histories may continue to learn differently, even when the groups are equated in terms of strategy use.

G. Memory Strategies Taught Do Not Necessarily Become Transformed into Expert Strategies

Children who become experts at certain tasks often have learned simple strategies and, thorough practice, discover ways to modify them into more efficient and powerful procedures (Schneider, 1993). In particular, the proficient learner uses higher-order rules to eliminate unnecessary or redundant steps to hold increasing amounts of information. The LD child, in contrast, may learn most of the skills related to performing an academic task and perform appropriately on that task by carefully and systematically following prescribed rules or strategies. Although LD children can be taught strategies, some studies suggest that the difference between LD (experts in this case) and non-LD children is that the latter have modified such strategies to become more efficient (Swanson & Cooney, 1985). It is plausible that the LD child remains a novice in learning new information because he or she fails to transform memory strategies into more efficient forms (see Swanson & Rhine, 1985).

H. Strategy Instruction Must Operate on the Law of Parsimony

A "number of multiple-component packages" of strategy instruction have been suggested for improving LD children's functioning. These components have usually encompassed some of the following: skimming, imagining, drawing, elaborating, paraphrasing, using mnemonics, accessing prior knowledge, reviewing, orienting to critical features, and so on. No doubt there are some positive aspects to these strategy packages:

1. These programs are an advance over some of the studies that are seen in the LDs literature as rather simple or "quick-fix" strategies (e.g., rehearsal or categorization to improve performances).
2. These programs promote a domain skill and have a certain metacognitive embellishment about them.
3. The best of these programs involved (a) teaching a few strategies well rather than superficially, (b) teaching students to monitor their performance, (c) teaching students when and where to use the strategy to enhance generalization, (d) teaching strategies as an integrated part of an existing curriculum, and (e) teaching that includes a great deal of supervised student practice and feedback.

The difficulty of such packages, however, at least in terms of theory, is that little is known about which components best predict student performance, nor do they readily permit one to determine why the strategy worked. The multiple-component approaches that are typically found in a number of LD strategy intervention studies must be carefully contrasted with a component analysis approach that involves the systematic combination of instructional components known to have additive effect on performance. As stated by Pressley (1986, p. 140), good strategies are "composed of the sufficient and necessary processes for accomplishing their intended goal, consuming as few intellectual processes as necessary to do so."

X. SUMMARY AND CONCLUSION

In summary, we have briefly characterized research on memory and LD. Our knowledge of LD individuals' memory somewhat parallels our knowledge about the differences between older and younger children's memory. The parallel relies in effortful processing, the focus on cognitive strategies, the development of a knowledge base, and the awareness of one's own memory processes. Most memory research emanates from an information-processing framework. Earlier research tends to emphasize the integration of information across modalities (visual-auditory) and perception (visual memory), whereas more recent studies tend to focus on the representation, control, and executive process (e.g., strategies) of memory. Current research on memory is beginning to examine the interaction of structures and process on performance. Most of the current research is occurring in the area of working memory. The limitations of previous models are highlighted as well as recent trends in memory research on students with LD. A number or principles related to memory strategy instruction have emerged that have direct application to the instruction of children and adults with LD. Some of these principles are related to (a) the purposes of strategies, (b) parsimony with regard to the number of processes, (c) individual differences in strategy use and performance, (d) learner constraints, and (e) the transfer of strategies into more efficient processes.

APPENDIX: CLASSIFICATION OF MEMORY STRATEGIES[a]

Categorical Information: Teachers might direct students to use taxonomic information (e.g., pictures accompanying a category) or to analyze the item into smaller units (e.g., looking for interitem associations).

Elaboration: Students are instructed to use elements of the stimulus material and assign meaning by, for instance, making up a phrase or sentence, making an analogy, or drawing a relationship based on specific characteristics found in the stimulus material.

General Aids: In contrast to specific aids, teachers recommend the same general aid for a variety of different problems. These aids are designed and used to serve a general reference purpose. Examples include the use of dictionaries or other reference works.

Imagery: This strategy usually consists of nonspecific instructions to remember by taking a mental picture of something or to maintain or manipulate them in the mind.

[a]Adapted from Moely et al. (1986).

Metamemory: Teachers instructing this strategy tell students that certain procedures will be more helpful for studying and remembering than others. The strategy frequently includes giving hints about the limits of memory, asking students about the task factors that will influence ease of remembering, or helping them understand the reasons for their own performance. Teachers can also tell students that they can devise procedures that will aid their memory or indicate the value of using a specific strategy.

Orienting (attention):   These strategies direct student's attention to a task. For example, teachers may instruct children to "follow along" or "listen carefully" during lessons.

Rehearsal: Students are told to rehearse verbally or to write, look at, go over, study, or repeat the stimuli in some other way. The children may be instructed to rehearse items just once, a finite number of times, or an unlimited number of times.

Specific Aids for Problem-Solving and Memorizing: This strategy involves the use of specific aids in problem solving or memorizing. For example, teachers may tell children to use blocks or other counters to represent addition or subtraction operations in a concrete way.

Specific Attentional Aids: This strategy is similar to the attention strategy, but students are instructed to use objects, language, or a part of their body in a specific way to maintain orientation to a task.

Transformation: Transformation is a strategy suggested by teachers for converting unfamiliar or difficult problems into similar or simpler ones that can then be remembered more easily. Transformations are possible because of logical, rule-governed relationships between stimulus elements.

References

Aaron, P. G. (1993). Is there a visual dyslexia? *Annals of Dyslexia, 43,* 110–124.

Anderson, J. (1990). *Cognitive psychology and its implications.* New York: Freeman.

Atkinson, R., & Shiffrin, R. (1968). Human memory, a proposed system and its control processes. In K. Spence & J. Spence (Eds.), *The psychology of learning and motivation: Advances in research and theory* Vol. 2 (pp. 85–195). New York: Academic Press.

Baddeley, A. D. (1976). *The psychology of memory.* New York: Basic Books.

Baddeley, A. D. (1986). *Working memory.* London: Oxford University Press.

Baddeley, A. D. (1992). Working memory: The interface between memory and cognition. *Journal of Cognitive Neuroscience, 4,* 281–288.

Baddeley, A. D., & Hitch, G. (1974). Working memory. In G. H. Bower (Ed.), *The psychology of learning and motivation* Vol. 8 (pp. 47–90). San Diego: Academic Press.

Baddeley, A., Logie, R., Nimmo-Smith, T., & Brereton, J. (1985). Components of fluent reading. *Journal of Memory & Language, 24,* 119–131.

Baker, J. G., Ceci, S. J., & Hermann, N. D. (1987). Semantic structure and processing: Implications for the learning disabled child. In H. L. Swanson (Ed.), *Memory and learning disabilities* (pp. 83–110). JAI Press, Greenwich, Connecticut.

Bauer, R. H. (1977). Memory processes in children with learning disabilities: Evidence for deficient rehearsal. *Journal of Experimental Child Psychology, 24,* 415–430.

Bauer, R. H. (1979a). Memory processes in children with learning disabilities: Evidence for deficient rehearsal. *Journal of Experimental Child Psychology, 24,* 415–430.

Bauer, R. H. (1979b). Memory, acquisition, and category clustering in learning disabled children. *Journal of Experimental Child Psychology, 27,* 365–383.

Bauer, R. H., & Emhert, J. (1984). Information processing in reading-disabled and nondisabled children. *Journal of Experimental Child Psychology, 37,* 271–281.

Bauer, R. H., & Peller-Porth, V. (1990). The effect of increased incentive on free recall by learning-disabled and nondisabled children. *The Journal of General Psychology, 117,* 447–462.

Bisiacchi, P. S., Cipolotti, L., & Denes, G. (1989). Impairment in processing meaningless verbal material in several modalities: The relationship between short-term memory and phonological skills. *The Quarterly Journal of Experimental Psychology, 41A,* 293–319.

Bjorklund, D. F. (1985). The role of conceptual knowledge in the development of organization in children's memory. In C. J. Brainerd (Ed.), *Basic processes in memory development* (pp. 103–134). New York: Springer-Verlag.

Bjorklund, D. F., Coyle, T. R., & Gaultney, J. F. (1992). Developmental differences in the acquisition and maintenance of an organizational strategy: Evidence for the utilization deficiency hypothesis. *Journal of Experimental Child Psychology, 54,* 434–448.

Bjorklund, D. F., & Schneider, W. (1996). The interaction of knowledge, aptitude, and strategies in children's memory performance. In H. W. Reese (Ed.), *Children's strategies: Contemporary views of cognitive development* (pp. 93–128) Hillsdale, NJ: Erlbaum.

Bjorklund, D. F., Schneider, W., Cassel, W. S., & Ashley, E. (1994). Training and extension of a memory strategy: Evidence for utilization deficiencies in the acquisition of an organizational strategy in high- and low-IQ children. *Child Development, 65,* 951–965.

Blumenthal, S. H. (1980). A study of the relationship between speed of retrieval of verbal information and patterns of oral reading errors. *Journal of Learning Disabilities, 3,* 568–570.

Borkowski, J. G., Carr, M., Rellinger, E. A., & Pressley, M. (1990). Self-regulated strategy use: Interdependence of metacognition, attributions, and self-esteem. In B. F. Jones (Ed.), *Dimensions of thinking: Review of research* (pp. 53–92). Hillsdale, NJ: Erlbaum.

Borkowski, J. G., Estrada, M., Milstead, M., & Hale, C. A. (1989). General problem-solving skills: Relations between metacognition and strategic processing. *Learning Disability Quarterly, 12,* 57–70.

Borkowski, J. G., & Muthukrishna, N. (1992). Moving metacognition into the classroom: "Working models" and effective strategy teaching. In M. Pressley, K. R. Harris, & J. T. Guthrie (Eds.), *Promoting academic competence and literacy in school* (pp. 477–501). Toronto: Academic Press.

Borkowski, J. G., Weyhing, R. S., & Carr, M. (1988). Effects of attributional retraining on strategy-based reading comprehension in learning-disabled students. *Journal of Educational Psychology, 80,* 46–53.

Bowey, J. A., Cain, M. T., & Ryan, S. M. (1992). A reading-level design study of phonological skills underlying fourth-grade children's word reading difficulties. *Child Development, 63,* 999–1011.

Brainerd, C. J., & Gordon, L. (1994). Development of verbatim and gist memory for numbers. *Developmental Psychology, 30,* 163–177.

Brainerd, C. J., Kingma, J., & Howe, M. L. (1986). Long-term memory development and learning disability: Storage and retrieval loci of disabled/nondisabled differences. In S. J. Ceci (Ed.), *Handbook of cognitive, social, and neuropsychological aspects of learning disabilities* Vol. 1 (pp. 161–184). Hillsdale, NJ: Lawrence Erlbaum.

Brainerd, C. J., Reyna, V. F. (1990a). Gist is the grist: Fuzzy-trace theory and the new intuitions. *Developmental Review, 10,* 3–47.

Brainerd, C. J., & Reyna, V. F. (1990b). Can age × learnability interactions explain the development of forgetting? *Developmental Psychology, 26,* 194–203.

Brainerd, C. J., & Reyna, V. F. (1991). Acquisition and forgetting processes in normal and learning-disabled children: A disintegration/redintegration theory. In J. Obrzut & G. W. Hynd (Eds.), *Neuropsychological foundations of learning disabilities* (pp. 147–175). New York: Academic Press.

Brainerd, C. J., Reyna, V. F., Howe, M. L., & Kingma, J. (1990). The development of forgetting and reminiscence. *Monographs of the Society for Research in Child Development, 53* (3–4, Whole No. 222).

Bronner, A. F. (1917). *The psychology of special abilities and disabilities.* Boston: Little, Brown.

Brown, A. L. (1975). The development of memory: Knowing, knowing about knowing, and knowing how to know. In H. Reese (Ed.), *Advances in child development and behavior* (Vol. 10). New York: Academic Press.

Brown, A. L., & Campione, J. C. (1981). Inducing flexible thinking: The problem of access. In M. Friedman, J. P. Das, & N. O'Connor (Eds.), *Intelligence and learning* (pp. 515–530). New York: Plenum Press.

Brown, A. L., & Palincsar, A. S. (1988). Reciprocal teaching of comprehension strategies: A natural history of one program for enhancing learning. In J. Borkowski & J. P. Das (Eds.), *Intelligence and cognition in special children: Comparative studies of giftedness, mental retardation, and learning disabilities.* New York: Ablex.

Brown, R., Pressley, M., Van Meter, P., & Schuder, T. (1996). A quasi-experimental validation of transactional strategies instruction with low-achieving second-grade readers. *Journal of Educational Psychology, 88,* 18–37.

Bruck, M. (1992). Persistence of dyslexics' phonological awareness deficits. *Developmental Psychology, 28,* 874–886.

Bryan, T. (1972). The effect of forced mediation upon short-term memory of children with learning disabilities. *Journal of Learning Disabilities, 5,* 605–609.

Campione, J. C., Brown, A. L., & Ferrara, F. A. (1982). Mental retardation and intelligence. In R. I. Sternberg (Ed.), *Handbook of human intelligence* (pp. 392–490). New York: Cambridge.

Cantor, J., & Engle, R. W. (1993). Working memory capacity as long-term memory activation: An individual differences approach. *Journal of Experimental Psychology: Learning, Memory, and Cognition, 18,* 972–992.

Case, R., Kurland, D. M., & Goldberg, J. (1982). Operational efficiency and the growth of short-term memory span. *Journal of Experimental Child Psychology, 33,* 386–404.

Ceci, S. J. (1984). Developmental study of learning disabilities and memory. *Journal of Experimental Child Psychology, 38,* 352–371.

Ceci, S. J., Ringstrom, M. D., & Lea, S. E. G. (1980). Coding characteristics of normal and learning-disabled 10 year olds: Evidence for dual pathways to the cognitive system. *Journal of Experimental Psychology: Human, Learning, & Memory, 6,* 785–797.

Cermak, L. (1983). Information processing deficits in learning disabled children. *Journal of Learning Disabilities, 16,* 599–605.

Cohen, J. (1969). *Statistical power analysis for the behavioral sciences.* San Diego, CA: Academic Press.

Conners, C. K., Kramer, K., & Guerra, F. (1969). Auditory synthesis and dichotic listening in children with learning disabilities. *Journal of Special Education, 3,* 163–170.

Conrad, R. (1964). Acoustic confusion in immediate memory. *British Journal of Psychology, 55,* 75–84.

Cooper, H., & Hedges, L. C. (1994). *Handbook on research synthesis.* New York: Russell Stage.

Dallego, M. L., & Moely, B. E. (1980). Free recall in boys of normal and poor reading levels as a function of task manipulation. *Journal of Experimental Child Psychology, 30,* 62–78.

Daneman, M., & Carpenter, P. A. (1980). Individual differences in working memory and reading. *Journal of Verbal Learning Verbal Behavior, 19,* 450–466.

Dawson, M. H., Hallahan, D. P., Reeves, R. E., & Ball, D. W. (1980). The effect of reinforcement and verbal rehearsal on selective attention in learning-disabled children. *Journal of Abnormal Child Psychology, 8,* 133–144.

Dempster, F. N. (1985). Short-term memory development in childhood and adolescence. In C. J. Brainerd & M. Pressley (Eds.), *Basic processes in memory development: Progress in cognitive development research* (pp. 209–248). New York: Springer.

Dempster, F. N., & Cooney, J. B. (1982). Individual differences in digit span, susceptibility to proactive interference, and aptitude/achievement test scores. *Intelligence, 6,* 399–416.

Denckla, M. B., & Rudel, R. G. (1974). Rapid "automatized" naming of pictured objects, colors, letters, and numbers by normal children. *Cortex, 10,* 186–202.

Eden, G. F., Stein, J. F., Wood, H. M., & Wood, F. B. (1995). Temporal and spatial processing in reading disabled and normal children. *Cortex, 31,* 451–468.

Elbert, J. C. (1984). Short-term memory encoding and memory search in the word recognition of learning-disabled children. *Journal of Learning Disabilities, 17,* 342–345.

Engle, R. W., Cantor, J., Carullo, J. J. (1992). Individual differences in working memory and comprehension: A test for four hypotheses. *Journal of Experimental Psychology: Learning, Memory and Cognition, 18,* 972–992.

Flavell, J. (1979). Metacognition and cognitive monitoring. *American Psychologist, 34,* 906–911.

Flavell, J. H., Beach, D. R., & Chinsky, J. M. (1966). Spontaneous verbal rehearsal in memory task as a function of age. *Child Development, 37,* 283–299.

Gathercole, S. E., & Baddeley, A. D. (1993). *Working memory and language.* Hove (UK): Erlbaum.

Geary, D. C., & Brown, S. C. (1991). Cognitive addition: Strategy choice and speed-of-processing differences in gifted, normal, and mathematically disabled children. *Developmental Psychology, 27,* 398–406.

Gelzheiser, L. M. (1984). Generalization from categorical memory tasks to prose by learning disabled adolescents. *Journal of Educational Psychology, 76,* 1128–1138.

156 H. L. Swanson, J. B. Cooney, and T. E. O'Shaughnessy

Gelzheiser, L. M., Cort, R., & Shephard, M. J. (1987). Is minimal strategy instruction sufficient for LD children? Testing the production deficiency hypothesis. *Learning Disability Quarterly, 10,* 267–276.

Gelzheiser, L. M., Solar, R. A., Shepherd, M. J., & Wozniak, R. H. (1983). Teaching learning disabled children to memorize: Rationale for plans and practice. *Journal of Learning Disabilities, 16,* 421–425.

Geschwind, N. (1962). The anatomy of acquired disorders of reading. In J. Money (Ed.), *Reading disability: Progress and research needs in dyslexia* (pp. 115–129). Baltimore: Johns Hopkins Press.

Goyen, J. D., & Lyle, J. (1971). Effect of incentives upon retarded and normal readers on a visual-associate learning task. *Journal of Experimental Child Psychology, 11,* 274–280.

Goyen, J. D., & Lyle, J. (1973). Short-term memory and visual discrimination in retarded readers. *Perceptual and Motor Skills, 36,* 403–408.

Gruneberg, M. M., & Sykes, R. (1969). Acoustic confusion in long term memory. *Acta Psychologica, 29,* 293–296.

Guthrie, J. T., & Goldberg, H. K. (1972). Visual sequential memory in reading disability. *Journal of Learning Disabilities, 5,* 41–46.

Guttentag, R. E. (1984). The mental effort requirement of cumulative rehearsal: A developmental study. *Journal of Experimental Child Psychology, 37,* 92–106.

Haines, D. J., & Torgesen, J. K. (1979). The effects of incentives on rehearsal and short-term memory in children with reading problems. *Learning Disability Quarterly, 2,* 48–55.

Hall, J., Wilson, K., Humphreys, M., Tinzmann, M., & Bowyer, P. (1983). Phonemic-similarity effects in good vs. poor readers. *Memory & Cognition, 11,* 520–527.

Hallahan, D. P., & Reeve, R. (1980). Selective attention and distractibility. In B. Keogh (Ed.), *Advances in special education* (pp. 141–182). Greenwich, CT: JAI Press.

Harnishfeger, K. K., & Bjorklund, D. F. (1994). A developmental perspective on individual differences in inhibition. *Learning & Individual Differences, 6,* 331–357.

Harris, K. R., Graham, S., & Pressley, M. (1992). Cognitive behavioral approaches in reading and written language: Developing self-regulated learners. In N. N. Singh & I. L. Beale (Eds.), *Current perspectives in learning disabilities: Nature, theory, and treatment* (pp. 415–451). New York: Springer-Verlag.

Hasselhorn, M. (1992). Task dependency and the role of category typicality and metamemory in the development of an organizational strategy. *Child Development, 63,* 202–214.

Hinshelwood, J. (1917). *Congenital word blindness.* London: Lewis.

Howe, M. L., Brainerd, C. J., & Kingma, J. (1985). Storage-retrieval processes of normal and learning disabled children: A stages-of-learning analysis of picture-word effects. *Child Development, 56,* 1120–1133.

Howe, M. L., Brainerd, C. J., & Kingma, J. (1989). Localizing the development of ability differences in organized memory. *Contemporary Educational Psychology, 14,* 336–356.

Howe, M. L., O'Sullivan, J. T., Brainerd, C. J., & Kingma, J. (1989). Localizing the development of ability differences in organized memory. *Contemporary Educational Psychology, 14,* 336–356.

Hulme, C. (1992). *Working memory and severe learning difficulties-Essays in cognitive psychology.* East Sussex, UK: Lawrence Erlbaum Associates.

Johnson, R. S., Rugg, M., & Scott, T. (1987). Phonological similarity effects, memory span and developmental reading disorders. *British Journal of Psychology, 78,* 205–211.

Just, M. A., & Carpenter, P. A. (1992). A capacity theory of comprehension: Individual differences in working memory. *Psychological Review, 99,* 122–149.

Kee, D. W. (in press). Development differences in associative memory: Strategy use, mental effort, and knowledge-access interaction. In H. W. Reese (Ed.), *Advances in child development and behavior* (Vol. 25). New York: Academic Press.

Klapp, S. T., Marshburn, E. A., & Lester, P. T. (1983). Short-term memory does not involve the "working-memory" of intellectual processing: The demise of a common assumption. *Journal of Experimental Psychology: General, 112,* 240–264.

Koorland, M. A., & Wolking, W. D. (1982). Effect of reinforcement on modality of stimulus control in learning. *Learning Disabilities Quarterly, 5,* 264–273.

Krupski, A., Gaultney, J. F., Malcolm, G., & Bjorklund, D. F. (1993). Learning disabled and nondisabled children's performance on serial recall tasks: The facilitating effect of knowledge. *Learning & Individual Differences, 5,* 199–210.

Kussmaul, A. (1877). Disturbances of speech. *Cyclopedia of Practical Medicine, 14,* 581–875.

Lee, C. P., & Obrzut, J. E. (1994). Taxonomic clustering and frequency association as features of semantic memory development in children with learning disabilities. *Journal of Learning Disabilities, 27,* 454–462.

Lehman, E. B., & Brady, K. M. (1982). Presentation modality and taxonomic category as encoding dimensions from good and poor readers. *Journal of Learning Disabilities, 15,* 103–105.

Lorsbach, T. C., Sodoro, J., & Brown, J. S. (1992). The dissociation of repetition priming and recognition memory in language/learning-disabled children. *Journal of Experimental Child Psychology, 54,* 121–146.

Lucangeli, D., Galderisi, D., & Cornoldi, C. (1995). Specific and general transfer effects following metamemory training. *Learning Disabilities Research & Practice, 10,* 11–21.

Male, D. R. (1996). Metamemorial functioning of children with moderate learning difficulties. *British Journal of Educational Psychology, 66,* 145–157.

Manis, F. R. (1985). Acquisition of word identification skills in normal and disabled readers. *Journal of Educational Psychology, 27,* 28–90.

Mann, V. A., Cowin, E., & Schoenheimer, J. (1989). Phonological processing, language comprehension, and reading ability. *Journal of Learning Disabilities, 22*(2), 76–89.

Mastropieri, M. A., Scruggs, T. E., Levin, J. R., Gaffney, J., & McLoone, B. (1985). Mnemonic vocabulary instruction for learning disabled students. *Learning Disability Quarterly, 8,* 57–63.

Mazer, S. R., McIntyre, C. W., Murray, M. E., Till, R. E., & Blackwell, S. L. (1983). Visual persistence and information pick-up in learning disabled children. *Journal of Learning Disabilities, 16,* 221–225.

McBride-Chang, C., Manis, F. R., Seidenberg, M. S., Custodio, R., & Doi, L. M. (1993). Print exposure as a predictor of word reading and reading comprehension in disabled and nondisabled readers. *Journal of Educational Psychology, 85,* 230–238.

McIntyre, C. W., Murray, M. E., Coronin, C. M., & Blackwell, S. L. (1978). Span of apprehension in learning disabled boys. *Journal of Learning Disabilities, 11,* 13–20.

Miller, P. H. (1990). The development of strategies of selective attention. In D. F. Bjork-lund (Ed.), *Children's strategies: Contemporary views of cognitive development* (pp. 157–184). Hillsdale, NJ: Lawrence Erlbaum Associates.

Miller, P. H., Haynes, V. F., DeMarie-Dreblow, D., & Woody-Ramsey, J. (1986). Children's strategies for gathering information in three tasks. *Child Development, 57,* 1429–1439.

Miller, P. H., & Seier, W. L. (1994). Strategy utilization deficiencies in children: When, where, and why. In H. W. Reese (Ed.), *Advances in child development and behavior* Vol. 25 (pp. 107–156). New York: Academic Press.

Miller, P. H., Woody-Ramsey, J., & Aloise, P. A. (1991). The role of strategy effortfulness in strategy effectiveness. *Developmental Psychology, 27,* 738–745.

Miyake, A., Carpenter, P. A., & Just, M. A. (1994). A capacity approach to syntactic com-prehension disorders: Making normal adults perform like aphasic patients. *Cognitive Neuropsychology, 11,* 671–717.

Miyake, A., Just, M., & Carpenter, P. (1994). Working memory constraints on the resolu-tion of lexical ambiguity. *Cognitive Neuropsychology, 33,* 175–202.

Moeley, B., Hart, S. S., Santulli, K., Leal, L., et al. (1986). How do teachers teach memo-ry skills? *Educatonal Psychologist, 21* (1–2), 55–71.

Monroe, M. (1932). *Children who cannot read.* Chicago: University of Chicago Press.

Montague, M. (1992). The effects of cognitive and metacognitive strategy instruction on the mathematical problem solving of middle school students with learning disabilities. *Journal of Learning Disabilities, 25,* 230–248.

Montague, M. (1993). Student-centered or strategy-centered instruction: What is our pur-pose? *Journal of Learning Disabilities, 26,* 433–437.

Morgan, W. P. (1896). A case of congenital word blindness. *British Medical Journal, 2,* 1378–1379.

Morrison, F. J., Giordani, B., & Nagy, J. (1977). Reading disability: An information pro-cessing analysis. *Science, 196,* 77–79.

Neisser, U. (1967). *Cognitive psychology.* Appleton-Century-Crofts: New York.

O'Shaughnessy, T. E., & Swanson, H. L. (in press). A metaanalysis of memory research and learning disabilities: Support for lag or deficit hypothesis? *Learning Disability Quar-terly.*

Ornstein, P. A., & Naus, M. J. (1978). Rehearsal processes in children's memory. In P. A. Ornstein (Ed.), *Memory development in children.* Hillsdale, NJ: Erlbaum.

Orton, S. T. (1925). "Word-blindness" in school children. *Archives of Neurology and Psy-chiatry, 14,* 581–615.

Orton, S. T. (1937). *Reading, writing, and speech problems in children.* New York: Norton.

Pennington, B. F., Van Orden, G. C., Kirson, D., & Haith, M. M. (1991). What is the causal relation between verbal STM problems and dyslexia? In S. A. Brady & D. P. Shankweil-er (Eds.), *Phonological processes in literacy* (pp. 173–186). Hillsdale, NJ: Erlbaum.

Pressley, M. (1991). Can learning disabled children become good information processors? How can we find out? In L. Feagans, E. Short, & L. Meltzer (Eds.), *Subtypes of learn-ing disabilities* (pp. 137–162). Hillsdale, NJ: Erlbaum.

Pressley, M. (1994). Embracing the complexity of individual differences in cognition: Studying good information processing and how it might develop. *Learning & Individ-ual Differences, 6,* 259–284.

Pressley, M., Borkowski, J. G., & Schneider, W. (1987). Cognitive strategies: Good strategy users coordinate metacognition and knowledge. *Annals of Child Development, 4,* 89–129.

Pressley, M., Cariglia-Bull, S. D., Schneider, W. (1987). Short-term memory, verbal competence, and age as predictors of an imaginary structural effectiveness. *Journal of Experimental Child Psychology, 43,* 194–211.

Samuels, S. J. (1987). Information processing and reading. *Journal of Learning Disabilities, 20,* 18–22.

Santiago, H. C., & Matos, I. (1994). Visual recognition memory in specific learning-disabled children. *Journal of the American Optometric Association, 65,* 690–700.

Schneider, W. (1993). Acquiring expertise: Determinants of exceptional performance. In K. A. Heller, F. J. Monks, & A. H. Passow (Eds.), *Research and development of giftedness and talent.* New York: Pergamon.

Scruggs, T. E., & Mastropieri, M. A. (1989). Mnemonic instruction of LD students: A field-based evaluation. *Learning Disability Quarterly, 12,* 119–125.

Seidenberg, M. S. (1989). Reading complex words. In G. N. Carlson & M. Tanenhaus (Eds.), *Linguistic structure in language processing* (pp. 53–105). New York: Kluver Academic Publishers.

Senf, G. M., & Feshbach, S. (1970). Development of bisensory memory in culturally deprived, dyslexic and normal readers. *Journal of Educational Psychology, 61,* 461–470.

Shah, P., & Miyake, A. (1996). The separability of working memory resources for spatial thinking and language processing: An individual differences approach. *Journal of Experimental Psychology: General, 125,* 4–27.

Shankweiler, D., Liberman, I. Y., Mark, S. L., Fowler, L. A., & Fischer, F. W. (1979). The speech code and learning to read. *Journal of Experimental Psychology: Human, Learning, & Memory, 5,* 531–545.

Shulman, H. G. (1971). Similarity effects in short term memory. *Psychological Bulletin, 75,* 389–415.

Siegel, L. S. (1993). Phonological processing deficits as the basis of a reading disability. Special Issue: Phonological processes and learning disability. *Developmental Review, 13,* 246–257.

Siegel, L. S. (1993). The cognitive basis of dyslexia. In M. Howe & R. Pasnak (Eds.), *Emerging themes in cognitive development* (pp. 33–52). New York: Springer-Verlag.

Siegel, L. S., & Linder, B. A. (1984). Short-term memory processing in children with reading and arithmetic learning disabilities. *Developmental Psychology, 20,* 200–207.

Siegel, L. S., & Ryan, E. S. (1988). Development of grammatical sensitivity, phonological, and short-term memory skills in normally achieving and learning disabled children. *Developmental Psychology, 24,* 28–37.

Siegel, L. S., & Ryan, E. B. (1989). The development of working memory in normally achieving and subtypes of learning disabled children. *Child Development, 60,* 973–980.

Sipe, S., & Engle, R. (1986). Echoic memory processes in good and poor readers. *Journal of Experimental Psychology: Learning, Memory, and Cognition, 12,* 402–412.

Stanovich, K. E. (1990). Concepts in developmental theories of reading skill: Cognitive resources, automaticity, and modularity. *Developmental Review, 10,* 72–100.

Stanovich, K. E., & Siegel, L. S. (1994). Phenotypic performance profile of children with reading disabilities: A regression based test of the phonological-core difference model. *Journal of Educational Psychology, 86,* 24–53.

Swanson, H. L. (1977). Nonverbal visual short-term memory as a function of age and dimensionality in learning disabled children. *Child Development, 45,* 51–55.

Swanson, H. L. (1978). Verbal coding effects on the visual short term memory of learning disabled and normal readers. *Journal of Educational Psychology, 70,* 539–544.

Swanson, H. L. (1983a). A study of nonstrategic linguistic coding on visual recall of learning disabled and normal readers. *Journal of Learning Disabilities, 16,* 209–216.

Swanson, H. L. (1983b). Relations among metamemory, rehearsal activity and word recall in learning disabled and nondisabled readers. *British Journal of Educational Psychology, 53,* 186–194.

Swanson, H. L. (1984a). Effects of cognitive effort and word distinctiveness on learning disabled and nondisabled readers' recall. *Journal of Educational Psychology, 76,* 894–908.

Swanson, H. L. (1984b). Semantic and visual memory codes in learning disabled readers. *Journal of Experimental Child Psychology, 37,* 124–140.

Swanson, H. L. (1986). Do semantic memory deficiencies underlie disabled readers encoding processes? *Journal of Experimental Child Psychology, 41,* 461–488.

Swanson, H. L. (1987a). Verbal-coding deficits in the recall of pictorial information by learning disabled readers: The influence of a lexical system. *American Educational Research Journal, 24,* 143–170.

Swanson, H. L. (1987b). Information processing and learning disabilities: An overview. *Journal of Learning Disabilities, 20,* 3–7.

Swanson, H. L. (1988). Learning disabled children's problem solving: Identifying mental processes underlying intelligent performance. *Intelligence, 12,* 261–278.

Swanson, H. L. (1989). The effects of central processing strategies on learning disabled, mildly retarded, average, and gifted children's elaborative encoding abilities. *Journal of Experimental Child Psychology, 47,* 370–397.

Swanson, H. L. (1991). A subgroup analysis of learning-disabled and skilled readers' working memory: In search of a model of reading comprehension. In L. Feagans, E. Short, & L. Meltzer (Eds.), *Subtypes of learning disabilities: Theoretical perspectives and research* (pp. 209–228). Hillsdale, NJ: Erlbaum.

Swanson, H. L. (1992). Generality and modifiability of working memory among skilled and less skilled readers. *Journal of Educational Psychology, 64,* 473–488.

Swanson, H. L. (1993a). Executive processing in learning-disabled readers. *Intelligence, 17,* 117–149.

Swanson, H. L. (1993b). Working memory in learning disability subgroups. *Journal of Experimental Child Psychology, 56,* 87–114.

Swanson, H. L. (1994). Short-term memory and working memory. Do both contribute to our understanding of academic achievement in children and adults with learning disabilities? *Journal of Learning Disabilities, 27,* 34–50.

Swanson, H. L., Ashbaker, M., & Lee, C. (1996). The effects of processing demands on the working memory of learning disabled readers. *Journal of Experimental Child Psychology.*

Swanson, H. L., & Berninger, V. (1995). The role of working memory in skilled and less skilled readers' comprehension. *Intelligence, 21,* 83–108.

Swanson, H. L., Cochran, K., & Ewers, C. (1989). Working memory and reading disabilities. *Journal of Abnormal Child Psychology, 17,* 745–756.

Swanson, H. L., Cochran, K. F., & Ewers, C. A. (1990). Can learning disabilities be determined from working memory performance. *Journal of Learning Disabilities, 23,* 59–68.

Swanson, H. L., & Cooney, J. (1985). Strategy transformations in learning disabled children. *Learning Disability Quarterly, 8,* 221–231.

Swanson, H. L., Cooney, J. D., & Overholser, J. D. (1988). The effects of self generated visual mnemonics on adult learning disabled readers' word recall. *Learning Disabilities Research, 4,* 26–35.

Swanson, H. L., & Rathgeber, A. J. (1986). The effects of organizational dimension on memory for words in learning-disabled and nondisabled readers. *Journal of Educational Research, 79,* 155–162.

Swanson, H. L., Reffel, J., & Trahan, M. (1990). Naturalistic memory in learning disabled and skilled readers. *Journal of Abnormal Child Psychology, 19,* 117–148.

Swanson, H. L., & Rhine, B. (1985). Strategy transformations in learning disabled children's math performance: Clues to the development of expertise. *Journal of Learning Disabilities, 18,* 596–603.

Tarver, S. G., Hallahan, D. P., Kauffman, J. M., & Ball, D. W. (1976). Verbal rehearsal and selective attention in children with learning disabilities: A developmental lag. *Journal of Experimental Child Psychology, 22,* 375–385.

Torgesen, J. K., & Goldman, T. (1977). Rehearsal and short-term memory in second grade reading disabled children. *Child Development, 48,* 56–61.

Torgesen, J. K., & Houck, D. G. (1980). Processing deficiencies of learning disabled children who perform poorly on the digit span subtest. *Journal of Educational Psychology, 72,* 141–160.

Torgesen, J. K., Rashotte, C. A., Greenstein, J., & Portes, P. (1991). Further studies of learning disabled children with severe performance problems on the Digit Span Test. *Learning Disabilities Research & Practice, 6,* 134–144.

Vellutino, F. R. (1979). *Dyslexia: Theory and research.* Cambridge, MA: MIT Press.

Vellutino, F., Scanlon, D. M., & Spearing, D. (1995). Semantic and phonological coding in poor and normal readers. *Journal of Experimental Child Psychology, 59,* 76–123.

Wadsworth, S. J., DeFries, J. C., Fulker, D. W., Olson, R. K., & others. (1995). Reading performance and verbal short-term memory: A twin study of reciprocal causation. *Intelligence, 20,* 145–167.

Waller, T. G. (1976). Children's recognition memory for written sentences: A comparison of good and poor readers. *Child Development, 47,* 90–95.

Waterman, B., & Lewandowski, L. (1993). Phonological and semantic processing in reading disabled and nondisabled males at two age-levels. *Journal of Experimental Child Psychology, 55,* 87–103.

Wilhardt, L., & Sandman, C. A. (1988). Performance of nondisabled adults and adults with learning disabilities on a computerized multiphasic cognitive memory battery. *Journal of Learning Disabilities, 21,* 179–185.

Willows, D. M., Corcos, E., & Kershner, J. R. (1993). Perceptual and cognitive factors in disabled and normal readers' perception and memory of unfamiliar visual symbols. In S. F. Wright & R. Groner (Eds.), *Facts of dyslexia and its remediation. Studies in visual information processing,* Vol. 3 (pp. 163–177). Amsterdam, Netherlands: North-Holland/Elsevier Science Publishers.

Wong, B. Y. L. (1978). The effects of directive cues on the organization of memory and re-call in good and poor readers. *Journal of Educational Research, 72,* 32–38.

Wong, B. Y. L. (1982). Strategic behaviors in selecting retrieval cues in gifted, normal achieving and learning disabled children. *Journal of Learning Disabilities, 15,* 33–37.

Wong, B. Y. L. (1991). Assessment of metacognitive research in learning disabilities: The-ory, research, and practice. In H. L. Swanson (Ed.), *Handbook on the assessment of learning disabilities* (pp. 265–284). Austin, TX: PRO-ED.

Wong, B. Y. L., & Jones, W. (1982). Increasing metacomprehension of learning disabled and normal achieving students through self-questioning training. *Learning Disability Quarterly, 5,* 228–240.

Worden, P. E. (1986). Comprehension and memory for prose in the learning disabled. In S. J. Ceci (Ed.), *Handbook of cognitive social and neuropsychological aspects of learn-ing disabilities* Volume 1, (pp. 241–262). Hillsdale, NJ: Erlbaum.

CHAPTER 5

Language Problems: A Key to Early Reading Problems

Virginia Mann

I. INTRODUCTION: THE LINK BETWEEN READING PROBLEMS AND LANGUAGE PROBLEMS

Why do some children become poor readers? Why do they fail so miserably in the very same classrooms where most children succeed? Learning to read is a task that poses a considerable difficulty for between 4 and 10% of children who are diagnosed as dyslexic or reading-disabled because their reading problems cannot be blamed on a lack of general intelligence, motivation, or adequate classroom experience.

Over the course of the following pages, my intent is to introduce and justify one very successful approach to explaining early reading problems. This approach is guided by the assumption that reading is first, and foremost, a language skill, and it raises the possibility that many instances of reading problems are the consequence of language problems. I will begin in section II by offering a rationale for associating reading problems with language problems. Section III will turn to reviewing some of the many interesting results which this rationale has engendered, section IV will consider some explanations and implications for remediation, and section V will offer some concluding remarks.

Psychologists, educators, and neurologists have all, in one way or another, tried to identify the basis of early reading difficulty. Although they have not always stated so explicitly, their efforts have been guided by some basic assumptions about reading and the demands that it makes upon children's perceptual and cognitive abilities. A basic review of the assumptions that link reading skill to spoken language skill will be offered in section II, which (a) discusses how the English alphabet "writes language" by mapping onto the morphophonological structure of spoken English and (b) reviews some experimental evidence about the spoken language skills that play a role in skilled reading. Section III turns to the real substance of the chapter, the two basic areas of spoken language skill that are linked to poor reading: (a) language processing and (b) language awareness. It will offer a survey of research that links early reading difficulty to problems within each area, prefaced by a few comments about some of the less successful accounts of early reading problems that have been entertained in the past. Section IV will present (a) some plausible explanations of the language problems that underlie reading problems and (b) some fruitful directions for remediating the language deficiencies that impede poor beginning readers. Section V concludes the chapter with a brief summary and some concluding remarks.

II. WHY SPOKEN LANGUAGE IS SO CRITICAL TO READERS

Two pieces of background information can start us on our path towards understanding the role of language problems in poor reading. One concerns how writing systems transcribe the units of spoken language; the other concerns how skilled readers depend upon certain language skills. We often think of reading as a "visual" skill, yet it is so much more. Reading involves perceiving, recognizing, remembering, and interpreting the various letters and the words, sentences, etc. which they form. Readers cannot interpret letters, words, sentences, and paragraphs unless they make some type of mapping between written language and spoken language.

A. How Writing Systems Represent Language

The history and diversity of writing systems is quite a fascinating topic to consider, and Hung and Tzeng (1981) and Watt (1989) offer some interesting discussions. All writing systems use symbols to represent the units of spoken language. Which type of unit is being represented determines the type of writing system: ideography, logography, syllabary, or alphabet. Ideas are represented by ideographies (petroglyphs or road signs), morphemes are represented by logographies (the Chinese writing system and Japanese Kanji), syllables are represented by syllabaries (the Hebrew writing system and the Japanese Kana), whereas phonemes are represented by alphabets.

Different systems make different demands on the beginning reader because of the differences in the type of the unit they transcribe. The beginning reader has some appreciation of the units that his or her writing system is representing; otherwise it will be difficult to understand how written words relate to their spoken language counterparts (for discussion, see Hung & Tzeng, 1981; Liberman, Liberman, Mattingly, & Shankweiler, 1980). Because alphabets represent phonemes, someone who wishes to learn how the English alphabet functions should be sensitive to the fact that spoken language can be broken down into phonemes. As we shall see in section III.D, there is much evidence that this "sensitivity," referred to as "phoneme awareness," is a trait of successful beginning readers, yet a problem for many young children and for poor readers, in particular.

1. The English Alphabet: a Morphophonological Transcription

Alphabets represent phonemes, the minimal units of sound that we sometimes refer to as consonants and vowels. The English writing system is, at base, an alphabet. However, it does not provide the consistent one-to-one mapping of letter to phonemes that one finds in Spanish, for example. Rather, the mapping between letters and phonemes often involves a deeper, more abstract level of linguistic representation, which has been referred to as morphophonological because it combines phonemes (units of sound) and morphemes (units of meaning). This mapping is said to correspond most closely to the way in which linguists believe that words are abstractly represented in an ideal speaker-hearer's mental dictionary, or lexicon.

According to linguistic theory (see Chomsky, 1964), words are represented in the mental lexicon in terms of the basic units of meaning that we refer to as morphemes, as well as in terms of phonemes. When we produce or perceive language, linguists presume that we convert the morphophonological representations of the words in our lexicons into to the less abstract, phonetic representations with which we are more familiar (i.e., the words we speak and hear). This conversion involves an ordered series of phonological rules that alter, insert, or delete phonemes. Presumably we use these rules without consciously knowing that we do so; we manipulate morphological representations, morphemes, and phonemes without being aware of their existence.

For the reader of English, the problem is this: If the writing system maps onto the mental lexicon, it will sometimes fail to represent the phonetic representations with which we are more familiar. A given letter will not always map onto the same sound. As an example, witness the spellings of word pairs such as *atom–atomic, heal–health, relate–relation*. In each pair, the common spelling of base and derived form captures the relatedness of their meanings. But in order for there to be a common spelling, certain letters or letter sequences must represent more than one phoneme. Liberman et al. (1980) discuss the spelling of *heal–health* as an example of how morphophonological transcription operates. The digraph "*ea*" to transcribe the vowels in *heal* and *health,* preserving their abstract morphological and phonological similarity, while blurring certain phonetic distinctions. Insofar as the letter sequences in "heal" and "health" stand for the morphophonological and representations of these words, they can provide a means of access to lexical information, including each word's meaning and grammatical properties. To pronounce a written word, readers who have received the appropriate morphophonological representation need only apply the phonological rules of their language—the same rules that otherwise exist for the perception, pronunciation, and comprehension of "heal" and "health" in normal speech.

This account of the English orthography is, of course, somewhat idealized. Sometimes words are transcribed at a shallower, more phonetic level than the morphophonological ideal, hence the different spelling of the vowels in *well* and *wealth*. Sometimes, too, the spelling of a word seems neither phonetically nor phonologically principled, as in the spelling of *sword*. Certain of these exceptions have the advantage of disambiguating homophones, others are historically based, but their existence does not seriously undermine Chomsky's claim about the basic operating principle of the English orthography (Liberman et al., 1980). The important point to be remembered is that the English alphabet represents phonemes and morphemes and there is a certain trade-off between these two types of representation.

2. Virtues of Alphabetic Systems

Why should English be transcribed with an alphabetic system? Why should a system transcribe both phonemes and morphemes? Are there any advantages to using an alphabetic orthography and to the deeper morphophonological system, in particular? One general benefit of alphabets stems from the fact that they transcribe phonemes as opposed to syllables or words. The transcription of phonemes greatly reduces the number of symbols which a child must learn to recognize and reproduce. Consider the ease of learning the 26 letters of the English alphabet as opposed to learning the two to three thousand characters needed to read a newspaper written in the Chinese logography.

There is another virtue to alphabets. Aside from being economical, they are highly productive. In alphabets, the relation between written words and spoken words is highly rule-governed. Knowledge of the rules that relate letter sequences to phonemes, morphemes, and their pronunciations, allows the reader to read not only highly familiar words, but also less familiar ones like "skiff" or "ablution," and even nonsense words like "atishnet" or "trilabial." Consider that a skilled reader of the Chinese logography must have memorized thousands of distinct characters—and even then may encounter difficulty in reading a new word. In contrast, a skilled reader of English need know only a limited set of phoneme-to-grapheme correspondences and the phonological rules of his or her spoken language in order to "decode" most words on the page (and any phonologically plausible nonword like "bliggle").

There is also a benefit to the English morphophonological system, as opposed to the more transparent alphabetic systems used in Spanish and Serbo-Croatian. This benefit stems from the fact that, by transcribing a deep, relatively abstract level of phonological structure where morphemes as well as phonemes are represented, the English writing system helps convey cues to meaning as well as to sound. If one recognizes *"heal"* in *"health"* or *"atom"* in *"atomic"*, or *"relate"* in *"relation"* then it can facilitate the recovery of that word's meaning. Another advantage to the transcription of morphemes is that it can avoid the need to create different spelling patterns for people who speak with different accents. Were English to use a more "shallow" alphabet, speakers from Boston would spell "cot" and "cart" the same way, speakers from the South would spell "pen" and "pin" the same, speakers from Brooklyn would spell "oil" and "earl" the same—imagine all of the inconveniences this could cause.

This is not to imply that there is anything inherently undesirable about reading a more shallow alphabet, a syllabary, or a pure logography. Ultimately, the utility of a given orthography rests upon the nature of the spoken language it transcribes. For example, a logography is appropriate for Chinese because it allows people to read the same text even though they cannot understand each other's speech. Likewise, for Japanese, the Kana syllabaries are quite well suited to the hundred or so syllables in the Japanese language. English, however, has less profound dialectical variation than Chinese, and the English language employs more than a thousand syllables. Hence, an alphabet is appropriate, and it would be less efficient and even a disservice to present the English writing system otherwise. But to reap the benefits of alphabetic transcription, the child who is learning to read must possess some appreciation of phonemes, morphemes, and the rules that manipulate them.

3. Phoneme Awareness: A Special Requirement of Alphabetic Systems

Alphabets may have clear advantages, but they nonetheless pose an obstacle for poor readers. Why should this be? Poor readers might have problems distinguishing and remembering the various letter shapes. They might have problems with processing spoken language and with understanding their teachers' instructions. They might lack an awareness of the linguistic units that the written words represent. But why would we want to distinguish between language processing and language awareness? If children can process spoken language, shouldn't they also know about the units of that language?

The answer to this question involves a distinction between linguistic and metalinguistic knowledge. We use linguistic knowledge when we process a language, we use metalinguistic knowledge to introspect upon the properties of that language—the units, rules, and representations that are a tacit, unconscious part of our processing ability. To read English, would-be readers must go one step further than merely being a speaker/hearer of their language, they must have an explicit, "metalinguistic" awareness of certain aspects of their language, phonemes, in particular (Mattingly, 1972).

Readers of English cannot be aware of this relationship between printed and spoken words unless they are aware of phonemes; unless they are sensitive to the fact that words can be broken down into phoneme-sized units, the letter–phoneme correspondences will be useless. This sensitivity is not something that we use in the normal activities of speaking and hearing, although we use it in certain secondary language activities such as appreciating verse (i.e., alliteration), making jokes (e.g., What did the baby banana say to its mother? I don't peel too good . . .), and talking in secret language (i.e., Pig-Latin). This sensitivity is commonly referred to as phoneme awareness.

One slight problem with the term phoneme awareness is that it is often used interchangeably with several other terms: phonological awareness, metalinguistic awareness, and linguistic awareness, to name a few. By using the term phoneme awareness we confine the issue to sensitivity about phonemes. Phonological awareness would also include sensitivity to syllables, morphemes, and the phonological rules that operate upon them, linguistic awareness and metalinguistic awareness would further include sensitivity to syntax (i.e., grammar), semantics (i.e., meaning), pragmatics, and their rules. These broader levels of awareness are of interest in their own right, and could be an interesting topic for research. To date, however, awareness of phonemes has been most often studied. Section III.D reviews how phoneme awareness is directly related to beginning readers' progress.

B. Language Skills That Skilled Readers Use

An appreciation of the English alphabet offers one form of evidence about the importance of spoken language skills to reading, highlighting the importance of language awareness and phoneme awareness in particular. A second source of evidence comes from studies of skilled readers. These show a clear involvement of certain spoken language processing skills in the skilled reading of words, sentences, and paragraphs. Such studies are important to consider, not only because they show that reading is really quite "parasitic" upon spoken language processes, but because they have inspired certain studies of the differences between good and poor beginning readers.

1. Language Skills and Word Recognition

The question of whether or not written words must be recoded into some type of silent speech has been a topic in much of the research on the psychology of skilled reading. It has especially preoccupied those who study the processes that make it possible to recognize the words of our vocabulary, a process often referred to as lexical access or word perception (for recent reviews of how readers gain lexical access, see Berent & Perfetti, 1995; Underwood & Batt, 1996, or Van Orden, 1987, for reviews). Under some circumstances, silent speech does not appear necessary for word recognition (i.e., lexical access). Some words may be directly perceived as visual units, instead of being decoded into a string of phonemes. But there is also clear evidence implicating at least some speech code involvement in word perception, making many psychologists favor a "dual-access" or "parallel race horse" model in which both phonetic and visual access occur in parallel. Others believe that the speech code or phonetic route may be most heavily used in the case of less frequent words and unfamiliar ones, with the visual or whole-word route as most important for very familiar words and words with irregular spelling patterns (Seidenberg, 1985). Still, others regard speech processes as playing an early, dominant role in all lexical access (van Orden, 1987; Rayner, Sereno, Lesch, & Pollatsek, 1995).

Regardless of how a word is recognized, the mental lexicon of words contains the morphophonological representation of each word in the readers' vocabulary, and that representation is the key to realizing the word's semantic extensions (its meaning) and its syntactic properties (its part of speech: noun, action verb, etc.), as well as its pronunciation. Hence it is appropriate that English speakers transcribe spoken words in terms of their morphophonological representations. It may not be necessary to recode print into a speech code in the process of gaining lexical access and it may not even be feasible, but morphophonological recoding clearly must occur, else the reading of phrases, sentences, and so on would not be possible.

2. Language Skills and the Reading of Sentences and Paragraphs

From the point of word perception onward, the involvement of speech processes in reading is quite clear (Perfetti & McCutchen, 1982). First of all, there is considerable evidence that short-term or working memory for written material involves recoding the material into some kind of silent speech, or phonetic representation. This type of representation is used whether the task requires temporary memory for isolated letters, printed nonsense syllables, and printed words. In all of these cases, both the nature of the errors that subjects make in recalling such material, and the experimental manipulations that help or hurt their memory performance have shown us that a phonetic representation is being used. That is, subjects are remembering the items in terms of the consonants and vowels that form the name of each item, rather than the visual shape of the letters, the shape of the words, and so on (see, for example, Baddeley, 1978; Conrad, 1964, 1972; Levy, 1977). It is further the case that subjects appear to rely on phonetic representation when they are required to comprehend sentences written in either alphabetic (Kleiman, 1975; Levy, 1977; Slowiaczek and Clifton, 1980) or logographic orthographies (Tzeng, Hung and Wang, 1977). This is one reason why we may observe such significantly high correlations between reading and listening comprehension across a variety of languages and orthographies, including English (see Curtis, 1980; Daneman & Carpenter, 1980; and Jackson & McClelland, 1979), Japanese, and Chinese (Stevenson, Stiegler, Lucker, Hsu, & Kitamura, 1982).

Thus it is apparent that, regardless of the way in which the reader recognizes each word, the processes involved in reading sentences and paragraphs place certain obvious demands on temporary memory, and temporary memory for language appears to make use of phonetic representation in working memory. The fact that readers make active use of a phonetic representation is important to keep in mind. In section III.C I will discuss how problems with phonetic representation are often found among poor beginning readers, in the form of short-term memory problems.

III. LANGUAGE PROBLEMS AS CAUSES OF EARLY READING PROBLEMS

Without spoken English, there would be nothing for the English orthography to transcribe; the well-known difficulties of deaf readers attest to the importance of spoken language skills for successful reading. But deaf children are not the only ones for whom deficient language abilities are a cause of reading problems. As we shall see shortly, many of the normally hearing children who are poor readers also suffer from spoken language problems, and although their problems are considerably more subtle than those of the deaf, they are no less critical. However, before discussing this fact, I will review some of the previously held theories about the cause of reading problems and some of the general evidence that points to a link between reading and language problems. I will then summarize the language skills needed by beginning readers before turning to a more detailed survey of various forms of evidence about the two types of language skill that are lacking in poor readers and are typical of kindergarten children who will become poor readers in the early elementary grades.

A. The Problem of Specific Reading Difficulty

One way to discover the problems that limit success in learning to read is to examine the differences between children who become poor readers and those who become skilled readers. We have now developed some ideas about where to look for those differences, namely in language processing and phoneme awareness. But before turning to a survey of research in each of these two areas, a bit more background is in order. It is appropriate to consider some of the ways in which psychologists and educators have tried to explain reading disability in the past. We might also ask if there are any indications that a linguistic account of poor reading will be more successful than some of the previously popular theories have been.

1. Some Less Successful Accounts of Poor Reading

As Rutter (1978) has noted, learning to read is a specific example of a complex learning task that correlates about 0.6 with IQ. Yet a low IQ cannot be the sole basis of reading problems, since there are children who are backwards in reading ability but average in intelligence (Rutter & Yule, 1973). Children who possess a seemingly adequate IQ (typically 90 or higher) but nonetheless encounter reading problems are said to have a specific reading difficulty, as their actual reading ability lags between 1 and 2 years behind that which is predicted on the basis of their age, IQ, and social standing. For these children, something other than general intelligence must be the primary "cause" of many instances of poor reading.

In attempting to discover the cause of early reading problems, many early theories were biased by an assumption that influenced psychologists and educators alike. That assumption stemmed from the view that reading is first and foremost a complex visual skill that demands differentiation and recognition of visual stimuli. Owing to it, models of skilled reading have often been biased toward clarification of how readers see and recognize the various letter and word shapes, and many studies of the cause of poor reading tried to blame early reading difficulty on some problem in the visual domain. Recently however, visual theories of reading disability have become less and less popular, for it seems that, at best, only a few of the children who are poor readers actually suffer from perceptual malfunctions that somehow prevent recognition, differentiation, or memory of visual forms. In short, visual skills do not reliably distinguish between children who differ in reading ability (see: Rutter, 1978; Stanovich, 1982a; and Vellutino, 1979, for recent reviews of these findings), so visual problems would not seem to be the primary cause of many instances of reading problems.

Let me follow Mann and Brady (1988) in mentioning two pieces of supporting evidence that show just how unfair it is to blame the majority of early reading problems on visual problems. First, 5 to 6-year-old children who were identified as having deficient visual perception and/or visuomotor coordination skills show no more instances of reading difficulty at age 8 to 9 than do matched controls who possess no such deficits (Robinson & Schwartz, 1973). Second, although it is true that all young children tend to confuse spatially reversible letters such as "b,d,p,g" until they are 7 or 8 years old (Gibson, Gibson, Pick, & Osser, 1962), letter and sequence reversals actually account for only a small proportion of the reading errors that are made by children in this age range. Even children who have been formally diagnosed as dyslexic make relatively few letter and sequence reversal errors (Fisher, Liberman, & Shankweiler, 1977).

Theories that placed emphasis on cross-modal integration have also been popular at one time or another (Birch & Belmont, 1964; see reviews by Benton, 1975; Rutter & Yule, 1973). Their misconception was that reading involved translating visual information into auditory information, and that this cross-modal match was the source of the problem. Such theories have met much the same fate as theories that emphasized visual deficiencies as the cause of reading problems. When investigators carefully examined the behavior of skilled readers, they realized that the translation was not directly from visual to auditory information. Instead, visual information was first translated into an abstract linguistic code. When they considered children's ability to map between information presented to the visual and auditory modalities they also began to realize that an abstract linguistic code was often the basis for the cross-modal integration. Finally, researchers began to realize that, when visual-auditory integration problems were present, then so were auditory-auditory problems and even visual-visual ones. Thus the poor readers' problems with visual-auditory integration have come to be viewed as one of the many consequences of a more general linguistic coding problem that hurts integration within modalities as well as between them (see Vellutino, 1979, for a review).

Other theories have suffered from similar attempts to explain an observation about poor readers in terms that are somehow too general. For example, certain theories were preoccupied by the fact that reading involves remembering an ordered sequence of letters in a word and of words in a sentence. Hence it was suggested that poor sequential-order memory (Corkin, 1974) or poor short-term memory (Morrison, Giordani, & Nagy, 1977) might be a cause of poor reading. A focus on memory problems was not a bad direction for theories to take, but some other observations about the specific pattern of poor readers disabilities and abilities indicate that some refinements are in order. Good and poor readers do not differ on all tasks that require temporary memory of items or their order. Good and poor beginning readers are equivalent, for example, in ability to remember faces (Liberman, Mann, Shankweiler, & Werfelman, 1982) or visual stimuli that cannot readily be assigned verbal labels (Katz, Shankweiler, & Liberman, 1981; Liberman et al., 1982; Swanson, 1978). Only when the to-be-remembered stimuli can be linguistically coded do children who are poor readers consistently fail to do as well as good readers (Liberman et al., 1982; Katz et al., 1981; Swanson, 1978).

Various other general or visual accounts of reading disability have been offered in the literature (see, Carr, 1981, for a review). These tend to be inadequate because they fail to explain why poor readers often do as well as good readers on nonlinguistic tasks, yet lag behind good readers in performance on many linguistic tasks. (For reviews, see Stanovich, 1982a,b; Vellutino, 1979). For the sake of brevity, such general accounts will not be discussed here. Instead, I turn to the more positive task of reviewing evidence that links language and reading problems.

2. A Language-Based Perspective May Offer a Better Account

The previous paragraphs mentioned several studies that demonstrate that good and poor readers are distinguished by their performance on certain linguistic tasks, but not by their performance on comparably demanding nonlinguistic ones (as shown by Brady, Shankweiler, and Mann, 1983; Katz et al., 1981; Liberman et al., 1982; Mann & Liberman, 1984; Swanson, 1978, for example). That evidence receives further support from a consideration of the frequency of reading difficulties in children with various sorts of handicaps. As Rutter (1978) observes, whereas children deficient in visual-perceptual and/or visual-motor skills do not encounter reading difficulty any more frequently than matched controls (Money, 1973; Robinson & Schwartz, 1973), children deficient in speech and language skills encounter reading problems at least six times more often than controls do (Ingram, Mason, & Blackburn, 1970; Mason, 1976). But we can ask whether there is a more fine-grained analysis of the language problems found among poor readers. Are some areas of language skill more problematic than others?

B. Two Types of Language Skills That Are Essential to Beginning Readers

What skills does a child need in order to learn to read well? Obviously, would-be readers need to possess the visual skills that allow them to differentiate and remember the various letter shapes. They also need language processing skills in order to be able to perceive and recognize the teacher's words, and to combine them into phrases, sentences, and paragraphs, as well as in order to meet the requirements of skilled reading discussed in section II.B. Finally, they will need to possess phoneme awareness, as discussed in II.A, if they are to make any real sense of the way in which the alphabet works.

1. Language Processing Skills

Beginning readers should possess language processing skills at four different levels. First of all, they need the speech perception skills that make it possible to distinguish the words of their vocabulary, the difference between cat and hat, for example. They also need vocabulary skills and morphological skills, although they need not necessarily possess mature morphophonological representations in their lexicons, given some evidence that the experience of reading, in and of itself, serves to stimulate and further morphological and phonological development (Moskowitz, 1973). Beginning readers should also have an adequate linguistic short-term memory, since this is not only critical to skilled readers but also supports retention of sufficient words to understand sentences and paragraphs. Finally, they should further be able to recover the syntactic and semantic structure of phrases and sentences (although their mastery of these aspects of language, like their mastery of phonology, may be facilitated by the experience of reading (Goldman, 1976).

2. Phoneme Awareness

Language processing skills, however, are only one aspect of the language skills needed by would-be readers of English. As was noted in section II.A, the English orthography requires that successful readers not only be able to process spoken language, but also be conscious of certain abstract units of that language—phonemes, in particular. Otherwise the alphabet will make no sense as a transcription of spoken English. Whereas sophistication about words is sufficient for learning a logography, and sophistication about words and syllables is sufficient for syllabaries, children must know about these units and also about phonemes if the alphabet is to make sense and if they are to use it to its fullest advantage.

Section II.A had hinted that phoneme awareness might pose a problem, but why should this be the case? One reason is that phonemes are quite abstract units of language, considerably more abstract than either words or syllables. We reflexively and unconsciously, perceive them when we listen to the speech stream, because we have a neurophysiology uniquely and elegantly adapted to that purpose (see A. Liberman, 1982). Yet phonemes cannot be mechanically isolated from each other, or produced in isolation (Liberman, Cooper, Shankweiler, & Studdert-Kennedy, 1967) as can syllables and words. There are some very interesting indications that infants may distinguish phonemes (see Miller & Eimas, 1983, for a review of the speech perception capabilities of infant listeners) and preschool-aged children most certainly employ phonetic representation when holding linguistic material in short-term memory (Alegria & Pignot, 1979; Eimas 1975). Yet these are automatic, "tacit" aspects of language-processing ability, and the child who knows his or her language well enough to perceive and remember phonemes can still be blissfully unaware of the fact that these units exist—much the same way that you and I are blissfully unaware of the rods and cones that allow us to see.

So there is a problem with using written language: the tacit must also become explicit. Successful beginning readers must not only know the difference between words like cat and hat, and how to hold these words in memory. They must further possess the realization that each word can be broken down into phonemes, so that they may appreciate the fact that, aside from referring to different objects, cat and hat differ in one phoneme, namely the first, and share a final phoneme which is the initial one in top. Otherwise the alphabet will remain a mystery to them, and its virtues unrealized.

C. Language Processing Skills and Poor Reading

Since the mid-1970s, there has been considerable activity in the psychology of early reading problems, and study after study has uncovered some link between difficulties in learning to read, and difficulties with some aspect of spoken language processing. Such a link is clearly established beyond question, not only in English but in Swedish (Lundberg, Oloffson, & Wall, 1980) and in Japanese (Leong & Tamaoka, 1995) and Chinese as well (Stevenson et al., 1982). In the case of English, there have also been considerable attempts to more precisely specify the nature of the language problems that typify poor beginning readers. These attempts can be organized in terms of the four levels of language processing that were identified in section III.A.1 as being important to beginning reading: speech perception, vocabulary skills, working memory, and syntax and semantics.

1. Speech Perception

The possibility that some aspect of speech perception might be a special problem for poor readers receives support from a study by Brady, Shankweiler, and Mann (1983). Their research considered a group of beginning readers who did not differ from each other in age, IQ, or audiometry scores but strongly differed in reading ability. The children were asked to identify spoken words or environmental sounds under a normal listening condition, and under a noisy condition, and the performance of the good and poor readers was compared. The results indicated that the good and poor readers were equally able to identify environmental sounds, whatever the listening condition. As long as the words were not masked by noise, the good and poor readers performed equivalently on these items, as well, but the poor readers made almost 33% more errors than the good readers when they were asked to identify the spoken words in the noisy condition. This result implies, as other research has suggested (Goetzinger, Dirks, & Baer, 1960), that poor readers have difficulties with speech perception when the listening conditions are less than optimal.

Another suggestion to this effect comes from studies that compare the categorical perception of synthetic speech stimuli by good and poor beginning readers. In such studies, categorical perception was evident in both groups of subjects, yet the poor readers differed from the good readers either in failing to meet the level of inter-category discrimination predicted on the basis of their identification responses or in failing to give as consistent identification responses (Brandt & Rosen, 1980; Godfrey, Syrdal-Lasky, Millay, & Knox, 1981; for a review see Mody, Studdert-Kennedy, & Brady, in press). These findings have been interpreted as the reflection of deficient speech perception processes on the part of poor readers. (But they may also relate to a problem with remembering speech sounds, because memory plays an obvious role in discrimination tasks, and in many identification tasks, as well; see Mody et al., in press).

2. Vocabulary Skills

There are quite a few indications that reading ability is related to certain vocabulary skills, depending upon how reading ability is measured and what type of vocabulary skill is at issue. Reading ability can be measured in terms of the ability to read individual words (decoding) or in terms of the ability to understand the meaning of sentences and paragraphs (comprehension). In the case of beginning readers, decoding and comprehension tests are correlated quite highly, implying that children who differ on one type of test will usually differ on the other as well. Still, there are cases in which the two types of tests identify different groups of good and poor readers that may lead researchers to different conclusions about the cause of poor reading (see Stanovich, 1988, for discussion). Vocabulary skill is a case in point; future research may uncover other cases as well.

Vocabulary skills are also tested with two different types of test. One type is recognition vocabulary tests like the Peabody Picture Vocabulary Test (PPVT), which requires the child to point to a picture that illustrates a word. Recognition vocabulary has sometimes been related to early reading ability (see Stanovich, Cunningham, & Feeman, 1984), although it is not always a very significant predictor (see Wolf & Goodglass, 1986). The utility of this test may depend upon how reading ability is measured, as the relationship seems stronger for tests of reading comprehension like the Reading Survey of the Metropolitan (see Stanovich, Nathan, & Zolman, 1988) than for tests of word recognition like the Word Identification and Word Attack tests of the Woodcock (see Mann & Liberman, 1984).

The other type of vocabulary test is naming or productive vocabulary tests like the Boston Naming Test, which requires the child to produce the word that a picture illustrates. Productive vocabulary gives clearer indications of a link between reading ability and vocabulary skill, and there is evidence that this link exists whether reading skill is measured in terms of decoding or comprehension. Performance on the Boston Naming Test predicted both the word recognition and the reading comprehension ability of kindergarten children far more accurately than did performance on the PPVT (Wolf, 1984; Wolf & Goodglass, 1986). In one study of the naming speed among dyslexic individuals, the performance of 17-year-olds was closest to that of 8-year-old normal children for colors, digits, letters, and pictures of common objects (Fawcett & Nicolson, 1994). Tests of continuous naming (sometimes called rapid automatization naming), which require children to name a series of repeating objects, letters, or colors, have also shown that children who are poor readers require longer to name the series than good readers do (see, for example, Denckla & Rudel, 1976; Blachman, 1984; Wolf, 1984). Performance on these tests bears an interesting relationship to the success of certain remediation measures (Torgesen & Davis, 1996), as shown in section IV.B.1.

A causal link between naming problems and reading problems is indicated by the discovery that performance on naming tests can predict future reading ability (for a review, see Bowers & Wolf, 1993). Wolf (1984) has noted that, whereas continuous naming tests using objects and colors are predictive of early problems with word recognition, problems with rapid letter recognition and retrieval play a more prolonged role in the reading of severely impaired readers, even in reading comprehension. In my laboratory, my students and I have used a test of letter naming ability in our longitudinal studies of kindergarten children (Mann, 1984; Mann & Ditunno, 1990) and have consistently found that kindergartners who take longer to name a randomized array of the capital letters are significantly more likely to perform poorly on word decoding tests and comprehension tests that are administered in first grade. It further seems that present letter naming predicts future reading ability more consistently than present reading ability predicts future letter naming ability (for relevant evidence, see Mann & Ditunno, 1990, and also see Stanovich et al., 1988). Thus it is likely that something other than a lack of educational experience is preventing these children from naming the letter names as fast as other children can, and that "something" could be a problem with productive vocabulary skills.

Another pertinent piece of evidence about the vocabulary problems of poor readers comes from a study by Katz (1982), who found that children who perform poorly on a decoding test are particularly prone to difficulties in producing low-frequency and polysyllabic names, and suggested that, for such words, these children may possess less phonologically complete lexical representations than good readers do. On the basis of his research, he further suggests that, because poor readers often have access to aspects of the correct phonological representation of a word, even though they are unable to produce that word correctly, their problem may be attributable to phonological deficiencies in the structure of the lexicon rather than to the process of lexical access, per se.

3. Working Memory

The observation that poor readers perform less well than good readers on a variety of short-term memory tests has given rise to one of the more fruitful lines of research in the field (for reviews, see Brady & Shankweiler, 1991; Mann & Brady, 1988). It has often been noted that poor readers tend to perform less well on the digit span test and are deficient in the ability to recall in order strings of letters and nonsense syllables or words, whether the stimuli are heard or seen. Poor readers even fail to recall the words of spoken sentences as accurately as good readers do (see Jorm, 1979, and Mann, Liberman, & Shankweiler, 1980, for references to these effects). Evidence that these differences are not merely consequences of differences in reading ability has come from a longitudinal study that showed that problems with recalling a sequence of words can precede the attainment of reading ability, and may actually serve to presage future reading problems (Mann & Liberman, 1984; see Rohl & Pratt, 1995, for a review).

In searching for an explanation of this pattern of results, researchers turned to the research on skilled readers that was discussed in section II.B, and to its indication that linguistic materials like letters, words, and so on are held in working memory through use of phonetic representation. Drawing upon this indication, Liberman, Shankweiler and their colleagues (Shankweiler, Liberman, Mark, Fowler, & Fisher, 1979) were the first to suggest that the linguistic short-term memory difficulties of poor readers might reflect a problem with using this type of representation. Several experiments have offered support for this hypothesis. These show that, when recalling letter strings (Shankweiler et al., 1979), word strings (Mann, Shankweiler, & Smith, 1980; Mann & Liberman, 1984) and sentences (Mann et al., 1980), poor readers are much less sensitive than good readers to a manipulation of the phonetic structure of the materials (i.e., the density of words that rhyme). Indeed, good readers can be made to appear like poor readers when they are asked to recall a string of words in which all of the words rhyme (such as bat, cat, rat, hat, mat), whereas poor readers perform at the same level whether the words rhyme or not. This observation has led to the postulation that poor readers—and children who are likely to become poor readers—are for some reason less able to use phonetic structure as a means of holding material in short-term memory (Mann et al., 1980; Mann & Liberman, 1984; Shankweiler et al., 1979).

One might ask, at this point, whether poor readers are avoiding phonetic representation altogether, or merely using it less well. We have obtained little evidence that poor readers employ a visual form of memory instead of a phonetic one (Mann, 1984), although there have been indications that they may place greater reliance on word meaning (Byrne & Shea, 1979). Evidence that poor readers are attempting to use phonetic representation has been found in the types of errors that they make as they attempt to recall or recognize spoken words in a short-term memory task (Brady et al., 1983; Brady, Mann, & Schmidt, 1987). These errors reveal that poor readers make use of many of the same features of phonetic structure as good readers do. In short, there is evidence that they make the same sort of phonetically principled errors—they merely make more of them.

4. Syntax and Semantics

Do poor readers have a problem with the syntax (the grammar) and the semantics (the meaning) of language in addition to their problem with speech perception, vocabulary, and using phonetic structure in short-term memory? The observation that poor readers cannot repeat sentences as well as good readers has led to some obvious questions about these higher level language skills and their involvement in reading problems.

Quite a few studies have examined the syntactic abilities of poor readers. There is an accumulating body of evidence that poor readers do not comprehend certain types of sentences as well as good readers do (see Mann, Cowin, & Schoenheimer, 1989, for a review). It has been shown that good and poor readers differ in both the ability to repeat and to comprehend spoken sentences that contain relative clauses such as, "The dog jumped over the cat that chased the monkey," (Mann, Shankweiler, & Smith, 1985). They also perform less well on instructions from the Token Test, such as "Touch the small red square and the large blue triangle" (Smith, Mann and Shankweiler, 1986). Indeed, following multistep directions was recently found to be one of the most consistently reported problems reported by parents of children with learning disabilities (Blumsack, Lewandowski, & Waterman, 1997). Children with reading problems also are less able to distinguish the meaning of spoken sentences like, "He showed her bird the seed" from "He showed her the birdseed," which uses the stress pattern of the sentence (its "prosody") and the position of the article "the" to mark the boundary between the indirect object and the direct object.

In searching to explain these and other sentence comprehension problems that typify poor readers, my colleagues and I have been struck by the fact that all of the problematic sentences in one way or another create processing demands on children's ability to hold a series of words in working memory. When we examined the results of the studies mentioned above, we found little evidence that the poor readers were having trouble with the grammatical structures being used in the sentences that caused them problems. In fact, the structures were often ones that young children master within the first few years of life and ones that the poor readers could be shown to understand if the sentence was short enough (see Mann et al., 1989, for a discussion). Instead we found much evidence that the comprehension problems were predominantly due to the working memory problem discussed in the previous section. It seems as if poor readers are just as sensitive to syntactic structure as good readers. The reason why they fail to understand sentences is that they cannot hold an adequate representation of the sentence in short-term memory (see Gottardo, Stanovich, & Siegel, 1996; Mann et al., 1985; Mann, Cowin, & Schoenheimer, 1989; Smith, Macaruso, Shankweiler, & Crain, 1989).

Another type of sentence comprehension task that is a problem for poor readers might at first glance seem to indicate a syntactic impairment. This is the sentence completion task used by Mahony (1994) and in Singson, Mahony, & Mann (in press) to test children's sensitivity to derivational suffixes. The task requires children to choose which word best completes a sentence, such as "He was blinded by the ———: bright, brighten, brightly, brightness." Poorer readers, both children and adults, perform less well on this test than normal readers, and they do so whether they are reading the sentences or hearing them aloud, and whether the word that fills in the blank is a real word or an appropriately derived word like "froodness." Here the important thing to note is that the task requires using morphological suffixes to distinguish among nouns, verbs, and adjectives. The poorer readers are probably failing because they lack sufficient knowledge of derivational morphology and not because they have a problem with syntax, per se. Given our previous discussion in section II.A about the morphophonological nature of the English alphabet, it is quite reasonable that problems with morphology would associate with poor reading. Others have also noted this association at a variety of different ages (Carlisle & Nomanbhoy, 1993; Leong, 1989; Elbro, 1989); what we are finding particularly striking in our own research is that morphological skills relate to both comprehension and decoding of written language.

At present, then, although it is clear that poor readers do have sentence comprehension problems, there is little reason to think that their difficulties reflect a problem with the syntax of language. Problems with working memory and problems with morphology seem to be more likely sources of difficulty. Goldman (1976) is correct in noting that such syntactic differences as have been reported among good and poor readers could be either the cause of reading difficulty or a consequence of different amounts of reading experience. It is also worth noting that such deficits as do exist are relatively subtle, with poor readers merely performing like somewhat younger children than the good readers.

As for the question of semantic impairments among poor readers, there is no reason to presume any real deviance exists. If anything, poor readers place greater reliance on semantic context and semantic representation than good readers do, perhaps in compensation for their other language difficulties (see Stanovich, 1982b, for a review, and also see Byrne & Shea, 1979; Simpson, Lorsbach, & Whitehouse, 1983).

D. Phoneme Awareness and Reading Problems

Possessing adequate phonetic perception and working memory skills, an adequate mental lexicon, and the ability to recover the syntactic and semantic structure of utterances is only part of the requirement of becoming a successful reader. As was noted in section II.B, optimal use of the alphabet also requires that readers go beyond their tacit, unconscious language processing abilities to achieve an awareness of phonemes. Let us now turn to studies that address this second requirement of learning to read an alphabetic orthography.

1. Evidence from the Analysis of Reading Errors

The errors that a person makes can be informative about the difficulties that produce those errors, and oral reading errors have offered an important source of evidence about the cause of reading problems. As noted earlier, such errors do not tend to involve visual confusions and letter or sequence reversals to any appreciable degree. What they did appear to reflect is a problem with integrating the phonological information that letter sequences convey. Hence, children often tend to be correct as to the pronunciation of the first letter in a word, but have more and more difficulty with subsequent letters, and a particular problem with vowels as opposed to consonants. For more detailed presentation of these findings and their implications, the reader is referred to papers by Shankweiler and Liberman (1972) and Fisher et al. (1977) and also to a paper by Russell (1982), which suggests that deficient phoneme awareness may account for the reading difficulties of adult dyslexics.

2. Evidence from Tasks That Measure Awareness Directly

Most of the studies of phoneme awareness have concerned tasks that measure phoneme awareness through language games that manipulate the phonemes within in a word in one way or another. The use of a variety of different counting tasks, elision, deletion, similarity judgments, etc. by a variety of different researchers has revealed that phoneme awareness develops later than phonetic perception and the use of phonetic representation and remains a chronic problem for those individuals who are poor readers (for reviews, see Adams, 1990; Elbro, 1996; Yopp, 1988).

Research involving such tasks began with a study by Liberman and her colleagues that asked whether a sample of 4, 5, and 6-year-olds could learn to play syllable counting games and phoneme counting games in which the idea was to tap the number of syllables or phonemes in a spoken word (Liberman, Shankweiler, Fisher, & Carter, 1974). It was discovered that none of the 4-year-old children could tap the number of phonemes in a spoken word, while half of them managed to tap the number of syllables. Only 17% of the 5-year-olds could tap phonemes, while, again, about half of them could tap syllables. Among the 6-year-olds, however, 90% of the children could tap syllables, and 70% were able to tap phonemes. From such findings about children's sensitivity to the number of phonemes and syllables in spoken words, it is clear that the awareness of phonemes and syllables develops considerably between the ages of 4 and 6. It is also clear that awareness of phonemes is slower to develop than awareness of syllables. Finally, both types of awareness markedly improve at just the age when children are learning to read (Liberman et al., 1974).

Numerous experiments involving widely diverse subjects, school systems, and measurement devices have shown a strong positive correlation between a lack of awareness about phonemes and current problems in learning to read (see, for example, Alegria, Pignot and Morais, 1982; Fox and Routh, 1976; Liberman et al., 1980; Lundberg et al., 1980; Perfetti, 1985; Yopp, 1988). Pertinent to our focus on phoneme awareness, many studies of problems with phoneme segmentation in the kindergarten year consistently predict reading problems in first grade and beyond (see, for example, Blachman, 1984; Mann, 1993; Torgesen et al., 1994). In one examplary study, a kindergarten battery of tests that assessed phoneme awareness accounted for 66% of the variance in children's first-grade reading ability (Stanovich, Cunningham, & Cramer, 1984). We shall return to this topic in section IV.B.1. There is also evidence that lack of awareness about syllables is associated with reading disability (Katz, 1986), including evidence from studies of kindergarten children that problems with syllable segmentation (Mann and Liberman, 1984) can presage future reading difficulty, which indicated that 85% of a population of kindergarten children who went on to become good readers in the first grade correctly counted the number of syllables in spoken words, whereas only 17% of the future poor readers could do so (Mann & Liberman, 1984). Treiman and her colleagues have discussed the hierarchical role of syllable awareness, onset-rime awareness, and phoneme awareness as determinants of early reading ability (see, for example, Treiman & Zukowski, 1991, 1996). So the problem may be even more basic than an insufficient awareness of phonemes; it may involve insufficient awareness of phonological structures, more generally.

Given the well-established link between phoneme awareness and early reading ability, some researchers have suggested that there can be interesting refinements to our conceptualization of phoneme awareness. Stanovich (1991), for example, has made a distinction between tasks that require phonological sensitivity and those that require a fully explicit phonological awareness. Sensitivity refers to the ability to recognize rhyme and alliteration, whereas fully explicit awareness requires the ability to explicitly manipulate phonemes: counting, identifying, noting order, and locating position are all tasks that require explicit awareness. Phonological sensitivity is required for early reading acquisition, and fully explicit awareness is facilitated by reading acquisition. Torgesen, Wagner, and their colleagues (Torgesen & Davis, 1996; Torgesen, Wagner, & Rashotte, 1994; Wagner, Torgesen, Laughon, Simmons & Rashotte, 1993) have further refined the notion of fully explicit awareness by focusing our attention on the distinction between phoneme segmentation, which is the ability to analyze words into phoneme-sized units, and phoneme blending, which is the ability to blend letter sounds (cuh-ah-tuh) into words ("cat"). These are two related but separate abilities: for example, both are involved in reading acquisition, both require explicit analysis of phonemes, letter-sound knowledge, and working memory. However, each has a different relationship to lexical access, which is demanded by blending but not segmentation. From this view it should come as no surprise that measures of phoneme awareness are often highly intertwined, and researchers are just beginning to consider the differences between them. Nonetheless, the role of metalinguistic abilities in reading acquisition can still be differentiated from the role of language processing abilities (see, for example, Rohl & Pratt, 1995).

IV. EXPLANATIONS OF THE LANGUAGE PROBLEM AND DIRECTIONS FOR REMEDIATION

Having surveyed some, though certainly not all, of the many findings that link reading difficulty to problems with language skills, we are now in an appropriate place to consider related lines of research that concerns the causes of the language problems that lead to reading problems and the most effective means of remediation. There are both theoretical and practical matters at stake in such research, for if we knew why poor readers are deficient in certain language skills, then we might be able to more effectively diagnose the deficiencies and prevent them if not soften their blow.

A. Hypotheses about the Cause of the Language Problems that Typify Poor Readers

Much of the available literature on the causes of language processing problems is centered on what I will refer to as constitutional causes. These involve factors that are somehow intrinsic to the child, such as brain structure, genetic makeup, and rate of physical development. Problems with phoneme awareness have also been explained in these terms, but it has been more common to attribute a lack of phoneme awareness to a lack of sufficient experience, such as insufficient exposure to instruction in the use of an alphabetic writing system. As representative but by no means exhaustive examples of theories that place the cause of a child's language problems within the child's constitution, I have chosen three theories that need not be taken as mutually exclusive. For example, an account that postulates subtle differences in the brains of poor readers may help to explain why the language development of many poor readers seem delayed, and why they are so resistant to remediation.

1. Constitutional Explanations

One of the first constitutional accounts of reading disability was offered by Orton (1937) in his now famous theory of strephosymbolia. Orton erroneously thought mirror reversals were the predominant symptom of reading disability, and he attributed them to insufficiently developed cerebral dominance. This insufficiency was manifest, according to Orton, in such abnormalities of lateral preference as mixed dominance.

Orton's theory has given rise to considerable research. On the one hand, it has been falsified by findings that reading difficulty is not associated with any particular pattern of handedness, eyedness, or footedness (see Rutter, 1978, for a review). It has also motivated quite a number of studies of cerebral lateralization for language processing among good and poor readers, with mixed results. Some such studies have provided evidence that poor readers show a reversal of the normal anatomical asymmetries between the left and right hemispheres, in conjunction with a lower verbal IQ (Hier, LeMay, Rosenberger, & Perlo, 1978). Others have reported that poor readers may show a lack of cerebral dominance for language processing (see, for example, Keefe & Swinney, 1979; Zurif & Carson, 1970). But there can, at best, be only a weak association between abnormal lateralization and poor reading, since not all of the individuals who display abnormal cerebral lateralization are poor readers (Hier et al., 1978). It must also be recognized that several other studies have failed to find that good and poor readers differ in the extent or direction of the lateralization for language processing (Fennel, Satz, & Morris, 1983; McKeever & van Deventer, 1975).

a. The Geschwind-Behan-Galaburda Cerebral Lateralization Account All in all, the data are not particularly supportive of Orton's thesis about incomplete cerebral dominance as the explanation of reading difficulty. Yet, Orton may still have been correct in the spirit, if not the letter, of his explanation. Given the wealth of evidence that the left hemisphere is the mediator of language processing (in the majority of individuals), and given this chapter's evidence that language processes are deficient among poor readers, then it is reasonable to suppose that some anatomical or neurochemical abnormality of the left hemisphere is involved in early reading difficulty. This is the position taken in the Geschwind, Behan, and Galaburda theory of cerebral lateralization (see Geschwind & Galaburda, 1987), a theoretical account of handedness and cerebral lateralization that, among other things, views developmental dyslexia as a consequence of slowed development of the left hemisphere. The slowed development is postulated to be a consequence of early exposure to the hormone testosterone, which explains the greater instance of reading problems among young boys. Geschwind and Galaburda (1987) offer support for their theory from a variety of sources, including autopsies of the brains of several adult dyslexics and population studies that indicate a certain profile of disabilities (language problems), abilities (spatial skills), and other traits (left handedness, allergies) that distinguish the population of dyslexics from the general population. Some recent evidence, however, challenges this theory. There are claims that the ratio of male-to-female dyslexics is actually quite close to 1:1, and there are claims that handedness, immune disorders, and dyslexia are not always correlated (for reviews, see Bryden, McManus, & Bulman-Flemin, 1994; Feldman, Levin, Fleischman, & Jallard, 1995; Flannery & Liederman, 1995, for a rebuttal, see Hugdahl, 1994).

b. Tallal's Auditory Temporal Processing Account A second neuropsychological account owes to Tallal (1980; Tallal et al., 1996), who regards the phonological difficulties of poor readers as a symptom of an underlying auditory temporal processing deficit. She suggests that an inability to recognize the very short-duration sounds of speech is at the root of some poor readers' phonological difficulties. In her view, the left hemisphere is specialized for the rapid auditory temporal processing that is essential to speech processing and the phonological deficits seen among some dysphasic children and some dyslexic children are due to left-hemisphere-based deficits in auditory temporal processing. For support she draws upon several sources, predominantly upon studies of dysphasic children but also upon some research involving aphasic adults and reading impaired children. She and her colleagues have shown that some spoken-language-impaired children show deficits in performance on discrimination and temporal order judgment of long versus short stimuli separated by long versus short intervals, and in performance in identifying synthetic speech in which the relevant cues involve rapidly changing acoustic spectra (for reviews and a more detailed account, see Farmer & Klein, 1995, and also see Tallal et al., 1996). They have developed a training program that gives experience with "stretched" speech, and this program is reported to improve the language skills of some language-learning-impaired children (Merzenich et al., 1996).

However, Tallal's hypothesis is considerably challenged by the research of Studdert-Kennedy and Mody (see Studdert-Kennedy & Mody, 1995; Mody, Studdert-Kennedy, & Brady, in press). They make several criticisms, each of which is compelling. Perhaps most compelling of all is their study of a group of impaired readers selected on the basis of having made many errors in Tallal's tonal order judgment task. These children showed problems with tonal order judgment, but only when the stimuli were highly similar pairs of syllables. Moreover, although the children had problems with discriminating similar speech sounds (i.e., "ba" and "da") their problems did not extend to nonspeech analogs of the rapidly changing parts of the difficult syllables, nor did they extend to another speech task that involved brief transitional cues. Thus Mody and Studdert-Kennedy conclude that although poor readers have problems with speech perception and with accessing a speech code (as was noted in section III.C), this has nothing to do with auditory temporal processing, in general, so much as with phonological skills. In their view, any constitutional problem is specific to the domain of language and phonological rather than general and auditory.

c. The Maturational Lag Account   Another constitutional explanation regards the language problems of poor readers as the consequence of a maturational lag in development (see, for example, Fletcher et al., 1981) which may be specific to language development (Mann & Liberman, 1984). Maturational lag has been offered to explain a range of problems among poor readers, including their word decoding problems (Stanovich, 1988), their speech perception difficulties (Brandt & Rosen, 1980), their problems with phonetic representation in temporary memory and phoneme awareness (Mann & Liberman, 1984) and their sentence comprehension problems (Byrne, 1981; Mann et al., 1989). Such theories are also providing an interesting account of adolescent learning disability, as well (Wong, Wong, & Blenkinsop, 1989).

Maturational lag theories have the virtue of providing a ready explanation of one of the more common findings in the field, namely, that the performance of poor readers never really deviates from that of good readers, but merely involves more of the kinds of errors typical of slightly younger children (Mann et al., 1989). They are also consistent with the observation that boys encounter reading problems more often than girls, since boys mature less rapidly than girls do. It has been suggested that a slower rate of physical maturation is associated with a pattern of mental abilities in which spatial processing skills are superior to language (Waber, 1977). If so, there should be disproportionately many boys with lesser language skills among children at a given age.

One difficulty with the concept of maturational lag is that it does not explain why only certain language difficulties tend to be found among poor readers. Perhaps the lag is confined to one area of language skill, and I shall have more to say about the identity of this area in the final section of this paper. Another problem with maturational lag is that the language processing difficulties of poor readers often persist beyond early childhood to adolescence (McKeever and van Deventer, 1975) and beyond (Feldman et al., 1995; Jackson and McClelland, 1979; Scarborough, 1984). That is, the language processing skills of poor readers may never really "catch up" to those of good readers (Elbro, 1996). Perhaps the concept of a lag in development will need to be refined to allow for the possibility that language development in poor readers is not only delayed but also reaches a premature plateau. In this regard it is interesting to note the results of a recent longitudinal study of children with reading disabilities (Francis, Shaywitz, Steubing, & Shaywitz, 1996) in which the analysis centered on the age and level at which reading scores plateaued. The reading-disabled children resembled normal children in the age at which they plateaued, they simply plateaued at a lower level. This lower level implies some type of deficit above and beyond a maturational lag.

2. Experiential Factors

Rutter and Madge (1976) have noted that poor reading and low verbal intelligence tend to associate with low socioeconomic status and large family size. In discussing their findings about "cycles of disadvantage," these investigators note that both genetic and environmental influences are to be held responsible. Let us now turn to some of the evidence that the environment can play an important role in the language skills that are important to reading. The language environment must surely be important to the child's development of speech perception, vocabulary, working memory, and so on, as well as in the development of an awareness of phonemes. To date, there is virtually no research on whether poor readers' deficient language processing skills are the consequence of insufficient language experience. However, there is a wealth of evidence about the role of experience in the development of phoneme awareness (see Morais, 1991, for a review).

In considering the role of the environment in the development of phoneme awareness, let us first return to the spurt in phoneme awareness that occurs at age 6 (Liberman et al., 1974). Why should such a spurt occur? Phoneme awareness is a cognitive skill of sorts, and, as such, must surely demand a certain degree of intellectual maturity. Yet, 6 is the age at which most children in America begin to receive instruction in reading and writing, and there is reason to suspect that not only may phoneme awareness be important for the acquisition of reading, being taught to read may at the same time help to develop phoneme awareness (see, for example, Alegria, Pignot, & Morais, 1982; Liberman et al., 1980; Morais, Carey, Alegria, & Berenson, 1979).

One source of evidence that phoneme awareness depends upon instruction comes from studies of illiterate adults. Such adults appear unable to manipulate the phonetic structure of spoken words (Morais et al., 1979). Other evidence comes from studies of children receiving different types of reading instruction. In Belgium, first graders taught largely by a phonics method did spectacularly better on a task requiring phoneme segmentation than did first graders taught by a largely whole-word method (Alegria et al., 1982). Still other evidence comes from training studies (see section B.2), which improve phoneme awareness by an average of one standard deviation (see Torgesen & Davis, 1996). It would seem that awareness of phonemes can be lacking when there has been no formal reading instruction, and that it is enhanced by methods of reading instruction that direct the child's attention to the phonetic structure of words, and it may even depend on such instruction.

However, experience alone cannot be the only factor behind some children's failure to achieve phoneme awareness. This is aptly shown by a finding that among a group of six-year-old skilled readers and 10-year-old disabled readers who were matched for reading ability, the disabled readers performed significantly worse on a phoneme awareness task, even though they would be expected to have had more reading instruction than the younger children (Bradley & Bryant, 1978). Likewise, in other research on phoneme awareness, between one-quarter and one-third of subjects have failed to benefit from explicit training (Lundberg, 1988; Torgesen & Davis, 1996). Here it could be argued that a constitutional factor, such as a basic problem with language skill or a problem with phonological processes, limits the attainment of phonological sophistication. Pennington and his colleagues (Pennington, Van Orden, Kirson, & Haith, 1991) have offered some new and interesting evidence that deficient phoneme awareness is the primary trait of individuals who are familial dyslexics. As we shall see shortly, Torgesen and Davis (1996) offer evidence that the ability to spell nonwords, along with general verbal ability and the ability to rapidly access phonological representations are significant predictors of kindergarten children's ability to profit from training in blending and segmentation.

B. Practical Applications: Predicting and Remediating the Language Problems behind Reading Problems

The research surveyed by this chapter will probably become most interesting to those directly concerned with learning-disabled children when I approach the problem of how to predict reading problems, and how to decrease their severity if not prevent them altogether. Some excellent research has actually addressed the link between basic research and practical application, and some representative findings are summarized next.

1. Predicting Reading Problems

One of the practical benefits of research that has asked whether language problems are the cause or consequence of reading problems concerns screening devices for identifying children at risk for early reading problems. Such phonological processing skills as the ability to rapidly access the names of objects and the ability to make effective use of phonetic representation in working memory have been shown to be effective kindergarten predictors of first-grade reading success and beyond (see, for example, Blachman, 1984; Mann & Liberman, 1984; Mann, 1984; Mann & Ditunno, 1990; Rohl & Pratt, 1995). But by far and away the most successful predictors of future reading ability are measures of phonological awareness. There is a variety of evidence that various tests of phoneme awareness can predict the future reading ability of kindergarten children (Stanovich, Cunningham, & Cramer, 1984; Stanovich, Cunningham, & Feeman, 1984; for a recent review, see Torgesen & Davis, 1996). We and others have obtained evidence that tests of phoneme and syllable awareness are consistently better predictors of reading ability than tests of language processing (Mann & Ditunno, 1990; Rohl & Pratt, 1995; Torgesen, Wagner, & Rashotte, 1994; Yopp, 1988).

A variety of different measures of phoneme awareness have been used to predict future reading ability, including similarity judgments and oddity judgments, counting tests, and so on. My students and I have had some success in developing an invented spelling test in which we ask preliterate children to try to write some familiar words. As first noted by Read (1986), preliterate children's spellings are quite unconventional, but show considerable creativity and considerable awareness of the fact that words can be broken down into smaller phonological units. When we score those responses in terms of their ability to capture the sound of the word the child is trying to spell, we find this score to be a very successful kindergarten predictor of first-grade reading ability (for discussion of the test, see Mann, Tobin, & Wilson, 1987; Mann & Ditunno, 1990; Mann, 1993; Torgesen & Davis, 1996). The final decisions about which type of test to use may depend upon the age of the children. There is some evidence from the research of Torgesen and his colleagues (Torgesen et al., 1994) that the phoneme awareness skills that predict success in the first grade may differ from those that predict success in the second grade. Their research shows that among kindergartners, phoneme analysis (i.e., the ability to identify the phonemes within words) has the strongest causal relation to first-grade reading ability. Among first graders, however, phoneme synthesis (i.e., the ability to blend separately presented phonemic segments into a word) has the strongest causal relation to second-grade reading ability.

Although there are age-related differences in the skills that relate to reading ability, and hence in the type of test that should be included in a screening battery, there is also considerable stability of individual differences in phonological awareness. These differences appear to be enduring characteristics of individual children, at least in the elementary grades, and sadly enough, enduring problems with phonological awareness are a trait of children with reading problems.

2. Remediating Language Problems

Just as the prospects were brightest for using phoneme awareness in order to predict future reading problems, the brightest prospects for remediation of language problems are offered by research that has shown that various types of training can facilitate phoneme awareness. Some very interesting and very practical advice is available on how to facilitate phoneme awareness and have it promote reading (Bradley & Bryant, 1985; Blachman, 1984, 1989; Blachman, Ball, Black, & Tangel, 1994; Cunningham, 1990; Goswami & Bryant, 1990; Liberman, 1982; Liberman, Shankweiler, Blachman, Camp, & Werfelman, 1980; Liberman, 1982; Torgesen & Davis, 1996). I will briefly summarize some of that research and its implications; what is particularly noteworthy is its inclusion of children that have historically low achievement in reading (from low income, inner-city classrooms, etc.).

Blachman and her colleagues (see, for example, Blachman, 1984, 1989; Blachman, Ball, Black, & Tangel, 1994) have been developing some very clever ways of promoting phoneme awareness. Teachers of preschool children as young as 3 years will find that Blachman makes some interesting observations about how word play with nursery rhymes can help to promote phoneme awareness. Kindergarten and first-grade teachers and reading specialists will be interested in the variety of tasks that Blachman uses to promote phoneme awareness and ultimately link it to reading. One that I find particularly appealing is a progressive series of "say-it-and-move-it" segmentation activities. In this series, the children learn to use disks to represent each of the phonemes in a word and ultimately learn to connect the sound segments represented by the disks to the letters of the alphabet. An 11-week course of training in this test, coupled with training in other segmentation-related activities and in letter name and letter sounds yielded significant improvements on kindergarten reading and spelling measures in low-income, inner-city classrooms (Blachman et al., 1994).

That we should pay attention not only to the activities but also to the type of instruction that we use is the very important point made by Cunningham and illustrated in one of her most recent studies (Cunningham, 1990). In her view, activities that encourage phoneme awareness will be the most beneficial to reading when the children learn how these activities are beneficial to reading. The validity of this view is illustrated with a study in which Cunningham compared two groups of kindergarten and first-grade children who were taught phoneme segmentation and blending tasks. Relative to children who did not learn such tasks, the children who received a "skill and drill" approach to learning had some advantage in learning to read. However, the greatest advantage was seen when children received a method of instruction that helped them to appreciate the value, application, and utility of phoneme awareness to reading. On the flipside of this, Ball and Blachman (1988) report that teaching letters and letter sounds to preschoolers was much less efficient than teaching letters and sounds in combination with phoneme segmentation.

A third area of particular importance to remedial efforts involves some very recent research by Torgesen and Davis (1996), who have united the study of kindergarten screening and preschool training. Their study asks which skills might best predict kindergartners' responses to a 12-week course of training in phonological awareness (four 20-minute sessions per week). Their pretraining measures examined measures of language processing, phoneme awareness, nonword reading and nonword spelling; their training involved game-like procedures to improve both phoneme analysis/segmentation and synthesis. Approximately 26% of the posttraining improvement in segmentation was predicted by two variables: performance on Stanford-Binet vocabulary and performance on a version of the invented spelling test mentioned in the previous section. Almost 100% of the posttraining improvement in blending was predicted by performance on the same invented spelling test and a test that required rapid access to phonological representations (i.e., rapid naming of digits).

Several things are underscored by Torgesen and Davis's research. First of all, segmentation and blending should be thought of as separate but correlated abilities, and both deserve separate screening and remediation efforts. Second, there are certain children who have less well-developed phoneme awareness skills, who are less efficient in accessing phonological representations, and who lack knowledge of the letter names and sounds. Third, the children who are deficient in these language skills are particularly resilient to the benefits of training. Torgesen and Davis suggest that these children may profit from longer, more explicit, and more intensive training procedures than the 8–12-week courses typically found in the literature (Torgesen & Davis, 1996).

V. SUMMARY AND CONCLUDING REMARKS

This chapter has proceeded from a consideration of the importance of certain language skills to reading, to a survey of evidence that links problems with these language skills to early reading disability, to a consideration of some plausible origins of these problems. By way of conclusion, I first offer a generalization about the type of language problems that cause dyslexia and reading problems more generally and then speculate about the prospects for the future prediction and remediation of reading problems.

A. The Phonological Core Deficit: A Language-Oriented Perspective on Reading Problems

This survey of the literature on the relation between language processing skills and reading problems indicates that poor readers—and children who are likely to become poor readers—tend to have problems with phoneme awareness and also with three aspects of language processing skill: (a) speech perception under difficult listening conditions, (b) vocabulary, especially when vocabulary is measured in terms of naming ability, and (c) using a phonetic representation in working memory. There is a logical interrelation between these difficulties, for they all involve phonological processes that concern the sound pattern of language. Hence we may speculate that the cause of many instances of reading disability is some problem within the phonological system, something that has been referred to as the "phonological core deficit" (see Stanovich, 1988, see also Mann, 1986, and Elbro, 1996, for other theories that postulate a phonological basis to the problem).

In this chapter the emphasis has been on the language problems of reading-disabled children, in general, and there has been no attempt to differentiate between dyslexic children and so-called garden variety poor readers. That is because there seems to be no sound reason for distinguishing the two groups; recent reviews have seriously discredited the use of a discrepancy between IQ and reading ability as a definitive characteristic that sets dyslexic children and their difficulties apart from other poor readers and their difficulties (see Fletcher, Francis, Rourke, Shaywitz, & Shaywitz, 1992; Francis et al., 1996). From the perspective of present research, the two groups of children seem to form a continuous distribution, both have problems with the phonological skills of primary interest in this paper, and the phonological core deficit seems just as characteristic of dyslexic children as of "garden variety" poor readers (see Stanovich, 1988 and also, Shankweiler et al., 1995). To date, receptive vocabulary is the only language measure that has distinguished the two groups of children (which may account for the lack of consensus about the role of receptive vocabulary problems in reading, as discussed in section III.C.2). All other differences between dyslexic and garden-variety poor readers seem to involve real-world knowledge and strategic abilities: The dyslexic children possess superior skills in these nonlinguistic areas, hence the discrepancy between their IQ and their reading ability, whereas the garden variety poor readers may show a developmental delay in these skills as well as in their phonological ones (see Stanovich, 1988, and Stanovich & Siegal, 1994).

If we accept the lack of distinction between dyslexic children and other poor readers, we can turn to a more and more accurate description of the phonological core deficit and its role in the reading problems of different groups of children. Elbro (1996) hypothesizes that the problem of poor readers may lie in a lack of distinctiveness between phonological representations in the mental lexicon, and he discussed various ways in which this hypothesis might be tested. Although an appreciably large-scaled study of nearly 1500 children has supported the phonological core deficit model (Siegel, 1993), there may ultimately be different problems or different clusters of problems for different children. In this regard it is interesting to remember Pennington and his colleagues' observation that the language problems of familial adult dyslexics tend to be restricted to phoneme awareness, whereas nonfamilial dyslexics demonstrate problems with phonetic representation in working memory as well as problems with phoneme awareness (Pennington et al., 1991).

There is also the question of whether the phonological core deficit account can accommodate all of the many findings about poor readers. Some recent evidence about poor readers' problems with morphological aspects of language, for example, suggests that both phonology and morphology are deficient. In fact, morphological problems may become an important variable above and beyond the well-attested problems with phoneme awareness, once we consider children in the later elementary grades (Singson, Mahony, & Mann, in press).

B. Practical Applications and Implications for Future Research

As we come closer and closer to identifying the linguistic problems associated with specific reading difficulty we also come closer to more effective treatment of those problems. For example, if a developmental delay in language development is the cause of reading difficulty, then perhaps we should attempt to identify children at risk for such a delay, and consider delaying beginning reading instruction until a point in time when those children have language skills that are more optimal. Yet we would not want to delay all of education—math, geography, etc.—for it is far from clear that poor readers, especially dyslexic ones, are deficient in those areas of development that support the ability to learn other types of curriculum (see Mann et al., 1989; Stanovich, 1988).

Current evidence suggests that both phonological processing and phoneme awareness play a causative role in reading ability. As noted earlier, there have been almost no attempts to discover ways of remediating deficient phonological processing skills. We might want to consider researching the possibility that certain types of environmental enrichment can decrease the extent of these children's language processing problems, and pursue research to that effect. Fortunately, there are quite bright prospects for remediation of deficient phoneme awareness. As we have seen, there is a diverse body of research that has shown that various types of training can facilitate phoneme awareness. Elsewhere my colleagues and I and others have suggested that the best favor we can do for all children is to use such training procedures that promote phoneme awareness so that we may impart the secrets of the alphabetic principle as early as possible (Ball & Blachman, 1988; Liberman, 1982; Liberman & Mann, 1980; Mann, 1986). Some very interesting and very practical advice on how to facilitate phoneme awareness is currently available from the work summarized in section IV.B.2. Researchers have developed a variety of word games, nursery rhymes, and other prereading activities that encourage the child's awareness of the way in which words break down into phonemes, some of these are even becoming available in the form of computer programs. Now that such methods are available, we may turn to the question of how best to increase the phoneme awareness of those 20–30% of children who have failed to profit from the training studies of the past.

A final implication of the information reviewed in this chapter concerns the type of instructional program that is most optimal for all children, good and poor readers alike. Had we shown that some general language ability is the primary determinant of reading ability vs. disability, then "whole-language" approaches to literacy, with their emphases on meaning and language experience rather than on skills development, would seem appropriate. The evidence, however, suggests that phonological aspects of language are the more important source of variance, and phoneme awareness is particularly important. This would argue for a preschool and early literacy environment that emphasizes the sounds of language and fosters training in phoneme awareness. In short, the use of phonics-oriented methods of instruction is most clearly favored by research on reading (see Adams, 1990; Chall, 1979; Chaney, 1990).

Acknowledgments

The author gratefully acknowledges the help of Maria Singson and Diane Zimmerle Schonberg for their helpful comments on earlier drafts and for their help in finding appropriate references. This chapter was prepared while the author was on leave at the University of Venice.

References

Adams, M. J. (1990). *Beginning to read: thinking and learning about print.* Cambridge, MA: M.I.T. Press.

Alegria, J., Pignot, E., & Morais, J. (1982). Phonetic analysis of speech and memory codes in beginning readers. *Child Development, 10,* 451–456.

Alegria, J., & Pignot, E. (1979). Genetic aspects of verbal mediation in memory. *Memory and Cognition, 50,* 235–238.

Baddeley, A. D. (1978). The trouble with levels: A Reexamination of Craik and Lockhardt's framework for memory research. *Psychological Review, 85,* 139–152.

Ball, E. W., & Blachman, B. A. (1988). Phoneme segmentation training: Effect of reading readiness. *Annals of Dyslexia, 38,* 208–225.

Benton, A. (1975). *Developmental dyslexia: Neurological aspects.* In W. J. Freelander (Ed.), *Advances in neurology*: Volume 7. (pp. 1–47) New York: Raven Press.

Berent, I., & Perfetti, C. A. (1995). A rose is a REEZ: The two-cycles model of phonology assembly in reading English. *Psychological Review, 102,* 146–184.

Birch, H. G., & Belmont, L. (1964). Auditory-visual interpretation in normal and retarded readers. *American Journal Ortho Psychology, 34,* 852–861.

Blachman, B. (1984). Relationship of rapid naming and language analysis skills to kindergarten and first-grade reading achievement. *Journal of Educational Psychology, 76,* 610–622.

Blachman, B. (1989). Phonological awareness and word recognition: Assessment and intervention. In A. G. Kamhi & H. W. Watts (Eds.), *Reading disabilities: A developmental language perspective* (pp. 133–158). Boston, MA: College Hill.

Blachman, B. A., Ball, E. W., Black, R. S., & Tangel, D. M. (1994). Kindergarten teachers develop phoneme awareness in low-income, inner-city schools. *Reading and Writing, 6,* 1–18.

Blumsack, J., Lewandowski, L., & Waterman, B. (1997). Neurodevelopmental precursors to learning disabilities: A preliminary report from a parent survey. *Journal of Learning Disabilities, 30,* 228–237.

Bowers, P. G., & Wolf, M. (1993). Theoretical links among naming speed, precise timing mechanisms and orthographic skills in dyslexia, *Reading and Writing, 5,* 69–85.

Bradley, L., & Bryant, P. (1985). *Rhyme and reason in reading and spelling.* Ann Arbor: University of Michigan Press.

Bradley, L., & Bryant, P. E. (1978). Difficulties in auditory organization as a possible cause of reading backwards. *Nature, 271,* 746–747.

Brady, S., Mann, V., and Schmidt, R. (1987). Errors in short-term memory for good and poor readers. *Memory & Cognition, 15,* 444–453.

Brady, S., & Shankweiler, D. (1991). *Phonological processes in literacy.* Hillsdale, NJ: Erlbaum.

Brady, S., Shankweiler, D., & Mann, V. (1983). Speech perception and memory coding in relation to reading ability. *Journal of Experimental Child Psychology, 35,* 345–367.

Brandt, J., & Rosen, J. J. (1980). Auditory phonemic perception in dyslexia: Categorical identification and discrimination of stop consonants. *Brain and Language, 9,* 324–337.

Bryden, M. P., McManus, I. C., & Bulman-Flemin, M. B. (1994). Evaluating the empirical support for the Geschwind-Behan-Galaburda model of cerebral lateralization. *Brain and Cognition, 26,* 103–167.

Byrne, B., & Shea, P. (1979). Semantic and phonetic memory in beginning readers. *Memory and Cognition, 7,* 333–338.

Carlisle, J. F., & Nomanbhoy, D. M. (1993). Phonological and morphological awareness in first graders. *Applied Psycholinguistics, 14,* 177–195.

Carr, T. H. (1981). Building theories of reading ability: On the relation between individual differences in cognitive skills and reading comprehension. *Cognition, 9,* 73–114.

Chall, J. (1979). The great debate: Ten years later with a modest proposal for reading stages. In L. Resnick & P. Weaver (Eds.), *Theory and practice of early reading* (Vol. 1, pp. 29–55). Hillsdale, NJ: Erlbaum.

Chaney, C. (1990). Evaluating the whole language approach to language arts: The pros and cons. *Language, Speech and Hearing Services in Schools, 21,* 244–249.

Chomsky, N. (1964) Cor (Ed.) *Comments for project literacy meeting.* Project Literacy Report *No. 2* (pp. 1–8). Reprinted in M. Lester, *Transformational Grammar.* New York: Holt Rinehardt and Winston.

Conrad, R. (1964). Acoustic confusions in immediate memory. *British Journal of Psychology, 55,* 75–84.

Conrad, R. (1972). Speech and reading. In J. F. Kavanagh & I. G. Mattingly (Eds.), *Language by ear and by eye: The relationships between speech and reading.* Cambridge, MA: MIT Press.

Corkin, S. (1974). Serial-order deficits in inferior readers. *Cortex, 12,* 347–354.

Cunningham, A. E. (1990). Explicit versus implicit instruction in phoneme awareness. *Journal of Experimental Child Psychology, 50,* 429–444.

Curtis, M. E. (1980). Development of components of reading skill. *Journal of Educational Psychology, 72,* 656–669.

Daneman, M., & Carpenter, P. A. (1980). Individual differences in working memory and reading. *Journal of Verbal Learning and Verbal Behavior, 19,* 450–466.

Daneman, M., & Case, R. (1981). Syntactic form, semantic complexity and short-term memory: Influences on children's acquisition of new linguistic structures. *Developmental Psychology, 17,* 367–378.

Denckla, M. B., & Rudel, R. G. (1976). Naming of object drawings by dyslexic and other learning-disabled children. *Brain and Language, 3,* 1–15.

Eimas, P. D. (1975). Distinctive feature codes in the short-term memory of children. *Journal of Experimental Child Psychology, 19,* 241–251.

Elbro, C. (1996). Early linguistic abilities and reading development: A review and a hypothesis. *Reading and Writing, 8,* 453–485.

Elbro, C. (1989). *Morphological awareness in dyslexia.* Unpublished manuscript, University of Copenhagen, Institute for General and Applied Linguistics, Copenhagen.

Fawcett, A. J., & Nicolson, R. I. (1994). Naming speed in children with dyslexia. *Journal of Learning Disabilities, 27,* 641–646.

Feldman, E., Levin, B. E., Fleischmann, J., Jallard, B. (1995). Gender differences in the severity of adult familial dyslexia. *Reading and Writing, 7,* 155–161.

Fennell, E. B., Satz, P., & Morris, R. (1983). The development of handedness and dichotic ear asymmetries in relation to school achievement: A longitudinal study. *Journal of Experimental Child Psychology, 35,* 248–262.

Fisher, F. W., Liberman, I. Y., & Shankweiler, D. (1977). Reading reversals and developmental dyslexia: A further study. *Cortex, 14,* 496–510.

Flannery, K. A., & Liederman, J. (1995). Is there really a syndrome involving the co-occurrence of neurodevelopmental disorder, talent, non-righthandedness and immune disorder among children? *Cortex, 31,* 503–515.

Fletcher, J. M., Satz, P., & Scholes, R. (1981). Developmental changes in the linguistic performance correlates of reading achievements. *Brain and Language, 13,* 78–90.

Fletcher, J. M., Francis, D. J., Rourke, B. J., Shaywitz, S. E., & Shaywitz, B. A. (1992). The validity of discrepancy-based definitions of reading disabilities. *Journal of Learning Disabilities, 25,* 555–561.

Fox, B., & Routh, D. K. (1976). Phonemic analysis and synthesis as word-attack skills. *Journal of Educational Psychology, 69,* 70–74.

Francis, D. J., Shaywitz, S. E., Stuebing, K. K., Shaywitz, B. A., et al. (1996). Developmental lag versus deficit accounts of reading disability: A longitudinal, individual growth curves analysis. *Journal of Educational Psychology, 88,* 3–17.

Geschwind, N., & Galaburda, A. M. (1987). *Cerebral lateralization.* Cambridge, MA: Bradford Books.

Gibson, E. J., Gibson, J. J., Pick, A. D., & Osser, R. (1962). A developmental study of the discrimination of letter-like forms. *Journal of Comparative and Physiological Psychology, 55,* 897–906.

Godfrey, J. L., Syrdal-Lasky, A. K., Millay, K. K., & Knox, C. M. (1981). Performance of dyslexic children on speech perception tasks. *Journal of Experimental Child Psychology, 32,* 401–424.

Goetzinger, C., Dirks, D., & Baer, C. J. (1960). Auditory discrimination and visual perception in good and poor readers. *Annals of Otology, Rhinology and Laryngology, 69,* 121–136.

Goldman, S. R. (1976). Reading skill and the Minimum Distance Principle: A comparison of listening and reading comprehension. *Journal of Experimental Child Psychology, 22,* 123–142.

Goswami, V., & Bryant, P. (1990). *Phonological Skills and Learning to Read,* East Sussex: Lawrence Erlbaum Asoc., Ltd.

Gottardo, A., Stanovich, K. E., & Siegel, L. S. (1996). The relationships between phonological sensitivity, syntactic processing and verbal working memory in the reading performance of third-grade children. *Journal of Experimental Child Psychology, 63,* 563–582.

Hier, D., LeMay, M., Rosenberger, P., & Perlo, V. (1978). Developmental dyslexia. *Archives of Neurology, 35,* 90–92.

Hugdahl, K. (1994). The Search continues: Causal relationships among dyslexia, anomalous dominance and immune functions. *Brain and Cognition, 26,* 267–285.

Hung, D. L., & Tzeng, O. J. L. (1981). Orthographic variations and visual information processing. *Psychological Bulletin, 90*, 377–414.

Ingram, T. T. S., Mason, A. W., & Blackburn, I. (1970). A retrospective study of 82 children with reading disability. *Developmental Medicine and Child Neurology, 12*, 271–281.

Jackson, M., & McClelland, J. L. (1979). Processing determinants of reading speed. *Journal of Experimental Psychology: General, 108*, 151–181.

Jorm, A. F. (1979). The cognitive and neurological basis of developmental dyslexia: A theoretical framework and review. *Cognition, 7*, 19–33.

Katz, R. B. (1986). Phonological deficiencies in children with reading disability: Evidence from an object naming task. *Cognition, 22*, 225–257.

Katz, R. B., Shankweiler, D., & Liberman, I. Y. (1981). Memory for item order and phonetic recoding in the beginning reader. *Journal of Experimental Child Psychology, 32*, 474–484.

Keefe, B., & Swinney, D. (1979). On the role of hemispheric specialization in developmental dyslexia. *Cortex, 15*, 471–481.

Kleiman, G. (1975). Speech recoding in reading. *Journal of Verbal Learning and Verbal Behavior, 14*, 323–339.

Leong, C. K. (1989). Productive knowledge of derivational rules in poor raeders. *Annals of Dyslexia, 39*, 94–111.

Leong, C. K., & Tamaoka, K. (1995). Use of phonological information in processing Kanji and Katakana by skilled and less skilled Japanese readers. *Reading and Writing, 7*, 377–393.

Levy, B. A. (1977). Reading: Speech and meaning processes. *Journal of Verbal Learning and Verbal Behavior, 16*, 623–638.

Liberman, A. M. (1982). On finding that speech is special *American Psychologist, 37*, 148–167.

Liberman, A. M., Cooper, F. S., Shankweiler, D., & Studdert-Kennedy, M. (1967). Perception of the speech code. *Psychology Review, 74*, 431–461.

Liberman, I. Y. (1982). A Language-oriented view of reading and its disabilities. In H. Mykelburst (Ed.), *Progress in learning disabilities*, Vol. 5 (pp. 81–101). New York: Grune and Stratton.

Liberman, I. Y., Liberman, A. M., Mattingly, I. G., & Shankweiler, D. (1980). Orthography and the beginning reader. In J. Kavanagh & R. Venezky (Eds.), *Orthography, Reading and Dyslexia*. Baltimore: University Park Press.

Liberman, I. Y., Mann, V. A., Shankweiler, D., & Werfelman, M. (1982). Children's memory for recurring linguistic and non-linguistic material in relation to reading ability. *Cortex, 18*, 367–375.

Liberman, I. Y., & Mann, V. A. (1980). Should reading remediation vary with the sex of the child? In A. Ansara, N. Geschwind, A. Galaburda, N. Albert, & N. Gartrell (Eds.), *Sex differences in dyslexia* (pp. 151–168). Towson, MD: The Orton Society.

Liberman, I. Y., Shankweiler, D., Blachman, B., Camp, L., & Werfelman, M. (1980). Steps towards literacy. Report prepared for Working Group on Learning Failure and Unused Learning Potential. President's Commission on Mental Health, Nov. 1, 1977. In P. Levinson & C. H. Sloan (Eds.), *Auditory processing and language: Clinical and research perspectives* (pp. 189–215). New York: Grune & Stratton.

Liberman, I. Y., Shankweiler, D., Fisher, F. W., & Carter, B. (1974). Explicit syllable and phoneme segmentation in the young child. *Journal of Experimental Child Psychology, 18,* 201–212.

Liberman, I. Y., Shankweiler, D., Liberman, A. M., Fowler, C., & Fisher, F. W. (1977). Phonetic segmentation and recoding in the beginning reader. In A. S. Reber & D. Scarborough (Eds.), *Towards a psychology of reading: The proceedings of the CUNY Conference* (pp. 207–226). Hillsdale, NJ: Lawrence Earlbaum Associates.

Lundberg, I., Oloffson, A., & Wall, S. (1980). Reading and spelling skills in the first school years predicated from phoneme awareness skills in kindergarten. *Scandinavian Journal of Psychology, 21,* 159–173.

Lundberg, I. (1988). Preschool prevention of reading failure: Does training in phonological awareness work? In R. L. Masland & M. W. Masland (Eds.), *Prevention of reading failure* (pp. 163–176). Parkton, MD: York Press.

Mahony, D. L. (1994). Using sensitivity to word structure to explain variance in high school and college level reading ability. *Reading and Writing, 6,* 19–44.

Mann, V. A. (1984). Longitudinal prediction and prevention of early reading difficulty. *Annals of Dyslexia, 34,* 117–136.

Mann, V. A. (1993). Phoneme awareness and future reading ability. *Journal of Learning Disabilities, 26,* 259–269.

Mann, V. A. (1986). Why some children encounter reading problems: The contribution of difficulties with language processing and linguistic sophistication to early reading disability. In J. K. Torgesen & B. Y. Wong (Eds.), *Psychological and Educational Perspectives on Learning Disabilities* (pp. 133–159). New York: Academic Press.

Mann, V. A., & Brady, S. (1988). Reading disability: The role of language deficiencies. *Journal of Consulting and Clinical Psychology, 56,* 811–816.

Mann, V. A., & Ditunno, P. (1990). Phonological deficiencies: Effective predictors of reading problems. In G. Pavlides (Ed.), *Dyslexia: Neurophysiological and learning perspectives* (pp. 105–131). Wiley & Sons: New York.

Mann, V. A., Cowin, E., & Shoenheimer, J. (1989). Phonological processing, language comprehension and reading ability. *Journal of Learning Disabilities, 22,* 76–89.

Mann, V. A., & Liberman, I. Y. (1984). Phonological awareness and verbal short-term memory: Can they presage early reading success? *Journal of Learning Disabilities, 17,* 592–598.

Mann, V. A., Liberman, I. Y., & Shankweiler, D. (1980). Children's memory for sentences and word strings in relation to reading ability. *Journal of Experimental Child Psychology, 8,* 329–335.

Mann, V. A., Shankweiler, D., & Smith, S. T. (1985). The association between comprehension of spoken sentences and early reading ability: The role of phonetic representation. *Journal of Child Language, 11,* 627–643.

Mann, V. A., Tobin, P., & Wilson, R. (1987). Measuring phonological awareness through the inverted spellings of kindergarten children. *Merrill-Palmer-Quarterly, 33,* 365–396.

Mason, W. (1976). Specific (developmental) dyslexia. *Developmental Medicine and Child Neurology, 9,* 183–190.

Mattingly, I. G. (1972). Reading, the linguistic process, and linguistic awareness. In J. F. Kavanagh & I. G. Mattingly (Eds.), *Language by ear and by eye: The relationship between speech and reading* (pp. 133–148). Cambridge, MA: MIT Press.

McKeever, W. F., & van Deventer, A. D. (1975). Dyslexic adolescents: Evidence of impaired visual and auditory language processing associated with normal lateralization and visual responsivity, *Cortex, 11,* 361–378.

Merzenich, M. M., Jenkins, W. M., Johnston, P., Schreider, C., Miller, S. L., & Tallal, P. (1996). Temporal processing deficits of language-learning impaired children ameliorated by training. *Science, 271,* 77–80.

Miller, J. L., & Eimas, P. D. (1983). Studies on the categorization of speech by infants. *Cognition, 13,* 135–166.

Mody, M., Studdert- Kennedy, M., & Brady, S. (in press). Speech perception deficits in poor readers: Auditory processing or phonological coding? *Journal of Experimental Child Psychology.*

Money, J. (1973). Turner's syndrome and parietal lobe functions. *Cortex, 9,* 387–393.

Morais, J. (1991). Constraints on the development of phonological awareness. In S. Brady and D. Shankweiler (Eds.) *Phonological Processes in Literacy.* Hillsdale, NJ: Erlbaum.

Morais, J., Cary, L., Alegria, J., & Berenson, P. (1979). Does awareness of speech as a sequence of phonemes arise spontaneously? *Cognition, 7,* 323–331.

Morrison, F. J., Giordani, B., & Nagy, J. (1977). Reading disability: An information processing analysis. *Science, 196,* 77–79.

Moskowitz, B. A. (1973). On the status of vowel shift in English. In T. Moore (Ed.), *Cognitive development and acquisition of language* (pp. 223–260). New York: Academic Press.

Orton, S. T. (1937). *Reading, writing and speech problems in children.* New York: Norton.

Pennington, B. F., Van Orden, G., Kirson, D., & Haith, M. (1991). What is the causal relation between verbal STM problems and dyslexia? In S. A. Brady & D. P. Shankweiler (Eds.), *Phonological processing skills in literacy* (pp. 173–186). Hillsdale, NJ: Erlbaum.

Perfetti, C. A. (1985). *Reading skill.* Hillsdale, NJ: Erlbaum.

Perfetti, C. A., & McCutchen, D. (1982). Speech processes inreading. Speech and Lanauge: *Advances in Basic Research and Practice, 7,* 237–269.

Rayner K., Sereno, S. C., Lesch, M. F., & Pollatsek, A. (1995). Phonological codes are automatically activated during reading: Evidence from an Eye Movement Priming Paradigm. *Psychological Science, 6,* 26–32.

Read, C. (1986). *Children's Creative spelling.* London: Routledge & Kegan Paul.

Robinson, M. E., & Schwartz, L. B. (1973). Visuomotor skills and reading ability: A longitudinal study. *Developmental Medicine and Child Neurology, 15,* 280–286.

Rohl, M., & Pratt, C. (1995). Phonological awareness, verbal working memory and the acquisition of literacy. *Reading and Writing, 7,* 327–360.

Russell, G. (1982). Impairment of phonetic reading in dyslexia and its persistence beyond childhood—research note. *Journal of Child Psychology and Child Psychiatry, 23,* 459–475.

Rutter, M. (1978). Prevalence and types of dyslexia. In A. L. Benton & D. Pearl (Eds.), *Dyslexia: An appraisal of current knowledge* (pp. 3–28). New York: Oxford Press.

Rutter, M., & Madge, N. (1976). *Cycles of disadvantage: A review of research.* London: Heinemann Educational.

Rutter, M., & Yule, W. (1973). The concept of specific reading retardation. *Journal of Child Psychiatry, 16,* 181–198.

Scarborough, H. S. (1984). Continuity between childhood dyslexia and adult reading. *British Journal of Psychology, 75,* 329–348.

Seidenberg, M. S. (1985). The time course of phonological activation in two writing systems. *Cognition, 19,* 1–30.

Shankweiler, D., Crain, S., Katz, L., Fowler, A. E., Liberman, A. E., Brady, S. A., Thornton, R., Lundquist, E., Dreyer, L., Fletcher, J. M., Stuebing, K. K., Shaywitz, S. E., & Shaywitz, B. A. (1995). Cognitive profiles of reading-disabled children: Comparisons of language skills in phonology, morphology and syntax. *Psychological Science, 6,* 149–156.

Shankweiler, D., & Liberman, I. Y. (1972). Misreading: A search for the causes. In J. F. Kavanagh & I. G. Mattingly (Eds.), *Language by ear and by eye: The relationships between speech and reading* (pp. 293–318). Cambridge, MA: MIT Press.

Shankweiler, D., Liberman, I. Y., Mark, L. S., Fowler, C. A., & Fisher, F. W. (1979). The speech code and learning to read. *Journal of Experimental Psychology: Human Perception and Performance, 5,* 531–545.

Siegel, L. S. (1993). Phonological processing deficits as the basis of a reading disability. *Developmental Review, 13,* 246–257.

Simpson, G. B., Lorsbach, T. C., & Whitehouse, D. (1983). Encoding and contextual components of word recognition in good and poor readers. *Journal of Experimental Child Psychology, 35,* 161–171.

Singson, M., Mahony, D., & Mann, V. (in press). The relation between reading ability and morphological skills: Evidence from derivational suffixes. *Reading and Writing.*

Slowiaczek, M. L., & Clifton, C. (1980). Subvocalization and reading for meaning. *Journal of Verbal Learning and Verbal Behavior, 19,* 573–582.

Smith, S. T., Macaruso, P., Shankweiler, D., & Crain, S. (1989). Syntactic comprehension in young poor readers. *Applied Psycholinguistics, 10,* 429–454.

Smith, S. T., Mann, V. A., & Shankweiler, D. C. (1986). Spoken sentence comprehension by good and poor readers: A study with the Tolus Test. *Cortex, 22,* 627–632.

Spring, C. (1976). Encoding speech and memory span in dylexia children. *Journal of Special Education, 10,* 35–40.

Stanovich, K. E. (1991). Changing models of reading and reading acquisition. In L. Rieben and C. A. Perfetti (Eds.), *Learning to read: Basic research and its implications* (pp. 19–32). Hillsdale, NJ: Erlbaum.

Stanovich, K. (1982a). Individual differences in the cognitive processes of reading: I. Word decoding. *Journal of Learning Disabilities, 15,* 485–493.

Stanovich, K. (1982b). Individual differences in the cognitive processes of reading: II. Text-level processes. *Journal of Learning Disabilities, 15,* 549–554.

Stanovich, K. (1988). Explaining the differences between the dyslexic and the garden-variety poor reader: The phonological-core variable difference model. *Journal of Learning Disabilities, 21,* 590–604.

Stanovich, K. E., Cunningham, A. E., & Cramer, B. B. (1984a). Assessing phonological awareness in kindergarten children: Issues of task comparability. *Journal of Experimental Child Psychology, 38,* 175–190.

Stanovich, K. E., Cunningham, A. E., & Freeman, D. J. (1984b). Intelligence, cognitive skills and early reading progress. *Reading Research Quarterly, 19,* 278–303.

Stanovich, K. E., Nathan, R. G., & Zolman, J. E. (1988). The developmental lag hypothesis in reading: Longitudinal and matched reading-level comparisons. *Child Development, 59,* 71–86.

Stanovich, K. E., & Siegel, L. S. (1994). Phenotypic performance profile of children with learning disabilities: A regression-based test of the phonological-core variable-difference model. *Journal of Educational Psychology, 86,* 24–53.

Stevenson, H. W., Stiegler, J. W., Lucker, G. W., Hsu, C-C, & Kitamura, S. (1982). Reading disabilities: The case of Chinese, Japanese and English. *Child Development, 53,* 1164–1181.

Studdert-Kennedy, M., & Mody, M. (1995). Auditory-temporal perception deficits in the reading-impaired: A critical review of the evidence. *Psychonomic Bulletin & Review, 2,* 508–514.

Swanson, L. (1978). Verbal encoding effects on the visual short-term memory of learning-disabled and normal children. *Journal of Educational Psychology, 70,* 539–544.

Tallal, P. (1980). Auditory temporal perception, phonics and reading disabilities in children. *Brain and Language, 9,* 182–198.

Tallal, P., Miller, S. L., Bedi, G., Byma, G., Wang, X., Nagarajan, S. S., Schreider, C., Jenkins, W. M., & Merzenich, M. M. (1996). Language comprehension in language-learning impaired children improved with acoustically modified speech. *Science, 271,* 81–84.

Thomas, C. C. (1905). Congenital "word blindness" and its treatment. *Opthalmoscope, 3,* 380–385.

Torgesen, J. K. (1977). Memorization processes in reading-disabled children. *Journal of Educational Psychology, 69,* 551–578.

Torgesen, J. K., & Davis, C. (1996). Individual difference variables that predict response to training in phonological awareness. *Journal of Experimental Child Psychology, 63,* 1–21.

Torgesen, J. K., & Hoack, D. J. (1980). Processing deficiencies of learning-disabled children who perform poorly on the digit span test. *Journal of Educational Psychology, 72,* 141–160.

Torgesen, J. K., Wagner, R. K., & Rashotte, C. A. (1994). Longitudinal studies of phonological processing and reading. *Journal of Learning Disabilities, 27,* 276–286.

Treiman, R., & Zukowski, A. (1991). Levels of phonological awareness. In S. Brady & D. Shankweiler (Eds.), *Phonological processes in literacy* (pp. 67–83). Hillsdale, NJ: Erlbaum.

Treiman, R., & Zukowski, A. (1996). Children's sensitivity to syllables, onsets, times and phonemes. *Journal of Experimental Child Psychology, 61,* 193–215.

Tzeng, O. J. L., Hung, D. L., & Wang, W. S-Y. (1977). Speech recoding in reading Chinese characters. *Journal of Experimental Psychology: Human Learning and Memory, 3,* 621–630.

Underwood, G., & Batt, V. (1996). *Reading and understanding: An introduction to the psychology of reading.* London: Blackwell.

Van Orden, G. C. (1987). A rows is a rose: Spelling, sound and reading. *Memory & Cognition, 15,* 181–198.

Vellutino, F. R. (1979). *Dyslexia: Theory and research.* Cambridge, MA: MIT Press.

Waber, D. P. (1977). Sex differences in mental abilities, hemispheric lateralization, and rate of physical growth at adolescence. *Developmental Psychology, 13,* 29–38.

Wagner, R., Torgesen, J. K., Laughon, P., Simmons, K., & Rashotte, C. (1993). The development of young readers' phonological processing ability. *Journal of Educational Psychology, 85,* 83–103.

Watt, W. C. (1989). Getting writing right. *Semiotica, 75,* 279–315.

Wolf, M. (1984). Naming, reading and the Dyslexics: A longitudinal overview. *Annals of Dyslexia, 34,* 87–115.

Wolf, M., & Goodglass, H. (1986). Dyslexia, dysnomia and lexical retrieval: A longitudinal investigation. *Brain and Language, 28,* 159–168.

Wong, B. Y. L., Wong, R., & Blenkinsop, J. (1989). Cognitive and metacognitive aspects of learning-disabled adolescents' composing problems. *Learning Disability Quarterly, 12,* 300–322.

Yopp, H. K. (1988). The validity and reliability of phonemic awareness tests. *Reading Research Quarterly, 23,* 159–177.

Zurif, E. B., & Carson, G. (1970). Dyslexia in relation to cerebral: dominance and temporal analysis. *Neuropsychologia, 8,* 351–361.

CHAPTER 6

Visual Processes in Learning Disabilities

Dale M. Willows

I. INTRODUCTION

This chapter describes the visual perception and visual memory abilities of individuals who have difficulties in processing written language. A very high proportion of those designated as learning disabled (LD) might more accurately be termed written-language-disabled, because their most salient difficulties are manifested in the areas of reading, spelling, handwriting, and written composition. Many LD individuals may also be language-disabled in a more general sense, showing problems in their receptive and expressive aural/oral language processes as well as in the written domain. Many others, however, seem to function very well in the aural/oral domain but they have great difficulty when dealing with print. Despite the fact that spelling, handwriting, and written composition difficulties are almost invariably involved, the term reading-disabled is commonly used to refer to those individuals who have written-language disabilities. There are many variants on this term including, specific reading disability, developmental reading disability, congenital reading disability, dyslexia, specific dyslexia, developmental dyslexia, and so on, but because there are no satisfactory distinctions in the definitions of these terms, the term reading disability will be used here to encompass them all.

Although listening, speaking, reading, and writing are all language processes, the latter two are distinct from the former by virtue of the fact that they involve a visual symbol system. For skilled readers and writers the visual symbols in the writing system are so familiar that it is very difficult for them to recall a time when printed words were just meaningless marks on the page. However, for beginning readers and writers, young or old, this is exactly the case. The person who is just starting to learn to read and write must differentiate and remember the symbols in their writing system, be they alphabetic like the Arabic system, logographic like the Chinese, or syllabic like the Cree.

If people differ from each other in their abilities to perceive, discriminate, identify, and remember visual symbols (as they differ from each other in virtually every other area of cognitive/linguistic functioning), then it might be expected that those who have weaknesses in these visual abilities would have trouble learning the symbol system of their written language, and as a consequence might become disabled in their learning to read and write. Despite this obvious possibility, the topic of visual processes in reading and writing disabilities is a very controversial one. This chapter explores why clinicians and educators have long considered visual processing deficits to be potential contributing factors in written language disabilities, and what current research has to say about the relation between visual processing deficits and reading disabilities. The chapter also addresses why some theorists and researchers dismiss the importance of visual factors in written language disabilities, and why others believe that progress toward an understanding of reading disabilities is being hampered by a failure to consider the possibility of a contribution by visual processing factors.

The chapter begins by considering the visual demands of learning to read, write, and spell. It then goes on to present clinical case studies and correlational evidence that seem to support the long-standing belief that visual processing weaknesses play some role in written language disabilities. The next section presents a review of the key basic research in the area, beginning with a discussion of a central point of controversy—whether reading disabilities are caused by one or more types of processing deficit. The research review covers a large number of studies that compare the visual processing abilities of disabled and normal readers. One major group of studies examines the initial stages of visual processing (visual perception) and another group of studies deals with later processing stages (visual memory). The chapter concludes with a discussion of the implications of the findings concerning visual processing deficits and reading disabilities for future research directions and practical applications.

II. VISUAL COMPONENTS IN READING AND WRITING

Before considering potential areas of visual processing difficulty among the reading disabled, the visual processing demands of learning to read, spell, and write are examined. To understand what the child, or anyone just beginning to learn the written form of a language, is faced with, consider the messages printed in Figure

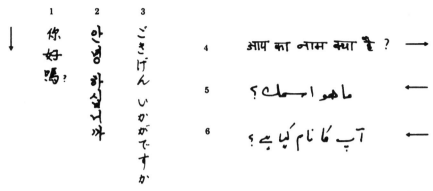

Figure 6.1 Samples of the written languages of Chinese (1), Korean (2), Japanese (3), Hindi (4), Arabic (5), and Urdu (6).

6.1. Unless you are familiar with the written languages of Chinese (1), Korean (2), Japanese (3), Hindi (4), Arabic (5), or Urdu (6), all of the characters and words in Figure 6.1 are just meaningless marks on the page. In fact, all six writing samples represent highly meaningful expressions: the first three languages all ask the question, "How are you?" and the latter three ask, "What is your name?" Despite the fact that the content of the messages is familiar, novice readers of the language (whether fluent in the oral language or not) must learn to pay close attention to the visual information on the page in order to extract the underlying meaning. For more experienced readers of these languages, the visual component is processed unconsciously and effortlessly, and may seem to be of little or no importance. For the beginner, the visual task of dealing with written language involves several types of demands, including the following:

1. Accurate visual perception of letters and words
2. Visual analysis of letter forms and the extraction of invariant features (so that variations of handwriting and type style will not interfere with reading)
3. Visual discrimination between similar forms in the writing system (in the English lower-case alphabet, letter pairs such as "h" and "n," "f" and "t," "b" and "d," "c" and "e" have a high degree of visual similarity)
4. Visual memory for the patterns of individual letters, of letter-strings (such as "ph," "ght," "oi," "th," "ing") that make up orthographic (i.e., spelling) patterns of the language, and of whole words, both to recognize them for reading and to recall or "revisualize" them for writing
5. Visual-spatial and scanning ability to track print from left to right and top to bottom on the page (or, whatever direction is appropriate for the writing system involved)

6. Visual-motor ability to reproduce letters and words in writing

7. Visual-linguistic integration to associate letters and words with sounds and word meanings.

(See Corcos & Willows, 1993; Dunn-Rankin, 1978; Gibson & Levin, 1975; Rayner & Pollatsek, 1989; Rosner, 1996; Vernon, 1971; Willows & Watson, 1998.)

The above demands are present for all novice readers, but, over time, with maturation and reading experience, most individuals master them. The extent to which the visual demands of reading and writing serve as a barrier to progress may vary considerably from one individual to another.

III. CLINICAL CASE STUDIES

A. Historical Perspectives

The earliest evidence suggesting that individual differences in visual processing abilities might be a basis for some reading disabilities comes from clinical reports before the turn of the century. In 1895, James Hinshelwood, a Scottish opthalmologist with a special interest in neurology, began to present his observations of individuals who exhibited a mysterious phenomenon, the sudden loss of reading ability. This acquired word-blindness, as Hinshelwood described it, is a condition in which an individual with normal vision is no longer able to interpret written or printed language, because of some brain injury. A series of fascinating clinical cases, in which the ability to recognize faces and objects was retained but the ability to read words was lost, led Hinshelwood to conclude that the "inability to read was . . . not due to any failure of visual power, but to a loss of the visual memory for words and letters" (Hinshelwood, 1917: 3).

On the basis of Hinshelwood's descriptions of acquired word-blindness, the medical community raised the possibility that there might be cases of congenital word-blindness in which an individual was impaired in her or his ability to process letters and words from birth. Pringle Morgan published a brief note in the *British Medical Journal* in 1896 describing a 14-year-old boy who might represent such a case. It was Hinshelwood's book (1917), *Congenital Word-Blindness,* however, that clearly described what seemed to be convincing evidence of congenital word-blindness. With its thorough and perceptive case histories, it outlines what has now come to be known as "specific dyslexia," "specific reading disability," or, simply, "reading disability." The case descriptions in Hinshelwood's book match very well those currently reported by educators and clinicians.

A few years later, in 1925, Dr. Samuel Orton, a medical doctor with a special interest in neurology (who is now considered by many to be the father of the field of reading disabilities), published an article on "Word-Blindness in School Chil-

Nick   9 years

ABcbEF GhiὐKIMnoP arStu-vW xys

12ξμ56<8Pⅰ0

David   10 years

p ddcᵇᵉ🝔ghiὐklmnopₐ

rstuᵛwxyℓ

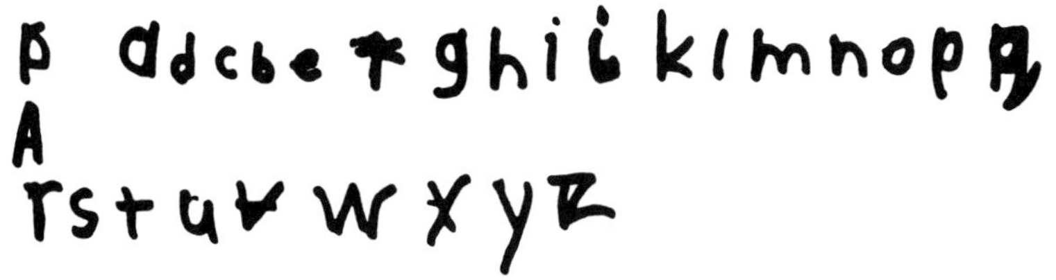

Figure 6.2   Examples of the "reversal errors" that clinicians often observe in the writing of reading-disabled children.

dren" (Orton, 1925). In it he described a range of phenomena associated with congenital word-blindness, with a particular emphasis on the confusions of letter and word orientation ("b" and "d," "was" and "saw"), the so-called reversal errors that clinicians often observe in the reading and writing of children with reading disabilities (e.g., see Figure 6.2). Based on his observations of word-blindness, which he preferred to call strephosymbolia (twisted symbols), Orton developed a theory of reading disability that also focused on visual processes.

In order to understand why these early clinicians formulated visual processing interpretations of reading disabilities, it is instructive to read Hinshelwood's original descriptions of cases of congenital word-blindness. The discrepancy between the children's oral/aural language facility and their specific weaknesses in processing visual symbols is consistent with present-day observations. One such case is presented below.

> Case I.—In March 1900 a boy, aged 11 years, was brought to me at the Glasgow Eye Infirmary by his father, who gave the following history: This boy had been at school for four and a half years, but was finally sent away, because he could not be taught to read. His father informed me that he was a considerable time at school before his defect was noticed, as he

had such an excellent memory that he learned his lessons by heart; in fact, his first little reading book he knew so well that whenever it came to his turn he could from memory repeat his lesson, although he could not read the words. His father also informed me that in every respect, unless in inability to read, the boy seemed quite as intelligent as any of his brothers or sisters. His auditory memory was excellent, and better than that of any of the other members of the family. When a passage was repeated to him aloud, he could commit it to memory very rapidly. When I first saw the boy and his father at the Eye Infirmary, I asked them to call at my house and I wrote down the address on an envelope. A few days thereafter the father could not find the envelope, but the boy at once told him my address correctly, having remembered it from hearing me state it once. When I examined the boy, he seemed a smart and intelligent lad for his years. He knew the alphabet by heart, repeating it rapidly and correctly. He could recognize by sight, however, only a very few letters, and these not with any degree of certainty, after being four and a half years at school. He could spell [aloud] correctly most simple words of one syllable, such as "cat," "dog," "man," "boy," etc., but he could not recognize by sight even the simplest and commonest words such as "the," "of," "in," etc. He had no difficulty in recognizing all other visual objects such as faces, places and pictures. On each page of the little primer in which I tested him, there was a picture of some object, which was followed by some simple letterpress about it. He at once recognized and named the pictures, e.g. "a cat," "a dog." I would then ask him to spell [aloud] the word, which he nearly always did correctly. On asking him to pick out the word "cat" on the page, he was unable to do it. I repeated this experiment with the same result on page after page of the little primer. On testing him with figures [numbers] I found that he could repeat from memory fluently and correctly numbers up to a hundred. He could also perform mentally simple sums of addition. He could not, however, recognize all the figures by sight, but he knew them better than the letters, and recognized a greater number of them. (Hinshelwood, 1917: 45–46)

In the next section, a summary of common clinical characteristics of reading-disabled children based on more recent reports is presented. From a comparison of the case above with this more recent clinical profile it should be evident that Hinshelwood's term congenital word-blindness was undoubtedly describing present-day specific dyslexia or reading disability.

B. A Clinical Profile

Consistent with the thoughtful observations of Hinshelwood and Orton, the case reports of clinicians observing the patterns of difficulties in the reading, writing, and spelling of reading-disabled children have confirmed over the last 70 to 80 years that a substantial proportion of these individuals seem to have difficulties with the visual demands of the tasks. Although there are good reasons to exercise great caution in interpreting subjective clinical reports that have not been confirmed through properly controlled experimental testing (Nisbett & Ross, 1980; Stanovich, 1992), there is a type of information available in clinical case studies that is extremely difficult to test directly with controlled research. Clinicians and educators who often work with the same individuals over weeks, months, and even years have an opportunity to observe patterns in the abilities and learning of reading-disabled individuals that short-term laboratory studies cannot assess. Only well-conceived longitudinal studies that follow the same children for an extended period can begin to capture the complex patterns of development over time. Few such studies exist.

A review of clinical reports suggests a common profile or pattern of difficulties in the reading and writing of many LD individuals over time, a pattern that seems to support the importance of some type of visual component processes. Students who experience great difficulty in their written language acquisition, irrespective of whether they manifest any sign of processing difficulties in their aural/oral language (indeed, some may have superior oral language abilities), often show the following characteristic set of problems as they are learning to read and write:

1. In reading:
   a. difficulty learning to recognize letters and numbers
   b. confusion between similar-looking letters and words
   c. great difficulty recognizing words "by sight"
   d. overreliance on context for word recognition
   e. failure to analyze the internal structure of words
   f. slow word-by-word reading
2. In writing:
   a. difficulty learning how to form letters
   b. confusion between similar-looking letters
   c. mirror-image printing of letters and numbers
   d. difficulty in remembering "how words look" to spell them
   e. phonetic spelling, based on the sounds in words

Aspects of this profile have been confirmed in a large number of clinical case reports and studies (e.g., Boder, 1973; Farnham-Diggory, 1978; Golick, 1984; Kaufman, 1980; Money, 1966; Rawson, 1982; Saunders, 1962; Simpson, 1979; Spache, McIlroy, & Berg, 1981; Willows, 1996; Willows & Terepocki, 1993). A comparison of the above pattern of difficulties manifested by many disabled readers with the earlier section on the "visual demands" of learning to read suggests that there is considerable overlap between the two lists. That is, the difficulties of disabled readers seem to involve visual perceptions and visual memory of printed symbols. It is no wonder, then, that early workers in the field, such as Hinshelwood and Orton, focused on visual factors.

IV. CLINICAL, NEUROPSYCHOLOGICAL, AND SUBTYPING RESEARCH

A. Standardized Psychometric Tests

During the 1960s a considerable number of studies related children's development of visual-perceptual and visual-motor abilities to their development of reading skill. Much of this research relied on standardized paper-and-pencil psychometric measures such as the Bender Visual-Motor Gestalt Test, the Frostig Developmental Test of Visual Perception, and the Memory-for-Designs test. For example, several studies examined the relation between performance on the Bender Test and scores on tests of reading achievement. Based on such evidence researchers reported a significant correlation between poor analysis of complex visual patterns and reading difficulties (e.g., Crosby, 1968; Lachmann, 1960). Moreover, some studies were predictive. The perceptual ability tests were administered before the children began learning to read, so inadequacy in reading could not have caused their poor visual analysis abilities (e.g., de Hirsch, Jansky, & Langford, 1966; Smith & Keogh, 1962).

This type of correlational evidence resulted in the development of visual discrimination exercises for the express purpose of improving reading skills (Frostig, 1968). Such training programs, often involving discriminating between geometric shapes, were notoriously unsuccessful because their effects were specific to the training stimuli and did not generalize to letters and words (Cohen, 1967; Rosen, 1966). One important conclusion that these training studies provide is that the type of training required to improve reading achievement is not a generic training of perceptual abilities but rather must be a more specific training of reading skills (e.g., letter and word recognition). An additional conclusion is that researchers must be careful in their interpretation of correlational findings. This caution is as important in the interpretation of present-day findings as it was 30 years ago. Evidence of a significant correlation between levels of performance on tests of perceptual skills, or any other type of processing, and reading achievement should not be assumed to reflect a causal link.

Performance on standardized psychometric tests is often open to a variety of interpretations because, although the test may be called a "visual" test and may seem to be assessing some sort of visual ability, other types of factors such as verbal abilities and attentional processes may also be involved over and above what the test purports to measure. Although current research continues to employ standardized psychometric measures to examine the possible role of visual processes in reading disability, such tests are usually used in conjunction with more controlled experimental tasks designed to assess "purer" visual processes.

B. Visual Deficit Subtypes

Over the last 30 years some researchers, primarily clinicians and neuropsychologists, have investigated the possibility that groups of reading-disabled children might be subdividable into relatively homogeneous subgroups or subtypes. That is, different types of processing deficits might play a role in the reading disabilities of different groups of reading-disabled individuals. Subtyping research usually involves administering a battery of tests (standardized and/or experimental) to groups of LD individuals. Based on a variety of methodological and statistical approaches researchers have come up with two, three, or more classifications of reading disabilities, often including a visual deficit subtype, variously labeled visual dyslexic (Johnson & Myklebust, 1967), dyseidetic (Boder, 1973), visual-perceptual (Denkla, 1977), visual-spatial (Bakker, 1979; DeFries & Decker, 1982), and visual perceptual-motor (Satz & Morris, 1981).

Particularly compelling have been studies in which researchers have attempted to reduce the subjectivity that has characterized clinical subtyping procedures by utilizing statistical subtyping techniques involving multivariate analyses (e.g., Doehring, Hoshko & Bryans, 1979; Lyon & Watson, 1981; Petrausskas & Rourke, 1979). Such studies are designed to categorize reading-disabled individuals more objectively into relatively homogeneous subtypes based on different patterns of processing difficulties. In one recent study of this type, Watson and Willows (1995) examined the score profiles of 50 unsuccessful readers (including 25 high-risk first graders and 25 older disabled readers) on a battery of 19 cognitive, linguistic, and achievement measures. Using cluster and Q-type factor analyses, Watson and Willows compared the score profiles of the resulting three subtypes with that of an appropriately-matched group of 25 successful readers. All three subtypes of unsuccessful readers exhibited deficits relative to successful readers on measures of symbolic-phonological processing and memory. Two of the subtypes, representing two-thirds of the subjects in the sample of unsuccessful readers, also exhibited deficits on visual and visual-motor measures.

Common patterns of difficulty among disabled readers in dealing with linguistic, phonological, visual, and other processing demands of written language are now well documented in the subtyping literature (Feagans & McKinney, 1991; Hooper & Willis, 1989). Based on this literature, it seems that three main possibilities exist with respect to the role of visual processing in reading disability. First, it may be that deficient visual analysis skills characterize a true subgroup of individuals whose reading difficulties are, in part, caused by this deficit. Second, it may be that visual processing differences within LD groups reflect individual variation in these processes within the normal population and have little or no role in causing reading disabilities. This possibility was highlighted in studies reported by McKinney, Short, and Feagans (1985) and Korhonen (1991), in which fairly significant numbers of control subjects (normal readers) clustered with the subgroup involving visual processing deficits. Third, it may be that it is only when visual processing weakness occurs in combination with another processing deficit (or deficits) that it is of consequence. Vellutino, Scanlon, and Tanzman (1991) have theorized that different subtypes of poor readers may be defined by the weighting associated with the processing deficit or deficits occurring. Whereas a single processing deficiency of sufficient magnitude by itself may interfere with reading performance, another processing deficiency less critical to reading performance may be tolerated until it occurs in combination with a second deficiency or multiple deficiencies. This interpretation of reading disability may account for the visual processing weakness that characterized some normal readers.

V. BASIC EXPERIMENTAL RESEARCH

A. Unitary or Multiple Factors

The above issue of whether reading disabilities are the result of one, or more than one type of processing problem has been a major source of contention between theorists over the years. There are those who have argued that all reading disabilities are a result of subtle and not-so-subtle linguistic processing deficits (e.g., Mann, 1984; Swanson, 1984; Vellutino, 1979). Others, however, have contended that there may be a variety of factors contributing to reading disabilities (e.g., Malatesha & Dougan, 1982; Rayner & Pollatsek, 1989), with different reading-disabled individuals being more or less affected by linguistic, visual, and other types of processing deficits.

Those who have maintained that the unitary cause of reading disability is some type of underlying language processing deficit used as the basis for their argument (a) that there is an enormous amount of evidence relating language and memory problems in phonological coding, syntax, and semantics to reading disabilities and (b) that there is a large body of evidence indicating that there are no visual processing differences between disabled and normal readers (Stanovich, 1982, 1985; Vellutino, 1979, 1987). Those who have questioned the unitary causation position have argued instead for a multiple causation position, suggesting either that there are different subtypes of reading disabilities, or that two or more areas of processing weakness in combination may underlie reading disabilities. All multiple causation theorists agree with unitary causation theorists that research evidence clearly shows that linguistic/phonological processing and memory factors are involved in most, if not all cases of reading disability, but they have questioned the validity of the second conclusion: that a large body of evidence indicates that there are no visual processing differences between disabled and normal readers (Di Lollo, Hanson, & McIntyre, 1983; Doehring, 1978; Fletcher & Satz, 1979a, 1979b; Gross & Rothenberg, 1979; Lovegrove, Martin, & Slaghuis, 1986; Willows, Kruk, & Corcos, 1993b). Rather, especially over the last 10–15 years, on the basis of evidence demonstrating the existence of basic visual processing differences between disabled and normal readers, they have argued that, in addition to linguistic/phonological factors, there may also be visual-perceptual and/or visual-memory factors involved in causing reading disabilities.

The basic research reviewed in this section reflects directly on this main point of dispute between unitary and multiple factor theorists. It deals with the question of whether disabled and normal readers demonstrate differences in their basic visual-perceptual and visual-memory processes.

B. Methodological Considerations

1. Operational Definitions

Throughout this section on basic research, the term reading disability will be defined by the conventional discrepancy definition that includes the following elements:

1. Reading performance of 2 or more years below what is expected for an individual's age and general level of cognitive ability[1]
2. Evidence of at least normal cognitive ability as reflected by scores on standardized IQ tests and/or areas of school achievement that do not involve written language
3. Normal educational opportunity to learn to read
4. No organic deficiencies of vision or hearing
5. No behavioral or emotional disorders

Virtually all of the studies examining the role of visual processes in reading disabilities have compared the performance of a group of disabled readers with that of normally achieving readers. Although most researchers have adopted an acceptable definition of reading disability, some have not. Because the operational definition of the groups of readers (i.e., how they are selected) is key to the interpretation of the data produced by research, this review focuses on studies that provide evidence of having met the conventional discrepancy definition for selecting the reading-disabled group and also of having employed an appropriate comparison group of nondisabled "normal" readers that differs from the disabled readers

---

[1]For children who are below the age of 8, and therefore cannot be more than 2 years below grade level, it is commonly accepted in research to designate an individual who is at least 1 year below age/grade at age 7 or at least six months below age/grade expectation at age 6 as being reading disabled.

on measures of written language (e.g., reading, spelling) but that is similar to them on factors such as age and general cognitive ability.

2. Language-Labeling Confounds

Although intuitively it might seem that the most direct way of assessing for visual processing differences between disabled and normal readers would be to test them with letters and words, there are serious problems with such an approach. In view of the fact that phonological coding and linguistic processing deficits undoubtedly play a very significant role in reading disabilities (as Mann has clearly shown, Chapter 5, this volume), an important factor to consider in defining experimental tasks thought to be assessing visual processes is whether performance on the task may involve the use of phonological-coding/linguistic processes that are confounded with the visual processes of interest. Some studies attempting to assess visual processes in reading disability may inadvertently have been assessing other processes as well as visual factors. Most studies in which the goal has been to assess visual factors free of phonological/linguistic/verbal confounds have avoided this pitfall by employing stimuli that are very difficult to label verbally, or by using procedures in which performance could not be affected by verbal labeling, or by taking precautions of both types. This review reports only studies that have attempted to exclude the possibility that the "visual" task could have been performed by labeling the stimuli. Thus studies that report the performance of subjects who apparently have visual processing strengths or weakness on a task but who in fact might have relied on linguistic/verbal rather than visual processes to complete it are not included in this review.

3. "Levels" of Visual Processing

Probably because of the long-standing views of clinicians and educators that reading disabilities have some underlying basis in visual processes, there has been a great deal of basic research attempting to examine the possibility that visual processing deficits play some role in reading disabilities. This research, which generally fits within an information-processing framework, has involved a wide range of methodologies. To understand the current status of our knowledge about visual processing, it is essential to review the research within the context of the types of methodologies involved.

The type of visual process investigated varies from one study to another. To understand the need to examine different aspects or levels of visual processing it is helpful to consider that from the instant a visual stimulus reaches the eye, the visual information begins to undergo "processing," proceeding from the retina to the visual cortex, to various association areas of the brain. It is possible that deficits in any or all of the levels of visual processing might have some role in reading, spelling, and writing disabilities. Some researchers have focused their efforts on understanding the earlier levels of visual processing, immediately after the information has entered the visual system, while others have been more interested in later levels of processing in which higher cognitive processing may play a greater role. Some studies simply require that subjects indicate when they see a stimulus on a screen, whereas others may require that subjects correctly recognize what they saw at some later point or even that they be able to reproduce accurately what they saw. Because the interpretation of any particular study depends on the level of processing demanded in the experimental task, the studies reviewed in the following sections are roughly organized from earlier to later levels of visual processing.

C. Visual Perceptual Processes

Clinical observations that disabled readers seem to confuse similar-looking letters and words in their reading and writing suggest that in comparison with normal readers, they may have some underlying difficulty in basic visual perception. A large number of studies have been undertaken to investigate this possibility. These studies have attempted to determine whether disabled and normal readers differ in their perception of visual stimuli in the early stages of processing before higher level cognitive processes have had time to come into play.

Much of the research comparing the early stages of visual information processing of disabled and normal readers has involved two main techniques: temporal integration tasks and backward masking tasks. These tasks are used to determine whether disabled and normal readers differ in how quickly they can perceive and extract information from a visual stimulus. Because visual information processing occurs at very rapid rates, highly sophisticated procedures are required in this type of research. Tachistoscopes (T-scopes), oscilloscopes, and computer presentation technologies have been used to control the time intervals, measured in thousandths of a second (msec).

1. Temporal Integration

The visible trace of a stimulus persists for a fraction of a second after the stimulus has been removed from view. The duration of this visible persistence can be measured by presenting two stimuli in very close temporal sequence and assessing whether the stimuli have been perceived as two separate stimuli or as a single stimulus. There are two main types of temporal integration task that have been used to compare the initial stages of visual information processing in disabled and normal readers. One type involves the presentation of two different stimuli with a variable time interval, the interstimulus interval (ISI), between them. The minimum length of ISI required for a person to perceive the two stimuli as separate is considered to reflect the duration of the visible persistence of the first stimulus. This is often referred to as the "separation threshold." An example may make this procedure clearer. In a well-known study by Stanley and Hall (1973), groups of disabled readers and normal readers were shown the pairs of stimuli in Figure 6.3. To begin with,

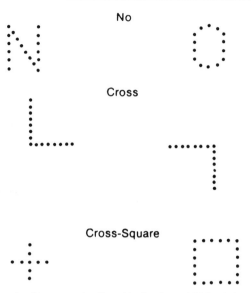

Figure 6.3 The three sets of two-part stimuli used by Stanley and Hall (1973) to investigate temporal integration of visual information.

each pair of stimuli was presented simultaneously so that they would be perceived as a single image. It can be seen from the examples in Figure 6.3 that if each pair of stimuli were displayed simultaneously in the same location they would combine to make the word NO, a cross, and a cross within a square, respectively. Next the procedure involved increasing, by very small steps (20 msec), the time interval between each pair of stimuli until the child reported that she or he saw two shapes instead of one. The results of Stanley and Hall's research indicated that the disabled readers' separation threshold before they reported seeing two separate images was significantly longer than that of the normal readers. This pattern of results showing longer visual persistence among the reading disabled was found in other studies using similar procedures (Lovegrove & Brown, 1978; Stanley, 1975).

A second type of temporal integration task has involved the presentation of two identical stimuli (such as two identical straight lines or sets of parallel lines called "gratings") in close temporal sequence, also to assess the visible persistence of the first stimulus. The task begins by presenting the two stimuli simultaneously and then the ISI is increased by very small steps until the subject reports that the stimulus is flashing rather than constant. Using this type of temporal integration task, researchers have amassed considerable evidence also indicating that disabled readers have longer visible persistence than normal readers (Di Lollo, Hanson, & McIntyre, 1983; Lovegrove, Billing, & Slaghuis, 1978; O'Neill & Stanley, 1976). The evidence suggests that the processing deficit is not at the level of the retina but occurs later in processing, at the level of the visual cortex (Slaghuis & Lovegrove, 1985; Slaghuis & Lovegrove, 1986). Moreover, it has been reported that 75% of disabled readers in a series of studies of early visual processing exhibited evidence of such deficits (Lovegrove et al., 1986). An impressive program of research has been undertaken attempting to clarify the nature of the processing mechanisms involved in these early visual processing deficits among disabled readers (Badcock & Lovegrove, 1981; Lovegrove, 1996; Lovegrove, Heddle & Slaghuis, 1980b; Lovegrove, Bowling, Badcock & Blackwood, 1980a; Lovegrove, Martin, Bowling, Blackwood, Badcock & Paxton, 1982; Martin & Lovegrove, 1984).

2. Backward Masking

When the onset of one visual stimulus, called the target, is followed almost immediately by the onset of another visual stimulus (known as a masking stimulus, or, simply a mask), the second stimulus interferes with the processing of the first. This effect is known as backward masking. Whereas the temporal integration tasks described earlier are thought to provide an index of the visible persistence of a stimulus after its termination, backward masking tasks are thought to provide a measure of the rate of information pick-up in the initial stages of visual information processing. In a typical backward masking experiment a target stimulus (a figure or letter) is briefly presented, then a mask is presented, and then a test stimulus is presented. The task involves a same–different paradigm (i.e., test format), such that one key is pressed to indicate that the test stimulus is the same as the target or another key is pressed to indicate that it is different. On every trial there is a 50/50 chance of a "same" or "different" response being correct. The time interval between the onsets of the target and the mask, the stimulus onset asynchrony (SOA), is systematically varied. The SOA level at which a subject is able to perform at 75% accuracy is the criterion threshold. The results of several experiments comparing performance on backward masking tasks have shown that disabled readers process visual information more slowly (they require a longer SOA to reach the criterion threshold) than normal readers (Di Lollo et al., 1983; Lovegrove & Brown, 1978; Mazer, McIntyre, Murray, Till, & Blackwell, 1983; O'Neill & Stanley, 1976; Stanley & Hall, 1973).

Overall, then, the pattern of results from both types of temporal integration task and from studies involving backward masking suggests that disabled readers may have some sort of temporal processing deficit relative to normal readers of similar age and IQ (Farmer & Klein, 1995). There is also some indication that this visual processing deficit may diminish with increasing age (Badcock & Lovegrove, 1981; Di Lollo et al., 1983; Lovegrove & Brown, 1978).

3. Relation to Reading Processes

There are some researchers who argue that the types of methodologies used to assess early visual processing differences between disabled and normal readers "are remote from the perceptual conditions facing a child learning to read" (Hulme, 1988, p. 373.), but there are others who argue just as persuasively that the types of measures of visual perception described here are more sensitive and powerful approaches to comparing the visual-perceptual functioning of disabled and normal readers (Di Lollo et al., 1983; Gross & Rothenberg, 1979; Lovegrove et al., 1986). Other types of procedures may be confounded with higher cognitive processes (e.g., verbal labeling, rehearsal, cognitive strategies). Moreover, evidence from studies of letter, number, and word perception, stimuli that are more closely related to reading, seems to confirm that disabled readers require stimuli to be exposed for a longer duration than normal readers in order to produce a given level of correct responding (e.g., Allegretti & Puglisi, 1986; Gross, Rothenberg, Schottenfeld, & Drake, 1978; Stanley, 1976).

What role, if any, early visual processing deficits might have in reading disabilities is clearly the matter of central importance, however. Disabled–normal reader differences do not indicate a causal link between early visual processing deficits and reading disabilities, but theorists have explored such a possibility. Two theories have generated attention and controversy. One involves a direct causal link between early visual processing deficits and reading disabilities; another involves a temporal processing deficit as a mediating factor contributing to both visual and phonological processing deficits, one or both of which might have a causal role in reading disabilities.

The first of these two, the transient deficit theory, is based on a model of how the visual system processes information that has the visual characteristics of print. This model postulates two mutually inhibitory systems or "channels": a sustained channel that is specialized for pattern analysis and detail, and a transient channel that shuts off the sustained response when there is flicker or movement, as in eye movements (Breitmeyer, 1993). There is evidence of a neurological basis for these two systems, with specialized cell pathways corresponding to sustained (parvocellular pathways) and transient (magnocellular pathways) channels (Lehmkuhle, 1993). The transient deficit theory holds that for the disabled reader, the persisting image of a previously read word (i.e., visible persistence) is not as efficiently suppressed by the transient visual system as it is in normal readers. Consequently, this image overlaps with the next word brought into view, creating distortions during reading (Breitmeyer, 1993). Empirical support for this "sluggish" transient visual system has come from physiological, psychophysical, and behavioral research (e.g., Livingstone, Rosen, Drislane, & Galaburda, 1991; Lovegrove & Williams, 1993).

The second theory attempting to explain the link between early visual processing deficits and reading disabilities postulates a generalized deficit in rapid temporal processing (the processing of short-duration stimuli presented in rapid succession) that affects both auditory and visual input (Farmer & Klein, 1995; Slaghuis, Lovegrove, & Davidson, 1993; Tallal, Sainburg, & Jernigan, 1991). Figure 6.4 illustrates a simple model of how Farmer and Klein (1995) propose that a

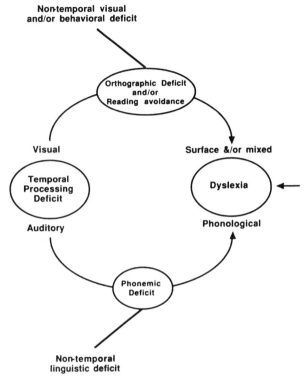

Figure 6.4 A simplified view of the potential pathways to dyslexia from a temporal processing deficit in either the visual or auditory modality from Farmer and Klein (1995). Reprinted with permission.

temporal processing deficit in the auditory and/or visual domains might operate to contribute to reading disabilities.

4. Consistency of Findings and Interpretations

Not all studies using temporal integration and backward masking tasks have produced the same patterns of early visual processing differences between disabled and normal readers reported here. A few older studies have been repeatedly cited in the literature as sources of contrary evidence (e.g., Arnett & Di Lollo, 1979; Fisher & Frankfurter, 1977; Morrison, Giordani, & Nagy, 1977). Methodological and statistical limitations have, however, been raised concerning these findings (Willows et al., 1993b).

More recently, the results of a number of studies have challenged the "sluggish transient system" interpretation of disabled/normal reader differences in tasks attempting to assess early visual processes. Kruk and Willows (1993) explored potential effects of a transient deficit on letter and word recognition in backward masking tasks that more closely approximate reading situations than previous research. Although the results confirmed once again that disabled readers perform less accurately than normal readers on tasks involving brief exposures of visual stimuli (both alphabetic and nonalphabetic), they were not consistent with a transient deficit interpretation because the differences were unrelated to the SOA (the time between the onset of the stimulus and the mask). In addition, a series of studies by Walther-Müller (1995) raised questions about the incidence of early visual processing deficits among disabled readers and about the role such deficits might have as a contributing factor in reading disabilities.

The "general temporal processing deficit" interpretation of the link between early visual processing deficits and reading disabilities has been disputed, as well. Rayner, Pollatsek, and Bilsky (1995) have argued that the incidence of visual processing deficits is very low and that the temporal processing deficit hypothesis presented by Farmer and Klein (1995) is too vague.

5. A Controversial Visual Intervention

Undoubtedly the most controversial recent work has concerned the role of wavelength of light (i.e., color) on visual processes in reading. Some basic researchers have argued that color can affect early visual processes by facilitating or inhibiting the transient visual system (Breitmeyer & Williams, 1990; Williams, LeCluyse, & Littell, 1996), and a practitioner independently reported that disabled readers' performance was improved through the use of colored overlays (transparencies) or tinted eyeglasses (Irlen, 1983).

Irlen (1991), a clinician, has claimed that a substantial proportion of disabled readers suffer from a perceptual dysfunction, Scotopic Sensitivity Syndrome (SSS), that contributes to their reading difficulties. Irlen has also reported that individually prescribed colored lenses or overlays can relieve symptoms of SSS and improve reading performance. These lenses are tinted filters which, according to Irlen, operate to eliminate specific light frequencies that would otherwise bring about a variety of perceptual disorders that adversely affect reading. Irlen developed a screening procedure to detect SSS, and established the Irlen Institute for training professionals in this technique. There are now Certified Irlen Screeners around the world prescribing colored lenses to individuals found to have SSS, according to their tests. At this point the Irlen technique has been widely publicized in the popular media as an intervention for individuals with reading disabilities.

In recognition of a need for careful study of the utility of Irlen Lenses, an entire issue of the *Journal of Learning Disabilities* (December 1990) was devoted to investigations and critical reviews on the subject. The intervention has been studied by a number of researchers examining its effect on word matching, word discrimination, reading rate, reading comprehension, and scores on standardized measures of reading ability (Blaskey et al., 1990; O'Connor, Sofo, Kendall, & Olsen, 1990;

Robinson & Conway, 1990; Robinson & Miles, 1987; Tyrrell, Holland, Dennis, & Wilkins, 1995). The findings from these investigations are mixed and inconclusive. The theoretical basis for scotopic sensitivity syndrome, and for the utility of the lenses in offsetting adverse effects on visual processing in disabled readers has been criticized on the grounds of imprecision, inaccuracy, and inconsistency with what is known about reading disability (Stanley, 1990). The empirical evidence, too, has been questioned for the validity of the methodology used in investigating the claims of improvement resulting from the use of the lenses (Parker, 1990; Sumbler & Willows, 1994; Willows & Sumbler, 1994). The only clear conclusion at this point is that findings are mixed and more carefully controlled research is needed. If the intervention is effective in improving reading, it may well be via some indirect route, such as through a reduction of visual discomfort, which in turn may result in more practice reading (Tyrrell et al., 1995).

6. Conclusions Concerning Early Visual Processes

Returning to the question of whether disabled readers differ from normal readers in their visual-perceptual processes, the answer seems to be in the affirmative. Clearly the performance of disabled and nondisabled readers differs on a range of tasks intended to assess early visual information processes.

In answer to the more fundamental question of whether perceptual deficits are one of the causes of reading disability, the answer is far from clear at this point. They may or may not have any causal role in reading disabilities. There is a possibility that they could have some direct causal role in the perception, discrimination, and analysis of the visual features of letters and words; or, they might reflect some more basic underlying processing differences between disabled and normal readers, such as temporal processing, which in turn might have some causal role in reading disabilities; or they might be an epiphenomenon, with no causal role in reading at all. At this point "the jury is still out."

D. Visual Memory Processes

In order to remember the letters and groups of letters that characterize the spelling patterns and words of the language—to recognize them for reading and to recall them for writing and spelling—an individual must be able to retain a record of them in memory and have easy access to that stored information.

After visual information has passed from the very brief visual persistence level to a short-term memory storage level, the information must be processed further in long-term memory if it is to be retained for later recognition and recall (Craik & Lockhart, 1972; Rayner & Pollatsek, 1989). A variety of experimental procedures have been used to determine whether there are differences between disabled and normal readers at these later processing stages. Most of the studies designed to investigate visual memory differences between disabled and normal readers have employed one of four main types of task, involving visual recognition memory, reproduction from visual memory, visual-visual paired-associate learning, and serial learning of visual designs. All of these types of tasks are designed to investigate how well individuals remember visual information that they have perceived, in order to recognize or reproduce it from memory later.

1. Visual Recognition Memory

In order to recognize words with speed and accuracy, a reader must be able to make use of information such as the overall shape of words. A series of investigations by Lyle and Goyen was designed to examine how accurately disabled readers and normal readers recognize unfamiliar visual stimuli that resemble "word contours" or "word shapes." Sample stimuli from their research are shown in Figure 6.5. In five experiments Lyle and Goyen, using tachistoscopic procedures, presented a series of different word shapes to disabled and normal readers (Goyen & Lyle, 1971a, 1971b; Goyen & Lyle, 1973; Lyle & Goyen, 1968; Lyle & Goyen, 1975). Shortly after the presentation of each word-shape target, one of two test formats was used. In one test situation a set of several test word shapes was presented and the child's task was to select the target stimulus she or he had just seen. In the other test format, involving a same-different paradigm, the child had to press one key to indicate whether she or he thought the test letter was the same as the target or another key if she or he thought it was different. Lyle and Goyen were interested not only in determining whether disabled readers differed from normal readers in their visual recognition of the word shapes, but also in whether younger children (age 6 to 8 years) in the two reading groups differed from older (age 8 to 10). In addi-

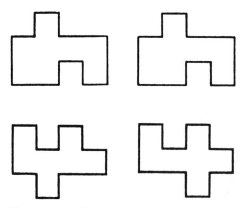

Figure 6.5 Samples of "word contours" used as stimuli in the research by Lyle and Goyen. The top pair are identical (same); the bottom pair are nonidentical (different).

tion they wanted to know whether the exposure duration of a word shape (ranging from .10 of a sec to 5.0 secs) and the degree of similarity among the set of test alternatives affected accuracy of responding.

The results of Lyle and Goyen's research showed clearly that, at the younger age level, disabled readers were less accurate in recognizing word shapes than were normal readers. Such differences were not found at the older age level. These differences between disabled and normal readers were found at the shorter stimulus duration rates (.10 sec and 1.0 sec) but not at longer ones (5.0 secs). Consistent with the findings of the studies described in the previous sections, Lyle and Goyen conclude from their research that

> the perceptual deficit manifested by young [disabled] readers on tachistoscopic tasks involves the input or processing of visual information at rapid exposures. The relative deficit of young [disabled] readers appears to arise not through short-term memory deficits or difficulty in discriminating between alternatives on response cards but through incomplete analysis of the tachistoscopically presented stimulus, so that certain distinctive features or their interrelationships are not taken into account. (1975, p. 675–676)

More recently, Willows, Corcos, and Kershner (1993a) conducted a study of children's visual recognition memory for unfamiliar visual symbols (letters from the Hebrew alphabet), using a same–different paradigm in a "computer game" format. Disabled and normal readers at three age levels (6, 7, and 8 years) were tested. On each trial in the "computer game" the child was shown a target stimulus selected randomly from a pool of 18 Hebrew letters (shown in Figure 6.6, in 6 sets of 3). After a brief interval they were shown the test stimulus; either the same letter again or a different, but similar-looking, letter from the same set. The child had to press one key to indicate that the test item was the same as the target and another if it was different. The delay between the target and test stimuli was varied to determine whether disabled readers' visual processing difficulty was at the level of initial input or whether it was a result of some memory difficulty. The results of this research were consistent with Lyle and Goyen's findings: reading-disabled children were less accurate and slower in their visual recognition performance. Moreover, there was a developmental pattern (i.e., the effect was greater among younger than older disabled readers) and the deficit appeared to be at the level of initial visual perception rather than visual memory.

Taken together then, the pattern of results from studies of visual recognition that involve rapid stimulus presentation is clear and consistent. Younger disabled readers make more errors and are slower at responding than normal readers of similar age and IQ. The disabled readers' difficulty seems to occur at the initial input stage rather than at a later storage stage. In other words, the findings of these studies that

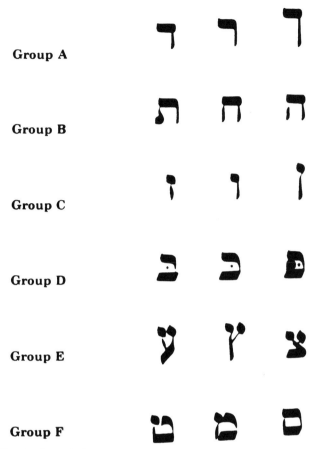

Figure 6.6 The stimulus pool of 18 Hebrew letters, grouped in six visually distinct sets of three visually similar items, used in the visual recognition studies of Willows et al. (1993a).

assessed both early and later stages of processing add to the evidence of early visual information-processing differences between disabled and normal readers.

2. Reproduction from Visual Memory

In learning to read and write the child must attend to and remember the visual information in the symbols in order to recognize them for reading and reproduce them for writing. A very widely cited series of studies was undertaken by Vellutino and his colleagues to investigate the possibility of visual memory differences between disabled and normal readers. These studies all involved having children view difficult-to-label visual shapes or strings of letters from the Hebrew alphabet, and then after the stimuli had been removed, "copy" them from memory. The performance of younger and older disabled and normal readers was compared. Based on the findings of the three key studies (Vellutino, Pruzek, Steger, & Meshoulam, 1973a; Vellutino, Smith, Steger, & Kaman, 1975b; Vellutino, Steger, Kaman, & DeSetto, 1975c) involving the ability to reproduce unfamiliar visual shapes from memory, Vellutino and his colleagues concluded that "In all these investigations, poor readers performed as well as normals in short- and long-term memory of Hebrew letters and words—symbols unfamiliar to both groups" (Vellutino, Steger, Moyer, Harding, & Niles, 1977, p. 57).

Other evidence, however, suggests that there may be disabled–normal reader differences in a draw-from-memory task (Lyle, 1968). In that research, Lyle compared the abilities of large samples of disabled and normal readers to draw unfamiliar visual patterns from memory using the Memory-for-Designs test. The results showed that the disabled were significantly inferior to the normal readers in their reproductions of the designs. Moreover, the previously mentioned findings by Willows et al. (1993a) showing disabled–normal reader differences in visual recognition (a less demanding task than reproduction from visual memory) of Hebrew letters, the type of stimuli used in the Vellutino et al. studies, suggest that caution is warranted in drawing definitive conclusions at this point.

The evidence reported by Vellutino and his colleagues on reproduction from visual memory does not contradict that from research on early stages of processing, since all of the studies by Vellutino and his colleagues involved "long" stimulus exposures. In the studies using Hebrew letters as stimuli, for example, the children examined the string of letters for 3 to 5 secs. These are longer exposure durations than those at which the research on visual perception found disabled–normal reader differences in performance.

3. Visual–Visual Paired-Associate Learning

In the context of attempting to compare disabled and normal readers' ability to associate unfamiliar visual shapes with sounds and words, as the child must do in learning to read, Vellutino and his colleagues undertook research in which they had disabled and normal readers learn to associate pairs of unfamiliar visual designs with each other. These studies also involved having the children associate visual designs with verbal responses, but this visual–verbal association aspect of the research is concerned with the children's ability to use verbal labels, and is essentially irrelevant to questions about visual perception and memory processes. Thus, only the visual–visual paired-associate tasks are discussed here. In these tasks the child was shown pairs of difficult-to-label shapes, such as those in Figure 6.7, and was told "to try to remember what two designs go together" (Vellutino, Steger, & Pruzek, 1973b, p. 117). On test trials the children were shown one of each stimulus pair and required to select its mate from a set of five choices. In both experiments Vellutino and his colleagues found no differences between disabled and normal readers' ability to associate visual designs with each other (Vellutino, Harding,

Training series

Visual stimulus   Response template

Figure 6.7   Samples of the pairs of difficult-to-label shapes used in the visual–visual paired-associate learning research by Vellutino et al. (1977).

Phillips, & Steger, 1975a; Vellutino, Steger, & Pruzek, 1973b). These results have been interpreted as additional evidence that there are no visual processing differences between disabled and normal readers.

The consistency of these results, using a visual–visual paired-associate task, with the earlier findings, using a reproduction from visual memory task, appears to add weight to Vellutino et al.'s (1977) conclusion that there are no disabled–normal reader differences on tasks designed to measure visual memory. The results do not contradict the evidence on visual perception, however. The disabled and normal readers in these studies were in an older age range, between about 9.5 and 12.5 years of age, and the stimulus presentation rates were relatively slow.

4. Serial Learning of Visual Designs

Following from the work of Vellutino and his colleagues, Swanson also undertook a series of studies designed to compare disabled and normal readers' abilities to remember difficult-to-label visual shapes under conditions in which verbal labels were either excluded or included. Swanson used a probe-type serial memory task in which he presented six nonsense shapes such as those shown in Figure 6.8. Again, the task involving the use of verbal labels, although interesting, is not relevant to the present discussion about visual memory processes. Only the unnamed condition is discussed here. In the unnamed condition a set of six cards, each with a different shape printed on it, was placed face down in front of the child. From left to right, each of the cards was then turned up for a few seconds and then turned down again. A probe (one of the six shapes) was then shown and the child had to point to the card in the row in front of her or him that matched the probe. Their task was essentially a visual-spatial task, because they were shown a probe and they had to remember where they had seen it. In three experiments involving children from 7 to 12 years of age, Swanson consistently found no differences between disabled and normal readers in serial memory for unnamed stimuli (Swanson, 1978, 1982, 1983).

Other research examining visual-spatial memory has produced a different pat-

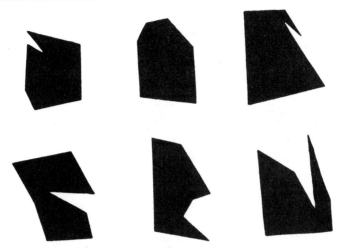

Figure 6.8   The six nonsense shapes (unnamed condition) used by Swanson in his studies involving a visual serial learning task.

tern of results, however. Willows et al. (1993a) presented strings of Hebrew letters to 6- to 8-year-old disabled and normal readers in a computer game. After each string of three visually distinct letters (each of the three was taken from a different set in Figure 6.6), one of the same three letters was shown in one of the three spatial positions that the original string had occupied. The child's task was simply to press one of two keys to indicate whether the letter was in the same or a different position from the one she or he had just seen it in. The results on both accuracy and response speed measures indicated that disabled readers were less able than normal readers to remember visual-spatial information. The disabled–normal reader differences were greater at the younger age levels.

5. Statistical Limitations

Although the failure to find disabled–normal reader differences on tasks tapping visual memory is a consistent pattern in the studies by both Vellutino and Swanson, several other researchers have been critical of the "no difference" conclusions from their findings. They argue that some of the studies have statistical ceilings and floors that prevent finding disabled–normal differences, especially among the younger readers, even if such differences actually exist (Doehring, 1978; Fletcher & Satz, 1979a, Gross & Rothenberg, 1979; Satz & Fletcher, 1980; Singer, 1979; Willows et al., 1993b). These statistical problems are very serious because they result in "no difference" conclusions when real differences may exist. If, for example, 10-year-old disabled and normal readers were compared on their ability to read first-grade level words, all children might read the words almost perfectly, that is, their performance might be at a statistical ceiling. Conversely, if 6-year-old disabled and normal readers were compared on their ability to read fifth-grade level words, all of the children might do very poorly, their performance being at the statistical floor. A failure to find disabled–normal reader differences with such tasks might simply indicate that the tasks were too easy (ceiling effect) or too difficult (floor effect) to detect differences.

6. Conclusions Concerning Later Visual Processes

The answer to the question of whether there are visual memory differences between disabled and normal readers is still uncertain. The evidence with respect to older children is fairly consistent. It seems quite unlikely that there are visual memory differences between older (over age 8) disabled and normal readers on the types of tasks reviewed here. At the younger age level, however, the possibility of some sort of developmental lag in visual memory still exists. There is evidence to suggest that younger disabled readers have difficulty in remembering visual information in a variety of task types. It may be that these difficulties are due to differences in early perceptual processes, since most of the studies that have found differences in visual memory tasks have involved brief stimulus presentation rates, whereas studies that have failed to find such differences have usually presented stimuli at slower rates. Further carefully done research is required to clarify the relation between later visual processes and reading disability, particularly in younger children (up to age 8).

VI. CONCLUSIONS AND FUTURE DIRECTIONS

A. Research Directions

The conclusion of the unitary deficit theorists that disabled readers have no visual processing difficulties appears to have been premature. There may be more to reading disabilities than the phonological coding and linguistic problems that have been well established in the literature. It is incumbent on researchers to explore all factors that may contribute to reading disabilities and not to limit themselves to those that may seem to fit with currently popular models.

Ultimately the goal of research examining the visual processing of readers of different ability levels is to determine the role that visual processes play in learning to read and in reading failure. However, establishing whether a weakness in any particular processing ability is causal in reading acquisition or reading failure is a difficult problem. Nearly all of the research examining the strengths and weaknesses of children who differ in reading ability is correlational in nature. It can tell us which factors are related to levels of reading ability, but it cannot tell us why. There is very little research on reading disabilities that can validly be interpreted as demonstrating a causal link between a particular processing deficit and reading failure. Deficits in some well-documented correlates of reading ability, such as phonemic awareness, have been suggested as causes of reading disability, but even these have not passed crucial experimental tests (Bryant & Goswami, 1987; Hulme, 1987) demonstrating a causal link.

Future research examining the relation between visual processing deficits and reading disability should focus particular attention on the possibility of visual memory deficits among reading-disabled children in the age range from 6 to 8 years. In addition, future research should explore other potential causal factors that might account for the relation between visual deficits and reading disabilities. Perhaps, as Farmer and Klein (1995) have argued, both visual and phonological/linguistic deficits may reflect a more basic "root cause," such as a temporal processing deficit. The challenge for future researchers is to explain how basic processing weaknesses of various types may be related to each other or may interact in causing reading disabilities.

Another topic deserving of research attention is the role of visual deficits in the processing of various types of orthographic information, both different orthographies (i.e., writing systems) and orthographic (i.e., spelling) patterns within alphabetic writing systems (Willows & Geva, 1995). For example, if visual processing deficits have some role in written language disabilities then they might be expected to affect the type and incidence of disabilities in countries with more visually confusing symbol systems.

B. Practical Implications

If some disabled readers have delays or deficits in their visual processing abilities, such weaknesses could be a factor in their apparent difficulties in differentiating between similar-looking letters and words; especially in analyzing and remembering the orthographic patterns in words and in processing letters and words at rapid rates in text. Clinical observations and case reports, correlational evidence from studies using standardized psychometric instruments, and visual deficit subtypes from clinical and neuropsychological studies all point to some relation between visual processing deficits and reading disabilities. Evidence from information-processing research involving basic visual perception and visual memory also suggests that there is some connection between visual processing deficits and reading disabilities. At this point, however, the potential role of visual processing weaknesses in written language problems is not well enough understood to draw confident conclusions about practice.

Clinicians and educators in the LD field should certainly keep an open mind about the possibility that visual processing deficits contribute in some way to reading disabilities. Prudence would dictate that both assessment approaches and teaching techniques should be devised on the assumption that the reading-disabled child may have some difficulty in coping with the visual demands of the task. The findings indicating that younger disabled readers (6 to 8 years of age) may be more likely to have some sort of visual perceptual and/or visual memory deficits are worthy of special note. The visual demands of the beginning stages of reading acquisition are probably more significant than those at later stages of reading acquisition when linguistic processes may play a greater role (Chall, 1996; Vernon, 1977).

References

Allegretti, C. L., & Puglisi, J. T. (1986). Disabled vs nondisabled readers: Perceptual vs higher-order processing of one vs three letters. *Perceptual and Motor Skills, 63,* 463–469.

Arnett, J. L., & Di Lollo, V. (1979). Visual information processing in relation to age and to reading ability. *Journal of Experimental Child Psychology, 27,* 143–152.

Badcock, D., & Lovegrove, W. (1981). The effects of contrast, stimulus duration, and spatial frequency on visible persistence in normal and specifically disabled readers. *Journal of Experimental Psychology: Human Perception and Performance, 7,* 495–505.

Bakker, D. J. (1979). Hemispheric differences and reading strategies: Two dyslexias? *Bulletin of the Orton Society, 29,* 84–100.

Blaskey, P., Scheiman, M., Parisi, M., Ciner, E. B., Gallaway, M., & Selznick, R. (1990). The effectiveness of Irlen filters for improved reading performance: A pilot study. *Journal of Learning Disabilities, 23,* 604–612.

Boder, E. (1973). Developmental Dyslexia: A diagnostic approach based on three atypical reading-spelling patterns. *Developmental Medicine and Child Neurology, 15,* 663–687.

Breitmeyer, B. (1993). Sustained (P) and transient (M) channels in vision: A review and implications for reading. In D. M. Willows, R. Kruk, & E. Corcos (Eds.), *Visual processes in reading and reading disabilities* (pp. 95–110). Hillsdale, NJ: Lawrence Erlbaum Associates.

Breitmeyer, B. G., & Williams, M. C. (1990). Effects of isoluminant-background color on metacontrast and stroboscopic motion: Interactions between sustained (P) and transient (M) channels. *Vision Research, 30*(7), 1069–1075.

Bryant, P. E., & Goswami, U. (1987). Development of phonemic awareness. In J. Beech & A. Colley (Eds.), *Cognitive approaches to reading* (pp. 213–244). Chichester, UK: Wiley.

Chall, J. S. (1996). *Stages of reading development* (2nd ed.). Orlando, FL: Harcourt Brace.

Cohen, R. (1967). Remedial training of first grade children with visual perceptual retardation. *Reading Horizons, 45,* 60–63.

Corcos, E., & Willows, D. M. (1993). The role of visual processes in good and poor readers' utilization of orthographic information in letter strings. In S. Wright & R. Groner (Eds.), *Studies in visual information processing: Facets of dyslexia and its remediation* (pp. 95–106). Amsterdam: North Holland Elsevier.

Craik, F. I. M., & Lockhart, R. S. (1972). Levels of processing: A framework for memory research. *Journal of Verbal Learning and Verbal Behavior, 11,* 671–684.

Crosby, R. M. N. (1968). *Reading and the dyslexic child.* London: Souvenir Press.

DeFries, J. C., & Decker, S. N. (1982). Genetic aspects of reading disability: A family study.

In R. N. Malatesha & P. G. Aaron, (Eds.), *Reading disorders: Varieties and treatments* (pp. 255–280). Toronto: Academic Press.

de Hirsch, K., Jansky, J. J., & Langford, W. S. (1966). *Predicting reading failure.* New York, NY: Harper & Row.

Denkla, M. B. (1977). Minimal brain dysfunction and dyslexia: Beyond diagnosis by exclusion. In M. Blaw, I. Rapin, & M. Kinsbourne (Eds.), *Topics in child neurology* (pp. 223–268). New York: Spectrum.

Di Lollo, V., Hanson, D., & McIntyre, J. S. (1983). Initial stages of visual information processing in dyslexia. *Journal of Experimental Psychology: Human Perception and Performance, 9,* 923–935.

Doehring, D. G. (1978). The tangled web of behavioral research on developmental dyslexia. In A. L. Benton & D. Pearl (Eds.), *Dyslexia: An appraisal of current knowledge* (pp. 123–135). New York: Oxford University Press.

Doehring, D. G., Hoshko, I. M., & Bryans, B. N. (1979). Statistical classification of children with reading problems. *Journal of Clinical Neuropsychology, 1,* 5–16.

Dunn-Rankin, P. (1978). Visual characteristics of words. *Scientific American, 238*(1), 122–130.

Farmer, M. E., & Klein, R. M. (1995). The evidence for a temporal processing deficit linked to dyslexia: A review. *Psychonomic Bulletin and Review, 2*(4), 460–493.

Farnham-Diggory, S. (1978). *Learning disabilities: A psychological perspective.* Cambridge, Mass.: Harvard University Press.

Feagans, L. V., & McKinney, J. D. (1991). Subtypes of learning disabilities: A review. In L. V. Feagans, E. J. Short, & L. J. Meltzer (Eds.), *Subtypes of learning disabilities: Theoretical perspectives and research* (pp. 3–31). Hillsdale, NJ: Lawrence Erlbaum Associates.

Fisher, D. F., & Frankfurter, A. (1977). Normal and disabled readers can locate and identify letters: Where's the perceptual deficit? *Journal of Reading Behavior, 9,* 31–43.

Fletcher, J. M., & Satz, P. (1979a). Unitary deficit hypotheses of reading disabilities: Has Vellutino led us astray? *Journal of Learning Disabilities, 12*(3), 155–159.

Fletcher, J. M., & Satz, P. (1979b). Has Vellutino led us astray? A rejoinder to a reply. *Journal of Learning Disabilities, 12*(3), 168–171.

Frostig, M. (1968). Education of children with learning disabilities. In H. R. Myklebust (Ed.), *Progress in learning disabilities* (pp. 234–266). New York: Grune & Stratton.

Gibson, E. J., & Levin, H. (1975). *The psychology of reading.* Cambridge, MA: MIT Press.

Golick, M. (1984). *Characteristics of developmental dyslexia: Implications for models of skilled performance.* Unpublished manuscript, McGill University, Montreal.

Goyen, J. D., & Lyle, J. G. (1971a). Effect of incentives and age on the visual recognition of retarded readers. *Journal of Experimental Child Psychology, 11,* 266–273.

Goyen, J. D., & Lyle, J. G. (1971b). Effect of incentives upon retarded and normal readers on a visual-associate learning task. *Journal of Experimental Child Psychology, 11,* 274–280.

Goyen, J. D., & Lyle, J. G. (1973). Short-term memory and visual discrimination in retarded readers. *Perceptual and Motor Skills, 36,* 403–408.

Gross, K., & Rothenberg, S. (1979). An examination of methods used to test the visual perceptual deficit hypothesis of dyslexia. *Journal of Learning Disabilities, 12,* 670–677.

Gross, K., Rothenberg, S., Schottenfeld, S., & Drake, C. (1978). Duration threshold for letter identification in left and right visual fields for normal and reading-disabled children. *Neuropsychologia, 16*, 709–715.

Hinshelwood, J. (1895). Word-blindness and visual memory. *Lancet, 2*, 1564–1570.

Hinshelwood, J. (1917). *Congenital word-blindness.* London: H. K. Lewis & Co.

Hooper, S. R., & Willis, W. G. (1989). *Learning disability subtyping.* New York, NY: Springer-Verlag.

Hulme, C. (1987). Reading retardation. In J. Beech & A. Colley (Eds.), *Cognitive approaches to reading* (pp. 245–270). Chichester, England: Wiley.

Hulme, C. (1988). The implausibility of low-level visual deficits as a cause of children's reading difficulties. *Cognitive Neuropsychology, 5*, 369–374.

Irlen, H. (1983, August). *Successful treatment of learning disabilities.* Paper presented at the 91st Annual Convention of the American Psychological Association, Annaheim, California.

Irlen, H. (1991). *Reading by the colors.* Garden City Park, CA: Avery.

Johnson, D. J., & Myklebust, H. R. (1967). *Learning disabilities: Educational principles and practices.* New York: Grune & Stratton.

Kaufman, N. L. (1980). Review of research on reversal errors. *Perceptual and Motor Skills, 51*, 55–79.

Korhonen, T. (1991). Neuropsychological stability and prognosis of subgroups of children with learning disabilities. *Journal of Learning Disabilities, 24*, 48–57.

Kruk, R., & Willows, D. M. (1993). Toward an ecologically valid analysis of visual processes in dyslexic readers. In S. Wright & R. Groner (Eds.), *Studies in visual information processing: Facets of dyslexia and its remediation* (pp. 193–206). Amsterdam: North Holland Elsevier.

Lachmann, F. M. (1960). Perceptual-motor development in children retarded in reading ability. *Journal of Consulting Psychology, 24*, 427–431.

Lehmkuhle, S. (1993). Neurological basis of visual processes in reading. In D. M. Willows, R. Kruk, & E. Corcos (Eds.), *Visual processes in reading and reading disabilities* (pp. 77–94). Hillsdale, NJ: Lawrence Erlbaum Associates.

Livingstone, M. S., Rosen, G. D., Drislane, F. W., & Galaburda, A. M. (1991). Physiological and anatomical evidence for a magnocellular defect in developmental dyslexia. *Proceedings of the National Academy of Sciences, 88*, 7943–7947.

Lovegrove, W. (1996). Could a transient visual system deficit play a role in reading disability? In R. P. Garzia (Ed.), *Vision and reading* (pp. 177–191). St. Louis, MO: Mosby.

Lovegrove, W., & Brown, C. (1978). Development of information processing in normal and disabled readers. *Perceptual and Motor Skills, 46*, 1047–1054.

Lovegrove, W., Billing, G., & Slaghuis, W. (1978). Processing of visual contour orientation information in normal and disabled reading children. *Cortex, 14*, 268–278.

Lovegrove, W., Bowling, A., Badcock, D., & Blackwood, M. (1980a). Specific reading disability: Differences in contrast sensitivity as a function of spatial frequency. *Science, 210*, 439–440.

Lovegrove, W., Heddle, M., & Slaghuis, W. (1980b). Reading disability: Spatial frequency specific deficits in visual information store. *Neuropsychologia, 18*, 111–115.

Lovegrove, W., Martin, F., Bowling, A., Blackwood, M., Badcock, D., & Paxton, S. (1982). Contrast sensitivity functions and specific reading disability. *Neuropsychologia, 20*, 309–315.

Lovegrove, W., Martin, F., & Slaghuis, W. (1986). A theoretical and experimental case for a visual deficit in specific reading disability. *Cognitive Neuropsychology, 3,* 225–267.

Lovegrove, W., & Williams, M. C. (1993). Visual temporal processing deficits in specific reading disability. In D. M. Willows, R. Kruk, & E. Corcos (Eds.), *Visual processes in reading and reading disabilities* (pp. 311–329). Hillsdale, NJ: Lawrence Erlbaum.

Lyle, J. G. (1968). Performance of retarded readers on the Memory-for-Designs test. *Perceptual and Motor Skills, 26,* 851–854.

Lyle, J. G., & Goyen, J. D. (1968). Visual recognition, developmental lag, and strephosymbolia in reading retardation. *Journal of Abnormal Psychology, 73,* 25–29.

Lyle, J. G., & Goyen, J. D. (1975). Effect of speed of exposure and difficulty of discrimination on visual recognition of retarded readers. *Journal of Abnormal Psychology, 84,* 673–676.

Lyon, R., & Watson, B. (1981). Empirically derived subgroups of learning disabled readers: Diagnostic characteristics. *Journal of Learning Disabilities, 14,* 256–261.

McKinney, J. D., Short, E. J., & Feagans, L. (1985). Academic consequences of perceptual-linguistic subtypes of learning disabled children. *Learning Disabilities Research, 1,* 6–17.

Malatesha, R. N., & Dougan, D. R. (1982). Clinical subtypes of developmental dyslexia: Resolution of an irresolute problem. In R. N. Malatesha & P. G. Aaron, (Eds.), *Reading disorders: Varieties and treatments* (pp. 69–92). Toronto: Academic Press.

Mann, V. (1984). Reading skill and language skill. *Developmental Review, 4,* 1–15.

Martin, F., & Lovegrove, W. (1984). The effects of field size and luminance on contrast sensitivity differences between specifically reading disabled and normal children. *Neuropsychologia, 22,* 73–77.

Mazer, S. R., McIntyre, C. W., Murray, M. E., Till, R. E., & Blackwell, S. L. (1983). Visual persistence and information pick up in learning disabled children. *Journal of Learning Disabilities, 16*(4), 221–225.

Money, J. (1966). Case 1: Space-form deficit. In J. Money (Ed.), *The disabled reader: Education of the dyslexic child* (pp. 263–276). Baltimore, MD: Johns Hopkins Press.

Morgan, W. P. (1896). A case of congenital word-blindness. *British Medical Journal, 2,* 1378.

Morrison, F. J., Giordani, B., & Nagy, J. (1977). Reading disability: An information-processing analysis. *Science, 19,* 77–79.

Nisbett, R., & Ross, L. (1980). *Human inference: Strategies and shortcomings of social judgment.* Englewood Cliffs, NJ: Prentice-Hall.

O'Connor, P. D., Sofo, F., Kendall, L., & Olsen, G. (1990). Reading disabilities and the effects of colored filters. *Journal of Learning Disabilities, 23,* 597–603, 620.

O'Neill, G., & Stanley, G. (1976). Visual processing of straight lines in dyslexic and normal children. *British Journal of Educational Psychology, 46,* 323–327.

Orton, S. T. (1925). "Word-blindness" in school children. *Archives of Neurology and Psychiatry, 14,* 581–615.

Parker, R. M. (1990). Power, control, and validity in research. *Journal of Learning Disabilities, 23*(10), 613–620.

Petrauskas, R. J., & Rourke, B. P. (1979). Identification of subtypes of retarded readers: A neuropsychological, multivariate approach. *Journal of Clinical Neuropsychology, 1,* 17–37.

Rawson, M. B. (1982). Louise Baker and the Leonardo Syndrome. *Annals of Dyslexia, 32,* 289–304.

Rayner, K., & Pollatsek, A. (1989). *The psychology of reading.* Englewood Cliffs, NJ: Prentice Hall.

Rayner, K., Pollatsek, A., & Bilsky, A. B. (1995). Can a temporal processing deficit account for dyslexia? *Psychonomic Bulletin and Review, 2*(4), 501–507.

Robinson, G. L. W., & Conway, R. N. F. (1990). The effects of Irlen colored lenses on students' specific reading skills and their perception of ability: A 12-month validity study. *Journal of Learning Disabilities, 23,* 588–597.

Robinson, G. L., & Miles, J. (1987). The use of colored overlays to improve visual processing: A preliminary survey. *The Exceptional Child, 34,* 65–70.

Rosen, C. (1966). An experimental study of visual perceptual training and reading achievement in first grade children. *Perceptual and Motor Skills, 22,* 979–986.

Rosner, J. (1996). Reading readiness. In R. P. Garzia (Ed.), *Vision and reading* (pp. 49–69). St. Louis, MO: Mosby.

Satz, P., & Fletcher, J. M. (1980). Minimal brain dysfunctions: An appraisal of research concepts and methods. In H. E. Rie & E. D. Rie (Eds.), *Handbook of minimal brain dysfunctions: A critical view* (pp. 669–715). New York: Wiley.

Satz, P., & Morris, R. (1981). Learning disability subtypes: A review. In F. J. Pirozzolo & M. C. Wittrock (Eds.), *Neuropsychological and cognitive processes in reading* (pp. 109–144). New York: Academic Press.

Saunders, R. E. (1962). Dyslexia: Its phenomenology. In J. Money (Ed.), *Reading disability.* Baltimore, MD: Johns Hopkins Press.

Simpson, E. (1979). *Reversals: A personal account of victory over dyslexia.* Boston, MA: Houghton Mifflin.

Singer, H. (1979). On reading, language and learning. *Harvard Educational Review, 49,* 125–128.

Slaghuis, W. L., & Lovegrove, W. J. (1985). Spatial-frequency-dependent visible persistence and specific reading disability. *Brain and Cognition, 4,* 219–240.

Slaghuis, W. L., & Lovegrove, W. J. (1986). The effect of physical flicker on visible persistence in normal and specifically disabled readers. *Australian Journal of Psychology, 38,* 1–11.

Slaghuis, W. L., Lovegrove, W. J., & Davidson, J. A. (1993). Visual and language processing deficits are concurrent in dyslexia. *Cortex, 29,* 601–615.

Smith, C. E., & Keogh, B. K. (1962). The group Bender-Gestalt as a reading readiness screening test. *Perceptual and Motor Skills, 15,* 639–645.

Spache, G. D., McIroy, K., & Berg, P. C. (1981). *Case studies in reading disability.* Boston, MA: Allyn and Bacon, Inc.

Stanley, G. (1975). Two-part stimulus integration and specific reading disability. *Perceptual and Motor Skills, 41,* 873–874.

Stanley, G. (1976). The processing of digits by children with specific reading disability (dyslexia). *British Journal of Educational Psychology, 46,* 81–84.

Stanley, G. (1990). Rose-coloured spectacles: A cure for dyslexia? *Australian Psychologist, 25*(2), 65–76.

Stanley, G., & Hall, R. (1973). Short-term visual information processing in dyslexics. *Child Development, 44,* 841–844.

Stanovich, K. E. (1982). Individual differences in the cognitive processes of reading: 1. Word decoding. *Journal of Learning Disabilities, 15,* 485–493.

Stanovich, K. E. (1985). Explaining the variance in terms of psychological processes: What have we learned? *Annals of Dyslexia, 35,* 67–96.

Stanovich, K. E. (1992). *How to think straight about psychology* (3rd ed.). New York, NY: HarperCollins.

Sumbler, K., & Willows, D. M. (1994, November). *Visual processing characteristics of disabled readers diagnosed with Scotopic Sensitivity Syndrome.* Paper presented at the 1994 Annual Conference of the Orton Dyslexia Society, Los Angeles.

Swanson, L. (1978). Verbal encoding effects on the visual short-term memory of learning disabled and normal readers. *Journal of Educational Psychology, 70*(4), 539–544.

Swanson, L. (1982). Verbal short-term memory encoding of learning disabled, deaf, and normal children. *Learning Disability Quarterly, 5,* 21–28.

Swanson, L. (1983). A study of nonstrategic linguistic coding on visual recall of learning disabled readers. *Journal of Learning Disabilities, 16*(4), 209–216.

Swanson, L. (1984). Semantic and visual memory codes in learning disabled readers. *Journal of Experimental Child Psychology, 37,* 124–140.

Tallal, P., Sainburg, R. L., & Jernigan, T. (1991). The neuropathology of developmental dysphasia: Behavioral, morphological and physiological evidence for a pervasive temporal processing disorder. *Reading and Writing, 3,* 363–377.

Tyrrell, R., Holland, K., Dennis, D., & Wilkins, A. (1995). Colored overlays, visual discomfort, visual search and classroom reading. *Journal of Research in Reading, 18*(1), 10–23.

Vellutino, F. R. (1979). *Dyslexia: Theory and research.* Cambridge, MA: The M. I. T. Press.

Vellutino, F. (1987). Dyslexia. *Scientific American, 256*(3), 34–41.

Vellutino, F. R., Scanlon, D. M., & Tanzman, M. S. (1991). Bridging the gap between cognitive and neuropsychological conceptualizations of reading disability. *Learning and Individual Differences, 3,* 181–203.

Vellutino, F. R., Pruzek, R., Steger, J. A., & Meshoulam, U. (1973a). Immediate visual recall in poor and normal readers as a function of orthographic-linguistic familiarity. *Cortex, 9,* 368–384.

Vellutino, F. R., Steger, J. A., & Pruzek, R. (1973b). Inter- versus intra-sensory deficiency in paired-associate learning in poor and normal readers. *Canadian Journal of Behavioural Science, 5,* 111–123.

Vellutino, F. R., Harding, C. J., Phillips, F., & Steger, J. A. (1975a). Differential transfer in poor and normal readers. *Journal of Genetic Psychology, 126,* 3–18.

Vellutino, F. R., Smith, H., Steger, J. A., & Kaman, M. (1975b). Reading disability: Age differences and the perceptual deficit hypothesis. *Child Development, 46,* 487–493.

Vellutino, F. R., Steger, J. A., Kaman, M., & DeSetto, L. (1975c). Visual form perception in deficient and normal readers as function of age and orthographic linguistic familiarity. *Cortex, 11,* 22–30.

Vellutino, F. R., Steger, J. A., Moyer, B. M., Harding, S. C., & Niles, C. J. (1977). Has the perceptual deficit hypothesis led us astray? *Journal of Learning Disabilities, 10,* 54–64.

Vernon, M. D. (1971). *Reading and its difficulties: A psychological study.* Cambridge, UK: The University Press.

Vernon, M. D. (1977). Varieties of deficiency in reading processes. *Harvard Educational Review, 47,* 396–410.

Walther-Müller, P. U. (1995). Is there a deficit of early vision in dyslexia. *Perception, 24,* 919–936.

Watson, C., & Willows, D. M. (1995). Information processing patterns in specific reading disability. *Journal of Learning Disabilities, 28*(4), 216–231.

Williams, M. C., LeCluyse, K., & Littell, R. (1996). A wavelength specific intervention for reading disability. In R. P. Garzia (Ed.), *Vision and reading* (pp. 283–305). St. Louis, MO: Mosby.

Willows, D. M. (1996). Assessment and programming for reading and writing difficulties. In R. P. Garzia (Ed.), *Vision and reading* (pp. 249–282). St. Louis, MO: Mosby.

Willows, D. M., Corcos, E., & Kershner, J. (1993a). Perceptual and cognitive factors in dyslexics' and normal readers' perception and memory of unfamiliar visual symbols. In S. Wright & R. Groner (Eds.), *Studies in visual information processing: Facets of dyslexia and its remediation* (pp. 163–178). Amsterdam: North Holland Elsevier.

Willows, D. M., Kruk, R., & Corcos, E. (1993b). Are there differences between disabled and normal readers in their processing of visual information? In D. M. Willows, R. Kruk, & E. Corcos (Eds.), *Visual processes in reading and reading disabilities* (pp. 265–285). Hillsdale, NJ: Lawrence Erlbaum.

Willows, D. M., & E. Geva. (1995). What is visual in orthographic processing? In V. W. Berninger (Ed.), *The varieties of orthographic knowledge II: Relationships to phonology, reading, and writing* (pp. 355–376). Dordrecht, The Netherlands: Kluwer Academic Publishers.

Willows, D. M., & Sumbler, K. (1994, November). *Effect of Irlen colored overlays on reading speed, accuracy, and comprehension.* Paper presented at the 1994 Annual Conference of the Orton Dyslexia Society, Los Angeles.

Willows, D. M., & Terepocki, M. (1993). The relation of reversal errors to reading disability. In D. M. Willows, R. Kruk, & E. Corcos (Eds.), *Visual processes in reading and reading disabilities* (pp. 31–56). Hillsdale, NJ: Lawrence Erlbaum.

Willows, D. M., & Watson, C. (1998). Diagnosis and remediation in reading. In D. A. Wagner, R. L. Venezky, & B. V. Street (Eds.), *Literacy: An international handbook.* New York, NY: Garland Publishing.

CHAPTER 7

Social Competence of Students with Learning Disabilities

Tanis Bryan

I. RATIONALE

In just a few decades the field of learning disabilities (LD) has made amazing progress in establishing services for children, training teachers to provide these services, and developing a research base to help us understand the nature of LD. This research base has accumulated evidence that a significant number of children with LD are likely to have problems in the social domain. In response, efforts to revise and refine the definition of LD have included social problems (Association for Children and Adults with Learning Disabilities, 1985; Kavanagh & Truss, 1987). Although alterations in the federal definition of LD included in P.L. 94 142 and I.D.E.A. are unlikely, estimates of the percentages of students with problems in the social domain indicate many students with LD experience problems gaining acceptance from their peers. Studies have found that 35% (Baum, Duffelmeyer, & Geelan, 1988) to 59.1% (Kistner & Gatlin, 1989) of children with LD have social problems with about half rejected and half ignored by classmates (Stone & LaGreca, 1990). Furthermore, the identification of social dysfunction among students with LD occurs at about the same rate irrespective of age and school and community settings. This suggests that the problems of younger children are not being addressed as they persist into junior high and senior high levels (Baum et al., 1988). Although professionals and parents have acknowledged that many children and adolescents with LD experience significant difficulties in acquiring the social skills necessary to be considered socially competent by others, these problems are not being adequately addressed.

Because current practices in assessment and interventions for students with LD stress academic skills, it is important to pause and consider why problems in the social domain demand our attention. First, across cultures, peer relationships are second only to parent relationships in their importance for child development. Abundant evidence attests to the centrality of peer interaction in children's development of reasoning in personal, societal, and moral domains of knowledge (Turiel, 1983). Abundant evidence also links problems in peer relationships to problems in school achievement (Parker & Asher, 1987), problems many years later in mental health and adjustment, and, in combination with aggression, adult criminality (Parker & Asher, 1987; Cowen, Pederson, Babigion, Izzo, & Trost, 1973).

Second, teaching and learning are social events. Classroom interactions and relationships between students, teachers, and classmates influence academic progress. Indeed, measures of self-concepts are better predictors of achievement gains in spelling, arithmetic, and written language than IQs (Kershner, 1990). Children who feel good about themselves and are confident in their ability to cope with school demands are more likely to be successful students. Third, social problems play a role in the referral and identification of children as LD. Poor academic achievement by itself may not prompt teachers to make special education referrals (Ysseldyke, Algozzine, Shinn, & McGue, 1982), but poor academic progress plus teachers' judgments of "teachability" (e.g., not paying attention, being disorganized, not responding to directions, not getting along with others; Keogh, 1983; T. Bryan, Bay, Shelden, & Simon, 1990) will generate referrals to special education. Thus, although social problems are not included in the federal definition of LD, and children are not explicitly referred for social problems, children's classroom behavior appears to be a decisive factor in the referral process.

Third, parents of students with LD have long campaigned for recognition of problems in the social domain (Bader, 1975). Parent concern is reflected in the 1985 definition of LD developed by the Association for Children and Adults with Learning Disabilities (ACLD), which includes this statement: "throughout life the condition can affect self-esteem, education, vocation, socialization, and/or daily living activities" (p. 2). Parental concerns have been legitimized by evidence that social difficulties may persist beyond the elementary and secondary school years. High school students and postsecondary adults with LD have indicated that they experience significant social problems (Gregory, Shanahan, & Walberg, 1986; White, 1985), and that these problems extend to the workplace (Minskoff, Sautter, Hoffmann, & Hawks, 1987). Professionals in the field should not ignore the observations, concerns, and complaints of parents and persons with LD as they seek help for such problems.

Fourth, LDs have been conceptualized as problems in information processing (attention, perception, memory, language) that affect children's thinking, speaking, and listening. These processes are required for almost everything we do. Hence, to limit our concern to information processing in reading and math and to ignore their importance in social interactions limits the likelihood that we can help children, or grow in our understanding of the nature of LD. It is of therapeutic and heuristic importance to consider how problems in attention, memory, perception, and the like affect children's social development.

A major objective in writing this chapter is to convince readers that the social problems of students with LD demand professional attention. When such problems are evident they have implications for life-long adjustment at home, on the job, and in the community. Even though teachers increasingly are aware of students' needs for social skills interventions, many teachers do not feel comfortable or prepared to teach social skills. Indeed, Baum et al.'s (1988) survey of resource teachers found that only 25% felt adequately prepared, 56% felt fair or poorly prepared, and over 18% indicated they had no preparation to teach social skills. This chapter will provide the necessary background for understanding the scope and specific nature of the problems many students with LD have in the social domain.

II. MODEL OF SOCIAL COMPETENCE AND OBJECTIVES

A. Definitions

Social competence refers to an evaluation that a person has performed a task adequately; behavior is socially competent if it results in positive social outcomes for people (Gresham, 1986). Vaughn and Hogan (1990) defined social competence as a multidimensional construct consisting of positive relations with others, accurate and age-appropriate social cognition, absence of maladaptive behaviors, and effective social skills. Social skills refer to specific behaviors an individual exhibits to perform competently on a task (Gresham, 1986). Definitions of social skills include (a) a peer-acceptance definition, in which children who receive positive ratings or are popular with peers are defined as socially skilled; (b) behavioral definition, in which specific behaviors are operationalized for assessment; and (c) social validity definition, in which social skills are behaviors demanded by the particular situation.

This chapter examines the social competence and social skills of students with LD. A broad view of social competence is taken, one that includes students affective states, self-concepts, and attributions because these feelings and beliefs influence social behavior. Thus, the chapter is organized around five categories of research that have delineated the problems many students with LD experience in becoming socially competent (cf. Pearl, T. Bryan, & Donahue, 1980; Margalit, 1994; Tur-Kaspa & Bryan, 1994). The five categories are (a) affective status (e.g., depression, anxiety), (b) children's beliefs (e.g., self-concept, attributions), (c) children's social competence (i.e., peer judgments and loneliness), (d) social skills (e.g., perception, cognition), and (e) maladaptive behaviors (e.g., hyperactivity, aggression; T. Bryan, 1997).

At the end, readers should have an understanding of the various factors that make up social competence, and how students with LD are vulnerable in the following areas:

1. Anxiety and depression
2. Self-concepts and attributions
3. Making friends and loneliness
4. Social perceptual, cognitive, and behavioral skills
5. Hyperactivity, aggression, teasing, and bullying.

II. STUDENTS' AFFECTIVE STATUS

A. Definition of Affect and Emotion

Although theories about human behavior have recognized the interrelationships of cognition, affect, and will (i.e., motivation) for centuries; affect and emotions have been pretty much ignored in education and psychology. Briefly, emotions are strong feelings that interrupt other behaviors and are expressed behaviorally or in facial expressions (Isen, 1984). Affect is much milder and less intense feelings and moods. Affect is more pervasive and does not interrupt our thoughts and behaviors. Until quite recently, research on human behavior has examined cognition independent of affect and emotion. Similarly, teachers have perceived themselves as primarily responsible for curriculum and instruction. The fact is that affective states, even mild ones that we are not aware of, influence a broad range of cognitive and social processes.

B. Depression, Anxiety, and Suicide

Affect has a significant effect on learning and social behavior. Thus it is important to recognize that many students with LD report experiencing more negative affect, such as depression and anxiety, than nondisabled (NLD) students (T. Bryan, Sonnefeld, & Greenberg, 1981; Cohen, 1985; Maag & Behrens, 1989; Maag & Behrens, 1994; Margalit & Heiman, 1986). Based on the Children's Depression Inventory (CDI; Kovaks, 1992) and the Child Anxiety Scale (CAS; Gillis, 1980), adolescents with LD demonstrate higher anxiety levels, more frequent and more serious bouts of depression, and higher rates of suicide than NLD adolescents (Huntington & Bender, 1993). Dalley, Bolocofsky, Alcorn, & Baker (1992) found that 7.7% of NLD, but 23.8% of students classified LD exhibited clinical levels of depressive symptomatology. Contradictory evidence, however, was reported by Maag and Reid (1994) and McPhail (1993). Maag and Reid (1994) found that the prevalence of depression for both adolescents with and without LD was 10%. McPhail (1993) had students rate their levels of affect, activation, cognitive efficiency, and self-esteem every 40 min to 2 h in response to electronic pagers. Students with LD reported feeling more positive and active during school, and no different after school than their peers.

C. Affect Influences Learning and Social Behavior

Although we have to account for contrary evidence, the impact of depression and suicide are such that we cannot ignore evidence that finds these students at greater risk. Teachers and parents should take very seriously indications of severe depression. In addition, affective states that are not life threatening have significant effects on learning and social behavior. Positive (mild) affect improves the amount and rate of learning, whereas negative affect retards learning and memory. It is believed that happiness induces higher levels of activation and faster and more efficient information-processing strategies, whereas sad moods may cause children to become more withdrawn and inattentive (Isen & Means, 1983). Affect also influences children's social behaviors with other children (Barden, Garber, Duncan, & Masters, 1981). Children who experience depression have been found to have poor social relationships (Spence, 1991). Part of the problem is that people prefer to be around happy people and avoid depressed people. Positive and negative emotions are nearly as contagious as colds and flus. Thus, not only does negativity make one feel bad, it depresses learning, and other people are reluctant to interact with depressed people.

D. Implications for Teaching

The good news is that positive affect can be self-induced. The results of studies conducted with children with LD, behavior disorders, and normally achieving students have shown that having children close their eyes and think of something that makes them very happy for about a minute has significantly positive effects on children's social problem solving (T. Bryan, Sullivan, & Mathur, in press), performance (e.g., doing math problems T. Bryan & Bryan, 1991), and learning (e.g., doing the coding subtest on the WISC-R; Yasutake & T. Bryan, 1994). Classroom teachers can start the day, or a lesson, or introduce the positive mood induction prior to a test. Compare results with students' performance under regular conditions. Forty-five seconds: it's worth a try.

IV. LEARNING-DISABLED STUDENTS' SELF-PERCEPTIONS AND BELIEFS

A. Overview of Self-Perceptions

Self-perceptions, a multidimensional construct, are included in this model of social competence because they influence behavior in academic and social domains. The degree to which we are self-confident, happy, and positive has an impact on how much effort we spend learning, and how we present ourselves to others. Consequently our self-perceptions shape others' responses to us. A great deal of attention has been paid to self-perceptions of students with LD. Research on students with LD has examined self-concept, self-esteem, and attributions.

B. Self-Concept

Self-concept refers to a person's awareness of his or her own characteristics and the ways in which he or she is like and unlike others (McCandless & Evans, 1973). Studies using the Piers-Harris Self Concept Scale (Piers & Harris, 1969) have found that students with LD rated themselves more negatively than NLD classmates (e.g., Jones, 1985; Rogers & Saklofske, 1985; Margalit and Zak, 1984), but other studies reported no differences (Boersma, Chapman, & Maguire, 1979; Silverman & Zigmond, 1983). Margalit and Zak (1984) used factor analysis to sort out this inconsistency, and found students with LD scored worse than NLD children on one of three factors—self-dissatisfaction. Jones (1985) found that students with LD differ on their estimations of intellectual abilities, social status, physical appearance, and attributes but not on social popularity, anxiety, and happiness and satisfaction. Using the Coopersmith Self-Esteem Inventory, Rosenberg and Gaier (1977) found students with LD differ from NLD classmates on the social self-peer scale by rating themselves as less easy to like, less fun to be with, and less popular with peers, but a study by Winne, Woodlands, and Wong (1982) found they differed only on the School/Academic subscale.

Harter's Perceived Competence Scale for Children (Harter, 1985) has children rate their scholastic competence, social acceptance, athletic competence, physical appearance, behavioral conduct, and global self-worth. Students with LD rate themselves lower on all scales than NLD students; they perceive themselves as having less ability in both academic and nonacademic areas and report having lower-self esteem than NLD classmates (Kistner and Osborne, 1987). However, Vaughn and Haager (1994) examined self-concepts of low achievers, and average/high achievers and students with LD prior to and following identification across kindergarten through fifth grades using the Harter and Pike (1984) and Harter scales (Harter, 1985). Students with LD showed a decline in academic self-perceptions between kindergarten and first grade, and students with LD and low achievers perceived themselves as lower in cooperation than higher achieving classmates. There were no other group differences on academic, global, or social self-perception across the four grades.

The Student's Perception of Ability Scale (Chapman, 1985; Boersma et al., 1979) measures students' perceptions of their general ability, arithmetic ability, reading and spelling ability, penmanship and neatness, confidence in academic ability, and general school satisfaction. Students with LD score lower than their NLD classmates, except for ratings of penmanship and neatness on this scale (Hiebert, Wong, & Hunter, 1982; Chapman, 1985). In a longitudinal study conducted over a 2-year period, Chapman (1988) reported that students with LD have relatively little confidence in their ability and expect to achieve at lower levels in comparison to NLD classmates. When students with LD experience success, they see it as being caused by a teacher's assistance or easy work. By and large, the results of self-concept studies indicate that children's decrements in academic self-concept occur by age 8 or 9 and remain relatively stable through at least Grade 10 (Chapman, 1988).

1. Self-Concepts of Subgroups

One of the criticisms of LD research is that the samples represent heterogeneous groups of children. Thus results could reflect characteristics of a particular subgroup of students with LD rather than LD in general. Durrant, Cunningham, and Voelker (1990) hypothesized that subgroups of LD students with behavior disorders account for the negative self-concepts found in studies of students with LD. In their study, non-behavior-disordered groups scored higher than behavior-disordered groups in cognitive, social, and general self-concept. The non-behavior-disordered LD group did not differ from the non-LD group. The results also showed that cognitive and social self-concept are as strongly related to behavioral factors as they are to achievement level. Bender and Golden (1990) used cluster analysis to identify five groups of students with LD on the basis of language and visually based cognitive ability, reading achievement, behavior, and self-concept. Two of the five subgroups had serious problems with self-concept. One group, which included 23% of the sample, had the lowest score on language-based cognitive ability, very low scores on self-perceptions of intellectual status, and popularity. The second group included 10% of the sample and was described as a behaviorally disordered group masquerading as LD. These students were superior to the others on cognitive and reading variables, but had major problems in behavior and self-concept.

2. Value Placed on Academics

Because students with LD sometimes score high on global measures of self-concept but low on academic self-concept, the degree to which they define academic achievement as important has been questioned. Clearly the value they place on school learning might influence their willingness to persist, especially on difficult material. Thus it is important that students with LD do not discount the importance of academic achievement regardless of their self-perceived lack of competence in the academic domain (Clever, Bear, & Juvonnen, 1992; Smith & Nagle, 1995).

3. Social Comparisons and School Placement

The integration of students with LD into regular classrooms has been based in part on the presumed stigma associated with segregation into self-contained classrooms. The presumption is that segregation has a negative impact on students' self-concepts. But self-perceptions are derived in part from social comparisons. Children with disabilities in mainstream classrooms may perceive themselves more negatively when they compare themselves with higher achieving classmates; they may perceive themselves more favorably when their references are other children with disabilities. Thus, several studies have examined the impact of special education and regular class placements on students self-concepts.

Two studies suggest that placement in segregated classes does not have a negative impact on self-concepts. Battle and Blowers (1982) found that students in special education classes had greater gains in self-perception than students in regular classes. Morvitz and Motta (1992) found that self-esteem of students in self-contained classes was not lower than students in regular classes. But, Leondari (1993) found that self-concepts of third- to sixth-grade Greek children in special education classes were more negative than children in regular classes on academic self-concept and global self-worth. Similarly, Beltempo and Achille (1990) found that third- and fourth-grade Canadian students in maximum special education placement (70% of the time) had lower self-concepts that persisted across time than children in the partial placement (30% of the time) and NLD groups. They also found students in resource programs were significantly lower than the regular class students. McKinney and Feagans (1984) showed that children with LD receiving interventions showed no improvement or declined in academic achievement. Renick and Harter (1989) reported that students with LD in a resource room program over the third through eighth grades gradually came to see themselves as less academically competent than their non-disabled peers; however when they based their self-evaluations on other students in the resource room, their perceived competence remained constant over that period. Smith and Nagle (1995) found that third- and fourth-grade children with LD rated themselves as less competent than did NLD students in intelligence, academic skills, behavior, and social acceptance. Furthermore, these differences were not related to the length of time they had received special education services, nor whether they compared themselves to regular or resource room peers. Clever, Bear, and Juvonen (1992) reported children with LD in full-time integrated classrooms held lower self-perceptions of academic achievement and behavioral conduct than NLD children.

4. Summary

There continues to be great interest, international in scope, in the construct of self-concept of students with LD. It is notable that investigators are using multivariate techniques; that is, they are trying to examine how self-concept relates to other factors of hypothesized importance (e.g., subgroups, values, class placement). Studies of self-concept represent a test of public policy as investigators examine self-concepts of students in different class settings. Unfortunately, the results are not consistent. Contradictory findings may result from many factors, for instance (a) age differences, (b) levels of academic achievement, (c) socioeconomic status and ethnicity, (d) and the social ecology of these classrooms (e.g., teachers attitudes and behaviors toward students with LD). Also there is some question about the link between low achievement in general and negative self-concepts (Haager & Vaughn, 1995). In addition, the reliability and validity of the measures used also influence outcomes. Much of the variability in these studies could be attributed to imperfections in the measures used. The construct of self-concept is broad and includes many factors. Although investigators have attempted to control for these factors by developing measures of specific categories, there is still much room for measurement error. At this point it seems safe to say that in general students with LD in self-contained, resource, and fully integrated regular classrooms are at risk for negative self-concepts in academic and perhaps social domains.

C. Self-Esteem

Self-esteem refers to the value a person puts on oneself and one's behavior (e.g., one's judgments about one's goodness or badness). Studies of self-esteem focus on perception of self-worth (e.g., "I am able to do things as well as most other people." "I take a positive attitude toward myself." "At times I think I am no good at all."). Studies of self-esteem have not found differences between elementary and junior high school students with LD and normal achieving students (Lincoln & Chazan, 1979; Winne et al., 1982). Using the Rosenberg Self-Esteem Scale (Rosenberg, 1965), appropriate for use with older students, Pearl, Bryan, and Donahue (1980) reported that females with LD may have lower self-esteem than males with LD, but Tollefson et al. (1982) found no group differences. However, in a large national survey of high school seniors in which 439 of 26,147 identified themselves as LD, the LD reported lower estimates of adjustment (e.g., "I'm satisfied with myself") than classmates (Gregory et al., 1986). A study of LD adults, 18–36 years old, indicated that problems in self-esteem and confidence ranked high in their concerns (White, 1985). Similarly, interviews with LD adults found that three of the five problems most frequently mentioned are self-image, affect, and motivation (along with hyperactivity and organization; Buchanan & Wolf,

1986). As with children, however, not all studies of adults have found differences between persons with and without LD (Lewandowski & Arcangelo, 1994).

D. Attributions and Locus of Control

Learning academic and social skills also are influenced by outcome expectations, or beliefs concerning the outcomes of one's actions. Attributions and locus of control are used to describe a person's explanations for outcomes. People's beliefs about the causes of events in their lives mediate their behavior (Bandura, 1982). People who assume that their outcomes result from their personal attributes (e.g., their ability, their effort) are said to have an internal locus of control; people who assume that their outcomes result from forces external to themselves (e.g., task difficulty, luck) have an external locus of control. The distinctions between internal and external locus of control are further refined by the temporalness of the attribution. Some attributions are seen as stable (e.g., attributions about ability); others are seen as temporal (e.g, attributions about effort). Attributions that are stable are perceived as less alterable than are temporal attributions. For example, if one does badly on a test it is important to attribute poor performance to alterable (e.g., effort) rather than stable (e.g., ability) causes because it is possible to increase one's effort but presumably not one's ability. Distinctions also are made about generalizability (e.g., I did badly on this math test, therefore I'll do badly on *all* math tests vs. I did badly on this math test but I'll do better the next time). Clearly it is better to interpret bad outcomes as alterable and limited in scope and time.

1. Attributions for Academic Outcomes

Several studies have examined LD students' attributions for outcomes in academic situations. A frequently used measure of attributions is the Intellectual Achievement Responsibility Scale (IAR; Crandall, Katkovsky, & Crandall, 1965). On this scale, children select either an internal (e.g., ability, effort) or external (e.g., luck) explanation in response to descriptions of hypothetical success and failure outcomes. Children are scored for their responses to the success and failure outcomes. A second instrument asks children to rate the importance of effort, ability, task difficulty, and luck for each selected domain (e.g., doing well or poorly in reading or math, getting along or not getting along with others; Pearl, Bryan, & Donahue, 1980).

Children and adolescents with LD consistently have been found to differ from normal-achieving classmates in their explanations for their successes and failures. Students with LD tend to be internal in their attributions for failure but are less likely than normal-achieving classmates to become internal in their attributions for success. Students with LD are more likely to believe that when they do well, it is because someone was nice to them or the work was easy; but when they do badly they believe it is because they are not smart. NLD students are more likely to attribute failure to lack of effort (Aponik & Dembo, 1983; Hallahan, Gajar, Cohen, & Tarver, 1978; Jacobsen, Lowery, & DuCette, 1986; Kistner, Osborne, & LeVerrier, 1988; Pearl, 1992; Tollefson et al., 1982). Not taking personal credit for success yet blaming oneself for failure is a devastating interpretation of outcomes.

Dalley et al. (1992) classified high school students with and without LD as "successful" and "unsuccessful" based on their grade point averages. The adolescents were administered measures of attributions, depression, and social competency. Students with LD showed higher depressive symptomatology, more maladaptive attributions, higher dysfunctional attitudes, and reported themselves less socially competent than NLD peers. The unsuccessful students with LD accounted for these differences. Dalley et al. suggest that unsuccessful students with LD had in effect failed twice, first by their placement in special education and second by their continuing limited success in the LD classroom. The combination of the LD placement and doing poorly in that placement were critical factors in contributing to negative self-judgments and feelings.

2. Attributions and Classroom Behavior

Kistner et al. (1988) examined the link between young children's attributions, academic progress, and teacher's ratings of behavior. In a 2-year longitudinal study of children in grades three through eight, attributions of failure to insufficient effort were positively related to achievement gains, whereas attributions of failure to lack of ability were negatively related to academic progress. Children's IQ scores were not related to children's attributions, but teacher ratings of children's classroom behavior were related. Children who tended to attribute their difficulties to insufficient effort were rated as more successful students, as more capable of independent classwork, and as demanding less time from the teacher. Children's attributions of failure to insufficient ability was related to teacher judgments of less success, less independence, and more demands for help from the teacher. On the follow-up study, the children with LD were less likely than normal-achieving classmates to attribute failure to insufficient effort and more likely to attribute failure to insufficient ability on one of two scales. On the second scale (the Intellectual Achievement Responsibility—IAR), LD and NLD children's attributions for success and failure became significantly more internal across the 2-year period. The Dalley et al. and Kistner et al. studies are important because they show that students' attributions about achievement are related to their academic progress across time and teacher ratings of their classroom behaviors.

3. Attributions and Social Relationships

Attribution research also has examined how people's beliefs influence their social behavior. Lonely adults and children tend to exhibit a nonadaptive pattern of attributions wherein they attribute social success to external and unstable causes and social failure to internal and stable causes (Anderson, Horowitz, and French, 1983;

Asher, Parkhurst, Hymel, & Williams, 1990). Bukowski and Ferber (1987) showed that poorly accepted children who blamed themselves for social failure were lonelier than poorly accepted children who viewed social failure as externally caused. Aggressive-rejected children tend to blame others in their interpretations of events; whereas submissive-rejected children tend to be more self-blaming. Students with LD have lower expectations for social success than nondisabled students (Sobol, Earn, Bennett, & Humphries, 1983; Tur-Kaspa & Bryan, 1994). Thus, the choices made by children with LD in social situations may reflect their interpretations of the causes of social success and failure.

4. Attributions and Behavior Problems

Durrant (1993) hypothesized that behavior problems are the source of maladaptive attributions by students with LD. Durrant (1993) classified students with LD, 8 to 13 years, into three groups: non-behavior-disordered, externalizers (e.g., conduct problems, antisocial tendencies, attention difficulties) and externalizers/internalizers (e.g., anxiety, depression, withdrawal). Based on open-ended interview questions, children with LD but no behavior disorders were more likely than NLD students to attribute their failures to insufficient motivation (e.g., "I wasn't interested."). Children with LD who were externalizers were more likely to blame other people for their failures than other children. The children with LD displaying both externalizing and internalizing symptoms attributed successes to luck more frequently than did the externalizing children with LD.

5. Attributions and Stimulant Medication

Many children with learning and behavior problems are given stimulant medication. Whalen and Henker (1986) questioned whether medicated children would attribute changes in their behavior to the stimulant and thus believe they have less control over outcomes, and consequently exert less effort to learn. Allen and Drabman (1991) compared the attributions of two groups of students with LD, one receiving medication and one not receiving medication. Boys who were not taking medication reported more internal-effort attributions in failure situations than boys who were taking medication. Boys with LD who were not treated with medication were more likely to believe that poor academic performance was the result of not having tried hard enough.

6. Teaching Styles Interact with Children's Attributions

As in the case of self-concepts, investigators have begun to explore how situation and instructional factors might influence students' attributions. Two studies demonstrated that teachers instructional strategies interact with students' beliefs to influence achievement outcomes. Pascarella and Pflaum (1981) exposed students with LD and normal-achieving students to one of two types of reading instruction. In the high-structure program, teachers corrected reading errors and confirmed correct responses during specially designed reading lessons. In the low-structure program, teachers encouraged children to determine the adequacy of their responses. Using pre- and posttreatment measures of reading, they found that children with LD and poor readers with high scores on internality benefited more from the low-structure teaching strategy, whereas children with LD and poor readers with low scores on internality benefited more from the high-structure teaching strategy. In the same vein, Bendell, Tollefson, & Fine, (1980) had junior high males with LD do their spelling assignment in either a high- or a low-structured condition. In the high-structured condition, students were directed to trace words they felt they had missed, write them three times, and say the word and the letter to themselves each time they wrote it. In the low-structured situation, students were given no specific study procedure but were reinforced with a nickel for each correctly spelled word. The results were that students high on internal locus of control did better in the low-structure situation, whereas students low on internal locus of control did better in the high-structure situation.

7. Teacher Feedback Influences Children's Attributions

Other studies have examined how teachers' feedback to children about their performance influences children's ideas about their self-worth. Stipek and Daniels (1988) compared kindergarten and fourth-grade children's perceived competence in classrooms that differed in evaluative feedback. In one group of classrooms, feedback was based on normative criteria and was made very salient and public. In the second type of classroom, normative evaluation was de-emphasized and infrequent. For instance, in the classrooms in which normative evaluation was salient, assignments were graded with checks, stars, and happy and sad faces or letter grades; "A" papers were placed on bulletin boards; and students were given positive or negative feedback after tests, sometimes verbally. In the classrooms in which normative evaluation was de-emphasized, instructional groups were flexible; comments, but not grades, were given on assignments and report cards; the curriculum was individualized; comparisons with others were discouraged; children were encouraged to seek help from classmates; and projects frequently were completed in groups.

Kindergartners in classes in which normative feedback was salient rated their competence lower than did kindergartners in classes in which normative evaluation was de-emphasized. However, kindergartners were more optimistic in their predictions for future academic achievement than fourth graders. Type of evaluative feedback did not affect the fourth graders, but the kindergartner's self-ratings were like the fourth-graders in the classrooms that emphasized feedback evaluation. Thus, the decline associated with age in children's perceptions of competence (Benenson & Dweck, 1986) already may have occurred. This study is important because it demonstrates how children's self-concepts for academic achievement can be significantly influenced at an early age by teachers' evaluative feedback.

E. Programs to Help Students Acquire Positive Self-Perceptions

1. Self-Concept Training

Programs to help children acquire positive self-concepts have not been effective. A meta-analysis by Prout and DeMartino (1986) suggested that group treatments in school may be more effective than individual interventions, but the lack of positive significant findings in carefully designed studies indicate little support for the effectiveness of such programs (Laconte, Shaw, & Dunn, 1991).

2. Attribution Training

Efforts to help children acquire adaptive attributions and self-efficacy have been much more successful than efforts to improve self-concepts. Attribution training studies have focused on (a) changing children's beliefs about the causes of success and failure, (b) increasing children's willingness to persist on difficult tasks, and (c) improving children's task performance. The basic steps in attribution training involve engaging the student in an academic task, giving the student interpretive feedback about the causes of his or her performance, and encouraging the student to make the same interpretation. Some studies have focused on effort feedback (e.g., "You've been working hard."), others on ability feedback ("You're good at this."), and some have used a blend of the two (cf. Borkowski, Weyhing, & Carr, 1988; Schunk, 1984, 1988; Dohrn & Bryan, 1994). Further, classroom teachers (Thomas & Pashley, 1982), parents (Dohrn & Bryan, 1994), and older students with LD acting as tutors for younger children (Yasutake, Bryan, & Dohrn, 1996) have been coached to serve as attribution trainers. Teachers, parents, and tutors had significant impacts upon the recipients of attribution statements. In addition, parents of students with LD developed more positive views of their children, and students with LD acting as tutors acquired more positive self-beliefs as a result of "preaching" to younger children. Thus, attribution training has been effectively moved out of laboratory settings and into the home and classroom. Attribution feedback combined with teaching specific task strategies leads children to persist on difficult tasks, to acquire adaptive beliefs about the causes of their performance, and to make academic achievement gains.

3. Self-Efficacy Training

Attributions refer to people's explanations for outcomes. Based on these explanations people make decisions about what they can and cannot do. Self-efficacy is the next step in this self-judgmental process. Self-efficacy refers to personal beliefs about one's capabilities to organize and implement actions necessary to attain designated levels of performance (Bandura, 1982). Self-efficacy is acquired through experience, attribution feedback from parents and teachers (e.g., "You can do this"), observing models, and physiological indices (e.g., anxiety). Self-efficacy influences choices of activities. Students avoid, or exert little energy on tasks for which they have a low sense of self-efficacy. Self-efficacy originally was studied in therapies to help people with phobias (e.g., snakes) overcome anxiety and cope with threatening activities (Bandura, 1982).

Dale Schunk (1989) used a self-efficacy model to conduct a systematic series of studies to help students' with low reading and math achievement. The proposition was that students' sense of self-efficacy for learning is influenced as they work on tasks by cues that signal how well they are learning. In Schunk's series, students were pre- and posttested on self-efficacy, skill, and persistence. Self-efficacy was measured by having students estimate their capabilities for solving different problems. In different studies, Schunk manipulated (a) strategy verbalization (i.e., prior to applying it versus just receiving strategy instruction; (b) attributional feedback about effort and/or ability ("You're been working hard"), (c) the influence of different models (e.g., peer versus teacher, coping versus skilled models, coping models demonstrate the fears and deficits of the students but gradually improve their performance and gain self-confidence; mastery models demonstrate faultless performance from the outset); (d) goal setting (i.e., students set specific performance goals versus teachers setting goals); and (e) rewards.

The results of these studies showed that (a) remedial readers, grades 2 to 4, who verbalized a strategy prior to applying it had higher reading comprehension, self-efficacy, and ability attributions than students given the strategy (Schunk and Rice, 1985); (b) observing peer models enhanced self-efficacy and performance more than teacher or no models (Schunk & Hanson, 1985); (c) specific performance goals enhanced math achievement and self-efficacy more than no goals, irrespective of whether the goals were self- or teacher established; (d) providing ability feedback for early successes led to higher ability attributions and posttest self-efficacy and skill (Schunk, 1984); (e) the timing of attributional feedback is important—feedback that links children's *prior* achievements with effort and ability (rather than exhortations regarding future achievement) are more effective; (f) performance-contingent rewards lead to high skill and self-efficacy compared with task-contingent and unexpected rewards (Schunk, 1983).

F. Implications for Teaching

The importance of self-perceptions in student achievement has been recognized for many years. Attempts to help children acquire positive self-concepts, however, have been largely ineffectual. At home and in the classroom, these efforts have consisted largely of parents' and teachers' exhortations to students. Exhortations, however, are the weakest form of influence. The results of the more recent attribution and self-efficacy training are much more promising. Both are cost-effective, easy to integrate into the curriculum, and require no special equipment, materials, or training. Because children's attributions and self-efficacy mediate their responsiveness to instruction, it is important that teachers and parents help children interpret success and failure outcomes as caused by controllable factors. Teachers and parents should model statements that attribute success to trying hard and getting smarter. Children should be directed to verbalize strategies for problem solving, to make attributional statements and be reinforced for doing so. Exhortations to try harder should be used only when the teacher is reasonably certain that the child has not put forth his or her best effort. If the child is trying hard, and the teacher misperceives the child's effort, the child will probably experience feelings of frustration and helplessness. Criticism should be prescriptive, directing children on how to solve the problem. Children interpret prescriptive feedback as a sign that the teacher or parent believes they are capable of doing better work. It is important that the parent and teacher give the child credit where credit is due and not take personal credit for the child's success. Social comparisons with other children should be de-emphasized and children's progress put in the context of learning new strategies, trying hard, and getting smarter.

V. A FRIEND: JUDGMENTS OF SOCIAL COMPETENCE OF STUDENTS WITH LEARNING DISABILITIES

A. Peer Social Status

Social status is defined as judgments made by significant others (e.g., classmates, teachers, parents). Peer judgments, as early as third grade, have been linked to social adjustment many years later (Parker and Asher, 1987). Although there are important developmental and gender differences in the ways that children relate to one another, good friends communicate care and concern, provide help in time of need, share intimate feelings and thoughts, and spend enjoyable time together (Parker and Asher, 1993). At least 30 studies have assessed peer ratings of students with LD. Although there are exceptions, the majority have reported that students with LD are less well accepted by their peers than their classmates (Ochoa and Palmer, 1995).

In trying to understand the social status of students with LD, we should consider that several variables influence children's social status. For one, low achievement often is related to lower social status among peers (Bursuck, 1989; Haager & Vaughn, 1995; LaGreca & Stone, 1990). Second, other characteristics, such as behavior problems, also generate peer rejection (Durrant, 1993). Third, the amount of time in the classroom influences how well students are known by classmates (LaGreca & Stone, 1990). Fourth, the degree to which there is a fit between the child's personality and the "personality" of the class influences peer status; for instance, hyperactive children are more likely to be popular in a class of hyperactive than laid-back children, whereas laid-back children are more likely to be popular among laid-back than hyperactive classrooms (Wright, Giammarino, & Parad, 1986). Finally, teachers' attitudes and behavioral interactions with students influence classmates' evaluations (Grolnick & Ryan, 1990; Vaughn & Haager, 1994).

B. Self-Perceptions of Loneliness

Studies of social status are typically based on sociometric measures. Over the past decades two sociometric measures, the Nomination and the Peer Rating Scale, have dominated studies of children's friendships (Parker & Asher, 1987). But sociometrics require a great deal of time and are not feasible for classroom teachers to use (although they were invented for this purpose by Moreno, 1934). The model presented here suggests examining social status from the perspective of the individual child. Recent studies by Margalit (Margalit, 1994; Margalit & Efrati, 1994) have examined children's self-perceived ratings of loneliness. Loneliness is defined as the unpleasant experience that occurs when children perceive a discrepancy between the desired and achieved patterns of their social networks (Peplau & Perlman, 1982). Loneliness may result from (a) the unsatisfied need for intimate relationships with a small number of good friends, (b) the unfulfilled expectations of belonging to a larger and desired social group, and (c) difficulty staying alone and being engaged in enjoyable solitary activities (Margalit, 1994).

Using the Loneliness and Social Dissatisfaction Questionnaire (Asher et al., 1990), Margalit's studies have demonstrated that children with LD and reading disorders are more likely to experience loneliness than nondisabled children. The result is that these children tend to spend time watching television, overeating, waiting for someone to telephone, and feeling sorry for themselves. Not all students respond this way. Some students like to engage in solitary activities, such as hobbies and computer games. Although it is desirable that children be able to entertain themselves, the issue is whether they choose to self-entertain or do so because they have no friends.

Peer and self-ratings are useful for identifying children who are having problems making friends. But we have noted that many factors influence peer and self-judgments. Neither peer nor self-ratings provide information about the reasons a particular child may be experiencing problems making friends. Low academic achievement may be a significant factor for many children with social problems. But there is a subset of students with LD who are experiencing problems because of social skills deficits. In order to help these children, we must identify the specific social skills that contribute to their social difficulties. In order to develop effective social skills interventions for these children, we must first figure out what deficits in social skills these children experience. For this, we turn to an assessment of the child's social cognitive skills and behaviors.

VI. SOCIAL SKILLS

A. Definition

Social skills are "the specific overt and cognitive behaviors required to produce positive outcomes from interactions with others and positive judgments of social competence" (Spence, 1991, p. 149).

B. Model of Social Skills

Many social skills are required to be socially competent. Models of social skillfulness have been developed based on comparisons of children with high versus low social status. The model used here was developed and tested by Dodge and his colleagues (cf. Coie & Dodge, 1983; Dodge, 1986; Dodge & Frame, 1982). This model assumes that children come to a particular situation or task with a biologically determined set of response capabilities and a database (i.e., their memories of past experiences and a set of goals). In this chapter, children's affect, self-perceptions (attributions and self-perceived effiacy), and social status are seen as significant components of children's database, influencing the way children process social cues in the environment.

The Dodge model assumes that this information processing occurs in sequential steps: each necessary for competent responding. When children act inappropriately it could be because of deficits or biases in perception, understanding, or interpretation of environmental cues. Deviant outcomes may result from dysfunction at a particular step or a combination of steps. A distinction also is made between skill deficits and performance deficits (Gresham & Elliott, 1989). Children with skill deficits do not have the necessary perceptual, cognitive, and/or behavioral skills. Children with performance deficits have the skills but fail to use them at acceptable levels, presumably because they lack motivation to do so. In the following sections, the research on the social skills of students with LD is summarized. The discussion is organized using the steps in the Dodge model.

C. Step 1: Encoding Social Cues

1. Definition

Children encode—attend to and perceive—social cues in the environment. They learn to focus on important cues, ignore irrelevant cues, and organize information for recall by chunking, rehearsal, and mnemonic devices. The first step in a social interaction requires the ability to perceive and identify vocal, facial, and bodily expressions. Nonverbal behaviors such as smiling, eye contact, and body posture play an important role in encoding; they communicate our feelings about the other person, the situation, the message, the desire to continue or terminate the interaction, and whether the exchange is going well or badly. Normally developing children as young as 3 years can identify affective states based on facial and bodily gestures and vocalizations, although their skillfulness in identifying subtle cues increases with age (Gross & Ballif, 1991) through adulthood (Jarvis & Justice, 1992).

2. Encoding Deficits/Nonverbal Learning Disabilities

The term *nonverbal LD* was coined by Johnson and Myklebust (1967) to describe children who have a major problem in encoding social cues. Rourke and colleagues (cf. Harnadek & Rourke, 1994; Rourke, 1989) describe a nonverbal LD syndrome that consists of significant deficits in social perception, social judgment, and social interaction skills. Also part of the syndrome are problems in tactile perception, psychomotor coordination, nonverbal problem solving, adapting to novel and complex situations, and mechanical arithmetic.

What evidence supports the hypothesis that students with LD have problems in encoding social cues? Wiig and Harris (1974) showed adolescents with and without LD tapes of a young female's nonverbal expressions of anger, embarrassment, fear, frustration, joy, and love. The adolescents with LD were less skilled at labeling the emotions than the NLD adolescents, which Wiig and Harris attributed to reduced visual-motor organization.

The Profile of Nonverbal Sensitivity (PONS; Rosenthal, Hall, Archer, DiMatteo, & Rogers, 1977) has been used to assess perception of nonverbal communication. On the PONS, subjects are shown a 45-min black-and-white videotape containing 220 items, each a 2-sec clip of a young woman portraying an emotional response. Three visual presentations (face, body, figure) and two auditory presentations (scrambled speech and electronically filtered speech) are shown, both alone and in combination. The subject views or listens to each clip and chooses one of two descriptions as the correct description of the scenario. Children with LD perform less accurately than NLD classmates on the PONS (Axelrod, 1982; Bryan, 1977; Hall & Richmond, 1985; Jackson, Enright, & Murdock, 1987). Stone and LaGreca (1984) hypothesized that group differences were the result of attention problems rather than differences in perception of nonverbal communication. They used the PONS, but prior to each clip reminded students to pay careful attention. The students with LD and NLD did not differ in their accuracy on the PONS.

One study examined encoding skills by presenting a scenario describing a social problem and then asking LD, average-achieving, and low-achieving students to explain what happened (Tur-Kaspa & T. Bryan, 1994). Students with LD scored lower on encoding than did average-achieving and low-achieving students. In addition, students with LD generated significantly more insertions of extraneous information than did average-achieving students.

3. Encoding Deficit or Developmental Lag?

Because Gerber and Zinkgraf (1982) found that social perception improved with age in children with LD, a number of studies examined age differences in social perception. Jackson, Enright, and Murdock (1987) used the PONS and found that children improve in social perception with age. However, NLD students at 3 age levels (11, 14, 17) performed better than students with LD. Holder and Kirkpatrick (1991) found children with LD to be less accurate in interpreting emotions from facial expressions and to take more time identifying specific emotions. Younger children required more time to interpret fear and anger, and boys spent more time interpreting happiness. Nabuzoka and Smith (1995) studied children with and without LD at 3 age levels (6, 9, 11 years) using photographs of facial expressions and posture cues and video recordings of gesture cues. NLD children identified facial expressions and posture cues more accurately than did children with LD. On gesture cues there were differences only for the younger and middle groups. Children with LD did show increased accuracy over a 1-year period. Although children with LD did relatively better interpreting gesture cues, few reached ceiling, whereas most NLD children did so on these measures and were near adult scores on the others. Jarvis and Justice (1992) assessed social perception and self-concept of junior and senior high school and college students with and without LD. After listening to taped recordings of actors in happy, angry, anxious, and sad interactions, subjects were asked how the actors felt and why. NLD students scored higher than LD students in each grade on happiness, anger, and anxiety, and college students scored higher than junior and senior high school students. The ability to correctly assess anger increased more across age for NLD than for students with LD. Furthermore, there was a significant correlation between the social perception and self-concept scores. The more socially sensitive the subject was, the higher was his or her self-concept.

4. Encoding and Social Status

Do measures of social perception relate to social status and behavior? Stilliadis and Wiener (1989) administered the Test of Social Inference (TSI) (Edmonson, DeJung, Leland, & Leach, 1974), the Social Perception Behavior Rating Scale (SPBRS; Maheady, Maitland, & Sainato, 1984) and a Peer Acceptance Scale to students in grades 4, 5, and 6. Students with LD scored worse than NLD classmates on both measures of social perception. Social perception scores on the SPBRS, but not the TSI, were highly correlated with peer acceptance.

5. Summary

What is significant about these studies? First, the studies examined presumably heterogeneous students with LD, not students identified as having nonverbal LD. It is likely that subgroups of students with LD account for LD–NLD group differences, but whether the subgroups have a nonverbal syndrome (Rourke, 1989), behavior problems (Durrant, 1993), attention problems (LaGreca & Stone, 1990), or some other unifying characteristic remains to be determined. Second, using still photographs to assess social encoding can be criticized because social events are dynamic, many cues are available simultaneously, and they take place within a social context that provides additional information. At the same time, however, in real-life interactions, social cues often are very subtle, take place very, very quickly, and contradictory cues can be present at the same time. Hence, interpreting still photographs may be a much easier task than interpreting nonverbal cues in real-life situations. If group differences are found on the simpler task, it seems reasonable that group differences would be found on more complex tasks. Furthermore, studies that used more realistic presentations through video recordings and scenarios of social situations also get differences between students with and without LD. Third, as reported by Tur-Kaspa and Bryan, social encoding discriminates students with LD from low-achieving students. Fourth, the differences between LD and NLD students do not appear to reflect a developmental lag. Although students with LD perform better as they age, high school and college students with LD perform worse than comparable NLD adults.

D. Mental Representation and Interpretation

Once cues have been encoded, children integrate the cues with past experiences and interpret the cues. Step 2 reflects children's understanding of the social situation. A variety of ways have been used to assess whether students with LD have problems in mental representation and interpretation.

1. Perspective-Taking Skills

One approach has been to examine children's perspective taking, the ability to understand how others would see or interpret social events. Measures of perspective taking typically provide the child with information about a social situation and then ask the child to report how someone else who has less or different information would interpret the situation. Dickstein and Warren (1980) and Bruck and Hebert (1982) measured cognitive, affective, and perceptual perspective taking. Each measure had egocentric questions that required children to respond from their own perspective and nonegocentric questions that required children to take a point of view that differed from their own. The cognitive task measured ability to predict the thoughts of others; the affective task to predict anther's feelings, and the perceptual task, the ability to take the visual perspective of others. Dickstein and Warren (1980) found no group differences between children ages 5 to 11 and NLD children 5 to 9 years on the egocentric questions. But on the nonegocentric questions, the LD performed more poorly than the NLD children. Although children with LD improved with age, they were no better at age 10 than they had been at age 8. Bruck and Hebert (1982) replicated Dickstein and Warren's results, and also found that students with LD performance could not be attributed to hyperactivity. Pearl and Cosden (1982) used segments from televised soap operas. Junior high students with LD performed more poorly than NLD classmates in making inferences about the televised characters' feelings and intentions. Weiss (1984) used videotapes of 4–16-sec scenes that depicted different social interactions between 2 or 3 boys: neutral, friendly, cooperative, teasing, horseplay, fighting, or angry. Subjects, 11–15 year old, aggressive and nonaggressive males with LD and NLD described the scenes and rated them on a scale (very, very friendly to very, very unfriendly). Both groups of males with LD viewed the scenarios as more unfriendly than the NLD groups. Pearl, T. Bryan, Fallon, and Herzog (1988) found that middle school students with LD were less skilled than NLD students in their ability to detect lies. One study failed to find differences. Maheady et al. (1984) presented a 30-min scenario showing 20 natural sequences of social interactions. Viewers answered an interpretive question about the people in the scene; for example, which of two women playing with a baby is the mother? There were no differences between 7–11- and 13–17-year-old LD, emotionally disturbed and NLD males; only a group of educable mentally retarded children made fewer correct responses.

2. Moral Development, Altruism, and Ingratiation

A different approach to assessing, Mental Representation and Interpretation has examined attitudes and views on such diverse topics as moral principals, altruism, and ingratiation. The most well-known model of moral development, developed by Lawrence Kohlberg (Kohlberg, Colby, Gibbs, Spicher-Dubin, & Power, 1978), is an age-stage model with six levels of moral reasoning assessed in the moral judgment interview (Kohlberg et al., 1978). A study of 8- and 9-year-old males found no differences between students with and without LD (Fincham, 1977), but a study of older males, 14.3–18.5 years, found males with LD resembled those of younger NLD children aged 10–14.

Children's altruism was assessed in a questionnaire about giving money to charity, doing good deeds for others, and the like. Children with LD did not differ from NLD students in their understanding of the "shoulds." However, on a questionnaire that asked students whether they would conform to peer pressure to engage in prosocial and antisocial actions, the students with LD indicated greater willingness than NLD students to conform to pressure on the antisocial scenarios (T. Bryan, Werner, & Pearl, 1982). Similar results were found in a series conducted by James Bryan (J. Bryan et al., 1981; J. Bryan & Sonnefeld, 1981). In these studies, children's attitudes toward how best to ingratiate peers, parents, teachers, and adults were tested. Students with LD showed no deficits in their knowledge concerning the social desirability of various ingratiation tactics addressed to different audiences; however, they indicated that they might select less socially desirable strategies than NLD children.

3. Summary

Students with LD appear to understand the principles governing morals, altruism, and ingratiation as well as their peers. Group differences emerge when asked how they might respond in social situations involving these principles. The students with LD indicate greater willingness to violate social norms. Whether they actually do so remains to be tested. It seems likely that their actual responses are influenced by the accuracy of their social perceptions of the situation. Based on the Maheady et al. data, they should not experience problems, but the results of the other studies suggest that their actual responses may be significantly influenced by the complexity of the social scenarios and the level of comprehension demanded by the social interaction. Students with LD performed worse than other students when required to make inferences based on subtle verbal and behavioral cues. Perhaps students with LD will not differ from NLD classmates when the social situation is familiar, the stimuli concrete, and/or the response is well known. Perhaps deficits in Encoding and Mental Representation are more likely when the situation is complex, intentions are communicated through nonverbal, subtle behaviors, and/or inferences about antecedents, intentions, and consequences must be made.

Although these studies need to be replicated, to find that children and adolescents with LD are not skilled at understanding others' points of view, or detecting lies, may misinterpret social interactions as unfriendly, and indicate they would choose undesirable options in social situations should be viewed seriously. These data provide a trail to follow for understanding the specific reasons why some students with LD may have problems becoming socially skillful and gaining acceptance from significant others.

E. Step 3. Response Search

1. Definition

Once children have represented and encoded the information in a meaningful way, they engage in a generative process of searching for possible behavioral responses. Popular children have been found able to generate more possible ways of responding in social situations than less popular children (Asher, 1983).

2. Generating Alternative Solutions

Students with LD have been found less skilled than NLD students in the quantity and quality of strategies chosen to resolve hypothetical, peer-related social situations (Carlson, 1987); less skilled in development of "sophisticated" goals (Oliva & LaGreca, 1988). Elementary, middle, and high school students with LD perform more poorly than NLD children in generating alternative solutions (Silver & Young, 1985; Toro, Weissberg, Guare, & Liebenstein, 1990; Tur-Kaspa & Bryan, 1994).

3. Role Plays

Another approach to assessing children's response search has been to involve children in social problem-solving role plays. Silver and Young (1985) compared LD, low-achieving, and NLD eighth-grade boys, and Schneider and Yoshida (1988) compared LD with NLD junior high school students. The measures included Means-Ends Problem Solving (Platt & Spivack, 1975), Social Interaction Role Play Assessment (Waddell, 1984), and the Awareness of Consequences Test (Platt & Spivack, 1975). In both studies, the males with LD scored lower than normal-achieving males.

4. "Scripts"

Pearl, Bryan, Fallon, and Herzog (1991) found differences favoring NLD adolescents in a study of adolescents' "scripts" for situations in which adolescents might be requested to engage in illegal, inappropriate acts. Students with LD expected others to make their pitch using simple requests, whereas NLD students expected requests that stressed the payoff to the listener, minimized the negative consequences, and maximized the positive consequences of the act. The adolescents with LD also showed less insight about suggestions to engage in illegal activities as they suggested fewer reasons why someone should accept or refuse the request and suggested fewer scenarios for what might happen if such a response were made. These data suggest that the notion of teaching children to "just say no" terribly misrepresents the problem because, as described by the NLD adolescents, invitations to engage in illegal or inappropriate behavior are seldom straightforward. To protect students from being led down the proverbial garden path, they not only need strategies for responding, but also for understanding the invitation.

5. Summary

Various ways of defining response search have found that students with LD also exhibit problems in generating multiple choices for response, role playing various ways of responding, and understanding why various responses are appropriate.

F. Step 4: Response Decision

1. Definition

As children consider the various ways they might respond, they evaluate the potential consequences of each choice and estimate the probability of favorable outcomes. In making a decision, children also take into account the environmental context and their own behavioral capabilities.

2. Choices Made by Students with LD

Students with LD response decisions are one of the most enigmatic areas in the study of their social competence. It appears that students with LD understand social norms and morals as well as NLD students (J. H. Bryan, Sonnefeld, & Greenberg, 1981; J. H. Bryan and Sonnefeld, 1981). However, when asked how they would actually respond, students with LD select social strategies that they themselves had identified as inappropriate (J. H. Bryan et al., 1981; T. Bryan et al., 1982; Tur-Kaspa & T. Bryan, 1994).

We are hard pressed to explain why students with LD indicate they would choose a less than optimal response in various social situations. Our best guess is that their social choices are influenced by their affective states, their attributions about their likely success in social situations, and/or their social status. As described earlier, we know that affect and attributions mediate people's decisions. Nonetheless, at this point we cannot determine whether inappropriate response decisions reflect cognitive, affective, attributional, or some other problem, nor do we have adequate assessments regarding what students would actually do if confronted with these situations.

G. Step 5. Enactment

1. Definition

When a response has been selected, children proceed to act it out. The Enactment step requires that one monitor the effects of one's behavior on the environment and regulate behavior accordingly. Enactment requires communication skills and the ability to enact a behavioral script. There is good reason to suspect that problems in communicative competence affect the enactment of students with LD. Language deficits are part of the definition of LD and language skills are fundamental in social discourse.

2. Communicative Competence of Students with LD

Students with LD have been found less skilled than their classmates in a variety of situations that have demanded different forms of communicative competence. For instance, they have been found to be less tactful in situations that require delivering bad news (Pearl, 1992). Students with LD were less likely to cushion bad news in statements that would soften the blow; they were more direct. Students with LD appear to be less persuasive (T. Bryan et al., 1981) in situations requiring they convince their classmates to make choices they had made. Students with LD were more likely to agree, less likely to disagree, and less likely to argue their case than their classmates. In a simulation of a television talk show, students with LD acting as host asked fewer questions of their guests, and their questions were less likely to be open-ended (a good strategy for eliciting longer responses from one's partner than questions that elicit "yes" or "no" answers (T. Bryan et al., 1981). In referential communication tasks, students with LD have been found to be less skillful communicators than NLD students (Donahue et al., 1982). Tur-Kaspa and Bryan (1994) found average-achieving students outperformed students with LD and low-achieving students in role playing competent solutions to social problems.

H. Implications for Teaching

It is likely that cursory observations of peer interactions would be unlikely to arouse concern for students' with LD communication skills. Because students with LD participate as much as other children in social exchanges, classroom teachers probably will not notice that they selectively use certain strategies. Being agreeable and letting others talk and make decisions is certainly adaptive behavior, at least under most conditions. But consider that it is cognitively and linguistically easier to agree than to argue one's position. It is easier to formulate a direct question ("Do you like *Home Improvement?*") than an open-ended query ("How do you feel about crime on television?"). But we all know that it is important to learn how to be persuasive, how to be tactful, and how to present our own position on issues. It is very important that children learn how to defend themselves verbally, how to carry on a disagreement, how to give and respond to negative feedback and evaluations, and how to express feelings and judgments in socially appropriate ways. These are life-long skills that are important at home and in the community. Thus, students with language and/or cognitive limitations may develop good strategies for interacting with others, but they will be at a disadvantage when they need to present an opposing argument, give negative feedback, be persuasive, and "stand up" for their views and wishes.

Again, there are a number of plausible reasons for these findings. LD students' performance may be related to deficits in cognition or communication skills. It also may be that children who have low social status play a more passive social role because the more popular children are allowed to play more active and dominant roles in the their social groups.

VII. MALADAPTIVE BEHAVIORS

A. Teacher Ratings

A number of maladaptive behaviors such as attention deficits and hyperactivity and aggression have important consequences for children's social status and personal adjustment. Because these behaviors wreak havoc in the lives of many children with LD, and are predictive of life-long problems in adjustment, they are singled out for attention. Teacher ratings of the social competence and behavior of students with LD, based on the Behavior Problem checklist (BPC; Epstein, Cullinan, & Rosemier, 1983; Bursuck, 1989), the Teacher Temperament Questionnaire (Keogh, 1983), the Walker-McConnell Scale of Social Competence and Adjustment (Walker & McConnell, 1988, 1991), and the Social Skills Rating Scale for

Teachers (SSRS-T; Gresham & Elliott, 1989) indicate that students with LD have a variety of problems in the personality (e.g., nervousness, fearfulness, lack of interpersonal competencies) and conduct (e.g., disruptiveness, aggression, and acting-out behaviors) domains. Among younger males and females with LD the problems seem to relate to attention deficits. Older students with LD are more likely to show predelinquent behavior problems (e.g., "stays out at night") than younger children. Teachers rate students with LD lower on task orientation and higher on acting-out behavior, distractibility, and disturbed peer relations. There also is a subset of students with LD with problems of shyness and withdrawal (Bender & Golden, 1990). Silver (1990) claims that about one-third of children and adolescents diagnosed as having conduct disorder and young adults diagnosed as having personality disorder have unrecognized or poorly treated LD. Haager and Vaughn (1995) indicate that students with LD and low achievers are rated by teachers as having poorer social skills and more behavior problems than higher achieving classmates. Thus, it is not clear as to whether these behavior problems are characteristic of "LDness" per se or low academic achievement.

B. Classroom and Playground Observations

Research on the social competence of students with LD has included observational studies of their behavior in the classroom and on the playground. The results of the classroom observations studies indicate that compared with NLD classmates, children with LD are more likely to be off-task and to interact with teachers (Feagans & McKinney, 1981; McKinney & Speece, 1986). Social competence in the classroom requires not only appropriate peer-interaction skills but also such behaviors as being on-task, completing work, and gaining attention appropriately.

1. Observations in the Lunchroom, Gym, and Playground

Levy and Gotlieb (1984), reported that boys and girls with LD had difficulties interacting with classmates on the playground. The girls appeared to hover on the group's perimeter while the boys seemed to flit in and out of groups without joining in. Mainstream children played significantly less frequently with children with LD on the playground, and this was more marked in the older than the younger children. Children with LD reported that they were teased and bullied more than NLD classmates, but the differences did not show up in playground observations. In contrast to bullying, children did not consider teasing as a cause of great distress.

With the exception of attention, there appears to be no observational behavioral evidence that students with LD exhibit conduct and personality problems. Most of the observation studies, however, have focused on young children. Epstein and colleagues (1983) have suggested that attention deficits in young children may evolve into conduct problems later. Also classroom observations are unlikely to detect low-frequency behaviors. Personality problems may be subtle or based on inferences teachers make following many observations of the child in different situations. Conduct problems may be infrequent, or students would be labeled emotional or behavior disordered, not LD.

The discrepancy between teachers and peer ratings and observations may be a measurement problem. Low-frequency or significant behaviors may not occur when the observations are being done, or may not show up in data analyses based on behavior frequencies. It also should be noted that classroom observation studies focus primarily on on- and off-task behaviors, not social interactions. In addition, the interactions that take place among children, especially as they grow older, are not accessible to adults. Children's social interactions become increasingly private. In the classroom, where children's opportunities to interact are limited, social communications are whispered or conducted out of adult view. And, as pointed out earlier, many children with LD adopt communication strategies that are appropriate but mask their communication deficiencies.

VIII. THE LAST WORD

This chapter summarized a great deal of research conducted within the last 15 years. The information was organized into five categories that represent a model of sorts of "what counts" in the social lives of students with LD. The results of the studies suggest that even though students with LD appear to acquire adequate knowledge of social norms, they evidence problems in virtually every category of social well-being; that is, affective, self-concept and attributions, and social skills. Not all students with LD have problems in the social domain, and headway has been made in identifying subgroups of social problems, and in developing screening devices to identify children at risk or in need of help in the social domain. However, we must be cautious in applying the results of this research to individual children with LD because we do not yet have good instruments for diagnosing the specific social skills as defined in the Dodge model. (e.g., encoding/perception; interpretation, comprehension, response decision/cognition; enactment/behavior).

There were topics beyond the scope of this chapter, such as gender differences and the relationship of social skills to IQ. These are important issues. IQ typically has no relation, or a very small but significant relationship to measures of social competence. IQ cannot be used as an explanation for differences between students with and without LD. Gender differences, when found, indicate that girls are at greater risk for problems in the social domain than boys, but this is not a consistent finding. Because there are important differences in the way females and males interact socially, this is an issue that deserves further attention.

Also understated in this chapter is the importance of the social ecology on children's social development and status. Mothers attributions and ratings of their child as fitting into the family's expectations relate to child behaviors in the classroom. For instance, children with LD whose mothers perceive a poor fit have less positive behavior and poorer achievement over the elementary school years (Feagans, Merriweather, & Haldane, 1991). Teachers differ in their tolerance of long hair, swearing, and messiness. Peer status is influenced by the fit between the individual's personality and the personality of the group (Wright et al., 1986). Thus, judgments of social competence are affected by characteristics of the person making the judgments as well as the person being judged. The appropriateness of social behaviors is defined to some degree by the social context in which they occur.

As Vaughn and Haager (1994) point out, students with LD in their studies did not suffer from a decline in self-concepts across time. Based on classroom observations, they attribute this finding to the supportive environment provided in participating schools. Much can be done by teachers to offset the impact of LD in children's self-perceptions and peer relationships. Teachers' attributions and feedback can help children acquire adaptive explanations for their performance. Teachers also can establish cooperative, nurturing standards for children so that children help each other and individual differences in academic and social abilities are minimized. Given the prevalence and seriousness of problems in the social domain, teachers need to acquire the skills to facilitate the development of social perception, cognition, communicative competence, and social acceptance of students with LD. Although youngsters with LD who experience severe problems in affect or in the acquisition of social skills may need individual therapy or social skills training, there are many ways teachers can help these children in the normal course of instruction. Teachers may be reluctant to prioritize social skills interventions at the expense of academic goals, but social skills training can be integrated into the curriculum such that teachers can address academic and social needs at the same time (T. Bryan & Bryan, 1996). It is important that research continue to identify the dynamics of social problems, but in the meantime, teachers can use the extant data to alleviate many of the social problems students with LD experience in classrooms.

Readers also should understand that there are limits in our knowledge. Although inroads are being made in identifying subgroups of children with LD who have different kinds of social problems, we know little about the origins of social problems. Are they the result of information-processing deficits, the outcome of the LD experience, or motivational? In addition, we are limited in the availability of reliable and valid assessment measures. Many of the measures were developed for use in research, and are not applicable for clinical use. Thus, we have few reliable ways of assessing social skills for the purposes of designing individualized interventions. It follows that we have much to learn about interventions. We need interventions that meet the specific problems of individual children; interventions that are transportable to students in different classroom settings; and perceived by teachers in general and special education classrooms as enhancing, rather than interfering with, academic instruction. Although we have much to learn, we have made substantial progress in outlining the social problems of students with LD, and in developing strategies and curriculum (T. Bryan & Bryan, 1996) that teachers can use to help ameliorate social problems in the classroom.

References

Allen, J. S., & Drabman, R. S. (1991). Attributions of children with learning disabilities who are treated with psychostimulants. *Learning Disability Quarterly, 14,* 74–79.

Anderson, C. A., Horowitz, L., and French, R. (1983). Peer rejection and loneliness in people. *Journal of Personality and Social Psychology, 45,* 127–136.

Aponik, D. A., & Dembo, M. H. (1983). LD and normal adolescents' causal attributions of success and failure at different levels of task difficulty. *Learning Disability Quarterly, 6,* 31–39.

Asher, S. R. (1983). Social competence and peer status: Recent advances and future direction. *Child Development, 54,* 1427–1433.

Asher, S. R., Parkhurst, J. T., Hymel, S., & Williams, G. A. (1990). Peer rejection and loneliness in childhood. In S. R. Asher & J. D. Coie, (Eds.), *Peer rejection and loneliness in childhood,* (pp. 253–272). Cambridge: Cambridge University Press.

Asher, S. R. & Renshaw, P. D. (1981). Children without friends: Social knowledge and social skill training. In S. R. Asher & J. M. Gottman (Eds.), *The development of children's friendships* (pp. 273–296). New York: Cambridge University Press.

ACLD definition of the condition: Specific learning disabilities (1985). ACLD Newsbriefs, No. 158, 1–3.

Axelrod, L. (1982). Social perception in learning disabled adolescents. *Journal of Learning Disabilities, 15,* 610–613.

Bader, B. W. (1975). *Social perception and learning disabilities.* Des Moines, IA: Moon Lithographing & Engraving.

Bandura, A. (1982). Self-efficacy: Toward a unifying theory of behavior change. *Psychological Review, 84,* 191–215.

Barden, C. R., Garber, J., & Duncan, W. S. (1981). Cumulative effects of induced affective states in children: Accentuation, inoculation, and remediation. *Journal of Personality and Social Psychology, 40,* 750–760.

Battle, J., & Blowers, R. (1982). A longitudinal comparative study of the self-esteem of students in regular and special education classes. *Journal of Learning Disabilities, 15,* 100–102.

Baum, D. D., Duffelmeyer, & Geelan, M. (1988). Resource teacher perceptions of the prevalence of social dysfunction among students with learning disabilities. *Journal of Learning Disabilities, 21,* 380–381.

Bendell, D., Tollefson, N., & Fine, M. (1988). Interaction of locus-of-control orientation and the performance of learning disabled adolescents. *Journal of Learning Disabilities, 13*, 32–35.

Bender, W. M., & Golden, L. B. (1990). Subtypes of students with learning disabilities as derived from cognitive, academic, behavioral, and self-concept measures. *Learning Disability Quarterly, 13*, 183–194.

Beltempo, J., & Achille, P. A. (1990). The effect of special class placement on the self-concept of children with learning disabilities. *Child Study Journal, 20*, 81–102.

Benenson, J., & Dweck, C. (1986). The development of trait explanations and self-evaluations in the academic and social domains. *Child Development, 57*, 1179–1187.

Boersma, F. J., Chapman, J. W., & Maguire, T. O. (1979). The student's perception of ability scale: An instrument for measuring academic self-concept in elementary school children. *Education, Psychology, Measurements, 39*, 1035–1041.

Borkowski, J. G., Weyhing, R. S., & Carr, M. (1988). Effects of attributional retraining on strategy-based reading comprehension in learning-disabled students. *Journal of Educational Psychology, 80*, 46–53.

Bruck, H., & Hebert, M. (1982). Correlates of learning disabled students' peer-interaction patterns. *Learning Disabilities Quarterly, 5*, 353–362.

Brumback, R. A., & Staton, D. R. (1983). Learning disability and childhood depression. *American Journal of Orthopsychiatry, 53*, 269–281.

Bryan, J. H., & Sonnefeld, J. (1981). Children's social ratings of ingratiation tactics. *Journal of Learning Disabilities, 5*, 605–609.

Bryan, J. H., Sonnefeld, J., & Greenberg, F. (1981). Children's and parents' views about ingratiation tactics. *Learning Disability Quarterly, 4*, 170–179.

Bryan, T. (1977). Children's comprehension of nonverbal communication. *Journal of Learning Disabilities, 10*, 501–506.

Bryan, T. (1997). Assessing the personal and social status of students with learning disabilities. *Learning Disabilities Research and Practice, 12*, 63–76.

Bryan, T., Bay, M., Shelden, C., & Simon, J. (1990). Teachers and at-risk students stimulated recall of instruction. *Exceptionality, 1*, 167–179.

Bryan, T., & Bryan, J. (1991). Positive mood and math performance. *Journal of Learning Disabilities, 24*, 490–494.

Bryan, T., & Bryan, J. (1996, April). *Amazing discoveries: The social science curriculum.* Paper presented at the Learning Disabilities Association conference, Orlando, FL.

Bryan, T., Donahue, M., & Pearl, R. (1981). Learning disabled children's peer interactions during a small-group problem-solving task. *Learning Disabilities Quarterly, 4*, 13–22.

Bryan, T., Sullivan, K., & Mathur, S. (1996). The impact of positive mood on learning. *Learning Disabilities Quarterly, 19*, 153–162.

Bryan, T., Werner, M., & Pearl, R. (1982). Learning disabled students' conformity responses to prosocial and antisocial situations. *Learning Disabilities Quarterly, 5*, 344–352.

Buchanan, M., & Wolf, J. S. (1986). A comprehensive study of learning disabled adults. *Journal of Learning Disabilities, 19*, 34–38.

Bukowski, W. M., & Ferber, J. S. (1987, April). *A study of peer relations, attributional style, and loneliness during early adolescence.* Paper presented at the biennial meeting of the Society for Research in Child Development, Baltimore.

Bursuck, W. (1989). A comparison of students with learning disabilities to low achieving and higher achieving students on three dimensions of social competence. *Journal of Learning Disabilities, 22,* 188–194.

Carlson, C. I. (1987). Social interaction goals and strategies of children with learning disabilities. *Journal of Learning Disabilities, 20,* 306–311.

Chapman, J. W. (1985). *Self-perceptions of ability, learned helplessness and academic achievement expectations of children with learning disabilities.* Unpublished manuscripts, Education Department, Massey University, Massey, New Zealand.

Chapman, J. W. (1988). Cognitive-motivational characteristics and academic achievement of learning disabled children: A longitudinal study. *Journal of Educational Psychology, 80,* 357–365.

Clever, A., Bear, G., & Juvonen, J. (1992). Discrepancies between competence and importance in self-perceptions of children in integrated classes. *Journal of Special Education, 26,* 125–138.

Cohen, J. (1985). Learning disabilities and adolescence: Developmental considerations. *Adolescent Psychiatry, 12,* 177–196.

Coie, J. D., & Dodge, K. A. (1983). Continuities and changes in children's social status: A five year longitudinal study. *Merrill-Palmer Quarterly, 29,* 261–281.

Cowen, E., Pederson, A., Babigion, M., Izzo, L. D., & Trost, M. A. (1973). Long-term follow-up of early detected vulnerable children. *Journal of Consulting Clinical Psychology, 41,* 438–446.

Crandall, V. C., Katkovsky, W., & Crandall, F. J. (1965). Children's beliefs in their own control of reinforcements in intellectual-academic situations. *Child Development, 36,* 91–109.

Dalley, M. B., Bolocofsky, D. N., Alcorn, M. B., & Baker, C. (1992). Depressive symptomatology, attributional style, dysfunctional attitude, and social competency in adolescents with and without learning disabilities. *School Psychology Review, 21,* 444–458.

Dickstein, E. B., & Warren, D. R. (1980). Role-taking deficits in learning disabled children. *Journal of Learning Disabilities, 13,* 33–37.

Dodge, K. A. (1986). A social information processing model of social competence in children. In M. Perlmutter (Ed.), *Cognitive perspective on children's social and behavioral development: The Minnesota Symposia on Child Psychology,* Vol. 18 (pp. 77–125). Hillsdale, NJ: Lawrence Erlbaum Associates.

Dodge, K. A., & Frame, C. L. (1982). Social cognitive biases and deficits in aggressive boys. *Child Development, 53,* 620–635.

Dohrn, E., & Bryan, T. (1994). Attribution instruction. *Teaching Exceptional Children, 26,* 61–63.

Donahue, M., & Bryan, T. (1984). Communicative skills and peer relations of learning disabled adolescents. *Topics in Language Disorders, 4,* 10–21.

Durrant, J. E. (1993). Attributions for achievement outcomes among behavioral subgroups of children with learning disabilities. *Journal of Special Education, 27,* 306–320.

Durrant, J. E., Cunningham, C. E., & Voelker, S. (1990). Academic, social, and general self-concepts of behavioral subgroups of learning disabled children. *Journal of Educational Psychology, 82,* 657–663.

Edmonson, B., DeJung, J., Leland, H., & Leach, E. (1974). *The test of social inference*. New York: Educational Activities.

Epstein, M. H., Cullinan, D., & Rosemier, R. (1983). Behavior problem patterns among the learning disabled: Boys aged 6–11. *Learning Disability Quarterly, 6*, 305–311.

Feagans, L., & McKinney, J. D. (1981). The pattern of exceptionality across domains in learning disabled children. *Journal of Applied Developmental Psychology, 1*, 313–328.

Feagans, L. V., Merriwether, A. M., & Haldane, D. (1991). Goodness of fit in the home: Its relationship to school behavior and achievement in children with learning disabilities. *Journal of Learning Disabilities, 24*, 413–420.

Fincham, F. A. (1977). Comparison of moral judgment in learning disabled and normal achieving boys. *Journal of Psychology, 96*, 153–160.

Gerber, P. J., & Zinkgraf, S. A. (1982). A comparative study of social-perceptual ability in learning disabled and non-handicapped students. *Learning Disability Quarterly, 5*, 374–378.

Gillis, J. S. (1980). *Child Anxiety Scale manual*. Champaign, IL: Institute for Personality and Ability Testing, Inc.

Gregory, J. F., Shanahan, T., & Walberg, H. J. (1986). A profile of learning disabled twelfth-graders in regular classes. *Learning Disabilities Quarterly, 9*, 33–42.

Gresham, F. M. (1986). Conceptual and definitional issues in the assessment of children's social skills: Implications for classification and training. *Journal of Clinical Child Psychology, 15*, 3–15.

Gresham, F. M., & Elliott, S. N. (1989). Social skills assessment technology for LD students. *Learning Disability Quarterly, 12*, 141–152.

Grolnick, W. S., & Ryan, R. M. (1990). Self-perceptions, motivation, and adjustment in children with learning disabilities: A multiple group comparison study. *Journal of Learning Disabilities, 23*, 177–184.

Gross, A. L., & Ballif, B. (1991). Children's understanding of emotion from facial expressions and situations: A review. *Developmental Review, 11*, 368–398.

Haager, D., & Vaughn, S. (1995). Parent, teacher, peer, and self-reports of the social competence of students with learning disabilities. *Journal of Learning Disabilities, 28*, 205–215.

Hall, C. W., & Richmond, B. O. (1985). Non-verbal communication, self-esteem and interpersonal relations of LD and non-LD students. *Exceptional Child, 32*, 87–91.

Hallahan, D. P., Gajar, A. H., Cohen, S. B., & Tarver, S. G. (1978). Selective attention and locus of control in learning disabled and normal children. *Journal of Learning Disabilities, 11*, 231–236.

Harnadek, M. C. S., & Rourke, B. P. (1994). Principal identifying features of the syndrome of nonverbal learning disabilities in children. *Journal of Learning Disabilities, 27*, 144–154.

Harter, S. (1985). Processes underlying the construction maintenance, and enhancement of the self-concept in children. In J. Suls & A. Greenwald, (Eds.), *Psychological perspectives on the self*, Vol. 3 (pp. 137–181). Hillsdale, NJ: Lawrence Erlbaum.

Harter, S., & Pike, R. (1984). The pictorial scale of perceived competence and social acceptance for young children. *Child Development, 55*, 1969–1982.

Hiebert, B., Wong, B., & Hunter, M. (1982). Affective influences on learning disabled adolescents. *Learning Disability Quarterly, 5,* 334–388.

Holder, H. B., & Kirkpatrick, S. W. (1991). Interpretation of emotion from facial expressions in children with and without learning disabilities. *Journal of Learning Disabilities, 24,* 170–177.

Huntington, D. D., & Bender, W. N. (1993). Adolescents with learning disabilities at risk: Emotional well-being, depression, suicide. *Journal of Learning Disabilities, 26,* 159–166.

Isen, A. M. (1984). Toward understanding the role of affect in cognition. In R. S. Wyer, Jr., & T. K. Srull (Eds.), *Handbook of motivation and cognition,* Vol. 3 (pp. 179–236). Hillsdale, NJ: Lawrence Erlbaum.

Isen, A. M., & Means, B. (1983). Positive affect as a variable in decision making. *Social Cognition, 2,* 18–31.

Jackson, S. C., Enright, R. D., & Murdock, J. Y. (1987). Social perception problems in learning disabled youth: Developmental lag versus perceptual deficit. *Journal of Learning Disabilities, 20,* 361–364.

Jacobsen, B., Lowery, B., & DuCette, J. (1986). Attributions of learning disabled children. *Journal of Educational Psychology, 78,* 59–64.

Jarvis, P. A., & Justice, E. M. (1992). Social sensitivity in adolescents and adults with learning disabilities. *Adolescence, 27,* 977–988.

Johnson, D. J., & Myklebust, H. (1967). *Learning disabilities: Educational principles and practices.* Orlando, FL: Grune & Stratton.

Jones, C. J. (1985). Analysis of the self-concepts of handicapped students. *Remedial and Special Education, 6,* 32–36.

Kavanagh, J. R., & Truss, T. J. (1987). *Learning disabilities: Proceedings of the National Congress,* Parkton, MD: York.

Kazdin, A. E. (1990). Childhood depression. *Journal of Child Psychology and Psychiatry, 31,* 121–160.

Keogh, B. K. (1983). Individual differences in temperament: A contributor to the personal-social and educational competence of learning disabled children. In J. D. McKinney & L. Feagans (Eds.), *Current topics on learning disabilities,* Vol. 1 (pp. 33–56). Norwood, NJ: Ablex.

Kershner, J. R. (1990). Self-concept and IQ as predictors of remedial success in children with learning disabilities. *Journal of Learning Disabilities, 23,* 368–374.

Kistner, J. A., & Gatlin, D. F. (1989). Sociometric differences between learning-disabled and nonhandicapped students: Effects of sex and race. *Journal of Educational Psychology, 81,* 118–120.

Kistner, J. A., & Osborne, M. (1987). A longitudinal study of LD children's self evaluations. *Learning Disability Quarterly, 10,* 258–266.

Kistner, J. A., Osborne, M., & LeVerrier, L. (1988). Causal attributions of learning-disabled children: Developmental patterns and relation to academic progress. *Journal of Educational Psychology, 80,* 82–89.

Kohlberg, L., Colby, A., Gibbs, J., Spicher-Dubin, B., & Power, C. (1978). *Assessing moral stages: A manual, preliminary edition,* July Cambridge: Center for Moral Education, Harvard University.

Kovacs, M. (1992). *Children's depression inventory (CDI)*. North Tonawanda, NY: Multi-Heath Systems, Inc.

Laconte, M. A., Shaw, D., & Dunn, I. (1991). The effects of a rational-emotive affective education program for high-risk middle school students. *Psychology in the Schools, 30,* 274–281.

La Greca, A. M., & Stone, W. L. (1990). LD status and achievement: Confounding variables in the study of children's social status, self-esteem, and behavioral functioning. *Journal of Learning Disabilities, 23,* 483–490.

Leondari, A. (1993). Comparability of self-concept among normal achievers, low achievers and children with learning difficulties. *Educational Studies, 19,* 357–371.

Levy, L., & Gottlieb, J. (1984). Learning disabled and non-learning disabled children at play. *Remedial and Special Education, 5,* 43–50.

Lewandowski, L., & Arcangelo, K. (1994). The social adjustment and self-concept of adults with learning disabilities. *Journal of Learning Disabilities, 27,* 598–605.

Lincoln, A., & Chazan, S. (1979). Perceived competence and intrinsic motivation in learning disability children. *Journal of Clinical Child Psychology, 8,* 213–216.

Maag, J. W., & Behrens, J. T. (1989). Depression and cognitive self-statements of learning disabled and seriously emotionally disturbed adolescents. *The Journal of Special Education, 23,* 17–27.

Maag, J. W., & Reid, R. (1994). The phenomenology of depression among students with and without learning disabilities: More similar than different. *Learning Disabilities Research and Practice, 9,* 91–103.

Maheady, L., Maitland, G., & Sainato, D. (1984). The interpretation of social interactions by mildly handicapped and nondisabled children. *Journal of Special Education, 18,* 151–159.

Margalit, M. (1994). *Loneliness among children with special needs: Theory, research, coping and interaction.* New York: Springer-Verlag.

Margalit, M., & Efrati, M. (1994, August). *Loneliness and coherence among children with reading difficulties.* Paper presented at the International Academy of Research in Learning Disabilities, Tromso, Norway.

Margalit, M., & Heiman, T. (1986). Learning disabled boys' anxiety, parental anxiety and family climate. *Journal of Clinical Child Psychology, 15,* 248–253.

Margalit, M., & Zak, I. (1984). Anxiety and self-concept of learning disabled children. *Journal of Learning Disabilities, 17,* 537–539.

McCandless, B. R., & Evans, E. D. (1973). *Children and youth: Psychological development.* Hinsdale, IL: Dryden.

McKinney, J. D., & Feagans, L. (1984). Academic and behavioral characteristics of learning disabled children and average achievers: Longitudinal studies. *Learning Disability Quarterly, 7,* 251–265.

McPhail, J. C. (1993). Adolescents with learning disabilities: A comparative life-stream interpretation. *Journal of Learning Disabilities, 26,* 617–629.

Minskoff, E. H., Sautter, S. W., Hoffmann, F. J., & Hawks, R. (1987). Employer attitudes toward hiring the learning disabled. *Journal of Learning Disabilities, 20,* 53–57.

Moreno, J. L. (1934). Who shall survive? *Nervous and Mental Disease Monograph No. 58,* Washington, D.C.

Morrison, G. M., Forness, S. R., & MacMillan, D. L. (1983). Influences on the sociometric ratings of mildly handicapped children: A path analysis. *Journal of Educational Psychology, 75,* 63–74.

Morvitz, E., & Motta, R. W. (1992). Predictors of self-esteem: The roles of parent–child perceptions, achievement, and class placement. *Journal of Learning Disabilities, 25,* 72–80.

Nabuzoka, D., & Smith, P. K. (1995). Identification of expressions of emotions by children with and without learning disabilities. *Learning Disabilities Research & Practice, 10,* 91–101.

Ochoa, S. H., & Palmer, D. J. (1995). A meta-analysis of peer rating sociometric studies with learning disabled pupils. *Journal of Special Education, 29,* 1–19.

Oliva, A. H., & LaGreca, A. M. (1988). Children with learning disabilities: Social goals and strategies. *Journal of Learning Disabilities, 21,* 301–306.

Parker, J. G., & Asher, S. R. (1987). Peer relations and later personal adjustment: Are low-accepted children at risk? *Psychology, Bulletin 102*(3), 357–389.

Parker, J. G., & Asher, S. R. (1993). Friendship and friendship quality in middle childhood. *Developmental Psychology, 29,* 611–621.

Pascarella, E. T., & Pflaum, S. W. (1981). The interaction of children's attribution and level of control over error correction in reading instruction. *Journal of Educational Psychology, 73,* 533–540.

Pearl, R. (1992). Psychological characteristics of learning disabled students. In N. N. Singh & I. L. Beale (Eds.), *Learning disabilities: Nature, theory,, and treatment* (pp. 96–125). New York: Springer Verlag, Inc.

Pearl, R., Bryan, T., & Donahue, M. (1980). Learning disabled children's attributions for success and failure. *Learning Disability Quarterly, 3,* 3–9.

Pearl, R., Bryan, T., Fallon, P., & Herzog, A. (1991). Learning disabled students' detection of deception. *Learning Disabilities Research & Practice, 6,* 12–16.

Pearl, R., & Cosden, M. (1982). Sizing up a situation: LD children's understanding of social interactions. *Learning Disability Quarterly, 5,* 371–373.

Peplau, L. A., & Perlman, D. (1982). Perspectives on loneliness. In L. A. Peplau & D. Perlman (Eds.), *Loneliness: A sourcebook of current theory, research and therapy* (pp. 1–18). New York: Wiley.

Piers, E., & Harris, D. (1969). *The Piers–Harris children's self-concept scale.* Nashville: Counselor Recordings and Tests.

Platt, J. J., & Spivack, G. (1975). *Manual for the means-ends problem solving procedure (MEPS): A measure of interpersonal cognitive problem-solving skill.* Philadelphia: Hahnemann Community Health/Mental Retardation Center, Department of Health Services.

Prout, H., & DeMartino, R. (1986). A meta-analysis of school based studies of psychotherapy. *Journal of School Psychology, 24,* 285–292.

Renick, M. J. (1985). *The development of learning disabled children's self-perceptions.* Bethesda: National Institute of Child Health and Human Development.

Renick, M. J., & Harter, S. (1989). Impact of social comparisons on the developing self-perceptions of learning disabled students. *Journal of Educational Psychology, 81,* 631–638.

Rogers, H., & Saklofske, D. H. (1985). Self-concept, locus of control and performance expectations of learning disabled children. *Journal of Learning Disabilities, 18,* 273–278.

Rosenberg, B. S., & Gaier, E. L. (1977). The self-concept of the adolescent with learning disabilities. *Adolescence, 12,* 490–497.

Rosenberg, M. (1965). Society and the Adolescent Self Image. Princeton, N.J.: Princeton University Press.

Rosenthal, R., Hall, J., Archer, D., DiMatteo, M. R., & Rogers, P. L. (1977). The PONS Test: Measuring sensitivity to nonverbal cues. In P. McReynolds (Ed.): *Advances in Psychological Assessment,* Vol. 4 (pp. 179–221). San Francisco: Jossey-Bass.

Rourke, B. P. (1989). Nonverbal learning disabilities: The syndrome and the model: New York: Guilford Press.

Schreider, M., & Yoshida, R. K. (1988). Interpersonal problem-solving skills and classroom behavior adjustment in learning-disabled adolescents and comparison peers. *Journal of School Psychology, 26,* 25–34.

Schunk, D. H. (1983). Developing children's self-efficacy and skills: The roles of social comparative information and goal settings. *Contemporary Educational Psychology, 8,* 76–86.

Schunk, D. H. (1984). Sequential attributional feedback and children's achievement behaviors. *Journal of Educational Psychology, 76,* 1159–1169.

Schunk, D. H. (1988). Self-efficacy and cognitive achievement: Implications for students with learning problems. *Journal of Learning Disabilities, 22,* 14–22.

Schunk, D. H., & Hanson, A. R. (1985). Peer models: Influence on children's self-efficacy and achievement. *Journal of Educational Psychology, 77,* 313–322.

Schunk, D. H., & Rice, J. M. (1985). Verbalization of comprehension strategies: Effects on children's achievement outcomes. *Human Learning, 4,* 1–10.

Silver, D. S., & Young, R. D. (1985). Interpersonal problem-solving abilities, peer status and behavioral adjustment in learning disabled and non-learning disabled adolescents. *Advances in Learning and Behavioral Disabilities, 4,* 201–223.

Silver, L. B. (1990). Attention deficit-hyperactivity disorder: Is it a learning disability or a related disorder. *Journal of Learning Disabilities, 23,* 394–377.

Silverman, R., & Zigmond, N. (1983). Self-concept in learning disabled adolescents. *Journal of Learning Disabilities, 16,* 478–482.

Smith, D. S., & Nagle, R. J. (1995). Self-perceptions and social comparisons among children with LD. *Journal of Learning Disabilities, 28,* 364–371.

Sobol, M. P., Earn, B. M., Bennett, D., & Humphries, T. (1983). A categorical analysis of the social attributions of learning-disabled children. *Journal of Abnormal Child Psychology, 11,* 217–218.

Spence, S. H. (1991). Developments in the assessment of social skills and social competence in children. *Behaviour Change, 8,* 148–166.

Stilliadis, K., & Wiener, J. (1989). Relationship between social perception and peer status in children with learning disabilities. *Journal of Learning Disabilities, 22,* 624–629.

Stipek, D. J., & Daniels, D. H. (1988). Declining perceptions of competence: A consequence of changes in the child or in the educational environment? *Journal of Educational Psychology, 80,* 352–356.

Spivack, G., Platt, J. J., & Shure, M. B. (1976). *The problem-solving approach to Adjustment: A guide to research and intervention.* San Francisco: Jossey-Bass.

Stone, W. L., & La Greca, A. M. (1984). Comprehension of nonverbal communication: A reexamination of the social competencies of learning-disabled children. *Journal of Abnormal Child Psychology, 12,* 505–518.

Stone, W. L., & La Greca, A. M. (1990). The social status of children with learning disabilities: A reexamination. *Journal of Learning Disabilities, 23,* 32–37.

Thomas, A., & Pashley, B. (1982). Effects of classroom training on LD students' task persistence and attributions. *Learning Disability Quarterly, 5,* 133–144.

Tollefson, H., Tracy, D. B., Johnsen, E. P., Buenning, M., Farmer, A., & Barke, C. R. (1982). *Attribution patterns of learning disabled adolescents. Learning Disabilities Quarterly, 5,* 14–20.

Toro, P. A., Weissberg, R. P., Guare, J., & Liebenstein, N. L. (1990). A comparison of children with and without learning disabilities on social problem-solving skill, social behavior, and family background. *Journal of Learning Disabilities, 23,* 115–120.

Turiel, E. (1983). *The development of social knowledge.* Cambridge: Cambridge University Press.

Tur-Kaspa, H., & Bryan, T. (1994). Social attributions of students with learning disabilities. *Exceptionality, 4,* 229–244.

Tur-Kaspa, H., & Bryan, T. (1994). Social information processing of students with learning disabilities. *Journal of Learning Disabilities Research and Practice, 9,* 12–23.

Vaughn, S., & Haager, D. (1994). Social competence as a multifaceted construct: How do students with learning disabilities fare? *Learning Disability Quarterly, 17,* 253–266.

Vaughn, S. R., & Hogan, A. (1990). Social competence and learning disabilities: A prospective study. In H. L. Swanson & B. K. Keogh (Eds.), *Learning disabilities: Theoretical and research issues* (pp. 175–191). Hillsdale, NJ: Erlbaum.

Waddell, J. (1984). The self-concept and social adaptation of hyperactive children in adolescence. *Journal of Clinical Child Psychology, 13,* 50–55.

Weiss, E. (1984). Learning disabled children's understanding of social interactions of peers. *Journal of Learning Disabilities, 17,* 612–614.

White, W. J. (1985). Perspectives on the education and training of learning disabled adults. *Learning Disabilities Quarterly, 86,* 231–236.

Wiig, E. H., & Harris, S. P. (1974). Perception and interpretation of nonverbally expressed emotions by adolescents with learning disabilities. *Perceptual and Motor Skills, 38,* 239–245.

Winne, P. H., Woodlands, M. H., & Wong, B. Y. L. (1982). Comparability of self-concept among learning disabled, normal and gifted students. *Journal of Learning Disabilities, 15,* 470–475.

Wright, J. C., Giammarino, M., & Parad, H. (1986). Social status in small groups: Individual-group similarity and the social "misfit." *Journal of Personality and Social Psychology, 50,* 523–536.

Yasutake, D., & Bryan, T. (1995). The impact of positive mood induction on learning and performance of students with learning disabilities. *Learning Disabilities Research and Practice, 10,* 38–45.

Yasutake, D., Bryan, T., & Dohrn, E. (1996). Effects of combining peer tutoring and attribution training on students' perceived self-competence. *Remedial and Special Education, 17*, 83–91.

Ysseldyke, J. E., Algozzine, B., Shinn, M., & McGue, M. (1982). Similarities and differences among low achievers and students labeled learning disabled. *Journal of Special Education, 16*, 73–85.

CHAPTER 8

Metacognition and Learning Disabilities

Deborah L. Butler

I. INTRODUCTION

Metacognition is a concept with "fuzzy boundaries" (Borkowski, 1992; Brown, 1987; Campione, Brown, & Connell, 1988). Since its historical inception, considerable debate has centered on just what aspects of students' cognition should be described as metacognitive (e.g., Borkowski, Estrada, Milstead, & Hale, 1989; Brown, 1987; Corno, 1986; Wong, 1991). In early definitions, for example, the term was employed to describe sets of distinct, if interrelated, constructs, including various aspects of students' knowledge and beliefs about cognition, students' active orchestration of cognitive activities during learning, and/or students' reflective awareness of knowledge and processing activities (Brown, 1987; Campione et al., 1988; Wong, 1991). In spite of this definitional conundrum, abundant research attests to the usefulness of metacognitive constructs to understanding effective learning (Brown, 1987). In the field of learning disabilities (LD), metacognitive theory has contributed substantially both to understanding students' underlying processing problems and to guiding development of instructional approaches that promote academic success (Wong, 1991).

This chapter provides a theoretical review of the relevance of metacognition to the field of LD. To increase definitional clarity, the first section presents a conceptual analysis of metacognition, building from early definitions toward a summary of current extensions to metacognitive theory. The second section establishes the importance of metacognition to the LD field, describing both the contributions

Learning about Learning Disabilities, Second Edition   277

and boundaries of metacognitive theory to understanding students' learning difficulties. The chapter closes with a discussion of implications for intervention.

II. DEFINING METACOGNITION

The emergence of metacognition as a central concept in educational research can be associated with researchers' ongoing quest to describe and promote strategic learning and problem solving. It has long been recognized that strategic learning requires not only automatic application of well-learned processing routines in the contexts of familiar tasks, but also flexible adaptation of strategies in the face of task variants (Borkowski, 1992; Butler, 1995; Reeve & Brown, 1985; Resnick & Glaser, 1976). Yet, in the mid-1970s, researchers observed that students often failed to spontaneously call upon extant knowledge about strategies to aid memory performance when not explicitly cued to do so. Flavell (1976) characterized these problems as "production deficiencies," because although students had knowledge about appropriate memory-enhancing strategies (e.g., about rehearsal strategies and how to use them), they failed to actively and strategically bring that knowledge to bear during learning tasks (so that they did not actually rehearse when trying to remember information). Flavell (1976) offered problems in metacognition as an explanation for these production deficiencies. And, in the years since Flavell's original introduction of the term, increasingly encompassing definitions of metacognition have emerged to explain why students fail to coordinate use of knowledge and cognitive processes when facing a range of learning tasks (e.g., Borkowski et al., 1989; Brown, 1987; Corno, 1986; 1992; Wong, 1991).

In early discussions of metacognition, three types of explanations for students' strategic performance deficits were commonly proposed (Campione et al., 1988). First, building on memory research in the early 1970s, Flavell (1976) originally explained production deficiencies as emerging from problems in students' metacognitive knowledge about their own memory processes (i.e., metamemorial knowledge). His definition of metacognition emphasized the influence of students' knowledge and beliefs about cognition on their strategic approaches to tasks (Flavell's 1976; 1987). In contrast, while recognizing the importance of students' knowledge about cognition on problem-solving performance, Ann Brown (1978, 1980) suggested that strategic performance deficits also can be associated with problems in students' coordination and control of the cognitive processes they engage. Therefore, a second focus in early definitions of metacognition was on students' self-regulation of cognitive processes, including their "coordination and control of deliberate attempts to learn or solve problems" (Brown, 1980, p. 78). Finally, common to both Brown's and Flavell's conceptions of metacognition was an emphasis on the importance of students' "ability to reflect upon both their knowledge and management processes" (Campione et al., 1988, p. 94).

Varying emphases across these early definitions led to some confusion about what metacognition entails, and to questioning whether subsuming such diverse constructs under a common label is even meaningful (see Brown, 1987). However, perhaps more important than providing a singular definition of metacognition is establishing a coherent framework for relating the various metacognitive components that shape students' strategic approaches to tasks. Certainly, not all aspects of strategic performance are metacognitive, and it remains useful to explore the family resemblances (Brown, 1987) between theoretical constructs that have prompted the use of that term. Further, emerging explanations for students' deficient strategic performance continue to amend metacognitive theory by articulating components that might be subsumed under the label (e.g., Boekaerts, 1995; Borkowski et al., 1989; Corno, 1986; 1992; 1994) and that help to explain when, how, and why students are strategic.

Thus, the remainder of this section provides an integrative review of emerging conceptions of metacognition, with the aim of distilling key concepts regarding the relationships between metacognitive components and students' strategic performance. To begin, the three key constructs included in early definitions are clarified, focusing sequentially on students' (a) metacognitive knowledge, (b) metacognitive processes (i.e., regulation of cognition), and (c) conscious reflection on knowledge or learning processes. Then, recent extensions to metacognitive theory are described.

A. Metacognitive Knowledge

Flavell (1976) originally defined metacognition as "one's knowledge concerning one's own cognitive processes and products or anything related to them" (p. 232). He identified three types of knowledge about memory processes that influence students' approaches to learning: how to engage a cognitive process (e.g., how to use a rehearsal strategy for memorizing), where to employ the process (e.g., what internal and external resources are available to support memory storage), and when to employ the process (what situations call for active and deliberate attempts to learn, store, or retrieve). He argued that production deficiencies arise when students have adequate knowledge about how to employ a process, but lack understanding about where or when the process can most profitably be used.

In 1987, Flavell elaborated on this original description to identify three types of metacognitive knowledge that impact on students' strategic approaches to tasks: knowledge of person, task, and strategy variables. Person variables reflect understandings about "what human beings are like as cognitive organisms" (p. 22). These understandings can be intraindividual (what students know about themselves as learners), interindividual (what students know about themselves relative to others), or universal (what students believe to be true of all learners). For example, a student may believe that she[1] is good in English but poor at math (an in-

---

[1]To avoid gender bias, use of the pronouns "he" and "she" are used alternately throughout the text.

traindividual perception), that she is a better writer than most of her classmates but slower at reading (an interindividual perception), and that all learners have difficulty when trying to express ideas in writing (a universal perception). Students' beliefs about person variables mediate the approaches they adopt toward tasks. For example, if a student believes she is terrible at math, she may exert less effort in trying to learn, particularly when encountering obstacles (Bandura, 1993). In contrast, if she believes that writing is a demanding process for everyone, not just her, she may be more likely to persevere at the task.

Flavell (1987) defined knowledge about task variables as students' understanding about relationships between task characteristics and associated processing demands. For example, with experience, students generally learn that memorizing a poem verbatim requires different learning approaches than does analyzing the same poem to extract themes. Finally, students' knowledge of strategy variables is their knowledge of cognitive procedures for accomplishing learning tasks. Again, Flavell (1976) differentiated between knowledge about how, when, and where strategies could be used. Similarly, Paris and his colleagues (e.g., Cross & Paris, 1988) described three types of strategy knowledge: declarative (about features of a strategy), procedural (how to use the strategy), and conditional (when and where the strategy is useful). Like Flavell (1976), they suggested that independent strategy use in new situations requires knowledge of each of these three types. Borkowski et al. (1989) also distinguished specific strategy knowledge (all that you know about a particular strategy and its usefulness) from general strategy knowledge (knowledge that use of cognitive strategies in general enhances learning). They proposed that general strategy knowledge energizes students to use strategies when facing a variety of tasks.

Flavell (1987) emphasized that students' knowledge of person, strategy, and task variables interact to influence approaches to learning. For example, effective learners recognize that, given their relative strengths and weaknesses in relation to the demands of a particular task, certain strategic approaches are more likely to be successful. Strategic learning therefore requires coordination of knowledge and beliefs related to cognition and learning processes. Researchers (e.g., Flavell, 1987; Paris & Byrnes, 1989; Wong, 1991) have suggested that students develop metacognitive understandings over time as they interpret their cognitive and metacognitive experiences with tasks (Flavell, 1987). Consistent with this suggestion, Brown (1987) has described metacognitive knowledge as generally "stable, statable, often fallible, and often late developing" (p. 67). Metacognitive knowledge is stable because students develop conceptions about processing that they tend to maintain over time; it is statable because it derives from students' conscious reflection on processing activities and abstraction of understandings in describable terms; it is fallible because it is based on inferences and interpretations that can certainly be wrong (e.g., as when a student misperceives task requirements); and it is late developing because it requires that learners have reached developmental levels sufficient to be able to "step back and consider their own cognitive processes as objects of thought and reflection" (p. 68).

B. Metacognitive Processes

Although Flavell (1976) is generally credited with recognizing the importance of metacognitive knowledge to students' strategic approaches to tasks, he also identified students' regulation of cognitive processing as central to metacognition. He wrote that "metacognition refers, among other things, to the active monitoring and consequent regulation and orchestration of these [cognitive] processes in relation to the cognitive objects or data on which they bear, usually in the service of some concrete goal or objective" (p. 232). Nonetheless, it was Ann Brown (1978; 1980) who most thoroughly addressed the role of metacognitive processes in problem-solving performance. And, in the past two decades, Brown and her colleagues (1987; Baker & Brown, 1984; Campione & Brown, 1990; Reeve & Brown, 1985) have extended application of metacognitive constructs from their identification in memory research to domains such as reading (Baker & Brown, 1984; Brown, 1980; Palincsar & Brown, 1984; 1988; Reeve & Brown, 1985) and mathematics (Brown, Campione, Ferrara, Reeve, & Palincsar, 1991; Campione & Brown, 1990; Campione et al., 1988).

Underlying various descriptions of metacognitive processes is the key proposition that effective learners actively manage, orchestrate, coordinate, control, and self-regulate their approaches to learning. Within that general frame, various specific activities have been labeled metacognitive, such as analyzing the problem at hand, understanding what is required, allocating attention, planning and sequencing problem-solving activities, monitoring, checking, evaluating success, testing (and reality testing), revising, and modifying or terminating activities strategically (Brown, 1978; 1980; Reeve & Brown, 1985; Wong, 1991). It has been suggested that these metacognitive processes are central to strategic performance (Brown, 1978; 1980; 1987) and play a key role as "mediators of learning and transfer" (Campione & Brown, 1990, p. 149).

To clarify the role of metacognitive processes in task performance, consider the relationship between cognitive and metacognitive strategies that might be employed by a strategic writer. An effective writer competently employs an array of cognitive strategies for successfully completing writing tasks. Cognitive strategies have been defined as procedures that help learners achieve a concrete goal (Flavell, 1987; Wong, 1991). In this context, examples of cognitive strategies for writing might include brainstorming ideas, creating an outline, free writing a first draft, or carefully rereading the text for grammatical errors. In contrast, students employ metacognitive processes (or strategies) to orchestrate their engagement in the process of writing. Metacognitive processes might include analyzing the writing task to determine what is required, making plans regarding which writing strategies to use given perceived task demands (e.g., determining whether brainstorm-ing is necessary), monitoring the success of strategic efforts (e.g., judging whether enough ideas were generated during brainstorming), and selecting remedial strate-gies to redress observed gaps in progress (e.g., deciding that more research is nec-essary to gather ideas). Strategic writers (and learners, more generally) flexibly shift between cognitive and metacognitive activities while engaged in learning tasks.

Note that it is not always straightforward to classify particular learning activi-ties as cognitive or metacognitive (Brown, 1987). This is partly because a given strategy might act as a cognitive or metacognitive activity, depending on the func-tion it serves. As Brown (1987) explains, an activity such as looking for main points during reading can be classed as a cognitive strategy, if it serves the goal of reading for meaning, or as a metacognitive strategy, if it is used to self-test com-prehension. Thus, identifying metacognitive processes requires attention to the function that specific activities serve in particular contexts. Activities are only metacognitive when they are used to self-regulate approaches to tasks.

C. Awareness and Conscious Reflection

A thorny issue in definitions of metacognition centers on the role of conscious awareness in students' strategic learning activities (Brown, 1987). On the one hand, conscious awareness of knowledge and strategic processing has been ac-corded a central role in strategic performance. For example, metacognition has been defined as "the deliberate conscious control of one's own cognitive actions" and as the understanding of knowledge "in terms of awareness and appropriate use" (Brown, 1980, p. 453). Similarly, Reeve and Brown (1985) described aspects of metacognition as an "individual's ability to understand and manipulate their own cognitive processes" (p. 343). Finally, as noted earlier, Campione et al. (1988) highlighted that common across definitions of metacognition is an emphasis on students' "ability to reflect upon both their knowledge and management process-es" (p. 94). Building from this perspective, researchers have identified as metacog-nitive a range of knowledge and activities that require conscious awareness. For example, during reading, students comprehend when they understand what is read, while metacomprehension requires students' awareness of whether they under-stood. Strategic learners are thought to possess "an awareness of what skills, strate-gies, and resources are needed to perform a task effectively" (Baker & Brown, 1984, p. 22). Strategic learning also requires students' awareness of what they do and do not know and their flexible access to metacognitive and cognitive knowl-edge as they direct their learning activities. Thus, metacognition has generally been associated with students' reflective awareness about knowledge in tandem with conscious deliberation during learning.

On the other hand, researchers acknowledge that self-regulation sometimes proceeds outside of conscious awareness. First, even young children have been shown to be planful and problem-solving (Brown, 1987; Reeve & Brown, 1985; Vygotsky, 1978), although they have trouble articulating descriptions about the cognitive processes they engage. Indeed, Brown (1987) has described metacognitive processes as "relatively unstable, not necessarily statable, and relatively age independent" (p. 68), suggesting that all active learning may involve elements of self-regulation, even if individuals cannot express understandings about cognitive processing in words. Second, researchers generally agree that much intelligent behavior occurs rapidly, automatically, and outside of conscious awareness. For example, expert readers often are not even aware of self-monitoring activities until a comprehension problem occurs (Brown, 1980). Only when problems arise do proficient readers shift from fluent cognitive processing (reading for meaning) and on-line monitoring to metacognitive activities that require conscious reflection (allocating attention to identify the comprehension difficulty and possible debugging strategies).

This apparent conflict underscores the complexity of strategic performance and the multifaceted nature of constructs that have been associated with metacognition. And, resolution of the conflict requires teasing apart related concepts and considering how metacognition develops. For example, consider the problem of automatic versus deliberative processing. Researchers have characterized the development of expertise as a movement from slower, sequential, and effortful processing to the gradual mastery and automatizing of increasingly familiar routines. Corno (1986) suggests that "automation of metacognition is generally regarded as adaptive in conceptions of self-regulated learning" (p. 334). Thus, effective learners appear to conduct much cognitive processing outside of conscious awareness, particularly when problems are familiar and appropriate processes are routine. This outside-of-awareness processing includes execution of both cognitive strategies and elements of executive processing associated with metacognition (e.g., strategy selection and self-monitoring). These latter activities are metacognitive because they serve to regulate students' approaches to tasks (e.g., identifying comprehension problems).

At the same time, the hallmark of strategic learning is students' ability to bring automatic processes to conscious awareness when more deliberate processing is called for, as in cases when comprehension breaks down during reading, or when facing a task that is not completely familiar. By definition, problem solving is required in those situations "in which an individual is called upon to perform a task not previously encountered and for which externally provided instructions do not specify completely the mode of solution" (Resnick & Glaser, 1976, p. 209). And in these situations, it is students' active and deliberative attempts to transfer strategy use across contexts or tasks that defines strategic processing, rather than the automatic implementation of well-learned routines (Brown, 1978; Reeve & Brown, 1985). So, given that conceptions of metacognition were developed to explain problems in strategic performance in novel contexts or tasks (i.e., to explain production deficiencies), it is not surprising that definitions have focused on the role of deliberate activities in problem-solving performance. While performance in familiar tasks may require flexible shifts between unconsciously and consciously directed processing, difficult or unfamiliar tasks require students' reflective orchestration of problem-solving activities.

Another source of confusion regarding the status of conscious awareness in definitions of metacognition stems from important differences between metacognitive knowledge and metacognitive processes. For example, although even young children self-direct learning activities (i.e., implement metacognitive processes), children's ability to reflect on and consciously describe aspects of cognition (i.e., metacognitive knowledge) develops with age (Brown, 1987; Reeve & Brown, 1985). That is, although young children planfully manipulate their environment and engage in problem solving (Brown, 1987; Reeve & Brown, 1985; Vygotsky, 1978), metacognitive understandings about those learning activities only start to develop when students consciously interpret cognitive and metacognitive experiences to make sense of learning (Flavell, 1987). Metacognitive knowledge emerges in tandem with developmental changes that permit students to see themselves as active cognitive agents, to think about cognitive means and goals, to reflect on their cognitive processes, and to participate in tasks, like reading, that invite self-regulation (Flavell, 1987). The implication is that, if one equates metacognition with students' ability to articulate metacognitive knowledge about learning, then conscious awareness is prerequisite. But, if one allows that young children actively self-direct learning, then metacognitive processes would appear to be operative before students are able to consciously reflect on their activities (Reeve & Brown, 1985). At the same time, metacognitive processing no doubt improves as students learn to consciously guide cognitive activities in light of emerging understandings about learning (Reeve & Brown, 1985). Ultimately, effective learners integrate metacognitive knowledge and processes to coordinate what they know about learning with what they actually do (Brown, 1978).

D. Extensions to Metacognitive Theory: Cognition, Motivation, and Volition

The preceding discussion illuminates interrelationships among the three key components in early definitions of metacognition: metacognitive knowledge, metacognitive processes, and students' awareness and conscious reflection on their knowledge and learning activities. These metacognitive components have been very useful in explaining many of the performance failures experienced by students with academic difficulties (Baker & Brown, 1984; Campione & Brown,

1990; Wong, 1985; 1991). Yet, in the past decade, researchers have also identified important gaps in prevailing models of metacognition. Expanded models have emerged to provide more complete explanations of influences on students' strategic approaches to tasks.

1. Motivational Beliefs

Numerous researchers have emphasized the importance of motivational beliefs to strategic task engagement (Bandura, 1993; Brown, 1978; Paris & Byrnes, 1989; Schunk, 1994; Wong, 1991; Zimmerman, 1989; 1994; 1995). For example, Borkowski (1992) stressed that "every important cognitive act has motivational consequences, and, furthermore, these consequences potentiate further self-regulated actions" (p. 253). Thus, motivation's relationship with strategic processing is bidirectional: motivational beliefs influence students' strategic approaches to tasks, while students' accumulating experiences with learning shape motivational beliefs (Borkowski, 1992; Borkowski et al., 1989).

Two types of motivational beliefs have received particular attention in discussions of self-regulation: perceptions of self-efficacy and attributional beliefs. Self-efficacy is defined as "personal beliefs about one's capabilities to learn or perform skills at designated levels" (Schunk, 1994, p. 75). Students' perceptions of self-efficacy have been linked with their selection of goals, choice of learning activities, effort expenditure, and task persistence (Bandura, 1993; Schunk, 1994). Attributions are students' beliefs about factors responsible for learning outcomes (Schunk, 1994; Weiner, 1974). For example, students can attribute a good grade on a test to factors such as ability, the amount of time and effort devoted to studying, the strategies used to prepare, luck, or teacher charity. Like perceptions of self-efficacy, students' attributions influence strategic processing (Schunk, 1994). For example, a student may be more likely to increase learning activities in the face of unsatisfactory progress if he believes more effort will lead to better performance.

It could be argued that students' motivational beliefs, such as perceptions of self-efficacy and attributions for performance, are akin to metacognitive knowledge. In fact, students' perceptions of task-specific self-efficacy may be closely related to the understandings they construct about themselves as learners and their strengths in relation to others (i.e., intra- and interindividual person variables, respectively). Furthermore, like other metacognitive understandings, students construct motivational beliefs based on successive experiences with tasks (Paris & Byrnes, 1989). Thus, understanding strategic learning requires appreciating the way in which motivational beliefs both shape and are shaped by students' learning experiences. Recognition of the central role of motivational beliefs in sustaining strategic performance has prompted development of models of self-regulation and metacognition that integrate cognitive and motivational influences (e.g., Boekaerts, 1995; Borkowski et al., 1989; Garcia & Pintrich, 1994; Schunk, 1994; Zimmerman, 1989; 1994).

2. Volitional Processes

Successful performance requires more than motivation, metacognition, and use of cognitive strategies. As Zimmerman (1995) aptly noted, "it is one thing to possess metacognitive knowledge and skill, but another thing to be able to self-regulate its use in the face of fatigue, stressors, or competing attractions" (p. 217). Thus, in the past decade, researchers have analyzed the requirements on students to manage competing goals, distractions, intrusions, waning motivation, and potentially debilitating emotional states (e.g., anxiety) so as to protect engagement in learning. Both Brown (1980) and Flavell (1987) alluded to these kinds of challenges in their discussions of metacognition. For example, Brown (1980) identified students' need to recover from disruptions or distractions, while Flavell (1987) recognized that metacognitive experiences are both cognitive and affective. However, only recently have researchers systematically articulated classes of metacognitive processes that effective learners use to sustain their strategic activities (Corno, 1986, 1992, 1993, 1994; Schunk, 1994; Zimmerman, 1995).

For example, Corno (1986, 1992, 1993, 1994) defined volitional processes as strategies students use to sustain focus and maintain effortful striving towards goals. Corno (1992, 1994) differentiates between motivational and volitional processes: "Volition picks up where motivation leaves off. Motivation denotes commitment, and volition denotes follow-through" (1994, p. 230). Corno (1986) identified six classes of volition control processes: Attention control processes are used to profitably direct attention, for example, by focusing attention on learning goals rather than the potential consequences of failing in front of one's peers; encoding control processes involve "holding information in working memory long enough to influence action" (p. 337); information-processing control processes are used to recognize when to initiate and sustain cognitive approaches to tasks (i.e., buckling down to the task at hand); motivation control strategies are used to sustain motivation in tasks, for example, by setting short-term goals or promising oneself rewards for finishing; emotion control strategies assist students to control negative affect, for example by breathing deeply to control anxiety; and environmental control processes involve taking active steps to modify environmental conditions (e.g., turning down the television) to enhance one's attention to learning. What these different strategies have in common is a focus on protecting and directing learning activities so that desired goals or intentions (motivation) can be positively achieved (using cognitive processes). These processes can be classified as metacognitive because they are used to regulate engagement in tasks.

3. An Integrated View of Metacognition: Cognition, Motivation, and Volition

In sum, in the past two decades, descriptions of the range of knowledge, beliefs, and strategic activities that underlie successful problem solving have become increasingly differentiated and complex. Early models of metacognition explained mature strategic performance in terms of students' active and contextually appropriate coordination of multiple types of knowledge while deliberately orchestrating use of cognitive strategies and skills. Emerging models add to this mix understandings about how students' motivational beliefs shape their strategic activities, and about how students' coordination of motivation, knowledge, and skill is dependent on their recognizing threats to task engagement and utilizing volition control strategies to sustain motivation and to protect their focus on learning.

III. METACOGNITION AND LEARNING DISABILITIES

Substantial research exists documenting metacognition's key role in successful task performance, for students with and without LD. This section focuses on contributions of metacognitive theory to explaining the academic performance of students with LD. First, the impact of metacognition on LD students' academic achievement is established. Second, limitations to metacognitive explanations for LD students' performance are outlined.

A. Metacognition, Effective Learning, and Problems of Students with LD

Research has uncovered metacognitive deficiencies for learners of all ages, even experienced students at the college level (e.g., Pressley & Ghatala, 1988; Walczyk & Hall, 1989). At the same time, research also suggests that the metacognitive problems of students with LD are often more pronounced than those of more successful peers. Excellent summaries of research on the metacognitive processing of LD, poor, and/or normally achieving learners are available (e.g., Baker & Brown, 1984; Corno, 1994; Englert, 1990; Jacobs & Paris, 1987; Licht, 1993; Paris & Byrnes, 1989; Van Haneghan & Baker, 1989; Wong, 1985; 1986; 1991), and those discussions are not reproduced here. Instead, attention is focused on illustrating common metacognitive deficiencies of all learners and how metacognitive theory has advanced understanding of the underachievement of students with LD.

 To review, metacognitive learners orchestrate learning to manage academic success. They employ metacognitive processes such as analyzing tasks, setting goals, planning, selecting and implementing strategies, monitoring progress, redressing observed gaps in performance, and managing motivation and emotions (Brown, 1987; Butler & Winne, 1995; Corno, 1986; 1994; Wong, 1991; Zimmerman, 1989; 1994). Simultaneously, students' metacognitive knowledge and motivational beliefs mediate their approaches to tasks (Bandura, 1993; Borkowski et al., 1989; Paris & Byrnes, 1989). Unfortunately, students often uphold understandings or beliefs that undermine task performance. Further, many students have difficulty engaging metacognitive processes to actively manage their performance in tasks. Selected examples of these metacognitive difficulties are described in more detail below.

1. Recognizing Task Requirements

Efficient learners are aware of task requirements and direct their learning efforts accordingly (Wong, 1985). In fact, it has been argued that understanding task demands is pivotal in strategic learning because students base all further efforts on the demands they perceive (Butler & Winne, 1995). For example, active learners set goals, select strategies, and monitor progress in light of performance criteria they extract from task understandings (Butler & Winne, 1995). It is not surprising, then, that Wong (1985, 1991) has associated an impoverished understanding about tasks with the low achievement of students with LD.

Consistent with that hypothesis O'Shea and O'Shea (1994) demonstrated that cuing students with or without LD to keep task purpose in mind (e.g., to read for meaning) improves comprehension performance, particularly if students are also provided with a strategy to assist comprehension. Similarly, Wong, Wong, and LeMare (1982) showed that LD and non-LD students' understanding of task requirements affects performance outcomes. Specifically, across two studies, they compared the comprehension and recall of 5th to 7th grade students with and without LD under two conditions. In the first condition, students were provided with explicit information about the requirements of upcoming tests (e.g., to study pre-paragraph questions as models for questions on a comprehension test). In the second condition, students were given general instructions about how to read and study (e.g., to think about what a passage was about and whether they liked it or not). Wong et al. (1982) found that providing explicit task information resulted in improved comprehension and recall scores. Further, when students' expectations matched the tests they received, they rated the tasks as easier and expressed less frustration. Wong et al. (1982) concluded that task understandings influence performance outcomes for both LD and non-LD learners. Further, they suggest that clear communication by teachers regarding expectations is critical, particularly for students with LD.

Unfortunately, students often have difficulty identifying task requirements. This difficulty stems in part from inadequate conceptions about tasks. For example, a substantial body of research has shown that younger and poorer readers are less aware of the purpose of reading, focusing more on decoding words or reading accurately than on extracting meaning from text (Baker & Brown, 1984; Jacobs & Paris, 1987; Pazzaglia, Cornoldi, & De Beni, 1995; Wong, 1985). As a result, they tend to adopt strategies for reading that promote word-by-word comprehension rather than identifying main ideas (Baker & Brown, 1984). Similarly, research has shown that students with LD focus on mechanical, rather than substantive, aspects of writing (Englert, 1990; Graham, Schwartz, & MacArthur, 1993). For example, Wong, Wong, and Blenkinsop (1989) compared the writing performance and metacognitive conceptions about writing of adolescents with LD (in 8th and 11th grade) to those of their normally achieving peers (in 6th and 8th grade). They found that, in contrast to normally achieving 8th graders, adolescents with LD produced shorter essays that were rated lower on five dimensions: interestingness, clarity in communication of goals, word choice, organization, and cohesion. Further, students with LD were more likely to equate the process of writing with idea generation or structural precision. Wong et al. (1989) concluded that, unlike normally achieving peers who emphasized the role in writing of higher-order processes such as planning or organization, students with LD focused on lower-level processes such as idea generation and spelling. And, if students perceive writing to be about spelling correctly and using correct grammar, rather than communicating coherently to a particular audience, then the goals they set and the strategies they use will be driven by that understanding.

Wong et al.'s (1982) research suggested that providing students with explicit information about tasks positively impacts performance. However, it is also incumbent on students to actively interpret task demands. As Winne and Marx (1982) aptly noted, students' responses to teacher-assigned tasks are based on their perceptions of tasks, not by the instructions as given. Therefore, although it is helpful for instructions to be as explicit as possible (Garner, Alexander, & Chou Hare, 1991), it is nonetheless critical that students be proficient and accurate at interpreting task requirements. But, whereas good learners actively clarify task demands so as to establish a purpose for learning (Baker & Brown, 1984; Wong, 1985; 1991), students with LD often fail to recognize the importance of analyzing task requirements. For example, Butler (1994, 1997, in press) has found that adult students with LD often misinterpret tasks and so misdirect their learning activities. To illustrate this problem, she presents an example of a student named Nancy[2] who, as part of an Early Childhood Education program, had been asked to observe children in a daycare center and to answer a series of questions (Butler, 1994). However, instead of writing a targeted response to the assigned questions, Nancy prepared for her instructor a chronological description of her experiences at the center. Butler concluded that, like many other students across studies, Nancy's difficulties derived in part from inadequate attention to deciphering the demands of the task, in spite of having been provided with explicit instructions (including a sheet describing specific marking criteria). When Nancy was cued to actively read and interpret her assignment, she quickly realized her mistake.

2. Selecting and Implementing Strategies

Once effective learners determine task requirements, they select appropriate strategies for accomplishing goals. However, younger learners, poor achievers, and LD students often experience problems in strategy selection and use. These problems may arise due to faulty or incomplete knowledge about learning or about strate-

---

[2]All names are fictional.

gies (Englert, 1990; Jacobs & Paris, 1987; Wong, 1985; 1986; 1991) or to problems in selecting strategies to match task demands (Wong, 1985; 1991), mobilizing strategy use (Brown, 1978; Torgesen, 1977; Wong, 1991), implementing learning strategies efficiently (Englert, Raphael, Anderson, Gregg, & Anthony, 1989; Montague, Maddux, & Dereshiwsky, 1990), and/or adapting strategies for use across tasks (Swanson, 1990; Wong, 1994).

For example, research suggests that students with LD have less sophisticated metacognitive understandings about strategies. In a series of studies, Englert and her colleagues studied the metacognitive knowledge of students with LD regarding the writing process (e.g., Englert et al., 1989; Englert, Raphael, Fear, & Anderson, 1988; Englert, Stewart, & Hiebert, 1988; Englert & Thomas, 1987). Based on a summary of this line of research, Englert (1990) concluded that students with LD generally differ from non-LD students in terms of their awareness of writing strategies and how to regulate the writing process. For instance, students with LD tend to use external cues (e.g., teacher judgments, mechanical features of the text, length of the paper) to judge when they are finished and are less sensitive to audience needs when crafting or editing their writing. Similarly, as described earlier, Wong et al. (1989) found that, when compared with non-LD peers, adolescents with LD focused more on lower-level than on higher-level processes when describing how they write. Ineffectual or faulty strategy knowledge has also been observed in the domain of reading. For example, younger and poorer readers have less knowledge about strategies for decoding and comprehending (Wong, 1986). Similarly, older and good readers are more aware of variables that impact on reading, strategies for improving reading, and the utility of different strategies under different circumstances (Jacobs & Paris, 1987).

Lower achieving students also have difficulty coordinating their learning activities in light of task requirements (Butler & Winne, 1995; Wong, 1991). For example, while good readers adjust their learning strategies to address different purposes for reading (i.e., skimming vs. studying), poor readers are less likely to modify reading approaches in light of different goals (Baker & Brown, 1984; Wong, 1985). Poorer learners also have trouble selecting the best strategies for meeting task requirements (Wong, 1991). For example, when describing their approaches to math problem solving, students with LD report using as many strategies as non-LD peers, but they describe using lower-level strategies focused on computation rather than higher-level strategies focused on problem representation (Montague, 1997). It is important to note that LD students do not completely lack knowledge about strategies for various tasks (Wong, 1991). Rather, their knowledge is not well developed or appropriately matched to task demands.

3. Monitoring and Adjusting Performance

Effective learners actively monitor their learning and the success of the strategies they employ. For example, expert readers keep track of comprehension levels and employ debugging strategies to repair comprehension deficiencies (Bereiter & Bird, 1985). In contrast, less effective learners, such as students with LD, are less likely to assess their progress accurately or remediate performance failures (Baker & Brown, 1984; Wong, 1985; 1991). These problems in metacognitive monitoring can sometimes be linked to faulty conceptions about tasks (Butler, 1994; 1997; Butler & Winne, 1995). As Brown (1978) noted "inadequate checking will be manifested at any age if the student does not fully comprehend the nature of the task" (p. 104). Problems may also stem from students' lack of awareness of their own level of knowledge (i.e., about what they do and do not know; Baker & Brown, 1984; Brown, 1978; Wong, 1985), use of less sophisticated standards for judging performance (Baker & Brown, 1984; Van Haneghan & Baker, 1989; Zabrucky & Moore, 1989), failures to actively self-interrogate to discern understanding (Wong & Jones, 1982; Wong, 1985), and/or failure to implement strategies to remediate performance difficulties (Baker & Brown, 1984; Wong, 1985, 1986).

For example, research on readers' comprehension monitoring has shown that younger and less proficient students have difficulty detecting errors in text (Baker, 1984; Wagoner, 1983). Baker (1984) attributed these problems to developmental differences in students' abilities to use multiple standards to monitor reading comprehension. Following on Baker's earlier work (Baker, 1984; Baker & Brown, 1984), Zabrucky and Moore (1989) recently examined the ability of 4th-, 5th-, and 6th-grade students identified as poor, average, or good readers to use three types of standards when detecting inconsistencies in texts. (Note that the researchers excluded students with comprehension scores more than 2 years below grade level, thereby excluding many students who might be identified as LD). These were lexical standards (i.e., judging the meaningfulness of words), external consistency standards (i.e., consistency of text information with prior knowledge about the world), and internal consistency standards (i.e., consistency of information across sentences within the text). Consistent with previous research, they found developmental shifts in children's ability to use the three standards, so that lexical, external consistency, and internal consistency standards appeared to be progressively more difficult to use. Poor readers' performance resembled that of the youngest children, and only good readers improved in their error detection when given explicit explanations about the three kinds of standards. These findings suggest that young and poor readers have more difficulty monitoring comprehension using a variety of standards. Further, based on this line of research, Zabrucky and Moore (1989) caution against taking a unidimensional view of students' monitoring abilities (i.e., suggesting generally that students do or do not monitor). They argue instead that assessing monitoring requires attending to the range of standards against which performance might be judged.

Interestingly, Van Haneghan and Baker (1989) extended this line of research to explore students' monitoring in the area of mathematics. They identified three standards against which students might monitor comprehension when solving problems in math: calculational accuracy, appropriate choice of an operation for completing the problem, and sensibility of the question in terms of prior knowledge. Based on a review of previous research, they argue that students with LD often have difficulty differentiating between correctly and incorrectly solved problems and tend to evaluate their work using only calculational standards. Further, they report findings from one study that examined students' ability to detect errors in completed problems using the three types of standards. Based on the results from that study, they conclude that younger learners and lower achievers are more likely to use superficial standards when detecting errors and that low achievers are more likely than higher achievers to use just one standard for checking or to utilize incorrect or inaccurate standards.

4. Motivation and Emotions

Students with LD often differ from non-LD peers in their perceptions about themselves as learners and in their motivational beliefs (Borkowski, 1992; Licht, 1993; Wong, 1991). As a result, researchers have called for attention to the interplay between metacognition, cognition, and motivation when accounting for the academic performance of students with LD. For example, Pazzaglia et al. (1995) emphasized the role in performance of students' emotions, intuitions, experiences, self-perceptions, and beliefs. They conducted two studies comparing good and poor readers' metacognitive knowledge about reading, attributions, and self-perceptions. In the first study they found differences between LD and non-LD 6th graders in their conceptions about reading tasks, sensitivity to text characteristics, knowledge about reading strategies, and error detection (taken as an index of monitoring), although they failed to find group differences in attributional patterns. In the second study (with 2nd to 6th graders) they found differences between poor and good comprehenders in their self-evaluations of how well they read, how much they like reading, and what factors contribute to reading success.

Montague (1997) recently summarized five studies investigating the interplay between affect and cognition in the domain of mathematical problem solving. Three of the studies were descriptive and investigated group differences in students' judgments about the importance of math problem solving, attitudes towards math, and self-perceptions of math performance. Results generally showed that 6th-, 7th-, and 8th-grade students with LD valued mathematics as highly as did other children. However, they expressed less positive attitudes toward math than did average students, rated their general math performance significantly lower than did average, high-achieving, or gifted students (studies 1 and 2), and rated their problem-solving performance lower than did gifted students (study 3). Interestingly, when examining students' actual problem-solving performance, results showed that, although students with LD described the math problems as more difficult than did average or gifted students, they spent *less* time solving the problems and performed more poorly. This finding suggests that LD students' poor perceptions of their math ability may undermine their persistence in tasks (Montague, 1997).

Finally, Chapman (1988) compared the academic self-concepts, academic locus of control, and achievement expectations of 11-year-old students with and without LD. He found that students with LD had lower self-perceptions on each of these variables and that group differences maintained over a 2-year period. Note, however, that the participants in Chapman's study were identified as LD or non-LD for the purposes of the research. They had not been identified as LD in schools, nor did they receive remedial instruction targeted at remediating performance or motivational difficulties. More encouragingly, Montague (1997) found that students' self-perceptions of their math performance improved after participating in strategy-based interventions.

Although much research has documented the generally poor self-perceptions of students with LD, Licht (1993) cautions that it is nonetheless important to recognize individual differences. Not all students with LD develop systems of self-perceptions that undermine motivation. For example, Pintrich, Anderman, and Klobucar (1994) failed to find differences in self-efficacy, intrinsic motivation, or anxiety between 5th graders with and without LD, although they did observe group differences in metacognitive awareness about reading and comprehension performance. Further, Pintrich et al. (1994) argue that, given potential differences in metacognition and motivation across students with LD, it may be more useful to identify clusters of similar students based on a combination of cognitive and motivational variables. In their study they used a cluster analysis to identify three groups of students with different profiles of scores: Cluster 1 included students who were high on comprehension, metacognition, and motivation (mostly students without LD); Cluster 2 included students who were low in comprehension and metacognition but high in intrinsic motivation (all students with LD); and Cluster 3 included students low on intrinsic motivation but average on comprehension and metacognition (a mix of LD and non-LD students). Although the variables that best distinguished between the three groups (i.e., that were statistically reliable after the clustering) were metacognitive awareness and comprehension, Pintrich et al. (1994) argue for understanding individual differences in terms of both motivational and metacognitive variables. Equivalent achievement outcomes may be attained by students with different constellations of beliefs, strategies, and skills.

B. Limitations to a Metacognitive Perspective on LD

Metacognitive theory has clearly contributed to a fuller description of the processing problems of students with LD. At the same time, it is important to consider the contributions of metacognitive theory in perspective (Wong, 1991). In particular, we need to remember that not all of the problems of students with LD are metacognitive. Further, it is also important to examine the implications of observed metacognitive deficits for conceptual definitions of LD.

1. Metacognitive Deficits in Perspective

As early as 1977, Torgesen called for research into the "metavariables" identified by Flavell as a potential explanation for achievement deficits of students with LD. He cautioned against ascribing observed problems in performance to neurologically based processing problems in attention, short-term memory, perceptual skills, or other areas without ruling out alternative explanations based on students' strategic approaches to tasks. Similarly, Wong (1985) argued for extending research into LD students' performance beyond consideration of specific ability deficits. She has argued persuasively for the relevance of theories of metacognition for more comprehensively understanding LD students' academic achievement (Wong, 1985, 1986, 1987, 1991).

At the same time, Wong (1991) cautioned against overextending metacognitive theory when accounting for achievement by students with LD. Even a broader view of metacognition that encompasses motivational and volitional processes is insufficient to account completely for students' performance difficulties. For example, students' basic processing problems in areas such as visual perception, phonological coding, and memory influence performance in important respects (e.g., Mann, 1991; Swanson, 1990; Willows, 1991). Understanding and remediating performance difficulties requires attending to the interaction between lower- and higher-level processes. Further, students' successful performance is also highly dependent on domain-specific knowledge (Alexander, 1995; Alexander & Judy, 1988; Bos & Anders, 1990). For example, students' domain knowledge interacts with their knowledge about strategies to shape cognitive and metacognitive processing (Alexander & Judy, 1988). Thus, accounting for LD students' performance difficulties requires keeping in focus the role of metacognition in relation to other influences on performance (of which basic processing skills and domain knowledge are two examples). Successfully remediating performance deficits requires dovetailing metacognitive intervention with instructional approaches that appropriately address a full range of needs.

2. Metacognitive Deficits: A Primary or Secondary Problem?

Conceptual definitions of LD consistently hinge on certain core concepts: that students with LD have average to above average potential; that they have specific, rather than generalized processing deficits; and that the processing problems underlying students' performance problems are neurologically based (Stanovich, 1986a; Torgesen, 1991; Wong, 1991). Stanovich (1986a) argued that the "assumption of specificity" is central to these conceptions of LD. This assumption holds that LD students' unexpectedly low performance on a task (such as reading) in light of their potential can be accounted for by problems in basic processes required by that task and not by more generalized cognitive deficits.

Detection of metacognitive deficits in students with LD has the potential to threaten several of these core concepts (Wong, 1991). For example, metacognition and adaptive problem solving have been associated consistently with potential (e.g., Brown, 1978; Campione & Brown, 1990; Resnick & Glaser, 1976; Stanovich, 1986a). Therefore, if students with LD have metacognitive deficits, can we maintain that they have average to above-average potential? Further, findings that faulty metacognition accounts in part for performance difficulties threatens the assumption of specificity (Stanovich, 1986a; Wong, 1991), if those metacognitive problems are pervasive rather than localized. These conceptual problems are compounded if we assume that metacognitive processes, like more basic processing problems, are also neurologically based. If metacognitive deficits are a first-order (with a direct neurological origin) rather than a second-order problem (deriving from other first-order problems in interaction with experiences), then how should we differentiate students with LD from students with cognitive disabilities or their normally achieving counterparts? Is it simply a matter of degree, so that on a continuum of potential, students with LD fall in the low average range (Wong, 1991)? Or, can we maintain that there is something qualitatively unique about the cognitive processing of students with LD?

A potential solution to these conflicts can be found by examining the origins of metacognition. Wong (1991) suggests that we think of LD students' metacognitive deficits as a second-order, rather than a first-order problem. That is, rather than representing an innate limitation to potential deriving from neurologically based problems in executive processing, the metacognitive problems of students with LD may emerge over time based on an interaction between delimited processing problems and successive experiences with tasks. Following on Stanovich (1986a, 1986b). Wong (1991) argues that students with specific processing deficits may experience early failure on culturally valued tasks (such as reading). This failure may undermine confidence and motivation, leading to task avoidance. Lack of success coupled with task avoidance reduce students' opportunities to learn. And, because metacognition only develops through experiences with tasks, students with LD fail to build metacognitive knowledge or processes that promote more successful performance. Over time, performance gaps widen. Whereas more successful peers build domain knowledge and acquire metacognition, thereby accelerating learning achievements, students with LD fall farther and farther behind. Without appropriate motivation and metacognition, students with LD fail to profit from successive learning experiences.

Development of metacognition by students with LD also may be limited by the kinds of tasks they experience in school. Researchers have argued that the metacognitive "deficits" observed in many learners reflect a logical abstraction of knowledge and skills based on the learning activities to which they are typically exposed (Campione et al., 1988; Lave, Smith, & Butler, 1988; Palincsar & Klenk, 1992; Schoenfeld, 1988; Van Haneghan & Baker, 1989). These experiences lead students to construct naive or inappropriate models of self-regulated learning that interfere with mature performance in tasks (Bereiter & Scardamalia, 1987; Corno, 1995). For example, Schoenfeld (1988) provides excellent examples of how math activities in schools lead to a suspension of sense-making, thereby undermining students' understanding about the nature of mathematics. Similarly, Campione et al. (1988) outline how students' experiences in school lead to construction of sub-optimal metacognition. They argue that, in reading, instruction in decoding at the expense of comprehension leads students to think of the goal of reading as decoding; in writing, early emphasis on mechanics rather than communication leads students to equate successful writing with neatness; and in math, emphasizing algorithms before understanding coupled with practice in decomposed skills leads students to think of math as applying algorithms and obtaining correct answers. Thus, it may be that some common instructional practices inadvertently lead students to develop inert knowledge (Campione et al., 1988; Bereiter & Scardamalia, 1985), faulty conceptions about tasks, and ineffective metacognitive processes (Campione et al., 1988; Lave et al., 1988; Palincsar & Klenk, 1992; Schoenfeld, 1988).

Students with LD are particularly at risk in this regard, because the specific processing problems they experience make it even more likely that the tasks they are given will emphasize basic skills at the expense of higher level processing (Campione et al., 1988; Palincsar & Klenk, 1992). As Campione et al. (1988) explain, "this emphasis on skill training is stressed to an even greater degree for low-achieving students, those for whom explicit instruction in understanding is particularly important" (p. 96). The result for students with LD is development of fragmented domain knowledge, faulty understandings about tasks, and difficulties with monitoring and self-regulation.

IV. INSTRUCTIONAL IMPLICATIONS

At the outset of this chapter, it was proposed that theories of metacognition emerged in response to educators' ongoing attempts to describe and promote strategic learning and problem solving. And, to this point in the chapter, discussion has focused on describing the role of metacognition (in conjunction with motivation, cognition, basic skills, and domain knowledge) in students' strategic performance as well as the implications of metacognitive theory for understanding LD. This last section takes up the question of how one should promote strategic processing, based on what we have learned. A great deal of intervention research has been done investigating instructional approaches designed to promote strategic learning by low-achieving students or by students with LD (e.g., Borkowski & Muthukrishna, 1992; Butler, 1995; in press; Ellis, 1993; Englert, Raphael, Anderson, Anthony, & Stevens, 1991; Graham & Harris, 1989; Harris & Graham, 1996; Palincsar & Brown, 1994; Pressley, El-Dinary, et al., 1995; Pressley, El-Dinary, et al., 1992; Schumaker & Deshler, 1992). A thorough discussion of that literature is beyond the scope of this chapter. Instead, this section simply outlines instructional implications that derive from metacognitive research and then highlights five instructional models developed to promote strategic performance.

A. General Instructional Implications

The research reviewed in this chapter has numerous implications for instruction. In this section, some of the more critical implications are outlined. Based on the research described so far, instructors should observe the following:

1. Establish tasks and instructional environments that promote students' construction of optimal conceptions of tasks and learning processes (Doyle, 1983; Garner et al., 1991; Schoenfeld, 1988). For example, set up math activities to emphasize math as a sense-making activity (Schoenfeld, 1988). Or, support students to build skills and strategies in the context of meaningful reading, so that the nature of reading activities (i.e., reading for meaning) is continually emphasized (Palincsar & Klenk, 1992). Critique approaches to remedial instruction in this light (Campione et al., 1988).
2. Actively support students to construct metacognitive understandings by encouraging analysis of metacognitive experiences (Butler, 1995; Borkowski et al., 1989; Ellis, 1993) and mindful reflection about learning processes (Wong, 1994).
3. Support students to modify motivational beliefs as they observe improvements in performance associated with the effortful use of strategies (Borkowski, Weyhing, & Carr, 1988; Reid & Borkowski, 1987; Schunk & Cox, 1986).
4. Explicitly support students' development of metacognitive and motivational processes in tandem with instruction in cognitive strategies (Brown, 1978; Butler, 1995; Campione et al., 1988; Harris & Graham, 1996; Sawyer, Graham, & Harris, 1992). Explicitly support volition control as part of self-regulation (Corno, 1994).
5. Consider individual differences in patterns of metacognitive knowledge, metacognitive processes, motivation, domain-specific knowledge, and basic processing skills to target instruction efficiently and effectively (Butler, 1995; in press; Montague, 1993; Pintrich et al., 19994; Swanson, 1990).

B. Instructional Approaches Designed to Promote Metacognition: Examples

Many current discussions exist regarding the qualities of effective instruction likely to promote, not only students mastery of task-specific strategies, but also their independent coordination of knowledge and cognitive processes across contexts and tasks (i.e., maintenance and transfer) (e.g., Butler, 1995; Ellis, 1993; Garner et al., 1991; Harris & Pressley, 1991; Pressley, El-Dinary, et al., 1992; Wong, 1994). These discussions seek to articulate how to support students' transition from other-regulated performance (i.e., mediated by teachers or peers) to self-regulation (i.e., self-mediated performance). In recognition of this literature (and to direct interested readers' attention to excellent resources), this section briefly highlights five empirically validated instructional models. Note that research demonstrating the efficacy of these models underscores the importance of metacognitive theory to understanding learning difficulties experienced by students with LD. This follows because interventions that draw on metacognitive theory have been consistently associated with improvements in LD students' understandings, beliefs, strategy use, and performance.

The instructional models highlighted below tend to share four key characteristics. First, most models simultaneously attend to cognitive, metacognitive, and motivational processes during instructional intervention. Second, instruction in metacognition is embedded in the context of meaningful work, so that the nature of strategic learning as a means to an end (rather than as an end in itself) is abundantly clear (e.g., Butler, 1995; Harris & Graham, 1996; Palincsar & Klenk, 1992; Pressley, El-Dinary, et al., 1995). Third, many of the models emphasize the important role of social interaction in students' development of self-regulation (e.g., Butler, 1995; Palincsar & Brown, 1988; Pressley, El-Dinary, et al., 1995; Pressley, El-Dinary et al., 1992). It is hypothesized that engaging students in collaborative problem solving promotes discussion about cognitive processing and construction of metacognitive understandings. Further, effective approaches to self-regulation can be modeled by teachers and peers during interactive discussions. Fourth, in most approaches, instruction is calibrated to address individuals' needs, and, while instructors guide individuals' strategic processing in early stages of instruction (teacher-mediation), they gradually cede control of learning processes to students to encourage self-mediation (Brown, 1987; Butler, 1995; Ellis, 1993; Palincsar & Brown, 1988).

1. Reciprocal Teaching

Reciprocal teaching was originally introduced by Palincsar and Brown (1984; 1988) as a model for promoting strategic reading. In the original applications of the model, students were taught four reading comprehension strategies that fostered metacognitive processing (i.e., monitoring of performance): summarizing, questioning, clarifying, and predicting. Then, teachers and students met in cooperative groups to jointly construct understandings about texts. Within that context, teachers and students took turns leading discussions wherein they implemented the learned strategies in the service of reading for meaning. At first, the classroom teacher supported students to take turns as leaders and to guide the group's reading activities. Over time, however, the teacher's support was faded as students became more able to direct their reading activities more independently. Much research exists documenting the efficacy of reciprocal teaching as a model for promoting reading comprehension (see Palincsar & Brown, 1984; Reeve & Brown, 1985; Brown et al., 1991). More recently, the reciprocal teaching model has been adapted for promoting listening comprehension, content learning (e.g., in science), and problem-solving in math (e.g., Brown et al., 1991; Campione et al., 1988).

2. Attributional Retraining

In recognition of the interdependence between students' motivational processes and self-regulation, approaches to instruction have been designed to enhance students' motivational beliefs (i.e., perceptions of self-efficacy and/or attributions) (e.g., Borkowski & Muthukrishna, 1992; Borkowski et al., 1988; Borkowski et al., 1986; Schunk & Cox, 1986). For example, in attributional retraining, instructors provide students with effort-related feedback (i.e., feedback that highlights the role of effortful strategy use in learning) in tandem with instruction targeted at executive processing. Considerable research has shown the efficacy of attributional retraining for improving the perceptions of self-efficacy, attributional patterns, and performance of low-achieving students and/or students with LD (e.g., Borkowski et al., 1988; Borkowski, Weyhing, & Turner, 1986; Groteluschen, Borkowski, & Hale, 1990; Reid & Borkowski, 1987).

3. Strategic Content Learning

Recently, Butler (Butler, 1993, 1995) proposed Strategic Content Learning (SCL) as a model for promoting development of self-regulation by students with LD. In SCL, students work collaboratively with instructors to complete classroom work. However, rather than teaching specific learning strategies as a springboard for instruction, instructors begin by completing a functional assessment of students' extant metacognition (i.e., knowledge and self-regulation). Then, building from what students already know, instructors guide students to approach learning tasks strategically (i.e., to analyze task requirements, set clear goals, select and implement strategies, monitor progress, and revise activities as required) and to reflect on their cognitive processing. In the context of interactive discussions, students are supported to reflect on, evaluate, and revise processes, metacognitive knowledge, and motivational beliefs. In a series of studies, Butler (1993, 1995, 1996, 1997, in press) has implemented SCL as a model for providing individualized support to postsecondary students with LD. Results from her studies have shown consistent gains in participants' task performance, metacognitive understandings, perceptions of self-efficacy, and attributional patterns. Further, evidence suggests that students not only develop new task-specific strategies associated with better performance, but that they also learn how to construct, test out, and revise strategies for themselves. Further research is required, however, to test the broader applicability of the approach (e.g., in group-based applications and with younger students).

4. Self-Regulated Strategy Development

Karen Harris and Steve Graham (Graham & Harris, 1989; Graham, Harris, & MacArthur, 1993; Harris & Graham, 1996; Sawyer et al., 1992) have developed an approach to promoting strategic writing that they call Self-Regulated Strategy Development (SRSD). They identify three goals underlying the SRSD approach, which are to support students to master higher level cognitive processes associated with successful writing, to promote reflective self-regulation of writing performances, and to develop positive attitudes regarding the writing process and themselves as writers (Case, Mamlin, Harris, & Graham, 1995). In a recent text, they also provide a comprehensive description of how the SRSD approach can be implemented longitudinally in regular classroom environments to support students' development of metacognition and motivation supportive of strategic writing (Harris & Graham, 1996). In support of their comprehensive instructional model (too complex to do justice to here), Graham and Harris have assembled copious empirical evidence demonstrating the positive impact of their approach on the writing performance, perceptions of self-efficacy, metacognitive understandings about writing, strategy usage, and transfer of students with LD (see Case et al., 1995, for a recent review).

5. Transactional Strategies Instruction

As a last example of a comprehensive instructional model that draws on metacognitive theory, Pressley and his colleagues (Pressley, Brown, El-Dinary, & Afflerbach, 1995; Pressley, El-Dinary, et al., 1995; Pressley, El-Dinary, et al., 1992) have developed an approach to teaching reading comprehension that they call transactional strategies instruction. Like the Harris and Graham model (1996), transactional strategies instruction is a long-term, multidimensional model that combines instruction in task-specific strategies with complementary instructional activities (such as collaborative implementation of strategies in cooperative groups) designed to promote self-directed processing, construction of metacognitive understandings, and development of positive motivational beliefs. And, like the other models described in this chapter, empirical evidence attests to the benefit of incorporating the instructional model into regular classroom instruction (see Pressley, Brown et al., 1995; Pressley, El-Dinary et al., 1992; Pressley, Schuder, Bergman, & El-Dinary, 1992).

V. CONCLUSION: METACOGNITION AND LEARNING DISABILITIES

The research reviewed in this chapter has established both the benefits and boundaries of applying metacognitive theory to the field of LD. On the one hand, research clearly indicates that students with LD have deficits in metacognition and motivation that undermine successful performance, and that comprehensive instructional models targeted at improving metacognition have a positive impact on strategic learning and problem solving. Practically speaking, then, metacognitive theory provides excellent guidance to practitioners regarding how to assess and address the learning difficulties associated with LD. At the same time, a range of interacting factors are implicated in the academic underachievement of students with LD, including (a) students' specific and localized processing problems; (b) the nature of many school tasks and remedial instruction; (c) the erosion of motivation that accompanies repeated failure experiences; (d) accumulating gaps in domain-specific knowledge; and (e) the underdevelopment of metacognitive knowledge and processes. These factors interact to perpetuate negative learning experiences, which in turn exacerbate motivation problems, metacognitive deficits, and knowledge losses. Breaking this cycle requires intervention supportive of students' needs at multiple levels. It is necessary, but insufficient, to target instruction at development of metacognitive knowledge and skills. Students also need help to recognize, circumvent, and address specific processing problems. Learning environments must be carefully structured to reinforce productive learning and metacognition, and basic skill instruction must constructively contribute to students' emerging conceptions about learning.

Acknowledgments

I would like to thank Bernice Wong for her helpful suggestions concerning earlier drafts of this chapter.

References

Alexander, P. A. (1995). Superimposing a situation-specific and domain-specific perspective on an account of self-regulated learning. *Educational Psychologist, 30,* 189–193.

Alexander, P. A., & Judy, J. E. (1988). The interaction of domain-specific and strategic knowledge in academic performance. *Review of Educational Research, 58,* 375–404.

Baker, L. (1984). Children's effective use of multiple standards for evaluating their comprehension. *Journal of Educational Psychology, 76,* 588–597.

Baker, L., & Brown, A. L. (1984). Cognitive monitoring in reading. In J. Flood (Ed.), *Understanding reading comprehension: Cognition, language, and the structure of prose.* (pp. 21–44). Newark, DE: International Reading Association.

Bandura, A. (1993). Perceived self-efficacy in cognitive development and functioning. *Educational Psychologist, 28,* 117–148.

Bereiter, C., & Bird, M. (1985). Use of thinking aloud in identification and teaching of reading comprehension strategies. *Cognition and Instruction, 2,* 131–156.

Bereiter, C., & Scardamalia, M. (1985). Cognitive coping strategies and the problem of "inert" knowledge. In S. F. Chipman, J. W. Segal, & R. Glaser (Eds.), *Thinking and learning skills: Research and open questions* (pp. 65–80). Hillsdale, NJ: Erlbaum.

Boekaerts, M. (1995). Self-regulated learning: Bridging the gap between metacognitive and metamotivational theories. *Educational Psychologist, 30,* 192–200.

Borkowski, J. G. (1992). Metacognitive theory: A framework for teaching literacy, writing, and math skills. *Journal of Learning Disabilities, 25,* 253–257.

Borkowski, J. G., Estrada, M. T., Milstead, M., & Hale, C. A. (1989). General problem-solving skills: Relations between metacognition and strategic processing. *Learning Disability Quarterly, 12,* 57–70.

Borkowski, J. G., & Muthukrishna, N. (1992). Moving metacognition into the classroom: "Working models" and effective strategy teaching. In M. Pressley, K. R. Harris, & J. T. Guthrie (Eds.), *Promoting academic competence and literacy in school* (pp. 477–501). Toronto: Academic Press.

Borkowski, J. G., Weyhing, R. S., & Carr, M. (1988). Effects of attributional training on strategy-based reading comprehension in Learning-Disabled Students. *Journal of Educational Psychology, 80,* 46–53.

Borkowski, J. G., Weyhing, R. S., & Turner, L. A. (1986). Attributional retraining and the teachings of strategies. *Exceptional Children, 53,* 130–137.

Bos, C. S., & Anders, P. L. (1990). Interactive teaching and learning: Instructional practices for teaching content and strategic knowledge. In T. Scruggs & B. Y. L. Wong (eds.), *Intervention research in learning disabilities* (pp. 116–185). New York: Springer-Verlag.

Brown, A. L. (1978). Knowing when, where and how to remember: A problem of metacognition. In R. Glaser (Ed.), *Advances in Instructional Psychology* (pp. 77–165). Hillsdale, NJ: Erlbaum.

Brown, A. L. (1980). Metacognitive development and reading. In R. J. Spiro, B. C. Bruce, & W. F. Brewer (Eds.), *Theoretical issues in reading comprehension: Perspectives from cognitive psychology, linguistics, artificial intelligence, and education* (pp. 453–481). Hillsdale, NJ: Erlbaum.

Brown, A. L. (1987). Metacognition, executive control, self-regulation, and other more mysterious mechanisms. In F. E. Weinert & R. H. Kluwe (Eds.), *Metacognition, motivation, and understanding* (pp. 65–116). Hillsdale, NJ: Erlbaum.

Brown, A. L., Campione, J. C., Ferrara, R. A., Reeve, R. A., & Palincsar, A. S. (1991). Interactive learning and individual understanding: The case of reading and mathematics. In L. T. Landsmann (Ed.), *Culture, schooling, and psychological development: Human development,* Vol. 4 (pp. 136–170). Norwood, NJ: Ablex Publishing Co.

Butler, D. L. (1993). *Promoting strategic learning by adults with learning disabilities: An alternative approach.* Unpublished doctoral dissertation, Simon Fraser University, Burnaby, BC.

Butler, D. L. (1994). From learning strategies to strategic learning: Promoting self-regulated learning by post secondary students with learning disabilities. *Canadian Journal of Special Education, 4,* 69–101.

Butler, D. L. (1995). Promoting strategic learning by post secondary students with learning disabilities. *Journal of Learning Disabilities, 28,* 170–190.

Butler, D. L. (1996, April). *The strategic content learning approach to promoting self-regulated learning.* Paper presented at the annual meeting of the American Educational Research Association, New York, NY.

Butler, D. L. (1997, March). *The roles of goal setting and self-monitoring in students' self-regulated engagement in tasks.* Paper presented at the annual meeting of the American Educational Research Association. Chicago, IL.

Butler, D. L. (in press). A strategic content learning approach to promoting self-regulated learning. In B. J. Zimmerman & D. Schunk (Eds.), *Developing self-regulated learning: From teaching to self-reflective practice.* New York: Guildford Publications, Inc.

Butler, D. L., & Winne, P. H. (1995). Feedback and self-regulated learning: A theoretical synthesis. *Review of Educational Research, 65,* 245–281.

Campione, J. C., & Brown, A. L. (1990). Guided learning and transfer: Implications for approaches to assessment. In N. Frederiksen, R. Glaser, A. Lesgold, & M. G. Shafto (Eds.), *Diagnostic monitoring of skill and knowledge acquisition* (pp. 141–172). Hillsdale, NJ Erlbaum.

Campione, J. C., Brown, A. L., & Connell, M. L. (1988). Metacognition: On the importance of understanding what you are doing. In R. I. Charles & E. A. Silver (Eds.), *The teaching and assessing of mathematical problem solving,* Vol. 3 (pp. 93–114). Hillsdale, NJ: Erlbaum.

Case, L. P., Mamlin, N., Harris, K. R., & Graham, S. (1995). Self-regulated strategy development: A theoretical and practical perspective. In T. Scruggs & M. Mastropieri (Eds.), *Advances in learning and behavioural disabilities,* Vol. 9 (pp. 21–46). Greenwich, Conn: JAI Press.

Chapman, J. W. (1988). Cognitive-motivational characteristics and academic achievement of learning disabled children: A longitudinal study. *Journal of Educational Psychology, 80,* 357–365.

Corno, L. (1986). The metacognitive control components of self-regulated learning. *Contemporary Educational Psychology, 11,* 333–346.

Corno, L. (1992). Encouraging students to take responsibility for learning and performance. *The Elementary School Journal, 93,* 69–83.

Corno, L. (1993). The best laid plans: Modern conceptions of volition and educational research. *Educational Researcher, 22*(2), 14–22.

Corno, L. (1994). Student volition and education: Outcomes, influences, and practices. In D. H. Schunk & B. J. Zimmerman (Eds.), *Self-regulation of learning and performance: Issues and educational applications* (pp. 229–251). Hillsdale, NJ: Erlbaum.

Corno, L. (1995). Comments on Winne: Analytic and systemic research are both needed. *Educational Psychologist, 30,* 201–206.

Cross, D. R., & Paris, S. G. (1988). Developmental and instructional analyses of children's metacognition and reading comprehension. *Journal of Educational Psychology, 80,* 131–142.

Doyle, W. (1983). Academic work. *Review of Educational Research, 53,* 159–199.

Dweck, C. S. (1986). Motivational processes affecting learning. *American Psychologist, 41,* 1040–1048.

Ellis, E. S. (1993). Integrative strategy instruction: A potential model for teaching content area subjects to adolescents with learning disabilities. *Journal of Learning Disabilities, 26,* 358–383, 398.

Englert, C. S. (1990). Unraveling the mysteries of writing instruction through strategy training. In T. Scruggs & B. Y. L. Wong (Eds.), *Intervention research in learning disabilities* (pp. 186–223). New York: Springer-Verlag.

Englert, C. S., Raphael, T. E., Anderson, L. M., Anthony, H. M., & Stevens, D. D. (1991). Making strategies and self-talk visible: Writing instruction in regular and special education classrooms. *American Educational Research Journal, 28,* 337–372.

Englert, C. S., Raphael, T. E., Anderson, L. M., Gregg, S. L., & Anthony, H. M. (1989). Exposition: Reading, writing, and the metacognitive knowledge of learning disabled students. *Learning Disabilities Research, 5,* 5–24.

Englert, C. S., Raphael, T. E., Fear, K. L., & Anderson, L. M. (1988). Students' metacognitive knowledge about how to write informational texts. *Learning Disability Quarterly, 11,* 18–46.

Englert, C. S., Stewart, S. R., & Hiebert, E. H. (1988). Young writers' use of text structure in expository text generation. *Journal of Educational Psychology, 80,* 143–151.

Englert, C. S., & Thomas, C. C. (1987). Sensitivity to text structure in reading and writing: A comparison between learning disabled and non-learning disabled students. *Learning Disability Quarterly, 10,* 93–105.

Flavell, J. H. (1976). Metacognitive aspects of problem solving. In L. B. Resnick (Ed.), *The nature of intelligence* (pp. 231–235). Hillsdale, NJ: Erlbaum.

Flavell, J. H. (1987). Speculations about the nature and development of metacognition. In F. E. Weinert & R. H. Kluwe (Eds.), *Metacognition, motivation, and understanding* (pp. 21–64). Hillsdale, NJ: Erlbaum.

Garcia, T., & Pintrich, P. R. (1994). Regulating motivation and cognition in the classroom: The role of self-schemas and self-regulatory strategies. In D. H. Schunk & B. J. Zimmerman (Eds.), *Self-regulation of learning and performance: Issues and educational applications* (pp. 127–153). Hillsdale, NJ: Erlbaum.

Garner, R., Alexander, P. A., & Chou Hare, V. (1991). Reading comprehension failure in children. In B. Y. L. Wong (Ed.), *Learning about learning disabilities* (pp. 238–307). San Diego: Academic Press.

Graham, S., & Harris, K. R. (1989). Components analysis of cognitive strategy instruction: Effects on learning disabled students' compositions and self-efficacy. *Journal of Educational Psychology, 81,* 353–361.

Graham, S., Harris, K. R., & MacArthur, C. A. (1993). Improving the writing of students with learning problems: Self-regulated strategy development. *School Psychology Review, 22,* 656–669.

Graham, S., Schwartz, S. S., & MacArthur, C. A. (1993). Knowledge of writing and the composing process, attitude toward writing, and self-efficacy for students with and without learning disabilities. *Journal of Learning Disabilities, 26,* 237–249.

Groteluschen, A. K., Borkowski, J. G., & Hale, C. (1990). Strategy instruction is often insufficient: Addressing the interdependency of executive and attributional processes. In T. Scruggs & B. Y. L. Wong (Eds.), *Intervention research in learning disabilities* (pp. 81–101). New York: Springer-Verlag.

Harris, K. R., & Graham, S. (1996). *Making the writing process work: Strategies for composition and self-regulation.* Cambridge, MA: Brookline.

Harris, K. R., & Pressley, M. (1991). The nature of cognitive strategy instruction: Interactive strategy construction. *Exceptional Children, 57,* 392–404.

Jacobs, J. E., & Paris, S. G. (1987). Children's metacognition about reading: Issues in definition, measurement, and instruction. *Educational Psychologist, 22,* 255–278.

Lave, J., Smith, S., & Butler, M. (1988). Problem solving as an everyday practice. In R. I. Charles & E. A. Silver (Eds.), *The teaching and assessing of mathematical problem solving,* Vol. 3 (pp. 61–81). Hillsdale, NJ: Erlbaum.

Licht, B. G. (1993). Achievement-related beliefs in children with learning disabilities: Impact on motivation and strategic learning. In L. M. Meltzer (Ed.), *Strategy assessment and instruction for students with learning disabilities: From theory to practice* (pp. 195–220). Austin, TX: Pro-Ed.

Mann, V. (1991). Language problems: A key to early reading problems. In B. Y. L. Wong (Ed.), *Learning about learning disabilities* (pp. 129–162). San Diego: Academic Press.

Montague, M. (1993). Student-centered or strategy-centered instruction: What is our purpose? *Journal of Learning Disabilities, 26,* 433–437.

Montague, M. (1997). Student perception, mathematical problem solving, and learning disabilities. *Remedial and Special Education, 18,* 46–53.

Montague, M., Maddux, C. D., & Dereshiwsky, M. I. (1990). Story grammar and comprehension and production of narrative prose by students with learning disabilities. *Journal of Learning Disabilities, 23,* 190–197.

O'Shea, L. J., & O'Shea, D. J. (1994). A component analysis of metacognition in reading comprehension: The contributions of awareness and self-regulation. *International Journal of Disability, Development, and Education, 41,* 15–32.

Palincsar, A. S., & Brown, A. L. (1984). Reciprocal teaching of comprehension-fostering and comprehension monitoring activities. *Cognition and Instruction, 1,* 117–175.

Palincsar, A. S., & Brown, A. L. (1988). Teaching and practicing thinking skills to promote comprehension in the context of group problem solving. *RASE, 9*(1), 53–59.

Palincsar, A. S., & Klenk, (1992). Fostering literacy learning in supportive contexts. *Journal of Learning Disabilities, 25,* 211–225, 229.

Paris, S. G., & Byrnes, J. P. (1989). The constructivist approach to self-regulation and learning in the classroom. In B. J. Zimmerman & D. H. Schunk (Eds.), *Self-regulated learning and academic achievement: Theory, research, and practice* (pp. 169–200). New York: Springer-Verlag.

Pazzaglia, F., Cornoldi, C., & De Beni, R. (1995). Knowledge about reading and self-evaluation in reading disabled children. In T. Scruggs & M. Mastropieri (Eds.), *Advances in learning and behavioural disabilities,* Vol. 9 (pp. 91–117). Greenwich, Conn: JAI Press.

Pintrich, P. R., Anderman, E. M., & Klobucar, C. (1994). Intraindividual differences in motivation and cognition in students with and without learning disabilities. *Journal of Learning Disabilities, 27,* 360–370.

Pressley, M., Brown, R., El-Dinary, P. B., & Afflerbach, P. (1995). The comprehension instruction that students need: Instruction fostering constructively responsive reading. *Learning Disabilities Research and Practice, 10,* 215–224.

Pressley, M., El-Dinary, P. B., Brown, R., Schuder, T., Bergman, J. L., York, M., & Gaskins, I. W. (1995). A transactional strategies instruction Christmas carol. In A. McKeough, J. Lupart, & A. Marini (Eds.), *Teaching for transfer: Fostering generalization in learning,* (pp. 177–213). Mahwah, NJ: Erlbaum.

Pressley, M., El-Dinary, P. B., Gaskins, I. W., Schuder, T., Bergman, J. L., Almasi, J., & Brown, R. (1992). Beyond direct explanation: Transactional instruction of reading comprehension strategies. *The Elementary School Journal, 92,* 513–555.

Pressley, M., & Ghatala, E. S. (1988). Delusions about performance on multiple-choice comprehension tests. *Reading Research Quarterly, 23,* 454–464.

Pressley, M., Schuder, T., Bergman, J. L., & El-Dinary, P. B. (1992). A researcher-educator collaborative interview study of transactional comprehension strategies instruction. *Journal of Educational Psychology, 84,* 231–246.

Reeve, R. A., & Brown, A. L. (1985). Metacognition reconsidered: Implications for intervention research. *Journal of Abnormal Child Psychology, 13,* 343–356.

Reid, M. K., & Borkowski, J. G. (1987). Causal attributions of hyperactive children: Implications for training strategies and self-control. *Journal of Educational Psychology, 76,* 225–235.

Resnick, L. B., & Glaser, R. (1976). Problem solving and intelligence. In L. B. Resnick (Ed.), *The nature of intelligence* (pp. 205–230). Hillsdale, NJ: Erlbaum.

Sawyer, R. J., Graham, S., & Harris, K. R. (1992). Direct teaching, strategy instruction, and strategy instruction with explicit self-regulation: Effects on the composition skills and self-efficacy of students with learning disabilities. *Journal of Educational Psychology, 84,* 340–352.

Scardamalia, M., & Bereiter, C. (1987). Knowledge telling and knowledge transforming in written composition. In S. Rosenberg (Ed.), *Advances in applied psycholinguistics, Vol. 1: Disorders of first-language development* (pp. 142–175). Cambridge: Cambridge Univeristy Press.

Schoenfeld, A. H. (1988). Problem solving in context(s). In R. I. Charles & E. A. Silver (Eds.), *The teaching and assessing of mathematical problem solving,* Vol. 3 (pp. 82–92). Hillsdale, NJ: Erlbaum.

Schumaker, J. B., & Deshler, D. D. (1992). Validation of learning strategy interventions for students with learning disabilities: Results of a programmatic research effort. In B. Y. L. Wong (Ed.), *Contemporary intervention research in learning disabilities: An international perspective* (pp. 22–46). New York: Springer-Verlag.

Schunk, D. H. (1994). Self-regulation of self-efficacy and attributions in academic settings. In D. H. Schunk & B. J. Zimmerman (Eds.), *Self-regulation of learning and performance: Issues and educational applications* (pp. 75–99). Hillsdale, NJ: Erlbaum.

Schunk, D. H., & Cox, P. D. (1986). Strategy training and attributional feedback with learning disabled students. *Journal of Educational Psychology, 78,* 201–209.

Stanovich, K. E. (1986a). Cognitive processes and the reading problems of learning-disabled children: Evaluating the assumption of specificity. In J. K. Torgesen & B. Y. L. Wong (Eds.), *Psychological and educational perspectives on learning disabilities* (pp. 87–131). New York: Academic Press.

Stanovich, K. E. (1986b). Matthews effect in reading: Some consequences of individual differences in the acquisition of literacy. *Reading Research Quarterly, 21,* 360–406.

Swanson, H. L. (1990). Instruction derived from the strategy deficit model: Overview of principles and procedures. In T. Scruggs & B. Y. L. Wong (Eds.), *Intervention research in learning disabilities* (pp. 34–65). New York: Springer-Verlag.

Torgesen, J. K. (1977). The role of non-specific factors in the task performance of learning disabled children: A theoretical assessment. *Journal of Learning Disabilities, 10,* 27–34.

Torgesen, J. K. (1991). Learning disabilities: Historical and conceptual issues. In B. Y. L. Wong (Ed.), *Learning about learning disabilities* (pp. 3–37). New York: Academic Press.

Van Haneghan, J. P., & Baker, L. (1989). Cognitive monitoring in mathematics. In C. B. McCormick, G. E. Miller, & M. Pressley (Ed.), *Cognitive strategy research: From basic research to educational applications* (pp. 215–238). New York: Springer-Verlag.

Vygotsky, L. S. (1978). *Mind in society.* Cambridge, MA: Harvard University Press.

Wagoner, S. A. (1983). Comprehension monitoring: What it is and what we know about it. *Reading Research Quarterly, 17,* 328–346.

Walczyk, J. J., & Hall, V. C. (1989). Effects of examples and embedded questions on the accuracy of comprehension self-assessments. *Journal of Educational Psychology, 81,* 435–437.

Weiner, B. (1974). An attributional interpretation of expectancy-value theory. In B. Weiner (Ed.), *Cognitive views of human motivation* (pp. 51–69). New York: Academic Press.

Willows, D. M. (1991). Visual processes in learning disabilities. In B. Y. L. Wong (Ed.), *Learning about learning disabilities* (pp. 163–193). New York: Academic Press.

Winne, P. H., & Marx, R. W. (1982). Students' and teachers' views of thinking processes for classroom learning. *Elementary School Journal, 82,* 493–518.

Wong, B. Y. L. (1985). Metacognition and learning disabilities. In T. G. Waller, D. Forrest-Pressley, & E. MacKinnon (Eds.), *Metacognition, cognition and human performance* (pp. 137–180). New York: Academic Press.

Wong, B. Y. L. (1986). Metacognition and special education: A review of a view. *Journal of Special Education, 20,* 9–29.

Wong, B. Y. L. (1987). How do the results of metacognitive research impact on the learning disabled individual? *Learning Disability Quarterly, 10,* 189–195.

Wong, B. Y. L. (1991). The relevance of metacognition to learning disabilities. In B. Y. L. Wong (Ed.), *Learning about learning disabilities* (pp. 231–256). New York: Academic Press.

Wong, B. Y. L. (1994). Instructional parameters promoting transfer of learned strategies in students with learning disabilities. *Learning Disability Quarterly, 17,* 110–120.

Wong, B. Y. L., & Jones, W. (1982). Increasing metacomprehension in learning disabled and normally achieving students through self-questioning training. *Learning Disability Quarterly, 5,* 228–240.

Wong, B. Y. L., Wong, R., & Blenkinsop, J. (1988). Cognitive and metacognitive aspects of learning disabled adolescents' composing problems. *Learning Disability Quarterly, 12,* 300–322.

Wong, B. Y. L., Wong, R., & LeMare, L. (1982). The effects of knowledge of criterion task on comprehension and recall in normally achieving and learning disabled children. *Journal of Educational Research, 76,* 119–126.

Zabrucky, K. & Moore, D. (1989). Children's ability to use three standards to evaluate their comprehension of text. *Reading Research Quarterly, 24,* 336–352.

Zimmerman, B. J. (1989). A social cognitive view of self-regulated academic learning. *Journal of Educational Psychology, 81,* 329–399.

Zimmerman, B. J. (1994). Dimensions of academic self-regulation: A conceptual framework for education. In D. H. Schunk & B. J. Zimmerman (Eds.), *Self-regulation of learning and performance: Issues and educational applications* (pp. 3–21). Hillsdale, NJ: Erlbaum.

Zimmerman, B. J. (1995). Self-regulation involves more than metacognition: A social cognitive perspective. *Educational Psychologist, 30,* 217–221.

Assessment and Instructional Aspects of Learning Disabilities

CHAPTER 9

Early Reading and Instruction

Lynn M. Gelzheiser and Diane M. Wood

I. INTRODUCTION

Most children classified as learning disabled (LD) are poor readers. They have not made satisfactory progress given instruction in a traditional general education classroom. This chapter focuses on children with reading disabilities; specifically, those who are failing or have failed to master basic word attack skills, in spite of average intelligence. These children do not adequately construct meaning from the written symbols in their environment. In order to develop into proficient readers, they are in need of direct instruction in letter-name knowledge, phonological awareness, and word attack strategies, as well as repeated meaningful exposures to print (Torgesen, in press).

Certain characteristics and experiences are warning signals that children may later have difficulty in learning to read. Because reading makes many language-based demands, children initially classified as preschoolers with speech or language disabilities are at increased risk to be later classified as LD and receive special education services in Language Arts (Bloom, 1980). Because English requires the reader to map letters to individual sounds, children who lack the ability to attend to sounds in words (phonological awareness) are known to be at risk for reading failure (Liberman, Shankweiler, Fischer & Carter, 1974). Such a deficit may be caused by an underlying problem in coding sounds in memory (Wagner, Torgesen, & Rashotte, 1994); may be related to fluctuating hearing loss due to otitis media or recurring ear infections (Silva, Chalmers & Stewart, 1986); or may reflect a lack of experience with activities that draw attention to sounds (e.g., nursery rhymes) (MacLean, Bryant, & Bradeley, 1987). Children who enter school without prior exposure to books (Heath, 1983), and/or without mastering many letter names (Bond & Dykstra, 1967) have also been shown to be at risk for early reading failure.

We shall begin with an overview of reading and the development of reading competence. We then describe typical problems of and remedial strategies for reading-disabled students at emergent literacy and beginning reader stages, focusing on the skills related to phonological awareness, letter-name knowledge, letter-sound correspondences, phonic analysis, word recognition, and context use.

Readers read for four purposes: to acquire information and understanding, to enjoy literature, to analyze others' point of view, and for social interaction (New York State Education Department, 1996). Decoding and other word attack skills are tools that allow the reader to accomplish these purposes. A balanced beginning reading program allows students to master word attack skills and fosters reading for meaningful purposes. In this chapter, we will discuss the word attack portion of a balanced reading program.

II. WHAT IS READING?

According to Gough and Hillinger (1980), learning to read is not a natural act. In English, the alphabetic code (that is, the relationship between letters and sounds) is both abstract and complex. Furthermore, text provides multiple cues (visual, contextual, and structural) to the reader. The hallmark of mature reading is the ability to attend to, interpret, and utilize all of these cues in a coordinated, relatively effortless fashion. Such expertise allows the reader to devote attention and cognitive resources to comprehension (LaBerge & Samuels, 1974).

Letters on the page comprise a first set of cues to the reader. Often, these are referred to as "visual cues." Single letters, regular groupings of letters known as orthographic patterns (e.g., "tion"), and even whole words may cue the reader to the sounds of word parts or words. The reader can only utilize visual cues if he or she attends to them. In order for the beginning reader to interpret visual cues, a second requirement is that he or she possess knowledge of how the visual symbol corresponds with sound. In time, after the reader has had many, many opportunities to process letters, he or she begins to build associations among letters that frequently co-occur in English. For example, the reader learns to recognize "th" as an acceptable orthographic pattern (Adams, 1990; Seidenberg & McClelland, 1989). "Tq" would not be learned because it is not encountered in reading English. Similarly, syllables are "seen" as units with experience. Mature readers appear to recognize such orthographic patterns and automatically access the sounds and meaning they represent. In subsequent sections, we describe how instruction can be used to encourage careful attention to visual cues, and provide knowledge of letter–sound correspondences. We then discuss how, after mastery of these skills, strategies to encourage recognition of orthographic patterns can be developed.

Given the importance of the visual cue system, at one time reading disability was thought to stem from a visual disorder (Johnson & Myklebust, 1967). More recent research confirms that decoding places great demands on the phonological (sound) system (Vellutino, 1979). Decoding requires mapping sounds to letters. In order to interpret visual cues, the reader must carefully attend to the sound structure of words. For many disabled readers, their difficulty in acquiring word attack skills seems to result from a phonological coding deficit. Later, we describe how instruction can facilitate attention to component sounds, or phonological awareness.

In text, every word is surrounded by a context of other words. If a word is not recognized, the context provides cues as to the part of speech and likely meaning of the word. That is, if the reader guesses at an unknown word, he or she can then use contextual cues to evaluate whether or not the guess is syntactically acceptable, and/or whether the idea makes sense (Smith, 1971). Just as with visual cues, the reader must learn to attend to context cues. The reader must also possess knowledge of language structure to interpret syntactic context cues. To evaluate whether a word "makes sense" in context requires adequate knowledge of the topic discussed in the text. In a later section, we describe how instruction can encourage students to utilize contextual cues.

A final cue system consists of structural cues. Print is structured according to conventions; in English, it is written from left to right, top of page to bottom. Pictures and words convey interconnected ideas. Most often, each paragraph has a central idea. Stories and expository text are each organized in a predictable fashion. Subsequently, we describe how instruction can ensure that students attend to structural cues, and have the knowledge needed for their interpretation.

III. THE DEVELOPMENT OF READING PROFICIENCY

Learning to read has been characterized as a series of stages (Chall, 1983). In each stage, the child is encouraged to attend to the cues in text, and acquires knowledge and strategies that enable him or her to interpret visual, contextual, or structural cues. Students with reading disabilities pass through these stages more slowly than normally achieving students. Reading instruction should be sequenced to acknowledge the unique accomplishments of each stage of reading acquisition.

A. Prereading and Emergent Literacy

During Chall's (1983) prereading stage (which typically occurs from birth through kindergarten), children learn to speak and understand language. During the later years of this stage, which reading experts refer to as a period of emergent literacy (e.g., Teale & Sulzby, 1986), children make connections between the listening and speaking and the symbolic aspects of language: reading and writing. During this period, parents or caregivers spend many hours reading storybooks and pointing out signs to children. Children observe their parents reading newspapers, mail, novels, and writing letters, notes, checks, and so on. These experiences enable children to learn that print is a medium for communication, and to begin to understand the purposes of reading and writing (Durkin, 1966; Teale & Sulzby, 1986). They learn to expect written language and events in books to make sense. Another major accomplishment of the prereading stage is that children acquire a fund of knowledge about the world. Children's acquisition of language, knowledge, and understanding of the purposes of reading are critical to their later competence as readers. In particular, this knowledge will later allow students to make strategic use of context cues in text.

Early instruction during the emergent literacy period teaches children to use the simplest structural cues. Children raised in print-rich environments learn how to hold a book, to analyze pictures, and to turn the pages from front to back. These skills are often referred to as "concepts about print" (Clay, 1985).

Finally, it is during the emergent literacy stage that students must acquire two prerequisites needed to interpret the visual cues present in text. At this stage, children learn the names of the letters, and often recognize certain salient words such as their own name and logos for favorite products (e.g., McDonald's, Barney). Most critically, during this stage children begin to acquire phonological awareness, that is, the ability to focus attention on individual sounds (called phonemes) in spoken words. It is only by attending to these individual sounds that children can later learn how the sounds are represented by letters. Listening to and reciting nursery rhymes, and attempts at invented spelling are common experiences that encourage preschoolers to attend to sounds in words.

B. Beginning Reading Stage

For typical readers, grades one and two have been characterized as a beginning reading stage (Chall, 1983). Children in this stage acquire a variety of word attack skills that enable them to use visual cues proficiently; they also begin to use context cues.

For readers of English, a first task of the beginning reading stage is learning that our written system is indeed a code. Words in English are not written in an arbitrary fashion but according to an alphabetic principle. Beginning readers must learn that letters have a regular and predictable relationship with sounds. The strategic reader takes advantage of the alphabetic principle, using letter–sound relationships to simplify the reading process (Gough & Hillinger, 1980). (The alternative is to memorize thousands of words as wholes!) Furthermore, since each letter plays a meaningful role in representing sounds, the beginning reader must learn that for accuracy it is necessary to attend to every letter. Vellutino and Scanlon (1986) characterized this as an "analytic attitude" toward reading.

Of course, an analytic attitude is not sufficient; the beginning reader must also learn the specific sounds represented by letters or letter groups. Acquiring this knowledge is the primary instructional task with beginning readers. It is a difficult task in English, because letters and letter combinations often represent more than one sound.

During this stage, the beginning reader's frequent encounters with phonetically regular text lay a foundation. If the reader carefully attends to letters, these experiences enable him or her to build a base of orthographic knowledge (Adams, 1990; Seidenberg & McClelland, 1989; Share, 1995). That is, the beginning reader is slowly recording in memory the predictable ways that letters are grouped in English. The repeated exposure and study provided during this stage will later enable the reader to recognize orthographic patterns, common syllables, and small words.

Readers at this stage learn to utilize context cues to assist in gaining meaning from print. If a word is not recognized, context may provide cues as to the part of speech of the word. Context can be used by the reader to judge the reasonableness of their efforts to "sound out" or guess an unknown word (Smith, 1971).

C. Fluency Stage

For students who successfully negotiate the beginning reading stage, the next stage is fluency (typically grades 2 and 3). Chall (1983) aptly characterized this stage as "ungluing from print." Rather than laborious, letter-by-letter analysis, decoding at this stage requires less conscious attention, and is more automatic. Students appear to recognize common orthographic patterns, frequently used syllables, and even short words. Word attack and context use strategies are deployed in an integrated, flexible fashion at this stage, and support orthographic pattern recognition.

Fluent readers have practiced word attack and context use strategies so extensively that they seem almost automatic. These activities do not require much mental effort. Fluent readers' attention can thus be directed towards comprehension (LaBerge & Samuels, 1974; Perfetti, 1985).

IV. READING INSTRUCTION DURING EMERGENT LITERACY

A. Concepts about Print

1. Research

Young children start to develop print awareness and concepts about print long before they begin to read. Children are developing an understanding of print conventions as they discern that print differs from other graphics and that print can be read or spoken. Children who have greater exposure to written language in their preschool years have an advantage over children who enter school with little or no literacy experience (Clay, 1985). If parents or caretakers read to them daily, children listen to approximately 1,000 hours of storybook reading prior to first grade (Adams, 1990).

2. Assessment

The Concepts About Print Test (CAPS) was developed to provide teachers with a guide to the knowledge children have about print and to inform teachers what to teach next about reading (Clay, 1985). CAPS assess book-handling skills, knowledge of directionality of print, and print awareness knowledge. CAPS is a component of the Diagnostic Survey, which is a broader instrument used for determining which "operations and strategies" a child uses while reading text (Clay, 1985).

CAPS is easily administered in 5 to 10 min in one sitting. The book-handling skills require a child to indicate the front cover of a book, that a left page is read before the right page, and that print contains the author's message. CAPS correlate with other reading readiness measures and with achievement tests (Clay, 1985).

Directionality concepts assessed involve the child pointing to indicate where the print begins on a page, showing that print is read from left to right, demonstrating the use of return sweep at the end of a line of print, tracking print from the bottom of a left page to the top of a right page, and showing concept of word by matching speech to print with one-to-one correspondence. Print awareness concepts contain tasks as the letter level, at the word level, and for punctuation.

3. Tips and Activities

Storybook reading or lap reading provides children with exposure to print. Both the quantity of reading material and the selection of books are important (Adams, 1990). It is important that storybook reading be interactive. Discussion and open-ended questions at appropriate points in a story will further engage a child and increase his or her attention and/or curiosity about written language. Encouraging children to explore letters, words, and punctuation and their relationships sets the stage for developing print concepts.

One of the most overt ways of fostering book handling, directionality of text, and print concepts is to model these concepts and skills during reading through fingerpointing and discussion. The use of big books or lap reading will help to emphasize concepts explicitly. When reading books to students, the use of fingerpointing can make directionality of text and concept of word in print observable.

As young children "read and reread" predictable books from memory, sometimes called "independent reenactments" (Sulzby & Teale, 1991), they learn many of the concepts of print naturally. Rereading familiar books allows opportunity to examine different aspects of print and meaning each time through.

Fingerpoint reading helps children develop a concept of a word in print. Teachers can model fingerpoint reading or children can fingerpoint using memorized texts, but the texts must contain multisyllabic words in order to determine whether emergent readers have mastered the concept. Other ways to teach the concept of word in print or word boundaries are to have students count the number of words on a sentence strip or cut sentence strips into individual words. Concept of word in print is also fostered when children write.

B. Phonological and Phonemic Awareness

1. Research

When we converse we attend to the meaning of language. When children are in the process of learning to read, they need also to attend to the sounds of language. Most children with reading disabilities have difficulty understanding this concept (National Center to Improve the Tools of Educators [NCITE], 1996). Phonological awareness, the attention to the sounds of language, facilitates reading acquisition. It appears to be an essential precursor to the ability to map graphemes to phonemes, which in turn is an important requisite to reading (Vellutino, 1991).

Phonological awareness is a well-documented predictor of reading achievement. Performance on tasks of rhyming (MacLean, Bryant, & Bradley, 1987), syllable detection (Mann & Liberman, 1984), separating words by onsets and rimes (Treiman, 1985), and isolating and/or manipulating phonemes (Ball & Blachman, 1991; Lundberg, Olofsson, & Wall, 1980; Stanovich, Cunningham, & Cramer, 1984; Tunmer & Nesdale, 1985) are related to subsequent reading achievement. Kindergarten performance on phonological awareness tasks has been used to predict word attack, word identification, and text comprehension measures of reading achievement at the end of first grade and throughout the elementary school years (Share, Jorm, MacLean, & Matthews, 1984; Vellutino & Scanlon, 1987; Wagner & Torgesen, 1987).

Phonological awareness is a general term that is used to describe the knowledge that the sounds of words are distinct from the words' meanings. Ability to rhyme words, say the whole word when told the parts of a compound word or the syllables of a word, and distinguishing onset and rime are phonological awareness tasks. Phonemic awareness refers to the conscious recognition of individual phonemes in words (e.g., /k/ /a/ /t/ are the phonemes of the word cat). Phonemes are the smallest units of speech sounds.

A continuum of phonological/phonemic awareness tasks has been delineated and provides a framework detailing which rudimentary components of phonological awareness precede phonemic awareness and phoneme manipulation (Adams, 1990). Some phonological awareness abilities are typically developed prior to reading acquisition, some develop in tandem with beginning reading, and more advanced abilities require some level of reading competence for successful performance (Adams, 1990; Bryant & Goswami, 1987; Stanovich et al., 1984).

Rhyming tasks are often mastered prior to reading. They are among the easiest phonological awareness tasks that have been performed successfully by 4-year-old children. Some 3-year-old children are able to produce rhymes when given target words and detect rhymes and alliteration (MacLean et al., 1987). However, children who enter school with speech and language difficulties and/or little experiential background or exposure to print may have difficulty performing these tasks.

Phonological tasks that involve subunits of words are often performed by children in early stages of reading acquisition. Natural intraword boundaries are formed between onsets, the initial consonant(s), and rimes, the vowel and the letter(s) that follow (Treiman, 1985). Children in grades kindergarten, one, and two have shown a proclivity toward separating syllables on the basis of onsets and rimes (Goswami, 1986; Treiman, 1985). Onsets are composed of the initial consonant or consonant cluster in words (e.g., "d" in dog, "cr" in crown). Rimes are composed of the vowel and any remaining letters (e.g., "e" in she, "ake" in take). All words and syllables have rimes, but not all words and syllables have onsets (e.g., ate, in). Onset-rime tasks seem to be more difficult than syllable awareness tasks and easier than phonemic awareness tasks for kindergarten children (Treiman, 1985).

Phonemic segmentation are among the more difficult phonemic awareness tasks. Indeed, most students who can perform phoneme segmentation tasks have mastered rudimentary reading skills. Phonemic awareness tasks involve counting phonemes, substituting phonemes, separating phonemes, saying phonemes in reverse order, and other manipulations. Students who are ready to perform phoneme awareness tasks typically know all or most of the letters of the alphabet. The performance of 6-year-old students on segmentation tasks, such as phoneme tapping, is a good predictor of subsequent reading achievement (Tunmer & Nesdale, 1985).

2. Assessment

Several published tests are available for assessing phonological awareness. A phoneme segmentation test is available by reproduction from Yopp (1995). The Yopp-Singer Test of Phoneme Segmentation (Yopp, 1995) is straightforward to give, score, and interpret. The test can be administered in 5–10 minutes. The examiner is expected to model phoneme segmentation on several training items. There are 22 test items and children are to be given feedback on each. The test was normed on second-semester kindergarten children for whom the mean score was about 11 correctly segmented items. Last, it has data to support its reliability and validity.

For students with reading disabilities, it is probably best to devise an informal test that starts with nursery rhyme recitation, rhyme oddity tasks, and saying whole words from parts (e.g., Recite three to five nursery rhymes. Given four pictures, select the one that doesn't rhyme. When two separate words are given, pronounce the compound word as a whole.) If students are deficient in these basic phonological skills, then instruction must begin at this level.

3. Tips and Activities

Please note that all phonological and many phonemic awareness activities can and should be done without print, as the object is for children to listen to and examine the sounds of words. The use of pictures and/or manipulatives is advisable to reduce memory load for children with LD. Two dimensions determine the levels of difficulty of phonological-phonemic awareness tasks: the size of the unit under analysis, and the position of the sound. Word, syllable, and rhyme activities are easier than onset-rime tasks, which in turn are easier than activities that involve separating words into individual phonemes. At the same time, it is easiest for young children to attend to beginning sounds, next they attend to final sounds, and finally they attend to the medial sounds in words. The goal of phonemic awareness activities is for children to understand that words are made of phonemes and to be able to hear and manipulate the phonemes of words. Not all children will need to do all of the activities listed to be successful at phoneme segmentation. This sequence of tasks is articulated for those students who move slowly from rhyming and word-level awareness to phonemic awareness.

Rhyming tasks that are at the easiest level of phonological awareness include nursery rhyme recitation, rhyme oddity, rhyme supply, and rhyme choice tasks. After children have memorized some common nursery rhymes, rhyming words can be substituted to change these well-known favorites to funny or silly versions (e.g., Jack fell down and broke his "town").

Rhyme oddity involves a child selecting which word or picture out of three or four does not rhyme with the others. In rhyme supply tasks, the teacher provides a target word and asks the child to provide a rhyming word. Listening activities books often contain category rhyme supply tasks by color, animal, furniture, food, and so on.

Other phonological awareness tasks involve the use of words and syllables. Children can be asked to distinguish which pronounced word is longer than the other. They can put the compound word components or syllables together to say the word the fast way. When doing this type of task, the teacher should hesitate about 1 sec between word parts (e.g., "Say foot—(1 sec.)—ball" or "say ham—(1 sec.)—burg—(1 sec.)—er"). Activities at the syllable level include tapping, snapping, or clapping the number of syllables in a word or breaking the word down and saying its syllables.

The next level of phonological/phonemic awareness activities involve onset and/or rime manipulation. Easy-level phonemic awareness tasks include having students listen for and identify words that begin or end with a salient sound. In general, beginning phonemes are easiest to identify, followed by ending sounds and finally medial sounds. In one of the easier tasks at this level, children are asked to substitute the initial consonant of a given word and produce the new word (e.g. "Say 'beat' with /s/."). Initial consonant deletion requires students to omit the beginning sound and pronounce the rime (i.e., "Remove the initial phoneme and say shout" which results in "out"). For matching initial consonant sounds, children listen to and repeat a target word and then choose one of the next three words heard which shares the initial sound.

Phonemic awareness tasks at a moderate level of difficulty involve activities with final consonants and isolating and saying the initial phonemes of a word. Matching final consonant sounds can be done auditorily using a similar format to matching initial consonant sounds above, but it will be easier for students if pictures are present. Display several pictures and have students select the picture containing the final consonant that matches the target word. To make it easier for a child to supply the initial consonant, the teacher pronounces a pair of words (e.g., cat—at) and the student has to break off the initial phoneme and say it (e.g., /k/).

Teach students to blend phonemes into words, starting with blending initial sound to the rime. Blend two- and three-phoneme words next and continue to blend the phonemes of longer words as children meet with success at each level of difficulty and have opportunity to practice new skills. It is appropriate to present letters starting with this activity.

Phoneme segmentation tasks have students break words into individual phonemes. Note that letters and phonemes are not interchangeable (e.g., "with" has four letters, but only three phonemes). Phoneme segmentation tasks include saying each phoneme separately, and tapping, snapping, or clapping the number of phonemes. Blocks can be used to represent the number of phonemes. Putting markers in boxes is another way to portray phonemes. This task is made more challenging if students are asked to use a different color marker for each distinct sound.

4. Printed Materials and Software

The Phonological Awareness Kit (Robertson & Salter, 1995) is designed for use with children in kindergarten through grade three. The program contains phonological awareness activities and phonetically controlled reading and spelling exercises that are meant to supplement the classroom reading program.

The Phonological Awareness Training for Reading program (Torgesen & Bryant, 1994) was designed to be used with small groups of students who are in the second semester of kindergarten or with students in grades one or two who are at risk for reading disability. It includes activities for rhyming, sound blending, phoneme segmentation, and reading and spelling.

The Phonological Awareness Kit contains a coherent sequence of phonological/phonemic activities, sample lessons, attractive materials, and an assessment component. The Phonological Awareness Training for Reading program does not contain a sufficient range of activities. This program uses a restricted set of letters and no activity uses all 14 letters that are introduced. One advantage of the Phonological Awareness Training for Reading program is that it includes instruction on awareness of mouth and tongue positions for phoneme production, which is beneficial for students with articulation and/or auditory discrimination difficulties.

Daisy Quest and Daisy's Castle are interactive software programs that were designed to develop phonological awareness abilities and have been used successfully with preschoolers, kindergartners, and first-grade disabled readers (Barker & Torgesen, 1995). Daisy Quest contains activities for teaching recognition of rhyming words and identifying words with the same sounds in the initial, medial, or final positions of words. Daisy's Castle is a sequel that includes onset and rhyme activities, phoneme segmentation awareness, and phoneme counting activities.

C. Letter-Name Knowledge

1. Research

Letter-name knowledge is frequently reported as the best predictor of reading in longitudinal studies that begin with preschool or kindergarten-aged children (Adams, 1990; Badian, 1982; Butler, Marsh, Sheppard & Sheppard, 1985; Robinson, 1990; Scanlon, Vellutino, Small, Spearing, & Wharton-McDonald, 1993; Share et al., 1984; Stevenson & Newman, 1986; Vellutino & Scanlon, 1987). It is hypothesized that latter-name knowledge is critical for two reasons.

First, it is an indicator that a child has been raised in a print-rich environment. Through repeated exposure, the child has learned the letters and acquired an understanding of their purpose. This hypothesis is supported by research showing that just teaching letter names to nonreaders does not provide children with the concepts typically gleaned from experience with print (Adams, 1990).

A second hypothesis about letter-name knowledge is that it is an indicator of learning ability. The underlying abilities that are required for letter-name knowledge are comparable to the basic learning skills needed to learn to read. Children who have learned letter names have shown capability in linguistic coding ability, visual-auditory learning, verbal working memory, visual ability, and visual memory ability (Wood, 1995). When children have learned the names of letters, they have associated names with the respective written symbols, they can retrieve and hold a letter's name in working memory, they can visually discriminate the shapes of letters, and they can retrieve these visual symbols from memory. It is not surprising that children who have demonstrated these abilities have been successful in learning to read.

Speed and accuracy of letter and object naming differentiate between good and disabled readers (Adams, 1990; Vellutino et al., 1996). This suggests that the thoroughness of letter learning and facility with linguistic abilities are important prerequisites for reading acquisition and development to occur. One large-scale study showed that middle-class first graders who entered kindergarten deficient in letter naming and other linguistic abilities subsequently had considerable difficulty acquiring reading skills despite one-to-one tutoring efforts (Vellutino et al., 1996).

2. Assessment

Letter-name knowledge can be assessed with teacher-made or standardized tests. Standardized tests only sample the student's letter-naming ability, in order to provide scores that indicate the child's standing relative to his age/or grade peers. Teacher-made tests will provide more complete information of student knowledge that is useful for planning instruction and assessing progress.

One measure of letter-name knowledge is the ability of a child to sing or chant the alphabet. This should be done by a child in such a manner that each letter is distinctly articulated and "lmnop" is not said as if it were one letter or word. Another way to assess letter-name knowledge is to determine whether a child can finger-point the alphabet while reciting it with one-to-one correspondence.

Several ways of assessing letter identification for accuracy include students naming upper case and lower case letters out of sequence and students writing letters from dictation. When students point to the letter named by the examiner this is an indication of letter recognition.

In order to assess fluency with letter-name knowledge students can be asked to complete verbal letter sequences (e.g., The examiner says "h,i,j,—" and pauses for student to give the next letter) or sequence letter cards. Letter sequencing can also be done with the entire alphabet using lower-case letters or upper-case letters or it can be a matched sequencing of both cases of letters. Using letter cards is easier than completing verbal letter sequences.

3. Tips and Activities

Children should be taught to sing or chant the alphabet from memory prior to learning to recognize the letter symbols. This reduces the memory load and it helps children to peg the visual symbol to the names that they have learned auditorily. For children who have had little experience with print prior to school, beginning with the letters in their names makes the learning personalized and provides motivation. Children who don't recognize their names should be taught to spell them first and match the letters to a model or sequence letters in their names.

When working with children with reading disabilities, teachers should not try to teach upper and lower case letters at the same time. Consideration of student age, grade, learning rate and memory capacity should be determinants of which to teach first, lower-case letter names, upper-case letter names, or letter sounds. Upper-case letters are more distinct visually than the lower-case letters, but lower-case letters are more predominant in text. For children with limited memory capacity, learning the letter sounds prior to learning letter names may expedite reading acquisition.

When teaching letter names, it is best to separate letters that are visually similar from one another (e.g., m,n,h,r; b,d,p,q; v,w). Children should learn one of the confusing pair of letters rather well and several other letters before the second letter of the pair is introduced (Carnine, Silbert, & Kameenui, 1997).

For students who have had little experience with print, letter puzzles, tactile letters, letter and sound Bingo- or Lotto-type games are useful activities. These students often readily learn the letters of their own names as well as those of pets and loved ones.

For children who need a multisensory approach to learning letter names, the use of sandpaper letters, Lauri puzzle letters, clay-formed letters, chocolate sauce or pudding, and fingerpaints will provide tactile stimulation. To help children form letters that they can feel, write with primary crayons on plain newsprint that is on top of a piece of plastic window screen.

D. Logographic Word Recognition: Beginning the Transition to Reading

In their early encounters with text, children often develop rudimentary reading-like strategies. When young children first make connections with environmental print, they remember salient features of logos or signs that are familiar to them, rather than letter sequences or spellings of words (Adams, 1990). Thus, the golden arches may be the portion of the McDonald's sign that cues a child to say, "Look, Mom! There's McDonald's."

Emergent readers in the logographic phase of reading are focusing on arbitrary features of signs or logos or letter shapes, but not linking these to the sounds of the letters (Ehri, 1992). Their attention may be drawn to the graphics, the stylized typeface, the color pattern, or letter shapes. When 5-year-olds were shown the print taken from logos they could "read" in context, and asked to read the print outside of its usual environment, these children were no longer able to read the same signs (Masonheimer, Drum, & Ehri, 1984).

Emergent readers' renditions of environmental print are often approximate rather than exact. Young children in the logographic stage are making associations between visual aspects of letters and word meanings. Ehri (1992) explains that these associations deteriorate easily without practice because these children haven't acquired thorough letter-name knowledge, and the visual cues they rely on to remember words are arbitrary and incomplete. Not surprisingly, logographic readers often confuse words that have many letters in common or similar word configurations.

When letter-name knowledge is solid and letter-sound associations and phonemic awareness are developing, emergent readers enter a phase of reading in which they focus on initial and final sounds in words and on letter names (Tunmer, Herriman, & Nesdale, 1988). Ehri (1992) calls this phonetic cue reading, because beginning readers are starting to use letter-sound associations to remember words.

At this stage, the use of letter names alone are sufficient to form tentative associations between the letters and the pronunciation of a word because many letter names contain their phonemes. Soon, children are able to use the beginning and ending sounds of a word to assist in its identification, but they do not match letters and sounds with one-to-one correspondence for the entire word. They are developing a system that is more reliable than logographic reading, yet their attempts at reading words by sight continue to result in systematic errors. Accuracy occurs only during the beginning reading stage, as children start using the alphabetic principle and decoding each letter to identify the sound it represents (Ehri, 1992).

V. INSTRUCTION DURING THE BEGINNING READING STAGE

A. Research on Disabled Readers and Beginning Reading

In comparison to normally developing readers, many disabled readers have difficulty in learning to use the visual cues of letters and letter groups to decode words. Vellutino and Scanlon (1991) reported that 83% of second-grade disabled readers were deficient in their ability to read regular words, where letters or letter groups correspond to sounds. More strikingly, by sixth grade, 70% of disabled readers still lacked word attack skills. A smaller group lacked context use strategies.

Armed with this knowledge, a special education teacher can proceed in several ways. First, he or she should be certain of his or her own conscious knowledge of word attack strategies. Many teachers lack this knowledge (Moats, 1995), and thus cannot provide well-structured instruction for their students. Second, a special education teacher should design the instructional program for disabled readers after carefully and comprehensively assessing word attack skills. Most disabled readers will do poorly on such an assessment and will require remediation of their word attack skills.

A third approach is early intervention. As we described earlier, there is converging evidence that disabled reading is a consequence of failing to acquire phonological awareness and word attack skills. Experts have argued that this evidence suggests a need for early intervention. Specifically, these experts recommend that early assessment be used to identify students deficient in phonological awareness or word attack skills. As soon as students fall behind their peers, intensive, one-to-one intervention should be implemented. Such early intervention in phonological awareness and word attack skills has been shown to be effective (Blachman, 1987; Torgesen, in press; Vellutino et al., 1996). Research suggests that early intervention allows many children to make up their deficits, and to acquire age-appropriate reading skills (Vellutino et al., 1996).

B. Correspondences between Single Letters and Sounds

1. Curriculum

Although decoding programs vary in the scope and sequence of skills taught, most begin by teaching the most common sound for each letter. This instruction has two purposes. First, it illustrates the alphabetic principle, that is, in English discrete sounds are represented by letters (or letter groups). As we noted earlier, if children are to become strategic readers, they must understand and utilize this principle. Adams (1990) has argued that the fundamental goal of instruction in letter–sound correspondences is to teach students to attend to each letter and its relationship to sound.

A second reason for letter–sound instruction is that as soon as students learn a few letter–sound correspondences, they can be taught the strategy of "sounding out" short, regular words. Sounding out means working from left to right, students say the most common sound for each letter. They then blend these sounds to produce a word. Sounding out is an appropriate strategy for regular words that follow patterns such as vowel consonant (VC, e.g., up); consonant-vowel-consonant (CVC, e.g., cat); and longer words containing blends (e.g., blend, stand).

Note that the sounding-out strategy will not work for many words (e.g., "the"). Sounding out letter-by-letter cannot be used with words that include groups of letters that represent sounds (e.g., "th" in "the") and/or the less common sound of the letter ("e" in "the"). Strategies for letter groups and irregular words are typically taught after the student has attained proficiency with sounding out (Carnine et al., 1997).

We have observed some teachers who begin teaching letter–sound correspondences with "A" and proceed to "Z." Other teachers sequence the letters according to the literature they would like students to read. Carnine et al. (1997) have provided research evidence for the most effective way to sequence the letter–sound curriculum. They documented that the letter–sound curriculum should be sequenced following two rules: (a) begin with common, useful letters; and (b) sequence the letters so as to avoid confusion.

If your decoding curriculum begins with the most common, useful letters, your students will be better equipped for sounding out. Knowledge of the sounds of the most common letters will enable students to sound out a larger body of words. Typically, common consonants and the short vowels are introduced before the less common consonants (e.g., z, j, w).

To avoid confusing the beginning reader, the teacher should initially separate similar letters (Carnine et al., 1997). In addition to the letters with similar shapes (discussed in the letter name knowledge section) it is critical to separate letters with similar sounds (/f/, /v/, /t/; /b/, /d/, /p/; /p/, /k/, /g/; /m/, /n/; /i/, /e/; /o/, /u/). Note that some letters (e.g., b, d) both look and sound similar.

Finally, because one goal of letter sound instruction is acquisition of the sounding out strategy, Carnine et al. (1997) have recommended that the letters that are least confusing to blend be taught first. The easiest consonants to blend are the continuous consonants (e.g., /s/, /m/). Their sounds can be held indefinitely, and are readily blended with the next letter. Examples of easy-to-blend words that begin with continuous consonants are fat, lamp, or nap.

Beginning readers may become confused if they are asked to blend stop consonants in the initial position. None of the stop consonants (/b/, /c/, /d/, /g/, /h/, /j/,

/k/, /p/, /q/, /t/, /x/) can be produced without the addition of a vowel sound (schwa). This "extra" phoneme must be ignored while blending, a process that is often confusing! (Note that if this extra sound comes at the end of the word [e.g., sub] it does not pose a difficulty for most readers).

2. Assessment

Assessment of letter–sound correspondence knowledge and mastery of the sounding out strategy may be done for two purposes: (a) to plan instruction, and (b) to document pupil progress. The same approach to assessment may be used for either purpose.

We use informal, curriculum-referenced assessment for these purposes. A first step is to establish which letters the student has been taught, to determine whether the sounding-out strategy has been taught, and to identify the types of words the student should be able to sound out. We assume that students have not mastered what they have not been taught.

To assess letter name knowledge, students can be shown the instructed letters in isolation, and asked to produce the most common sound of the letter. Letter–sound associations can be assessed by having students name a word that begins with a particular letter, or by having them point to or circle the picture that begins with the sound given or the letter shown. Children need to be able to look at a letter and associate its sound in order to sound out words.

To assess mastery of a sounding-out strategy, students can be asked to sound out regular words that follow (VC (e.g., at), CVC (e.g., cat), CVCC (e.g., camp), and CCVCC (e.g., stamp) patterns. Some words should begin with stop consonants and others with continuous consonants. Words that cannot be sounded out letter by letter (e.g., that, said, bake) should not be included in an assessment of letter–sound knowledge and sounding out.

This assessment can be given prior to remediation, to establish the student's present level of functioning. After remediation or early intervention, it may be repeated to document progress. Daily probes of particular letter groups or word types can be used to monitor lesson effectiveness.

Error analysis should focus on that which is often challenging or confusing to beginning readers. Does the student make errors with less common letters? Does the student have particular difficulty with visually or auditorily confusable letters? Does the student have difficulty sounding out words with stop consonants in the initial position? Are longer words more difficult than shorter words for the student to sound out?

For the beginning reader, the initial sound in a word is the most prominent. Research in reading and spelling supports that children find it easier to deal with the initial sound of a word, then the final sound, and finally the medial sounds of words. Thus, it is common for children to make the majority of their decoding errors with the medial sound.

3. Methods for Teaching Single Letter–Sound Correspondences

Reading-disabled students require explicit, systematic intensive teaching, with a maximum amount of interaction with the teacher (Haring & Bateman, 1977). This approach has been termed direct instruction. Direct instruction of letter–sound correspondences begins with gaining and maintaining student attention. Students are seated to ensure eye contact with the teacher, and engaging materials are used (e.g., colorful letters, puppets). The lesson begins with the teacher modeling the sound that the new letter represents. Students are then guided to produce the sound of the letter, in small groups and individually. Prompts may be used initially (e.g., the group prompts individual students, the teacher whispers the sound), but prompts are faded and independent performance is expected as students gain proficiency. Each day, previously taught letters are reviewed. After mastery in isolation, confusable letters are contrasted and reviewed together. Feedback is provided promptly.

Oftentimes, teachers pair a picture with a letter (e.g., apple for /a/), so that students can use the picture to help them remember the most common sound of the letter. Ehri, Deffner, and Wilce (1984) developed Mnemonics for Phonics to make it even easier for students to recall the sound represented by the letter. They integrated the picture with the letter (e.g., the house was drawn under the hump in the h; the letter is highlighted in the picture), thus providing students with a mnemonic to assist memorization. It is critical that the letter shape be prominent both in terms of being visually distinct and fundamental to the picture (e.g., a bold-faced "f" forms the stem and leaf veins of a flower). Children first name the letter, picture, and give the sound. The letter and picture name are gradually dropped, so that students just look at the letter and give the correct sound. Students learned their letter sounds faster using these mnemonics.

Children can also create personalized sounds books to help them learn letter–sound correspondences. One letter of the alphabet is on each page. The child draws a picture exemplifying the initial sound or cuts and pastes pictures. These provide a permanent record that the child can read over and over again to build the necessary sound associations and to distinguish the name of the letter, a picture that begins with the sound, and the sound association in isolation.

4. Methods for Teaching Sounding out and Blending

Sounding out requires the reader to give the sound for each letter of the word, and then to blend these distinct sounds to form a recognizable word. Many of the phonemic awareness activities described earlier can now be linked to print, to facilitate acquisition of this strategy.

It is important to model sound blending for students. The key concept in sound blending is to say each sound without stopping, thus blending each sound to the next sound in a word using the same breath of air. Initially, teach children to sound blend words in which the beginning consonant sound is continuous. It is easier to blend the sounds in the word "mat" than "pat" because /m/ is a continuous sound and /p/ is a stop sound. It is difficult to pronounce stop sounds in isolation because we tend to add a vowel sound when we try to isolate stop sounds.

There are several ways to teach children to blend consonant-vowel-consonant words that begin with stop sounds. One way to sound blend the word "pat" is to isolate and extend the short vowel sound for /a/, then rhyme the /p/ to produce /pa/ and finally add the /t/ to pronounce "pat." This method is recommended for children who are emergent readers and can only attend to one letter at a time. Another way to teach children to blend a word such as "pat" is to have them blend the /a-t/ sounds, hold "at" in working memory and then rhyme "at" to say "pat." The use of iteration, the oral repetition of the stop consonant several times in succession before sound blending the rest of the word, provides an alternate method of sustaining the stop sound without distorting its sound (e.g., /p-p-p-p-a-a-t/) (Lewkowitz, 1980).

Children who have difficulty sound blending tend to stop between each sound, thus producing a series of punctuated sounds. They do not hear the word in its slowly pronounced elongated form. This can be corrected by teaching children to blend without stopping between sounds, but you may need to go back to blending just two sounds and work up to three- and four- letter words.

Game formats can be used to practice sound blending. One game involves cards with onsets or rimes (common phonograms). Each player selects an onset card and a rime card and blends the sounds to decode the complete word and then decides if the combination results in a real word or a nonsense word. Points can be given both for pronouncing the resultant 'word' and for determining whether it is a real word or a nonsense word.

Writing and invented spelling facilitate decoding ability. Decoding is acquired more rapidly when teachers encourage children to write using invented spellings (Clarke, 1988; Ehri, 1989; Ellis & Cataldo, 1990). This is believed to occur because invented spelling encourages children to attend to phonemes, and then to relate them to letters.

C. Correspondences between Letter Groups and Sounds

1. Curriculum

In English, there are four types of letter groups that have a predictable relationship with sounds: (a) vowel (ai) and consonant (th) digraphs are defined as two letters that represent a single sound; (b) vowel diphthongs (oy) are two vowels that each contribute to the production of a distinctive sound; (c) L-controlled (hold) and r-controlled (car) vowels indicate that the sound of the vowel is changed when followed by an "l" or "r"; finally, (d) "silent e" words follow a vowel-consonant-silent e pattern, and the first vowel makes the long sound (e.g., lake). Experts do not agree as to whether these should be taught directly as rules, or whether students should be encouraged to "discover" these generalizations through teacher-structured tasks. It may be that each approach is effective, for some students.

Each of these phonic patterns is regular (print corresponds to sound in a predicable fashion) but cannot be sounded out letter-by-letter. Instead, students must learn to attend to larger groups of letters. Carnine et al. (1997) refer to this strategy as phonic analysis.

A sequence for teaching letter groups should follow the same guidelines as was used for single letters (Carnine et al., 1997). Rather than teaching the letter groups in alphabetical order or in an order derived from literary themes, it is best to teach useful letter groups first, and to separate letter groups that are confusing (sh, ch; oo, ou; ar, ur, or) because they are similar in the way they look and sound. Carnine et al. note that most students are not confused by letter groups that make the same sound (ee, ea) so that these do not need to be separated.

2. Assessment

Curriculum-referenced assessment of knowledge of letter group–sound correspondences and a phonic analysis strategy begins with an analysis of the curriculum. Which letter groups have been taught? Has a phonic analysis strategy been taught? It is reasonable to assume that students have not mastered that which has not been taught.

For an initial assessment of knowledge of letter group–sound correspondences and phonic analysis, the special education teacher should construct a survey that includes one or two words for each correspondence (some of the letter patterns in isolation may also be included). The results of the survey can be used to identify those correspondences that have been mastered. Probes (five or more words of one type, e.g., maid, stain, bait, paid, rain) can be designed and administered to distinguish letter groups that need review or instruction. It is also useful to design probes that contrast CVC and silent e pairs (e.g., can and cane). Because there are many exceptions to these correspondences (often called "outlaws" e.g., said, have, deaf) be sure to proofread your assessment and eliminate any words that are not phonetically regular. Probes can be readministered after remediation or early intervention, to document pupil progress.

Another approach is to ask students to sort words, according to criteria of their own choosing. This should indicate whether students "see" the phonic patterns.

Error analysis should attend to letter groups that are confusing. Some students will read regular words as if they were "outlaws" (e.g., so that maid rhymes with said).

3. Methods for Teaching Correspondences between Letter Groups and Sounds

Letter groups are efficiently taught using direct instruction. After gaining student attention, the teacher models the sound produced by the letter group in isolation, and in regular words. Guided practice with ample feedback is provided, then students are expected to read these words independently.

Word sorts are an activity that allow students to practice attending to letter groups. Word sorts require close examination of the contrasting letter groups for reading and sorting the words accurately. The teacher generates word cards and specifies the criteria for sorting (e.g., Have students read and sort into groups with similar endings. Use words that end with -ake, -ail, and -ay).

4. Methods for Teaching a Phonic Analysis Strategy

The phonic analysis strategy should be taught directly. Effective strategy instruction always begins by teaching students what the strategy is, and the circumstances where the strategy is and is not useful (Brown, Bransford, Ferrara, & Campione, 1983). Students should be told explicitly that many phonic patterns in English cannot be sounded out letter-by-letter, but need to be "attacked" as groups of letters. Students should be provided with models of words where they must "step back" and attend to groups of letters. Students should also be reminded that while many words are regular, others are not. Students should be encouraged to use context cues to help them to identify "outlaws."

The teacher should model the phonic analysis strategy, guide its use, provide prompting and feedback as needed, and gradually move students to independent performance. As new letter groups are introduced, use of the phonic analysis strategy should be scaffolded by the teacher. That is, as students struggle with new applications, the teacher may need to model, guide, or prompt again. A teacher who scaffolds provides just enough support for students to succeed (Tharp & Gallimore, 1988).

We like to replicate materials from the Glass Analysis for Decoding Only program (Glass & Glass, 1976) for student practice of phonic analysis. The teacher writes "—aid" on an index card; a series of initial letter cards (l, m, p, r) are attached to this bottom card with a ring on the left. The student flips the initial letter cards to read "laid," "maid," "paid," "raid." If the ring is placed on the right, a set of words with different endings can be practiced (e.g., "rain," "rate," "ray"). Making the letter groups concrete in this way is a simple reminder to students that the phonic analysis strategy requires attention to letter groups.

D. Sight Words

1. Research

In addition to phonics instruction, disabled readers often need help in building a repertoire of words they can recognize on sight. Word recognition is equally important for phonetically regular and irregular words, although these two types of words may be introduced differently.

Sight words are words that a reader knows immediately upon presentation. There is no hesitation to decode, to discriminate, or to recall the words; they are read with ease. Accuracy and automaticity are critical. They allow reading with fluency and comprehension of what is read. When children learn to read words automatically, their attention is available for processing and comprehending text. Sight words consist of all types of words that have been read a sufficient number of times to establish connections in long-term memory (Ehri, 1992).

Children who are proficient in decoding words learn sight words with greater ease than children who have difficulty decoding (Ehri, 1991; Jorm & Share, 1983). The development of word recognition skill leads to increases in reading comprehension (Biemiller, 1970; Stanovich, 1985).

Children tend to learn most easily the words that are meaningful to them (e.g., their names, names of pets, mom, dad). They learn words that interest them and in which they know the meanings. Words with strong emotional charge and words that invoke imagery are words that children want to learn (Harris & Sipay, 1990). Content words (nouns, verbs, adjectives, adverbs) are learned more easily than function words (prepositions, connectors), but many function words are high-frequency words.

High-frequency words are words that appear often in print. Many of the high-frequency words are phonetically irregular and are learned more easily by whole-word methods than by decoding. Thirteen high-frequency words account for 25% of the words in text (a, and, for, he, is, in, it, of, that, the, to, was, you) (Johns, 1981). They should be among the first words that children learn to read.

Among the more popular high-frequency word lists for beginning readers are the Dolch Basic Sight Vocabulary List, Fry's Instant Words, the Harris-Jacobson graded word lists, and Eeds' Bookwords. There are many words that overlap on these lists. All of the lists target readers in the primary grades, except for the Harris-Jacobson lists, which continue through grade eight. However, the lists were developed using different methods and have unique features. You may find a certain list to be more appropriate for a particular student dependent on student ability, reading style, and need. The reading materials you are using may also help you select a list.

Dolch (1939) compiled a list of 220 words, excluding nouns, that account for over 50% of words in student texts. The Dolch Basic Sight Vocabulary List is divided into Easier 110 and Harder 110. When the list was devised, guidelines indicated that the Easier 110 words should be mastered by mid-second grade and the entire list of 220 by third grade. A more recent analysis by Harris and Jacobson (1982) indicated that the 220 Dolch words appear earlier in contemporary reading basals. Approximately 150 of these words are incorporated in preprimer and primer level basals and only 21 words remain to be introduced in second grade. The Easier 110 contain 12 of the 13 high-frequency words that account for 25% of the words in text.

There are 300 words in Fry's (1980) Instant Words list. They constitute 65% of all words in text. One hundred words should be mastered at the end of each grade for grades one through three. The first thirteen words on list one are the words that account for 25% of the words in print. Function words and content words comprise the list and six common suffixes are indexed as well.

Harris-Jacobson (1982) prepared word lists for grades 1–8 using words from student textbooks. These lists contain nouns as well as many of the high-frequency words from the Dolch lists, however they are more extensive than the Dolch lists. Twelve of the 13 high-frequency words that comprise one-quarter of the words in text are found on the Pre-primer list.

Eeds (1985) entered all of the words from 400 children's literature books that had been recommended as suitable for beginning readers. The final list contains 227 of the most frequent words. Guidelines that influenced word selection were that compound words were entered as two separate words (grand and mother for grandmother), only the base of inflected words appear on the list (go for goes, going), only the base word was entered if pronunciation was unaffected (did for didn't). The least common words on the list appeared in print 20 times. The 13 high-frequency words are contained on this list.

Eeds's Bookwords would be an appropriate match for teachers who are teaching reading using a literature-based approach. Teachers should add the compound words and inflected words to the base words to have a complete listing. Fry's Instant Word List has appeal as a well-rounded list for students reading at a primary level (grades 1–3) because both nouns and function words are incorporated, common suffixes are listed, and it contains many high-frequency words. The Dolch Basic Sight Vocabulary List has stood the test of time in terms of frequency, but is most useful for first-grade-level readers. The Harris-Jacobson word lists are the most comprehensive and are the only lists that provide basic vocabulary words beyond the primary level.

Sight words can be taught in isolation or in context. When words are taught in context, children learn more about their syntactic and semantic qualities. When words are taught in isolation or in lists, children learn more about their orthographic qualities (Ehri & Wilce, 1980).

2. Assessment

Teachers should pretest sight words using words from high-frequency lists. First select the list that is appropriate for the student. If reading level is unknown, then start at the beginning of the list and continue until 10 errors in a row or until the end of the list is reached. Remember to mark only the words read with accuracy and automaticity as correct.

For children with few sight words, it is often easiest to put the words on index cards and flip through cards, rather than having students read off a lengthy list. Have a copy of the list ready to mark words that are automatic. Note the words that a child gets right by sounding out; these are the some of the words that should be introduced next.

It is best to ask the student to attempt each word. Do not pronounce words for a student during testing. When students who are not risk takers are given the option to pass on unknown words, they will use that option frequently, and it may result in an underestimation of sight vocabulary. Further, student errors are an important guide to the teacher. A record of miscues should be analyzed for error types and used to plan instructional interventions.

3. Methods for Teaching Sight Words

Flash cards or word cards are an instructional tool for teaching sight words. In order to keep interest high and learning at a premium, have students practice known words with unknown words. For emerging readers, introduce new words at a ratio of 4:1 known to unknown initially. As unknown words become known, add a new word and remove a well-known word. Save the known words and review them periodically, weekly for students with few sight words and then at longer intervals.

When children have gained a sight vocabulary of at least 20 words, have children practice making sentences using the words, writing them in sentences, or making compound words. You can also make up short repetitive stories for the children to read using their known sight words. Sight words can also be written in phrases or short sentences for children to practice in context.

High-frequency words that carry little meaning (i.e., function words) should be taught in context to help students associate them with something meaningful. They can be accompanied with pictorial aids (e.g., for "of," a piece of pizza) or mnemonics (e.g., There is a hen in when). Once a word has been connected to its meaning, the association must be practiced.

The Drill Sandwich developed by Coulter and Barrilleaux (as cited in Tucker & Gickling, 1995) is a powerful method for increasing sight vocabulary. It involves a folding-in strategy that builds new sight vocabulary and reinforces known words simultaneously. Unknown words are sandwiched between known words with a ratio of 80% known and 20% challenge. Children can practice their cards alone or with a peer. When they read them to the teacher, the teacher can reinsert the unknown words several times through so the child gets to practice the unknown words more frequently than the known. For disabled readers who know 30 or fewer sight words, start with three or four known words and one challenge word until sight vocabulary increases and gradually increase the number of words being practiced. Other activities involve having the students practice spelling the words and using them in sentences. Both can be done orally or in writing. As new words are added, well-known words are removed but saved for periodic review. Student cards can be stored in reclosable baggies.

Another method of teaching sight words was designed as a classroom activity that can be adapted for small group or individual readers. It is called Words on the Wall (Cunningham, 1995). High-frequency words are displayed on a wall or bulletin board and several new words are added weekly. Activities using the wall include finding words, writing words, and chanting the spelling of words. The word walls can be made portable for use with small groups or individuals by writing the words across opened file folders. Typically, words are displayed alphabetically for easy reference. Words can be selected from high-frequency lists or by student need. Difficult or confusable elements can be highlighted by using a different color marker for certain letters or color-coding words. The shape of the word can be accentuated by cutting around the letters on cards or tracing the configuration with a marker.

Reading easy books, repeated readings, and choral readings facilitate the development of sight word vocabularies. Games like Word Tic-Tac-Toe, Word-o or Word Bingo, Concentration, Sight Word Checkers, and Go Fish can be used to foster sight word growth.

Word Tic-Tac-Toe can be played on paper or on the chalkboard with two players. Just write the targeted words in each space on the grid. The players must read the word correctly before placing their X's and O's on the words.

Word-o and Word Bingo take their format from Bingo games. Write or type the words on cards in a five-by-five grid and have a separate set of individual word cards for the caller. The caller can hold up the card or read the word without showing it to the other players. Players put chips on the words that are called and the first player to cover five in a row and read the words that were covered wins.

Word concentration is played by writing pairs of words on 3 × 5-inch index cards. The cards are placed face down in rows. The object is to turn over two cards that match. Players take turns and read every card they turn over. For children with fewer than 50 sight words, concentration can be simplified by writing the 10 to 15 word pairs on two different colored cards. Thus, players turn over a yellow card and a green card to find each match. Flip chart markers do not show through the backside of index cards.

For Sight Word Checkers write the word on a checkerboard template or on cards that fit on a checkerboard. Be sure to put words on the black squares only. Play according to checkers rules with the addition of pronouncing the word that the player's checker lands on.

To play Go Fish with sight words make up packets of cards with the appropriate sight words. Note the words can be written two, three, or four times each. Pass out five cards for each player and place the remaining cards face down in a pool on the table. During a player's turn, the player asks another person for the match to a certain card. If the other player has it, he has to turn it over to the player who asked. If he does not have it, he says "Go Fish" and the player takes a card from the pool. The object is to get packets of cards and to get rid of all the cards in one's hand. This can also be adapted to play with rhyming cards.

Predictable books can be used to increase sight word vocabularies in beginning readers. Rhyme and repetition are frequently incorporated into predictable books making it easy and pleasurable for emerging readers to read and examine the reoccurring text over and over again. There are different types of predictable books: repetitive, repetitive-cumulative, familiar sequence, and predictable plot. One of the simplest is the repetitive book in which a sentence or phrase is repeated throughout much of the story (Bridge, 1979). The repetitive-cumulative predictable books use an add-on technique for phrases or sentences that become longer with each refrain. Familiar sequence predictable books are written using common series such as the alphabet, days of the week, enumeration, and so on. A fourth type of predictable book contains predictable plots or phrases that enable the young reader to foretell upcoming events in the story. For beginning readers, the repetitive-cumulative predictable book is most likely to contain the greatest number of recurrences of high-frequency words.

E. Context Use

1. Research

Research has shown that children do not automatically integrate context use and word attack strategies. Children come to school with the knowledge of language and the world that they need to make use of context cues. Thus, they typically begin reading by overrelying on context when they encounter an unfamiliar word (Biemiller, 1970; Weber, 1970). At this stage, their guess often ignores most or all of the letters. As children are taught to decode, they move to a second phase, where they use the letter cues to sound out and do not seem to care if what they read makes sense. It is only as both decoding and context use strategies become practiced that the child enters a third stage. Here, he or she produces guesses that utilize both visual and context cues. They make sense of the context and what is written.

As this progression suggests, mastery of a context use strategy alone is not sufficient. The reader must also acquire decoding skills. Readers encounter large numbers of unfamiliar or uncommon words (Carroll, Davies, & Richman, 1971). Typically, the least familiar words carry the greatest meaning (Finn, 1977–78). Guessing at these unfamiliar but critical words is unlikely to be as productive an approach as one that uses both decoding and context cues.

Most disabled readers have an acceptable or even well-developed ability to use context cues (Stanovich, 1980). In grade level materials, however, this ability may not be apparent because students cannot decode enough words to establish a context (Stanovich, 1984). These students will not require context use strategy instruction.

However, a small group of disabled readers will require explicit context use strategy instruction. These students are good decoders (e.g., they can decode at a third-grade level) who should be able to integrate decoding with context use. Often, these students are termed "word callers" as they decode with ease, but don't notice the meaning of what they read.

2. Assessment

Two approaches can be used to establish whether or not students require explicit instruction in context-use strategies. One is "miscue analysis." Students read a somewhat challenging passage aloud, and the teacher records their errors or "mis-cues," and notes whether or not students tend to self-correct. A chart is construct-ed of these errors. For each error, the teacher analyzes whether the miscue reflects use of (a) the visual cues (are 50% or more of the written letters reflected in the miscue?); (b) syntactic context (is the miscue grammatically acceptable?); and (c) meaning context (does the miscue make sense in the passage?). If most of a stu-dent's miscues do not show use of syntax or meaning, then context-use strategy instruction is needed. This recommendation may be disconfirmed by an analysis of student strengths, as exhibited by what is read correct and the presence of self-corrections.

Another approach to assessing context use is the cloze passage. A passage at the student's independent reading level is selected. The passage is retyped so that roughly every fifth word is replaced with a blank. The student must fill in the blank with the exact missing word. Salvia and Hughes (1990) note that this is a difficult task, and that only 50% accuracy is attained by good readers. Students who score well below this criterion may require instruction in context use strategies.

3. Instruction

Context use strategies should be practiced using materials that are meaningful to the student. That is, the teacher must establish that the student has the background knowledge needed to use the context.

The goal of context use instruction is for the student to ask him or herself "did what I just read make sense?" and to reread and self-correct if it did not. Many teachers inadvertently discourage students from using context. These teachers con-stantly ask "did that make sense?" or immediately correct errors before the student can self-correct. These students are prevented from learning to use context, be-cause their teachers are using it for them!

In these cases, students may acquire context use strategies if the teacher (a) pro-vides less feedback; (b) provides less specific feedback; or (c) delays feedback. The goal of these instructional modifications is to give the student the time and space to use the strategy independently.

In other cases, direct instruction in the strategy is required. As always, the teacher begins strategy instruction by defining the strategy, stating its purpose, and clarifying when and where the strategy should be used. It is helpful to remind stu-dents that not every error needs to be corrected. The focus of context use strategy instruction should be on self-correcting those errors that change the meaning of the text.

The teacher can model using a "think aloud" approach. The teacher reads aloud and makes errors. After the error, the teacher says (aloud) "did that make sense? No; I better go back and reread. Or, yes, it made sense, pat myself on the back and keep reading." As needed, the teacher rereads, reviews the context, and self-cor-rects. This model can be reinforced by having the student observe peers or listen to tapes of other students who read aloud, reflect, and self-correct. The student should then be encouraged to practice the strategy. Some students will need a signal (like a small flag made from a straight pin) to remind them to self-monitor. These can be placed at the end of the sentence initially; then less frequently, at the end of the paragraph, and then the page. Eventually all prompts should be faded, and the student expected to use the strategy independently.

VI. SUMMARY

Teachers of students with reading disabilities need to provide a balanced and comprehensive program of instruction. The reading curriculum for these students should include concepts about print, phonological and phonemic awareness, letter name knowledge, the correspondences between single letters and sounds, the correspondences between letter groups and sounds, and sight words. Futher, three critical strategies should be taught: sounding out, phonic analysis, and context use strategies. This curriculum will allow students to acquire proficiency in word attack and word recognition.

Because reading proficiency is acquired in stages, reading instruction must be appropriate for the student's level of performance. After individual assessment, appropriately tailored instruction will allow students to progress through the emergent literacy and beginning reading stages.

We have advocated that direct instruction and effective strategy instruction be used with reading-disabled students. These methods are recommended because they are explicit, and because they afford students ample opportunities for practice. It is only with extensive practice that students with reading disabilities will integrate the use of the visual, contextual, and structural cue systems. With extensive practice, decoding and word recognition skills will become tools that the students will use as he or she reads for meaning and enjoyment.

Acknowledgments

An earlier version of this chapter, authored by Lynn M. Gelzheiser and Diana Brewster Clark, appeared in the first edition of this text. We dedicate this chapter in memory of the late Dr. Clark, gratefully acknowledging her contributions to this work and her zeal to improve services to students with disabilities.

References

Adams, M. J. (1990). *Beginning to read: Thinking and learning about print.* Cambridge, MA: The MIT Press.

Badian, N. A. (1982). The prediction of good and poor reading before kindergarten entry: A four-year follow-up. *The Journal of Special Education, 16*(3), 309–318.

Ball, E. W., & Blachman, B. A. (1991). Does phoneme awareness training in kindergarten make a difference in early word recognition and developmental spelling? *Reading Research Quarterly, 26*(1), 49–66.

Barker, T. A., & Torgesen, J. K. (1995). An evaluation of computer-assisted instruction in phonological awareness with below average readers. *Journal of Educational Computing Research, 13*(1), 89–103.

Biemiller, A. (1970). The development of the use of graphic and contextual information as children learn to read. *Reading Research Quarterly, 6,* 76–96.

Blachman, B. A. (1987). An alternative classroom reading program for learning disabled and other low-achieving children. In W. Ellis (Ed.), *Intimacy with language: A forgotten basic in teacher education* (pp. 49–55). Baltimore: Orton Dyslexia Society.

Bloom, L. (1980). Language development, language disorders, and learning disabilities: LD3. *Bulletin of the Orton Society, 30,* 115–133.

Bond, G. L., & Dykstra, R. (1967). The cooperative research program in first-grade reading instruction. *Reading Research Quarterly, 2,* 5–142.

Bridge, C. (1979). Predictable materials for beginning readers. *Language Arts, 56*(5), 503–507.

Brown, A. L., Bransford, J. D., Ferrara, R. A., & Campione, J. C. (1983). Learning, remembering, and understanding. In J. H. Flavell & E. M. Markman (Eds.), *Handbook of child psychology* (4th ed., Vol. 3, pp. 77–166). New York: Wiley.

Bryant, P., & Goswami, U. (1987). Phonological awareness and learning to read. In J. R. Beech & A. M. Colley (Eds.), *Cognitive approaches to reading* (pp. 213–243). John Wiley & Sons Ltd.

Butler, S. R., Marsh, H. W., Sheppard, M. J., & Sheppard, J. L. (1985). Seven-year longitudinal study of the early prediction of reading achievement. *Journal of Educational Psychology, 77*(3), 349–361.

Carnine, D. W., Silbert, J., & Kameenui, E. J. (1997). *Direct instruction reading* (3rd. ed.). Upper Saddle River, NJ: Prentice-Hall.

Carroll, J. B., Davies, P., & Richman, B. (1971). *Word frequency book.* Boston: Houghton Mifflin.

Chall, J. S. (1983). *Stages of reading development.* New York: McGraw Hill.

Clarke, L. K. (1988). Invented versus traditional spelling in first graders' writings: Effects on learning to spell and read. *Research in the Teaching of English, 22*(3), 291–309.

Clay, M. M. (1995). *The early detection of reading difficulties* (3rd. ed.). Portsmouth, NH: Heinemann.

Cunningham, P. M. (1995). *Phonics they use* (2nd ed.). New York: Harper Collins.

Dolch, E. W. (1939). *A manual for remedial reading.* Champaign, IL: Garrard.

Durkin, D. (1966). *Children who read early: Two longitudinal studies.* New York: Teachers College Press.

Eeds, M. (1985). Bookwords: Using a beginning word list of high frequency words from children's literature K–3. *The Reading Teacher, 38,* 418–423.

Ehri, L. C. (1991). Learning to read and spell words. In L. Trieben & C. Perfetti (Eds.), *Learning to read: Basic research and its implications* (pp. 57–73). Hillsdale, NJ: Erlbaum.

Ehri, L. C. (1989). Movement into word reading and spelling: How spelling contributes to reading. In J. Mason (Ed.), *Reading and writing connections* (pp. 65–81). Boston, MA: Allyn & Bacon.

Ehri, L. C. (1992). Reconceptualizing the development of sight word reading and its relationship to recoding. In P. B. Gough, L. C. Ehri, & R. Treiman (Eds.), *Reading acquisition* (pp. 107–143). Hillsdale, NJ: Erlbaum.

Ehri, L. C., Deffner, N. D., & Wilce, L. S. (1984). Pictorial mnemonics for phonics. *Journal of Educational Psychology, 76,* 880–893.

Ehri, L. C., & Wilce, L. S. (1980). Do beginners learn to read function words better in sentences or in lists? *Reading Research Quarterly, 15,* 451–476.

Ellis, N., & Cataldo, S. (1990). The role of spelling in learning to read. *Language and Education, 4*(1), 1–28.

Finn, P. J. (1977–1978). Word frequency, information theory, and cloze performance: A transfer feature theory of processing in reading. *Reading Research Quarterly, 13,* 508–537.

Fry, E. (1980). The new instant word list. *The Reading Teacher, 34,* 284–289.

Glass, G. G., & Glass, E. W. (1976). *Glass analysis for decoding only: Teachers Guide.* Garden City, NJ: Easier to learn.

Goswami, U. (1986). Children's use of analogy in learning to read: A developmental study. *Journal of Experimental Child Psychology, 42,* 73–83.

Gough, P. B., & Hillinger, M. L. (1980). Learning to read: An unnatural act. *Bulletin of the Orton Society, 30,* 179–196.

Haring, N. G., & Bateman, B. (1977). *Teaching the learning disabled child.* Englewood Cliffs, NJ: Prentice-Hall.

Harris, A. J., & Jacobson, M. D. (1982). *Basic reading vocabularies.* New York: MacMillan.

Harris, A. J., & Sipay, E. R. (1990). *How to increase reading ability* (9th ed.). New York: Longman.

Heath, S. B. (1983). *Ways with words.* Cambridge: Cambridge University Press.

Johns, J. L. (1981). The development of the Revised Dolch List. *Illinois School Research and Development, 17,* 15–24.

Johnson, D. J., & Myklebust, H. R. (1967). *Learning disabilities.* New York: Grune and Stratton.

Jorm, A. F., & Share, D. L. (1983). Phonological recoding and reading acquisition. *Applied Psycholinguistics, 4,* 103–147.

LaBerge, D., & Samuels, S. J. (1974). Toward a theory of automatic information processing. *Cognitive Psychology, 6,* 293–322.

Lewkowitz, N. K. (1980). Phonemic awareness training: What to teach and how to teach it. *Journal of Educational Psychology, 72*(5), 686–700.

Liberman, I. Y., Shankweiler, D., Fischer, F. W., & Carter, B. (1974). Reading and the awareness of linguistic segments. *Journal of Experimental Child Psychology, 18,* 201–212.

Lundberg, I., Olofsson, A., & Wall, S. (1980). Reading and spelling skills in the first school years predicted from phonemic awareness in kindergarten. *Scandinavian Journal of Psychology, 21,* 159–173.

MacLean, M., Bryant, P., & Bradley, L. (1987). Rhymes, nursery rhymes, and reading in early childhood. *Merrill-Palmer Quarterly, 33*(3), 255–281.

Mann, V. A., & Liberman, I. Y. (1984). Phonological awareness and verbal short-term memory. *Journal of Learning Disabilities, 17*(10), 592–599.

Masonheimer, P. E., Drum, P. A., & Ehri, L. C. (1984). Does environmental print identification lead children into word reading? *Journal of Reading Behavior, 16,* 257–271.

Moats, L. C. (1995). The missing foundation in teacher education. *American Educator, 19,* 9–51.

National Center to Improve the Tools of Educators (1996). *Tips for teachers: Teaching reading to students with learning disabilities.* Washington, DC: U.S. Office of Special Education Programs.

New York State Education Department (1996). *Learning standards for english language arts.* Albany: The University of the State of New York.

Perfetti, C. A. (1985). *Reading ability.* New York: Oxford University Press.

Robertson, C., & Salter, W. (1995). *The phonological awareness kit.* E. Moline, IL: LinguiSystems.

Robinson, S. S. (1990). *Developmental spelling and other language predictors of reading achievement.* Ames: Iowa State University of Science and Technology. Research Institute for Studies in Education. (ERIC Document Reproduction Service No. 327 815).

Salvia, J., & Hughes, C. (1990). *Curriculum-based assessment.* NY: MacMillan.

Scanlon, D. M., Vellutino, F. R., Small, S. G., Spearing, D., & Wharton-McDonald, R. (1993, April). *Prediction of "Reading Disability" and progress in remediation using a kindergarten test battery.* Paper presented at the International Reading Association Annual Meeting, San Antonio, TX.

Seidenberg, M. S., & McClelland, J. L. (1989). A distributed, developmental model of word recognition and naming. *Psychological Review, 96,* 523–568.

Share, D. L. (1995). Phonological recoding and self-teaching: Sine qua noon of reading acquisition. *Cognition, 55,* 151–218.

Share, D. L., Jorm, A. F., Maclean, R., & Matthews, R. (1984). Sources of individual differences in reading acquisition. *Journal of Educational Psychology, 76,* 1309–1324.

Silva, P. A., Chalmers, D., & Stewart, I. (1986). Some audiological, educational, and behavioral characteristics of children with bilateral otitis media with effusion: A longitudinal study. *Journal of Learning Disabilities, 19*(3), 165–169.

Smith, F. (1971). *Understanding reading.* New York: Holt, Rinehart, and Winston.

Stanovich, K. E. (1980). Toward an interactive-compensatory model of individual differences in the development of reading fluency. *Reading Research Quarterly, 16,* 32–71.

Stanovich, K. E. (1984). The interactive-compensatory model of reading: A confluence of developmental, experimental, and educational psychology. *Remedial and Special Education, 5,* 11–19.

Stanovich, K. E. (1985). Explaining the difference in reading ability in terms of psychological processes: What have we learned? *Annals of Dyslexia, 35,* 67–96.

Stanovich, K. E., Cunningham, A. E., & Cramer, B. B. (1984). Assessing phonological awareness in kindergarten children: Issues of task comparability. *Journal of Experimental Child Psychology, 38,* 175–190.

Stevenson, H. W., & Newmann, R. S. (1986). Long-term prediction of achievement and attitudes in mathematics and reading. *Child Development, 57,* 646–659.

Sulzby, E., & Teale, W. (1991). Emergent literacy. In R. Barr, M. L. Kamil, P. Mosenthal, & P. D. Pearson (Eds.), *Handbook of reading research* Vol. II. (pp. 727–757). White Plains, NY: Longman, Inc.

Teale, W. H., & Sulzby, E. (Eds.) (1986). *Emergent literacy: Writing and reading.* Norwood, NJ: Ablex Printing.

Tharp, R. G., & Gallimore, R. (1988). *Rousing minds to life: Teaching, learning and schooling in social context.* New York: Cambridge University Press.

Torgesen, J. K. (in press). The prevention and remediation of reading disabilities. Evaluating what we know from research. *Academic Language Therapy Association Monographs.*

Torgesen, J. K., & Bryant, B. R. (1994). *Phonological awareness training for reading.* Austin, TX: PRO-ED.

Treiman, R. (1985). Onsets and rimes as units of spoken syllables: Evidence from children. *Journal of Experimental Child Psychology, 39,* 161–181.

Tucker, J. A., & Gickling, E. E. (1995, July). *Instructional Assessment: The search for what works in reading assessment and instruction.* Paper presented at Ravena-Coeymans-Selkirk Central School District, Selkirk, NY.

Tunmer, W. E., Herriman, M. L., & Nesdale, A. R. (1988). Metalinguistic abilities and beginning reading. *Reading Research Quarterly, 23,* 134–158.

Tunmer, W. E., & Nesdale, A. R. (1985). Phonemic segmentation skill and beginning reading. *Journal of Educational Psychology, 83*(4), 437–443.

Vellutino, F. R. (1979). *Dyslexia: Theory and research.* Cambridge, MA: MIT Press.

Vellutino, F. R. (1991). Introduction to three studies on reading acquisition: Convergent findings on theoretical foundations of code-oriented versus whole-language approaches to reading instruction. *Journal of Educational Psychology, 83*(4), 437–443.

Vellutino, F. R., & Scanlon, D. M. (1986). Experimental evidence for the effects of instructional bias on word identification. *Exceptional Children, 53,* 145–155.

Vellutino, F. R., & Scanlon, D. M. (1987). Phonological coding, phonological awareness and reading ability: Evidence from a longitudinal and experimental study. *Merrill-Palmer Quarterly, 33*(3), 321–365.

Vellutino, F. R., & Scanlon, D. M. (1991). The preeminence of phonologically based skills in learning to read. In S. A. Brady & D. P. Shankweiler (Eds.), *Phonological processes in literacy: A tribute to Isabelle Y. Liberman* (pp. 237–252). Hillsdale, NJ: Lawrence Erlbaum.

Vellutino, F. R., Scanlon, D. M., Sipay, E. R., Small, S. G., Pratt, A., Chen, R., & Denckla, M. B. (1996). Cognitive profiles of difficult-to-remediate and readily remediated poor readers: Early intervention as a vehicle for distinguishing between cognitive and experiential deficits as basic causes of specific reading disability. *Journal of Educational Psychology, 88,* 601–638.

Wagner, R. K., & Torgesen, J. K. (1987). The nature of phonological processing and its role in the acquisition of reading skills. *Psychological Bulletin, 101,* 192–212.

Wagner, R. K., Torgesen, J. K., & Raschotte, C. A. (1994). The development of reading-related phonological processing abilities: New evidence of bi-directional causality from a latent variable longitudinal study. *Developmental Psychology, 30,* 73–87.

Weber, R.-M. (1970). A linguistic analysis of first-grade reading errors. *Reading Research Quarterly, 5,* 427–451.

Wood, D. M. (1995). *A study of relationships among spelling instruction, student characteristics, and spelling stage.* (Doctoral dissertation, University at Albany, 1994). (University Microfilms No. DAO 72699).

Yopp, H. K. (1995). A test for assessing phonemic awareness in young children. *The Reading Teacher, 49*(1), 20–29.

CHAPTER 10

Fostering Reading Competence in Students with Learning Disabilities

Patricia A. Alexander, Ruth Garner, Christopher T. Sperl, and Victoria Chou Hare

I. INTRODUCTION

In today's information-rich world, academic success remains strongly dependent upon a learner's ability to acquire competence in reading and to apply that competence in the development of understanding in other domains of knowledge. The former has been referred to as "learning to read," and the latter as "reading to learn" (Austin & Morrison, 1963). Reading, under both circumstances, involves comprehension, the construction of meaning from written text. A multitude of factors, cognitive and noncognitive, must work in concert if students are to become successful readers (Garner, 1990; Wigfield, 1997). Similarly, a learner's ability to construct a principled body of knowledge from written language is an equally complex process predicated upon an array of cognitive, motivational, and strategic components (Wigfield & Guthrie, 1997). In this chapter, we take a closer look at these components, especially as they pertain to one particular segment of the school population—students with learning disabilities (LD). Our goal is to offer recommendations for educating students with LD, so as to promote their reading competence. Further, we want to consider ways that these students can be helped to achieve in other domains through effective reading.

Learning about Learning Disabilities, Second Edition   343

II. COMPETENCE IN READING: ACHIEVING
INDEPENDENT FUNCTIONING

What are the dimensions that seem to give rise to competent reading and how are these dimensions manifested in students with LD? At the very least, the construction of meaning from text depends on the interplay of (a) linguistic and metalinguistic knowledge; (b) conceptual understanding; (c) strategic ability; and (d) motivation for learning.

A. Linguistic and Metalinguistic Knowledge

Because reading requires access to and interpretation of written language, competent readers must be able to "break the code" (Goswami, 1988; Perfetti & Lesgold, 1979). That is to say, they must make sense of the symbols and systems of language. Linguistic knowledge encompasses learners' understanding of such fundamental code-breaking processes as phonological and orthographic awareness, graphophonemic patterning, syntax, and semantics (Diveta & Speece, 1990; Ehri, 1989; Lovett, Warren-Chaplin, Ransby, & Borden, 1990). Metalinguistic knowledge, which is likewise requisite for successful reading, entails the individual's cognizance of language concepts and conventions (Adams, 1990). Such concepts or conventions can include an understanding of what qualifies as a word, a sense of when and where certain language patterns or registers are appropriate, as well as an awareness of what it means to read or to comprehend. Research has consistently demonstrated that linguistic and metalinguistic knowledge must be sufficiently developed in readers to permit them to decode and encode print rapidly and accurately (Perfetti, 1985; Swanson & Berninger, 1995; Wagner & Torgeson, 1987).

Several chapters in this volume present detailed analyses of phonological and orthographic processes (Mann, chapter 5), including the role of such processes in early reading programs (Gelhzeiser & Wood, chapter 9). We acknowledge the importance of these components to reading acquisition and to comprehensive literacy programs for the learning disabled. Still, educators must continue to guard against children's overreliance on common phonological or orthographic codes (Baker & Zimlin, 1989; Swanson & Ramalgia, 1992), or learners' disregard of the "meaning-making" or aesthetics of text-processing (Paris & Myers, 1981; Rosenblatt, 1978). The literature is replete with studies that tell us that less skilled or younger readers equate decoding with comprehension (Baker & Zimlin, 1989; Moore & Zabrucky, 1989; Wagner, Spratt, Gal, & Paris, 1989). Baker's research (e.g., 1984a, 1984b, 1985) offers one explanation as to why children might have an illusion of understanding if they merely decode text successfully.

Specifically, Baker proposed that readers use at least three standards to evaluate their comprehension of text: lexical, syntactic, and semantic. The lexical standard operates at the level of the individual word, making attention to the context unnecessary. The syntactic standard requires sensitivity to grammatical constraints of language, whereas the semantic standard requires consideration of sentences and the surrounding context. It is the semantic standard that requires the most thorough processing of text and that is most important to effective comprehension. Baker found that younger and less-skilled readers often use the lexical standard of evaluation exclusively to judge their efforts at meaning making. More recently, Swanson and Ramalgia (1992) reported a similar overreliance on phonological codes among 13-year-olds with LD.

Still, some cause for optimism can be found in Baker and Zimlin's (1989) study. These researchers determined that children can be taught to evaluate their comprehension using multiple standards. Moreover, these instructional effects generalized to noninstructed standards and were maintained over time. It would seem, therefore, that educators should consider explicit instruction in both the linguistic *and* metalinguistic dimensions of reading for students with LD (Ehri & Wilce, 1985).

B. Conceptual Understanding

One of the most consistent findings to emerge from the reading research of the past several decades pertains to the powerful role that an individual's knowledge base plays in learning from text (Alexander & Murphy, in press, a; Anderson, Pichert, & Shirey, 1983; Anderson, Reynolds, Schallert, & Goetz, 1977). That is to say, the meaning that students construct from text is directly related to the framework of conceptual knowledge that they bring to that text. Conceptual knowledge is a term we use to designate all the knowledge that someone possesses about any specific concept or idea (Alexander, Schallert, & Hare, 1991). For example, when a young child reads the word "dog," she can bring to mind many understandings of this concept that developed in school and in out-of-school experiences. She may envision a four-legged animal that barks, for instance, and that likes to chase cats. As her schooling continues, the child's understanding of this and multitudes of other concepts are enriched and expanded.

In general, the richer the students' base of relevant conceptual knowledge, the better their comprehension and recall of text (Alexander, 1997b). Conversely, the processing of text dealing with unfamiliar concepts can complicate learners' ability to comprehend text, even if their linguistic skills seem adequate to the task (Stahl, Hare, Sinatra, & Gregory, 1991). Should either children's reading skills or their knowledge be seriously limited or mismatched with regard to the learning tasks before them, their progress toward competence will be threatened. When both reading abilities and knowledge are insufficient or poorly linked to the expectations and demands of school learning, children will find it increasingly difficult to thrive in schools (Alexander, 1997b). For this reason, children must have every opportunity to construct a foundation of conceptual knowledge *and* secure the basic processes of reading within a supportive and challenging environment.

According to Rumelhart (1980), difficulties in processing text due to conceptual knowledge can arise in three ways. First, readers may not have the appropriate concepts that facilitate their learning. Second, the learner may have the relevant knowledge but textual cues may be insufficient to activate that knowledge. Third, the reader may find an inconsistent, but plausible, interpretation than the one perhaps intended by the author. Let's use a simple text to illustrate these situations (Minsky, 1986):

> Mary was invited to Jack's party.
> She wondered if he would like a kite.

For one thing, there are potentially those individuals who know little about parties and for whom the concepts of gift giving suggested in these sentences are confusing. There are also individuals who have conceptual knowledge about parties, especially birthday parties, but have insufficient cues within the text to make this connection. Finally, we can envision a child who reads these sentences but who images some other event than a birthday party, leading to an alternative but reasonable interpretation.

How does this dimension of conceptual knowledge pertain specifically to reading competence among students with LD? Although specific research on this question is difficult to locate, there are several inferences that can be derived from the available data. First, given that the designation of LD is most often indicative of a IQ–performance gap (Swanson, 1991), we could speculate that some students in this population have difficulty accessing and utilizing their conceptual knowledge. Support for this contention can be found in several recent studies that have investigated the activation of prior knowledge in students with LD (Carr & Thompson, 1996; Dole, Valencia, Greer, & Wardrop, 1991; Snider, 1989).

Carr and Thompson (1996), for example, determined that students with LD benefited significantly more than same-age peers from experimenter activation of their relevant knowledge for rather unfamiliar passages. Just by asking these seventh and eighth graders what they knew about the topic, these researchers significantly increased what the students remembered from these texts. Thus, it would seem that students with LD may well have relevant knowledge that they fail to activate when appropriate.

It is also quite possible that the nature of these students' learning disabilities delimits their ability to use the textual cues effectively—leading them to misread the message that the author may have intended. For our earlier example of the birthday party, students may focus solely on the word "kites" and miss the reference to a party, resulting in a rather varied interpretation. Finally, it may be that the instruction provided to some students with LD could widen the gap between knowledge and reading performance (Borkowski, 1992; Palincsar & Klenk, 1992). That is, some reading programs may target only linguistic processes or self-regulatory strategies in a fairly decontextualized manner and at the expense of conceptual knowledge development (Englert & Palincsar, 1991; Garner, 1990).

Notable exceptions do exist, however. The apparent success of programs, like reciprocal teaching (Palincsar & Brown, 1984) and CSILE (Computer-Supported Intentional Learning Environments; Bereiter & Scardamalia, 1989), for instance, may be associated with their concurrent focus on comprehension strategies and subject-matter knowledge (e.g., science or social studies). In CSILE classrooms, for example, students are actively engaged in the joint construction of knowledge with learners in classrooms across the world. On-line technologies provide the linkages between these distant communities of learners. The catalyst for the writing and reading that occurs in these classrooms is the creation of a hypothetical civilization that must be effectively documented and described to others seeking to understand this diverse culture in relation to their own.

C. Strategic Ability

To achieve competence in reading, learners must function with an awareness of their behavior, monitor the cognitive aspects of their performance, establish their goals for learning, as well as regulate their efforts toward those goals. In short, competent readers must be active, strategic text processors (Elliott-Faust & Pressley, 1986; Garner, 1987; Garner & Alexander, 1989; Mathes, Fuchs, Fuchs, Henley, & Sanders, 1994). The term *strategy* refers to a special form of procedural knowledge. These procedures are intentionally and effortfully applied to remedy problems in understanding or to optimize performance (Alexander et al., 1991). There is ample evidence within the literature that younger and less able readers often fail to engage in the active, self-evaluative, and self-regulatory behavior that competent reading demands (Brown, Armbruster, & Baker, 1986; Garner, 1987; Markman, 1981). Rather, these younger and less able readers often look to others (e.g., teachers or parents) for direction and evaluation, fail to detect problems in the comprehension, and falter in their choice or execution of procedures that could augment their understanding. Moreover, even more than their same-age peers, students with LD have been characterized as interactive learners who do not monitor or oversee their reading performance (Borkowski, 1992; Sawyer, Graham, & Harris, 1992; Swanson, 1991; Torgeson, 1982).

The recognition of the critical role that strategic processing plays in competent reading and competent learning resulted in a plethora of strategy training studies during the 1970s and early 1980s (Alexander & Murphy, in press, a; Pressley, Brown, El-Dinary, & Afflerbach, 1995). Prototype studies during this period targeted singular cognitive or metacognitive procedures that were frequently presented in a scripted fashion and practiced in a somewhat ritualistic manner (e.g.,

Baumann, 1984; Brown & Day, 1983; Hare & Borchardt, 1984; Judy, Alexander, Kulikowich, & Willson, 1986; Meichenbaum, 1977). For example, Baumann (1984) used a direct instruction approach to teach sixth graders a strategy for identifying or constructing a main idea in paragraphs and passages. He developed eight 30-minute lessons that moved students systematically through the components of the strategy. Those receiving the treatment performed significantly better on the outcome measures that involved the recognition or production of main ideas than the comparison groups.

As with the Baumann (1984) investigation, the majority of these intervention studies showed gains for students trained in specific strategies, including children with LD. For example, Talbott, Lloyd, and Tankersley (1994) conducted a meta-analysis of reading comprehension intervention studies for students with LD. These researchers found that those students receiving training did significantly better on comprehension outcome measures than nontrained students in 87% of the 48 studies analyzed. However, the findings for maintenance and transfer of these trained strategies have been less impressive.

Since the period of the late 1980s, the research and interventions on strategic processing matured in various ways (Dole, Duffy, Roehler, & Pearson, 1991). First, the debate on the dominance of domain-specific knowledge or general strategies, exemplified by the point and counterpoint of Glaser (1984) and Sternberg (1985), gave way to the recognition that both dimensions are essential for competence (Alexander & Judy, 1988). At the heart of this debate was the argument, forwarded by Glaser, that general strategies are essentially weak alternatives that are employed when learners do not have knowledge of more particular and appropriate problem-solving strategies. The counterpoint, offered by Sternberg, was to demonstrate the power of general strategic processing, especially in those situations when the problem is more complex, real-world, or "fuzzy." Again, most cognitive researchers would now acknowledge the necessity of both forms of strategic processing to academic learning (Alexander, Graham, & Harris, in press).

Also, there was more attention paid to identification of core strategies, such as knowledge activation, self-interrogation, and summarization, which underlie effective reading and learning (Dole et al., 1991; Graham & Harris, 1989; Palincsar & Brown, 1987; Pressley, Johnson, Symons, McGoldrick, & Kurita, 1989). Further, it became more common for researchers to combine these core strategies into more comprehensive instructional approaches (e.g., Palincsar & Brown, 1984; Pressley, El-Dinary, Gaskins, Schuder, Bergman, Almasi, & Brown, 1992).

In addition, more consideration was given to the personalization of strategies based on situational and contextual factors, as well as on the characteristics of the learners themselves (Brown, Collins, & Duguid, 1989; Harris & Graham, 1996; Zaragoza & Vaughn, 1992). Part of this personalization involves the intentional shifting of responsibility for regulation from teacher to student during the instruction (Garner, 1992; Meichenbaum & Asarnow, 1979; Palincsar & Klenk, 1992), and a strong encouragement to students to treat strategies flexibly (Harris, 1996;

Pressley, Harris, & Marks, 1992; Wong, 1989). Yet another change in the nature of strategy instruction, and one that is evident in the LD literature, pertains to the expansion of self-evaluation and self-regulation to affective and motivation aspects of one's learning as well as to the cognitive dimensions (Pintrich & Schunk, 1996; Zimmerman, 1989). In the subsequent section, we look more closely at various motivational factors that have been strongly linked to reading competence.

D. Motivation for Learning

Recently, educational researchers have come to realize that academic learning cannot be treated as a coldly cognitive enterprise (Brown & Campione, 1990; Pintrich & Schrauben, 1992). That is, competence in reading, as with any demanding academic domain, is as much an investment of the spirit, as it is the mind (Alexander, 1997a; Alexander & Murphy, 1997; Paris & Cross, 1983). Children can have the requisite linguistic and metalinguistic knowledge, a conceptual framework, and a rich strategic repertoire. However, without a suitable goal (Nicholls, 1983), an interest in the topic or task at hand (Hidi, Baird, & Hildyard, 1982), a belief in themselves as learners (Bandura, 1993; Wylie, 1989), and a sense of self-control or self-determination (Deci & Ryan, 1991; Deci, Valleran, Pelletier, & Ryan, 1991), students may still never fully realize competence as readers. For this reason, the motivational dimensions of the reading process, including goal setting, individual interest, self-efficacy, and agency have garnered increasing attention in the literature (e.g., Guthrie, McCann, Hynd, & Stahl, in press; Guthrie, McGough, Bennett, & Rice, 1996; Pintrich & Schunk, 1996; Wigfield & Guthrie, 1997; Wigfield, & Karpathian, 1991).

1. Goals

There is a marked difference between *incidental* and *intentional* learning. Incidental learning is the spontaneous understanding that is reached in the course of everyday living and working, as when a child "discovers" that dogs and cats behave differently from observing these animals in their environs (Vygotsky, 1934/1986). Intentional learning, in contrast, "is an achievement resulting from the learner's purposeful, effortful, self-regulated, and active engagement" (Palincsar & Klenk, 1992, p. 212). In essence, intentional learning is goal-directed. It is evident that students engage in reading for many reasons (e.g., Schunk, 1991; Wigfield & Eccles, 1992; Wigfield & Harold, 1992). Sometimes a student's purpose is just to get the task done (Meece, Blumenfeld, & Hoyle, 1988). At other times, the goal may be to please those in authority or to look good to one's peers (Wentzel, 1991, 1993). There are also those students who operate under work avoidance goals (Meece & Holt, 1993); that is, trying to get by with the least amount of mental effort.

Of course, there are those learners who set out to learn all they can and to understand deeply. Overall, those who hold to such learning goals are more likely to achieve competence in reading than students with task completion, ego-social, or work avoidance goals (Dweck & Leggett, 1988). In their self-regulated strategy development (SRSD) model, Graham and Harris (1989) have purposefully incorporated a goal-setting component in their strategy training for students with LD. In this model, students with LD are helped to assess their reasons for engagement and to set realistic and positive goals for learning (Sawyer, Graham, & Harris, 1992). Graham and Harris (1989) found that this goal-setting component is essential for optimal acquisition and maintenance of students' strategic behavior.

2. Interest

Just as students' goals for reading can vary, so can the nature and intensity of the interest they show in the task before them. Hidi (1990) has used the term *text-based interests* to capture the type of interest that written materials might elicit in readers, as a consequence of the ideas, concepts, or portrayals they contain. In Hidi's estimation there are a variety of factors that contribute to the "interestingness" of a text, including its novelty or surprise. Likewise, Kintsch (1980) distinguished between emotional interest and cognitive interest with regard to text processing. Emotional interest deals with the feelings or reactions that a text can engender as a result of its inherent qualities, personal relatedness, or because of character identification. In this way, it relates to Hidi's concept of text-based interest. Cognitive interest, on the other hand, has more to do with stimulation of the readers' thinking than to their emotions.

Our own research (Alexander, 1997b; Alexander, Jetton, & Kulikowich, 1995; Garner, Brown, Sanders, & Menke, 1992; Garner, Gillingham, & White, 1989) has been concerned with two related characterizations of interest—situational interest and personal or individual interest. When students are situationally interested, they are drawn by aspects within the immediate situation, although the attraction is often fleeting (Hidi & Anderson, 1992; Schiefele, 1991; Wade, 1992). Schraw, Bruning, and Svoboda (1995) have identified several characteristics of situationally interesting texts. Those characteristics include ease of comprehension (i.e., how easy to remember), cohesion (i.e., its organization and clarity), vividness (i.e., its inclusion of exciting or vivid details), engagement (i.e., whether it is provocative or timely), emotiveness (i.e., whether it evokes strong emotions), and prior knowledge (i.e., its familiarity). The more of these characteristics a piece of text has, the more that students should find it situationally interesting.

There are also those enduring interests that readers carry with them from situation to situation and from text to text. These personal or individual interests can be related to students' vocations, or avocations. This form of interest is also in keeping with Dewey's (1913) notion of "motivating from within," and can become the catalyst for a reader's active pursuit of related knowledge and experiences. There is evidence that reader's personal interests are also associated with their knowledge, their goals, their willingness to exert strategic effort, and their persistence (Alexander, Kulikowich, & Schulze, 1994; Alexander, Murphy, Woods, Duhon, & Parker, 1997; Dweck & Leggett, 1988; Renninger, 1992). Moreover, when students have the opportunity to read texts that relate to their deep-seated interests, the influences of personally involving or potentially distracting or "seductive" (i.e., high interest/low importance) content is mitigated (Garner, Alexander, Gillingham, Kulikowich, & Brown, 1991).

Instructional programs that specifically attend to students' interests in an effort to build their literacy skills have reported marked improvements in students' reading and writing performance (Guthrie et al., 1996; Renninger & Wozniak, 1985). The framework for the Concept-Oriented Reading Instruction (CORI) program, developed by Guthrie et al. (1996), for example, begins with a concrete tangible experience (e.g., watching and documenting the transformation of caterpillars to butterflies). Students are then encouraged to identify and explore some personally important dimensions from that experience. Guthrie et al. have reported positive outcomes from the CORI program not only on students' reading and writing, but also their subject-matter knowledge and their motivations for reading.

3. Self-Efficacy and Agency

Achievement in reading cannot be attained *and* sustained unless the learner has a belief in his or her ability to process text competently. This is what Bandura (1977) and others (Bandura & Schunk, 1981; Schunk, 1990) refer to as self-efficacy. For many students with LD, difficulties in breaking the linguistic code, coupled with their placement in programs that stress decontextualized skills (McGill-Franzen & Allington, 1991), can have a detrimental effect on their feelings of efficacy. From these experiences, those identified as LD can derive nonoptimal expectations about their likelihood of success that can profoundly affect both the initiation and persistence of problem-solving behaviors (Borkowski, Carr, & Pressley, 1987).

Conditions within the regular classroom, such as social comparisons or academic competitions, can exacerbate the dilemma of low self-efficacy for students with reading difficulties (Ames, 1984). These students may come to feel that their learning difficulties are not malleable and outside of their control (Covington, 1985; Weiner, 1979). That is to say, these children's sense of agency or self-determination can be negatively impacted. *Agency* refers to the conception that individuals remain active agents in their learning (Deci & Ryan, 1991; Dworkin, 1988; Ryan, 1993). It is related to the notion of *self-determination*. When exhibiting self-determination, the student undertakes activities with a "full sense of wanting, choosing, and personal endorsement" (Deci, 1992, p. 44). Yet, if students feel that the circumstances are stable and beyond their control then they have no reason to demonstrate agency or self-determination.

The good news is that teachers can contribute to students' active, self-directed learning by creating meaningful and stimulating learning environments (e.g., Bereiter & Scardamalia, 1989; Brown & Campione, 1990; Brown & Palincsar, 1989; Cognition and Technology Group at Vanderbilt, 1990). In these environments, students are given opportunities to define their goals, to pursue their interests, and to take greater responsibility for their learning (e.g., Corno & Rohrkemper, 1985; deCharms, 1968; Zimmerman & Martinez-Pons, 1986, 1992). These effective learning environments, in effect, promote agency and self-determination among students. What is also positive news is that students tend to be more successful academically when they have the opportunity to pursue their own goals and interests (Amabile, 1983, 1990; Deci & Ryan, 1991). For this reason, these classroom communities that support agency among students, including those with LD, can also influence these learners' beliefs about their likelihood for continued success; that is, their self-efficacy (Harris, 1989; Sawyer et al., 1992).

In her study of classroom contexts that appear to motivate children's literacy for example, Turner (1995) found that open literacy tasks were the best predictors of first graders' motivations to engage. Turner defines open literacy tasks as those in which the children direct the instructional processes and specify the goals of learning. Open tasks are also sufficiently challenging to students and pertain to their interests. Under these instructional conditions, Turner found that the children used more reading strategies, persisted longer at the task, and were better able to control their attention regardless of other factors. Although Turner did not specifically address children with LD in this research, her instructional conditions seem consistent with those described by others in their work with students with LD (Harris & Graham, 1996; Pressley et al., 1992).

E. Summary

To become competent at the process of reading, students with LD must not only have the linguistic and metalinguistic abilities required to "break the code," but they must also possess a foundation of conceptual knowledge that brings meaningfulness to the print. Moreover, because reading is a demanding and complex undertaking, these students must come to the print with an arsenal of strategies that allow them to monitor and regulate themselves and their behaviors, as well as to remedy any gaps in their performance. Finally, these learners cannot truly realize competence in reading unless they believe that this end is within their grasp and have the goals, interests, and agency they need to sustain them on this developmental journey. Yet, competent reading is not the only academic aim for students with LD. These students must also have the ability and desire to apply the processes of reading to the building of a principled based of knowledge in other academic fields. Thus, we now turn to a consideration of "reading to learn."

III. READING FOR COMPETENCE: THE ACT OF KNOWLEDGE SEEKING

Achieving competence in reading is certainly a laudable goal for all students. Yet competence in reading is as much a means to an end as it is an end in and of itself. So much of the information that students need to attain competence in other academic fields, such as history, mathematics, or science, is accessible through the written word (Dole, Valencia, Greer, & Wardrop, 1991). Consequently, the ability and the willingness to locate, comprehend, and remember this information is critical for academic achievement. However, many students, including many identified as LD, never realize the success, to say nothing of the pleasure, that knowledge seeking through reading can afford. This may be due, in part, to the emphasis in classrooms on information getting (i.e., finding the answers to someone else's questions), rather than on knowledge seeking (i.e., search for knowledge for one's own purposes). This problem may be compounded by the limited guidance students receive in their efforts to seek knowledge.

Thus, even if they have the intention of building their understanding through text, students may not have the strategies for navigating through the sea of available information. This problem of informational navigation is exacerbated by the growing presence of nontraditional and nonlinear forms of written materials available to today's students, as in the form of hypermedia (Alexander, Kulikowich, & Jetton, 1994; Garner & Gillingham, 1996; Swanson & Trahan, 1992). So, what are the factors that contribute to individuals' desire and ability to build their understanding in academic domains and how do these factors relate to students with LD? Specifically, we want to explore several circumstances that seem especially relevant to the act of reading to learn: (a) understanding the forms and structures of text; (b) distinguishing more important from less important information; and (c) creating communities of knowledge seekers.

A. Understanding the Forms and Structures of Text

The texts that students encounter on a daily basis come in many forms and serve many purposes. Some texts have been written to tell a story. The label *narrative* is often applied to this class of written materials. The storybooks that children read are examples of narrative texts. Structurally, narratives often have generic elements that frame their stories, including characters, a setting, and a plot. These generic components have been referred to as story grammar (Mandler & Johnson, 1977; Trabasso, Secco, & van den Boek, 1984). Other texts seem primarily intended to inform the reader. The term *exposition* is typically used to designate this type of text. The textbooks that are used in many subject-matter classes are common examples of exposition found in schools. While the structure of exposition is less universal than for narratives and can vary from paragraph to paragraph, a few basic patterns reoccur. These patterns include description or simple listing; comparison/contrast; temporal sequencing; cause/effect; and problem/solution (Armbruster, 1984). Between these two categories of text, however, are a vast array of written materials that have characteristics both of narration and exposition. These have appropriately been called *mixed* texts (Hidi et al., 1982). Textbooks that include some storylike segments or biographies that have personally involving, storylike elements fit this category of mixed texts.

Understanding the various forms and structures of text can help students in their knowledge seeking by providing them with a global framework for identifying and managing their search. A number of research studies, including several targeting children with LD, have demonstrated the effectiveness of alerting students to these forms and structures (Dimino, Taylor, & Gersten, 1995; Englert & Mariage, 1990, 1991; Englert & Thomas, 1987; Griffin & Tulbert, 1995). Some researchers have recommended that students use these forms and structures as templates for organizing and summarizing information as they read. For example, Dimino et al. (1995) reviewed the research to ascertain the effectiveness of teaching students with LD about the common elements of narratives (i.e., story grammar). They determined that these students' comprehension was improved when they were explicitly taught a clear strategy for recognizing the generic components of narratives. Further, the researchers determined that students comprehended and recalled better when (a) these story grammar components were taught in an integrated fashion, (b) there was a gradual transfer of responsibility from the teacher to the student, and (c) specific attention was paid to self-monitoring. In another review, Griffin and Tulbert (1995) explored the utility of using graphic organizers for students with LD as they processed expository text. Overall, Griffin and Tulbert found that students trained to construct or use graphic organizers showed improved comprehension. This was true whether the graphic organizers were used prior to, during, or after reading.

Englert and colleagues (e.g., Englert & Mariage, 1990, 1991) have devised an instructional procedure known as POSSE to make the structure of expository text and children's prior knowledge central to classroom interactions. POSSE (i.e., predicting, organizing, searching, summarizing, and evaluating) draws heavily on reciprocal teaching (Palincsar & Brown, 1984) in the selection of reading strategies. As in reciprocal teaching, groups of students discuss and collaborate in sense making around expository text. Part of the instruction involves having students talk about and map common forms of expository text structures, including description, problem-solution, cause/effect, and compare/contrast. Englert and Mariage (1991) found that this instructional approach significantly improved the recall of expository text and the use of comprehension strategies among students with LD.

B. Distinguishing More Important from Less Important Information

Structure, however, does not refer solely to the global categories of text organization. It also entails that hierarchical structure of text segments that is formed from the distinction between main ideas, supporting ideas, and tangential information (Kintsch & van Dijk, 1978). The higher the segment is within this hierarchical structure, the more important it is held to be. Alexander and Jetton (1996) describe this distinction between more or less important content in text as *structural im-*

portance. There is ample evidence in the literature that many readers, including students with LD, have difficulty distinguishing between main ideas and details in what they read. This creates problems for them as they try to comprehend, organize, and remember what they process (Schellings, Van Hout-Wolters, & Vermunt, 1996).

Sometimes the "signaling" that authors insert in text can be a guide to readers who are attempting to separate the main concepts from less important or even irrelevant content (Meyer, Brandt, & Bluth, 1980). However, text is not always very considerate of readers (Armbruster, 1984) and can actually serve to lead less knowledgeable or skillful readers astray (Alexander & Jetton, 1996; Wade, 1992; Wade, Schraw, Buxton, & Hayes, 1993). Particularly during the 1980s, researchers devised various procedures to assist readers, including those with LD, to distinguish between main ideas and details and to construct summaries that reflect such differences (Baumann, 1984; Brown, Campione, & Day, 1981; Hare & Borchardt, 1984; Taylor & Beach, 1984).

What seems to add to these readers' problems in knowledge seeking is that there is frequently a divergence in what is important and what is interesting in text, especially for expository and mixed texts (Hidi et al., 1982). As we already noted, situational interest exerts a great deal of influence on readers, especially those who know little and care little about the topic at hand. Consequently, unless students have a strong base of relevant subject-matter knowledge when they read demanding exposition, they can find themselves drawn to information that is very interesting but structurally unimportant. Garner et al. (1989) have aptly labeled this phenomenon the "seductive detail" effect.

Alexander, Jetton, Kulikowich, and Woehler (1994) and Jetton and Alexander (1997) also found that conditions within the classroom may contribute to students' struggles to build a principled understanding from text. Specifically, what these studies determined was that teachers, especially those with less advanced subject-matter knowledge or pedagogical skills, give less structurally important information undue attention in their teaching and in their assessments. In effect, there were discrepancies between what was *structurally* important and what was *instructionally* important (Alexander et al., 1994; Schellings & Van Hout-Wolters, 1995). Further, when these two forms of importance were at odds, it was typically instructional importance that won out. The lesson for teachers, it would appear, is that they need to be sensitive to the power that their discussions and assessments have on students' learning and use that power to guide students toward relevant and important textual information.

C. Creating Communities of Knowledge Seekers

Beyond the conditions we have described, there appear to be two additional qualities of classroom communities that support students' knowledge seeking through text. The first is the opportunity for students to focus on complex and relevant problems that involve the search through a variety of linear and nonlinear text sources (Brown & Campione, 1990; Cognition and Technology Group at Vanderbilt, 1990; Guthrie et al., 1996). Nonlinear text sources are those associated with hypermedia, including videodisc technologies, e-mail, and the internet.

The second quality concerns students' collaboration and dialoguing around these intriguing and pertinent problems (Bereiter & Scardamalia, 1992; Garner, 1990, 1992; Palincsar & Klenk, 1992; Resnick, 1991). The on-line interactions between students around the theme of cultures, as promoted by the CSILE project (Bereiter & Scardamalia, 1989), or the creative hypermedia mathematical problem solving that results from the Jasper project (Cognition and Technology Group at Vanderbilt, 1990) build on both of these concerns. In effect, these classrooms seem to ignite and maintain student interests in learning and anchor instructional activities around demanding but personally relevant problems that link to the topic under study. Moreover, the students in these classrooms have occasions for self-determination and choice, and they are encouraged to share their thinking and learning with others who populate their community, as well as communities in distant locations (Bereiter & Scardamalia, 1989; Garner & Gillingham, 1996).

Some researchers suggest that collaborative groups be carefully orchestrated to reflect academic and cultural diversity (Slavin, 1987, 1991). Others seem more inclined to allow these groups to form naturally around shared interests and goals (Englert & Palincsar, 1991; Goldman & Newman, 1992; Torney-Purta, 1996). Regardless of such philosophical differences, advocacy for collaboration and dialoguing within classrooms is clearly on the rise and should be considered an essential component in reading for competence. With the call for inclusion in special educational programs, students with LD may have even more opportunities to engage in collaboration and dialoguing in classrooms. We see this as a positive trend.

D. Summary

Learning is a life-long undertaking and the ability to gain understanding through text is a significant aspect of that endeavor. In addition to the general dimensions that underlie competence in reading, such as linguistic knowledge, reading for competence involves a recognition that text comes in many forms and can serve many purposes. Competent learners have the ability to use the general structures of text to aid their pursuit of knowledge. They have also gained the ability to tell what is significant and relevant in text from information that is less important and irrelevant. Finally, knowledge seeking for all students is facilitated by creating communities where such an enterprise is valued and given prominence. In these communities, students with LD are actively, meaningfully, and collaboratively engaged in the pursuit of understanding of knowledge seekers, and see text in all its many forms as an avenue to that understanding.

IV. CONCLUDING THOUGHTS

In order to be considered educated in today's world, individuals must be able to read well. They must also be able to use their reading skills effectively to gain access to the wealth of knowledge that resides in text, whether that text is found in the pages of books or on-line. This is true for all students including those with LD. Still, it is clear that students with LD often find their journey toward competence more arduous than their peers without such disabilities. For this very reason, those dedicated to guiding the development of this special population must be even more diligent in their efforts to create learning environments that urge these students forward on the path toward competence in reading and in other academic domains. In short, they must chart an instructional course that aids students in developing the linguistic and metalinguistic knowledge, conceptual understanding, strategic abilities, and the motivation to learn that underlie competence in reading. Moreover, these educational guides must help students articulate their own aims in academic development. Finally, they must allow students, even those who may initially experience difficulties, reluctance, or trepidation, to become self-sufficient learners who sense the excitement and beauty of the journey toward understanding. Doubtless this will not be easy to accomplish, but the destination is unquestionably worth the effort.

References

Adams, M. J. (1990). *Beginning to reading: Thinking and learning about print.* Cambridge, MA: MIT Press.

Alexander, P. A. (1997a). Knowledge seeking and self-schema: A case for the motivational dimensions of exposition. *Educational Psychologist, 32,* 83–94.

Alexander, P. A. (1997b). Mapping the multidimensional nature of domain learning: The interplay of cognitive, motivational, and strategic forces. In M. L. Maehr & P. R. Pintrich (Eds.), *Advances in motivation and achievement* (Vol. 10, pp. 213–250). Greenwich, CT: JAI Press.

Alexander, P. A., Graham, S., & Harris, K. (in press). A perspective on strategy research: Pioneers and frontiers. *Educational Psychology Review.*

Alexander, P. A., & Jetton, T. L. (1996). The role of importance and interest in the processing of text. *Educational Psychology Review, 8*(1), 89–122.

Alexander, P. A., Jetton, T. L., & Kulikowich, J. M. (1995). Interrelationship of knowledge, interest, and recall: Assessing a model of domain learning. *Journal of Educational Psychology, 87,* 559–575.

Alexander, P. A., Jetton, T. L., Kulikowich, J. M., & Woehler, C. (1994). Contrasting instructional and structural importance: The seductive effect of teacher questions. *Journal of Reading Behavior, 26,* 19–45.

Alexander, P. A., & Judy, J. E. (1988). The interaction of domain-specific and strategic knowledge in academic performance. *Review of Educational Research, 58,* 375–404.

Alexander, P. A., Kulikowich, J. M., & Jetton, T. L. (1994). The role of subject-matter knowledge and interest in the processing of linear and nonlinear texts. *Review of Educational Research, 64,* 201–252.

Alexander, P. A., Kulikowich, J. M., & Schulze, S. K. (1994). How subject-matter knowledge affects recall and interest on the comprehension of scientific exposition. *American Educational Research Journal, 31,* 313–337.

Alexander, P. A., & Murphy, P. K. (in press, a). The research base for APA's learner-centered principles. In B. L. McCombs & N. Lambert (Eds.), *Issues in school reform: A sampler of psychological perspectives on learner-centered schools.* Washington, DC: The American Psychological Association.

Alexander, P. A., & Murphy, P. K. (in press, b). What cognitive psychology has to say to school psychology: Shifting perspectives and shared purposes. In C. R. Reynolds & T. B. Gutkin (Eds.), *The handbook of school psychology* (3rd ed.). New York: John Wiley & Sons.

Alexander, P. A., Murphy, P. K., Woods, B. S., Duhon, K. E., & Parker, D. (1997). College instruction and concomitant changes in students' knowledge, interest, and strategy use: A study of domain learning. *Contemporary Educational Psychology, 22,* 125–146.

Alexander, P. A., Schallert, D. L., & Hare, V. C. (1991). Coming to terms: How researchers in learning and literacy talk about knowledge. *Review of Educational Research, 61,* 315–343.

Amabile, T. M. (1983). *The social psychology of creativity.* New York: Springer-Verlag.

Amabile, T. M. (1990). With you, without you: The social psychology of creativity, and beyond. In M. A. Runco & R. S. Albert (Eds.), *Theories of creativity* (pp. 61–91). Newbury Park, CA: Sage Publications.

Ames, C. (1984). Achievement attributions and self-instructions under competitive and individualist goal structures. *Journal of Educational Psychology, 76,* 478–487.

Anderson, R. C., Pichert, J. W., & Shirey, L. L. (1983). Effects of reader's schema at different points in time. *Journal of Educational Psychology, 75,* 271–279.

Anderson, R. C., Reynolds, R. E., Schallert, D. L., & Goetz, E. T. (1977). Frameworks for comprehending discourse. *American Educational Research Journal, 14,* 367–381.

Armbruster, B. B. (1984). The problem of "inconsiderate text." In G. G. Duffy, L. R. Roehler, & J. Mason (Eds.), *Comprehension instruction: Perspectives and suggestions* (pp. 202–217). New York: Longman.

Austin, M. C., & Morrison, C. (1963). *The first R: The Harvard report on reading in elementary schools.* New York: Macmillan.

Baker, L. (1984a). Children's effective use of multiple standards for evaluating their comprehension. *Journal of Educational Psychology, 76,* 588–597.

Baker, L. (1984b). Spontaneous versus instructed use of multiple standards for evaluating comprehension: Effects of age, reading proficiency, and type of standard. *Journal of Experimental Child Psychology, 38,* 289–311.

Baker, L. (1985). How do we know when we don't understand? Standards for evaluating text comprehension. In D. L. Forrest-Pressley, G. E. MacKinnon, & T. G. Waller (Eds.), *Metacognition, cognition, and human performance,* Vol. 1. (pp. 155–205). Orlando, FL: Academic Press.

Baker, L., & Zimlin, L. (1989). Instructional effects on children's use of two levels of standards for evaluating their comprehension. *Journal of Educational Psychology, 81,* 340–346.

Bandura, A. (1977). Self-efficacy: Toward a unifying theory of behavioral change. *Psychological Review, 84,* 191–215.

Bandura, A. (1993). Perceived self-efficacy in cognitive development and functioning. *Educational Psychologist, 28,* 117–148.

Bandura, A., & Schunk, D. H. (1981). Cultivating competence, self-efficacy, and intrinsic interest through proximal self-motivation. *Journal of Personality and Social Psychology, 45,* 1017–1028.

Baumann, J. F. (1984). The effectiveness of a direct instruction paradigm for teaching main idea comprehension. *Reading Research Quarterly, 20,* 93–115.

Bereiter, C., & Scardamalia, M. (1989). Intentional learning. In L. B. Resnick (Ed.), *Knowing, learning, and instruction: Essays in honor of Robert Glaser* (pp. 361–392). Hillsdale, NJ: Lawrence Erlbaum Associates.

Borkowski, J. G. (1992). Metacognitive theory: A framework for teaching literacy, writing, and math skills. *Journal of Learning Disabilities, 25,* 253–257.

Borkowski, J. G., Carr, M., & Pressley, M. (1987). "Spontaneous" strategy use: Perspectives from metacognitive theory. *Intelligence, 11,* 61–75.

Brown, A. L., Armbruster, B., & Baker, L. (1986). The role of metacognition in reading and studying. In J. Oransanu (Ed.), *Reading comprehension: From research to practice* (pp. 49–75). Hillsdale, NJ: Lawrence Erlbaum Associates.

Brown, A. L., & Campione, J. S. (1990). Communities of learning and thinking, or a context by any other name. *Contributions to Human Development, 21,* 108–126.

Brown, A. L., Campione, J. S., & Day J. D. (1981). Learning to learn: On training students to learn from texts. *Educational Researcher, 10,* 14–21.

Brown, A. L., Collins, A., & Duguid, P. (1989). Situated cognition and the culture of learning. *Educational Researcher, 18*(1), 32–42.

Brown, A. L., & Day, J. D. (1983). Macrorules for summarizing texts: The development of expertise. *Journal of Verbal Learning and Verbal Behavior, 22,* 1–14.

Brown, A. L., & Palincsar, A. S. (1989). Guided cooperative learning and individual knowledge acquisition. In L. B. Resnick (Ed.), *Knowing and learning: Issues for a cognitive psychology of learning. Essays in honor of Robert Glaser* (pp. 393–451). Hillsdale, NJ: Lawrence Erlbaum Associates.

Carr, S. C., & Thompson, B. (1996). The effects of prior knowledge and schema activation strategies on the inferential reading comprehension of children with and without learning disabilities. *Learning Disability Quarterly, 19,* 48–61.

Cognition and Technology Group at Vanderbilt. (1990). Anchored instruction and its relationship to situated cognition. *Educational Researcher, 19*(6), 2–10.

Corno, L., & Rohrkemper, M. (1985). The intrinsic motivation to learn in classrooms. In C. Ames & R. Ames (Eds.), *Research on motivation in education: The classroom milieu* Vol. 2 (pp. 53–84). New York: Academic Press.

Covington, M. V. (1985). Strategic thinking and the fear of failure. In J. W. Segal, S. F. Chipman, & R. Glaser (Eds.), *Thinking and learning skills,* Vol. 1, (pp. 389–416). Hillsdale, NJ: Lawrence Erlbaum Associates.

deCharms, R. (1968). *Personal causation: The internal affective determinants of behavior.* New York: Academic Press.

Deci, E. L. (1992). The relation of interest to the motivation of behavior: A self-determination theory perspective. In K. A. Renninger, S. Hidi, & A. Krapp (Eds.), *The role of in-*

terest in learning and development (pp. 43–70). Hillsdale, NJ: Lawrence Erlbaum Associates.

Deci, E. L., & Ryan, R. M. (1985). *Intrinsic motivation and self-determination in human behavior.* New York: Academic Press.

Deci, E. L., & Ryan, R. M. (1991). A motivational approach to self: Integration in personality. In R. Dienstbier (Ed.), *Nebraska symposium on motivation, 1990* (pp. 237–288). Lincoln, NE: University of Nebraska Press.

Deci, E. L., Valleran, R. J., Pelletier, L. G., & Ryan, R. M. (1991). Motivation and education: The self-determination perspective. *Educational Psychologist, 26,* 325–346.

Dewey, J. (1913). *Interest and effort in education.* Boston: Riverside.

Dimino, J. A., Taylor, R. M., & Gersten, R. M. (1995). Synthesis of the research on story grammar as a means to increase comprehension. *Reading and Writing Quarterly: Overcoming Learning Disabilities, 11,* 53–72.

Diveta, S. K., & Speece, D. L. (1990). The effects of blending and spelling training on the decoding skills of young poor readers. *Journal of Learning Disabilities, 23,* 579–582.

Dole, J. A., Duffy, G. G., Roehler, L. R., & Pearson, P. D. (1991). Moving from the old to the new: Research on reading comprehension instruction. *Review of Educational Research, 61,* 239–264.

Dole, A. J., Valencia, S. W., Greer, E. A., & Wardrop, J. L. (1991). Effects of two types of prereading instruction on the comprehension of narrative and expository text. *Reading Research Quarterly, 26,* 142–159.

Dweck, C. S., & Leggett, E. L. (1988). A social-cognitive approach to motivation and personality. *Psychological Review, 95,* 256–273.

Dworkin, G. (1988). *The theory and practice of autonomy.* New York: Cambridge University Press.

Ehri, L. C. (1989). The development of spelling and its role in reading acquisition and reading disability. *Journal of Learning Disabilities, 22,* 356–364.

Ehri, L. C., & Wilce, L. S. (1985). Movement into reading: Is the first stage of printed word learning visual or phonetic? *Reading Research Quarterly, 20,* 163–177.

Elliott-Faust, D., & Pressley, M. (1986). How to teach comparison processing to increase children's short and long-term listening comprehension monitoring. *Journal of Educational Psychology, 78,* 27–33.

Englert, C. S., & Mariage, T. V. (1990). Send for the POSSE: Structuring the comprehension dialogue. *Academic Therapy, 25,* 473–487.

Englert, C. S., & Mariage, T. V. (1991). Making students partners in the comprehension process: Organizing the reading "posse." *Learning Disability Quarterly, 14,* 123–138.

Englert, C. S., & Palincsar, A. S. (1991). Reconsidering instructional research in literacy from a sociocultural perspective. *Learning Disabilities Research and Practice, 6,* 225–229.

Englert, C. S., & Thomas, C. C. (1987). Sensitivity to text structure in reading and writing: A comparison between learning disabled and non-learning disabled students. *Learning Disability Quarterly, 10,* 93–108.

Garner, R. (1987). *Metacognition and reading comprehension.* Norwood, NJ: Ablex.

Garner, R. (1990). When children and adults do not use learning strategies: Toward a theory of settings. *Review of Educational Research, 60,* 517–529.

Garner, R. (1992). Self-regulated learning, strategy shifts, and shared expertise: Reactions to Palincsar and Klenk. *Journal of Learning Disabilities, 25,* 226–229.

Garner, R., & Alexander, P. A. (1989). Metacognition: Answered and unanswered questions. *Educational Psychologist, 24,* 143–148.

Garner, R., Alexander, P. A., Gilingham, M. G., Kulikowich, J. M., & Brown, R. (1991). Interest and learning from text. *American Educational Research Journal, 28,* 643–659.

Garner, R., Brown, R., Sanders, S., & Menke, D. J. (1992). "Seductive details" and learning from text. In K. A. Renninger, S. Hidi, & A. Krapp (Eds.), *The role of interest in learning and development* (pp. 239–254). Hillsdale, NJ: Lawrence Erlbaum Associates.

Garner, R., & Gillingham, M. G. (1996). *Conversations across time, space, and culture.* Mahwah, NJ: Lawrence Erlbaum Associates.

Garner, R., Gillingham, M. G., & White, C. S. (1989). Effects of "seductive details" on macroprocessing and microprocessing in adults and children. *Cognition and Instruction, 6,* 41–57.

Glaser, R. (1984). Education and thinking: The role of knowledge. *American Psychologist, 39,* 93–104.

Goldman, S. V., & Newman, D. (1992). Electronic interactions: How students and teachers organize schooling over wires. *Interactive Learning Environments, 2*(1), 31–44.

Goswami, U. (1988). Orthographic analogies in learning to read: A developmental study. *Journal of Experimental Child Psychology, 42,* 73–83.

Graham, S., & Harris, K. R. (1989). Components analysis of cognitive strategy instruction: Effects on learning disabled students' composition and self-efficacy. *Journal of Educational Psychology, 81,* 353–361.

Griffin, C. C., & Tulbert, B. L. (1995). The effect of graphic organizers on students' comprehension and recall of expository text: A review of the research and implications for practice. *Reading and Writing Quarterly: Overcoming Learning Disabilities, 11,* 73–89.

Guthrie, J. T., McCann, A., Hynd, C., & Stahl, S. (in press). Classroom contexts promoting literacy engagement. In J. Flood, S. B. Heath, & D. Lapp (Eds.), *Handbook for literacy educators: Research on teaching the communications and visual arts.* New York: Macmillan.

Guthrie, J. T., McGough, K., Bennett, L., & Rice, M. E. (1996). Concept-oriented reading instruction: An integrated curriculum to develop motivations and strategies for reading. In L. Baker, P. Afflerbach, & D. Reinking (Eds.), *Developing engaged readers in school and home community* (pp. 165–190). Mahwah, NJ: Lawrence Erlbaum Associates.

Hare, V. C., & Borchardt, K. M. (1984). Direct instruction of summarization skills. *Reading Research Quarterly, 20,* 62–78.

Harris, K. R. (1989, March). *The role of self-efficacy in self-instructional strategy training and the development of self-regulated learning among learning disabled children.* Paper presented at the annual meeting of the American Educational Research Association, San Francisco.

Harris, K. R. (1996, April). *The state of strategy research: Is this old territory or are there new frontiers?* Symposium presented at the annual meeting of the American Educational Research Association, New York.

Harris, K. R., & Graham, S. (1996). *Making the writing process work: Strategies for composition and self-regulation.* Cambridge, MA: Brookline.

Hidi, S. (1990). Interest and its contribution as a mental resource for learning. *Review of Educational Research, 60,* 549–571.

Hidi, S., & Anderson, V. (1992). Situational interest and its impact on reading and expository writing. In K. A. Renninger, S. Hidi, & A. Krapp (Eds.), *The role of interest in learning and development* (pp. 215–238). Hillsdale, NJ: Lawrence Erlbaum Associates.

Hidi, S., Baird, W., & Hildyard, A. (1982). That's important but is it interesting? Two factors in text processing. In A. Flammer & W. Kintsch (Eds.), *Discourse processing* (pp. 63–75). Amsterdam: North-Holland.

Jetton, T. L., & Alexander, P. A. (1997). Instructional importance: What teachers value and what students learn. *Reading Research Quarterly, 32,* 290–308.

Judy, J. E., Alexander, P. A., Kulikowich, J. M., & Willson, V. L. (1988). Effects of two instructional approaches and peer tutoring on gifted and nongifted sixth graders' analogy performance. *Reading Research Quarterly, 23,* 236–256.

Kintsch, W. (1980). Learning from text, levels of comprehension, or: Why anyone would read a story anyway. *Poetics, 9,* 87–89.

Kintsch, W., & van Dijk, T. A. (1978). Toward a model of text comprehension and production. *Psychological Review, 85,* 363–394.

Lovett, M. W., Warren-Chaplin, P. M., Ransby, M. J., & Borden, S. L. (1990). Training the word recognition skills of reading disabled children: Treatment and transfer effects. *Journal of Educational Psychology, 82,* 769–780.

Mandler, J. M., & Johnson, N. S. (1977). Remembrance of things parsed: Story structure and recall. *Cognitive Psychology, 9,* 111–151.

Markman, E. M. (1981). Comprehension monitoring. In W. P. Dickson (Ed.), *Children's oral communication skills* (pp. 61–84). New York: Academic Press.

Mathes, P. G., Fuchs, D., Fuchs, L., Henley, A. M., & Sanders, A. (1994). Increasing strategic reading practice with Peabody classwide peer tutoring. *Learning Disabilities Research and Practice, 9,* 44–48.

McGill-Franzen, A., & Allington, R. L. (1991). The gridlock of low reading achievement: Perspectives on practice and policy. *Remedial and Special Education, 12*(3), 20–30.

Meece, J. L., Blumenfeld, D. C., & Hoyle, R. H. (1988). Students' goal orientation and cognitive engagement in classroom activities. *Journal of Educational Psychology, 80,* 514–523.

Meece, J. L., & Holt, K. (1993). A pattern analysis of students' achievement goals. *Journal of Educational Psychology, 85,* 582–590.

Meichenbaum, D. (1977). *Cognitive behavior modification: An integrative approach.* New York: Plenum Press.

Meichenbaum, D., & Asarnow, J. (1979). Cognitive behavior modification and metacognitive development: Implications for the classroom. In P. C. Kendall & J. D. Hollon (Eds.), *Cognitive-behavioral interventions: Therapy, research, and procedures* (pp. 11–35). New York: Academic Press.

Meyer, B. J., Brandt, D. H., & Bluth, G. J. (1980). Use of author's textual schema: Key for ninth-graders' comprehension. *Reading Research Quarterly, 16,* 72–103.

Minsky, M. (1986). *The society of mind.* New York: Simon and Schuster.

Moore, D., & Zabrucky, K. (1989). Verbal reports as measures of comprehension evaluation. *Journal of Reading Behavior, 21,* 295–307.

Nicholls, J. G. (1983). Conceptions of ability and achievement motivation: A theory and its implications for education. In S. G. Paris, G. M. Olson, & H. W. Stevenson (Eds.), *Learning and motivation in the classroom* (pp. 211–237). Hillsdale, NJ: Lawrence Erlbaum Associates.

Palincsar, A. S., & Brown, A. L. (1984). Reciprocal teaching of comprehension-fostering and monitoring activities. *Cognition and Instruction, 1,* 117–175.

Palincsar, A. S., & Klenk, L. (1992). Fostering literacy learning in supportive contexts. *Journal of Learning Disabilities, 25,* 211–225, 229.

Paris, S. G., & Cross, D. R. (1983). Ordinary learning: Pragmatic connections among children's beliefs, motives, and actions. In J. Bisanz, G. L. Bisanz, & P. Kail (Eds.), *Learning in children: Progress in cognitive development research* (pp. 137–169). New York: Springer-Verlag.

Paris, S. G., & Myers, M. (1981). Comprehension monitoring, memory, and study strategies of good and poor readers. *Journal of Reading Behavior, 13,* 5–22.

Perfetti, C. A. (1985). Reading ability. In R. J. Sternberg (Ed.), *Human abilities: Information-processing approach* (pp. 59–81). New York: W. H. Freeman.

Perfetti, C. A., & Lesgold, A. M. (1979). Coding and comprehension in skilled reading and implications for reading instruction. In L. B. Resnick & P. A. Weaver (Eds.), *Theory and practice of early reading,* Vol. 1 (pp. 57–84). Hillsdale, NJ: Lawrence Erlbaum Associates.

Pintrich, P. R., & Schrauben, B. (1992). Students' motivational beliefs and their cognitive engagement in classroom academic tasks. In D. Schunk & J. Meece (Eds.), *Student perceptions in the classroom* (pp. 149–183). Hillsdale, NJ: Lawrence Erlbaum Associates.

Pintrich, P. R., & Schunk, D. H. (1996). *Motivation in education: Theory, research, and applications.* Englewood Cliffs, NJ: Prentice Hall.

Pressley, M., Brown, R., El-Dinary, P. B., & Afflerbach, P. (1995). The comprehension instruction that students need: Instruction fostering constructively responsive reading. *Learning Disabilities Research & Practice, 10,* 215–224.

Pressley, M., El-Dinary, P. B., Gaskins, I., Schuder, T., Bergman, J., Almasi, L., & Brown, R. (1992). Beyond direct explanation: Transactional instruction of reading comprehension strategies. *Elementary School Journal, 92,* 511–554.

Pressley, M., Harris, K. R., & Marks, M. B. (1992). But good strategy instructors are constructivists! *Educational Psychology Review, 4,* 3–31.

Pressley, M., Johnson, C. J., Symons, S., McGoldrick, J. A., & Kurita, J. A. (1989). Strategies that improve memory and comprehension of what is read. *Elementary School Journal, 90,* 3–32.

Renninger, K. A. (1992). Individual interest and development: Implications for theory and practice. In K. A. Renninger, S. Hidi, & A. Krapp, (Eds.), *The role of interest in learning and development* (pp. 361–395). Hillsdale, NJ: Lawrence Erlbaum Associates.

Renninger, K. A., & Wozniak, R. H. (1985). Effect of interest on attentional shift, recognition, and recall in young children. *Developmental Psychology, 21,* 624–632.

Resnick, L. B. (1991). Shared cognition. In L. B. Resnick, J. M., Levine, & S. D. Teasley (Eds.), *Perspectives on socially shared cognition* (pp. 1 –20). Washington, DC: American Psychological Association.

Rosenblatt, L. M. (1978). *The reader, the text, the poem: The transactional theory of the literary work.* Carbondale, IL: Southern Illinois University Press.

Rumelhart, D. E. (1980). Schemata: The building blocks of cognition. In R. J. Spiro, B. C.

Bruce, & W. F. Brewer (Eds.), *Theoretical issues in reading comprehension* (pp. 33–58). Hillsdale, NJ: Lawrence Erlbaum Associates.

Ryan, R. M. (1993). Agency and organization: Intrinsic motivation, autonomy, and the self in psychological development. In J. Jacobs (Ed.), *Nebraska symposium on motivation,* Vol. 40 (pp. 1–56). Lincoln, NE: University of Nebraska Press.

Sawyer, R. J., Graham, S., & Harris, K. R. (1992). Direct teaching, strategy instruction, and strategy instruction with explicit self-regulation: Effects on the composition skills and self-efficacy of students with learning disabilities. *Journal of Educational Psychology, 84,* 340–352.

Schellings, G. L. M., & Van Hout-Wolters, B. H. A. M. (1995). Main points in an instructional text, as identified by student and by teachers. *Reading Research Quarterly, 30,* 742–756.

Schellings, G. L. M., Van Hout-Wolters, B. H. A. M., & Vermunt, J. D. (1996). Selection of main points in instructional texts: Influence of task demands. *Journal of Literacy Research, 28,* 355–378.

Schiefele, U. (1991). Interest, learning, and motivation. *Educational Psychologist, 26,* 229–323.

Schraw, G., Bruning, R., & Svoboda, C. (1995). Sources of situational interest. *Journal of Reading Behavior, 27,* 1–17.

Schunk, D. (1991). Self-efficacy and academic motivation. *Educational Psychologist, 26,* 207–231.

Slavin, R. E. (1987). Grouping for instruction in the elementary school. *Educational Psychologist, 22,* 109–128.

Slavin, R. E. (1991). Neverstreaming: Prevention and early intervention as an alternative to special education. *Journal of Learning Disabilities, 24,* 373–378.

Snider, V. E. (1989). Reading comprehension performance of adolescents with learning disabilities. *Journal of Learning Disabilities, 25,* 618–629.

Stahl, S. A., Hare, V. C., Sinatra, R., & Gregory, J. F. (1991). Defining the role of prior knowledge and vocabulary in reading comprehension. The retiring of number 41. *Journal of Reading Behavior, 23,* 487–508.

Sternberg, R. J. (1985). But it's a sad tale that begins at the end: A reply to Glaser. *American Psychologist, 40,* 571–573.

Swanson, H. L. (1991). Operational definitions and learning disabilities: An overview. *Learning Disability Quarterly, 14,* 242–254.

Swanson, H. L., & Berninger, V. (1995). The role of working memory in skilled and less skilled readers' comprehension. *Intelligence, 21,* 83–108.

Swanson, H. L., & Ramalgia, J. M. (1992). The relationship between phonological codes on memory and spelling tasks for students with and without learning disabilities. *Journal of Learning Disabilities, 25,* 396–407.

Swanson, H. L., & Trahan, M. F. (1992). Learning disabled readers' comprehension of computer mediated text: The influence of working memory, metacognition, and attribution. *Learning Disabilities Research and Practice, 7,* 74–86.

Talbott, E., Lloyd, J. W., & Tankersley, M. (1994). Effects of reading comprehension interventions for students with learning disabilities. *Learning Disability Quarterly, 17,* 223–232.

Taylor, B. M., & Beach, R. W. (1984). The effects of text structure instruction on middle-grade students' comprehension and production of expository text. *Reading Research Quarterly, 19,* 134–146.

Torgeson, J. K. (1982). The learning disabled child as an inactive learner: Educational implications. *Topics in Language and Learning Disabilities, 2,* 45–51.

Torney-Purta, J. (1996). Conceptual change among adolescents using computer networks and peer collaboration in studying international political issues. In S. Vosniadou, E. D. Corte, & H. Mandl (Eds.), *International perspectives on the design of technology-supported learning environments* (pp. 203–219). Mahwah, NJ: Lawrence Erlbaum Associates.

Trabasso, T., Secco, T., & van den Boek, P. (1984). Causal cohesion and story coherence. In H. Mandl, N. L. Stein, & T. Trabasso (Eds.), *Learning and comprehension of text* (pp. 83–111). Hillsdale, NJ: Lawrence Erlbaum Associates.

Turner, J. C. (1995). The influence of classroom contexts on young children's motivation for literacy. *Reading Research Quarterly, 30,* 410–441.

Vygotsky, L. (1986). *Thought and language.* A. Kozulin (Trans.). Cambridge, MA: MIT Press. (Original work published in 1934)

Wade, S. E. (1992). How interest affects learning from text. In K. A. Renninger, S. Hidi, & A. Krapp (Eds.), *The role of interest in learning and development* (pp. 255–277). Hillsdale, NJ: Lawrence Erlbaum Associates.

Wade, S. E., Schraw, G., Buxton, W. M., & Hayes, M. T. (1993). Seduction of the strategic reader: Effects of interest on strategies and recall. *Reading Research Quarterly, 28,* 93–114.

Wagner, D. A., Spratt, J. E., Gal, I., & Paris, S. G. (1989). Reading and believing: Beliefs, attributions, and reading achievement in Moroccan schoolchildren. *Journal of Educational Psychology, 81,* 283–293.

Wagner, R. K., & Torgeson, J. K. (1987). The nature of phonological processing and its casual role in the acquisition of reading skills. *Psychological Bulletin, 101,* 192–212.

Weiner, B. (1979). A theory of motivation for some classroom experiences. *Journal of Educational Psychology, 71,* 3–25.

Wentzel, K. R. (1991). Relations between social competence and academic achievement in early adolescence. *Child Development, 62,* 1066–1078.

Wentzel, K. R. (1993). Social and academic goals at school: Motivation and achievement in early adolescence. *Journal of Early Adolescence, 13,* 4–20.

Wigfield, A. (1997). Reading motives: A domain-specific approach to motivation. *Educational Psychologist, 32,* 59–68.

Wigfield, A., & Eccles, J. (1992). The development of achievement task values: A theoretical analysis. *Developmental Review, 12,* 265–310.

Wigfield, A., & Guthrie, J. T. (1997). Relations of children's motivation for reading to the amount and breadth of their reading. *Journal of Educational Psychology, 89,* 420–432.

Wigfield, A., & Harold, R. D. (1992). Teacher beliefs and children's achievement self-perceptions: A developmental perspective. In D. H. Schunk & J. L. Meece (Eds.), *Student perceptions in the classroom* (pp. 95–121). Hillsdale, NJ: Lawrence Erlbaum Associates.

Wigfield, A., & Karpathian, M. (1991). Who am I and what can I do? Children's self-concepts and motivation in achievement situations. *Educational Psychologist, 26*(3 & 4), 233–261.

Wong, B. Y. L. (1989). Musing about cognitive strategy training. *Intelligence, 13,* 1–4.

Wylie, R. C. (1989). *Measures of the self-concept.* Lincoln, NE: University of Nebraska Press.

Zaragoza, N., & Vaughn, S. (1992). The effects of process writing instruction on three 2nd-grade students with different achievement profiles. *Learning Disabilities Research and Practice, 7,* 184–193.

Zimmerman, B. J. (1989). A social cognitive view of self-regulated academic learning. *Journal of Educational Psychology, 81,* 329–339.

Zimmerman, B. J., & Martinez-Pons, M. (1986). Development of a structured interview for assessing student use of self-regulated learning strategies. *American Educational Research Journal, 23,* 614–628.

Zimmerman, B. J., & Martinez-Pons, M. (1992). Perceptions of efficacy and strategy use in the self-regulation of learning. In D. H. Schunk & J. L. Meece (Eds.), *Student perceptions in the classroom* (pp. 185–207). Hillsdale, NJ: Lawrence Erlbaum Associates.

CHAPTER 11

Reading, Spelling, and Writing Disabilities in the Middle Grades

Louisa C. Moats

I. READING DIFFICULTIES ARE WIDESPREAD AND DEBILITATING

Reading failure, in the view of researchers at the National Institutes of Child Health and Human Development (NICHD), constitutes not only an urgent challenge for our schools, but a public health problem with major consequences and costs (Alexander, 1996; Lyon, 1995a). To this end, the NICHD has spent over $120 million in research over the last 5 years to understand not only the causes but the consequences of reading problems and related cognitive, academic, social, behavioral, and emotional difficulties. It has become clear on the basis of longitudinal research that once students fall behind in the language-based skills of reading and writing, they usually do not catch up or become fluent readers unless intensive, expert help is available to them (Lyon, 1996; Torgesen, Wagner, Rashotte, Alexander, & Conway, 1997). About 80% of children who are behind in reading by the end of first grade are still significantly behind grade level by the fourth grade unless they receive specialized instruction (Juel, 1994; Lyon & Chhabra, 1996). The evidence is strong that these children become frustrated and drop out at higher rates than their classmates (Alexander, 1996). Because the social and economic consequences of reading failure are legion, schools have every justification for investing resources to reverse the tide of reading failure once students reach the middle grades.

How common is reading failure in the fourth grade? According to the 1994 National Assessment of Educational Progress, the only nation-wide test on which we can base such estimates in the United States, 44% of fourth graders read at "below basic" levels. This means they demonstrated little or no mastery of knowledge and skills necessary to perform work at each grade level. Only about 5–6% of these children should legitimately be classified as having severe, intrinsically based learning disorders (LD) (Lyon, 1996; Torgesen et al., 1997; Vellutino, Scanlon, Sipay, Small, Pratt, Chen, & Denckla, 1996). The others are likely to be suffering the consequences of inappropriate teaching, low standards, and/or disadvantageous environmental circumstances for learning to read.

Although these statistics can seem bleak, there is good news for educators: most cases of reading failure can be prevented or alleviated with early and sustained intervention that employs the lessons from research. Most reading problems do respond to preventive and appropriate treatment. The timing of intervention, however, is critical to related outcomes; the earlier children learn to read, the more likely it is that schooling will mitigate the effects of socioeconomic, racial, or cultural disadvantage. The longer problems go untreated, the lower the rate of success and the more time and effort are involved in reversing the course of failure (Lyon, 1996).

The cumulative effects of proficient and unproficient reading have been measured as early as beginning first grade. Children who read well by the end of first grade are exposed to far more text than children who read poorly. The better children read and the earlier children read, the more they will be exposed to new vocabulary and the richness of academic language in literature and textbooks (Cunningham & Stanovich, 1991). The advantages of this verbal exposure accumulate rapidly.

When children do not read well, their general knowledge, spelling ability, and vocabularies all suffer from lack of exposure to text and restricted experience with language. By the fourth grade, unless the teacher is very well trained, equipped, dedicated, and resourceful, children are repeatedly exposed to materials and assignments that are too difficult for them. Reading and writing become unrewarding experiences that lead to avoidance and lack of involvement, and certainly to reduced independent reading and writing (Cunningham & Stanovich, 1991; Stanovich, 1986, 1992). By fourth grade, students may have concluded beyond doubt that they are incapable of learning and often have become invested in avoiding, covering up, or compensating for their problems. In Stanovich's terms, the rich get richer and the poor get poorer, at least as far as reading is concerned (Stanovich, 1986). The middle-grade teacher is then faced with the challenge of remediating a reading disability and helping the student compensate for the cumulative deficits in vocabulary, background knowledge, language comprehension, writing, and study skills that have arisen from the core deficit in basic reading skill—that is, if the student is still invested in learning.

II. COMPONENTS OF READING AND READING DISABILITY

A large body of replicated, scientifically sound research has been conducted over the last 25 years that explains the nature of reading acquisition and the psycholinguistic and cognitive differences between good and poor readers. The research base for understanding reading disabilities consists of replicated findings from controlled studies that use sophisticated methodology to ensure the findings can be generalized or applied to a well-defined group of individuals (Adams, Treiman, & Pressley, 1996; Lyon & Chhabra, 1996). These studies have emanated from education and fields beyond education, including cognitive psychology, educational psychology, neuropsychology, medicine, and developmental psycholinguistics. Although no one would disagree that the purpose of reading is to gain meaning from print, and that reading is not simply the act of decoding the words, many studies have been devoted to the question of how important each of these basic functions is to reading. Given that 20% of the adult population in the United States is functionally illiterate (reading below the fourth-grade level) and more do not have the literacy skills to perform in the workplace (U.S. Office of Technology Assessment, 1993) learning to read is clearly not a natural skill for many individuals (Adams, Treiman, & Pressley, 1996). The nature of that difficulty and the effortful process many students experience as they learn to read is now understood far better than 20 years ago.

In a "simple view," reading is the product of decoding and comprehension (Gough, Juel, & Griffith, 1992). Decoding, or the ability to decipher the words represented by print, is certainly not the whole of reading. Comprehension—the ability to use background knowledge and linguistic knowledge to make sense out of a message—takes place in addition to ciphering or mapping the print onto speech. Each of these important domains, of course, can be further parsed into subskills and the interactions among those studied. However, these two basic domains of processing are quite distinguishable in reading: a person may be significantly more proficient at one component than the other.

For the beginning reader, no matter what the person's age, the first and most important task is learning to decipher the print with sufficient ease and fluency that meaning can be accessed. Reading for meaning depends on being able to read the words on the page. The necessity of decoding accuracy and fluency in proficient reading at all levels has been resoundingly confirmed by multiple studies (see reviews in Adams, 1990; Adams, Treiman, & Pressley, 1996; Gough, Ehri, & Treiman, 1992; Rayner & Pollatsek, 1989; Rieben & Perfetti, 1991; Vellutino & Scanlon, 1991). In addition, research has converged across disciplines and methodologies to demonstrate that critical prerequisite abilities enable children to learn word recognition skills. The most pivotal of those abilities is phonological sensitivity, for children and adults (Adams, 1990; Ball, 1993, 1994; Kamhi & Catts, 1989; Liberman, Shankweiler, & Liberman, 1989; Shankweiler, Lundquist, Dreyer, & Dickinson, 1996; Stanovich & Siegel, 1994).

The relationship between decoding and comprehension in accounting for overall reading skill changes as reading develops. If decoding is mastered, it becomes less of an issue in reading success. In the beginning stages, word identification is the major task of learning to read (Foorman, Francis, Shaywitz, Shaywitz, & Fletcher, 1997; Vellutino & Scanlon, 1991). Reasoning and comprehension skills are not nearly as important to beginning reading success as they become later in reading development. By the fourth-grade reading level, however, a child's overall reading score is accounted for much more by the child's comprehension capability—that is, if the child has learned to recognize separate words with proficiency. Although the vast majority of poor readers in the middle grades show persistent deficits in word recognition, another subgroup emerges for the first time with problems in comprehension of academic language. That subgroup of children learn the code easily enough, but they are not sufficiently familiar with word and text meaning to enter into the "reading to learn" phase without considerable additional instruction. Because reading is composed of decoding *and* comprehension skills, reading instruction in the middle grades must foster word recognition *and* the comprehension of text, ideally with an integrated, interesting approach.

A. What Distinguishes a Proficient Reader?

Good readers tend to develop phoneme awareness early and with relatively little effort (see the summaries in Adams, et al., 1996; Ball, 1993; Brady & Shankweiler, 1991). Good readers know, either implicitly or explicitly, how the letters in a printed word correspond to the sounds in the word, and if asked, can identify those relationships on a sound-by-sound basis (Share & Stanovich, 1995). Even though good readers appear to read words automatically or to process large "chunks" of print when they read, they can do this because they are able to rapidly and automatically associate phonemes or individual speech sounds with print units. Fluent reading is not, as might appear, propelled by semantic or syntactic processing of words in peripheral vision or by anticipatory guessing (see reviews by Adams, 1990; Adams, et al., 1996; Rayner & Pollatsek, 1989; Rieben & Perfetti, 1991; Share & Stanovich, 1995). Good readers develop automaticity, or the ability to read words as wholes with little conscious effort, and thus have available the cognitive resources needed to focus on comprehension. They are more likely, then, to be familiar with the language of text and to have better vocabularies.

B. Characteristics of Poor Readers in the Intermediate Grades

Poor readers at any age are characterized by overreliance on context and guessing strategies to read (Adams, 1990; Perfetti, 1995; Share & Stanovich, 1995). They do not *prefer* to guess at what words say, but rather they use guessing as a default strategy when the symbol-to-sound associations cannot be deciphered with accuracy or fluency. At the root of reading and spelling disability in the large majority of cases is limited phoneme awareness (Lyon, 1995a, 1995b; Share & Stanovich, 1995; Shaywitz, 1996). Although the great majority of students who do not learn to read easily have a primary problem with phonic decoding and fluent word identification, some students are characterized by a very slow rate of word recognition or naming speed. Those children are too dysfluent to make sense of what they read. Others have pronounced problems with short-term memory that cause great inconsistency in learning (Brady, 1991). Reading-disabled children at the intermediate level often become frustrated and avoidant unless they are making steady progress and are protected from inappropriate assignments. Not all poor readers have similar characteristics, however; there is individual variation in the associated symptoms that accompany a core deficit in linguistic processing (Share & Stanovich, 1995; Shaywitz, 1996).

Research in reading disorders is challenging because of the frequent coexistence of other developmental difficulties in children who read poorly. According to Lyon's recent summary of the NICHD work on classification and prevalence of childhood LD (Lyon, 1996), children with reading disabilities are twice as likely as other children to meet the diagnostic criteria for an attention deficit disorder (15% vs. 7%). Similarly, an individual with an attentional disorder is twice as likely as a member of the general population to demonstrate phonologically based reading problems (36% vs. 17%). Children with coexisting attentional and reading problems are more difficult to treat successfully. Boys are affected with attentional disorders three to four times more often than girls, although girls are affected with reading problems as frequently as boys. Boys, however, are referred for special services about four times more often than girls, most likely because their attentional and behavioral problems arouse their teachers' concern. For both sexes, reading difficulties are commonly associated with other weaknesses in language-related skills, as well as increasing problems with social, behavioral, and emotional adjustment. The overlap among conditions and the lack of clear definitional guidelines for some disorders constitute one of the greatest challenges for researchers investigating the many remaining questions regarding interventions for reading and writing disabilities (Lyon & Moats, 1997).

C. Dyslexia

The term *dyslexia* is accepted among reading scientists for individuals who have constitutionally based, unexpected difficulty learning to read and spell because of weaknesses in phonological processing and related language abilities (Lyon, 1995a,b; Shaywitz, 1996). The 20% prevalence rate for dyslexia is determined somewhat arbitrarily (Shaywitz, Escobar, Shaywitz, Fletcher, & Makuch, 1992) by selecting a point on the continuum of reading ability that seems to coincide with evidence for real-world functional impairment. Again, more children are affected by this disorder than are eligible for special education, and many must have their needs met through classroom-based programming. Within the population of children with diagnosed LD, however, at least 80% have a primary weakness in reading, and almost all of those have related deficits in spelling and writing. The core linguistic problem in dyslexia is quite unrelated to intelligence; that is why many very bright children cannot read well, and many children with intellectual ability below average are able to read. The reason the term *dyslexia* is preferred by many professionals is that it describes the broad-based "difficulty with words" that is manifest in spelling, formulation of ideas, vocabulary acquisition, ability to pronounce words, writing, and general language proficiency.

The relationship between phonological processing, reading, and spelling is a very close and interdependent one. As noted above, specific tests of the ability to detect and manipulate the syllables and individual speech sounds in words are among the most powerful markers of reading ability and disability at all ages. Phonological ability is highly heritable (Pennington, 1995); at the same time, it is modifiable through experience and instruction, even in older students. Children in the intermediate grades continue to show deficits in the ability to compare the sounds in words and analyze them on tests such as the Lindamood Auditory Conceptualization Test (Lindamood & Lindamood, 1979). For example, they may confuse similar words such as *Pacific* and *specific* or mispronounce words such as *simular* without awareness that their production is different from the target, or they may be unable to detect what speech sounds are omitted from a word they have attempted to spell. Most importantly, children may not benefit from instruction in phonics or spelling until they are phonemically aware, because the sound–symbol mapping instrinsic in an alphabetic writing system may remain a mystery to them. Children must realize that the segments of their own speech are represented by print before they can decode or spell reliably.

D. The Manifestations of Reading Disabilities in Older Students

The manifestations of dyslexia or specific reading disability change as children progress in their skill acquisition, although the core deficit in phonology, perception of language structure, and decoding persists to adulthood (Shankweiler et al.,

1996). In the middle grades, children may have acquired rudimentary word recognition and sound–symbol knowledge, but are likely to be slow, inaccurate, or inconsistent in the application of that knowledge. On a standardized test that allows comparison between word recognition and comprehension skills, they are typically lower in word recognition, especially nonsense word reading. They may continue to show weaknesses in related phonological skills, including recall of lists and facts, pronunciation of words, recall of names, and awareness of the individual sound segments in complex syllables. They may be able to use context to some extent to comprehend passages, but their comprehension will be limited by their inefficient recognition of the many content words that are vital for carrying meaning.

Children with persistent phonologically based problems will be very poor spellers, and their spelling will be marked by obvious deviations in representation of phonemes. Written language may be very constrained and marked by multiple spelling errors, little or no use of punctuation, inability to write in complete sentences, and poor elaboration of ideas. More specifically, speech sounds will often be omitted in consonant clusters or unaccented syllables, endings will be confused or left off, and sounds will be confused with one another (Moats, 1995). If the student reaches a third-grade level of spelling or more, errors are also likely to show poor internalization of other language structures, including syllable types and morphemes, such as compounds and derived words.

A subgroup of middle-grade students will have learned phonic decoding, but their reading will be marked by dysfluency or lack of automaticity. They will continue to try and sound out every word when they should be recognizing larger print units more rapidly. The inefficiency and labored quality of their reading is usually associated with avoidance, lack of persistence, and fatigue in carrying out written work. With these individuals, spelling tends to be phonetically accurate or decipherable, with fewer errors of speech sound confusion, omission or substitution, and more errors of orthographic representation—getting the right letters for the sounds (see Figure 11.1).

In this writing sample many kinds of linguistic confusions are evident that exemplify the nature of a specific reading/writing disability (dyslexia) in a sixth-grade student of high intellectual ability. Speech sound substitutions that represent poor differentiation of phoneme features include ATRUG/attracted (voicing confusion of /g/ and /k/) and LIVING/leaving (confusion of vowel placement). The liquid sound /r/ is left out when it occurs after a vowel and before a consonant as in SHAK/shark and STOM/storm. Word boundaries are not clear (ONA; BADSTOM). The grammatical morphemes called inflections are omitted in WAVE/waves, SHARK/sharks, KILL/killed, and ATRUG/attracted, and spelled phonetically in ROST/rushed. Command of sentence structure is limited to simple sentences strung together with "and," with little elaboration of descriptive or narrative elements. Letter formation difficulties include B/D substitutions, mixing of upper and lower case, and confusion of manuscript and cursive.

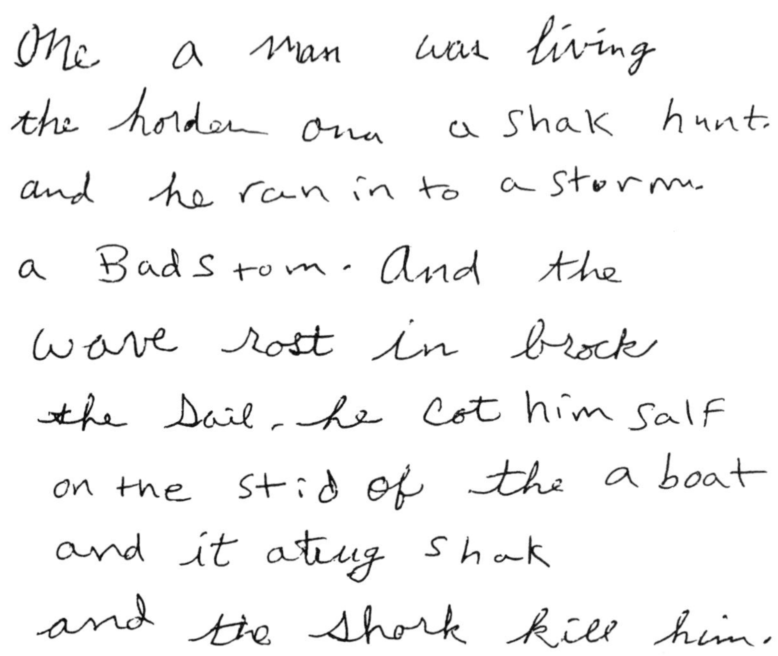

One a man was living the holder ona a shak hunt. and he ran in to a storm. a Badstom. And the wave rost in brock the sail. he cot him salf on the stid of the a boat and it ateug shak and the shork kill him.

Figure 11.1 Writing of a fourth-grade boy with dyslexia.

As this example illustrates, specific reading and writing problems in otherwise competent students are characterized by multiple difficulties with language processing at the levels of orthography, phonology, syntax, and morphology. Effective remediation, then, must address all levels of language organization in a deliberate, systematic fashion, using validated instructional principles.

III. COMPONENTS OF EFFECTIVE REMEDIATION

Unfortunately, the field of reading instruction as it pertains to both the regular classroom and special education programs has been polarized between those who assert that code-based instruction is best and those who assert that code-based instruction is harmful or unnecessary (McPike, 1995). This debate has been mirrored among researchers in LD who have argued variously for and against approaches that teach alphabetic coding and phonological skills. In the community of reading researchers who use scientific methodology, however, there is broad agreement that effective instructional programs at any level should include a number of interrelated components (Adams, 1990; Beck & Juel, 1995; Stanovich, 1994; Vellutino et al., 1996). Each of these components should be taught explicitly and systematically, albeit in a thematically unified way that relates skills to interesting text. The components include phonological awareness, letter recognition and formation, sound–symbol connections, opportunities to practice decoding in controlled texts, vocabulary building with an emphasis on word structure and morphology, instruction in comprehension strategies, and motivational techniques to foster independent reading (Foorman, Francis, Beeler, Winikates, & Fletcher, 1997; Torgesen et al., 1997; Vellutino et al., 1966).

Recent research on remediation with middle-grade poor readers has highlighted the necessity for informed, deliberate instruction in the language skills, which are most likely to cause the reading failure. Those pivotal skills that often require more attention and expertise in teaching the poor reader are phoneme analysis, sound–symbol decoding, fluency in word recognition and text reading, and the use of comprehension strategies. Spelling and writing skills are even more challenging to develop. The best programs teach each of these components explicitly, deliberately, and actively (Gaskins, Ehri, Cress, O'Hara, & Donnelly, 1996; Tunmer & Hoover, 1992; Vellutino, 1991). Balance in each day's lesson and in the overall program is achieved by apportioning instructional time for all the major elements of language arts, even for those children with more severe LD.

Given the need for comprehensiveness and balance in any reading program, the key finding in recent intervention studies is that the core phonological and linguistic deficits in reading disability cannot be successfully bypassed with "visual" teaching strategies. Contrary to earlier conceptions of LD (see Lyon & Moats, 1988, and Moats & Lyon, 1993, for historical overviews), results of well-designed studies are quite consistent in showing that direct work on the core deficit has the best chance of success with the most students. Although it has never been shown that one program is best for all learners, or that any program is equally successful with everyone, researchers have documented excellent gains in students receiving appropriate programming.

If instruction is complete and theoretically sound, intermediate grade children can achieve significant success. Lovett and her associates (Lovett, Borden, Lacerenza, Benson, & Brackstone, 1994) obtained strong gains in 35 hours of intensive instruction with 9-year-old children who were taught sound segmentation and blending for word decoding. Alexander, Anderson, Heilman, Voeller, and Torgesen (1991) gave 65 hours of intensive teaching to ten 10-year-old children with severe phonologically based LD and raised their standard score in phonic word attack from 77 to 98 (average). The approach emphasized direct, intensive, in-depth training in phonology and decoding.

Torgesen and his co-workers (1997) reporting the results of 2 years of an intervention study with poor readers who have weak phonological abilities, have demonstrated the power of intensive intervention in reversing the course of reading failure. Children already classified as having LD ($n = 31$), average age 10 years, entered the study with very poor phonological skills and reading skills at least 1.5 standard deviations below average. The progress of two groups was compared, when each group received teaching for 2 hours per day, 5 days a week, for 8 weeks. The first group was taught with the Lindamoods' Auditory Discrimination in Depth (Lindamood & Lindamood, 1984) approach, which stimulates phonological awareness by helping children discover the manner in which sounds are articulated. Self-reliance in making judgments of the identity, number, and sequence of speech sounds in words is emphasized. The program also provides direct instruction in sound–symbol correspondence and the application of those correspondences to reading and spelling. The second intensive program was an embedded phonics approach that also taught decoding but that emphasized the use of context clues to support phonic strategies, the recognition of sight words, the discovery of sounds in known words, and fluent reading of text.

Both groups made dramatic gains in phonic word attack and real-word reading, scoring at or close to grade level in these skills. Within groups, however, there was considerable variability in response to the intensive interventions. Some children progressed rapidly and dramatically; others progressed very slowly and seem to be among the very few students whose problems are intractable. The study will continue for several more years, collecting information about the long-term effects of these intensive approaches on variables such as fluent text reading, reading habits, and reading comprehension. How well the gains in word reading are maintained and what is needed to help the children generalize them to fluent, independent reading are still being investigated. Eighty hours of instruction were not enough to "cure" the more severe cases of phonologically based reading disability.

IV. PRINCIPLES OF INSTRUCTION

A. Phonological Skill and Phoneme Awareness

The ability to recognize words in print develops in stages or phases, but rests on a foundation of phoneme awareness (Ehri, 1994). Children may learn to recognize a limited vocabulary of whole words through incidental cues (Gough et al., 1992), but do not become proficient readers without attaining insight into the idea that the alphabet represents the segments in their own speech.

Phonemes are *sounds,* not letters. Phonemes exist in all languages: only some languages use alphabetic symbols or graphemes to represent them. Most of the world's existing languages have no writing, and many of those use logographic, ideographic, or syllabic writing systems. Phonemic writing is a late evolutionary achievement in human history; therefore it should not be surprising that phoneme awareness is unnatural for many students and that it requires direct instruction.

Phoneme awareness is best taught with explicit reference to the organization of the speech sound system. The vowel sounds in English, 15 common phonemes, can be arranged by place of articulation—high to low, front to back. Unfortunately, English has only six letters to represent vowel spellings (*a, e, i, o, u, y*), with the extra help of *w* in combinations. If phonic symbols are used to represent the phonemes, diacritical marks or vowel team spellings are necessary to represent the sounds. Figure 11.2 shows the vowel sounds in order by place of articulation.

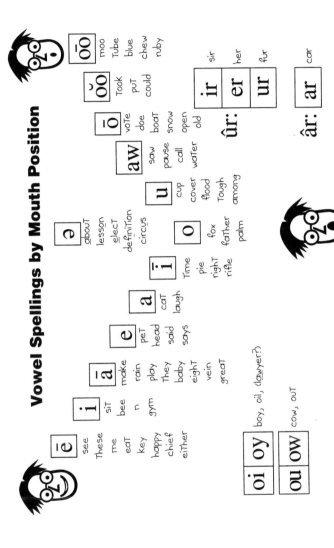

Figure 11.2 Vowel spellings by mouth position. Copyright © 1997 Comprehensive Reading Leadership Program (AB 3482).

	lips	lips/ teeth	tongue between teeth	tongue behind teeth	roof of mouth	back of mouth	throat
stop	/p/ /b/			/t/ /d/		/k/ /g/	
nasal	/m/			/n/		/ng/	
fricative		/f/ /v/	/th/ /th/	/s/ /z/	/sh/ /zh/		
affricate					/ch/ /j/		
glide						/y/	/wh/ /w/	/h/
liquid				/l/ /r/			

Figure 11.3   American English consonants. Copyright © 1997 Comprehensive Reading Leadership Program (AB 3482).

The diphthongs and r-controlled vowels are listed separately because they do not fit on the vowel chart. This chart can be used to clarify for students the sound, feel, appearance, spelling, and identity of the vowels.

English has 25 basic consonant sounds that also can be classified by place and manner of articulation (Figure 11.3). We also have too few letters to represent the consonants and must use letter combinations for some of the sounds. There are nine pairs of consonants that differ only in voicing, a critical feature that is sometimes difficult for students to perceive unless their attention is directly drawn to this feature. Some of the most effective approaches to instruction for older students teach the sounds by their articulatory features (quiet sound; noisy sound; nosey sound; windy sound, etc.).

B. Principles for Teaching Decoding

Awareness of individual sounds and the letters that represent them facilitates learning and remembering sight words (Ehri, 1994; Share & Stanovich, 1995). Thus, learning a sight vocabulary is not a separate skill but one that is definitely bolstered by knowing phonics. The rapid, fluent processing of larger units of print such as syllable patterns, meaningful roots, suffixes, and whole words occurs as a consequence of insight into the alphabetic principle and knowledge of sound–symbol correspondences. Learning the code well is an indispensable, unavoidable part of learning to read print with proficiency and must be part of any effective program in the middle grades if children are falling behind.

It has been known for some time that explicit classroom instruction that points to and teaches units of speech–print correspondence without waiting for children to intuit or discover them on their own, gets better results for more children more rapidly than nonexplicit or contextual approaches (Adams & Bruck, 1995; Chall, 1983; Foorman et al., in press; Torgesen et al., 1997; Tunmer & Hoover, 1992; Vellutino et al., 1996; Williams 1991) when such instruction is part of a comprehensive, balanced program. Many children can learn to recognize and use the code if instruction emphasizes pieces of syllables (onsets and rimes) or word families (Gaskins et al., 1996; Olson, Wise, Ring, & Johnson, 1997). However, these same studies emphasize that some children must have explicit teaching at the individual sound–symbol level to progress and cannot learn unless each element is established in memory like a brick in a foundation.

Effective teaching of the code enables children to gain access to meaning in print and to do so in the most efficient manner. Study of the sound–symbol system need not be boring; children can enjoy exploring words and discovering that they trust their word recognition skills. Effective instruction leads to insight about language structure that may generalize to other language activities, such as distinguishing similar vocabulary items, recognizing words by analogy, and recognizing word relationships. The principles include the following:

1. Model and practice.
2. Teach sound-symbol links directly, systematically, explicitly, and sequentially (scope and sequence is necessary).
3. Include phoneme awareness in beginning lessons.
4. Clarify the identity of sounds and symbols with labels.
5. Emphasize active, vocal response.
6. Teach high-frequency words as well as regular patterns.
7. Promote generalization: integrate skills into context.
8. Check for fluent application.

Proficient decoding permits comprehension of text, although many children will not automatically comprehend just because they can read the words. Various cognitive skills are involved in comprehension, which also need to be taught directly to children who do not "get the message" with ease.

C. Fluency and Automaticity

Like a child who rides a bike too slowly to keep it upright, a reader who reads too slowly will lose the meaning. Although the initial stages of reading for many students require sequential learning of skills, ample practice of those skills, and continual application of those skills, automaticity in word recognition must be acquired for meaning to be accessed.

Children vary in the amount of practice that is required for automaticity and fluency in reading to occur. Some need to read a word only once to recognize it again with greater speed; others need more than 20 exposures. The average child needs between 4 and 14 exposures to automatize recognition of a new word; children with LD may need up to 40 exposures to remember a new word. Therefore, it is vital that students read a large amount of text at their independent reading level, and that the text provides specific practice in the skills being learned (Beck & Juel, 1995; Samuels, Schermer, & Reinking, 1992). Reading simultaneously, rereading familiar material, alternate oral reading, and reading many books by the same writer are ways to build fluency. Brief 2-minute drills, if they are not overdone, to underline or locate a target word, syllable, or spelling pattern in an array can also be helpful in building automaticity.

D. Principles for Teaching Vocabulary

When middle-grade students do not read well, vocabulary must be taught through oral reading, oral discussion, or supported word study. Most of the words children need to know are encountered through text, not through casual conversation, television, or listening to adults talk, so reading to children often is critically important even in the middle grades. Reading aloud from material above grade level can help compensate for the gap that increases daily between the good readers and the poor readers in knowledge of "textbook" language. From fourth grade, knowledge of specific word meanings determines most of the variance in passage comprehension. Instruction should emphasize the relationships among words, not simply their definitions, and provide practice comparing word meanings, categorizing, and using words actively. Dictionary use should be encouraged as soon as children are able to read the guide words.

E. Comprehension

There is a sizable literature on the importance of teaching comprehension skills directly (Pressley et al., 1992). Many poor readers do not comprehend well because they do not know vocabulary meanings and do not read words with sufficient fluency; others do not have the experience with text organization and syntax to digest meanings. All of these skills need to be taught to students using validated strategies.

In teaching middle-grade students with reading difficulties, the teacher needs to be mindful of including comprehension instruction in the lessons even though the child may be progressing slowly with word recognition. The most critical skills for comprehension are the ability to summarize, predict, question, and clarify; these are learned best through active dialogue among students, overt modeling by the teacher, and explicit teaching of the component skills to be practiced in text reading (Adams, et al., 1996).

F. Spelling

The primary goal of spelling instruction should be to instill in the student the logic and organization of the spelling system. Words should represent patterns the student has already studied for reading, but include some "outlaw" words that must be memorized using multisensory tracing, writing, and saying techniques. Students with disabilities may need to study fewer words per week than other children, but the most important adaptation in their instruction should be the selection of words that are at the appropriate level of difficulty (Morris, Blanton, Nowacek, & Pierney, 1995). Spelling instructional level can be judged by using a developmental inventory of orthographic knowledge (Templeton & Bear, 1992).

Purposeful spelling instruction asks the student to identify the sounds and syllable patterns in words, examine orthographic patterns closely, notice the details of their structure, and look for patterns that work in the spelling system. Writing to dictation, if not overdone, provides needed practice and review of previously learned material. Learned words should then be used in many purposeful writing activities so that habits are developed for the words most often used in writing (see Moats, 1995, for full discussion of spelling). Instructional principles to maintain in instruction include the following:

1. Active study: sorting, dialogue, word building
2. Organized, systematic progression
3. Multisensory practice: see, say, feel, write
4. Emphasis on language structure (sounds, syllables, morphemes)
5. Frequent opportunities to write
6. Incentives to apply spelling in composition

Purposeful spelling instruction need not be passive, rote, or silent. Instruction that engages students in exploration of word relationships can involve parsing, comparison, and sorting of words into groups and discussion of word form. If children appreciate why words are spelled with certain letters, syllable patterns, and meaningful parts, they are more likely to notice and remember analogous constructions and avoid common errors. They are more likely to look for the sense in word form, and such insight generalizes to vocabulary and reading skill. Children must, in addition, practice memorization of some high-frequency irregular spelling words, gradually introduced a few at a time. Spelling instruction must afford children ample practice writing learned words in many contexts and incentives for children to proofread and correct their work.

Even with these techniques, middle-grade students with severe reading and writing difficulties are likely to need protection from unfair grading practices that overemphasize correct spelling in first drafts. Spelling is the most difficult literacy skill to develop in children with dyslexia, so expectations for improvement must be modest.

G. Written Expression

Even though students with specific reading difficulties struggle with handwriting, spelling, and composing, communicative writing can be expected of them from the outset. Initially, written expression may need to be accomplished through dictation or partnering with a student who can transcribe words. Students with writing disabilities may need extensive practice with sentence construction before they feel comfortable with more open-ended assignments. Questions, statements, exclamations, and imperatives can be learned, along with strategies for elaborating a subject and predicate. Reluctant writers may feel more secure if they are first given a mold to pour their words into and explicit models of what is required of them (Calfee, Chambliss, & Beretz, 1991). Providing structure need not stifle creativity and may bolster writing confidence. Most of all, structure or a framework for writing sentences and paragraphs gives students a scaffold on which to rest their ideas and relief from the complexity of this multidimensional language skill.

V. EXEMPLARY PROGRAMS FOR THE MIDDLE GRADES

A. *Language!*

Language! (Greene, 1995, 1996) is described as "the opposite of whole language" by its author. It is designed to be a comprehensive language study curriculum that employs direct concept teaching within a sequential, cumulative format. It teaches the elements of language at all levels, building from the parts to the whole, using deductive strategies. The complete *Language!* program can take up to 3 years to teach and can be the basis for an alternative language arts program in the middle grades. Each unit includes the following strands: phoneme awareness, decoding and encoding isolated words; varieties of word structures; reading sentences, paragraphs, and passages for meaning; understanding and using figurative language; applying principles of composition; pragmatic language use; abstract language interpretation; the grammatic structures of English and their interrelationships; the idioms and collocations of English; punctuation, capitalization, and mechanics in writing; morphology; vocabulary expansion; and expository and narrative writing. The instructional program is supplemented by a series of readers designed to provide practice in the skills being learned. The material is thematically appealing for middle-grade and high school level students.

In a pilot study, the *Language!* program was delivered to 45 adjudicated students between the ages of 13 and 17 for 22 weeks (Greene, 1996). A comparison group of 50 students, also assigned to programs for juvenile offenders, did not receive the program. Students in both groups were predominantly African American. Highly significant gains were recorded in oral reading rate and accuracy, reading comprehension, spelling, and word identification in the treatment group, with increases averaging about three grade levels over the 6 months of teaching. Standard scores in reading were 92 for the treatment group in word reading and 96 in comprehension (average), up from 74 and 82, respectively.

B. The Wilson Reading System

The Wilson Reading System (Wilson, 1996) reviewed in Clark and Uhry (1995) is another that was designed specifically for older students with significant reading problems. Based on Orton-Gillingham instructional principles, it is designed to teach language structure and basic reading using multisensory, cumulative, sequential techniques. It emphasizes the syllable as the basic unit for decoding and spelling. Sound associations are taught to automaticity and applied in reading decodable text, and there is constant review and practice in skills previously taught. The regularities of English orthography and the predictable patterns of language in general are emphasized from the beginning so that students can rely on their own knowledge to decipher unknown words in text.

Six basic syllable types are taught, including open, closed, r-controlled, vowel-consonant-e, vowel team, and consonant-le. As students read words, they scoop under the syllables instead of dividing them so that left-to-right progression is reinforced. A marking system is taught for classifying syllables before they are sounded. Tapping out words and spelling sounds on the fingers reinforce phonological awareness. Ample supplementary materials include sound and word cards; passages for dictation; and controlled vocabulary passages and stories for reading.

Although the Wilson Reading System has not been formally tested in a highly controlled study, the authors have collected their own efficacy data that reflect very strong gains by students in the program. Data were gathered on 220 student–teacher pairs, including 92 students in grades 3–4 and 128 in grades 5–12. All students had progressed poorly in other programs and were at least 2 years behind grade level. In 1 year, the average gain in these students was 4.5 grade levels in word attack and 1.5 grade levels in reading comprehension using the Woodcock Reading Mastery test.

C. The Lindamoods' Auditory Discrimination in Depth

Auditory Discrimination in Depth (Lindamood & Lindamood, 1979) and its companion program, Visualizing and Verbalizing, are designed by a former linguist and a speech pathologist, Charles and Patricia Lindamood, and their colleague, Nanci Bell. The program teaches the development of auditory conceptualization, which is the ability to identify the form, number, and sequence of speech sounds in words. With the goal of helping students become self-reliant in their judgments of sounds, the program teaches explicit labeling of articulatory gestures. Information about speech sounds is linguistically accurate and detailed; letter symbols are eventually introduced but not before students have learned to conceptualize the segments of speech by their place and manner of production. Spelling by sound is practiced before the emphasis turns to reading. Reading comprehension is enhanced by sequential, cumulative development of concept imagery in the Visualizing and Verbalizing program.

As cited above, several studies have yielded impressive results with severely disabled poor readers in the middle grades who received intensive tutorial instruction with Auditory Discrimination in Depth (ADD) (Alexander et al., 1991; Olson et al., in press; Torgesen et al., 1997). The techniques can also be modified for small groups in classrooms and even for whole class instruction. Training and preparation in the theory and techniques of the program are, however, essential for the practitioner. The Lindamood-Bell center is located in San Luis Obispo, California, but trainings are given in different locations nationally.

D. Words

For classroom use with poor readers and for a tutorial word study curriculum, Marcia Henry's Words and Patterns for Reading and Spelling (Henry, 1988; Henry & Redding, 1996) are also well conceived. They are organized around the layers of language that were preserved in English orthography (Figure 11.4). Designed for middle-grade instruction, the program teaches regular phonograms and syllable types but emphasizes the Latin and Greek layers of English morphology. Activities refer often to the texts students are using for reading.

E. Project Read

Project Read's Linguistics Kit, Comprehension Kit, and Written Expression Kit were designed by Mary Lee Enfield and Tori Greene (1996) to be delivered in the regular classroom by either mainstream or reading teachers. The programs teach the structure of English to students with language learning problems at the levels of sounds, words, sentences, and text organization. Systematic, direct, multisensory strategies are employed throughout the strands to make abstract language con-

	Sound	Syllable	Morpheme
Anglo-Saxon	**Consonants** - single - blends - digraphs **Vowels** - short/long - r-controlled - teams - diphthongs	6 types: closed open r-controlled c-le vowel team vce	compounds inflections
Romance (Latin)			prefixes suffixes roots plurals
Greek	y = /l/ *gym* ch = /K/ *chorus* ph = /f/ *sphynx*		**Combining forms** (scientific vocab.) (micro + meter) (psych + ology) **Plurals:** crises

Figure 11.4 Word study curriculum. Copyright © 1997 Comprehensive Reading Leadership Program (AB 3482).

cepts concrete. In Bloomington, Minnesota, where the programs have been implemented on a preventive basis with 25% of children in grades 1–3 and 12–15% of children in grades 4–6, only 1.8% of the population is coded as LD and the district's dropout rate has decreased from 13.8% to an average of 2% over the last 5 years (Enfield & Greene, 1996). Mainstream Project Read is far less expensive than special education pull-out models of service. More than 20 years of implementation in various cities have yielded similar data to support the program's effectiveness.

VI. CONCLUSION

No doubt, too many children are failing to learn to read in the primary grades. Their numbers exceed the most generous estimates of those who should qualify for special services as having LD. Their presence in our intermediate classrooms constitutes a challenge for mainstream educators as well as special educators.

Middle-grade children who cannot read or write well are not beyond help. Intensive, well-designed intervention that addresses the core linguistic deficits underlying reading failure has been shown to salvage most children, even if their early instruction was inadequate. Many children with phonological deficits, the largest group of those who read poorly, can respond to daily one-on-one instruction that is sustained for long enough periods. The instruction must be comprehensive, continuous, and inclusive of all the major components of reading (phoneme awareness, phonic decoding, fluency in text reading, vocabulary, comprehension, spelling, composition, related language concepts) to have the best chance of success. But the success of even the best designed program is highly dependent on the knowledge and the skill of the teacher, who must be well trained in a specific approach and supported in its implementation (Moats & Lyon, 1996).

Reading disabilities are not "mild" disorders. They are persistent, debilitating, and cumulative in their effects. Every major societal problem we face is greatly exacerbated by reading failure. It behooves us to provide informed, intensive teaching even in the middle grades when it is not too late to save young lives.

References

Adams, M. (1990). *Beginning to read: Thinking and learning about print.* Cambridge, MA: MIT press.

Adams, M. J., & Bruck, M. (1995). Resolving the 'Great Debate.' *American Educator, 19* (20), 7, 10–20.

Adams, M. J., Treiman, R., & Pressley, M. (1997). Reading, writing, and literacy. In I. Sigel & A. Renninger (Eds.), *Handbook of child psychology, Volume 4: Child psychology in practice* (pp. 275–276). New York: Wiley.

Alexander, A., Anderson, H., Heilman, P. C., Voeller, K. S., & Torgesen, J. K. (1991). Phonological awareness training and remediation of analytic decoding deficits in a group of severe dyslexics. *Annals of Dyslexia, 41,* 193–206.

Alexander, D. (1996). Learning disabilities as a public health concern. In S. Cramer & W. Ellis (Eds.), *Learning disabilities: Lifelong issues* (pp. 249–253) Baltimore: Paul H. Brookes.

Ball, E. (1993). Assessing phoneme awareness. *Language, Speech, and Hearing Services in the Schools, 24,* 130–139.

Beck, I., & Juel, C. (1995). The role of decoding in learning to read. *American Educator, 19* (8), 21–25, 39–42.

Brady, S. A. (1991). The role of working memory in reading disability. In S. A. Brady & D. P. Shankweiler (Eds.), *Phonological processes in literacy: A tribute to Isabelle Y. Liberman* (pp. 129–152). Hillsdale, NJ: Lawrence Erlbaum.

Brady, S. A., & Shankweiler, D. P. (Eds.) (1991). *Phonological processes in literacy: A tribute to Isabelle Y. Liberman* (pp. 129–152). Hillsdale, NJ: Lawrence Erlbaum.

Calfee, R., Chambliss, M., & Beretz, M. (1991). Organizing for comprehension and composition. In W. Ellis (Ed.), *All language and the creation of literacy* (pp. 79–93) Baltimore: Orton Dyslexia Society.

Chall, J. S. (1983). *Learning to read: The great debate.* New York: McGraw-Hill.

Clark, D. B., & Uhry, J. K. (1995). *Dyslexia: Theory and practice of remediation* (2nd ed.). Baltimore: York Press.

Cunningham, A. E., and Stanovich, K. E. (1991). Tracking the unique effects of print exposure in children: Associations with vocabulary, general knowledge, and spelling. *Journal of Educational Psychology, 83,* 264–274.

Ehri, L. C. (1994). Development of the ability to read words: Update. In R. Ruddell, M. Ruddell, & H. Singer (Eds.), *Theoretical models and processes of reading* (pp. 323–358). Newark, DE: International Reading Association.

Enfield, M. L., & Greene, T. (1996). *Project read.* Bloomington, MN: Language Circle. (P.O. Box 20631, 800-450-0343).

Foorman, B. R., Francis, D. J., Beeler, T., Winikates, D., & Fletcher, J. M. (1997). Early interventions for children with reading problems: Study designs and preliminary findings. *Learning Disabilities: A Multidisciplinary Perspective. 8,* 63–71.

Foorman, B. R., Francis, D. J., Shaywitz, S. E., Shaywitz, B., & Fletcher, J. (1997). The case for early intervention. In B. Blachman (Ed.), *Foundations of reading acquisition: Implications for intervention and dyslexia.* (pp. 243–264) Hillsdale, NJ: Lawrence Erlbaum.

Gaskins, I. W., Ehri, L. C., Cress, C., O'Hara, C., & Donnelly, K. (1996–97). Procedures for word learning: Making discoveries about words. *The Reading Teacher, 50,* 312–327.

Gough, P. B., Ehri, L. C., & Treiman, R. (Eds.) (1992). *Reading acquisition.* Hillsdale, NJ: Lawrence Erlbaum.

Gough, P. B., Juel, C., & Griffith, P. L. (1992). Reading, spelling, and the orthographic cipher. In P. B. Gough, L. C. Ehri, & R. Treiman (Eds.), *Reading acquisition* (pp. 35–48). Hillsdale, NJ: Lawrence Erlbaum.

Greene, J. (1995). *Language!* Longmont, CO: Sopris West.

Greene, J. (1996). Language!: Effects of an individualized structured language curriculum for middle and high school students. *Annals of Dyslexia, 46,* 97–121.

Henry, M. (1988). Beyond phonics: Integrated decoding and spelling instruction based on word origin and word structure. *Annals of Dyslexia, 38,* 258–275.

Henry, M., & Redding, N. (1996). *Patterns for reading and spelling.* Austin, TX: Pro-Ed.

Juel, C. (1994). *Learning to read and write in one elementary school.* New York: Springer-Verlag.

Kamhi, A. G., & Catts, H. W. (1989). Language and reading: Convergences, divergences, and development. In A. G. Kamhi & H. W. Catts (Eds.), *Reading disabilities: A developmental language perspective* (pp. 1–34). Needham Heights, MA: Little Brown.

Liberman, I. Y., Shankweiler, D., & Liberman, A. (1989). *The alphabetic principle and learning to read.* Bethesda, MD: U.S. Department of Health and Human Services, National Institutes of Child Health and Human Development.

Lindamood, C. H., & Lindamood, P. C. (1979). *Lindamood auditory conceptualization test.* Austin, TX: Pro-Ed.

Lindamood, C. H., & Lindamood P. C. (1984). *Auditory discrimination in depth.* Austin, TX: Pro-Ed.

Lovett, M. W., Borden, S. L., Lacerenza, T. D., Benson, N. J. & Brackstone, D. (1994). Treating the core deficits of developmental dyslexia: Evidence of transfer of learning after phonologically and strategy-based reading training programs. *Journal of Educational Psychology, 30,* 805–822.

Lyon, G. R. (1995a). Research initiatives in learning disabilities: Contributions from scientists supported by the National Institutes of Child Health and Human Development. *Journal of Child Neurology, 10,* 120–126.

Lyon, G. R. (1995b). Toward a definition of dyslexia. *Annals of Dyslexia, 45,* 3–27.

Lyon, G. R. (1996). Learning disabilities. *The Future of Children: Special Education for Students with Disabilities, 6,* 54–76.

Lyon, G. R., & Chhabra, V. (1996). The current state of science and the future of specific reading disability. *Mental Retardation and Developmental Disabilities Research Reviews, 2,* 2–9.

Lyon, G. R., & Moats, L. C. (1988). Critical issues in the instruction of the learning disabled. *Journal of Consulting and Clinical Psychology, 56,* 830–835.

Lyon, G. R., & Moats, L. C. (1997). Critical conceptual and methodological considerations in reading intervention research. *Journal of Learning Disabilities, 30,* 578–588.

McPike, L. (Ed.) (1995). Learning to read: Schooling's first mission. Special Issue, *American Educator, 19,* (2).

Moats, L. C. (1995). *Spelling: Development, disability, and instruction.* Baltimore: York Press.

Moats, L. C., & Lyon, G. R. (1993). Learning disabilities in the United States: Advocacy, science, and the future of the field. *Journal of Learning Disabilities, 26,* 282–294.

Moats, L. C., & Lyon, G. R. (1996). Wanted: Teachers with knowledge of language. *Topics in Language Disorders, 16,* 73–86.

Morris, D., Blanton, L., Blanton, W., Nowacek, J., & Perney, J. (1995). Teaching low-achieving spellers at their instructional level. *The Elementary School Journal, 96,* 163–177.

Olson, R. K., Wise, B., Ring, J., & Johnson, M. (1997). Computer-based remedial training in phoneme awareness and phonological decoding: Effects on the post-training development of word recognition. *Scientific Studies of Reading. 1,* 235–253.

Pennington, B. (1995). Genetics of learning disabilities. *Journal of Child Neurology, 10,* S69–S77.

Perfetti, C. (1995). Cognitive research can inform reading education. *Journal of Research in Reading, 18,* 106–115.

Pressley, M., El-Dinary, P. B., Gaskins, I., Schuder, T., Bergman, J. L., Almasi, J., & Brown, R. (1992). Beyond direct explanation: Transactional instruction of reading comprehension strategies. *Elementary School Journal, 92,* 511–554.

Rayner, K., & Pollatsek, A. (1989). *The psychology of reading.* Hillsdale, NJ: Lawrence Erlbaum.

Rieben, L., & Perfetti, C. A. (1991). Learning to read: Basic research and its implications. Hillsdale, NJ: Lawrence Erlbaum.

Samuels, S. J., Schermer, N., & Reinking, D. (1992). Reading fluency: Techniques for making decoding automatic. In S. J. Samuels & A. E. Farstrup (Eds.), *What research has to say about reading instruction* (2nd ed.) (pp. 124–145). Newark, DE: International Reading Association.

Shankweiler, D., Lundquist, E., Dreyer, L. G., & Dickinson, C. C. (1996). Reading and spelling difficulties in high school students: Causes and consequences. *Reading and Writing: An Interdisciplinary Journal, 8,* 267–294.

Share, D. E., & Stanovich, K. E. (1995). Cognitive processes in early reading development:

Accommodating individual differences into a mode of acquisition. *Issues in education: Contributions from educational psychology, 1,* 1–57.

Shaywitz, S. E. (1996). Dyslexia. *Scientific American, 275* (5), 98–104.

Shaywitz, S. E., Escobar, M. D., Shaywitz, B. A., Fletcher, J. M., & Makuch, R. (1992). Evidence that dyslexia may represent the lower tail of a normal distribution of reading ability. *New England Journal of Medicine, 326,* 145–150.

Stanovich, K. E. (1986). Matthew effects in reading: Some consequences of individual differences in the acquisition of literacy. *Reading Research Quarterly, 21,* 360–407.

Stanovich, K. (1994). Romance and reality. *The Reading Teacher, 47,* 280–291.

Stanovich, K. (1992). Speculations on the causes and consequences of individual differences in early reading acquisition. In P. Gough, L. Ehri, & R. Treiman (Eds.), *Reading acquisition* (pp. 307–342). Hillsdale, NJ: Lawrence Erlbaum.

Stanovich, K., & Siegel, L. C. (1994). Phenotypic performance profile of children with reading disabilities: A regression-based test of the phonological-core variable-difference model *Journal of Educational Psychology, 86,* 24–53.

Templeton, S., & Bear, D. (1992). *Development of orthographic knowledge and the foundations of literacy: A memorial Festschrift for Edmund H. Henderson.* Hillsdale, NJ: Lawrence Erlbaum.

Torgesen, J. K., Wagner, R. K., & Rashotte, C. A., Alexander, A. W., & Conway, T. (1997). Preventive and remedial interventions for children with severe reading disabilities. *Learning Disabilities: A Multidisciplinary Journal, 8,* 51–61.

Tunmer, W. E. & Hoover, W. (1992). Cognitive and linguistic factors in learning to read. In P. B. Gough, L. C. Ehri, & R. Treiman (Eds.), *Reading acquisition* (pp. 175–214). Hillsdale, NJ: Erlbaum.

United States Office of Technology Assessment. (1993). *Adult literacy and new technologies.* Washington, DC: U.S. Government Printing Office.

Vellutino, F. R. (1991). Introduction to three studies on reading acquisition: Convergent findings on theoretical foundations of code-oriented versus whole-language approaches to reading instruction. *Journal of Educational Psychology, 83,* 437–443.

Vellutino, F. R., & Scanlon, D. M. (1991). The preeminence of phonologically based skills in learning to read. In S. A. Brady & D. P. Shankweiler (Eds.), *Phonological processes in literacy* (pp. 237–252). Hillsdale, NJ: Lawrence Erlbaum.

Vellutino, F. R., Scanlon, D. M., Sipay, E., Small, S., Pratt, A. Chen, R. & Denckla, M. (1996). Cognitive profiles of difficult-to-remediate and readily remediated poor readers: Early intervention as a vehicle for distinguishing between cognitive and experiential deficits as basic causes of specific reading disability. *Journal of Educational Psychology, 88,* 601–638.

Williams, J. (1991). The meaning of a phonics base for reading instruction. In W. Ellis, (Ed.), *All language and creation of literacy* (pp. 9–19). Baltimore: Orton Dyslexia Society.

Wilson, B. (1996). *Wilson reading system.* Millbury, MA: Wilson Language Training. (175 West Main Street; 508-865-5699).

CHAPTER 12

Writing Instruction

Steve Graham, Karen R. Harris, Charles MacArthur, and Shirley Schwartz

I. INTRODUCTION

The purpose of this chapter is to review what is known about teaching writing to students with learning disabilities (LD). We begin by briefly considering what is known about the process of writing and how students with LD write. This is followed by specific instructional recommendations for teaching writing to students with LD. Whenever possible, recommendations are based on empirically validated procedures. We did not limit our discussion just to research-supported methods, however. Promising practices are emphasized as well.

II. THE NATURE OF WRITING

A. Skilled Writing

Although the path of writing development is complex and somewhat uncertain, scientists have identified at least four of the forces that play a vital role in this process (Alexander, in press; Graham & Harris, 1997a). Writing development depends upon knowledge of writing and writing topics, skills for producing and crafting text, processes for energizing and directing thoughts and actions, and strategies for achieving writing goals and overcoming obstacles. Each of these—knowledge, skill, will, and self-regulation—are evident in skilled writing.

Take for instance, knowledge of writing topics. Skilled writers typically generate more ideas than they need when writing, culling and eliminating less productive ones as they compose. Raymond Chandler, the popular mystery writer, for example, cut the first drafts of his stories in half as he edited them (Burnham, 1994). Perhaps more importantly, when skilled writers are not knowledgeable about a topic, they devise effective and sometimes ingenious methods for obtaining information. Sue Hubble, a writer of children's books about insects, indicated that at the start of a new writing project, she visits the Library of Congress and spends several weeks reading everything she can about her topic. She then talks to entomologists who are experts on the subject, and if she can find no expert, she obtains the needed information by raising and observing the insects of interest herself (Hubble, 1996).

Skilled writers are also adept at the basic skills for translating language into print, such as handwriting and spelling. These skills are so well mastered by most skilled writers that they have little or no influence on the writing process (Scardamalia & Bereiter, 1986). This is not the case for all of the skills involved in producing and crafting text, however. Writers must make decisions about word choice, textual connections, syntax, clarity, and so forth. This can be both taxing and time consuming, even for a skilled writer. The famed novelist, Vladimir Nabokov, indicated that his pencils outlasted his erasers, as he had rewritten, often several times, every word he ever published (Safire & Safire, 1992).

Many skilled writers further develop routines, rewards, or goals to motivate themselves to write. Jack Kerouac, author of *On the Road,* used a variety of rituals to help him compose, including kneeling and praying before starting to write and lighting a candle and composing by its light (Plimpton, 1967). Sophie Burnham, author of *For Writers Only,* indicated that she would promise herself an ice cream cone or a call to a friend as an inducement to finish a section she was working on (Burnham, 1994). Philip Dick, the famed science fiction writer, regulated his writing output by setting a goal to write two novels a year (Sutlin, 1989).

Finally, skilled writers employ a variety of strategies to help them achieve their writing goals and overcome difficulties they encounter while writing. These include strategies for planning, generating information, evaluating, revising, environmental structuring, and so forth. The popular children's writer, R. L. Stine, indicated he outlines every book in advance of writing it (Associated Press, 1995), whereas cult writer, William Volmann, noted that he carries a notebook everywhere—jotting down interesting observations that may later be used when writing (Streitfeld, 1994).

B. The Writing of Students with LD

In a recent *Peanut's* cartoon, Peppermint Patty is reading a report she has written to the class. The paper includes an initial sentence that the report is on wind, a second sentence that wind blows your hair around on the way to school, a third sentence that you don't have a comb when you get to school, and a final sentence indicating that this gives you something to write about when you can't think of anything else.

Peppermint Patty's approach to writing is similar to the approach employed by many students with LD. In contrast to more skilled writers, they employ an approach to composing that minimizes the role of planning, revising, and other self-regulation strategies (Graham, 1997; Graham & Harris, 1994a). Like Peppermint Patty, children with LD typically convert writing tasks into tasks of telling what one knows, doing little planning or reflection in advance or during writing (Graham, 1990; McCutchen, 1988). Information that is somewhat topic appropriate is gathered from memory and written down, with each preceding idea stimulating the generation of the next idea. Little attention is directed to the needs of the audience, the organization of text, the development of rhetorical goals, or the constraints imposed by the topic.

Children with LD differ from more skilled writers in several other important ways as well. One of the most striking differences involves their writing output. The papers of students with LD are inordinately short, containing little detail or elaboration, and once an idea is generated, they are very reluctant to discard it (Graham, Harris, MacArthur, & Schwartz, 1991).

There are several possible reasons why these children generate so little content when composing. One, they may be unknowledgeable or uninterested in the topics they write about. Two, they may terminate the composing process too soon, before accessing all they know. In one study (Graham, 1990), children with LD spent only 6 or 7 min writing an opinion essay, but when prompted to write more, generated 2 to 4 times more text, with at least half of the prompted material being new and useful. Three, they may lose or fail to generate possible content because of interference from poorly developed text production skills. In contrast to skilled writers, many students with LD struggle with the mechanics of writing, producing papers full of spelling, capitalization, punctuation, and handwriting miscues (Graham et al., 1991).

Another difference between skilled writers and students with LD centers on their knowledge about writing. Students with LD are less knowledgeable about writing and the writing process than their normally achieving peers (Englert, Raphael, Fear, & Anderson, 1988), and more likely to emphasize form, rather than substance, in their writing (Graham, Schwartz, and MacArthur, 1993). For instance, a student with LD who struggled with writing told us that good writers, "Spell all of their words correctly, make all of their letters the same height, and write neatly." In contrast, a good writer in his class told us that good writers, "Brainstorm ideas . . . then think about it and then write about it . . . look it over to see how to make it all fit right . . . then they do a final copy and go over that; and then if it is still not right, they do it again."

An important goal in writing instruction for students with LD, therefore, is to help them develop the knowledge, skills, and strategies used by more skilled writers. Methods for fostering confidence and motivation for writing are important as well, as children are unlikely to engage in the types of mental activities that epitomize skilled writing, if they do not value writing or what they write (Graham & Harris, 1994a). Impressive changes in the writing of students with LD have been obtained when instruction has emphasized the development of these factors (Berninger, Abbott, Whitaker, Sylvester, & Nolen, 1995; Englert et al., 1995; Englert et al., 1991; Graham et al., 1991; MacArthur, Graham, Schwartz, & Schafer, 1995). In the next section, we examine one approach to writing instruction that establishes conditions that are especially helpful in fostering the development of these processes, particularly motivation and self-regulation in writing.

III. THE PROCESS APPROACH TO WRITING

The process approach to writing is probably the most common method recommended by language experts for teaching writing today (Graham & Harris, 1994b). This instructional approach is based on a view that "good" writing involves the skillful use of planning, drafting, revising, and editing (Graves, 1983). It also places value on establishing authentic reasons for learning to write, and it emphasizes the communicative purpose of writing by creating a social context in which students write for real audiences. The process approach to teaching writing further provides for continuous, mutually responsive interactions between teachers and students. Personalized and explicit instruction, individually tailored, is used to promote the development of a variety of strategies and skills that are often difficult for students with LD to acquire (MacArthur, Graham, & Schwartz, 1993).

Despite the popularity of the process approach among experts, many writing programs for students with LD concentrate almost exclusively on practicing "basic" skills such as grammar, spelling, and handwriting. Although instruction in some of these skills are an important part of helping students develop writing competence, we agree with Emig (1978) that they are not the real basics of writing. In contrast, the process approach stresses higher order, self-regulatory processes, such as planning and revising and emphasizes the importance of writing to an audience. Students are perceived as having meaningful things to say and the teacher's role is to help students learn how to say them. This is, in large part, promoted through the use of writing conferences, peer-collaboration, modeling, and dialogues among students and teachers. The teacher functions as a facilitator creating an atmosphere (both nonthreatening and supportive) in which the writer can flourish, providing individually tailored assistance to students who will be functioning at different levels and working on different writing projects. Finally, in the process approach to writing, meaning is seen as more important than form and, thus, communication receives greater emphasis than correct spelling, grammar, and so forth.

A. An Example of the Process Approach

We have worked with a number of teachers who implemented a process approach to writing instruction with elementary and secondary students (MacArthur et al., 1995, 1993). The framework for operationalizing the process approach that the teachers used was Writers' Workshop (Atwell, 1987; Calkins, 1986). This approach includes four elements: time, ownership, response, and instruction (Graves, 1983). The rationale for each of these is described below.

1. Time

Students need to write frequently and regularly in order to become comfortable with writing and to develop their ideas. It is unrealistic to think that setting aside time once a week will help students with LD develop meaningful composing skills. A more productive schedule for young writers is to create time in each school day for composing. Opportunities for sustained writing allows students to work on the same piece of text over time and helps validate the idea that writing is a worthwhile activity.

2. Ownership

Permitting students to make decisions about their own work is a necessary condition to creating an environment where they will want to write. At least initially, this includes encouraging students to choose what to write about and deciding how they will revise their work. Self-selected topics increase the likelihood that students will write about subjects that interest and matter to them. By encouraging students to decide what they will write about, and what and how much they have to say about it, teachers increase the possibility that students will view themselves as being responsible for their own writing.

3. Response

A primary purpose in writing is to communicate. Writers' Workshop accentuates this aspect of writing by having students constantly share their work with each other. This allows each student to have an audience respond to the meaning of what they have written. Receiving regular, frequent responses to their texts help students learn what works in their writing and what doesn't. Reactions or responses to students' text can occur during teacher–student conferences (Vukelich & Leverson, 1987), a class or group sharing time (DiPardo & Freedman, 1988), or student–peer editor conferences (MacArthur, Schwartz, & Graham, 1991).

4. Instruction

Beyond structuring the classroom by providing regular time for writing and responses to writing, teachers using the Writers' Workshop can further facilitate competence in writing by structuring and directing what students do as they compose. The emphasis here is on providing support and instruction aimed at extending students' skills at carrying out the cognitive processes underlying effective writing. In essence, the teacher is a designer of the learning environment, capitalizing on "teachable moments" during conferencing, offering direct instruction in revising and evaluating text, and integrating assigned topics with self-selected topics to extend students' writing skills.

To illustrate one aspect of instruction during the Writers' Workshop, teachers may initially help students become comfortable with the basic processes involved in composing by creating a predictable routine for students to follow (Graham & Harris, 1988). First, students can be urged to concentrate on topic choice, planning, and content generation. Once a first draft is generated, students can then concentrate on revising their paper with a focus on content and organization. When students feel comfortable that their paper is complete, then editing for mechanical errors can take place. A routine of this nature primarily focuses students' efforts on content and meaning without forgetting that the paper will eventually need to be edited so that the reader will not be needlessly distracted by errors of mechanics and usage. As students master such a routine, they should further be encouraged to use the various processes more recursively, switching back and forth between them as the need arises.

It is not only critical that students become comfortable with the various stages involved in writing, they also need to develop effective strategies for executing these processes. Within a Writers' Workshop, one way teachers can help students develop these strategies is to model them and the thought processes involved in their execution. For instance, a teacher may demonstrate how to gather raw material, mentally rehearse ideas and images to write about, talk to others to gain information, or use brainstorming and webbing activities to generate content for a topic. Modeling will not be enough for most students with LD, however; they will need explicit instruction in applying writing strategies (see section IV, Strategy Instruction). Current research on teaching and learning suggests that this type of contextualized and explicit instruction is highly effective in promoting the development of cognitive and self-regulation skills central to academic success (Duffy & Roehler, 1986; Graham & Harris, 1997b; Harris & Graham, 1992).

B. Implementing a Writers' Workshop

Something that has been extremely striking to us in working with teachers implementing Writer's Workshop is that a process-centered classroom looks and sounds different than many traditional classrooms. First, the physical arrangement of the classroom varies considerably from the traditional setup. In a process classroom, space needs to be physically arranged for mobility and flexible seating. Students need space to write alone and with their peers, as well as a place to hold peer planning and revising conferences. In addition, teachers need to have areas in the classroom for holding individual conferences and for teaching strategies or skills to small groups of students. At any given time during the writing period, some students will be busy writing, others will be conferring with the teacher, while others will be meeting with peers to plan or revise their work.

A second difference involves the level of social interaction; in a process approach, writing does not take place in a vacuum; verbal discussion between participants is a central part of the process. It is assumed that talking with others encourages thinking and the discovery of new ideas. It is not unusual to find students talking in order to rehearse and expand their ideas, verbalize writing strategies and decisions, evaluate efforts, and affirm their membership in the writing community (Cox, 1988).

A third characteristic of the Writers' Workshop is the creation of a predictable set of routines designed to let students work with a minimum of teacher direction and at their own pace. The use of such a routine not only allows students to know what to expect during writing time, but makes it possible for teachers to conference with individual students and to offer instruction within a meaningful context–the student's own text.

Typically, in Writers' Workshop, writing time is divided into four components: status of the class, a mini-lesson, workshop proper, and closure (Atwell, 1987). Components can be thought of as modular (Calkins, 1986), and their sequencing is flexible to accommodate the needs of the students and teacher.

1. Status of the Class

In a brief period at the beginning of writing time, the teacher quickly checks with each student on what they are doing and/or planning to do. Establishing the status of the class allows the teacher to keep track of where each student is in the writing process. Not only does this allow students to articulate and formalize their intentions, but it gives the teacher an estimate of what student needs will be and helps the teacher keep track of student progress.

2. Mini-lessons

Mini-lessons are brief, usually 5-min lessons that expose students to information about writing. The lesson may focus on process skills (e.g., brainstorming), mechanical skills (e.g., punctuation), types of writing (e.g., parts of an opinion essay), or classroom procedures (e.g., criteria for group sharing). Instruction during mini-lessons is conducted in close association with the real writing activities that are going on in the classroom, and the teacher assumes an overt role, focusing the lesson on a particular aspect of writing. Thus, information is provided to students when they need it within the context of their current writing tasks.

3. Workshop Proper

Two-thirds of writers' workshop is devoted to actual writing. While the bulk of teachers' time is spent conferencing with individual students, teachers should spend some of this time writing themselves. By demonstrating that they are writers familiar with all the phases of the writing process, teachers can be an effective role model for their students. This also demonstrates that teachers value the utility and importance of writing.

Conferencing with students is probably the teacher's most critical role during writing time. Conferences are usually brief, ranging from a 30-sec check to see how things are going to a 5-min conversation about a completed draft or a particular problem. They may occur at any given point in the composing process. The teacher's task during a conference is to help writers extend their control over the writing process. An essential characteristic of all teacher–student conferences, no matter what the purpose, is responsive listening (Sowers, 1986). During conferences, the teacher responds as a reader and a coach, assisting the writer with the massive amount of decision making that goes on during writing.

Conferences are used for a wide range of purposes including, finding something to write about, generating content, editing a text, or reflecting on the writing process. Many times conferences are centered around content and begin with a brief, "How's it going?" This allows the student to maintain ownership of the text and at the same time allows the teacher to ask clarifying questions and help the student articulate problems and attempt solutions. Vukelich and Leverson (1987) report a strong relationship between conference discussion and text clarifications. Their research indicates that when novice writers use the information they've gained in teacher conferences to guide their text revisions, they typically make additions to the text. Through repeated cycles of conferencing, teachers gain enormous amounts of information about students' strengths and weaknesses, and students gain expertise and control over their writing. However, teachers must be careful to guard against the temptation to do too much of the work or to be dictatorial during conferences; this will only serve to make the student more (instead of less) dependent on the teacher.

4. Closure

Closure is a time for group sharing of work or discussion of what was accomplished during the writing period. It is important that much of what students write be shared, presented, or published so that students view writing as a meaningful way of telling others about their experiences and knowledge. Through group sharing, students learn what effect their words have on an audience. Similarly, during group dialogues students learn to critically assess their own and others' text and to respond effectively to their peers as writers. Nonetheless, teachers may need to give some consideration, at least initially, as to how to promote positive interchanges between students. The development of specific ground rules for providing feedback and the modeling of positive dialogues are two procedures that teachers should consider.

Publication projects can also be discussed during the closing part of the workshop. Students are motivated to communicate ideas and information by the knowledge that their writing will be shared with an audience, and they learn about their writing by predicting how the audience will respond. Publications can be as simple as an attractive bulletin board in the hallway or more elaborate such as a class magazine, a newsletter, or a book for the school library. Whatever method of publication is chosen, however, the emphasis should be on providing real and meaningful outlets for student writing.

C. Additional Comments

Several noteworthy features of the process approach to writing are frequent writing on authentic tasks aimed at a real audience, encouraging students to choose their own topics or develop unique interpretations of assigned topics, allowing students' to work together and at their own pace, providing a supportive and pleasant writing environment, and establishing a predictable writing routine that includes both planning and revising. Choice, authentic writing tasks, real audiences, ownership and control, working together, and a supportive environment all contribute to the development of students' interest in writing. In conjunction with a predictable writing routine, they also serve to induce self-regulatory behavior, such as planning and revising. When children value writing, for instance, they are more likely to use self-regulatory strategies such as planning and revising (Graham & Harris, 1997a, 1994a). These factors further influence children's acquisition of text production skills and their knowledge of the writing process. As children gain more experience writing, for example, they typically develop more fluent handwriting (Graham & Weintraub, 1996). Similarly, students gain knowledge about writing as they work together, sharing their writing efforts, talking about the process of creating them, and providing advice and feedback.

Despite its obvious advantages, critics contend that without modification and enhancements the process approach to writing instruction is not powerful enough to help all students (particularly those with LD) learn all the knowledge, skills, and strategies needed to write effectively (Graham & Harris, 1997, 1994b; Harris & Graham, 1994). One primary concern is that this approach relies too much on informal methods of teaching (e.g., learning through writing) and not enough on direct and explicit teaching methods. A considerable amount of research demonstrates that many students with LD do not acquire a variety of skills and strategies unless detailed and explicit instructions are provided (e.g, Brown & Campione, 1990). A second concern is that not enough attention is devoted to the development of text production skills. This was illustrated in a study by Reyes (1991), where students in a process writing classroom did not adopt models of conventional form in their writing even though their teacher modeled correct form, provided mini-lessons on how to apply correct form, and increased reading and writing activities.

This is not meant to imply that the process approach to writing is ineffective with students with LD. Instead, we believe that the advantages offered by this approach can be amplified by addressing the two criticisms noted above. More explicit teaching methods can be incorporated into the instructional routine and greater attention to the development of text production skills can be emphasized. The process approach to writing instruction can also be improved by taking advantage of recent technological advances. The remainder of the chapter examines explicit approaches for teaching self-regulation, knowledge, and skills in writing. The application of technology to writing instruction is also addressed.

IV. STRATEGY INSTRUCTION

As we indicated earlier, students with LD have difficulty with many of the self-regulatory processes, including planning and revising, considered critical to effective writing. An obvious means for addressing this problem is to confront it head on by explicitly teaching them to upgrade or even replace their existing writing strategies with more sophisticated ones, those requiring the same self-regulatory procedures used by skilled writers.

One well-known example of a program for explicitly teaching writing strategies to students with LD is the Cognitive Strategies Instruction in Writing program (CSIW) (Englert et al., 1991). In CSIW, "think sheets" that provide prompts for carrying out specific activities are used to direct students' actions during the following writing processes: planning, organizing information, writing, editing, and revising. For example, the think sheet for organizing information when writing directions for completing a task includes prompts to identify where the activity will take place, what materials are needed, and what steps are involved. To help students internalize the strategies and the framework incorporated in the "think sheets," a variety of features common to effective strategy instruction are used, including an emphasis on teachers modeling an inner dialogue on how to use the "think sheets"; assisted teaching in using the procedures until coaching is no longer needed; and guiding students to understand what they are learning, why it is important, and when it can be used. In a study including both students with LD and normally achieving students, the authors of CSIW found that their approach had a positive impact on expository writing.

Another example of strategy instruction in writing involves the work done by Wong and her colleagues (Wong, in press). Wong et al. (1994), for example, taught adolescents with LD how to use a variety of planning and revising strategies (i.e., searching memory for relevant topics and ideas, revisualizing events, reexperiencing emotions, detecting and diagnosing writing problems, and evaluating the clarity of the central theme of the paper) when writing reportive essays. To teach the strategies, the instructor first modeled their use and then helped students learn how to use them by providing collaborative assistance in their application. Instruction in these strategies resulted in more clearly written essays with better developed themes.

Writing strategies have also been taught to adolescents with LD by Deshler and his colleagues (Deshler & Schumaker, 1986). They have developed strategies for generating different types of sentences and paragraphs as well as a strategy for writing a theme, consisting of five paragraphs. Their mostly widely used writing strategy, however, is a self-directed routine for editing a paper for errors of capitalization, appearance, punctuation, and spelling. After learning to use this strategy, students with LD were able to detect and correct more mechanical errors in both their own writing and that of others (Schumaker et al., 1982).

A. Self-Regulated Strategy Development

We have also been involved in teaching writing strategies to students with LD, using an approach we refer to as self-regulated strategy development (SRSD). This approach is designed to help students master the higher level cognitive processes involved in composing; develop autonomous, reflective, self-regulated use of effective writing strategies; increase knowledge about the characteristics of good writing; and form positive attitudes about writing and their capabilities as writers (Harris & Graham, 1996).

These goals are achieved through various forms of support in the SRSD model.[1] One form of support is inherent in the writing strategies students are taught: a strategy provides structure that helps one organize and sequence behavior. A second form of support involves helping children acquire the self-regulation skills needed to use writing strategies successfully, manage the writing process, and replace unproductive behaviors with constructive ones. This includes teaching students to use self-regulatory procedures such as goal setting, self-assessment, and self-instructions.

Additional support is provided through the methods used to teach the writing strategies and accompanying self-regulation procedures. As students initially learn to use these processes, the teacher supports them through modeling, explaining, reexplaining, and assisting when necessary. This assistance is gradually withdrawn, as students become more able to use these processes independently. Writing capabilities are further strengthened by increasing students' knowledge about themselves, writing, and the writing process. Model compositions are used to introduce students to the characteristics of good writing. Goal setting, self-monitoring, and teacher feedback help students acquire knowledge of their writing capabilities and how to regulate the composing process.

1. Stages of Instruction

Six instructional stages provide the framework for SRSD (Harris & Graham, 1992, 1996). These stages provide a "metascript" or general guideline that can be re-

---

[1]Many of these same kinds of support are evident in the other strategy instructional approaches reviewed in this chapter.

ordered, combined, or modified to meet student and teacher needs. In some instances, a particular stage may not be needed at all. For example, students may have already acquired the background knowledge (stage 1) needed to use the writing strategies and self-regulation processes targeted for instruction. Similarly, the types of self-regulatory procedures (self-instructions, goal setting, self-monitoring, and so forth) taught to students is determined on an individual basis.

The first stage of instruction (Develop Background Knowledge) involves helping students develop the preskills, including knowledge of the criteria for good writing, needed to understand, acquire, and use the writing strategies targeted for instruction. During the second stage (Discuss It), students examine and discuss their current writing performance as well as the strategies they use to accomplish specific writing assignments. The target writing strategies are then introduced, and their purpose and benefits as well as how and when to use them are examined by the students. At this point, students are asked to make a commitment to learn the strategies and act as collaborative partners in this endeavor. The teacher may also decide to explore with students any negative or ineffective self-statements or beliefs that currently affects their writing.

In the third stage (Model It), the teacher models, while thinking aloud, how to use the writing strategies using appropriate self-instructions, including problem definition, planning, strategy use, self-evaluation, coping and error correction, and self-reinforcement statements. After analyzing the teacher's performance, teacher and students may collaborate on changing the strategies to make them more effective. Students then develop and record personal self-statements they plan to use during writing.

During stage four (Memorize It), the steps of the writing strategies, any mnemonics for remembering them, and personalized self-statements are memorized. Although students paraphrase the steps when memorizing them, care is taken to ensure the original meaning is maintained. This stage is not needed by all students, and is typically included for children who have severe memory problems.

In stage five (Support It), students and teachers use the strategies and self-instructions collaboratively to complete specific writing assignments. Self-regulation procedures, including goal setting and self-assessment, may be introduced at this time. Students set goals to improve specific aspects of their writing and use the strategies and self-instructional procedures to mediate their performance. They evaluate their success in meeting these goals by monitoring and evaluating their written products as well as what they do. During the final stage (Independent Performance), students use the strategies independently. If students are still using goal setting or self-assessment, they may decide to start fading them out. Students are also encouraged (if they are not already doing so) to say their self-statements covertly in "their head."

Procedures for promoting maintenance and generalization, including the use of self-reflection (see Graham, Harris, & Troia, in press), are integrated throughout the stages of instruction. These include identifying opportunities to use the writing strategy and self-regulation procedures, analyses of how these processes might need to be modified with other tasks and in new settings, and evaluation of the success of these processes during instruction and subsequent application.

To date, 20 studies using SRSD to teach writing strategies have been conducted. The model has been used to teach a variety of planning and revising strategies, including brainstorming (see Harris & Graham, 1985), self-monitoring of productivity (see Harris, Graham, Reid, McElroy, & Hamby, 1994), reading for information and semantic webbing (see MacArthur, Schwartz, Graham, Molloy, & Harris, 1996), generating and organizing writing content using text structure (see Graham & Harris, 1989; Sawyer, Graham, & Harris, 1992), goal setting (see Graham, MacArthur, & Schwartz, 1995; Graham, MacArthur, Schwartz, & Voth, 1992), revising using peer feedback (see MacArthur, Schwartz, & Graham, 1991), and revising for both mechanics and substance (see Graham & MacArthur, 1988). SRSD has led to changes and improvement in four aspects of students' performance: quality of writing, knowledge of writing, approach to writing, and self-efficacy (cf. Graham et al., 1991; Harris & Graham, 1996). Evaluations of SRSD by teachers and students have also been positive. An example of a writing strategy developed by one of our former students, Sue De La Paz (De La Paz & Graham, 1997a, 1997), and taught using the SRSD method is presented in Table 12.1.

B. Additional Comments

Although strategy instruction has been presented as a curricular option in and of itself (Deshler & Schumaker, 1986), we believe that it is much more powerful when it is integrated as part of the regular program. In the area of writing, for example, teaching students a peer-planning strategy that can be used as an integral

Table 12.1

A Strategy for Writing an Opinion Essay[a]

THINK:	Who will read this?
	Why am I writing this?
STOP:	Suspend judgment. (Generate ideas for each side of the issue.)
	Take a side. (Decide your position.)
	Organize ideas. (Select ideas to include and order them for writing.)
	Plan more as you write. (Continue planning while writing.)
DARE:	Remember:
	Develop your topic sentence.
	Add supporting ideas.
	Reject arguments for the other side.
	End with a conclusion.

[a]From De La Paz and Graham (1997a).

part of the process approach to writing provides an excellent means for promoting collaboration and improving students' planning skills (see MacArthur et al., 1991).

It should further be noted that well-taught and well-learned strategies may not be used regularly and effectively by students with LD (Graham et al., in press). Although students may possess the know-how, they may not possess the will to use the strategies or may use them in a mindless fashion (Wong, 1994). Consequently, teachers should consider students' goal orientations and attitudinal dispositions when developing and providing strategy instruction, and employ instructional procedures that facilitate mindful use of the inculcated strategies (see Graham et al., in press; Wong, 1994). It is equally important to monitor if students continue to use the strategies over time and if they adapt their use to new situations. Although provisions for promoting maintenance and generalization should be a routine part of good strategy instruction, teachers may need to use booster sessions to promote continued and adaptive strategy use (Harris & Graham, 1992).

There are at least three other issues that we would like to consider (Graham & Harris, 1993). First, we would encourage teachers to be sensitive to individual differences in children. Some students will benefit more from a specific strategy than other students, and the amount of instructional assistance needed to learn a strategy will vary among students (Pressley, Goodchild, Fleet, Zajchowski, & Evans, 1989). Second, although it would be tempting to suggest that students be taught a single, universal writing strategy for all writing tasks, we are hard pressed to identify a strategy that would be adequate to meet the wide variety of assignments and genres students are asked to write about. Instead, it would appear to be more reasonable to teach different strategies for different purposes. However, teachers need to give careful thought as to what strategies should be taught, as students will not be able to remember and execute an infinite number. Third, it is important to pay careful attention to what students internalize as a result of strategy instruction. They may modify an inculcated strategy making it less effective. Do not assume that students will use a strategy just as you planned.

V. KNOWLEDGE ABOUT WRITING

The most common means for acquiring knowledge about writing is through exposure to specific literary examples, either through reading or the presentation of models that embody a specific pattern. Although the practice of imitating written models can have a positive impact on writing, it should be used judiciously, as the effects are quite modest (Hillocks, 1984). Students also acquire some rhetorical knowledge through reading, but the extent of such learning is not known (Bereiter & Scardamalia, 1982). Consequently, teachers should play an active role in guiding the process of acquiring rhetorical knowledge through reading. As students read a particular book, for example, the teacher can encourage discussion, focusing attention on important features of text, such as the use of dialogue, plot development, foreshadowing, and so forth (Bos, 1988).

Students' knowledge about writing can also be increased through explicit instruction. Fitzgerald and Teasley (1986), for instance, reported that children who received instruction in narrative structure (i.e., specific story elements and their interplay) improved both the organization and quality of their papers. Fitzgerald and Markham (1987) obtained similar results for revising, indicating that students became more knowledgeable and effective revisers after receiving instruction on how to revise.

VI. METHODS FOR IMPROVING TEXT PRODUCTION SKILLS

There is a strong relation between the fluency and quality of children's writing and their proficiency with text production skills such as handwriting and spelling (Graham, 1990; Graham et al., in press). Moreover, efforts to improve such skills can also result in corresponding improvements in writing performance (Berninger, Vauhn, et al., in press). Consequently, we recommend that teachers devote instructional time to teaching both handwriting and spelling (Graham & Harris, 1988). Such instruction should not dominate the writing program, however, and should focus on those skills that are most likely to make difference.

A. Handwriting

The basic goals of handwriting instruction are to help students develop writing that is legible and can be produced quickly with little conscious attention. This involves teaching students an efficient pattern for forming individual letters as well as how to hold their pen or pencil and position the paper they are writing on (Graham, 1992). This does not require hours of time practicing individual letters. Instead, once a letter is introduced, students should spend a short time carefully practicing the letter, receive help as needed (including subsequent review), and evaluate their own efforts. Fluency in handwriting is best promoted through frequent writing, and develops gradually over time (Graham & Weintraub, 1996).

Ample research on effective conventional practices for teaching letter formation skills exists (Graham & Weintraub, 1996), and many of these practices along with a variety of traditional procedures that have not been empirically validated are appropriate for use with students with LD. According to Graham and Miller (1980), these include teacher modeling of the formation of the letter; comparing and contrasting features of the target letter with other letters that share common formational characteristics; visual and sometimes even physical prompts and cues to help guide the student in forming the letter; considerable practice in tracing, copying, and writing the letter from memory; corrective feedback and praise from the teacher regarding the student's effort in forming the letter; student's correction of malformed letters through the assistance of a visual aid or under the direction of the teacher; encouraging students to self-evaluate their efforts; and visual dramatization of student's progress through the use of charts or graphs. Available research with students with LD has shown that the astute use of a combination of these procedures is advantageous (Fauke, Burnett, Powers, & Sulzer-Azaroff, 1973; Robin, Armel, & O'Leary, 1975). Moreover, computerized handwriting programs can be profitably employed to help students with handwriting difficulties learn how to correctly form letters (see Graham & Weintraub, 1996). In contrast, having students overtly verbalize the steps in forming a letter as they are learning how to write it does not appear to be a viable instructional practice (Graham, 1983a).

In addition to having students write frequently, teachers can also seek to increase handwriting fluency through self-competition on timed exercises and through the use of reinforcement to increase motivation. Attempts to increase students' speed, however, must be balanced against any possible decreases in legibility. It is important to remember that handwriting fluency develops gradually. In some instances it may be possible to make more dramatic gains, if the student's slow rate of production is due to some interfering factor such as off-task behavior. For example, Hallahan, Lloyd, Kosiewicz, Kauffman, and Graves (1979) were able to increase the handwriting fluency of students with attention difficulties by cuing them to monitor their attentional behavior.

It is also important that students with LD develop the skills necessary to insure that the papers they turn in for class assignments are acceptable in appearance. Anderson-Inman, Pine, and Duetchman (1984) improved the appearance of students' writing by providing direct instruction in skills involving neatness coupled with self-monitoring in the use of those skills. Similarly, Blandford and Lloyd (1987) found that the appearance of the journal writing of students with LD were improved through the use of self-directed procedures for guiding and evaluating their sitting position and the formation and spacing of letters.

Before concluding this section on handwriting, several additional considerations need to be addressed. First, instructors should be sensitive to the special needs of left-handed writers. Special instructional provisions, such as having left-handed writers turn their papers somewhat clockwise and hold the pencil slightly farther back than right-handers do, should be common practice (see Graham & Miller, 1980). Second, only a few errors account for a large percentage of the illegibilities in children's writing (Horton, 1969). Once basic letter forms have been mastered, focusing remedial efforts on the most common types of errors (for example, malforming the letters, a,e,r, and t) often yield a high rate of return for a small amount of effort. Third, despite the common stereotype that students with LD are plagued by reversals, this proposition has not received much empirical support. If students are still making a considerable number of reversals after the age of 7 or 8 years of age, teachers should consider direct instructional methods for eliminating them. Finally, conflicting claims regarding the effectiveness of various forms of script with LD students have been made in the literature (see Graham, 1992; Graham & Miller, 1980). Although manuscript appears to have a slight edge over cursive writing for the general population (Graham & Miller, 1980), a recommendation for students with LD based on empirical evidence would be premature at this time. Furthermore, claims that slanted manuscript alphabets, such as D'Nealian alphabet, are superior to the traditional manuscript alphabet (characterized by upright letters that resemble type) are not substantiated by research (Graham, 1992, 1993/1994).

B. Spelling

The basic goal of spelling instruction is to help students become proficient and fluent in spelling words they are likely to use in their writing. This involves learning the common regularities and patterns underlying English orthography; the correct spelling of frequently used words; as well as strategies for studying new words, applying knowledge of spelling (e.g., spelling by analogy), and proofreading (Graham, Harris, & Loynachan, 1996). Frequent reading and writing contribute to spelling development, as they serve as a source for additional learning, a context for practicing newly learned skills, and a reminder on the importance of correct spelling in practical and social situations. Children also need to become familiar with external aids to spelling such as the dictionary, thesaurus, spell checkers, or asking another person for help.

Although a comprehensive body of research on effective conventional spelling practices exist (Cahen, Craun, & Johnson, 1971), most of it has focused on how to teach spelling vocabulary. Many of these procedures are recommended for use with students with LD (Graham & Miller, 1979), including presenting words to be studied in a list form rather than in sentences, pretesting spelling words and concentrating study only on the words missed, teaching students a systematic procedure for studying unknown words, having students correct their spelling tests under the direction of the teacher, using spelling games to promote interest, and concentrating spelling instruction on words most likely to be useful to students. Although teachers cannot directly teach students all of the words they are likely to use in their present and future writing (Wilde, 1990), they can teach students the words they are most likely to use as well as words they already use and misspell.

The typical approach to teaching spelling vocabulary is to have students learn 15 to 20 (often unrelated) words. On Monday, the spelling list is introduced, followed by a pretest on Tuesday. On Wednesday, students use the words in sentences, while on Thursday they practice phonic skills or the words missed on the pretest. On Friday a posttest is administered.

Three ways in which this common pattern can be made more effective for students with LD is to decrease the number of words to be learned each week, daily presentation and practice of a few words each day, and daily testing of the words to be learned (Bryant, Drabin, & Gettinger, 1981; Gettinger, Bryant, & Fayne, 1982; Rieth et al., 1975). We advise that the weekly spelling list for students with LD be limited to 6–12 words. Since such a recommendation likely means that students with LD are exposed to fewer spelling words, it is critical that the words they study yield a high rate of return (see Graham, Harris, & Loynachan, 1993, 1994, for lists of such words).

It is especially helpful if the words students with LD are asked to study are selected or arranged so that common orthographic patterns are emphasized. Children's spelling words for a particular week, for example, might contain words for two different spellings of long /o/: hope and road. Students can be asked to sort these words into groups with like sounds and spellings to discover the underlying patterns. They can then be asked to hunt for words with the same features in their writing and reading material (cf. Graham et al., 1996).

Although it is generally agreed that students should be taught a systematic procedure for studying new spelling words, this axiom appears to be especially significant for students with LD. Graham and Freeman (1986), for example, found that when students with LD were directed to study 15 spelling words in their usual manner, they learned the correct spelling of less than 20% of the words. There are a variety of word study techniques that are useful for these students (see Graham, 1983b, for examples). An effective word study technique should focus student's attention on the whole word, require pronunciation of the word, involve distributed practice in learning the word, and involve self-evaluation and correction of the practiced response. Forming a visual image of the word in addition to tracing or sounding out the word may be helpful for some students with LD. Although it is essential that students learn how to spell new words correctly, it is just as critical that they can produce the spellings quickly and with little conscious attention. As a result, weekly spelling units need to include interesting practice activities (such as games) designed to promote fluency in producing the correct spelling.

It is also advantageous to teach students with LD strategies for using the skills they already possess when trying to learn new spelling words or when trying to figure out the correct spelling of words they want to use in their writing. To illustrate, Englert, Hiebert, and Stewart (1985) taught students with LD how to use their knowledge of spelling patterns to spell new words. Not surprisingly, though, the impact of such a strategy is diminished if the student has few skills (e.g., word analysis skills) to draw upon (Wong, 1986).

Students with LD further need to learn how to regulate the process for studying new spelling words (Graham & Voth, 1990). Although teaching students to independently use a word-study procedure is a good first step, students need to progress beyond this elementary level, applying a broad array of self-regulation skills to spelling. For instance, study behavior and/or spelling performance can be improved by having students with LD monitor the number of times they practice spelling words (cf. Harris, 1986), assess their accuracy during study followed by self-administration of reinforcement contingent upon performance (Kapadia & Fantuzzo, 1988), and set goals on the number of words to be spelled correctly on weekly tests (McLaughlin, 1982). A classroom resource that is not often employed during traditional spelling instruction are the students themselves. Two potentially powerful means of using student resources are peer tutoring and cooperative study arrangements. The spelling performance of students with LD has been improved by providing them with a tutor or having them act as a tutor to other students (cf. Dineen, Clark, & Risley, 1977). Class-wide peer tutoring arrangements may be particularly useful, especially in mainstreamed classrooms (Maheady & Harper, 1987). In terms of cooperative group arrangements, Lew and Bryant (1984) found that placing each of the special needs children in a mainstreamed classroom into a different cooperative study group resulted in improved spelling performance for all students, and the teacher felt more confident about meeting the spelling needs of the whole class.

C. Sentence Production Skills

In addition to developing fluent handwriting and spelling skills, students need to develop proficiency in framing their text within a variety of sentence formats (e.g., expressing their thoughts within the context of a complex sentence). Sentence combining, the practice of building more complex sentences from simpler ones, has proven to be a highly effective technique for promoting such skills (Hillocks, 1984). Other traditional procedures for improving students' sentence-building skills include arranging and rearranging word cards to form sentences, completing sentences from which specific words or phrases have been deleted, and encouraging students to imitate the patterns in exemplary sentences. Despite the fact that these last three procedures are common staples in many writing programs, there is not much evidence to support their effectiveness even with normally achieving students (Graham, 1982).

The only systematic attempt that we are aware of to improve the sentence-writing skills of students with LD was conducted by Schumaker and Sheldon (1985). They developed a strategy designed to help students generate 14 different types of sentences. For each sentence type, students use a formula to guide the process of building the sentence and selecting words. In addition, students are taught to identify and define a host of grammatical structures that are relevant to the parts included in the various formulas. Unfortunately, we cannot recommend the use of this strategy for the majority of students with LD. First, there is little evidence to support the use of the procedures. Second, because of the amount of memorization required in learning to use the strategy and the complicated nature of some of the formulas, students may be especially susceptible to corruption and misuse of the strategy over time. Third, current research suggests that some of the practices incorporated within the strategy (e.g., identifying and defining various parts of speech) are not a necessary prerequisite to sentence writing.

VII. USE OF TECHNOLOGY

Computers can enhance the writing of students with LD in many ways. Word processing and related technology can support the basic skills of producing legible text with correct mechanics as well as the more complex cognitive processes of planning, drafting, and revising text and the social processes of collaboration and communication with an audience.

A. Word Processing

A recent meta-analysis of the extensive research on instructional use of word processing with normally achieving students (Bangert-Drowns, 1993) found a positive, though modest, impact on student writing. In another review (Cochran-Smith, 1991), the author indicated that the impact of word processing on students' writing processes and products depended on how effectively teachers took advantage of the capabilities of computers. In reviews of the research on word processing with students with LD, MacArthur (1988) concluded that word processing in combination with effective writing instruction can enhance the writing of students with LD.

Word processors offer several capabilities that may influence the writing process. First, they support the process of revision by easing the physical burden of recopying and the mess of erasing; text can be easily moved, deleted, added, or substituted. The editing capabilities of word processing can be a great boon to writers if they can take advantage of its capabilities. However, simple access to word processing has little impact on the revising behavior of students with LD, who generally have a limited view of revision as correcting errors (MacArthur & Graham, 1987).

To take advantage of the editing power of word processing, students with LD need instruction and support in learning to revise for meaning as well as errors. Process approaches to writing support revision through teacher conferences and peer response. The revising skills of students with LD can also be improved by instruction in strategies for evaluating and revising their writing. Several studies have combined word processing and strategy instruction in teaching revision, resulting in increases in the number of substantive and mechanical revisions made by students with LD as well as improvement in the quality of their texts (Graham & MacArthur, 1988; MacArthur et al., 1991; Stoddard & MacArthur, 1993). In the cooperative revision strategy developed by MacArthur et al. (1991), for example, students work in pairs using the following steps (expressed as directions to the peer editor):

1. LISTEN and READ along as the author reads the story.
2. TELL what it is about and what you liked best.
3. READ it to yourself and make NOTES about:
   a. CLARITY? Is there anything you don't understand?
   b. DETAILS? What information/details could be added?
4. DISCUSS your suggestions with the author.
5. Author: Make changes on the computer.

(Note that evaluation questions in step 3 can be tailored to the ability of the students and to ongoing instruction.)

In addition to supporting revision, word processors enhance publishing by making it possible to produce neat, printed work in a wide variety of professional-looking formats, including newsletters, illustrated books, business letters, and signs and posters. The motivation provided by printed publications may be especially important for students with LD who often struggle with handwriting and mechanics. For classrooms that have just one or two computers, the best use of that equipment may be for publishing projects. Students can work together on a class newsletter or other project, or they can select their best writing for inclusion in a literary magazine.

A third feature of word processing that is less often mentioned is the visibility of the screen. This visibility, together with the use of typing rather than handwriting, can facilitate collaborative writing among peers and scaffold interactions between teacher and student. Peers can work together sharing responsibility for generating ideas, typing, and revising since both can see and read the text easily, and typing does not identify separate contributions. The visibility of the screen also enables teachers to more easily observe students' writing processes and intervene when appropriate (Morocco & Newman, 1986). Using a large monitor or projection panel, teachers can model writing processes and strategies for planning and revising.

A final consideration in using word processing is that students must develop some proficiency in typing and learn to operate the software. Although typing can be considerably easier than handwriting for many students, students with LD should not be expected to develop typing skills without instruction and practice. A variety of software is available to provide such practice. In addition, to avoid frustration due to lost text and other problems, students should receive basic instruction in the proper operation of word-processing software.

B. Basic Writing Skills

The difficulties that students with LD have with basic writing skills or mechanics—spelling, capitalization, punctuation, and usage—are well documented. Computer tools, such as spelling and grammar checkers, speech synthesis, word prediction, and voice recognition, have potential to compensate for problems in these areas.

The most widespread tools to support basic writing skills are spelling checkers. Nearly all current word processors include integrated spelling checkers that scan a document for errors and suggest correct spellings. Spelling checkers will not, however, automatically result in error-free documents. We (MacArthur, Graham, Haynes, & DeLaPaz, 1996) found that students with LD were able to correct about one-third of their spelling errors using a spelling checker. The most significant limitation of spelling checkers was that they failed to identify about one-third of errors because the errors were other words correctly spelled, including homonyms and others (e.g., "whet" for "went"). Furthermore, spelling checkers suggested the correct spelling for only one-half to two-thirds of the errors that they did find. Finally, students with LD in this study sometimes failed to recognize the correct spelling in the list of suggestions provided, though this problem was not as common as the preceding difficulties. Instruction in strategies for using a spelling checker effectively (e.g., trying alternate spellings) may improve performance somewhat. In addition, students need to learn to use traditional aids like the dictionary in combination with spelling checkers. Despite their limitations, spelling checkers are clearly important tools for students with LD.

Speech synthesis, another tool with potential to enhance writing skills, includes software or hardware that translates text into speech. It does not sound as natural as digitized speech, which is recorded, but has the advantage that it can be used to speak any text. Word processors with speech synthesis capabilities enable students to hear what they have written and read what others have written. Speech synthesis may help students monitor the adequacy of their writing, including spelling and grammar. Although current research by Borgh and Dickson (1992) and MacArthur and Haynes (1996) found that the use of speech synthesis did not influence either the length or quality of papers produced by students with LD, additional research is needed to determine if this tool has a beneficial affect on other aspects of writing. Furthermore, improvements in the quality of speech synthesis may increase its effectiveness.

A third software tool, word prediction, has the potential to enhance the basic writing skills of students with severe spelling problems. Word prediction was originally developed for individuals with physical disabilities to reduce the number of keystrokes required to type words. As the user begins to type a word, the software predicts the intended word and presents a list of words from which the user can choose. Depending on the sophistication of the software, predictions are based on spelling, word frequency, individual word frequency, and syntax. Generally, speech synthesis is available to read the word choices. Students with severe spelling problems, who cannot realistically benefit from a spelling checker, may benefit from using word-prediction software. MacArthur (1996) found that word prediction resulted in substantial improvements in the readability of text produced by 7-year-old students with LD whose papers were initially difficult to read because of spelling errors.

A fourth computer tool that is often mentioned as an aid for students with LD is grammar or style checkers. Although many students with LD could benefit from the use of software that provides feedback on grammar and usage, available software is designed for older writers and often misses more basic grammatical and mechanical errors. Moreover, the feedback provided is often difficult to comprehend.

Finally, voice-recognition software designed to take dictation provides a tool that allows the writer to circumvent the mechanics of writing altogether (De La Paz & Graham, 1995). Unfortunately, current software has a variety of limitations (in addition to high cost) that undermine its effectiveness with students with LD. As the quality of voice-recognition software increases, however, we anticipate that it will provide a viable approach to composing for many students with LD.

C. Planning Processes

Outlining and semantic mapping are common strategies used by writers to organize ideas prior to writing. For students with LD, these writing strategies have been effective in improving the overall quality of their writing (Harris & Graham, 1996). Many word processors include outlining capabilities, and software is now available for semantic mapping. Advantages to using a computer-generated outlining or semantic-mapping program is that they are easier to revise and often more flexible than their paper counterparts.

The interactive capabilities of computers can further be used to develop programs that prompt writers to engage in planning processes. The most common programs present a series of questions based on text structures to help students generate ideas prior to writing. Although we are not aware of any research on such programs with students with LD, there is research indicating that simple text structure prompts may enhance the writing of students with LD (Montague, Graves, & Leavell, 1991).

The potential of multimedia software to enhance writing processes is just beginning to be explored as new tools are developed. For young children, composing often begins with drawing. Software that permits children to draw pictures and write about them can motivate students to write and help them generate ideas for stories. New CD ROM "books" provide a link between reading and writing activities; children read the books or have the computer read to them, and then write their own stories using pictures and words from the story. Older students can use more grown-up multimedia software that permits them to integrate visuals, sounds, and writing to create new forms of communication. Multimedia can also be used to provide background knowledge and as a research source for writing projects.

D. Collaboration and Communication on Networks

Computer networks, whether local area networks within a classroom or school or the internet, can offer expanded opportunities for collaborative writing and communication with diverse audiences. Two examples will illustrate some of the possibilities. Peyton and Batson (1986) used a network within a classroom to teach writing classes for deaf students in which all discussion and interaction were conducted in writing. For the deaf students, the network provided an immersion approach for mastering English. Similar networks have potential in writing instruction for students with LD by providing a natural connection between conversation and more formal writing. An entire prewriting class discussion can be captured for later use in writing. Riel (1985) used email to link students from diverse cultures in collaborative production of a newspaper. Since the students from Alaska and California did not share the same cultural knowledge, they had to struggle to communicate clearly, which provided opportunities to learn about writing and revising. The recent rapid expansion of internet resources has opened up new opportunities for communication and collaboration on writing projects.

VIII. WHAT ELSE CAN I DO?

In addition to the procedures already discussed, there are a number of other techniques that we believe have considerable potential for use with students with LD. Many of these procedures have only been field tested with normally achieving students. Thus, the challenge for teachers will be to effectively adapt these techniques for use with students with LD.

In a review of instructional research in writing, Hillock's (1984) indicated that writing can be enhanced by having students engage in free writing such as keeping a journal, apply specific criteria or questions to evaluate their own or others' writing, and participate in structured problem-solving writing tasks (for instance, analyzing situations that contain ethical problems and then developing arguments about those situations). It was also clear from this review that the most effective writing programs were those in which the objectives were clear and specified.

A variety of behavioral techniques have also been investigated as methods for improving specific features of children's writing; contingent reinforcement has been the primary behavioral technique of choice (Kerr & Lambert, 1982). To illustrate, in a study by Bording, Mclaughlin, and Williams (1984), the correct use of capitalization and punctuation in special education students' writing increased as a result of awarding free-time dependent upon performance on these skills. We found the results from this study intriguing because they suggest that poor writers' difficulties with the conventions of writing may be due, in part, to motivational factors. The error-prone papers produced by students with LD may also be a result of monitoring difficulties. In a study by Espin and Sindelar (1988), the percent of grammatical errors that students with LD identified increased (the percent of errors corrected did not) when they listened and viewed a passage in contrast to just reading it. In any case, both of these procedures provide viable means for reducing the number of mechanical errors in LD students' writing.

Other methods that may hold potential promise for improving the writing of students with LD include instructional efforts aimed at increasing creativity and systematic monitoring of student progress using curriculum-based measurement (CBM). Although the current research on creativity instruction is flawed experimentally, several investigators have reported gains in story writing performance as a result of such instruction (cf. Fortner, 1986). In terms of CBM, it is well established that handicapped students make greater achievement gains as a result of systematic monitoring of progress (Fuchs & Fuchs, 1986). It is possible that writing performance of students with LD can also be improved through the use of such procedures, as they may make teachers more aware of the effects of their instruction and the need to make modifications.

A final instructional technique that teachers may wish to use with LD students is dictation. For very young children who have very limited mechanical skills in writing, dictation provides an excellent method for helping children get their thoughts down on paper (De La Paz & Graham, 1995). Dictation may further be a viable alternative to writing for older students with LD, and even adults, who have not been able to automatize the basic writing skills. Although Gould (1980) found that college students could learn to dictate effectively with only a small amount of practice, persons with LD may benefit from more extended instruction in how to use dictation, especially planning their papers in advance of dictation (De La Paz & Graham, 1997b).

IX. WHAT NOT TO DO

One of the most robust findings in the research literature is that the study of traditional school grammar (i.e., definition of parts of speech, diagramming of sentences, etc.) does not improve the quality of students' writing (Graham, 1982). Likewise, the decontextualized study of usage and punctuation has little or no effect on what students write (Hillocks, 1984). Nonetheless, language arts textbook series place considerable emphasis on teaching these skills through the use of workbook activities, such as copying a sentence and correcting it by supplying the correct verb tense, punctuation, or capitalization (Bridge & Hiebert, 1985). Based on our current knowledge of what constitutes effective writing, the use of such materials cannot be recommended.

This does not mean that we believe that correct capitalization, punctuation, verb tense, the use of plurals, and so forth are not important. Rather, we believe that these skills are best developed within the context of real writing tasks (Graham & Harris, 1988). When specific errors occur in the child's writing or when the child asks how to use a particular form, this is the point at which such instruction should occur, when it will be meaningful and useful to the child. It should further be stressed that teachers need to use some restraint in terms of the amount of emphasis that they place on students' writing errors. The available evidence indicates that intensive evaluation (marking every error) may make students more aware of their limitations and less willing to write, resulting in poorer writing performance (Graham, 1982). Teachers would be well advised, therefore, to pinpoint only one or two types of errors made by the student at any one time, giving priority to errors that occur frequently and have the largest effect on obstructing the reader's understanding of text. The feedback that students receive should be explanatory, specific, and include suggestions for making corrections.

Because children's written language skills tend to be related to their oral language development, some experts recommend that oral language instruction should be an integral part of the writing program (cf. Golub, 1974). We have reservations about this recommendation, especially if written language instruction is delayed in favor of an oral language program. General language instruction has not been shown to result in improvements in students' writing, and after the elementary grades students do not write as they speak (see Graham, 1982, for additional information on this topic).

X. CONCLUDING COMMENTS

A school's success in teaching writing should be judged not only in terms of how well students develop the skills necessary for meeting academic and occupational demands, but also by the students' desire and ability to use writing for the purpose of social communication and recreation. In our efforts to improve the writing of students with LD, we do not want to lose sight of the critical goals of helping students learn to appreciate writing and to enjoy doing it. In this chapter we have presented a variety of procedures that, when applied in concert, should help students realize all of these goals. Foremost among these procedures are the process approach to writing, the application of computer technology, and the use of procedures for helping students develop basic text production skills as well as the higher order writing skills involved in planning and revising.

Finally, if we are to improve in any meaningful way how and what students with LD write, we must be dedicated to the importance of writing. Too often special education teachers have made writing instruction the step-child to reading or math. In allocating time for instruction, it is not unusual to find teachers giving maximum priority to teaching reading with little emphasis on teaching writing (Leinhart, Zigmond, & Cooley, 1980). Similarly, we have found through our own experiences in working with schools and teachers that they are often hesitant and sometimes resistant to allocating sufficient time for writing instruction; they often fear that making such a commitment will have negative consequence because students will get less of something *really important* like reading. We would argue that writing is as important as reading, especially in terms of school performance; it is the primary means by which students demonstrate their knowledge and the primary instrument by which teachers evaluate performance (Graham, 1982). Therefore, we would like to encourage teachers to provide at least 4 days of writing instruction a week, look for ways of promoting increased writing across the curriculum, and attempt to engage students in meaningful and purposive writing activities.

References

Alexander, P. (in press). Stages and phases of domain learning: The dynamics of subject-matter knowledge, strategy knowledge, and motivation. In C. Weinstein & B. Mc-Colombs (Eds.), *Strategic learning: Skill, will, and self-regulation*. Hillsdale, NJ: Erlbaum.

Anderson-Inman, L., Paine, S., & Deutchman, L. (1984). Neatness counts: Effects of direct instruction and self-monitoring on the transfer of neat-paper skills to nontraining settings. *Analysis and Intervention in Developmental Disabilities, 4,* 137–155.

Associated Press. (1995). This man gives children 'Goosebumps' and 'Fear Street.' *Valdosta Daily Times,* Dec 27, 1995, B 1.

Atwell, N. (1987). *In the middle: Reading, writing, and learning from adolescents.* Portsmith, NH: Heinmann.

Bangert-Drowns, R. L. (1993). The word processor as an instructional tool: A meta analysis of word processing in writing instruction. *Review of Educational Research, 63,* 69–93.

Bereiter, C., & Scardamalia, M. (1982). From conversation to composition: The role of instruction in a developmental process. In R. Glaser (Ed.), *Advances in instructional psychology* (Vol. 2, pp. 1–64). Hillsdale, NJ: Lawrence Erlbaum.

Berninger, V., Abbott, R., Whitaker, D., Sylvester, L., & Nolen, S. (1995). Integrating low- and high-level skills in instructional protocols for writing disabilities. *Learning Disability Quarterly, 18,* 293–310.

Berninger, V., Vaughn, K., Abbott, R., Abbott, S., Rogan, L., Brooks, A., Reed, E., & Graham, S. (in press). Preventing handwriting and compositional disability: Training in handwriting fluency and transfer to compositional fluency. *Journal of Educational Psychology.*

Blandford, B., & Lloyd, J. (1987). Effects of a self-instructional procedure on handwriting. *Journal of Learning Disabilities, 20,* 342–346.

Bording, C., McLaughlin, T., & Williams, R. (1984). Effects of free time on grammar skills of adolescent handicapped students. *Journal of Educational Research, 77,* 312–318.

Borgh, K., & Dickson, W. P. (1992). The effects on children's writing of adding speech synthesis to a word processor. *Journal of Research on Computing in Education, 24,* 533–544.

Bos, C. (1988). Process-oriented writing: Instructional implications for mildly handicapped students. *Exceptional Children, 54,* 521–527.

Bridge, C., & Hiebert, E. (1985). A comparison of classroom writing practices, teachers' perceptions of their writing instruction, and textbook recommendations on writing practices. *Elementary School Journal, 86,* 155–172.

Brown, A., & Campione, J. (1990). Interactive learning environments and the teaching of science and mathematics. In M. Gardner, J. Green, F. Reif, A. Schoenfield, A. di Sessa, & E. Stage (Eds.), *Toward a scientific practice of science education* (pp. 112–139). Hillsdale, NJ: Erlbaum.

Bryant, N. D., Drabin, I. R., & Gettinger, M. (1981). Effects of varying unit size on spelling achievement in learning disabled children. *Journal of Learning Disabilities, 14,* 200–203.

Burnham, S. (1994). *For writers only.* New York: Ballantine Books.

Cahen, L., Craun, M., & Johnson, S. (1971). Spelling difficulty a survey of the research. *Review of Educational Research, 41,* 281–301.

Calkins, L. M. (1986). *The art of teaching writing.* Portsmouth, NH: Heinemann.

Cochran-Smith, M. (1991). Word processing and writing in elementary classrooms: A critical review of related literature. *Review of Educational Research, 61,* 107–155.

Cox, C. (1988). *Teaching language arts.* Boston, MA: Allyn & Bacon, Inc.

De La Paz, S., & Graham, S. (1997a). Strategy instruction in planning: Effects on the writing performance and behavior of students with learning difficulties. *Exceptional Children, 63,* 167–181.

De La Paz, S., & Graham, S. (1997b). The effects of dictation and advanced planning instruction on the composing of students with writing and learning problems. *Journal of Educational Psychology, 89,* 203–222.

De La Paz, S., & Graham, S. (1995). Dictation: Application for writing with students with learning disabilities. In T. Scruggs & M. Mastroperi (Eds.), *Advances in learning and behavioral disabilities* (pp. 229–249, Vol. 9). Greenwich, CT: JAI Press.

Deshler, D. D., & Schumaker, J. B. (1986). Learning strategies: An instructional alternative for low-achieving adolescents. *Exceptional Children, 52,* 583–590.

Dineen, J. P., Clark, H. B., & Risley, T. R. (1977). Peer tutoring among elementary students: Educational benefits to the tutor. *Journal of Applied Behavior Analysis, 10,* 231–238.

DiPardo, A., & Freedman, S. (1988). Peer response group in the writing classroom: Theoretic foundations and new directions. *Review of Educational Research, 58,* 119–149.

Duffy, G. G., & Roehler, L. R. (1986). *Improving classroom reading instruction: A decision-making approach.* NY: Random House.

Emig, J. (1978). Hand, eye, brain: Some "basics" in the writing process. In C. Cooper & L. Odell (Eds.), *Research on composing.* Urbana, IL: National Council on Teachers of English.

Englert, C., Garmon, A., Mariage, T., Rozendal, M., Tarrant, K., & Urba, J. (1995). The early literacy project: Connection across the literacy curriculum. *Learning Disability Quarterly, 18,* 253–277.

Englert, C. S., Hiebert, E. H., & Stewart, S. R. (1985). Spelling unfamiliar words by an analogy strategy. *Journal of Special Education, 19,* 291–306.

Englert, C., Raphael, T., Anderson, L., Anthony, H., Steven, D., & Fear, K. (1991). Making writing and self-talk visible: Cognitive strategy instruction in writing in regular and special education classrooms. *American Educational Research Journal, 28,* 337–373.

Englert, C., Raphael, T., Fear, K., & Anderson, L. (1988). Students' metacognitive knowledge about how to write information texts. *Learning Disability Quarterly, 11,* 18–46.

Espin, C., & Sindelar, P. (1988). Auditory feedback and writing: Learning disabled and nondisabled students. *Exceptional Children, 55,* 45–51.

Fauke, J., Burnett, J., Poers, M., & Sulzer-Azeroff, R. (1973). Improvement of handwriting and letter recognition skills: A behavior modification procedure. *Journal of Learning Disabilities, 6,* 25–29.

Fitzgerald, J., & Markham, L. (1987). Teaching children about revision in writing. *Cognition and Instruction, 4,* 3–24.

Fitzgerald, J., & Teasley, A. (1986). Effects of instruction in narrative structure on children's writing. *Journal of Educational Psychology, 78,* 424–432.

Fortner, V. (1986). Generalization of creative productive-thinking training to LD students' written expression. *Learning Disability Quarterly, 9,* 274–284.

Fuchs, L., & Fuchs, D. (1986). Effects of systematic formative evaluation: A meta-analysis. *Exceptional Children, 53,* 199–208.

Gettinger, M., Bryant, N. D., & Fayne, H. R. (1982). Designing spelling instruction for learning disabled children: An emphasis on unit size, distributed practice, and training for transfer. *Journal of Special Education, 16,* 439–448.

Golub, L. (1974). How American children learn to write. *Elementary School Journal, 74,* 236–247.

Gould, J. (1980). Experiments on composing letters: Some facts, some myths, and some observations. In L. Gregg & E. Steinberg (Eds.), *Cognitive processes in writing* (pp. 97–127). Hillsdale: Lawrence Erlbaum.

Graham, S. (1997). Executive control in the revising of students with writing and learning difficulties. *Journal of Educational Psychology, 89,* 223–234.

Graham, S. (1993/1994). Are slanted manuscript alphabets superior to the traditional alphabet. *Childhood Education, 70,* 91–95.

Graham, S. (1992). Issues in handwriting instruction. *Focus on Exceptional Children, 25,* 1–14.

Graham, S. (1990). The role of production factors in learning disabled students' compositions. *Journal of Educational Psychology, 82,* 781–791.

Graham, S. (1983a). The effects of self-instructional procedures on LD students' handwriting performance. *Learning Disability Quarterly, 6,* 231–234.

Graham, S. (1983b). Effective spelling instruction. *Elementary School Journal, 83,* 560–568.

Graham, S. (1982). Composition research and practice. A unified approach. *Focus on Exceptional Children, 14,* 1–16.

Graham, S., Berninger, V., Abbott, R., Abbott, S., & Whitaker, D. (1997). Role of mechanics in composing of elementary school students: A new methodological approach. *Journal of Educational Psychology, 89,* 170–182.

Graham, S., & Freeman, S. (1986). Strategy training and teacher vs. student-controlled study conditions: Effects on learning disabled students' spelling performance. *Learning Disability Quarterly, 9,* 15–22.

Graham, S., & Harris, K. R. (1997a). It can be taught, but it does not develop naturally: Myths and realities in writing instruction. *School Psychology Review, 26,* 414–424.

Graham, S., & Harris, K. R. (1997b). Self-regulation and writing: Where do we go from here. *Contemporary Educational Psychology, 22,* 102–114.

Graham, S., & Harris, K. R. (1997c). Whole language and process writing: Does one approach fit all? In J. Lloyd, E., Kameenui, & D. Chard, (Eds.), *Issues in educating students with disabilities* (pp. 239–258). Hillsdale, NJ: Erlbaum.

Graham, S., & Harris, K. R. (1994a). The role and development of self-regulation in the writing process. In D. Schunk and B. Zimmerman (Eds.), *Self-regulation of learning and performance: Issues and educational applications* (pp. 203–228). New York: Lawrence Erlbaum.

Graham, S., & Harris, K. R. (1994b). Implications of constructivism for teaching writing to students with special needs. *Journal of Special Education, 28,* 275–289.

Graham, S., & Harris, K. R. (1993). Teaching writing strategies to students with learning disorders: Issues and recommendations. In L. Meltzer (Ed.), *Strategy and processing deficits in learning disorders* (pp. 271–292). Austin, TX: Pro-Ed.

Graham, S., & Harris, K. R. (1989). A components analysis of cognitive strategy instruction: Effects on learning disabled students' compositions and self-efficacy. *Journal of Educational Psychology, 81,* 353–361.

Graham, S., & Harris, K. R. (1988). Instructional recommendations for teaching writing to exceptional students. *Exceptional Children, 54,* 506–512.

Graham, S., Harris, K. R., & Loynachan, C. (1996). The Directed Spelling Thinking activity: Application with high frequency words. *Learning Disability Research and Practice, 11,* 34–40.

Graham, S., Harris, K. R., & Loynachan, C. (1994). The spelling for writing list. *Journal of Learning Disabilities, 27,* 210–214.

Graham, S., Harris, K. R., & Loynachan, C. (1993). The basic spelling vocabulary list. *Journal of Educational Research, 86,* 363–368.

Graham, S., Harris, K. R., MacArthur, C., & Schwartz, S. (1991). Writing and writing instruction with students with learning disabilities: A review of a program of research. *Learning Disability Quarterly, 14,* 89–114.

Graham, S., Harris, K. R., Troia, G. A. (in press). Writing and Self-Regulation: Cases From The Self-Regulated Strategy Development Model. In D. Schunk & B. Zimmerman (Eds.), *Developing self-regulated learners: From teaching to self-reflective practices.* New York: Guilford.

Graham, S., & MacArthur, C. (1988). Improving learning disabled students' skills at revising essays produced on a word processor: Self-instructional strategy training. *Journal of Special Education, 22,* 133–152.

Graham, S., MacArthur, C., & Schwartz, S. (1995). The effects of goal setting and procedural facilitation on the revising behavior and writing performance of students with writing and learning problems. *Journal of Educational Psychology, 87,* 230–240.

Graham, S., MacArthur, C., Schwartz, S., & Voth, T. (1992). Improving the compositions of students with learning disabilities using a strategy involving product and process goal setting. *Exceptional Children, 58,* 322–335.

Graham, S., Schwartz, S., & MacArthur, C. (1993). Learning disabled and normally achieving students' knowledge of the writing and the composing process, attitude toward writing, and self-efficacy. *Journal of Learning Disabilities, 26,* 237–249.

Graham, S., & Miller, L. (1980). Handwriting research and practice: A unified approach. *Focus on Exceptional Children, 13,* 1–16.

Graham, S., & Miller, L. (1979). Spelling research and practice: A unified approach. *Focus on Exceptional Children, 12,* 1–16.

Graham, S., & Voth, V. (1990). Spelling instruction: Making modifications for students with learning disabilities. *Academic Therapy, 25,* 447–457.

Graham, S., & Weintraub, N. (1996). A review of handwriting research: Progress and prospect from 1980 to 1994. *Educational Psychology Review, 8,* 7–87.

Graves, D. H. (1983). *Writing: Teachers and children at work.* Portsmouth, NH: Heinemann.

Hallahan, D. P., Lloyd, J. W., Kosiewicz, M., Kauffman, J. M., & Graves, A. (1979). Self-monitoring of attention as a treatment for a learning disabled boy's off-task behavior. *Learning Disability Quarterly, 8,* 27–36.

Harris, K. (1986). Self-monitoring of attentional behavior vs. self-monitoring of productivity: Effects on on-task behavior and academic response rate among learning disabled children. *Journal of Applied Behavior Analysis, 19,* 417–423.

Harris, K. R., & Graham, S. (1994). Constructivism: Principles, paradigms, and integration. *Journal of Special Education, 28,* 275–289.

Harris, K. R., & Graham, S. (1992). Self-regulated strategy development: A part of the writing process. In M. Pressley, K. Harris, & J. Guthrie (Eds.), *Promoting academic competence and literacy in school* (pp. 277–309). San Diego: Academic Press.

Harris, K. R., & Graham, S. (1985). Improving learning disabled students' composition skills: Self-control strategy training. *Learning Disability Quarterly, 8,* 27–36.

Harris, K. R., & Graham, Reid, R., McElroy, K., & Hamby, R. (1994). Self-monitoring of attention versus self-monitoring of performance: Replication and cross-task comparison studies. *Learning Disability Quarterly, 17,* 121–139.

Hillocks, G. (1984). What works in teaching composition: A meta analysis of experimental studies. *American Journal of Education, 93,* 133–170.

Horton, L. (1969). *An analysis of illegibilities in the cursive writing of 1,000 selected sixth-grade students.* Unpublished doctoral dissertation, Ohio State University, Columbus.

Hubble, S. (1996). News from an uncharted world. *Washington Post Bookworld,* p. 1.

Kapadia, S., & Fantuzzo, J. (1988). Effects of teacher- and self administered procedures on the spelling performance of learning handicapped children. *Journal of School Psychology, 26,* 49–58.

Kerr, M., & Lambert, D. (1982). Behavior modification of children's written language. In M. Hersen, R. Eisler, & P. Miller (Eds.), *Progress in behavior modification* Vol. 13 (pp. 79–108). San Diego: Academic Press.

Leinhart, G., Zigmond, N., & Cooley, W. (1980, April). *Reading instruction and its effects.* Paper presented at the Annual Meeting of the American Educational Research Association, Boston.

Lew, M., & Bryant, R. (1984). The effects of cooperative groups on regular class spelling achievement of special needs learners. *Educational Psychology, 4,* 275–283.

MacArthur, C. (1996). Using technology to enhance the writing processes of students with learning disabilities. *Journal of Learning Disabilities, 29,* 344–354.

MacArthur, C. A. (1988). The impact of computers on the writing process. *Exceptional Children, 54,* 536–542.

MacArthur, C. A., & Haynes, J. A. (1996, April). *Beyond word processing: Speech synthesis and word prediction for students with learning disabilities.* Annual conference of the Council for Exceptional Children, Orlando.

MacArthur, C., & Graham, S. (1987). Learning disabled students' composing with three methods: Handwriting, dictation, and word processing. *Journal of Special Education, 21,* 22–42.

MacArthur, C., Graham, S., Haynes, J., & De La Paz, S. (1996). Spelling checkers and students with learning disabilities: Performance comparisons and impact on spelling. *Journal of Special Education, 30,* 35–57.

MacArthur, Graham, S., & Schwartz, S. (1993). Integrating strategy instruction and word processing into a process approach to writing. *School Psychology Review, 22,* 671–681.

MacArthur, C., Graham, S., Schwartz, S., & Shafer, W. (1995). Evaluation of a writing instruction model that integrated a process approach, strategy instruction, and word processing. *Learning Disabilities Quarterly, 18,* 278–292.

MacArthur, C., Schwartz, S., & Graham, S. (1991). Effects of a reciprocal peer revision strategy in special education classrooms. *Learning Disabilities Research and Practice, 6,* 201–210.

MacArthur C., Schwartz, S., Graham, S., Molloy, D., & Harris, K. (1996). Integration of strategy instruction into whole language classrooms: A case study. *Learning Disabilities and Practice, 11,* 168–176.

Maheady, L., & Harper, G. (1987). A class-wide peer tutoring program to improve the spelling test performance of low-income, third- and fourth-grade students. *Education and Treatment of children, 10,* 120–133.

McCutchen, D. (1988). "Functional automaticity" in children's writing: A problem of metacognitive control. *Written Communication, 5,* 306–324.

McLaughlin, T. (1982). Effects of self-determined and high performance standards on spelling performance. A multi-element baseline analysis. *Child and Family Behavior Therapy, 4,* 55–61.

Montague, M., Graves, A., & Leavell, A. (1991). Planning, procedural facilitation, and narrative composition of junior high students with learning disabilities. *Learning Disabilities Research and Practice, 6,* 219–224.

Morocco, C. C., & Neuman, S. B. (1986). Word processors and the acquisition of writing strategies. *Journal of Learning Disabilities, 19,* 243–247.

Peyton, J. K., & Batson, T. (1986). Computer networking: Making connections between speech and writing. *ERIC/CLL News Bulletin, 10*(1), 1,5–7.

Plimpton, G. (Ed.) (1967). *Writers at work: the Paris* Review *interviews* (Third Series). New York: Viking Press.

Pressley, M., Goodchild, F., Fleet, J., Zajchowski, R., & Evans, E. (1989). The challenges of classroom strategy instruction. *Elementary School Journal, 89,* 301–342.

Reyes, M. (1991). A process approach to literacy using dialogue journals and literature logs with second language learners. *Research in the Teaching of English, 25,* 291–313.

Riel, M. M. (1985). The computer chronicles newswire: A functional learning environment for acquiring literacy skills. *Journal of Educational Computing Research, 1,* 317–337.

Rieth, H. J., Axelrod, S., Anderson, R., Hathaway, F., Wood, K., & Fitzgerald, C. (1974). Influence of distributed practice and daily testing on weekly spelling tests. *Journal of Educational Research, 68,* 73–77.

Robin, A. L., Armel, S., & O'Leary, D. K. (1975). The effects of self instruction on writing deficiencies. *Behavior Therapy, 6,* 178–187.

Safire, W., & Safire, L. (1992). *Good advice on writing.* New York: Simon & Schuster.

Sawyer, R., Graham, S., & Harris, K. R. (1992). Direct teaching, strategy instruction, and strategy instruction with explicit self-regulation: Effects on learning disabled students' compositions and self-efficacy. *Journal of Educational Psychology, 84,* 340–352.

Scardamalia, M., & Bereiter, C. (1986). Written composition. In M. Wittrock (Ed.), *Handbook of research on teaching* (3rd Ed., pp. 778–803). New York: MacMillan.

Schumaker, J., Deshler, D., Alley, G., Warner, M., Clark, F., & Nolan, S. (1982). Error monitoring: A learning strategy for improving adolescent performance. In W. M. Cruickshank & J. Lerner (Eds.), *Best of ACLD* (Vol. 3, pp. 179–183). Syracuse, NY: Syracuse University Press.

Schumaker, J., & Sheldon, J. (1985). *The sentence writing strategy*. Lawrence: University of Kansas.

Sowers, S. (1986). Reflect, expand, select: Three responses in the writing conference. In T. Newkirk & N. Atwell (Eds.), *Understanding writing: Ways of observing, learning and teaching* (pp. 123–129). Portsmouth, NH: Heinemann.

Stoddard, B., & MacArthur, C. (1993). A peer editor strategy: Guiding learning disabled students in response and revision. *Research in the Teaching of English, 27,* 76–103.

Streitfeld, D. (1994). Obscurely famous. *Washington Post,* April 10.

Sutlin, L. (1989). *Divine invasions: A life of Philip K. Dick.* NY: Harmony.

Vukelich, C., & Leverson, L. D. (1987). Two young writers: The relationship between text revisions and teacher/student conferences. In J. E. Readence & R. S. Baldwin (Eds.), *Research in literacy: Merging perspectives. Thirty-sixth Yearbook of the National Reading Conference* (pp. 281–286). Rochester, NY: National Reading Conference.

Wilde, S. (1990). Spelling textbooks: A critical review. *Linguistics and Education, 2,* 259–280.

Wong, B. (in press). Research on genre specific strategies in enhancing writing in adolescents with learning disabilities. *Learning Disability Quarterly.*

Wong, B. (1994). Instructional parameters promoting transfer of learned strategies in students with learning disabilities. *Learning Disability Quarterly, 17,* 100–119.

Wong, B. Y. L. (1986). A cognitive approach to teaching spelling. *Exceptional Children, 53,* 169–173.

Wong, B., Butler, D., Ficzere, S., Kuperis, S., Corden, M., & Zelmer, J. (1994). Teaching problem learners revision skills and sensitivity to audience through two instructional modes: Student-teacher versus student-student interactive dialogues. *Learning Disabilities Research and Practice, 9,* 78–90.

CHAPTER 13

Instructional Interventions for Students with Mathematics Learning Disabilities

Margo A. Mastropieri, Thomas E. Scruggs, and SuHsiang Chung

I. INTRODUCTION

In 1989, the National Council of Teachers of Mathematics (NCTM) published its *Curriculum and Evaluation Standards for School Mathematics.* These standards emphasized conceptual development through manipulative materials, learner-based knowledge construction, and the stimulation of deep understanding of mathematical concepts and procedures. Greatly de-emphasized was rote learning and computation. These standards are presently exerting substantial influence on mathematics education reform in the United States (Pressley & McCormick, 1995).

Unfortunately, many special education professionals have expressed concern about the NCTM standards as applied to students with learning disabilities (LD) (e.g., Hofmeister, 1993; Kameenui, Chard, & Carnine, 1996; Montague, 1996c; Rivera, 1993, 1997; Woodward, Baxter, & Scheel, 1997). These concerns are essentially based on fears that methods (e.g., "discovery," "inquiry") that require independent insight on the part of the learner will not be effective for students with LD, for whom insight or deductive inference can be relative weaknesses (Mastropieri, Scruggs, & Butcher, 1997). However, it also may be true that historically, special education professionals have overemphasized rote learning of facts and procedures, to the extent that students have had little opportunity to experience and practice mathematical reasoning (Cawley, Miller, & School, 1987).

Among the concerns mentioned are limited reference to students with LD, discussion of vague (or incompletely specified) theoretical constructs, and an emphasis on theory rather than substantive research findings. Bishop (1990) noted,

> It is a little surprising that there is not much reference to the research literature concerning mathematics learning and teaching. There is no impression of the existence of a substantial body of research on which, for example, the proposals in the Standards are based. (p. 366)

The NCTM standards in and of themselves make little reference to disability. The National Research Council's *Everybody Counts* (NRC, 1989), which seeks to describe a mathematics agenda for the United States, does address mathematics and students with disabilities; however, the discussion is brief and implicitly limited to individuals with physical disabilities:

> Mathematics requires only mental acuity for effective performance. Success in mathematics depends neither on physical skills nor on the physical means by which the worker communicates his or her results. (National Research Council, 1989, p. 23)

Even if this statement is applied solely to physical/sensory disabilities, it may not be entirely accurate. Advocates for the hearing-impaired (for whom mathematics may be an area of relative strength), for example, have suggested that the new standards' emphasis on printed English may have negative consequences because few prelingually deaf students achieve full competence in Standard English (Schroeder & Strosnider, 1997). Additionally, students with visual impairments may have difficulties with print and mathematical notation, and students with physical disabilities may exhibit problems with physical aspects of the new mathematics standards, such as manipulatives (e.g., Mastropieri & Scruggs, 1993).

Additionally, all individuals with intellectual or LD may not exhibit the "mental acuity" implicitly required by NRC. In this light, the NRC statement seems to dismiss rather easily those who may not possess such acuity. In the following section, we discuss the mathematics abilities of students with LD.

II. LEARNING DISABILITIES AND MATHEMATICS ACHIEVEMENT

Research has documented that students with LD can lag far behind other students in the area of mathematics. Scruggs and Mastropieri (1986) reported that a sample of 619 primary grade students with LD scored between the 18th and 34th percentile on the Total Math subtest of the Standard Achievement Test. Parmar, Cawley, and Frazita (1996) reported that a sample of 197 students with LD and behavioral disorders, in grades 3–8, scored as much as 4 years below their nondisabled peers on tests of math problem solving. McLeskey and Waldron (1990) reported that 64% of 906 students in the state of Indiana from ages 5–19 were achieving below grade level in mathematics.

Montague (1996b) summarized the types of difficulties many students with LD may exhibit in the area of mathematics (see also Miller & Mercer, 1997):

1. Memory and strategic deficits can differentially affect mathematics performance, causing some students to experience difficulty conceptualizing mathematical operations, representing and automatically recalling math facts, conceptualizing and learning algorithms and mathematical formulae, or solving mathematical word problems.
2. Language and communication disorders may interfere with students' functioning when they are expected to read, write, and discuss ideas about mathematics.
3. Deficiencies in processes and strategies specifically associated with solving mathematical word problems also can interfere with students' conceptual understanding of problem situations and how to address those situations mathematically.
4. Low motivation, poor self-esteem, and a history of academic failure can arrest a student's desire to value mathematics and to become confident in his or her ability to become mathematically literate (Montague, 1996b, p. 85).

Cawley, Fitzmaurice, Shaw, Kahn, and Bates (1979) described several contributing factors to poor math performance, including (a) problems related to other deficits, such as reading (see also Englert, Culatta, & Horn, 1987); (b) ineffective or inappropriate instruction; and (c) deficits in psychological processes, such as memory, attention, encoding, or organizational skills. DeBettencourt, Putnam, and Leinhardt (1993) described deficits of students with LD in understanding of derived strategies for basic facts. Researchers such as Montague (1996a,b,c) and Lucangeli, Coi, and Bosco (1997) have provided evidence that students with LD exhibit lower levels of metacognitive awareness in mathematics than normally achieving peers.

What intervention strategies have been previously shown to be effective with students with LD? Mastropieri, Scruggs, and Shiah (1991) reviewed research conducted between 1975 and 1989, the year the NCTM Standards were published. They located 30 intervention research studies that documented effective treatments involving reinforcement and goalsetting, specific strategies for computation and problem solving, mnemonic strategies, peer mediation, and computer-assisted instruction (CAI). Most intervention strategies focused on computation and employed direct instruction or behaviorally oriented treatments. However, no conclusions can be drawn about research that was conducted since 1989. Recently, Jitendra and Xin (1997) reviewed mathematics interventions for students with LD published between 1986 and 1995. Although some significant progress was noted in teaching mathematics, this review was not comprehensive, focusing instead on 14 individual studies concerned with word problem solving involving students with learning and other disabilities, students "at risk," and students receiving remedial instruction. Maccini and Hughes (1997) reviewed mathematics interventions for students with LD from 1988 to 1995, but confined their review to 20 studies that dealt specifically with adolescents.

The purpose of this chapter is to review and summarize intervention research on mathematics performance of students with LD in grades K–12, that has occurred since the research reported by Mastropieri et al., (1991). Such a review can provide important information on the present state of knowledge regarding mathematics interventions for students with LD, and how such information informs previous research, as well as NCTM standards. In addition, it is thought that such a review could provide direction for future research efforts in this area.

III. PROCEDURES

A systematic literature search was conducted through a computer-based database, Education Resources Information Center (ERIC) to locate articles published from 1988 to 1995. This search procedure used the following descriptors: research or intervention in mathematics, arithmetic, computation, problem solving, or word/ story problems in LD or mildly handicapped individuals. The reference lists of all obtained articles were examined for further sources. Previous reviews (e.g., Jitendra & Xin, 1997) were also examined for relevant sources. Finally, a hand search of relevant journals (e.g., *Journals of Learning Disabilities, Learning Disabilities Research & Practice, Exceptional Children*) was conducted.

Articles that met the following criteria were included: First, the target population involved students with LD enrolled in grades K–12. Second, the investigation examined the effects of interventions on mathematics performance. Third, articles were published from July 1988 through December 1996, in order to extend a previous review paper on mathematics interventions for students with LD, which reviewed studies published prior to July 1988 (Mastropieri et al., 1991).

Several articles that met some of the required characteristics were excluded from this review. For example, six articles were excluded because participants' disability areas were not specified (e.g., Moore & Carnine, 1989). Two were excluded from the initial pool of articles because students did not meet age specifications (Johnson, 1994; Zawaiza & Gerber, 1993). As the result of the search procedure, 38 articles were identified that met all selection criteria.

IV. OVERALL STUDY CHARACTERISTICS

A total of 780 LD students participated as subjects in the 38 investigations. The mean age of these samples ranged from 6.5 to 16.8 per group, and ranged in mean IQ from 74.99 to 99.5 per group. Of the total sample, 73.1% (570) were males. The majority of interventions were conducted in school settings, such as special education or general education classrooms, or computer labs.

Nineteen studies (50%) employed single subject designs, 15 studies (39%) employed experimental group comparison designs, and 4 studies (11%) employed pre–post group designs. All studies used criterion-referenced tests except one, which used a standardized test as a dependent measure. The studies considered in this review fell broadly into computation or problem-solving categories. Each of these categories is discussed in the following sections.

V. INTERVENTIONS ON COMPUTATION

Twenty-four (65%) of the identified studies focused on methods for improving the computation skills of students with LD. The computation studies included methods for developing proficiency in basic numeration concepts, facts, and operations (addition, subtraction, multiplication, and division) with whole numbers, fractions, or decimals.

A. Behavioral Approaches

1. Reinforcement

Pavchinski, Evans, and Bostow (1989) described an intervention with a 12-year-old student with LD to increase basic reading and math skills. Using a changing criterion design and a token reinforcement system, the student was presented with Dolch sight words, and a second set of measures consisting of a list of 220 simple arithmetic problems. Tokens earned for meeting the target criterion could be exchanged for privileges in the student's group home program. In a second experiment, the student studied the 95 most difficult multiplication and division problems. The authors concluded that the student made very substantial progress with the program.

2. Presentation Variations

Albers and Greer (1991) increased the number of three-term contingency trials (antecedent, response, consequence) in order to increase rates of correct responding on mathematics content in students with LD. In Experiment 1, the presentation of three-term contingency trials was increased by a factor of three (from .41 to 1.25 per minute) for two students. In Experiment 2, the treatment was applied differentially to written and vocal presentations for a third student with LD. Results of both experiments indicated that increasing the rate of three-term contingency trials resulted in an increase in correct responding while maintaining low levels of incorrect responding.

Koscinski and Gast (1993b) used a 4-sec constant time delay procedure (correct response was provided 4 sec after the stimulus presentation; see Koscinski & Hoy, 1993) to teach multiplication facts to five elementary grade students with LD. Responding was found to generalize to a paper-and-pencil task, horizontal number display, reverse fact, and ability to solve missing-factor problems.

Houten (1993) compared rote drill with a rule learning procedure in learning subtraction in three experiments with 8 students, 5 of whom were characterized as having LD. The rule taught was, then subtracting 7 or 9, "you simply add three/one to the number above the (seven/nine)" (p. 150). Data from alternating treatment designs revealed that students made greater progress in the rule condition. In the third experiment, students generalized their rule knowledge to a new problem.

Cooke, Guzaukas, Pressley, and Kerr (1993), in the second of three experiments, investigated the effects of interspersal drill and practice using a ratio of 30% new items to 70% review items, or 100% new items. Subjects were three 9- to 11-year-old students with LD. All three students made greater gains in the 30/70% condition.

3. Peer Mediation

Beirne-Smith (1991) investigated the effects of peer tutoring on acquisition of addition facts for elementary age students with LD. In one tutoring condition, related facts (second addend increased by one) were presented in sets of three; in a second condition, facts were presented randomly. Both treatments resulted in gains relative to a no-treatment control condition. However, differences were not observed in outcomes between the two tutoring conditions, for tutors or tutees.

Hawkins, Brady, Hamilton, Williams, Taylor (1994) investigated the use of peer guided practice or independent practice during instructional pauses from lecture in arithmetic computation to eight students classified as LD or severely emotionally disturbed. During 4-minute pauses, students either practiced in pairs or practiced independently. Although results from the treatment comparisons were mixed, students overall gained substantially from the intervention.

Fuchs et al. (1996) investigated the quality and effectiveness of students' (grades 2–4) mathematical explanations to 20 tutees with LD as a function of the ability of the tutor in mathematics. Their results indicated that high-achieving tutors were rated higher on conceptual and procedural characteristics as well as on overall quality, as compared with tutors of average ability. High-achieving tutors also were associated with higher performance of tutees, in that tutees with LD completed 91% of the arithmetic computation problems correctly with the high-achieving tutor, compared with 75% accuracy with average-achieving tutors.

4. Counting Money

Hastings, Raymond, and McLaughlin (1989) used task-analysis and direct instruction procedures to train seven students, including two with LD, to count money rapidly. After training, all students maintained 90% levels of accuracy, significantly improved their rates of counting, and maintained their skills across settings and time.

5. Homework Completion

Patzelt (1991) employed several behavioral techniques to increase the rate of mathematics homework completion by a 9-year-old student with LD. Homework completion increased substantially as a consequence of a 3-week behavioral contract and edible and social reinforcers, including reminder notices, a certificate of accomplishment, and verbal praise. The contract required the student to complete homework neatly, check homework with the teacher, and jointly complete a recording chart. Over time, the student became responsible for checking homework and monitoring the chart.

O'Melia and Rosenberg (1994) investigated the effectiveness of Cooperative Homework Teams (CHT) in increasing mathematics achievement. One hundred seventy-one middle-school students (including 160 students with LD and 11 students with emotional disturbance) were randomly assigned to a CHT or control condition. Students in the CHT condition were assigned to a team of three of four members, who met each morning to submit their math homework assignment to the student designated each day as a checker. The checker checked each student's work and reported the grades to the teacher. Analysis of results revealed that students in the CHT condition performed significantly higher than the control condition on homework completion and percentage correct on homework assignments, but not higher on a global measure of mathematics achievement.

6. Summary

Recent behavioral research has provided additional information on the positive effects of a variety of behavioral techniques on the math computation performance of students with LD. These techniques have included behavioral techniques such as presentation rate, drill and practice, direct instruction, cumulative review, reinforcement and behavioral contracting, commonly reported to be generally effective teaching strategies (Mastropieri & Scruggs, 1994). In addition, further information was provided on rule learning and peer mediation, including tutoring and cooperative homework teams.

B. Metacognitive Training

1. Self-Monitoring

Prater, Hogan, and Miller (1992) trained an adolescent with LD and behavioral disorders to use self-monitoring of on-task behavior to improve his academic functioning, including the area of mathematics. The student listened to an audio-cassette player with headphones. When a tone was heard, the student was instructed to ask himself, "Was I working?" and to record the answer. Visual cues of on-task behavior were provided. In the mainstream classroom, the student was instructed to self-record "whenever he thought of it" (p. 49). It was reported that the student's academic behavior improved both in the resource room and in the generalization setting.

2. Academic Strategies

Four studies used some variations of metacognitive training to enhance computation skills. Dunlap and Dunlap (1989) investigated the effects of error self-monitoring to improve subtraction with regrouping of three students with LD. A two-phase baseline was employed, in which students received instruction and incentives. Students' error patterns were then analyzed, and individualized self-monitoring checklists were developed. For example, for one student, a five-step checklist was developed (Dunlap & Dunlap, 1989, p. 311):

1. I copied the problem correctly.
2. I regrouped when I needed to (top number is bigger than the bottom).
3. I borrowed correctly (number crossed out is one bigger).
4. I subtracted all the numbers.
5. I subtracted correctly.

For another student, a four-step checklist was developed (Dunlap & Dunlap, 1989, p. 311):

1. I underlined all the top numbers that were smaller than the bottom.
2. I crossed out only the number next to the underlined number and made it one less.
3. I put a "1" beside the underlined number.
4. All the numbers on the top are bigger than the numbers on the bottom.

Students then worked on problems, and recorded a plus for performing each specific step and a minus for not performing a self-monitoring step on the checklist. If they failed to perform any specific step, they reworked the problems again. The results revealed that the students immediately improved their performance to 60–100% as self-monitoring checklists were employed. These students maintained their levels of performance after the checklists were removed.

Kamann and Wong (1993) investigated the effectiveness of self-statement instruction to reduce math anxiety in 10 students with LD (grades 4–7) when solving problems involving fractions. Ten normally achieving students served as a comparison group. The trainer demonstrated a self-talk procedure that consisted of positive, neutral, and negative statements. Oral and visual representation of poor self-talk that affects performance were presented to evoke awareness of students' maladaptive styles of thinking. Next, the coping strategies were introduced. The trainer modeled the strategies as outlined on two cue cards that described the steps in the coping process and the coping self-statements: situation assessment, identifying and controlling negative thoughts, coping thought, and reinforcement. The confronting/coping/controlling self-statements included the following (Kamann & Wong, 1993, p. 632).

> Don't worry. Remember to use your plan.
> Take it step by step—look at one question at a time.
> Don't let your eyes wander to other questions.
> Don't think about what others are doing. Take it one step at a time.
> When you feel your fears coming on . . . take a deep breath, think, "I am doing just fine. Things are going well."

The problems included deriving equivalent fractions, converting fractions, addition and subtraction of unit fractions and mixed fractions without regrouping, and multiplication and division of unit fractions. Students were encouraged to think aloud during the intervention with cue cards. Students were prompted if they ceased thinking aloud in 3 min. A booster session was provided for students. On the first, fourth, and sixth days of intervention, students redid a completed problem without using cue cards. Results indicated that although normally achieving students produced more positive and less negative self-statements than students with LD on the pretest, there was no substantial difference on posttest. Positive thinking had significant correlation on fraction performance on students with LD. Moreover, correct responses of students with LD increased approximately 32%. The intervention was apparently less successful for fourth graders.

Laird and Winton (1993) compared the effectiveness of three self-instructional checking procedures for math performance. Five students with LD were trained for multiplication and two others were trained for division. During baseline, students were taught to think aloud while solving problems. Three checking procedures were used during and after solving problems: (a) no-checking—not required to check, (b) end checking—check after solving problems, and (c) multichecking. Each procedure was randomly selected once in every block of three sessions. After the written and verbal demonstration of checking procedures, students were asked to verbalize for at least 12 min when solving problems. Prompts were given to ensure students followed the correct procedures in 4 sec intervals. When the most effective procedure was determined, three sessions each of the best procedure, follow-up, and best procedure again were implemented. For all students except one, multichecking was the most effective. Generalization effects were obtained. Although all students increased in accuracy, the division group performed higher than the multiplication group.

Wood, Rosenberg, and Carran (1993) studied the effects of tape-recorded self-instruction cues in a multiple baseline, single-subject design. Nine LD students were stratified to high, middle, and low achievement levels, and randomly assigned to one of three conditions. Students in the experimental condition were provided with ten-step self-instruction cues for solving addition and subtraction problems (e.g., point to the problem, read the problem, circle the sign, self-reinforce). Students then recorded these steps onto audiotape. Positive feedback was provided to students for correct responses and repeated remodeling and rehearsing for incorrect responses until students could correctly and independently use taped cues to apply the self-instruction procedure. The experimental group increased dramatically in accuracy, number of problems completed, and time to complete problems following the second self-instruction training session. No concurrent effects were observed for students assigned to observer or control conditions.

3. Summary

Interventions on a variety of metacognitive strategies to improve math computation skills of students with LD were largely effective, providing further evidence for general metacognitive deficits in students with LD (e.g., Scruggs & Brigham, 1990). In the research presently reviewed, effective metacognitive training was implemented in the areas of self-monitoring of on-task behavior, error self-monitoring, making positive affective self-statements, self-instructional checking procedures, and self-instruction of calculation procedures.

C. Use of Manipulatives and Metacognitive Training

Harding, Gust, Goldhawk, and Bierman (1993) investigated the effectiveness of a curriculum that employed manipulatives, pencil-and-paper activities, and verbal interaction to improve calculation of basic facts in eight students with LD, two students with emotional disturbance, and one student with mental retardation. Over an average of 32 instructional sessions, students increased substantially in their ability to calculate multiplication and division problems.

Miller and Mercer (1993a) investigated the effectiveness of a sequence of concrete-semiconcrete-abstract (CSA) instruction on math facts (see Mercer & Miller, 1992). In this study, there were five LD students, three "at-risk" students, and one educable mentally handicapped student who had math disabilities. One of three teachers taught three students in each of three math skills: (a) addition facts with sums from 10 to 18, (b) division facts with quotients from 0–9, and (c) coin sums amounting to as much as 50 cents. The teacher provided a verbal organizer, demonstrated the skill by think-aloud and modeling, provided guided practice with prompts, cues, and feedback, and provided independent practice. The instruction sequences progressed from concrete, semiconcrete, to abstract, on each instructional level. The concrete level instruction employed manipulatives; illustrations were provided on the semiconcrete level; on the abstract level, drawings were provided only when students could not recall the facts. Data were collected after every lesson and 1 week after treatment based on 1-minute probes on the abstract level.

The results were discussed with respect to "crossover effects," by which was meant the point at which correct responses exceeded incorrect responses on 1-min abstract probes. It was concluded that four students experienced crossover effects during concrete, and five students during semiconcrete level instruction. Further analysis manifested that students took 3–7 lessons to obtain crossover effects. The authors concluded that CSA was an effective means for teaching math computation.

Harris, Miller, and Mercer (1995) investigated the effect of using concrete-representational-abstract teaching sequence to improve multiplication skills in mainstream classrooms. Twelve students with LD and one emotionally disturbed student who were mainstreamed in six regular second-grade classrooms with a total of 99 nondisabled peers participated in this experiment.

Understanding of multiplication concepts were taught (lesson 1–3) to students by using concrete manipulatives with language parallel to that used in the problems. On the representational level (lesson 4–6), students were taught to use pictures of objects and tallies to solve problems. The mnemonic acronym DRAW was taught in the seventh lesson. Students were encouraged to use the DRAW (Discover the sign, Read the problem, Answer (or draw), check, and Write the answer) mnemonic to solve problems without using manipulatives, pictures, or tallies for the following three lessons.

Word problems and increasing computation rate began from lesson 11. In this lesson, students were taught a mnemonic device, FAST DRAW, which combined the FAST (Find what you're solving for, Ask yourself "What are the parts of the problem?", Set up the numbers, and Tie down the sign) device and previous learned DRAW device, to set up and solve word problems. During lessons 12 to 21, students independently practiced word problems with or without extraneous information and filled in blank spaces to create their own word problems. Results indicated that students with LD substantially increased their math performance, although not to the level of the normally achieving students.

1. Summary

Recent research has demonstrated the positive effects of the use of concrete, manipulative materials to increase computation ability. In many cases, students learned a progression of skills from concrete, to pictorial, and then to use of abstract numbers in solving computation problems.

D. Computer-Assisted Instruction

1. Drill and Practice

Koscinski and Gast (1993a) examined the effect of a CAI program incorporating constant time delay on student learning of multiplication facts. A 5-sec delay was employed after the initial prompt, after which time the correct answer appeared, if it has not been produced by the student. Screening was conducted to determine 15 unknown multiplication facts as the instructional target for six students with LD. Those facts were then divided into three sets of five facts each. Each of the five facts in a set were presented six times with 0-sec delay procedure, followed by a 5-sec delay procedure. Results indicated that all students mastered multiplication facts using the CAI procedure.

2. Games versus Drill

Bahr and Rieth (1989) examined the effect of two components of a CAI program on multiplication computation skill. Fifty students with LD participated in this investigation. The drill-and-practice and the instructional game components of a software program, *Math Blaster* (Eckert & Davidson, 1987), were administered alternatively for 3 weeks each. Students in the drill-and-practice condition had twice as many opportunities to respond correctly and received feedback on response accuracy. The instructional game condition required students to respond to problems quickly in order to keep playing and obtain higher scores. Students were tested with paper-and-pencil problems. No effect was observed between the two computer components. Inconsistent outcomes were observed among three schools.

The impact of the elements within a CAI program was assessed by Christensen and Gerber (1990). Thirty students with LD (grades 3–6), and 30 normally achieving students (grades 1–2) were stratified by ability and assigned at random to one of two computer programs. One was a commercial program employing a game-like format; the other was developed for this study and included "unadorned, straightforward drill" (p. 149). After 13 training sessions, it was reported that students with LD performed better on the unadorned program, whereas the effects were less consistent for the normally achieving students. The authors concluded that the game format may have had a distracting influence on the students with LD.

The relative effectiveness of drill versus game-type format in CAI on arithmetic fact learning was further evaluated by Okolo (1992a). Forty-one LD students were stratified to low- or high-aptitude levels based on mathematics aptitude scores, and then randomly assigned to either drill or game programs, derived from two separate sections of the Math Masters computer program (DLM, 1988). Results suggested that all conditions improved from pretest to posttest; however, learning did not differ as a function of condition, even though students responded more frequently in the drill condition. Students did not report different levels of satisfaction for either of the programs. Attitudes toward math did not change after the intervention; however, low-aptitude students who had been assigned to the game condition exhibited greater motivation to continue on math tasks after the intervention was completed.

3. Attributions

Okolo (1992b) compared CAI-based attribution or neutral feedback on the learning of multiplication facts by students with LD. Both groups used modifications of public-domain software for teaching multiplication facts. The attribution-re-training group received ability attribution feedback after each set of 5 problems (e.g., "You really know these"), and effort feedback after each set of 25 problem (e.g., "You are really trying hard," or, conversely, "You can get it if you keep try-ing"; p. 329). No change in reported attributions was observed in this study; how-ever, students in the attribution-retraining group significantly improved in multi-plication performance.

4. Goal Setting

Bahr and Rieth (1991) examined the differences between goal-assigned experi-mental conditions and a control condition in learning subtraction and multiplica-tion facts. Thirty-two students with LD, 13 educable mentally retarded students, and one seriously emotionally disturbed student were paired and assigned at ran-dom to cooperative, competitive, individualistic, and no goal conditions. Group or individual goals were assigned according to each group. The goal was to score at least 50% higher than baseline levels. In the cooperative condition, students re-ceived more points (10 vs. 5) for collectively meeting the criterion. In the indi-vidualistic condition, students received 10 points rather than 5 for meeting the cri-terion individually. In the competitive condition, students received 10 points for outscoring their partner, who earned 5 points. In the no-goal condition, students received 10 points for simply participating. After 12 10-min sessions imple-mented over a 4-week period, no differences were observed among conditions on math achievement, although some modest across-condition pre–posttest gains were noted.

Fuchs, Bahr, and Rieth (1989) investigated the effects of assigned versus self-selected goals, and contingent versus noncontingent game activities on the learn-ing of arithmetic computation. Twenty students with LD were provided with com-puter-assisted drill and practice. Half of the students were assigned performance goals, while the other half were allowed to select their own goals. Each of these groups was then divided into groups of students who received access to a video game contingent upon reaching their goal, or noncontingently (i.e., whether or not they met their goal). Results suggested that students who selected their own goals outperformed students who were provided with goals. No effect was observed for contingent versus noncontingent access to the video game.

5. Instructional Design Features

Kelly, Gersten, and Carnine (1990) compared the relative effectiveness of a math basal and videodisc software that incorporated specific instructional design fea-tures on computation with fractions for students with remedial high school stu-dents and students with LD. The major difference between the curricula, other than the technological approach, was the "provision of detailed, step-by-step strategies in the instructional design curriculum" (p. 25). Curriculum-based tests of items covered explicitly in both curricula revealed that students performed significantly higher in the videodisc condition.

6. CAI versus Teacher-Directed Instruction

Finally, Wilson, Majsterek, and Simmons (1996) compared rate of acquisition of multiplication facts under CAI (*Math Blaster*) versus teacher-directed, one-to-one instruction. The CAI program provided examples of previously unlearned multiplication facts, a controlled-practice component with a time delay of 3 to 10 sec (cf. Koscinski & Gast, 1993a), and a game-style practice activity. Teacher-directed instruction provided similar activities, including presentation of new facts, drill and practice, and a game-like activity. Using a single-subject, alternating treatments design, Wilson et al. (1996) concluded that all four students acquired more math facts under teacher-directed instruction, particularly after the first several sessions. Analysis of opportunities to respond to data revealed that students received more than double the total opportunities to respond in the teacher-directed condition. Wilson et al. (1996) concluded:

> The flexible and responsive nature of the teacher-directed condition allowed teachers to move at a quicker pace, remediate errors more immediately and differentially, and build fluency through greater opportunities for practice. (p. 389)

7. Summary

Several overall conclusions can be drawn from these investigations of CAI effectiveness with students with LD. First, students with LD typically benefit to some extent from CAI in math computation. Second, performance does not appear to vary overall as a function of drill or game-like programs; however, under some circumstances, games may be less effective. Third, effort and ability attributions delivered by computer may enhance computation performance. Fourth, different types of goal assignments (e.g., cooperative-competitive) may exert little relative influence on achievement; however, self-selected goals may enhance learning over assigned goals. Finally, one-to-one teacher-directed instruction may be more effective than CAI for acquisition of basic math facts.

VI. INTERVENTIONS ON PROBLEM SOLVING

A. Metacognitive and Strategy Training

1. Direct Instruction in Fact Families

Wilson and Sindelar (1991) examined the effects of three teaching procedures on math word-problem solving of 62 elementary age students with LD. Students were taught over a 3-week period in small groups under three instructional conditions.

In the first (sequence) condition, students were provided with instruction using a sequence of complexity of word problems (simple action, classification, complex action, and comparison), adapted from a basal series. In the second (strategy) condition, students were given instruction in the "fact family" concept (Silbert, Carnine, & Stein, 1981) and provided with a rule for solving problems (e.g., "When the big number is given, subtract"). In the third condition (strategy plus sequence), students were provided with both the fact family concept and a sequence of word problems. Analysis of posttests and follow-up tests revealed significant differences among conditions, generally favoring the strategy plus sequence condition over the strategy condition, which outperformed the sequence condition.

2. Diagrams and Key Words

Walker and Poteet (1989–1990) examined the effects of diagrammatic versus key word methods for solving one- and two-step addition and subtraction story problems on 70 sixth-, seventh-, and eighth-grade students with LD. The components of effective instruction procedures were used for both groups during 17 training sessions, including teacher demonstration of the strategy, guided and independent practice, daily formative evaluation, and a review of problems. For the key word group, the procedure included (a) use of the key word method to determine what is to be found, (b) locating information, (c) writing a number sentence, and (d) finding the answer. The diagrammatic method employed the following steps: (a) draw a diagram to represent the problem, (b) write a number sentence, and (c) solve the number sentence. No significant differences were found between the two methods. Neither of the two methods appeared to increase problem-solving performance substantially over pretest levels.

3. Manipulatives

The use of manipulatives in teaching problem solving was investigated by Marsh and Cooke (1996). After verbal (abstract) instructions for problem solving during baseline, Cuisenaire rods of different values and colors were introduced to solve one-step word problems. Students were guided in manipulating the Cuisenaire rods to understand and solve the problems. The dependent measure was the number of correct operations (e.g., addition, subtraction) selected for ten-item probes. After intervention, correct responding increased 58% to 77% for all students. One student could solve problems at the abstract level, while the others improved from the concrete level to the representational level.

Miller and Mercer (1993b) validated the effectiveness of a graduated word problem sequence strategy for teaching math problem solving. The experimental design consisted of three levels of instruction: concrete, semiconcrete, and abstract. Each level contained four instructional steps: (a) providing an advance organizer, (b) demonstrating and having students model skills, and (c) guided and (d) independent practice with feedback.

The word used in the word problems matched the manipulative objects in the concrete and semiconcrete levels (Miller & Mercer, 1993b). For example, if students were learning to subtract using cubes, the words "cubes" was used in the problem (p. 172):

$$
\begin{array}{r}
4 \text{ cubes} \\
-2 \text{ cubes} \\
\hline
\text{cubes}
\end{array}
$$

During the abstract level, the difficulty of word problems increased gradually from simple words, phases, and sentences, such as (p. 172):

$$
\begin{array}{r}
8 \text{ pieces of candy} \\
-8 \text{ pieces of candy sold} \\
\hline
\text{are left}
\end{array}
$$

to more elaborate sentences (p. 172):

$$
\begin{array}{l}
\text{Jennie had 4 pens.} \\
\underline{\text{She lost 2 of them.}} \\
\text{She has} \quad \text{pens left.}
\end{array}
$$

to having the student create his/her own word problems. Posttest scores suggested that the intervention had been effective, although students predictably scored lowest in creation of their own problems.

4. Schema Diagrams

Jitendra and Hoff (1995) evaluated the effects of schema-based instruction for one-step addition and subtraction word-problem solving. One third- and two fourth-grade students with LD whose difficulty involved using incorrect equations to solve word problems participated in this study. During the problem schemata phase, students learned how to recognize relations in the problem and to distinguish three types of problems (change, group, and compare). Students mapped features of situations onto the appropriate schemata diagrams after reading story situations. For example, in change problem, the procedure involved reading the change word (e.g., verb) to determine whether an increase or decrease had occurred to the beginning amount. When the ending amount was determined to be more than the beginning amount, the word "total" was written under the ending amount on the schema diagram; otherwise the word "total" was written under the beginning amount. When the total and one of the other numbers was known, using subtraction was appropriate; when the total was unknown and the other two numbers were known, using addition was appropriate. Students successfully applied this strategy to solve addition and subtraction word problems.

The results indicated that not only the overall percentage of correct word problems increased substantially over baseline, but also that at least some generalization was evident for all students. Students circled the keyword consistently, but were less likely to draw pictures. Students reported that they found the instruction beneficial.

5. Metacognitive Academic Strategies

Case, Harris, and Graham (1992) conducted an experiment to investigate the effects of self-regulated strategy use on mathematical problem solving. Participants were four fifth- and sixth-grade LD students who had addition, subtraction, and regrouping skills but who could not solve simple word problems using these skills. Steps used in problem-solving strategy were (a) imagine pictures, (b) identify and circle cue words/phrases, (c) draw pictures, (d) write math sentence and the answer. The self-regulated instruction included the procedures of defining problems, planning, strategy use, self-evaluation, and self-reinforcement.

Students learned how to identify the cue words or phrases in word problems using manipulatives and practiced until they could identify two of three problems. The strategies were learned by students through guided practice and independent practice, and prompts were withdrawn gradually during the intervention. Students were encouraged to discuss the strategy to their teachers and apply it to different subject areas. Both phase 1 (addition instruction) and phase 2 (subtraction instruction) employed the same procedure. The results indicated that the percentage of correct answers increased substantially, accompanied by a decrease in equation errors after intervention. Students circled words but did not draw pictures. Interpretation of interview data revealed positive perception of the strategy usage for both students and their teachers. However, maintenance effects of the intervention were mixed.

Montague (1992) assessed the effects of cognitive and metacognitive strategy instruction on mathematical problem solving. Six middle school students with LD were randomly assigned to one of two groups. Group 1 received cognitive strategy instruction (CSI) followed by metacognitive strategy (MCSI). Group 2 received the reverse instructional sequence.

Strategy training consisted of demonstration, guided practice, and testing sessions. Students in the CSI group learned seven cognitive processes (read, paraphrase, visualize, hypothesize, estimate, compute, and check) and the initial letters (RPV-HECC) by memory without being taught how to apply those processes. Metacognitive strategy training included self-instruction, self-questioning, and self-monitoring to monitor and control strategy usage. Students in the MCSI group learned to apply metacognitive activities to each cognitive process by using say, ask, and check activities without memorizing. Students practiced strategies in the second phase. If students provided less than seven correct answers on a 10-problem test, alternate guided practice sessions were provided to those students.

Results indicated that the combination of cognitive and metacognitive strategies may be more effective than either cognitive or metacognitive strategies alone. Students improved their performance on mathematical problem solving, but the sixth-grade students performed less well than the seventh- and eighth-grade students. In addition, a positive shift in attitude perception of performance and strategy knowledge on problem solving were evident.

Montague, Applegate, and Marquard (1993) evaluated the effectiveness on 2- to 4-step math problem solving on 72 junior high LD students. One group received training on cognitive strategies for problem solving; a second group received metacognitive training; a third group received a combination of cognitive and metacognitive strategy training. After 7 days of training, the first two experimental groups received an additional 5 days of training in the complementary component of the instructional program, while the third group received an additional 5 days of cognitive and metacognitive instruction. Although differences were not observed among conditions after training, all groups wee seen to benefit from training, with posttest and maintenance scores comparing favorably with those of a group of normally achieving peers.

6. Algebra Problems

Hutchinson (1993) investigated the effects of cognitive strategy instruction on algebra problem solving. Twenty adolescent students with LD were randomly assigned to either the instructional or comparison condition. Instructional condition students were provided with cognitive strategy training for representing and solving algebra word problems. Three types of word problems (relational, proportional, and two-variable) with each surface structure or story line (work, age, distance, money, and number) were used through the study. Each student in the instructional condition met with the instructor individually on alternate days for a period of 4 months. Students in the comparison condition received an equivalent amount of instruction in the resource room.

Students in the instructional condition were taught to apply the following self-questions for representing word problems (Hutchinson, 1993, p. 39):

1. Have I read and understood each sentence: Are there any words whose meaning I have to ask?
2. Have I got the whole picture, a representation, for this problem?
3. Have I written down my representation on the worksheet? (goal; unknown(s); known(s); type of problem; equation)
4. What should I look for in a new problem to see if it is the same kind of problem?

For solving algebra word problems, students were taught to ask themselves the following:

1. Have I written an equation?
2. Have I expanded the terms?
3. Have I written out the steps of my solution on the worksheet? (collected like terms; isolated unknown(s); solved for unknown(s); checked my answer with the goal; highlighted my answer).
4. What should I look for in a new problem to see if it is the same kind of problem?

Students were also provided with a structured worksheet to assist with organizing, representing, and solving problems.

Although individual students varied on the amount of material mastered, posttests, transfer, and maintenance tests all demonstrated very substantial gains relative to those of students in the comparison condition.

7. Summary

A number of recent research investigations examined the use of metacognitive strategy training on word problem solving by students with LD. Teaching fact families, providing schema, and training in multiple-step cognitive strategies proved to be very effective in increasing the problem-solving skills of students with LD in areas of arithmetic and algebra. The failure of one investigation to improve problem-solving performance using either key word strategies or diagrams, however, provides evidence that all training does not necessarily lead to success with students with LD. Important considerations for all types of instruction include rates of engagement and time on-task, teacher presentation variables, and continuous monitoring of progress toward final objectives (Mastropieri & Scruggs, 1994).

B. Computer-Assisted Instruction

Shiah, Mastropieri, Scruggs, and Fulk (1994–1995) described the development and implementation of a tutorial computer program to teach math problem solving to students with LD. The program included a digitized voice component to compensate for any accompanying reading disabilities. Students were trained to use the mouse to interact with the tutorial instruction and undertake guided practice solving problems.

Three versions of the program were developed. In the first version (animated picture), students were taught a seven-step strategy for solving the problem (i.e., read about the problem, think about the problem, decide the operation, write the math sentence, do the problem, label the answer, check every step, cf. Montague, Applegate, & Marquard, 1993). Students were instructed to click on each step in order with the mouse, and work the problem through with the computer. During the second step (think), an animated picture represented the problem to be solved. That is, for the problem, "Mr. Brown has 32 books. Mrs. Jones has 26 books. How many books do they have altogether?", the computer displayed two people holding books, then walking together to combine the books in one pile. Students then went to the next step, decide the operation, and to the following four steps. All objects in the problems (e.g., books) were drawn to be ambiguous with respect to number so that they could not be counted on the screen.

In the second condition (static picture), students received the identical instruction, except that a static, rather than animated picture was displayed during the "think about the problem" step. In the third (control) condition, students were shown a static picture of the problem during the "think" step, but received no specific training on the seven-step strategy.

Thirty elementary age students with LD who had scored 33% correct or lower on the problem-solving pretest were assigned at random to each of the three conditions. Each student received 40 min of individualized training across 2 days, followed by posttesting and a 1-week delayed test, using both computer and pencil and paper. It was found that all students, regardless of condition, made substantial progress from pre- to posttest; however, differences among conditions were not statistically significant, perhaps due to the relatively small number of subjects who had met preskill criteria, or the variability of student performance (Mastropieri et al., 1994–1995). Nevertheless, all versions of the program were found to be associated with substantial improvements from baseline levels. It was also noted that gains made on the computer did not readily transfer to pencil-and-paper problem solving, an issue that will need to be addressed in future research.

VII. DISCUSSION

A comprehensive review of research on mathematics instruction involving students with learning disabilities revealed that many of the topics of interest in research conducted prior to 1989 was still of interest in more recent years. It has generally been demonstrated that a variety of behavioral, cognitive, and metacognitive approaches have been found to be effective in improving both mathematical computation and mathematical problem solving in students with learning disabilities. Although many of the behavioral interventions represent replications of earlier studies, specific progress was noted from the studies reviewed by Mastropieri, Scruggs, and Shiah (1991), in several different areas.

First, research in metacognitive strategy training has revealed the effectiveness of such training across an expanding area of tasks, as well as types of training. Of particular interest in recent years is the research on algebra problem solving, and research on affectively oriented self-instruction. This research has extended our knowledge of the potential breadth of metacognitive training, with respect to types of intervention as well as and content area.

Second, some novel uses of peer mediation appeared to extend our knowledge of strategies relevant to math achievement. Using peers in goal-setting, and homework-monitoring capacities appeared to signal interesting departures from the previous (but effective) uses of peers as tutors of math facts. Of particular interest was the findings of Fuchs et al. (1996) regarding the relative performance of the tutees with LD as a function of the mathematics ability of the tutor.

Finally, several important features of CAI in mathematics were addressed. Although all of the research findings did not agree, it was interesting to note overall that although CAI generally increased the math functioning of students with LD, some specific features of CAI appeared to bear less strong association to achievement. For instance, outcomes of game versus drill formats appeared to be inconsistent, although both were seen to improve performance under some circumstances. In addition, competitive versus individualistic formats, and videogames as reward contingencies appeared to exert little effect on outcomes. Finally, animated versus static pictures, and tutorial versus practice formats appeared to exert little specific influence on mathematics learning. On the other hand, it may be that attributional feedback and goal setting may exert some positive influence on CAI in mathematics. In addition, the investigation by Shiah and colleagues demonstrates that tutorial strategy instruction on problem solving, with animated formats, can be incorporated within CAI, and understood independently by students with LD. It seems clear that research on CAI in math for students with LD is beginning to expand our knowledge of the possibilities of these practices.

Similar to the previous review of Mastropieri, Scruggs, and Shiah (1991), a very substantial number of investigations in the present review were concerned with calculation performance. This finding appears to contrast strongly with the expressed views of the National Research Council (1989) and the NCTM (1989), who have repeatedly argued against the emphasis on computation over conceptual development. In addition, some special education researchers have frequently argued that too much emphasis is placed on computation (e.g., Parmar, Cawley, & Frazita, 1996). However, it has been clearly demonstrated that students with LD frequently exhibit persistent difficulties mastering basic number facts and computational skills (Fleischner, Garnett, & Shepard, 1982; Garnett, 1992) a well as in simple verbal problem solving (Lerner, 1997; Montague & Bos, 1986).

Nevertheless, proportion of experiments published in a given area is not necessarily an indication of its proportion of use (or even of recommended proportion of use) in schools. Researchers may select topics for research based on many factors, including personal interest in the topic, compatibility with the researcher's methodological interests and skills, as well as the researcher's sense of the importance of the topic. In the present instance, the large proportion of studies focusing on computation may well be due to a combination of researchers' personal interest in improving computation, an awareness of the difficulties of students with LD in this area, and a general compatibility of computation with the largely behavioral perspective of special education researchers.

Even when word problem solving interventions have been conducted, they have tended to involve relatively simple and straightforward problems of the sort typically found in math workbooks (for an exception see Hutchinson, 1993). Such problems do not generally correspond to the NCTM (1989) emphasis on "word problems of varying structures" (p. 20), such as problems that require analysis of the unknown, problems that provide insufficient or incorrect data, problems that can be solved in more than one way, or that have more than one correct answer (see Baroody, 1987; Parmar, Cawley, & Frazita, 1996). If special education researchers have not undertaken such research, it may be out of concern that acquisition of more basic skills remains a problem for many students with LD, in conjunction with concerns for the validity of "discovery" or "inquiry" oriented paradigms for students with LD (Mastropieri, Scruggs, & Butcher, 1997). It is also true that constructivist researchers in mathematics education (e.g., Cobb, 1994) typically have not specifically examined the performance of students with LD.

Nevertheless, it does seem that additional research in solving different types of problems, perhaps using calculators to assist in calculations, would be helpful in the future, particularly as students with LD are included more in regular class instruction. The role of manipulatives in developing mathematical understandings has gotten underway, and more research seems appropriate in this area (Mercer, Jordan, & Miller, 1996). More basic research on, for example, number concepts of students with LD, and how these compare with normally achieving peers, could also provide important information for practice. Although work completed to date on CAI and peer mediation seems very promising, additional research in these areas may prove to be of particular importance in the future. Finally, it was disappointing to note that only one study addressed intervention procedures for higher level math, such as algebra. Since many students with LD do enroll (and no doubt, experience difficulty) in algebra or higher level mathematics courses, further research in this area seems quite warranted.

Overall, it can be stated that research in mathematics education for students with LD is progressing steadily. Future researchers and practitioners will be able to benefit greatly from the insights gained from the present research.

References

Albers, A. E., & Greer, R. D. (1991). Is the three-term contigency trial a predictor of effective instruction? *Journal of Behavioral Education, 1,* 337–354.

Bahr, C. M., & Rieth, H. J. (1991). Effects of cooperative, competitive, and individualistic goals on student achievement using computer-based drill-and-practice. *Journal of Special Education Technology, 11,* 33–48.

Bahr, C. M., & Rieth, H. J. (1989). The effects of instructional computer games and drill and practice software on learning disabled students' mathematics achievement. *Computers in the Schools, 6,* 87–101.

Baroody, A. J. (1987). *Children's mathematical thinking.* New York: Teachers College Press.

Beirne-Smith, M. (1991). Peer tutoring in arithmetic for children with learning disabilities. *Exceptional Children, 57,* 330–337.

Bishop, A. J. (1990). Mathematical power to the people. *Harvard Educational Review, 60,* 357–369.

Case, L. P., Harris, K. R., & Graham, S. (1992). Improving the mathematical problem-solving skills of students with learning disabilities: Self-regulated strategy development. *Journal of Special Education, 26,* 1–19.

Cawley, J. F., Fitzmaurice, A. M., Shaw, R. A., Kahn, H., & Bates, H. (1979). LD youth and mathematics: A review of characteristics. *Learning Disability Quarterly, 2,* 29–44.

Cawley, J. F., Miller, J., & School, B. A. (1987). A brief inquiry of arithmetic word-problem-solving among learning disabled secondary students. *Learning Disabilities Focus, 2,* 87–93.

Christensen, C. A., & Gerber, M. M. (1990). Effectiveness of computerized drill and practice games in teaching basic math facts. *Exceptionality, 1,* 149–165.

Cobb, P. (1994). Where is the mind? Constructivist and sociocultural perspectives on mathematical development. *Educational Researcher, 23*(7), 13–20.

Cooke, N. L., Guzaukas, R., Pressley, J. S., & Kerr, K. (1993). Effects of using a ratio of new items to review items during drill and practice: Three experiments. *Education and Treatment of Children, 16,* 213–234.

deBettencourt, L. U., Putnam, R. T., & Leinhardt, G. (1993). Learning disabled students' understanding of derived fact strategies in addition and subtraction. *Focus on Learning Problems in Mathematics, 15*(4), 27–43.

DLM (1988). *Math masters* [Computer Program]. Allen, TX: Author.

Dunlap, L. K., & Dunlap, G. (1989). A self-monitoring package for teaching subtraction with regrouping to students with learning disabilities. *Journal of Applied Behavior Analysis, 22,* 309–314.

Eckert, R., & Davidson, J. (1987). *Math blaster plus* [Computer software]. Torrance, CA: Davidson & Associates.

Englert, C. S., Culatta, B. E., & Horn, D. G. (1987). Influence of irrelevant information in addition word problems on problem solving. *Learning Disability Quarterly, 10,* 29–36.

Fleischner, J. E., Garnett, K., & Shepard, M. J. (1982). Proficiency in basic fact computation of learning disabled and nondisabled children. *Focus on Learning Problems in Mathematics, 4,* 47–55.

Fuchs, L. S., Bahr, C. M., & Rieth, H. J. (1989). Effects of goal structures and performance contingencies on the math performance of adolescents with learning disabilities. *Journal of Learning Disabilities, 22,* 554–560.

Fuchs, L. S., Fuchs, D., Karns, K., Hamlett, C. L., Dutka, S., & Katzaroff, M. (1996). The relation between student ability and the quality and effectiveness of explanations. *American Educational Research Journal, 33,* 631–664.

Garnett, K. (1992). Developing fluency with basic number facts: Interventions for students with learning disabilities. *Learning Disabilities Research & Practice, 7,* 210–216.

Harding, D. C., Gust, A. M., Goldhawk, S. L., & Bierman, M. M. (1993). The effects of the interactive unit on the computation skills of students with learning disabilities and students with mild cognitive impairments. *Learning Disabilities, 4,* 53–65.

Harris, C. A., Miller, S. P., & Mercer, C. D. (1995). Teaching initial multiplication skills to students with disabilities in general education classrooms. *Learning Disabilities Research & Practice, 10,* 180–195.

Hastings, F. L., Raymond, G., & McLaughlin, T. F. (1989). Speed counting money: the use of direct instruction to train learning disabled and mentally retarded adolescents to count money efficiently. *Journal of Special Education, 13,* 137–146.

Hawkins, J., Brady, M. P., Hamilton, R., Williams, R. E., & Taylor, R. D. (1994). The effects of independent and peer guided practice during instructional pauses on the academic performance of students with mild handicaps. *Education and Treatment of Children, 17,* 1–28.

Hofmeister, A. M. (1993). Elitism and reform in school mathematics. *Remedial and Special Education, 14*(6), 8–13.

Houten, R. V. (1993). Rote vs. rules: A comparison of two teaching and correction strategies for teaching basic subtraction facts. *Education and Treatment of Children, 16,* 147–159.

Hutchinson, N. L. (1993). Effects of cognitive strategy instruction on algebra problem solving of adolescents with learning disabilities. *Learning Disability Quarterly, 16,* 34–63.

Jitendra, A. K., & Hoff, K. E. (1995). *Schema-based instruction on word problem solving performance of students with learning disabilities.* East Lansing, MI: National Center for Research on Teacher Training. (ERIC Document Reproduction Service No. ED 381 990)

Jitendra, A. K., & Xin, Y. P. (1997). Mathematical word-problem-solving instruction for students with mild disabilities and students at risk for math failure: A research synthesis. *Journal of Special Education, 30,* 412–438.

Johnson, D. J. (1994). Clinical study of adults with severe learning disabilities. *Learning Disabilities, 5*(1), 43–50.

Kamann, M. P., & Wong, B. Y. L. (1993). Inducing adaptive coping self-statements in children with learning disabilities through self-instruction training. *Journal of Learning Disabilities, 26,* 630–638.

Kameenui, E. J., Chard, D. J., & Carnine, D. W. (1996). The new school mathematics and the age-old dilemma of diversity: Cutting or untying the Gordian knot. In M. C. Pugach & C. L. Warger (Eds.), *Curriculum trends, special education, and reform: Refocusing the conversation* (pp. 94–105). New York: Teachers College Press.

Kelly, B., Gersten, R., & Carnine, D. (1990). Student error patterns as a function of curriculum design: Teaching fractions to remedial high school students and high school students with learning disabilities. *Journal of Learning Disabilities, 23,* 23–29.

Koscinski, S. T., & Gast, D. L. (1993a). Computer-assisted instruction with constant time delay to teach multiplication facts to students with learning disabilities. *Learning Disabilities Research & Practice, 8,* 157–168.

Koscinski, S. T., & Gast, D. L. (1993b). Use of constant time delay in teaching multiplication facts to students with learning disabilities. *Journal of Learning Disabilities, 26,* 533–544, 567.

Koscinski, S. T., & Hoy, C. (1993). Teaching multiplication facts to students with learning disabilities: The promise of constant time delay procedures. *Learning Disabilities Research & Practice, 8,* 260–263.

Laird, J. L., J., & Winton, A. S. W. (1993). A comparison of self-instructional checking procedures for remediating mathematical deficits. *Journal of Behavioral Education, 3,* 143–164.

Lerner, J. (1997). *Learning disabilities: Theories, diagnosis, and teaching strategies* (7th ed.). Boston: Houghton Mifflin.

Lucangeli, D., Coi, G., & Bosco, P. (1997). Metacognitive awareness in good and poor math problem solvers. *Learning Disabilities Research & Practice, 12,* 209–212.

Maccini, P., & Hughes, C. A. (1997). Mathematics interventions for adolescents with learning disabilities. *Learning Disabilities Research & Practice, 12,* 168–176.

Marsh, L. G., Cooke, N. L. (1996). The effects of using manipulatives in teaching math problem solving to students with learning disabilities. *Learning Disabilities Research & Practice, 11,* 58–65.

Mastropieri, M. A., & Scruggs, T. E. (1994). *Effective instruction for special education.* Austin, TX: ProEd.

Mastropieri, M. A., & Scruggs, T. E. (1993). *A practical guide for teaching science to students with disabilities in inclusive settings.* Austin, TX: Pro-Ed.

Mastropieri, M. A., Scruggs, T. E., & Butcher, K. (1997). How effective is inquiry learning for students with mild disabilities? *Journal of Special Education, 31,* 199–211.

Mastropieri, M. A., Scruggs, T. E., & Shiah, S. (1991). Mathematics instruction with learning disabled students: A review of research. *Learning Disabilities Research & Practice, 6,* 89–98.

Mastropieri, M. A., Scruggs, T. E., Shiah, R. L., & Fulk, B. J. M. (1994–1995). Reflections on "The effects of computer assisted instruction on the mathematical problem solving of students with learning disabilities." *Exceptionality, 5,* 189–193.

McLeskey, J., & Waldron, N. L. (1990). The identification and characteristics of students with learning disabilities in Indiana. *Learning Disabilities Research, 5,* 72–78.

Mercer, C. D., Jordan, L., & Miller, S. P. (1996). Constructivistic math instruction for diverse learners. *Learning Disabilities Research & Practice, 11,* 147–156.

Mercer, C. D., & Miller, S. P. (1992). Teaching students with learning problems in math to acquire, understand, and apply basic math facts. *Remedial and Special Education, 13*(3), 19–35, 61.

Miller, S. P., & Mercer, C. D. (1997). Educational aspects of mathematics disabilities. *Journal of Learning Disabilities, 30,* 47–56.

Miller, S. P., & Mercer, C. D. (1993a). Using data to learn about concrete-semiconcrete-abstract instruction for students with math disabilities. *Learning Disabilities Research & Practice, 8,* 89–96.

Miller, S. P., & Mercer, C. D. (1993b). Using a graduated word problem sequence to promote problem-solving skills. *Learning Disabilities Research & Practice, 8,* 169–174.

Montague, M. (1992). The effects of cognitive and metacognitive strategy instruction on the mathematical problem solving of middle school students with learning disabilities. *Journal of Learning Disabilities, 25,* 230–248.

Montague, M. (1996a). Assessing mathematical problem solving. *Learning Disabilities Research & Practice, 11,* 238–248.

Montague, M. (1996b). Student perception, mathematical problem solving, and learning disabilities. *Remedial and Special Education, 18*(1), 46–53.

Montague, M. (1996c). What does the "New View" of school mathematics mean for students with mild disabilities? In M. C. Pugach & C. L. Warger (Eds.), *Curriculum trends, special education, and reform: Refocusing the conversation* (pp. 84–93). New York: Teachers College Press.

Montague, M., Applegate, B., & Marquard, K. (1993). Cognitive strategy instruction and mathematical problem-solving performance of students with learning disabilities. *Learning Disabilities Research & Practice, 8,* 223–232.

Montague, M., & Bos, C. (1986). Verbal math problem solving and learning disabilities: A review. *Focus on Learning Problems in Math, 8*(2), 7–21.

Moore, L. J., & Carnine, D. (1989). Evaluating curriculum design in the context of active teaching. *Remedial and Special Education, 10,* 28–37.

National Council of Teachers of Mathematics (1989). *Curriculum and evaluation standards for school mathematics.* Reston, VA: Author. (ERIC Document Reproduction Service No. ED 304 336)

National Research Council (1989). *Everybody counts: A report to the nation on the future of mathematics education.* Washington, DC: National Academy Press.

Okolo, C. M. (1992a). The effect of computer-assisted instruction format and initial attitude on the arithmetic facts proficiency and continuing motivation of students with learning disabilities. *Exceptionality, 3,* 195–211.

Okolo, C. M. (1992b). The effects of computer-based attribution retraining on the attributions, persistence, and mathematics computation of students with learning disabilities. *Journal of Learning Disabilities, 25,* 327–334.

O'Melia, M. C., & Rosenberg, M. S. (1994). Effects of cooperative homework teams on the acquisition of mathematics skills by secondary students with mild disabilities. *Exceptional Children, 60,* 538–548.

Parmar, R. S., Cawley, J. F., & Frazita, R. R. (1996). Word problem-solving by students with and without mild disabilities. *Exceptional Children, 62,* 415–429.

Patzelt, K. E. (1991). *Increasing homework completion through positive reinforcement.* East Lansing, MI: National Center for Research on Teacher Training. (ERIC Document Reproduction Service No. ED 343 306)

Pavchinski, P., Evans, J. H., & Bostow, D. E. (1989). Increasing word recognition and math ability in a severely learning-disabled student with token reinforcers. *Psychology in the Schools, 26,* 397–411.

Prater, M. A., Hogan, S., & Miller, S. R. (1992). Using self-monitoring to improve on-task behavior and academic skills of an adolescent with mild handicaps across special and regular education settings. *Education and Treatment of Children, 15,* 43–55.

Pressley, M., & McCormick, C. (1995). *Advances educational psychology for educators, researchers, and policymakers.* New York: HarperCollins.

Rivera, D. (1993). Examining mathematics reform and the implications for students with mathematics disabilities. *Remedial and Special Education, 14*(6), 24–27.

Rivera, D. (1997). Mathematics education and students with learning disabilities. *Journal of Learning Disabilities, 30,* 2–19.

Schroeder, B., & Strosnider, R. (1997). Box-and-whisker what? Deaf students learn—and write about—descriptive statistics. *Teaching Exceptional Children, 29*(3), 12–17.

Scruggs, T. E., & Brigham, R. (1990). The challenges of metacognitive instruction. *Remedial and Special Education, 11*(6), 16–18.

Scruggs, T. E., &°Mastropieri, M. A. (1986). Academic characteristics of behaviorally disordered and learning disabled children. *Behavioral Disorders, 11,* 184–190.

Shiah, R. L., Mastropieri, M. A., Scruggs, T. E., & Fulk, B. J. M. (1994–1995). The effects of computer assisted instruction on the mathematical problem solving of students with learning disabilities. *Exceptionality, 5,* 131–161.

Silbert, J., Carnine, D., & Stein, M. (1981). *Direct instruction mathematics.* Columbus, OH: Merrill.

Walker, D. W., & Poteet, J. A. (1989–1990). A comparison of two methods of teaching mathematics story problem-solving with learning disabled students. *National Forum of Special Education Journal, 1,* 44–51.

Wilson, C. L., & Sindelar, P. T. (1991). Direct instruction in math word problems; Students with learning disabilities. *Exceptional Children, 57,* 512–520.

Wilson, R., Majsterek, D., & Simmons, D. (1996). The effects of computer-assisted versus teacher-directed instruction on the multiplication performance of elementary students with learning disabilities. *Journal of Learning Disabilities, 29,* 382–390.

Wood, D. A., Rosenberg, M. S., & Carran, D. T. (1993). The effects of tape-recorded self-instruction cues on the mathematics performance of students with learning disabilities. *Journal of Learning Disabilities, 26,* 250–258, 269.

Woodward, J., Baxter, J., & Scheel, C. (1997). It's what you take for granted when you take nothing for granted: The problems with general principles of instructional design. In T. E. Scruggs & M. A. Mastropieri (Eds.), *Advances in learning and behavioral disabilities,* Vol. 11 (pp. 199–234). Greenwich, CT: JAI.

Zawaiza, T. B. W., & Gerber, M. M. (1993). Effects of explicit instruction on community college students with learning disabilities. *Learning Disability Quarterly, 16,* 64–79.

Social Competence of Students with Learning Disabilities: Interventions and Issues

Sharon Vaughn and Jane Sinagub

I. SCOPE AND OBJECTIVES

Students with learning disabilities (LD), by definition, experience learning problems that interfere with their academic success in the classroom. The established link between LD and social skills difficulties, however, has persuaded the U.S. Interagency Committee on Learning Disabilities (ICLD, 1987) to include social skills as an additional deficit area for identifying students with LD. The current ICLD definition of LD reflects the importance of social skills and suggests the need for social skills instruction for students with LD who have deficits in this area. In turn, the ICLD definition has influenced the National Joint Committee for Learning Disabilities to also include significant difficulties in the development and use of social skills as one area in which LD may manifest.

This chapter provides an overview of social skills and focuses on procedures for enhancing the social skills and peer acceptance of students with LD. Specific interventions developed for and evaluated with students with LD are described as are social skills interventions that can be used with students with other exceptionalities (e.g., emotional or behavioral disorders) as well as regular education students. The chapter also addresses issues that are relevant to the teaching of social

Learning about Learning Disabilities, Second Edition

453

skills to children and adolescents with LD. Finally, directions for future research in the area of social skills intervention for students with LD and other exceptionalities are discussed.

After reading this chapter, the reader will be able to address each of the following objectives:

Define social skills.
Explain why many students with LD need to be taught social skills.
Explain why teachers may not emphasize the teaching of social skills in their curricula for students with LD.
Describe the cognitive-social learning model.
Describe the interpersonal problem-solving model.
Compare and contrast characteristics of contextualist and deficit models of social skills.
Summarize the procedures and critical comments concerning empirically substantiated social skills interventions for students with LD: cooperative learning, mutual interest discovery, contextualist intervention, and a social skills program for adolescents.
Summarize procedures and critical comments regarding empirically substantiated social skills interventions with other special populations: peer social initiations, social decision making, and structured learning.
Explain several key issues related to teaching social skills to students with LD.
Discuss future directions for research in the area of social competence of students with LD and other exceptionalities.

II. OVERVIEW OF SOCIAL SKILLS

A. Why Teach Social Skills?

Why should we teach social skills to students with LD? These students are poorly accepted and more frequently neglected or rejected by their classmates than are their non-LD peers (NLD; i.e., average- and high-achieving students) (for review, see Haager & Vaughn, 1995; Stone & La Greca, 1990; Vaughn, Elbaum, & Schumm, 1997; Vaughn, McIntosh, Schumm, Haager, & Callwood, 1993; Wiener, 1987). And youngsters who experience peer rejection are at greater risk for a myriad of negative outcomes including later adjustment difficulties, school dropout, and loneliness (for review, see Kupersmidt, Coie, & Dodge, 1990; Parker & Asher, 1987). Rejection of students with LD, however, is not solely a function of their academic difficulties. For example, after observing students on videotape for only a few minutes, strangers, unaware of which students were LD and which NLD, were more likely to perceive the students with LD more negatively than the NLD students (Bryan & Perlmutter, 1979; Bryan & Sherman, 1980). In addition, a prospective study examining the social skills, peer acceptance, and self-perceptions of students with LD prior to their referral for LD found that students with LD prior to identification differed significantly from their NLD peers on social variables and behavior problems (Vaughn, Hogan, Kouzekanani, & Shapiro, 1990). More specifically, 8 weeks after entering kindergarten, students who were later identified as LD received low peer acceptance and high peer rejection ratings, and were also described by their teachers as displaying more attention problems than their NLD peers (Vaughn et al., 1990). Accordingly, not only are students with LD at greater risk than their NLD peers for low peer acceptance, but they display behaviors that interfere with their social adjustment (Vaughn & Haager, 1994; Vaughn & La Greca, 1988).

Due, at least in part, to the social deficits that characterize students with LD, these students are not well liked by their teachers or peers (for review, see Bos & Vaughn, 1997; Bryan, Bay, Lopez-Reyna, & Donahue, 1991). As a result, the incorporation of social skills instruction would seem an essential component of any successful intervention program for students with LD. In their meta-analysis, Swanson and Malone (1992) reported that only 16% of students with LD exhibit social skills comparable to their NLD peers. In a more recent meta-analysis by Kavale and Forness (1996), 75% of students with LD were found to exhibit social skills deficits. In a study involving resource room teachers (Baum, Duffelmeyer, & Geelan, 1988), almost 38% of the teachers perceived their students with LD to have deficits in social functioning. Yet these teachers reported that social skills instruction did not have a high priority in their curricula. In this same study, of the students identified as having social deficits, only 37% had goal statements related to social skill interventions included in their Individual Education Programs (IEPs). Thus, although teachers believe that many students are in need of social skills instruction, they do not address this need in the goals or objectives of students' IEPs.

Since peer relationships are highly valued by our society and associated with many positive outcomes, why is it that so few teachers teach interpersonal skills? It may be that teachers are aware that students with LD have social difficulties, but do not value social skills as an important element of the curricula. In other words, educators may view the teaching of social skills as "taking away" from the student's academic program. Conversely, some teachers may highly value the importance of teaching social skills, but because social skills are not valued by the school system and/or parents, they do not teach them.

Perhaps too, some teachers believe social skills are important and wish that their students demonstrated more prosocial behaviors, but do not believe it is the school's responsibility to teach social skills. These teachers believe social behaviors should be learned at home, and that it is the family's duty to ensure the acquisition and mastery of positive social behaviors. Also, some educators consider social skills something that is acquired incidentally in the process of "growing up." They think of social skills more as a "characteristic" of the youngster, rather than as behaviors that are amenable to change. Fortunately, many youngsters learn appropriate social behaviors without direct, systematic instruction. Social skills, however, are best strengthened through structured intervention programs.

Finally, the rationale that perhaps best represents the greatest number of educators is that social skills are not taught because teachers do not know how to teach them. Teachers take courses that focus on teaching language arts, math, reading, and the academic subjects for which they are responsible. Teachers may even take courses on how to structure and manage behaviors in the classroom. Very few teachers, however, take courses that provide opportunities for learning how to teach social skills to their students. Teaching social behaviors requires that the teacher understand the development and acquisition of social behavior. Few teachers have confidence that they understand the "scope and sequence" of social development and that they would be able to identify and teach the social skills needed by their students. Thus, part of the solution to providing social skills instruction for students with LD is to require related courses and field experiences in teacher training programs.

B. What Are Social Skills?

The issue of defining social skills has been approached by many researchers and proven to be an enigmatic task. According to Foster and Ritchey (1979), social skills are "those responses, which within a given situation prove effective, in other words, maximize the probability of producing, maintaining, or enhancing positive effects for the interaction" (p. 626) and, it should be added, without harm to others. Ladd and Mize (1983) define social skills as "children's ability to organize cognitions and behaviors into an integrated course of action directed toward culturally acceptable social or interpersonal goals" (p. 127). Their definition focuses on the importance of cognition, or what the person thinks, as well as her or his ability to implement behaviors as part of social skills. Finally, Haager and Vaughn (1997) state that social skills are "the pro-social and responding skills demonstrated across settings and persons. These include language, nonverbal reactions, and attitudes a person conveys to others. Social skills involve appropriate initiation and responsiveness to others" (p. 8).

In their model, Vaughn and Hogan (1990) have stressed the need to look at social skills as part of the higher order construct of social competence. This construct is multifaceted, encompassing several individual components. Although these components are described separately, it is the interaction among all of these elements that actually generates social competence. The four components included in this model are (a) positive relations with others (ability to get along with peers and adults), (b) accurate age-appropriate social cognition (ability to problem solve and recognize and monitor social situations), (c) absence of maladaptive behaviors (absence of noxious and serious behavior problems such as attention problems, acting out, and withdrawal), and (d) effective social skills (ability to initiate and respond appropriately to others). According to this model, social skills are but one component of social competence. The model proposed by Vaughn and Hogan (1990) provides the structure for the contextualist intervention described in Section IV, Empirically Substantiated Interventions with Other Special Populations.

C. Social Skills Models

1. Cognitive-Social Learning Model

Ladd and Mize (1983) proposed a cognitive-social learning model for social skills instruction. Based primarily on the work of Bandura (1978, 1982), this model posits that children form constructs about behaviors based on their observations and their interpretations of the consequences of implementing these behaviors. According to this model there are three basic objectives for instruction: enhancement of skill concepts, promotion of skillful performance, and promotion of skill maintenance and generalization. In order to accomplish these objectives, specific instructional techniques referred to as variables are required.

The first variable, instruction, is defined as providing information that illustrates the desired behavior or the expected performance standard. Instruction can occur in two forms: modeled or verbal. When instruction is modeled, the behavior is actually displayed or enacted through a role play, film, videotape, or vignette. When instruction is verbal, the concept or desired behavior is represented by and communicated through spoken language.

The second variable, rehearsal, involves acting and/or practicing a behavior until it reaches a standard or criterion. Rehearsal can be overt, as when the individual in fact practices that specified skill, or covert, as when the individual thinks about or rehearses in her or his mind how to perform a particular skill.

The third variable, feedback, is the opportunity to evaluate the extent to which the exhibited behavior corresponds with the target behavior. Feedback can be given by others or by the individual herself or himself.

In addition to the aforementioned instructional variables, the cognitive-social learning model delineates specific instructional procedures for teaching social skills. These procedures correspond directly with the objectives, and the relationship between the procedures and objectives can be seen in Table 14.1.

2. Interpersonal Problem-Solving Model

Having problems with others is an inevitable part of life. Learning to share, to handle teasing, and to cope with a bully are just a few of the many difficulties that face children from the time they are toddlers. To learn how to be a good problem solver is considered to be related to present and later adjustment and to be a buffer against

Table 14.1
Cognitive-Social Learning Model of Social Skills[a] Training

Training objective	Training procedure
Enhancement of skill concepts	A. Establish an intent to learn the skill concept. Provide an advance organizer. Stress the functional relevance of the concept. B. Define the skill concept in terms of its attributes. Convey concept meaning. Identify relevant and irrelevant attributes. C. Generate exemplars. Identify positive and negative examples. D. Promote rehearsal and recall of the skill concept. Encourage verbal rehearsal. Establish a memory code. E. Refine and generalize the concept. Correct misconceptions. Identify alternative applications.
Promotion of skillful performance	A. Provide opportunities for guided rehearsal. Request overt skill rehearsal. Conduct rehearsals in a sheltered context. B. Evaluation of performance by the instructor. Communicate performance standards. Provide feedback about the match between standards and performance. C. Foster skill refinement and elaboration. Recommend corrective action, including concept reformulation and skill modification.
Promotion of skill maintenance and generalization	A. Provide opportunities for self-directed rehearsal. Skill rehearsal in a series of contexts that approximate real-life situations. B. Promote self-initiation of performance. Encourage skill usage while withdrawing performance cues or aids. C. Foster self-evaluation and skill adjustment. Self-appraisals of skill performance. Self-monitoring of skill outcomes. Adoption of nondefeating self-attributes and affective states. Use of information from self-monitoring to modify performance.

[a]Reprinted from Ladd, G. W., & Mize, J. (1983). A cognitive-social learning model of social-skills training. *Psychological Review, 90*(2), 127–157. Copyright © 1983 by the American Psychological Association. Reprinted with permission.

the negative effects of stressful life events (Dubow, Tisak, Causey, Hryshko, & Reid, 1991).

The interpersonal problem solving (IPS) model focuses on teaching thought processes that are expected to mediate behavior. The assumption underlying this model is that if children learn how to think through problem situations this will influence how they act. The IPS model has received perhaps its most extensive evaluation through the work of Shure, Spivack, and colleagues, who studied the effects of IPS training programs on children and adolescents (Shure & Spivack, 1979, 1980; Spivack, Platt, & Shure, 1976). The success of their work encouraged others to utilize IPS programs with a range of youngsters, including aggressive and submissive children (Deluty, 1981; Vaughn , Ridley, & Bullock, 1984), elementary students (Elardo & Caldwell, 1978; McKim, Weissbar, Cowen, Gesten, & Rapkin, 1982; Vaughn & Lancelotta, 1990), students identified as emotionally disturbed (Amish, Gesten, Smith, Clark, & Stark, 1988), students identified as mentally retarded (Vaughn, Ridley, & Cox, 1983), and low-accepted students with LD (Vaughn, Lancelotta, & Minnis, 1988; Vaughn, McIntosh, & Spencer-Rowe, 1991). The IPS intervention has been found to be an effective model for increasing these students' social skills and their ability to generalize these skills to relevant situations and interpersonal interactions.

The key components of the IPS model include goal identification, alternative thinking, consequential thinking, and solution implementation. Goal identification teaches children to identify what they want as well as what others want. In the case of a problem situation, children are taught to identify their goals as well as the goals of involved others. This process starts with recognizing one's own feelings, learning how to prevent these feelings from leading to undesirable behaviors, and recognizing and coping with the feelings of others. Children are encouraged to identify goals that meet their needs and the needs of others involved in the problem situation.

The second component of the IPS model, alternative thinking, teaches one to generate a range of potential alternatives to problem situations. The emphasis is on generating as many different solutions as possible with little attempt at this point to evaluate the potential effectiveness of each solution. For example, when children offer a number of aggressive solutions (e.g., beating, hitting, kicking), the instructor indicates that they have many ideas for solutions that involve hurting others and encourages participants to suggest different alternatives, ones that do not focus on hurting. Emphasis is on finding alternatives that are safe and fair and that are good choices in the long run, rather than just the short run.

The third component, consequential thinking, emphasizes the importance of predicting the likely outcome of each generated possible alternative before selecting a particular alternative to a problem situation. Consequential thinking involves anticipating what would happen next if the student implemented a selected alternative. There are several important aspects to consequential thinking. One is that students are asked to consider who is involved in the problem situation, with the understanding that particular alternatives are effective with some people and ineffective with others. Another important aspect is to consider whether the solution will be effective in the long run or just in the short run. Lastly, students are asked whether or not the selected alternative is safe and fair. Thus, consideration for how the alternative will affect others is part of the intervention program. The final component involves the actual implementation of the chosen solution. Although the components are often taught separately, they are combined through applied practice (e.g., role plays).

3. Contextualist versus Deficit Models

Both the cognitive-social learning model and the IPS model assume that the primary source of social skills difficulties lies within the individual. Thus, teaching the child specific skills and behaviors solves the student's social skills problems. Forman (1987) argues that despite the fact that this deficit model is the most common model for remediating peer difficulties, what is needed to most effectively solve the social difficulties of students with LD is a contextualist model. The contextualist model emphasizes several principles for remediating the social difficulties of students with LD. First, other people from the child's context (environment), such as peers and family members, need to be involved. Second, the social difficulties need to be identified explicitly and, when possible, the source of the identification should be described. Third, the target students need to be motivated to make the necessary changes or to learn the targeted skills. Fourth, the intervention should be implemented in such a manner as to be able to respond to changes in the student's relationships with others, classroom, school, or family. The need for family involvement and support in providing intervention for students with LD is critical. Involving the family puts the problems in context and allows for a complete intervention program (Wilchesky & Reynolds, 1986). Fifth, the classroom teacher must be involved in monitoring the desired change.

The assumption underlying deficit-based approaches is that children and adolescents learn social skills from social skills instruction, resulting in improved relations with peers and adults. Research examining the effects of social skills interventions with students with LD have demonstrated few if any positive changes in peer ratings of acceptance. Even when positive behavioral changes are documented by trained observers (e.g., Northcutt, 1987), teachers and peers do not perceive these positive changes. In addition, when appropriate social behaviors are observed in controlled settings, such as during instruction, these changes usually do not generalize to more natural settings (Marchetti & Campbell, 1990; Mathur & Rutherford, 1991; Stokes & Osnes, 1986). Social skills instruction that is based on behavioral principles may hold great promise for youngsters with handicaps because it is performance-based (Gresham, 1984). The following instructional techniques stem from the behavioral model: instructions, modeling, prompts, rehearsal, feedback, reinforcement, and peer interaction (Brown & Odom, 1994).

In summary, it would seem the most successful and comprehensive social skills intervention would include components of both contextualist and behavioral models. Social skills interventions should not be implemented in isolation, but should utilize behavioral principles, and include significant others in the child's life, as well as demonstrate an awareness of the effects of the context on the youngster's acquisition and use of social skills.

III. INSTRUCTIONAL METHODS

Students with LD are disproportionately represented in the social status categories of neglected and rejected and underrepresented in the popular social status classification (e.g., Vaughn et al., 1990). The number of students with LD who are rejected by their peers is considerably greater than the number of NLD students who are rejected. In fact, approximately 50% of students with LD are identified as poorly accepted (Stone & La Greca, 1990; Vaughn et al., 1991). What this statistic means is that some students with LD are not at risk for adjustment difficulties associated with peer rejection. As a result, any social intervention should be tailored to the specific needs of the target student.

Since no single pattern of social difficulties represents all youngsters with LD (McIntosh, Vaughn, & Zaragoza, 1991; Vaughn, McIntosh, & Zaragoza, 1992), interventions must provide some form of assessment to ensure the social skills interventions will be directed toward the youngster's particular problems. For example, some students who are not well accepted by their peers and who have social skills problems may need specific instruction in one or more of the following basic skills: reducing inappropriate behaviors, accepting negative feedback, giving positive feedback, learning conversational skills, implementing interpersonal problem solving, and initiating contact/interaction with others.

The low peer acceptance of students with LD has been repeatedly documented. What has been significantly less documented are explanations for why many students with LD are poorly accepted. A prospective longitudinal study has examined students with LD prior to their identification in order to identify their characteristic social and academic patterns as compared with their low-, average-, and high-achieving peers (e.g., Vaughn & Hogan, 1994; Vaughn, Zaragoza, Hogan, & Walker, 1993). Initial results suggest that as early as 10 weeks into their kindergarten year, children later identified as LD are significantly different from even their low-achieving peers on measures of peer acceptance and attention problems (Vaughn et al., 1990). Efforts at grouping youngsters with LD with their NLD classmates, in order to encourage and promote positive peer interaction, failed to improve peer acceptance ratings. In fact, in some cases the peer acceptance ratings of the students with LD actually were lower after the grouping effort (for review, see McIntosh et al., 1991).

Similar findings were found in a study of students with LD educated in inclusion classrooms. The peer acceptance ratings of these students were lower than for average- and high-achieving students, but comparable to those for low-achieving students (Vaughn, Elbaum, & Schumm, 1996). One year after the students with LD had participated in the general education classroom full-time, the number who were disliked by their classmates actually increased from the fall to the spring of the academic year.

How students feel about their classmates is not as susceptible to change as one might like. Accordingly, even when students demonstrate improved social skills, and these changes are documented through behavioral observations, classmates either do not perceive the changes or the changes are not dramatic enough to alter their perceptions of the target student. In this chapter, an intervention that provides opportunities for students with LD and their NLD classmates to spend structured time together, getting to know each other better, is described. This procedure has resulted in increased peer ratings for the students who participated.

A. Empirically Substantiated Interventions with Students with LD

Four interventions will be discussed in this section: a social skills program for adolescents, a contextualist intervention, cooperative learning, and mutual interest discovery. An introduction to each intervention will be provided as well as procedures for implementing each intervention and evaluative comments.

1. A Social Skills Program for Adolescents

A Social Skills Program for Adolescents (ASSET) is designed to teach adolescents the social skills they need to interact successfully with peers and adults. The positive effects of implementing ASSET with adjudicated youth and youngsters with LD has been documented (Hazel, Schumaker, Sherman, & Sheldon-Wildgen, 1981). ASSET considers eight social skills fundamental to making and maintaining relationships with others. The following eight skills comprise the foundation of the program: giving positive feedback, giving negative feedback, accepting negative feedback, resisting peer pressure, problem solving, negotiation, following instructions, and making and maintaining conversation. Underlying this program is the belief that many youngsters do not exhibit desirable behaviors, not because they are not motivated to do so, but because they do not know how to perform them. This program has been developed to teach the social skills needed by adolescents to interact effectively with peers and adults. The teaching procedures used in the program are based on success, successive approximations, mastery, and multiple exemplars. Materials including videotapes of eight teaching sessions, skill sheets, home notes, and criterion checklists are available with the program. Following are the procedures for implementing ASSET:

Each lesson is taught in a small group and involves nine basic steps. Step one reviews previously learned skills including reviewing homework. Step two explains or describes the skill that is the focus of the lesson. Sometimes this is a review of the skill being taught or may be an overview of a new skill. Step three provides a rationale for the skill being taught. This step requires "hooking" the student into learning the skill by providing a convincing rationale for its importance. Step four is a discussion of example situations for using the target skill. When presenting examples of the situation, choose those that are specific and believable, and to which a teenager can relate. Students can also provide examples. Step five examines the steps or subskills necessary to carry out the target skill. A skill sheet provides the step-by-step sequence of subskills needed to effectively implement each target skill. Step six models the skill itself. Videotapes that provide a model of a student implementing particular skills are available with the program. Activities for students in the program to demonstrate and model specific skills are also provided. Step seven, verbal rehearsal, familiarizes the student with the sequence of steps associated with the target skill and provides a procedure for memorizing the steps in the sequence. Step eight, behavioral rehearsal and criterion performance, provides an opportunity for the student to practice the skills and demonstrate that the criterion for exhibiting each of the delineated skills is met. Step nine is the assignment of homework, and may include a home note for recording how the student practices and uses skills outside of the instructional setting, particularly at home. Within these nine steps, each of the eight skills are taught. At least one teaching session is needed to address each of the eight skills.

  a. Comments   In a study by Hazel, Schumaker, Sherman, and Sheldon (1982), eight students with LD were taught six of the eight skills delineated in the ASSET program: giving positive feedback, giving negative feedback, accepting negative feedback, resisting peer pressure, negotiation, and personal problem solving. Following program implementation, the students were tested, using behavioral role-play situations, on each of the six skills. Students with LD involved in the intervention demonstrated increases in the use of social skills during role plays. When compared with two other groups, NLD and court-adjudicated youth, the students with LD made only slight gains on cognitive problem solving.

  ASSET specifically delineates the subskills within each target skill, and thus it is useful to teachers who seek a structured curriculum for teaching social skills. It is advised that when teaching social skills to adolescents with LD, it is necessary to "apply the same careful systematic procedures used in teaching academic skills" (Zigmond & Brownlee, 1980, p. 82). ASSET provides the guidelines and curriculum for applying systematic procedures.

  Further research with the ASSET program is needed, however, to determine the extent to which skill acquisition demonstrated during structured situations (e.g., role plays) generalizes to nonstructured situations. For example, do students who display increased social skills in a role-play "testing" situation apply those same social skills in real-life settings? Also needed is further information on how target students perceive ASSET instruction. It is likely that students who believe the intervention is effective are more likely to apply and generalize the learned skills.

2. An Interpersonal Problem-Solving Intervention

Social skills need to be considered in light of the family, school, environment, classroom, peers, and other relevant issues. Fundamental to this perspective is the belief that teaching social skills in isolation is unlikely to provide significant and long-lasting change. A social strategy training program emphasizing a problem-solving approach has been developed and evaluated by Vaughn and colleagues (McIntosh, Vaughn, & Bennerson, 1995; Vaughn & Lancelotta, 1990; Vaughn et al., 1988; Vaughn et al., 1991). The following procedures outline this model:

1. A school-wide sociometric assessment is performed where each student rates her or his same-sex classmates on the extent to which he or she would like to be friends with them.
2. Students who receive few "friendship" votes and many "no friendship" votes form the rejected group; students with many friendship and few no friendship votes comprise the popular group.
3. Social skills trainers for each participating class include a rejected student with LD and a highly accepted NLD classmate.
4. The social skills trainers are removed from their classrooms several times (e.g., 2–3) each week for approximately 30 min each session to learn specific social skills strategies.
5. The first social skills strategy taught is the FAST strategy. The four steps associated with FAST follow (McIntosh et al., 1995):
   a. FREEZE AND THINK! Do not act too quickly. Stop and think: What is the problem?
   b. ALTERNATIVES? What are all of my possible solutions?
   c. SOLUTION EVALUATION. What are the likely consequences of each solution. What would happen next if I do . . . ? Select the best solution(s) for the long run as well as the short run.
   d. TRY IT! What do I need to do to implement the solution? If it does not work, what else can I try?
6. In addition to the FAST strategy, social skills trainers are taught to address solutions in terms of long-run and short-run consequences, and to accept negative feedback by learning the SLAM strategy (McIntosh et al., 1995). Coaching and role-playing are used to promote understanding of the lessons and to practice skills. The four components of the SLAM strategy follow:
   a. STOP! Stop whatever you're doing.
   b. LOOK! Look the person in the eye.

   c. ASK! Ask the person a question to clarify what she or he means.
   d. MAKE! Make an appropriate response to the person.
7. While social skills trainers are learning the social strategies, a problem-solving box (e.g., a decorated shoe box) is put into every classroom. This box is used by all of the students in the classroom to write problems they have with other children, at home, on the playground, and so on. The teacher and social skills trainers explain to the class that the purpose of the problem-solving box is to ask questions about problems they have in the classroom, on the playground, and at home. Problems submitted by students are used by social skills trainers and the entire class to practice their social problem-solving skills and for discussion.
8. After the social skills trainers have learned a particular strategy (e.g., FAST) and rehearsed it using real-life problems, they present the strategy to their classmates with backup and support from the researcher and classroom teacher.
9. In subsequent weeks, the social skills trainers leave the classroom for only one session per week, and review the skill strategy (e.g., FAST) with classmates at least once per week. These reviews include large-group explanations and small-group problem-solving exercises using the problems from the problem-solving box.
10. Social skills trainers are recognized in front of their classes or schools by the principal. Social skills trainers wear special buttons while at school that indicate that they are social skills trainers for that school. Students in the school are asked to consult these social skills trainers when they have interpersonal difficulties.

   a. Comments   The social strategy training program proposed by Vaughn and colleagues has been successfully conducted with a female student with LD in a case study design (Vaughn et al., 1988) as well as with a group of students with LD who were identified by their peers as socially rejected (Vaughn et al., 1991). Many of the students who participated in the intervention demonstrated increases in peer acceptance following the intervention. In the case study, the female student with LD who was identified as rejected at pretest was identified as popular at the posttest. In the group intervention, all 10 students with LD were identified as rejected at pretest with only 5 identified as rejected at posttest and follow-up. Students who participated in the intervention received significantly more positive nominations at posttest than at pretest. Future work needs to examine the characteristics of students with whom this intervention is successful and those with whom it is not successful. Initial evaluations with students with LD whose peer ratings were not improved following intervention suggest that students with LD who have acting-out and aggressive behavior problems are less likely to demonstrate changes in peer acceptance following intervention. Finally, this intervention has been used with elementary-aged students with LD, and the extent to which the model could be adapted and used with older youngsters is as yet unknown.

3. Cooperative Learning

Slavin, Madden, and Leavey (1984) have used a combination of cooperative learning and individualized programming in an intervention called Team Assisted Individualization (TAI). While the primary purpose of this intervention is to increase academic skill levels, cooperative learning has also been used to integrate students with and without disabilities and to increase the social acceptance of children in a group. Students work in heterogeneous groups and assist each other with directions and tasks as well as check each other's work. The cooperative atmosphere as well as the increased exposure to all students in the classroom is expected to increase peer acceptance. Johnson and Johnson (1986) suggest that classrooms can be organized so students work together in small groups or pairs with the emphasis on helping each other to accomplish goals and learn material. The elements necessary for cooperative learning to occur are provided in Table 14.2. Cooperative learning involves the following procedures:

1. High-, average-, and low-achieving students are assigned to four- or five-member teams. Students who are identified as receiving special education or resource help are assigned randomly to teams.
2. Students are pretested on the academic area of focus, and placed in an individualized program based on their performance on this test.
3. Students complete the following steps to finish their individualized academic area work.
   a. Students bring their work materials into pairs or triads within their teams.
   b. Students exchange answer sheets with partners.
   c. Students read instructions and begin work on skill sheets.
   d. When a student completes the first four problems, a partner is asked to check the answers. If the first four are correct, the student goes on to the next skill sheet. If any items are wrong, the student continues with the next problems. If the student needs assistance, the teacher will provide instructive feedback.
   e. When students complete the final skill sheet, they take an exam, which is scored by a teammate. If they pass the exam, they go to the next more difficult set of problems. If they do not pass, they are provided instruction from the teacher.
4. Teams that meet criteria are rewarded with certificates at the end of the week.
5. The teacher works with individuals or small groups of students on specific skills.

Table 14.2
Basic Elements for Enhancing Cooperative Learning[a]

1. Positive interdependence
   a. The goal of the group is to assure that all group members learn, often by producing a group project.
   b. Reward is linked to the overall achievement of the group, not the achievement of individuals within the group.
   c. For group members to achieve their goal, coordination of all group members is necessary.
2. Individual accontability
   a. To ensure that students work together and that each member of the group is responsible and learning, randomly select one student's work to represent the group.
   b. Ask students to select one student's work to represent the group.
3. Collaborative skills
   a. Teach students the skills they need to be successful at working cooperatively with others. These skills include decision making, role-taking, trust-building, and conflict management.
   b. Teach students leadership skills and the skills to be cooperative partners.
4. Group processing
   a. How well the group is functioning needs to be a focus of discussion. Which aspects of the group are functioning well and which aspects are not should be delineated by group members.
   b. The group should identify its goals and assess whether the group is making progress towards these goals.
5. Teacher's role during cooperative learning
   a. Monitor the students' behavior by making suggestions and asking questions that teach. Do not take over and attempt to solve students' problems for them; rather, teach them how to solve problems for themselves.
   b. Provide task assistance. If students are having difficulty with an assignment or project, provide needed assistance and background information.
   c. Intervene to teach collaborative skills. Assist students in acquiring and practicing skills that enhance cooperation.
   d. Provide closure to the lesson by reviewing the progress of each group.
   e. Evaluate each individual student's learning and assess how well each group as a whole functions.

[a]Identified by Johnson and Johnson (1986)

The peer acceptance of youngsters who participate in the TAI program increases; however, it may not be in response to the cooperative element of the program. In a comparison study between TAI and individualized instruction, students in the individualized instruction group demonstrated increases in peer acceptance that exceeded the increases of the TAI group when both groups were compared with a control (Slavin et al., 1984). There were no differences between the TAI group and the individualized instruction group, however, on either academic achievement or peer acceptance.

a. Comments   The effects of cooperative learning on the amount and type of interactions engaged in by students with learning and behavior problems in the regular classroom has been evaluated (Johnson, Johnson, Warring, & Maruyama, 1986). The effects of cooperative learning on the social competence of students with exceptionalities, however, has not been as thoroughly examined. One study with students classified as mentally retarded suggests that students instructed in collaborative skills engage in more positive interactions and fewer negative interactions than students not receiving such instruction (Putnam, Rynders, Johnson, & Johnson, 1989). The extent to which cooperative learning improves the social competence of students with exceptionalities other than mental retardation needs to be further investigated.

4. Mutual Interest Discovery

Mutual Interest Discovery is an approach developed by Fox (1980) and evaluated with students with LD (Fox, 1989). Central to this intervention is the premise that persons who have similar attitudes will be attracted to each other. In other words, knowing the ways you are like another person increases the likelihood you will like that other person. Mutual Interest Discovery provides structured activities for students with and without LD to get to know each other with the desired outcome being greater peer acceptance. This is accomplished through the following procedures:

1. Low-accepted students with LD are paired with NLD classmates.
2. Each pair of students works together on preassigned topics once a week for 40 min. The assignments involve interviewing each other on topics appropriate for their specific age group (e.g., entertainment, hobbies, sports).
3. Following the interview, students write three items they discovered they have in common with, or learned about, their partners.
4. Students then complete a brief art activity related to what they learned about their partners. At the bottom of the art assignment, each student writes two sentences about what she or he learned about her or his partner.
5. The completed art project is placed in a mutual art book which is added to each week.

a. Comments   The Fox (1989) study found that students who participated in the Mutual Interest Discovery intervention reported higher ratings of their partners over time than did students in a control group. Females were more responsive to a mutual interest group as opposed to an academic task group than were males, who responded about equally well to both groups. Students with LD rated their partners significantly higher than their partners rated them over time. However, students with LD who were involved in this program did receive higher ratings of social acceptibility following their involvement. This intervention, however, was not designed to teach social skills, so the effects of this intervention on the overall social skills of students with LD is left unanswered. This initial study does suggest that LD acceptance can be increased through mutual interest activities. Students with LD who participated in this study were in the lower half of the students in their class for peer acceptance prior to the intervention. The low peer acceptance of many students with LD may be a result of their being less well known to their classmates. Because Mutual Interest Discovery is a relatively easy intervention to implement, and it can be implemented in the regular classroom, providing mutual interest activities for all students paired with social skills instruction for target students may be a highly effective intervention.

IV. EMPIRICALLY SUBSTANTIATED INTERVENTIONS WITH OTHER SPECIAL POPULATIONS

A. Peer Social Initiations

Peer social initiations is an empirically validated approach to teaching social skills to young children with handicaps (for review, see Odom, McConnell, & McEvoy, 1992; Strain & Odom, 1986). The Early Childhood Social Skills Program uses the principles and procedures of peer social initiations to facilitate the development of positive interaction skills in preschoolers with and without social delays (Kohler & Strain, 1993). Although peer social initiations was not developed and evaluated with youngsters with LD specifically, it demonstrates the application of a highly replicated social skills intervention that shows promise for students with LD and other disabilities. The successful implementation of peer social initiations involves four components; they are as follows:

1. Selecting specific peer initiations that are most likely to yield a positive response from the student. Behaviors such as sharing, affection, and assistance are likely to receive positive responses from peers (Strain, 1983).
2. Arranging the physical environment to promote interaction requires that materials be available to facilitate interaction. For example, with preschoolers some materials such as wagons, cars, blocks, and house materials are likely to yield peer interactions, whereas materials such as puzzles, crayons, and paints are more likely to produce solitary play.
3. Instructing peers to implement the intervention requires selecting peers (confederates) that are desirable playmates as well as willing participants. Confederates practice and rehearse the initiation skills with the researcher prior to implementing them with a target peer. Confederates rehearse the intervention through multiple role plays in order to know what to do to encourage the stu-

Table 14.3

Session 1: Introduction to System-Share Initiation-Persistence[a]

Adult: "Today you are going to learn how to be a good teacher. Sometimes your friends in your class do not know how to play with other children. You are going to learn how to teach them to play. What are you going to do?"

Child: "Teach them to play."

Adult: "One way you can get your friend to play with you is to share. How do you get your friend to play with you?"

Child: "Share."

Adult: "Right! You share. When you share you look at your friend and say, 'Here,' and put a toy in his/her hand. What do you do?"[Repeat this exercise until the child can repeat these three steps.]

Child: "Look at friend and say, 'Here,'" and put the toy in his/her hand."

Adult: "Now, watch me. I am going to share with _____. Tell me if I do it right." [Demonstrate sharing.] "Did I share with _____? What did I do?"

Child: "Yea! _____ looked at _____, and said 'here _____' and put a toy in his hand."

Adult: "Right. I looked at _____ and said, 'here _____' and put a toy in his hand. Now watch me. See if I share with _____." [Move to the next activity in the classroom. This time provide a negative example of sharing by leaving out the "put in hand" component. Put the toy beside the role player.] "Did I share?" [Correct if necessary and repeat this example if child got it wrong.] "Why not?"

Child: "No. You did not put the toy in _____'s hand."

Adult: "That's right. I did not put the toy in _____'s hand. I have to look at _____ and say, 'here _____' and put the toy in his hand." [Give the child two more positive and two more negative examples of sharing. When the child answers incorrectly about sharing, repeat the example. Vary the negative examples by leaving out different components: looking, saying 'here,' putting in hand.]

Adult: "Now _____, I want you to get _____ to share with you. What do you do when you share?"

Child: "Look at _____ and say, 'here _____,' and put a toy in his hand."

Adult: "Now, go get _____ to play with." [For these practice examples, the role playing should be responsive to the child's sharing.] (To the other confederates:) "Did _____ share with _____? What did he/she do?"

Child: "Yes/No. Looked at _____, and said, 'here _____, and put a toy in his hand."

Adult: [Move to the next activity.] "Now, _____, I want you to share with _____."

Introduce Persistence

Adult: "Sometimes when I play with _____, he/she does not want to play back. I have to keep on trying. What do I have to do?"

Child: "Keep on trying."

Adult: "Right, I have to keep on trying. Watch me. I am going to share with _____. Now I want to see if I keep on trying." [Role player will be initially unresponsive.] [Teacher should be persistent until child finally responds.] "Did I get _____ to play with me?"

Child: "Yes."

Adult: "Did he want to play?"

Child: "No."

Adult: "What did I do?"

Child: "Keep on trying."

Adult: "Right, I kept on trying. Watch. See if I can get _____ to play with me this time." [Again, the role player should be unresponsive at first. Repeat above questions and correct if necessary. Repeat the example until the child responds correctly.]

---

[a]From Strain and Odom (1986). Reprinted by permission of the publisher.

dent to respond as well as what to do when the student does not respond. Table 14.3 provides a sample script for how to train confederates to implement a portion of the intervention.

4. Daily intervention sessions are the step-by-step process for structuring the interactions between the target student and the confederate. In a small group that includes a confederate and a target peer, the teacher describes the activities and materials available to conduct the activities. The student initiates the activity while the confederate is taken aside by the teacher and prompted as to which social initiations he or she should implement with the target student during the activity. The teacher prompts and reinforces the confederate and the target child for their interactions.

a. Comments The peer social initiations intervention has been systematically implemented across numerous settings and populations. It has been demonstrated to have a positive impact on both the confederates and the target students. Populations who have successfully participated in the intervention include preschool-aged handicapped youngsters, elementary-aged mentally retarded and behavior-disordered youngsters, and children with visual impairments. These positive outcomes include increases in positive social responses, increases in responses to initiations, increased length of social exchanges, and cross-setting generalization of responses.

One concern about this intervention, however, is the limited generalization and maintenance of treatment effects. A likely explanation is that the environments to which the students were returned did not have socially responsive peers to initiate and maintain the target behaviors. When responsive peers are present, generalization and maintenance effects have been documented (Shafer, Egel, & Neef, 1984).

Overall, this intervention is powerful and applicable in a wide range of settings. One of the strengths of this intervention is that it does not require a special curriculum or teacher's guide. Yet, because this intervention has not yet been systematically tested with students with LD, further research is needed before its efficacy with this population is known.

B. Social Decision Making

The Social Decision Making approach is a classroom-based intervention developed for children and adolescents that has been used in both regular and special education classes to teach decision making and interpersonal problem-solving skills (Elias & Clabby, 1989, 1992; Elias & Kress, 1994). The intervention focuses on three readiness areas (i.e., self-control, group participation, and social awareness) and eight steps for social decision making and problem solving. While the developers list the steps in a sequence, they acknowledge that decisions are not always made by strictly adhering to this sequence. The basic structure of the So-

Table 14.4

Basic Structure of the Social Decision-Making Approach[a]

When children or adolescents use their social decision-making skills, they are

A. Using self-control skills:
   1. Listening carefully and accurately,
   2. Following directions,
   3. Calming themselves down when upset or under stress, and
   4. Approaching and talking to others in a socially appropriate manner.

B. Using social awareness and group participation skills:
   1. Recognizing and eliciting trust, help, and praise from others,
   2. Understanding others' perspectives,
   3. Choosing friends wisely,
   4. Participating appropriately in groups, and
   5. Giving and receiving help and criticism.

C. Using critical thinking skills for decision making and problem solving:
   1. Noticing signs of feelings,
   2. Identifying issues or problems,
   3. Determining and selecting goals,
   4. Generating alternative solutions,
   5. Envisioning possible consequences,
   6. Selecting the best solution,
   7. Planning and making a final check for obstacles, and
   8. Noticing what happened and using the information for future decision making and problem solving.

---

[a]From Elias, M. J., Kress, J. S. Social decision-making and life skills development: A critical thinking approach to health promotion in the middle school. *Journal of School Health*. Vol. 64, No. 2, pp. 62–66, February 1994. Reprinted with permission. American School Health Association, Kent, Ohio.

cial Decision-Making approach is outlined in Table 14.4. The intervention guide is also replete with sample worksheets, directions for how to teach students to role-play, and many helpful teaching tips.

   a. Comments   Social Decision Making has been used in regular classes, special education classes, middle schools and even high schools. The associated skills have also been taught to parents (Clabby & Elias, 1986). Participating children and adults report high satisfaction. For example, children say they use what they learn in all aspects of their lives: with parents, siblings, and friends. Children entering middle school who did not participate in the problem-solving instruction identified such school stressors as peer pressure, academic demands, coping with authority figures, and becoming involved in substance abuse as significantly greater problems than did students who participated in the problem-solving instruction (Elias et al., 1986).

C. Structured Learning

Structured Learning, also referred to as skillstreaming, is a procedure for teaching prosocial skills to children (McGinnis & Goldstein, 1984; McGinnis, Goldstein, Sprafkin, & Gershaw, 1984) and adolescents (Goldstein, Sprafkin, Gershaw, & Klein, 1980). This format is designed for both handicapped and nonhandicapped students who have not learned to interact with others in socially appropriate ways. The procedure is designed to be used by teachers, social workers, psychologists, and school counselors.

Structured Learning is a psychoeducational, behavioral format for teaching prosocial skills based on four components: modeling, role-playing, performance feedback, and transfer of learning (Goldstein, 1993). Not one of these components alone is considered sufficient, but in combination are effective in teaching prosocial skills (Goldstein, Harootunian, & Conoley, 1994).

1. Modeling. The trainer describes the skill, provides a behavioral description of the steps that compose the skill, and role-plays these steps. Other models provide a portrayal of implementing the skill.
2. Role-playing. The trainer encourages the students to relate the skill modeled in step one to their own lives. Use of the skill in specific situations both present and future are discussed. Students then participate in role-plays that are coached and cued by the trainer. Observers are also encouraged to look for specific behaviors.
3. Feedback. Feedback occurs after each role-play and provides specific responses to the role-play. The trainer provides feedback on what aspects of the role-play were effective and provides encouragement. The trainer also models and role-plays skills that were not role-played effectively.
4. Transfer of learning. This provides opportunities to practice the steps and skills in real-life settings. One procedure for implementing this is the Homework Report, which requests detailed information on the consequences of implementing a skill sequence outside of the instructional setting.

The structured learning program designed for elementary students contains 60 prosocial skills arranged in five groups: classroom survival skills, friendship-making skills, skills for dealing with feelings, skill alternatives to aggression, and skills for dealing with stress. The five groups and skills that relate to each group are provided in Table 14.5. The structured learning skills for adolescents include 60 skills arranged in six groups. The six groups include beginning social skills (e.g., listening, saying "thank you," giving a compliment), advanced social skills (e.g., asking for help, following instructions, convincing others), skills for dealing with feelings (e.g., knowing your feelings, dealing with someone's anger, dealing with fear), skill alternatives to aggression (e.g., asking permission, negotiating, using

Table 14.5
Structured Learning: Prosocial Skills[a]

Group I. Classroom survival skills
 1. Listening
 2. Asking for help
 3. Saying "thank you"
 4. Bringing materials to class
 5. Following instructions
 6. Completing assignments
 7. Contributing to discussions
 8. Offering help to an adult
 9. Asking a question
 10. Ignoring distractions
 11. Making corrections
 12. Deciding on something to do
 13. Setting a goal
Group II. Friendship-making skills
 14. Introducing yourself
 15. Beginning a conversation
 16. Ending a conversation
 17. Joining in
 18. Playing a game
 19. Asking a favor
 20. Offering help to a classmate
 21. Giving a compliment
 22. Accepting a compliment
 23. Suggesting an activity
 24. Sharing
 25. Apologizing
Group III. Skills for dealing with feelings
 26. Knowing your feelings
 27. Expressing your feelings
 28. Recognizing another's feelings
 29. Showing understanding of another's feelings
 30. Expressing concern for another
 31. Dealing with your anger
 32. Dealing with another's anger
 33. Expressing affection
 34. Dealing with fear
 35. Rewarding yourself
Group IV. Skill alternatives to aggression
 36. Using self-control
 37. Asking permission
 38. Responding to teasing
 39. Avoiding trouble
 40. Staying out of fights
 41. Problem solving

continued

Table 14.5

(Continued)

42. Accepting consequences
43. Dealing with an accusation
44. Negotiating
Group V. Skills for dealing with stress
   45. Dealing with boredom
   46. Deciding what caused a problem
   47. Making a complaint
   48. Answering a complaint
   49. Dealing with losing
   50. Showing sportsmanship
   51. Dealing with being left out
   52. Dealing with embarrassment
   53. Reacting to failure
   54. Accepting no
   55. Saying no
   56. Relaxing
   57. Dealing with group pressure
   58. Dealing with wanting something that is not mine
   59. Making a decision
   60. Being honest

[a]From *Skillstreaming the Elementary School Child: A Guide for Teaching Prosocial Skills* (pp. 108–110) by E. McGinnis and A. P. Goldstein, 1984, Champaign, IL: Research Press. Copyright 1984 by the authors. Reprinted by permission.

self-control, keeping out of fights), skills for dealing with stress (e.g., making a complaint, standing up for a friend, responding to failure and persuasion, getting ready for a difficult conversation), and planning skills (e.g., deciding on something to do, setting a goal, making a decision, concentrating on a task).

a. Comments   Steps for teaching each of the 60 skills are provided within a "lesson" format that includes steps for performing the skill, notes for discussion about each step in the skill, suggested situations for role-playing the skill, and comments about the skill. A sample lesson is provided in Table 14.6. The lesson format provided for teaching each of the social skills can be readily used by teachers and other professionals interested in teaching social skills. While the program appears to hold promise, empirical reports of the efficacy of applying the lessons with students with LD have not been documented.

Table 14.6

Group I. Classroom Survival Skills[a]

Skill 1: Listening steps	Notes for discussion
1. Look at the person who is talking.	Point out to students that sometimes others may think someone is not listening, even though he/she really is. These steps are to show someone that you really are listening.
2. Remember to sit quietly.	Tell students to face the person and remember not to laugh, fidget, play with something, and so on.
3. Think about what is being said.	
4. Say, "yes," or nod your head.	
5. Ask a question about the topic to to find out more.	Discuss relevant questions (i.e., those that do not change topic).

Suggested Situations

School: Your teacher explains an assignment.
Home: Your parents are talking to you about a problem.
Peer group: Another student tells you of a TV program he/she watched or what he/she did over the weekend.

[a]From *Skillstreaming the Elementary School Child: A Guide for Teaching Prosocial Skills* (pp. 108–110) by E. McGinnis and A. P. Goldstein, 1984, Champaign, IL: Research Press. Copyright 1984 by the authors. Reprinted by permission.

D. Other Social Skills Interventions

Social skills instructional procedures have also been developed and tested with low-accepted, nonspecial education students. In a study by Bierman, Miller, and Stabb (1987), rejected males in grades one through three were assigned to one of four groups. The first group was provided with social skills instruction involving the description and practice of three target skills. The second group was considered a prohibition condition. The boys in this group were presented with a set of preestablished rules (e.g., no yelling) and received tokens (exchangeable for snacks at the end of the day) at random intervals provided they were not engaging in the prohibited behaviors. The third group received a combined treatment of skills instruction and prohibition. The last group was a no-treatment control condition. Students who participated in the combined intervention demonstrated the most stable behavioral improvements: decreases in negative behavior initiations, stable peer interactions, and decreases in negative peer responses. Central to this combined treatment are peer modeling and the teaching of conversational skills (i.e., self-expression, questioning, and leadership bids). Bierman's research (e.g., Bierman, 1986; Bierman & Furman, 1984) emphasizes the importance of these two components in any effective social skills intervention for youngsters.

Teaching, Learning, and Caring (TLC) (Vaughn, 1987; Vaughn & McIntosh, 1989) is a social skills intervention program designed to teach interpersonal problem-solving and social cognition to adolescents with emotional and behavioral problems and LD.

TLC was developed to teach the social behaviors frequently identified by parents, teachers, and counselors as problematic for many students with LD and emotional problems. These behaviors include impulsivity, inability to identify and respond to the affective states of others, difficulty generating a range of responses to problem situations, inability to evaluate and identify the likely consequences in a problem situation, problems initiating appropriate interactions, and problems responding appropriately to the initiations of others. Procedures for teaching appropriate social behaviors include modeling, role-playing real-life problems, and applying learned skills. Members of the participating group give positive and negative feedback about how well target students complete the role-play by applying the social skills. Systematic evaluation of the efficacy of this intervention with students with LD has not been reported. An overview of the TLC model is provided in Table 14.7.

Table 14.7
Overview of the TLC Model[a]

Core components	Prerequisite skill	Product/outcome
Goal identification	Recognizing goals of both self and others	
Empathy	Recognizing one's own feelings Recognizing the feelings of others	Integration–combining
Cue sensitivity	Awareness of verbal cues Awareness of nonverbal cues Awareness of environmental cues	skills to create an interpersonal problem-solving process that leads to
Alternative thinking	Alternative points of view-context versus content Alternative solutions to interpersonal problems	successful interpersonal skills
Consequential thinking	Cognitive predicting Role play/acting out	
Skills implementation	Cognitively describe steps Role playing	

[a]From Bos, C., & Vaughn, S. (1994). *Strategies for teaching students with learning and behavior problems* (3rd ed., p. 374). Allyn & Bacon: Heedham Heights, MA. Reprinted by permission of the publisher.

V. ISSUES

Many students with low peer status also experience poor academic performance. Because the correlation is not perfect, however, some children with low peer status will not perform poorly academically. Coie and Krehbiel (1984) examined the effects of academic tutoring on the social adjustment of rejected peers who also had academic problems. Rejected low-achieving students were assigned to one of four groups: academic tutoring, social skills instruction, combined academic tutoring and social skills, and a no-treatment control condition. The somewhat surprising results revealed that children in the academic tutoring conditions (both alone and combined) improved both in academic achievement and in social adjustment and maintained these gains up to a year later. The social skills instruction alone condition did have a positive effect on adjustment, but the gains were not evident at the 1-year follow-up. During the last decade we have come to understand the vital role social competence plays in healthy development and adjustment both in the short- and the long-term. The current state of knowledge, however, concerning which specific models for improving social competence work best with which populations and settings, remains polemic.

Those programs that are most effective are the ones that are tailored to the specific needs of the identified population (Coie, 1985). This notion of fitting the intervention to the requirements of the population needs to be further explored with students with LD whose social competence, for example, is associated with a number of areas that on the surface may appear unrelated to social competence (e.g., academic performance). If the goal is to increase the social acceptance of students, a model that solely emphasizes teaching social skills to the student in isolation is likely to be insufficient. Rather, models that include academic tutoring, peer involvement, social skills instruction, and perhaps even teacher training are needed. In addition, it may be necessary to develop specific interventions for youngsters with social skills difficulties based on whether they exhibit behavior problems. For example, youngsters with externalizing behavior problems (e.g., aggression) may need interventions that include prohibitions as well as social skills instruction.

An important issue in social skills interventions with students with LD is the use of NLD peers in the intervention. Sancilio (1987) reviewed the literature on peer interaction as a method of intervention with children and concludes that peers can serve as effective change agents with other peers, but the interventions need to be highly structured and focused on improving the target child's social skills. Peer interactions that emphasize increased peer contact without a structured intervention are less likely to be successful. Structured peer interactions usually take one of two forms: peers as social reinforcers or peers as trained initiators. As social reinforcers, peers may provide positive reinforcement such as, "good," and "I like playing with you when you share." Additionally, peers can be trained to ignore negative behaviors while still reinforcing positive behaviors (Solomon & Wahler,

1973). Peer interaction with social skills instruction is more effective than merely providing opportunities for peer interaction (Sancilio, 1987).

A second issue is the need for social skills interventions to be part of the curriculum rather than brief, one-shot interventions. In a discussion of their research involving a 6-week intervention with students with LD who had poor social skills, La Greca and Mesibov (1981) caution,

> It is not reasonable to expect that longstanding social problems can be entirely remediated within the span of six weeks, although definite inroads can be made. Thus, it is suggested that future investigators consider issues such as examining the effects of longer and more comprehensive intervention programs, as well as exploring the possibility of including social-skills instruction in the school curriculum, so that instruction can be accomplished on a regular, ongoing basis. (p. 238)

Reviews of social skills interventions with students with LD have yielded several guidelines for the successful implementation of these interventions (La Greca & Vaughn, 1992; McIntosh et al., 1991; Vaughn & La Greca, 1988).

A. Use Principles of Instruction

Procedures for teaching social skills are similar to those for effectively teaching other skills. First, the student needs to be motivated to learn the target skill (e.g., Goldstein et al., 1994). As with all instruction, it is difficult to teach students skills they are not interested in learning. Second, the student's social behaviors should be assessed in a variety of settings and through several methods, including observation. Before instruction is implemented, it is important to know explicitly which social behaviors are to be targeted, and in what settings the student may display the target behavior or other behaviors that may inhibit display of the target behavior. Third, after selecting appropriate social skills, the steps for performing the social skill need to be analyzed and described to the student. Fourth, the student needs to demonstrate knowledge of the steps that comprise the social skill. Fifth, the student needs to role-play the skill in controlled and naturalistic settings. Feedback and rehearsal are important aspects of role-playing. Sixth, students are taught to self-monitor and self-evaluate their progress and to generalize their newly learned skills to a variety of settings.

B. Teachers Must Interact with All Students in Ways That Communicate Acceptance

Teachers' perceptions of the students in their classes are communicated to all of the students in the room even when teachers believe they are concealing their opinions (Vaughn, McIntosh et al., 1993). Teacher's perceptions are a powerful force in the classroom and influence the attitudes of the students in their classrooms (Brophy, 1983). It is quite unlikely that any teacher truly feels equally positive about all of the students she or he teaches. It is possible, however, for teachers to communicate with all students in a manner that conveys acceptance. Most teachers do not realize the extent to which their tone, voice, expression, and style communicates to the child and to others in the room that the child is "OK" or "not OK".

Acceptance is communicated by the teacher through a classroom environment that supports all students. This classroom environment conveys a clear message that all students are valued. What occurs in classrooms in which all children are valued? Youngsters work cooperatively as well as in heterogeneous groups. Planned educational and social situations provide opportunities for all students to feel successful and appreciated. Neither teachers nor other students "put down" others. The teacher knows each student's area of expertise and capitalizes on what each student can do and knows. The teacher encourages students to appreciate the talents and abilities of their classmates.

C. Give All Students the Opportunity to Be the "Knower"

Positive self-perceptions and equally positive perceptions of others are strongly influenced by the extent to which a person is perceived as having something important to say or contribute. Students with LD are seldom placed in a role in which they demonstrate "knowing" or having something important to say or contribute. Because students with LD by definition demonstrate academic difficulties, it is not easy for teachers to find opportunities to allow them to be knowers.

The writing process approach (Graves, 1983) emphasizes the student as knower by having students write about what they know. When students with LD read their writing to others, the story they tell places them in the position of knower. The teacher and classmates ask questions about the story that only the target student can answer. Likewise, reciprocal teaching (Palinscar & Brown, 1984) provides a model for teaching reading comprehension through small-group instruction. Students are taught to lead groups, ask questions, and involve other students in the groups. Because group leadership is rotated among the students in the group, all students are provided opportunities to serve in the role of the knower.

D. Involve Peers, School Personnel, and the Community in Social Skills Instruction

Whenever possible, the school should have a model for social skills instruction; thus, communicating that it is a priority for the entire school. This does not mean that all students in the school need to be involved in a social skills intervention, but that the school provides support for those students who are involved. This might include articles written about the social skills program in PTA or student papers, awards given to students who successfully complete the social skills program, notes sent home to parents, or certificates of merit.

Most social skills programs are effective in altering target social skills but are less effective in improving the peer acceptance of target youngsters. Systematic involvement of peers in social skills instruction is an effective strategy for increasing peer acceptance.

VI. FUTURE DIRECTIONS FOR SOCIAL SKILLS INTERVENTION RESEARCH

Social skills interventions for students require further empirical evidence of their effectiveness for improving the social behavior of youngsters with specific disabilities (e.g., LD) as well as the acceptance and positive perceptions of these youngsters by significant others (e.g., peers, teachers, parents). In addition, the efficacy of these interventions on students' behavior in more natural settings (i.e., outside of the classroom or clinic) also needs to be evaluated. Finally, it can be difficult to assess the social functioning of at-risk youngsters. Many of the measures available have not been adequately tested and modified for use with youngsters with disabilities (Vaughn & Sinagub, 1997). The development of more adequate measures for assessing the self-concept, peer acceptance, social skills, and behavior adjustment of students with disabilities would enable researchers and practitioners to more accurately assess the specific area(s) at which social skills interventions should be targeted to meet the needs of individual students.

VII. SUMMARY

This chapter provides an overview of interventions designed to enhance the social skills and peer acceptance of students with LD. Background on why students need social skills interventions and what barriers might exist that discourage or prevent teachers from teaching social skills are also provided. Definitions of social skills and models that provide a background for applied social interventions are presented. The models for social intervention presented in this chapter include cognitive-social learning, interpersonal cognitive problem solving, and a comparison between the contextualist and deficit models of social skills.

Several interventions that have been conducted specifically with students with LD are described in detail. These interventions include a social skills program for adolescents, a contextualist intervention, cooperative learning, and Mutual Interest Discovery. Procedures for implementing these interventions as well as comments that might assist in knowing when and with whom to use the interventions are provided. In addition to social interventions implemented with populations with LD, social interventions that have been evaluated with other populations are also discussed.

Finally, this chapter provides an overview of issues relevant to teaching social skills to students with LD. The following guidelines for teaching social skills are addressed: use principles of effective instruction, interact with students in ways that communicate acceptance, give all students the opportunity to be the "knower," and involve peers, school personnel, and the community in social skills instruction.

References

Amish, P. L., Gesten, E. L., Smith, J. K., Clark, H. B., & Stark, C. (1988). Social problem-solving training for severely emotionally and behaviorally disturbed children. *Behavioral Disorders, 13*(3), 175–186.

Bandura, A. (1978). The self system in reciprocal determinism. *American Psychologist, 33,* 344–358.

Bandura, A. (1982). Self-efficacy mechanism in human agency. *American Psychologist, 37,* 122–147.

Baum, D., Duffelmeyer, F., & Geelan, M. (1988). Resource teacher perceptions of the prevalence of social dysfunction among students with learning disabilities. *Journal of Learning Disabilities, 21*(6), 380–381.

Bierman, K. L. (1986). Process of change during social skills training with preadolescents and its relation to treatment outcome. *Child Development, 57,* 230–240.

Bierman, K. L., & Furman, W. (1984). The effects of social skills training and peer involvement on the social adjustment of preadolescents. *Child Development, 55,* 151–162.

Bierman, K. L., Miller, C. L., & Stabb, S. D. (1987). Improving the social behavior and peer acceptance of rejected boys: Effects of social skill training with instructions and prohibitions. *Journal of Consulting & Clinical Psychology, 55,* 194–200.

Bos, C. S., & Vaughn, S. (1997). *Strategies for teaching students with learning and behavior problems* (4th ed.). Needham Heights, MA: Allyn & Bacon.

Brophy, J. (1983). Research on the self-fulfilling prophecy and teacher expectations. *Journal of Educational Psychology, 75,* 631–661.

Brown, W. H., & Odom, S. L. (1994). Strategies and tactics for promoting generalization and maintenance of young children's social behavior. *Research in Developmental Disabilities, 15*(2), 99–118.

Bryan, T., Bay, M., Lopez-Reyna, N., & Donahue, M. (1991). Characteristics of students with learning disabilities: A summary of the extant data base and its implications for educational programs. In J. Lloyd, N. Singh, & A. Repp (Eds.), *The regular education initiative: Alternative perspectives on concepts, issues, and models* (pp. 113–131). Sycamore, IL: Sycamore.

Bryan, T., & Perlmutter, B. (1979). Female adults' immediate impressions of learning disabled children. *Learning Disabilities Quarterly, 2,* 80–88.

Bryan, T., & Sherman, R. (1980). Immediate impressions of nonverbal ingratiation attempts by learning disabled boys. *Learning Disability Quarterly, 3,* 19–28.

Clabby, J. F., & Elias, M. J. (1986). *Teach your child decision making.* New York: Doubleday.

Coie, J. D. (1985). Fitting social skills intervention to the target group. In B. H. Schneider, K. H. Rubin, & J. E. Ledingham (Eds.), *Children's peer relations: Issues in assessment and intervention* (pp. 141–156). New York: Springer-Verlag.

Coie, J. D., & Krehbiel, G. (1984). Effects of academic tutoring on the social status of low-achieving, socially rejected children. *Child Development, 55,* 1465–1478.

Deluty, R. H. (1981). Alternative thinking ability of aggressive, assertive, and submissive children. *Cognitive Therapy and Research, 5,* 309–312.

Dubow, E. F., Tisak, J., Causey, D., Hryshko, A., & Reid, G. (1991). A two-year longitudinal study of stressful life events, social support, and social problem-solving skills: Contributions to children's behavioral and academic adjustment. *Child Development, 62,* 583–599.

Elardo, P. T., & Caldwell, B. M. (1978). The effects of an experimental social development program on children in the middle childhood period. *Psychology in the Schools, 16,* 93–100.

Elias, M. J., & Clabby, J. F. (1989). Social decision-making skills: A curriculum guide for the elementary grades. Rockville, MD: Aspen.

Elias, M. J., & Clabby, J. F. (1992). *Building social problem-solving skills: Guidelines from a school-based program.* San Francisco: Jossey-Bass.

Elias, M. J., Gara, M., Ubriaco, M., Rothbaum, P., Clabby, J., & Schuyler, T. (1986). Impact of a preventive school problem-solving intervention on children's coping with middle-school stressors. *American Journal of Community Psychology, 14*(3), 259–275.

Elias, M. J., & Kress, J. S. (1994). Social decision-making and life skills development: A critical thinking approach to health promotion in the middle school. *Journal of School Health, 64*(2), 62–66.

Forman, E. A. (1987). Peer relationships of learning disabled children: A contextualist perspective. *Learning Disabilities Research, 2*(2), 80–90.

Foster, S. L., & Ritchey, W. C. (1979). Issues in the assessment of social competence in children. *Journal of Applied Behavior Analysis, 12,* 625–631.

Fox, C. L. (1980). *Communicating to make friends.* Rolling Hills Estates, CA: Winch & Associates.

Fox, C. L. (1989). Peer acceptance of learning disabled children in the regular classroom. *Exceptional Children, 56,* 50–57.

Goldstein, A. P. (1993). Interpersonal skills training interventions. In A. P. Goldstein & C. R. Huff (Eds.), *The gang intervention handbook* (pp. 87–157). Champaign, IL: Research Press.

Goldstein, A. P., Harootunian, B., & Conoley, J. C. (1994). *Student aggression: Prevention, management, and replacement training.* New York: Guilford.

Goldstein, A. P., Sprafkin, R. P., Gershaw, N. J., & Klein, P. (1980). *Skillstreaming the adolescent.* Champaign, IL: Research Press.

Graves, D. H. (1983). *Writing: Teachers and children at work.* Portsmouth, NH: Heinemann.

Gresham, F. M. (1984). Social skills and self-efficacy for exceptional children. *Exceptional Children, 51*(3), 253–261.

Haager, D., & Vaughn, S. (1997). Assessment of social competence in students with learning disabilities (pp. 129–152). In D. Chard, E. J. Kameenvi, & J. W. Lloyd (Eds)., *Issues in educating students with disabilities*. Hillsdale, NJ: Lawrence Erlbaum.

Haager, D., & Vaughn, S. (1995). Parent, teacher, peer, and self-reports of the social competence of students with learning disabilities. *Journal of Learning Disabilities, 28*(4), 205–215, 231.

Hazel, J. S., Schumaker, J. B., Sherman, J. A., & Sheldon, J. (1982). Application of a group training program in social skills and problem solving to learning disabled and non-learning disabled youth. *Learning Disability Quarterly, 5,* 398–408.

Hazel, J. S., Schumaker, J. B., Sherman, J. A., & Sheldon-Wildgen, J. (1981). *ASSET: A social skills program for adolescents*. Champaign, IL: Research Press.

Interagency Committee on Learning Disabilities. (1987). *Learning disabilities: A report to congress*. Washington, DC: Department of Health and Human Services.

Johnson, D. W., & Johnson, R. T. (1986). Mainstreaming and cooperative learning strategies. *Exceptional Children, 52,* 553–561.

Johnson, D. W., Johnson, R. T., Warring, D., & Maruyama, G. (1986). Different cooperative learning procedures and cross-handicap relationships. *Exceptional Children, 53*(3), 247–252.

Kavale, K. A., & Forness, S. R. (1996). Social skill deficits and learning disabilities: A meta-analysis. *Journal of Learning Disabilities, 29*(3), 226–237.

Kohler, F. W., & Strain, P. S. (1993). The early childhood social skills program. *Teaching Exceptional Children, 25*(2), 41–42.

Kupersmidt, J. B., Coie, J. D., & Dodge, K. A. (1990). The role of poor peer relationships in the development of disorder. In S. R. Asher & J. D. Coie (Eds.), *Peer rejection in childhood* (pp. 274–308). Cambridge, UK: Cambridge University Press.

Ladd, G. W., & Mize, J. (1983). A cognitive-social learning model of social-skill training. *Psychological Review, 90*(2), 127–157.

La Greca, A. M., & Mesibov, G. B. (1981). Facilitating interpersonal functioning with peers in learning-disabled children. *Journal of Learning Disabilities, 14,* 197–199, 238.

La Greca, A. M., & Vaughn, S. (1992). Social functioning of individuals with learning disabilities. *School Psychology Review, 21*(3), 340–347.

Marchetti, A. G., & Campbell, V. A. (1990). Social skills. In J. L. Matson (Ed.), *Handbook of behavior modification with the mentally retarded* (2nd ed., pp. 333–355). New York: Plenum.

Mathur, S. R., & Rutherford, R. B. (1991). Peer-mediated interventions promoting social skills of children and youth with behavior disorders. *Education and Treatment of Children, 14,* 226–242.

McGinnis, E., & Goldstein, A. P. (1984). *Skillstreaming the elementary school child: A guide for teaching prosocial skills*. Champaign, IL: Research Press.

McGinnis, E., Goldstein, A. P., Sprafkin, R. P., & Gershaw, N. J. (1984). *Skillstreaming the elementary school child: A guide for teaching prosocial skills*. Champaign, IL: Research Press.

McIntosh, R., Vaughn, S., & Bennerson, D. (1995). FAST social skills with a SLAM and a RAP. *Teaching Exceptional Children, 28,* 37–41.

McIntosh, R., Vaughn, S., & Zaragoza, N. (1991). A review of social interventions for students with learning disabilities. *Journal of Learning Disabilities, 24*(8), 451–458.

McKim, B. J., Weissbar, R., Cowen, E. L., Gesten, E. L., & Rapkin, B. D. (1982). A comparison of the problem-solving ability and adjustment of suburban and urban third-grade children. *American Journal of Community Psychology, 10,* 155–169.

Northcutt, T. E. (1987). The impact of a social skills training program on the teacher-student relationship (Doctoral dissertation, University of Maryland, 1987). *Dissertation Abstracts International, 47,* A3712.

Odom, S. L., McConnell, S. R., & McEvoy, M. A. (1992). *Social competence of young children with disabilities: Issues and strategies for intervention.* Baltimore: Paul H. Brookes.

Palinscar, A. S., & Brown, A. L. (1984). Reciprocal teaching of comprehension fostering and comprehension monitoring activities. *Cognition and Instruction, 1*(2), 117–175.

Parker, J. G., & Asher, S. R. (1987). Peer relations and later personal adjustment: Are low accepted children at risk. *Psychological Bulletin, 102*(3), 357–389.

Putnam, J. W., Rynders, J. E., Johnson, R. T., & Johnson, D. W. (1989). Collaborative skill instruction for promoting positive interactions between mentally handicapped and nonhandicapped children. *Exceptional Children, 55*(6), 550–557.

Sancilio, M. F. M. (1987). Peer interaction as a method of therapeutic intervention with children. *Clinical Psychology Review, 7,* 475–500.

Shafer, H. S., Egel, A. L., & Neef, N. A. (1984). Training mildly handicapped peers to facilitate changes in the social interaction skills of autistic children. *Journal of Applied Behavior Analysis, 17,* 461–476.

Shure, M. B., & Spivack, G. (1979). Interpersonal cognitive problem solving and primary prevention: Programming for preschool and kindergarten children. *Journal of Clinical Child Psychology, 2,* 89–94.

Shure, M. B., & Spivack, G. (1980). Interpersonal problem solving as a mediator of behavioral adjustment in preschool and kindergarten children. *Journal of Applied Developmental Psychology, 1,* 29–44.

Slavin, R. E., Madden, N. A., & Leavey, M. (1984). Effects of cooperative learning and individualized instruction on mainstreamed students. *Exceptional Children, 50*(5), 434–443.

Solomon, R. W., & Wahler, R. G. (1973). Peer reinforcement control of classroom problem behavior. *Journal of Applied Behavior Analysis, 17,* 461–476.

Spivack, G., Platt, J. J., & Shure, M. B. (1976). The problem-solving approach to adjustment. San Francisco: Jossey-Bass.

Stokes, T. F., & Osnes, P. (1986). Generalizing children's social behavior. In P. S. Strain, M. J. Guralnick, & H. M. Walker, (Eds.), *Children's social behavior: Development, assessment, and modification* (pp. 407–443). Orlando: Academic Press.

Stone, W. L., & La Greca, A. M. (1990). The social status of children with learning disabilities: A reexamination. *Journal of Learning disabilities, 23,* 32–37.

Strain, P. S. (1983). Identification of peer social skills for preschool mentally retarded children in mainstreamed classes. *Applied Research in Mental Retardation, 4,* 369–382.

Strain, P. S., & Odom, S. L. (1986). Peer social initiations: Effective intervention for social skills development of exceptional children. *Exceptional Children, 52,* 543–551.

Swanson, H. L., & Malone, S. (1992). Social skills and learning disabilities: A meta-analysis of the literature. *School Psychology Review, 21,* 427–443.

Vaughn, S. R. (1987). TLC-Teaching, learning, and caring: Teaching interpersonal problem solving skills to emotionally disturbed adolescents. *Pointer, 31,* 25–30.

Vaughn, S., Erlbaum, B. E., & Schumm, J. S. (1997). *New research on inclusion: What are the social outcomes for students with learning disabilities?* Manuscript submitted for publication.

Vaughn, S., Erlbaum, B. E., & Schumm, J. S. (1996). The effects of inclusion on the social functioning of students with learning disabilities. *Journal of Learning Disabilities, 29*(6), 598–608.

Vaughn, S., & Haager, D. (1994). The measurement and assessment of social skills. In G. R. Lyon (Ed.), *Frames of reference for the assessment of learning disabilities: New views on measurement issues* (pp. 555–570). Washington, D.C.: Brookes.

Vaughn, S., & Hogan, A. (1990). Social competence and learning disabilities: A prospective study. In H. L. Swanson & B. K. Keogh (Eds.), *Learning disabilities: Theoretical and research issues* (pp. 175–191). Hillsdale, NJ: Lawrence Erlbaum.

Vaughn, S., & Hogan, A. (1994). The social competence of students with learning disabilities over time: A within individual examination. *Journal of Learning Disabilities, 27*(5), 292–303.

Vaughn, S., Hogan, A., Kouzekanani, K., & Shapiro, S. (1990). Peer acceptance, self-perceptions, and social skills of LD students prior to identification. *Journal of Educational Psychology, 82,* 101–106.

Vaughn, S., & La Greca, A. M. (1988). Social skills of LD students: Characteristics, behaviors, and guidelines for intervention. In K. Kavale (Ed.), *Handbook in learning disabilities* (pp. 123–140). San Diego: College Hill.

Vaughn, S., & Lancelotta, G. X. (1990). Teaching interpersonal social skills to low accepted students: Peer-pairing versus no peer-pairing. *Journal of School Psychology, 28*(3), 181–188.

Vaughn, S., Lancelotta, G. X., & Minnis, S. (1988). Social strategy training and peer involvement: Increasing peer acceptance of a female, LD student. *Learning Disabilities Focus, 4,* 32–37.

Vaughn, S., & McIntosh, R. (1989). Interpersonal problem solving: A piece of the social competence puzzle for LD students. *Journal of Reading and Writing Learning Disabilities, 4*(4), 321–334.

Vaughn, S., McIntosh, R., Schumm, J. S., Haager, D., & Callwood, D. (1993). Social status, peer acceptance, and reciprocal friendships revisited. *Learning Disabilities Research & Practice, 8*(2), 82–88.

Vaughn, S., McIntosh, R., & Spencer-Rowe, J. (1991). Peer rejection is a stubborn thing: Increasing peer acceptance of rejected students with learning disabilities. *Learning Disabilities Research & Practice, 6*(2), 83–88.

Vaughn, S. R., McIntosh, R., & Zaragoza, N. (1992). Social interventions for students with learning disabilities: Towards a broader perspective. In S. Vogel (Ed.), *Educational alternatives for students with learning disabilities* (pp. 183–198). New York: Springer-Verlag.

Vaughn, S. R., Ridley, C. A., & Bullock, D. D. (1984). Interpersonal problem-solving skills training with aggressive young children. *Journal of Applied Developmental Psychology, 5,* 213–233.

Vaughn, S. R., Ridley, C. A., & Cox, J. (1983). Evaluating the efficacy of an interpersonal skills training program with children who are mentally retarded. *Education and Training of the Mentally Retarded, 18,* 191–196.

Vaughn, S., McIntosh, R., Schumm, J. S., Haager, D., & Callwood, D. (1993). Social status, peer acceptance, and reciprocal friendships revisited. *Learning Disabilities Research & Practice, 8*(2), 82–88.

Vaughn, S., & Sinagub, J. M. (1997). Social assessment of at-risk populations: Implications for students with learning disabilities. In S. M. Clancy Dollinger & L. DiLalla (Eds.), *Assessment and intervention issues across the lifespan* (pp. 159–180). Hillsdale, NJ: Lawrence Erlbaum.

Vaughn, S., Zaragoza, N., Hogan, A., & Walker, J. (1993). A four-year longitudinal investigation of the social skills and behavior problems of students with learning disabilities. *Journal of Learning Disabilities, 26*(6), 404–412.

Wiener, J. (1987). Peer status of learning disabled children and adolescents: A review of the literature. *Learning Disabilities Research, 2*(2), 62–79.

Wilchesky, M., & Reynolds, T. (1986). The socially deficient LD child in context: A systems approach to assessment and treatment. *Journal of Learning Disabilities, 19*(7), 411–415.

Zigmond, N., & Brownlee, J. (1980). Social skills training for adolescents with learning disabilities. *Exceptional Education Quarterly, 12*, 77–83.

CHAPTER 15

Classrooms for Students with Learning Disabilities: Realities, Dilemmas, and Recommendations for Service Delivery

Jean B. Crockett and James M. Kauffman

> While a lecture was going on before a large class, a student in the back row fell unquietly asleep. The professor noticed the defection but continued with his remarks, more in sorrow than in anger. A few minutes later the boy recovered consciousness, and blurted out an apology. "No," said the professor, "it is I who should apologize to you—for not keeping you awake." (Peterson, 1946, p. 341)

Such civility may not be a hallmark of contemporary classrooms, but serving up instruction remains a challenging task. Today's teachers still cannot assume that students have any interest in what is being taught, or that their own, or their students', mere presence in the classroom eliminates boredom or day dreaming—or, more importantly, ensures learning. At the close of the 20th century, the job of the educator remains unchanged: to make tough decisions that guide the effective delivery of instruction to all students, front row or back, eager or reluctant.

Students with learning disabilities (LD) pose a particular challenge to educators who would seek, as Peterson suggests, to arouse and engage "their awakened, sym-

Learning about Learning Disabilities, Second Edition

pathetic, and co-operating faculties" (p. 341). These youngsters have in common the need for focused, intensive, and consistent instruction and often must double the efforts of their classmates to achieve an adequate level of performance (Garnett, 1996; Hallahan, Kauffman, & Lloyd, 1996). When defined as academic learners, students with LD often don't measure up, and their motivation in the classroom suffers (Wilson & David, 1994). "Because of the crowded conditions of classroom life and because of the surveillance of the teacher and of other students, trying to learn something while others are watching raises issues of maintaining 'face'" (Erickson, 1996, p. 99). Students need confidence that they will be respected and not shamed before a daily audience of teacher and classmates.

Erickson suggests that students' identities are fluid and their constructions shift across different learning configurations, or what he calls various academic task structures. When in alienating task structures, students disaffiliate with both the teacher and the classroom. "This is not to say the students don't learn—they are always learning, but not always what the teacher and school may want. Students are always 'on task.' The question is, which task, and for whose purposes?" (p. 100). Students and teachers interact through the social participation task structure, seeking and giving help, participating in classroom conversations, working individually and collectively, and fraternizing with each other. But it is the subject matter task structure that demands greater accountability through task completion, levels of difficulty, acquisition of knowledge, and requisite skills. Erickson contends that students wield the power to withhold classroom learning, and to construct personal identities that resist rather than affiliate with school: "This is to say that you can lead a horse (student) to water (learning environment) but you can't make it drink (learn)" (p. 101).

Our exploration of what special and regular classroom contexts are like for students with LD, and what the customary behaviors of these students and their teachers are within them, is intended to better clarify the connection between students and their learning environments. This chapter explores the nature of classrooms for students with LD by examining current realities and dilemmas of service delivery, legal parameters, and environmental contingencies that affect instruction. We look closely at what recent research suggests is happening in classrooms and whether these students are performing better as a result of efforts to redesign the structure of schools. Our concluding thoughts suggest what teachers can do to provide a more special education for their students with LD.

I. CLASSROOMS FOR STUDENTS
WITH LEARNING DISABILITIES

Providing service delivery to students with LD has been fraught with controversy about which students should be served, which curricula and instructional methodology should be used, and where instruction should be provided (Kauffman & Trent, 1991). Consequently, many educators in elementary and secondary schools are facing predicaments with regard to special education reform initiatives for which there are few blueprints. Administrators' skills, knowledge, and understanding are challenged as they attempt to accommodate increasing numbers of students with disabilities into general education classrooms while they cope with their own and their faculty's lack of preparation for educating students with special needs (Bailey, 1989; Kritsonis, 1992/3; Sage & Burrello, 1994; Scruggs & Mastropieri, 1996).

The international school reform movement, including initiatives in Canadian provinces, Europe, and Australia as well as the United States reflect similar rearrangements. Information is being shared globally as educators attempt to make classrooms more accommodating for their students with disabilities ("Special Educators Worldwide Work," 1995). Recently, in an internet post to SpedTalk, an electronic bulletin-board, a South African special educator asked for help in finding research to support his school's move toward more inclusive services. His question echoed Garnett's (1996): "Can the general education classroom be reshaped to allow for these youngsters to learn more, not simply to find a social niche?" (p. 25).

The international call for competitive standards, accountability, equity, and excellence for all students occurs simultaneously with concerns about opportunities to learn for those least equipped to compete. Most educators, while embracing greater participation in the mainstream, fear a loss of equity for students with LD unless they are provided with appropriate curriculum and instruction, supportive peer and teacher interactions, and suitable organization and management of their educational environments.

A. Current Realities of Service Delivery

American classrooms are currently experiencing unexpected growth. At a time when government funding is scarce and public confidence in the nation's schools is declining, the student population is growing as fast as it did in the 1960s. Six million more children are attending school now than were 10 years ago, and it is estimated that by 2025, the school population will increase from 49 million to 58 million children, a startling rise of 18% (Society, 1995). In addition to redesigning the schoolhouse, administrators must also adapt fiscally as well as instructionally to unexpected overcrowding, higher poverty rates, greater ethnic diversity, and increasing numbers of children with disabilities in regular classrooms.

According to the 18th Annual Report to Congress on the implementation of the Individuals with Disabilities Education Act (IDEA), 5.6 million children with disabilities from the ages of 3 through 21 received special education services in the 1995–96 school year (U.S. Department of Education, 1997). In the past 5 years, the percentages of school-age students with disabilities spending at least 80% of their day in regular classrooms has risen to 43%. This pattern of inclusion varies by age and represents nearly half of all students with disabilities ages 6 to 11, 33% of those ages 12 to 17, and 27% for those 18 to 21 (U.S. Department of Education, 1996). The pattern also varies by disability. Of the 2.5 million students with LD receiving services in the U.S. in 1994–95, 39% were assigned to regular classes for at least 80% of their instructional time. Frequently, it is the performance of these students in the general education setting that calls for a special instructional response.

B. Current Dilemmas of Service Delivery

"Before the 1960s, few public schools concerned themselves with students who, despite normal intellectual abilities and opportunities to learn, had significant problems with school achievement" (Zigmond et al., 1995, p. 531). Since the passage of federal legislation in 1975 and the emergence of the resource room design, there have been efforts to provide appropriate classroom instruction for students with LD alongside their nondisabled peers. However, the absence of consistent terminology and clear communication about several critical issues has hampered effective service delivery.

1. Definition of Learning Disability

Both Bateman (1992) and Keogh (1988) speak to the confusion between classification or identification of students with LD and the perplexing learning difficulties of these students that defy even the most effective known instructional strategies. The definition of LD is even more confusing if it is extended to include students who are educationally needy but not strictly defined as disabled. Many urban districts, short on resources and long on low-achieving students, use special education as a means of dealing with general education's nondisabled fallout. Gottlieb, Alter, Gottlieb, and Wishner (1994) describe many children in urban schools classified as LD as "having an acquired learning deficiency in all subject areas that is attributable to a variety of factors, but not to a learning disability the way it is conventionally defined" (p. 463).

Learning disabilities vary in type and range from mild to severe, and type and severity affect how instructional interventions will be approached in classrooms. In 1993, the Rehabilitation Services Administration categorized adults with LD as mildly disabled to distinguish their needs from others with severe, profound, or multiple disabilities. Mixing terms that have one meaning in habilitative services for seriously disabled adults with other terms connoting special instruction for children and youth, however, can lead to the unfortunate assumption that the educational needs of students with LD are mild and easily addressed (Mather &

Roberts, 1994). Reformers laboring under this untenable assumption may conclude that all students with LD can be educated appropriately in general education.

2. Variance among Students with LD and Students with Other Educational Disabilities

Although there is variability among students classified as LD, there is also variance between them and students with other special educational needs. Breaking down the term "mild disabilities" into its components better reflects the often varied outcomes of special education for students with LD, mental retardation (MR), behavior disorders (BD), or speech/language (S/L) disorders. In planning for service delivery, "disaggregating general from special education is not sufficient; students with disabilities must be disaggregated" (Kauffman, 1993, p. 11). Walker and Bullis (1991) noted that restructuring special education for inclusion "does not apply uniformly across handicapping conditions" (p. 76). This variability among groups and individuals with disabilities demands clear thinking regarding "how, and under what conditions, individual differences among learners can be accommodated" (Keogh, 1988, p. 20).

3. Differentiating Service Needs for Elementary and Secondary Students with LD

There are marked differences in the structure and curriculum of elementary and secondary schools in mission, teacher training, professional role perception, and opportunities for flexible programming. Even more striking are the differences in time for student contact, with the typical secondary teacher spending 50 min per day with a given student, and the typical elementary classroom teacher spending 350 min daily (Schumaker & Deshler, 1988). The importance of differentiating student characteristics and classroom environments developmentally is underscored in planning for service delivery. Not only do educational structures differ, but the inability of young children to use social comparison and normative information in the early grades could affect their sense of competence or vulnerability in instructional settings (Butler & Marinov-Glassman, 1994).

a. Definition of Inclusion   The following distinctions have been made among mainstreaming, integration, and inclusion, the terms most commonly used to indicate the instruction of students with disabilities alongside their nondisabled peers: (a) *mainstreaming* is defined as the placement of a student with a disability in a regular classroom for the express purpose of teaching an academic or special subject. Evidence from evaluations leads to the expectation that the special-needs student will achieve, with appropriate supports, at or about the level of his or her nondisabled peers; (b) *integration* is characterized by the placement of a student with a disability into a regular public school building where interaction, bolstered by necessary supports, can occur during nonacademic activities; (c) *inclusion* is most often described as the placement of a student, regardless of the level of disability, into an age-appropriate general education classroom in the local community school. All necessary supports are provided when inclusion is properly implemented including modification of curriculum, use of special education teachers, additional instructional and support staff, integrated related services, adaptive technology, instructional methodologies that support diversity, and team planning, which includes families, school personnel, students with and without disabilities, friends, and community members (New York State Regents, 1993).

Martin (1995) suggests that for those wishing to study it more scientifically, inclusion poses a challenge as there are many differing approaches to what bears the name. He notes that practices differ markedly from setting to setting and observes that "as a matter of public policy, a federal or state government, even a local school system, cannot responsibly adopt 'inclusion' without defining its proposed program" (p. 193). Skrtic (1991) describes four models, all of which agree that a restructured and unified system of special and general education should be "'flexible, supple and responsive', a 'totally adaptive system' in which professionals personalize instruction through 'group problem solving, . . . shared responsibility, and . . . negotiation', [but the models] disagree on which students should be integrated into the new system on a full-time basis" (p. 158). Some models propose the inclusion of literally all students with disabilities; others propose the inclusion of students for whom it is "appropriate."

C. Legal Foundations of Service Delivery Options

The legal parameters that guide service delivery for American students with LD are essentially the same as for other students whose educational rights are protected by Section 504 of the Rehabilitation Act (1973) and the Individuals with Disabilities Education Act (IDEA), the federal financing statute originally known as the Education for All Handicapped Children Act of 1975, Public Law 94–142. However, there are several notable additions for students with LD that highlight the role of professional collaboration. IDEA regulations emphasize a multidisciplinary partnership on the team that determines initial eligibility for LD services. Regulations stipulate that a team member other than the general education teacher must observe the child's academic performance in the regular classroom to determine whether the child is or is not achieving at a level commensurate with his or her age or ability even when provided with learning experiences appropriate to both age and ability (34 CFR 300.542). Basic to the definition of LD is the presence of a severe discrepancy between a student's ability and actual performance in language areas or mathematics that is not attributable to a visual, hearing, or motor impairment, mental retardation, emotional disturbance, or environmental, cultural, or economic disadvantage (34 CFR 300.541(a)(b)).

1. IEP: Individualized Education Program

Once a child has been found eligible to receive special education services, an IEP is developed based upon his or her unique educational needs. Only after this plan has been agreed upon should consideration be given to the student's placement (Bateman, 1996). Simply put, for any child with a disability, placements are to be (a) individualized; (b) based on availability of a full continuum of alternative placements that range from the regular classroom to a residential school; (c) consistent with the principles of the least restrictive environment; and (d) "secondary to the primary purpose of special education that is the provision of an appropriate program" (Bateman & Chard, 1995, p. 286).

2. FAPE: Free, Appropriate, Public Education

In writing the 1982 decision for the well-known *Hendrick Hudson District Board of Education v. Rowley* case, Supreme Court Justice Rehnquist declared that the standard for being "appropriate" could be met by a program developed in a procedurally correct manner, individualized, and reasonably calculated to provide the student with educational benefit. The degree of benefit is to be determined on a case by case basis—except in only one instance. When a student is placed in the regular classroom, all necessary aids and services are to be provided to enable him or her to achieve passing marks and legitimate passage from grade to grade. Bateman (1992) remarks that, realistically, districts mainstream perhaps millions of children with disabilities with no expectation of grade level performance or anything near the support needed to approach it. "The discrepancy between what the U.S. Supreme Court believes mainstreaming practice to be and what it actually is, is a mile wide and equally deep" (p. 30).

3. LRE: Least Restrictive Environment

The term Least Restrictive Environment appears only twice in the IDEA regulations, once as a column heading, and once in the following requirement: "In selecting the LRE, consideration is given to any potential harmful effect on the child or on the quality of services that he or she needs" (34 CFR 300.552(d). Bateman and Chard (1995) remark that, other than general requirements for an appropriate education, this is the only place the regulations refer to quality of services. Critical to the issue of service delivery is wording under this heading, which calls for children with disabilities to be educated with their nondisabled peers "to the maximum extent appropriate" (34 CFR 300.550 (b)(1)). Those who argue for cautious movement toward fuller inclusion take issue with others who substitute the phrase "to the greatest degree possible." Such conceptual distinctions represent more than semantic quibbles. They imply a vastly different regard for the law's intent and for its provision of a continuum of alternative placements beyond the regular classroom.

At the core of this quandary is the tension that exists in the law between offering an individually appropriate program, and doing so in a setting that offers interaction with nondisabled peers to the appropriate degree for each student with a disability. There is current confusion about whether the regular classroom in the neighborhood school is by definition the LRE (NASBE, 1992), or whether the setting that provides an appropriate education for a particular student and offers an appropriate degree of interaction for that student with nondisabled peers is, indeed, the LRE for that child (IDEA of 1997, 20 U.S.C. Sec 1401 et seq.). Can the LRE be identified as a specific place, or only as a setting in relation to an individual child? Is LRE an end in itself, or a means to an end? How educational leaders interpret the principles of LRE, with an emphasis on place or unique educational needs, has a significant effect on how schools will be structured and classrooms designed to address the needs of all students.

D. Individual Students and Classroom Environments

Zigler (1996) frames this difficult issue positively by asking, "What kind of transactions do we want to see in classrooms and how may disabilities affect these transactions?" (p. x). Keogh and Speece (1996) suggest looking inward and examining environmental variables, or the ecologies of classrooms, because they consider schooling to be both an influence on and a contributor to the risk status of all students, and to long-term outcomes for students with LD. They contend that "educational status is, in part at least, a function of 'goodness of fit' between child attributes and schooling demands, noting that for some children 'educational risk' changes relative to setting and to time" (p. 5).

Gottlieb, Alter, and Gottlieb (1991) define LRE as "that environment which imposes the fewest restrictions on a child's cognitive, emotional, and/or social development, regardless of the physical location of that environment" (p. 97). For them, individual assessment of the student and instructional placement are closely intertwined. They suggest that before a placement determination can be made, a minimum of information should be collected on the ecology of the general education classroom into which the child is scheduled to be placed. Morsink and Lenk (1992) also consider the selection of the LRE as a match between the learner's needs and the characteristics of the environment and state that determination of the LRE should be based on these issues: (a) making decisions on an individual basis based on the student's unique educational needs; (b) considering factors that can make an environment that appears to be less restrictive for a student actually more restrictive, such as a range of student variability and class size that stretch a classroom's limited tolerance for diversity, teacher attitudes and training, and impact on other students in the classroom; and (c) identifying factors of effective instruction that categorize any environment within the continuum of placements.

Various scales have been developed for use with students that attempt to match their individual attributes with characteristics of learning environments (Epstein, Quinn, & Cumblad, 1994; Greenwood, 1996; Vaughn & Schumm, 1996). Keogh and Speece (1996) underscore the importance of such eco-behavioral programming by suggesting that "children with LD are especially vulnerable to schooling effects, including changes in instructional and curricular demands and to teachers' expectations for performance" (p. 5).

II. WHAT HAPPENS IN CLASSROOMS?

Recent studies in both elementary and secondary schools provide a clearer picture of what special education is like for students with LD in the context of more inclusive programming. These snapshots of classroom ecologies provide descriptions of student and teacher interactions, curriculum and instruction, and the organization and management of resources from recent explorations of school reform.

A. Student and Teacher Interactions

1. Characteristics of the Students

Students with LD have more severe academic deficits than do their low-achieving peers (Kavale, Fuchs, & Scruggs, 1994). These students have well-documented problems in the classroom including (a) severe deficits in basic literacy and numeracy skills; (b) generalized failure and below-average performance in content areas such as science and social studies; (c) inadequate student-survival skills, such as study and test-taking skills, listening well, and taking notes; (d) pervasive lack of motivation and passive learning behaviors; and (e) inadequate interpersonal skills (Rieth & Polsgrove, 1994).

   In short, the primary characteristics of students with LD are delayed development of academic and social skills. These are also the primary criteria in determining whether students should be promoted or retained in grade level (McLeskey, Lancaster, & Grizzle, 1995). The outcomes of their instruction increase in importance, considering that "within conventional general education classrooms, these children previously have failed to achieve important literacy and numeracy goals, with 6 of 10 students with LD having been retained in at least one grade prior to their placement in special education" (L. Fuchs, 1996, p. 83). Wagner (1990) reported that of 531 adolescents with LD, 73% were at least 1 year older than their nondisabled classmates. Retention rates are high for students with LD despite the lack of research support for retention's effectiveness, regardless of its long-term negative effects, and in the face of evidence that it contributes to the school dropout problem (McLeskey, et al, 1995).

2. Characteristics of Teachers

In the United States, special education teachers are considerably younger than their general education counterparts. Almost half are younger than 40 years old, compared with 35% of regular educators. Approximately 90% of elementary general and special educators are female, but at the secondary level there is a considerable gender difference. Women comprise 77% of secondary special educators but only 53% of secondary general educators. The ethnic comparison of special and general educators is similar, but representation of African-American teachers is 25% higher in special education. A greater percentage of special educators hold a graduate degree, but their colleagues in general education have more years of teaching experience (Cook & Boe, 1995).

3. Beliefs and Behaviors of Students with LD and Their Teachers

For teachers, classrooms are academic environments; for students, classrooms are social environments where academic learning takes place. For teachers, completion of an academic task is influenced by the degree of student mastery. For students, completion of an academic task is influenced by what occurs in the social structure of the classroom (Reyes, 1996). Reyes points out that not only can students with LD withhold assent to learn in classrooms, but some appear not to know how to learn even when they want to.

In reviewing research on the classroom behavior of students with LD, Bulgren and Carta (1992) determined that these students behave the same in different educational settings. Off-task behavior is exhibited more often by students with LD than their nondisabled classmates, and the authors remarked on the significant relationship between this inappropriate behavior and poor academic progress. Adolescents with LD were found to demonstrate more passive, off-task behavior than do low-achieving classmates. During whole-group instruction, both groups are more likely to be passively off-task than during seatwork, when the requirements are more procedural and directive.

The behaviors of teachers toward students with LD in the regular classroom often indicate a difference in the type and quality of interactions compared to those experienced by nondisabled students. Although contrary to effective behavior management practice, teachers are more likely to ignore students with LD when they are working quietly on their work, yet interact with them when they are actively off-task and disruptive to classmates. In their interchange with students with LD, teachers tend to use more corrective behavior, longer and more frequent interactions with negative verbal or nonverbal behaviors than with other children. In one case, despite an intervention designed to decrease such interactions, elementary teachers did not reduce the quantity, only the negativity, of these interchanges. Teachers direct fewer academic questions or feedback to these students, and it is hypothesized that either teachers consider socialization rather than academic learning to be the primary goal of mainstreaming or they attribute achievement problems to inherent limitations in ability (Bulgren & Carta, 1992). In contrast, Vaughn and Schumm (1996) observe that many teachers treat students with LD much the same as others, posing a dilemma: "students were not singled out and certainly did not feel as though they were 'different' from others in the class. . . . students with LD could expect few accommodations and adjustments in assignments, teaching routines, expectations, homework, or testing" (p. 111).

Scruggs and Mastropieri (1995) suggest that concerns about stigmatization have been exaggerated and that such concerns are inconsistent with the perceptions of students with LD about their special education services. They report numerous interviews indicating that students often have a preference for the privacy of resource rooms, appreciation for individualized special education support, and increased self-esteem from increased outcomes achieved in separate, intensive instruction.

4. Teachers' Perceptions of Mainstreaming or Inclusion

There is general agreement that for students with disabilities to be served well in inclusive settings the regular education teacher must be supportive of both the principles and challenges of teaching them. Scruggs and Mastropieri (1996) reviewed 27 survey reports in which 9772 teachers were asked about their attitudes toward mainstreaming children with disabilities. These reports spanned the years 1958 to 1995 and included teachers from Canada, the United States, and Australia. Regardless of geography or chronology, the willingness of these educators seemed inversely related to the degree of additional classroom assistance such students might require. Only about one-fourth agreed that mainstreaming most students with disabilities was desirable. About the same number said they thought they had sufficient time, training, and resources to implement it successfully. Most responded that they lacked the skills or training in modifying instruction as well as the time and resources. Most wanted reduced class size, greater material and personnel support, and more time for planning and implementing instruction and collaborating with support staff. Full-time inclusion in the regular classroom met with strong negative response from two 1994 studies, with 80% of respondents in one report saying they felt coerced into full inclusion. The authors note that responses were surprisingly stable from the earliest to the most recent reports. There appeared to be no systematic relation between teachers' attitudes and publication date, lending support to the idea that "teachers regard students with disabilities in the context of procedural classroom concerns (which have improved little if any in recent decades), rather than in the context of social prejudice and attitudes toward social integration (which appear to have improved somewhat in recent decades)" (p. 71).

B. Instructional Interventions for Students with LD

1. Teaching Conditions

In addition to larger classes, teachers are currently responding to a wide range of instructional levels within general education, with estimates indicating that more than five grade levels are represented per classroom in some schools (Fuchs,

Fuchs, Hamlett, Phillips, & Bentz, 1994). Given current fiscal restraints, teachers
are not often supported when special education students are integrated. "In addition, this greater responsibility is not always accompanied with more intensive
preparation of teachers and administrators, increased educational support, more
manageable class sizes, or state of the art technology" (Roberts & Mather, 1995,
p. 50). Lieberman (1996) refers to increased demands on classroom teachers and
questions not the ideals but the strategy of full inclusion: "We are testing more, not
less. We are locking teachers into constrained curricula and syllabi more, not less
. . . The flexibility demanded by full inclusion is rarely encountered" (p. 17).

Roberts and Mather (1995) observe that "regular educators are not trained to
provide diversified instructional methods or to cope with the needs of diverse
learners" (p. 50). Similarly commenting on the infrequency with which general educators employ prereferral intervention strategies, Gottlieb et al. (1994) found that
other than knowing that these children needed one-to-one instruction, almost two-
thirds of the 206 referring classroom teachers could not indicate what resources
they would need. Only 16% indicated they could be trained with the necessary
skills to retain these children in their classes, and only 10% presented activities
that could reasonably be described as curriculum adaptation.

There is evidence that students with LD are not typically receiving needed support from general educators, who are more often concerned with conformity than
accommodations for individual students in the regular class (Bos & Vaughn, 1994;
Lieberman, 1996; Roberts & Mather, 1995). For example, in studying interventions that elementary and secondary teachers would be willing to use, Johnson and
Pugach (1990) and Ellet (1993), respectively, found that classroom teachers at both
levels highly ranked these general and nonspecific strategies: (a) encourage and
support attempts at academic improvement; (b) emphasize the good qualities of
behavior; (c) demonstrate difficult tasks; and (d) establish specific consequences
for appropriate behavior. In a study of 775 general educators, K-12, Schumm and
Vaughn (1992) also report that teachers are likely to make adaptations "on the
spot" during instruction rather than to plan for their use ahead of time. Information sources used for planning and adapting instruction most frequently come from
interactions with other teachers, parents, or directly with the student; resources
outside the classroom, such as other agencies or textual data from IEPs or psychological reports, are rarely used.

2. Teaching Practices

Effective teachers in general and special classes have been found to use the following elements of instruction: (a) teacher-directed instruction with individual
feedback; (b) student opportunities for active academic responses; (c) high rates
of contingent reinforcement; (d) adaptive teaching strategies to accommodate individual differences; (e) high rate of interaction among students, teachers, and
peers; (f) instruction at a brisk pace and in small steps; (g) progressive goals to

100% mastery; (h) structured lessons; (i) strategy instruction; j) computer-assisted instruction (Ellet, 1993; D. Fuchs & Fuchs, 1995a; Morsink & Lenk, 1992). Most of these practices have been validated using one-on-one or small group instruction in special education settings, but not in inclusive ones. Others, such as team teaching, consultant teacher, and cooperative learning have yet to be validated for students with LD in a regular class setting (D. Fuchs & Fuchs, 1995a).

Although grade levels or severity of learning problems are not consistently apparent in the studies they review, Bulgren and Carta (1992) examine certain "ecological events" such as the amount of engaged time students with LD spend in different instructional activities and structures across settings. These include regular and self-contained classrooms, a consulting-teacher classroom, or a resource room setting. Results suggest that although the structures of special education classrooms differ from general education classrooms, in either setting teachers allocate similar amounts of time to various instructional activities. There is no difference in opportunities for students to actively respond, although students in less restrictive settings are given more whole-group teaching structures, and students in more restrictive settings spend more time in individualized structures. There tends to be no difference in active student responses in the small-group structures used across settings.

In one study of effective methodology, an ecobehavioral analysis was used based on student achievement, analysis of the classroom behavior, and features of the class instruction that determined that direct instruction was found to be effective with students with LD in both a resource room and a regular classroom.

3. Teacher Acceptability

"Teacher acceptability refers to the extent to which teachers view a strategy as easy to use, effective, reasonable, fair, consistent with their teaching style and philosophy, and appropriate for their setting" (Gajria, Salend, & Hemrick, 1994, p. 236). In general, teachers are more likely to use practical strategies that are easy to implement, effective, and conducive to their classroom routine and teaching style.

Some general educators rate accommodations as more desirable than feasible. Schumm and Vaughn (1991) report that 93 teachers (25 elementary, 23 middle school, and 45 high school) identified as feasible those requiring no instructional or curricular changes and could be done with relative ease. Similarly, these teachers identified as desirable those adaptations that require them to reinforce and encourage students, establish personal rapport with them, respect mainstreamed students as individuals and involve them in whole class activities, establish appropriate routines, and adapt classroom management strategies. Adaptations considered least desirable and feasible included adapting long-range plans, modifying the physical environment, adapting regular materials, using alternative materials, adapting grading criteria, and providing individualized instruction. Schumm and Vaughn conclude that "teachers are willing to make accommodations that demonstrate acceptance of the student with LD, but less willing to make adaptations that require planning, instructional, or environmental adaptations" (Vaughn & Schumm, 1996, p. 109).

As a result of their extensive work in elementary and secondary classrooms with hundreds of teachers and students, Vaughn and Schumm have added a critical element to their fundamental research question. In addition to seeking the most effective practices for students with LD in the general education classroom, they now ask which ones are feasible to implement, likely to be used by teachers over time, and will positively influence the performance of all learners in the classroom, including average- and high-achieving students. "We have reframed the question because we have learned that teachers' beliefs about instruction focus on meeting the needs of the class as a whole and not on implementing specific instructional practices that will meet the needs of target students (e.g., students with LD)" (Vaughn & Schumm, 1996, p. 110).

C. Curricular Organization and Management

1. Appropriateness of the General Education Curriculum for Students with LD

The following three beliefs underlie the assumption that the general education curriculum is appropriate for students with LD: (a) this curriculum can be modified to meet the diverse needs and learning styles of all students; (b) teachers are able to assess students' needs and modify the curriculum accordingly; and (c) teacher training and in-service programs help teachers acquire the skills necessary to teach a diverse group of students (Roberts & Mather, 1995).

These assumptions beg critical questions: Can the curriculum be modified to meet the needs of all students? Can professional training positively affect teaching practice? Are teachers providing specialized instruction for individual students with LD as they attempt to offer an improved, personalized, and accommodating educational experience for all students? Such questions have practical merit. If an accommodating general education provides academic and social benefit to a student with LD so that he or she makes progress from grade to grade, then conceivably more students could be disenfranchised from mandated services, and more districts released from costly obligations (Zigmond, 1995).

The formal curriculum of a school denotes the plans made to guide learning, including the structures and practices to implement what is to be taught and learned (Pugach & Warger, 1993). Instructional practices flow from curricular imperatives dictating policies of class grouping, grade levels, grading practices, grade retention, and academic content. "Teaching to the middle" is a practice that may be appropriate only in classes of homogeneous students. "Many students do not have the ability to keep pace with the curriculum the way it is structured within the general education classroom and thus may experience a different kind of segregation—the exclusion from the basic right to learn" (Schumm et al., 1995, p. 335).

2. Content Coverage

Classroom life is frequently dominated by concerns about covering the curriculum. Even the practices of elementary and secondary classroom teachers considered to be effective with students with LD reflect these priorities: (a) planning for content coverage and classroom activities, not individual needs; (b) at the secondary levels, students with LD are expected to cover the same content and at the same pace as other students, although modifications are more likely to be made at the elementary level; (c) monitoring of students with LD occurs largely by checking on what they are doing with little systematic monitoring of understanding; and (d) success of lessons and time to introduce new content is based on the performance of the class as a whole and the amount of content coverage demanded by the curriculum. "The class moved on, whether the students understood the material or not" (Vaughn & Schumm, 1996, p. 111).

Extensive conversations with teachers suggest less concern with students' knowledge acquisition or the need for additional help or explanation, but with whether students demonstrate interest, create discipline problems, and enjoy the lessons. Many elementary teachers reflect a classroom ecology more supportive of social acceptance and self-esteem than of academic learning. Middle school teachers seem more concerned with content coverage and discipline problems. High school teachers refer to issues of fairness and concern that to identify or accommodate a handicap would make a student stand out and thus would not prepare him or her for the real world (Vaughn & Schumm, 1996).

Demands facing content area teachers in inclusive settings to cover the curriculum may serve as a barrier to full and effective implementation of strategy instruction beneficial to students with LD (Scanlon, Deschler, & Schumaker, 1996). This becomes an administrative issue and

> teachers need assurances from supervisors that when there are several special needs students in their classrooms they will not be held accountable for covering the full content of the curriculum. The first priority must be to ensure that the students succeed in learning the content that is covered. (Bos & Vaughn 1994, p. 445.)

3. Goal Setting

The general education curriculum is not often individualized, nor are instructional decisions based on assessment data. There is also little evidence of a relationship between IEP goals and subsequent instruction (Roberts & Mathers, 1995). Disturbing results of interviews conducted over 8–10 years by Gottlieb et al. (1991) indicate that fewer than 10% of general educators who had children with

LD in their classes had more than a perfunctory knowledge of the child's IEP. None had participated in a formal multidisciplinary conference regarding the child's progress. The majority of teachers had never seen the IEP, and a substantial percentage did not know what an IEP was. These authors ask, "How can we seriously maintain that a regular class placement is appropriate when the child study teams know little about the general education class, and the general education teacher knows little about the mainstreamed special education pupil?" (p. 101).

In special education settings, however, there is concern that too often the IEP becomes the only instructional guide, and instead of adapting the general curriculum for the student with LD, many special educators only address individualized goals (Pugach & Wagner, 1993; Sands, Adams, & Stout, 1995). There are few reported systematic investigations of how these goals are set for students' performance at the class, school, district, or state levels. Whether in a separate setting or a regular classroom, little is known about how special educators make decisions for their students' short- or long-term academic goals, and empirically guided methods of identifying appropriate goals are not available (Rieth & Polsgrove, 1994). In addition, these goals are often set in spring, months before final grades document the efficacy of the current program. This practice makes it difficult to set goals that are both attainable and ambitious. Fuchs, Fuchs, and Hamlett (1989) observe that goal standards often underestimate student performance and that special educators need prompting to raise them to realistic levels. In this way, "existing professional practices that lead to the establishment of underestimated performance goals for disabled students may be contributing inadvertently to the students' lack of academic progress" (Rieth & Polsgrove, 1994, p. 122).

D. Management of Student Diversity in Inclusive Settings

To attempt to manage engaging and effective instruction, collaborative and consultative staffing models have been developed, and several instructional models including cooperative learning, peer tutoring, and curriculum-based measurement (CBM) have been transplanted from special settings to regular classrooms. Most of the studies validating these practices for students with LD have been conducted in special education settings, suggesting limited assumptions for their success in regular classroom environments (D. Fuchs & Fuchs, 1995b; Schrag, 1994). For example, controversy surrounds the generalizability of cooperative learning research because many of the studies were conducted in special experimental classrooms. In sum, the studies bode optimistically for social benefits, but the academic progress of students with LD is not so clearly indicated (Schrag, 1994).

O'Connor and Jenkins (1996) captured the problems of managing time and providing individualized instruction through a cooperative learning model for second-grade readers. They observed that special educators expend their energies preparing students with LD to be able to participate in group activities in the regular class.

No special or general educators were seen working on skills likely to close the gap in reading levels between these students and their nondisabled peers. Nevertheless, a special educator supported the cooperative structure:

> Now we're talking about issues of socialization and self-esteem, and I don't think you can put a price on that, or a value on that. To me, what is important, is that these kids have some experience with that story before the class does. So when they go—they feel more a part of the classrooms. (p. 68)

These words cut to the heart of the issue of managing inclusive services for students with LD. According to O'Connor and Jenkins, "When there is only time for one, should special education focus primarily on providing extraordinary instruction or on facilitating participation?" (p. 68).

E. Results of Implementation of Inclusion Models

Zigmond and Baker (1995) conducted extensive case studies in six restructured schools to determine the nature of special education provided to elementary students with LD in regular classrooms. All of the classrooms they observed used popular practices considered supportive of inclusion, including learning strategy instruction, CBM, team teaching and teacher consultation, modified grading, phonics instruction and alternative reading strategies, peer tutoring, and cooperative learning. Expectations and assignments were also aligned with each school's curriculum, and special education support was provided by teachers who were veterans of pull-out service delivery who had been trained for their new roles and responsibilities.

Inclusion was interpreted and implemented differently in each school, with special-needs students either clustered or dispersed throughout classes. Two sites retained resource room support or alternative instruction during the school day. In the others, pull-out services were discontinued and all children were reintegrated into regular classrooms with the understanding that necessary supports and services would be provided there. In these schools, parents, teachers, and administrators expressed concern about meeting the remedial needs of students who were struggling with reading and math. Since teaching schedules had already been established, creative solutions for extra help included tutoring at lunchtime or before and after school. The need for pull-out support and its impact on extended-day schedules raise the question of realistically eliminating the requirement for a continuum of alternative placements.

Coteaching and collaborative staffing models did not address individual needs, even though extra planning time was built into professional schedules. Collaborative meetings were used to plan what and how something would be taught, rather than who would be taught it. Instructional decisions were neither personalized nor databased, nor were accommodations planned or individualized. Some teachers at grades 4–6 objected philosophically to adaptations, believing that students needed to learn to cope independently.

In all schools, one-to-one peer tutoring was used to increase active responses and provide support to students who could not manage classwork on their own. In some instances, paraprofessionals monitored and provided small group instruction, although only one site made provision for their training. The help provided by peer tutors and paraprofessionals was informal because specific assignments were not developed ahead of time by the teacher to ensure engagement or success. Baker and Zigmond (1995) raise concerns that "to economize, schools used peers, paras, and parents in instructional roles, the *least well trained* individuals to teach the *most difficult to teach!*" [italics in original] (p. 177).

1. Room for Improvement in Service Delivery

Results of these observations show room for improvement. They also suggest the need for a deeper professional understanding of required services for students with LD if general education teachers are to provide specially designed instruction. Bateman (1992) predicted that special education in the 1990s would focus on the all-important issues of curriculum. She stressed the need for schools to specify performance standards and to adopt instructional approaches and curricular materials that have been shown to be effective to that end. "As long as we are content for children to engage in certain activities or processes, without regard to outcome, we will continue to have large numbers of children failing" (p. 34).

III. OUTCOMES OF SERVICE DELIVERY MODELS FOR STUDENTS WITH LEARNING DISABILITIES

Given the foregoing, D. Fuchs and Fuchs (1995b) ask a basic question, "Can teaching methods that focus instructional decisions on individual students and that have been empirically validated by special education in special education settings be exported to mainstream classrooms to improve outcomes of students with severe learning problems?" (p. 528).

A. Student Outcome Data

Current evidence from inclusive classroom ecologies suggest that individualized instruction for students with LD does not travel well. To protect children from what he calls "well-intentioned experimentation," Martin (1995) writes that policymakers should not, as a scientific matter, use the general enthusiasm for inclusion and its adoption elsewhere as criteria for decision making. He calls for a study of student outcomes and an answer to the question, "Will inclusive programs provide more effective programming?" (p. 193).

Martin encourages "careful, systematic measurements on the child," including both achievement scores and specific measurement in areas of difficulty, as well as "sophisticated measures of self-concept and socialization" (p. 194). Jenkins et al. (1994) observe that although "'experiments in schooling' are on the increase, rarely are they accompanied by the kind of outcome-oriented research that is required for us to make progress in teaching and learning" (p. 357). For example, in at least one state, academic outcome data such as grades, grade retentions, and drop-out rates, which could be used to monitor the impact of increased inclusive programming, were not being collected systematically and summarized on a school or district basis for students with LD. Enabling outcome indicators—social acceptance in the regular class, satisfaction with class placement, attitude toward learning, and parental satisfaction—were the more frequently used measures (Houck & Rogers, 1994).

In an era of educational reform focused on improving and measuring results, decision makers struggle with the following questions: (a) Can the same outcomes be defined for all students, regardless of level of functioning? (b) Should outcomes be looked at on a system-wide basis, individual basis, or both? (c) Should outcomes for special education rest on different assessment systems from general education? (Bruininks, Thurlow, & Ysseldyke, 1992).

B. Research Designs

"Numerous studies of the effects of service delivery models have been done, but most of them have been so seriously flawed that the results are not reliable" (Hallahan et al., 1996, p. 452). Marston (1988) holds that outcome studies have been compromised by the means with which gains have been measured. For example, against whom should the student with disabilities be compared, and how should progress be assessed? Early studies on the effectiveness of regular class placement simply evaluated whether the experimental mainstreaming program yielded better academic achievement, social adjustment, or classroom behavior than the control resource room or self-contained class. In short, they measured the outcomes for students who were socially and academically stronger from the beginning with lower performing students in special education settings (Fuchs & Fuchs, 1995a).

Another oversimplification occurs when the results of program research are reported collectively as effective for all students without reporting the separate effects for students of different ability levels or disability classification (Hallahan et al., 1996). The often quoted meta-analysis of Carlberg and Kavale (1980) is frequently truncated and summarized by reporting the collective results of regular vs.

special class placement for students who are mentally retarded, emotionally and behaviorally disordered, and learning disabled. As a result, proponents of full inclusion cite Carlberg and Kavale as evidence that education in the regular class is more beneficial to students with disabilities than education in special settings. A closer analysis of the separate results reveals something else. For students with mental retardation, regular class placement was superior. However,"the average BD/ED or LD student in special class placement was better off than 61% of his/her counterparts in regular class" (Carlberg & Kavale, 1980, pp. 301–302).

In designing studies of educational programs in the mainstream, Gottlieb et al. (1991) pose two research questions essential to service delivery: (a) Do the main-streamed children function within a range of proficiency that the classroom teacher believes acceptable for the child to progress adequately and remain in the class? (b) Would similar outcomes emerge if the control group in the separate class setting received the bulk of attention and resources? The challenge would then become this: "Can we construct self-contained placements that are superior to integrated placements on a set of redefined dimensions? If we can, are mainstreamed environments still the preferred placement?" (p. 104).

Carnine (1994a) suggests that educational decision makers responsible for service delivery evaluate studies according to the following guidelines: (a) the manageability of the interventions; (b) the elements of their effectiveness; (c) principles of accountability; (d) clarity for replication; (e) equity; and (f) cost benefits. Unfortunately, results are not frequently published in a way that facilitates such analysis. The key is for researchers to report their results in a manner that fosters this practical use.

C. Empirical Studies

A search of the Psych Lit and ERIC databases reveals a vast amount of process literature on mainstreaming and inclusion, covering such topics as the characteristics and behavior of both teachers and students, instructional interventions, inclusive practices, classroom attributes, and professional collaboration. There are far fewer studies empirically documenting whether promising practices in inclusive programs are providing more effective programming for elementary and secondary school students with LD.

In 1988, the U.S. Department of Education issued a call for building-level models that restructured schools instructionally, organizationally, and administratively to provide services to special education students in the regular classroom. These major studies evaluated elementary school models where program effectiveness was to be outcome-based: special education students were to achieve better academic outcomes than in traditional, fragmented pull-out programs (Zigmond et al. 1995). The purpose of the present analysis is to review several themes that emerge in this literature from the late 1980s to the present considering the subjects and settings, instructional components, elements of effectiveness, manageability or potential for realistic implementation, and effects on educational outcomes.

1. School Structures: Resource Room or Regular Class Outcomes

Research examining the educational outcomes for students with LD in resource rooms or the regular classroom does not present conclusive evidence for preferred service delivery. As some have suggested, it "has actually done little but demonstrate the difficulty of doing such research" (Hallahan et al, 1996, p. 451).

Some studies have not used multiple variables or investigated multiple outcomes for students in their designs. Students and teachers have not been randomly assigned, and control groups have been established based upon an assumption that different schools are more alike than not because of demographic similarities rather than community ethic. Affleck, Madge, Adams, and Lowenbraun (1988) looked at academic benefits for students with LD in examining the Integrated Classroom Model (ICM), described as "a service delivery model for educating mildly handicapped children in integrated classrooms administered jointly by regular and special education personnel" (p. 340). They compared this with the resource room model to determine both its academic viability and cost effectiveness over a 3-year period in elementary schools in a suburban district. The investigation focused on the observation of "best practice" teaching behaviors and resultant student achievement of students with LD served full-time in regular classes. A control group of special education cohorts was established at a nearby school that used a resource model and housed no integrated classrooms (perhaps a relevant ecological variable in the school's culture). Both sets of teachers had equivalent backgrounds and all were eligible for the district's in-service development over the 3 years of the study. Results revealed no cost differential and no significant differences in academic outcomes for students with LD in the ICM or the resource room model. Resource room services were retained in the district and reintroduced to the inclusive school because data did not indicate that ICM should be the only model of service delivery available to mildly disabled students. It should be noted that ICM teachers are selected by principals and special education administrators and typically have years of experience and dual certification in both general and special education. Qualifications for providing individualized instruction and behavior management techniques must be met, ensuring strong performance and program effectiveness. It might be suggested that this program is one that does not hurt students, although it might without the stringent qualifications applied to the selection of teachers in this study.

Marston (1987–88) looks somewhat differently at the impact of regular and special education to examine the hypothesis that the delivery of special education services to children with learning difficulties using the resource model enhances their prospects for academic gains in reading when compared to placement in regular education classrooms. This study was done over one year and involved 272 stu-

dents with mild disabilities (LD, BD, MR) in grades 4 through 6 who were mostly male and in fourth grade. A single-subject design was used to assess each child's
reading progress first in the regular class and then in the resource room. A secondary purpose focused on the instructional components within both service
delivery models, and teachers were asked to identify which components best described their approach: one-to-one tutorial, home intervention, use of reinforcement, corrective feedback, cooperative learning, use of cues and explanation, increasing time on task, assigning homework, utilization of cognitive strategies, and
emphasis on drill and practice. Student outcomes were measured individually using slopes of improvement on weekly CBM (reading scores) to determine any differences. Average gain was much greater for students when they received special
education resource support than when they received reading instruction exclusively in the regular class. An analysis of the teachers' approaches indicates that
instruction in special education resource rooms is more intensive. However, this
outcome is confounded by self-reports. An interesting aspect of this investigation
is that students with disabilities are not compared to either low-achieving or average-achieving peers, but to themselves. Says Marston, "This reliance upon an assessment system designed to measure learning, rather than to reflect individual differences, creates an opportunity to implement more accurate effectiveness
research" (p. 24).

In comparing resource room with consultative services, Schulte, Osborne, and
McKinney (1990) designed a study with several unusual features: (a) participants
were randomly assigned to settings; (b) the consulting teachers had small case
loads of 12 to 14 students, and were not district employees. They had been hired
by the researchers. This factor contributes to the likelihood of a greater success
than was actually demonstrated, since interventions are more effective when they
are provided directly by those who have designed them (Talbott, Lloyd, & Tankersley, 1994). This investigation measured student outcomes in math, reading, written language, and reading/study skills of 67 students with LD and comparison
groups in grades one through four from 11 randomly selected elementary schools
in a large diverse school district serving more than 60,000 students. LD students
who received resource room services for reading or written language and had at
least average intelligence could participate. Parental permission, along with cooperation from the teacher assistance team, helped to address any IEP changes necessary to accommodate service deliveries, and children were assigned randomly
to the four different instructional settings: a resource room, for either 1 or 2 periods a day, or consultative services providing either direct service to the student in
class, or indirectly to the classroom teacher. Results indicate that students made
gains in all four settings. Overall academic gains were greatest for those students
assigned to the consultative direct service delivery model. However, when academic scores were looked at separately for reading, writing, and math, there were
no significant differences between either consultative model or resource room setting.

Deno, Maruyama, Espin, and Cohen (1990) examined whether school reform efforts occurring within general education are associated with increases in cognitive and affective development for students who are low achieving or who have mild disabilities. The relationship between school effectiveness variables and student achievement was examined, and a comparison was made of instructional outcomes in integrated programs with those in resource rooms. In all, 2604 students in grades 1–6 and 756 staff from 32 schools participated, and seven schools were targeted as inclusive for the sake of comparing organizational and instructional variables. Results show that staff perceptions of effectiveness were not strong indicators of student achievement. Inclusive schools perceived themselves to be more effective than did resource program schools, but academic scores did not differ significantly in either inclusive or resource program schools. Also, there was a significant correlation between perceived parental involvement and academic scores; however, no outcomes for students supported this.

Instructional outcomes in reading were also compared for 255 special education students and 523 low-achieving peers in eight inclusive schools and three schools with a conventional resource room model. This second section of the study contrasted complex program characteristics at the school level and within the reading program, in addition to measuring both academic and social outcomes for students with mild disabilities. Results indicate that instructional practices, as well as data collection on students and its use, differed between the special and regular settings. General educators tended not to differentiate instruction, while special educators were more knowledgeable about their students and mindful of data-driven decisions and individualized instruction. Educational outcome data must be interpreted conservatively because students with disabilities were not randomly assigned to programs. With this in mind, both low-achieving students and students with mild disabilities served in inclusive settings scored higher academically; however, special education students served in resource programs attained higher spelling scores. Whether in inclusive or special education settings, students with mild disabilities scored significantly lower in all academic areas than did the low-achieving students. In inclusive settings, they were not offered differentiated instruction. It should be noted that students' academic self-perceptions were not related to the type of service delivery model.

In summary, evidence in favor of resource room instruction in this study is not strong. It would be interesting to see how these students performed in the mainstream over time, and to observe what was occurring in the resource rooms before writing them off as ineffective. The authors of this study sum up the dilemma that inconclusive evidence presents for professionals responsible for providing service delivery to students with LD:

> Those wishing to develop policies supporting integrated programming of students with mild disabilities could use the data presented here to argue that special education students do better both socially and academically

in integrated programs. Conversely, those who believe that what makes special education "special" is the individual attention given by special education teachers to individual student characteristics will be happy with the findings that reading programs are more differentiated in resource programs. Our own conclusion is that the evidence is insufficient to confidently conclude that either approach is more appropriate. (p. 160)

2. Methodology in Restructured Schools: Outcomes for Students with LD

While results in a reform-based study gave this innovative school and collaborators at the University of Washington information for restructuring, the best practices used did not result in improved achievement, academically or socially. Jenkins, Jewell, Leicester, Jenkins, and Troutner (1991) sought to develop a variety of instructional methods for serving all children with mild handicaps and at-risk children within the mainstream that would improve reading, math, and written language outcomes and behavioral competency outcomes beyond the level observed in pull-out programs. Five hundred and forty-one students with mild disabilities (LD, MR, BD) from two schools received a variety of interventions, including cooperative learning and cross-age tutoring. However, the only significant difference in academic outcomes was the result of higher math scores in the comparison school where special education students received direct instruction through pull-out services or supplemental remedial instruction. Teachers were receptive to the in-class service model, but it created numerous problems:

Students with handicaps in this elementary school were distributed across many different classrooms, and basic skill instruction occurred at the same time in several of these classrooms, but specialists cannot be in two places at once. Whereas pull-out programs allow specialists to bring together students from several classrooms for daily instruction, strictly defined in-class models cannot realistically match that level of direct instruction from specialists. In-class models require that classroom teachers assume greater responsibility for instructing students with handicaps to compensate for the reduction in contact time between these students and specialists. (p. 319)

Most studies of mainstreaming and inclusion have explored the effects on students once they are in the regular classroom setting. There is little information about how best to help students move from one setting to another and how to sustain their success after the transition (Fuchs, Roberts, Fuchs, & Bowers, 1996). Fuchs, Fuchs, and Fernstrom (1993), in an initiative between Vanderbilt University and an urban southeastern school district, sought to implement and validate a collaborative process between special and general educators called Transenvironmental Programming. This reintegration process provides students with mild disabilities (LD, BD, S/L) four levels of support: an assessment of the behavioral and academic expectations in the receiving environment; instruction by a special educator in skills needed in the new environment; practice and use of these skills in the new setting; and evaluation in the mainstream to determine academic and social adjustment. Following instruction in self-contained and regular education settings, math outcomes were assessed for elementary students with mild disabilities in control and experimental groups and compared with low-achieving peers in the mainstream. Results indicate that the math progress of LD students prepared by special educators for transition to the mainstream outpaced progress made by the special education control group, but was significantly worse than that of low-achieving peers already in the regular class. This study had some unusual elements. There was much collaboration between special and general educators as well as numerous hours of support from four project staff in developing instructional interventions in the mainstream. All teachers involved were volunteers and special educators were given the incentive of a small stipend. Even with all of these facilitating factors, students with disabilities demonstrated no gains in the regular class, although they had made steady gains in the self-contained setting prior to transition. It is disturbing that in this and subsequent studies of transenvironmental programming experimental students with mild disabilities generally did not demonstrate academic gains once placed in regular education for instruction (D. Fuchs et al., 1996).

3. Outcomes of Special Education Service Delivery in Restructured Schools

These innovative and collaborative models of service delivery for students with LD at Vanderbilt University and The University of Washington developed a common database with a model of similar focus at the University of Pittsburgh in an effort to enhance information beyond the scope of individual studies. "Each of the three models focused on restructuring mainstream instruction to increase teachers' capacity to accommodate learning activities that met a greater range of student needs" (Zigmond et al. 1995, p. 535). Each was a university initiative with elementary schools that sought to alter their learning environments. At both Washington and Pittsburgh, the intent was to eliminate pull-out programming by assisting classroom teachers to better accommodate and manage instruction for students with LD. Transenvironmental Programming, to facilitate transition between environments, was the focus at Vanderbilt. In each model academic achievement was the critical outcome and the measure of effectiveness for special education service delivery. Since the achievement level of students with LD is typically well below their nondisabled peers, analysis focused on the size of the reading gains they registered. In order to maintain or reduce the gap, gains needed to match or exceed grade-level peers. Results indicate that after 1 year of fully integrated educational programs and services, the percentage of students who made average gains varied by site: Pittsburgh, 33%, Washington, 23%; Vanderbilt, 64%. Viewed across the three models, only 37% made average gains and 63% did not. Even more discouraging was that 40% of the LD sample made gains that were less than half the size of the grade-level averages. According to Zigmond et al. (1995). "Findings from these three studies suggest that general education settings produce achievement outcomes for students with learning disabilities that are neither desirable nor acceptable" (p. 539).

D. Conclusions Based on Outcomes

Since 1986, tremendous amounts of financial and professional support have undergirded all of these studies examining whether inclusive service delivery models provide more effective programming for students with LD. Yet, this review of research suggests that inclusive settings or even the practices hoped to enhance student success in the mainstream have not permitted these children to function at the level hoped for earlier by Gottlieb et al. (1991): "within a range of proficiency that the classroom teacher believes acceptable for the child to progress adequately and remain in the class." Although these studies are dominated by an academic focus far narrower than the range of social/behavioral needs essential to the inclusion of many students with LD, the acquisition of basic academic skills is where consideration must begin (Zigmond et al., 1995). Academic outcomes have been disappointing, shedding little light on a preferred learning environment for students who appear to do poorly wherever they are served. It could be argued that assumptions have been made about the comparability of various models and the ecological variables of the environments in which they were implemented.

To settle the score, a fair test is needed, and Zigmond et al. (1995) join Gottlieb et al. (1991) in calling for a comparison of enhanced general education with separate special education settings "that have had equal resources invested for the purposes of intensifying programs" (p. 540). Such an approach would acknowledge the urgency required in educating students with LD to address pervasive underachievement that threatens life-long goals.

E. Inclusion as a Reform Strategy

Gerber (1995) asks, "Why has special education in these schools been demoted from *program to service?* [italics in original]. . . . Why has the vague concept of 'participation,' rather than meaningful opportunity to learn, become the apparent objective of inclusion?" (p. 184). Has the overemphasis on service delivery in the least restrictive environment shifted focus away from specially designed instruction reasonably calculated to provide educational benefit to students with LD?

Murphy (1995) provides insight from a school-reform perspective and takes the position that inclusion is primarily an organizational, not an educational intervention. He sees it as related to significant changes in administrative thought that embrace beliefs that all children can learn and that schools are responsible, to a significant extent, for that outcome. Agreeing that results of inclusive programming should not be assumed and assessment of student outcomes should be pursued, Murphy acknowledges an inherent theoretical dilemma: "Organizational changes—whether of the macrolevel variety, such as the centralization or decentralization of governance and management, or of the more microlevel variety, such as student grouping—have not, do not now, and never will, predict organizational effectiveness" (p. 210). Such links have been elusive and unfruitful, suggesting the absence of a reliable technology of administration and teaching. Hoy (1994) observes that "We do not have a sound understanding of cause and effect in our study of teaching, administration, and organization. Rather, we have a competing array of intriguing theories, methods, and findings that remains inconclusive" (p. 196). Elmore, Peterson, and McCarthey (1996) point out that reforms, such as inclusion, are based on the shaky premise that changing structure changes practice: "Stripped to its essentials, school restructuring rests on a fundamental belief in the power of organizational structure over human behavior. In this belief, traditional school structures are the enemy of good teaching practice, and fundamental structural changes are the stimulus for new practices" (p. 4).

The major studies reviewed in this analysis report that inclusion does not improve students' educational outcomes for students with LD. In fact, much of what has been written suggests that instructional components, rather than educational setting, are more relevant to student success. Most studies also concur that in terms of providing intense and individualized instruction to students with special needs, teachers in general education might be willing, but are not quite up to speed. An important implication of these findings for reformers is that perhaps norms and behaviors of schools and teachers need to change before structures are redesigned. Such an approach "would require reformers to treat structural change as a more contingent and uncertain result of change in practice, rather than as a means of reaching new practice" (Elmore, 1995, p. 26).

IV. RECOMMENDATIONS TO PROVIDE BETTER SPECIAL EDUCATION TO STUDENTS WITH LEARNING DISABILITIES

The need to improve student learning has been a political rallying cry for the past decade, putting the pressure on educators and policy makers to distinguish between innovations and reforms. Carnine (1994b) describes innovation as part of the problem-solving process, not the solution to educational dilemmas: "An innovation succeeds when a change has been made; an educational reform succeeds when learning improves" (p. 1). In this spirit, the following recommendations are offered to better provide services for students with LD: (a) shift the focus from innovative structures to meaningful practice; (b) focus on specialized instruction and assessment of student progress; (c) implement IDEA fully; and (d) acknowledge both diversity *and* disability in designing educational programs.

A. Shift the Focus from Innovative Structures to Ethical and Meaningful Practice

In considering the current status in the move toward fuller inclusion, Cohen (1993) states that "we face a situation where any one or all of the actors have limited knowledge and differences in opinion about what is best for the child" (p. 266). Kauffman (1992) poses the following questions regarding the ethics of moving forward armed with limited knowledge:

> Under what conditions, if any, is an approach to education (or to child discipline, medical treatment, or any other human service) "right" even if it doesn't work? Can education or treatment be morally "right" if it provides no benefit, even if it does harm? Are we to assume that what is "right" for most students is "right" for all, regardless of benefit or harm in the individual case? (p. xv)

Children and youth with LD are reported in national data as the most integrated special education students in American classrooms (cf. U.S. Department of Education, 1996). However, high rates of failure suggest their presence in general education is not sufficient for them to benefit educationally. Lack of progress for this group of students in augmented general education settings as well as in special classrooms suggests a shift of focus beyond simplistic notions of placement or transformation of a monolithic bureaucracy. Given the severity of their academic difficulties, problems with social adjustment, and poor record of success, Schulte (1996) suggests that the issue be framed backwards by asking "what type and intensity of intervention is necessary to ensure that students with LD achieve commensurate with peers and, only when the limits of intervention have been determined, that we ask where high-quality services can be delivered" (p. 205). These steps are consonant with the prescriptions of the IDEA that require a sequence of decisions beginning with eligibility of a student for special education and progressing to development of the service plan, and only subsequently to determination of where it will be implemented to best suit the needs of the child (Bateman, 1996).

Keogh (1994) highlights the importance of considering which goals to achieve with students at which developmental stage, keeping in mind that various strategies addressing prevention, intervention, or both, cross the life span. Keogh's conceptualization of services would address four developmental periods: infancy/preschool; middle childhood; adolescence; and adulthood. Goals appropriate to one group of students with LD might not apply to others, while commonalties and linkages among goals might stress elements for smooth transitions in services from one level to another.

B. Focus on Instruction and Assessment of Student Progress

Martin (1995) finds neither a change in the philosophy nor the goals of including persons with disabilities necessary. He calls for improved, specialized instruction and services with "an acceptance of the obligation to measure what we do in terms that are important and significant to the total lives of our students: Do our programs meet the test of assisting students to attain postschool success and positive self-regard?" (p. 199). The key, he believes, is in demonstrating what is meant by "appropriate." "Where we've gone wrong in special education is that we haven't followed how kids have done. We have not interpreted 'appropriate' as empirically derived by student outcomes. We have used argument instead of data in making placement decisions" (E. Martin, personal communication, April 1996). By proceeding without data, the field has been susceptible to what Martin calls "the myth of mildness," that these students are not so tough to teach or so different in their educational needs. "Without data", he says, "all we have are assumptions."

C. Implement the IDEA Fully

1. Create Meaningful IEPs and Use Them

Creating and implementing IEPs is integral to service delivery for students with LD. Bateman (1996) describes the IEP process as the heart and soul of the IDEA, essential to the formulation of appropriate programming and the determination of the least restrictive environment for the child. As the law suggests, only when such a program is designed, with collaborative input, can appropriate instruction and placement follow. IEPs also need to be put to good use. Heufner (1994) points out that many courts have not given enough consideration to a close analysis of the student's educational needs, goals, and objectives when deciding placement cases but instead have restricted their judicial analysis to the part of the IEP dealing with recommended services. In the schools, poorly written and sloppily implemented IEPs contribute to underserved children and to a district's culpability in failing to provide them with "specialized, individualized instruction and services that confer appropriate benefit and produce progress" in the least restrictive environment (Heufner, 1994, p. 43).

2. Lubricate, Rather than Eliminate, the Continuum

A further recommendation is perhaps best described as the lubrication, rather than the elimination, of the continuum of alternative placements. An area that needs particular attention is that of improving the transition of individual students from one placement to another in either direction along this continuum, from most inclusive to most separate (D. Fuchs et al, 1996). Gillet (1995) calls for training practices to ensure this planned transition, training that addresses the following administrative concerns:

> What are the indicators? What are the preliminary steps? How are staff, parents, and students involved? How is the transitional planning conference conducted? What does the transition plan from one placement to another look like? What are best practices for monitoring and support activities that should be done and for what time period? (p. 57)

The focus for such planning should extend not just to the exiting of special education, but also to the receiving of more special services when necessary. Gillet makes good sense when she observes that this fluidity will be an increasing demand as children move from inclusive preschools and elementary programs to the differing and more complex academic and social demands at the middle and secondary levels. Local districts are advised to inform parents at the time of eligibility meetings that special education may not be needed throughout a student's educational career or that the service levels might vary along a continuum of placements. Exit criteria for passage from one placement on the continuum to another could be set as a goal that students, parents, and professionals could work toward together.

It may be de rigueur to call for radically redesigned schooling and an overstatement to call for its restructure. Nevertheless, there is little doubt that parts of the system need a metaphorical oil change. If special education research continues to discover increasingly workable techniques for the successful inclusion of students with LD in regular classes, then the gears of the continuum should be well greased so that no child gets stuck along the way.

D. Final Reflections: Acknowledging Both Diversity and Disability

In the United States, educational entitlements vary state by state. However, the IDEA makes a free, appropriate public education for students with disabilities a federal right—something it is *not* for all students. Gallagher (1981) calls this "vertical equity," or an attempt to correct discrimination by providing such students with an opportunity for equal access to educational benefits. Dessent (1987) uses the term "positive discrimination" to describe Britain's efforts to bolster the skills of students with disabilities. The current social ethic is far more critical of such affirmative actions now than in the past, spurring a backlash against special education costs and services.

As classrooms simultaneously attempt to cope with diversity and standards of excellence, educational consumers ask why children who disrupt instruction are allowed to remain in regular classes, and why children who achieve the least receive the greatest resources at the expense of average and above-average children who receive little individualized attention in overcrowded and undersupplied classrooms. Elrich (1996) observes that if it is suggested that children with LD possess a "special right to a nurturing and supportive educational environment and a greater per pupil expense than is accorded a non-LD child, the making of the political and moral debate that surrounds special education service levels today results" (p. 200). While advocating that a nourishing environment has universal value for all, Elrich takes the position that full inclusion without provision for separate settings is a prescription for disaster for some students with LD who need intensive instruction. For him, the root issue is to determine whether a student is not learning because of environmental, organic, or pedagogical reasons, and to base remediations on what is known about the cause.

There is evidence that many students benefit from approaches helpful to students with LD, and ample suggestion of their similar need for modifications. For example, in New York City, only about one-third of the high school students graduate in the customary 4 years. The majority require alternative approaches and schedules for completion (Carnine & Kameenui, 1990). The implication is that regular classrooms and curriculum designed for middle class students are failing many like those in another urban study, in which only 34% of the children in the elementary general education population were found to read at or above grade level (Gottlieb et al., 1994). Carnine and Kameenui see the larger issue as one of how to best educate students who are likely to fail in schools that have based instruction on models popular for children who do well. Rather than dismantling the special education system, and losing the organizational capability for specific research, professional preparation, and advocacy for students with LD, they recommend extending support to teachers who work mostly with students at risk for failure. They urge augmenting the mainstream by both reorganizing classroom instruction for these students and increasing the efficacy and professional pride of those who teach them. In this way, "mainstream programs for classrooms containing a majority of students with special needs—be they handicapped, economically disadvantaged, limited-English-speaking—should be tailored to the needs of those students, not to those of the advantaged minority" (p. 144).

Adjusting service delivery to the demanding realities of the current context of classroom diversity suggests a deliberative approach. It is hard to imagine how an impoverished or irrelevant general education program, increasingly inappropriate for many, could be considered the least restrictive environment for most students with LD. No one strategy or structure is likely to be uniquely applicable to all situations. Rather, effective service delivery would seem to depend more on the management concept that posits "for many problems, there are many solutions, but no optimal solutions" (Sherman, 1981, p. 25). Consequently, there is work to be done by educational decision makers on two fronts: first, "to provide the necessary support to make the special education setting as good as it can be before deciding to eliminate current models of special education altogether" (Scruggs and Mastropieri, 1995, p. 231); second, to make general education environments more responsive to the diversity of children they serve—front row or back, eager or reluctant.

References

Affleck, J. Q., Madge, S., Adams, A., & Lowenbraun, S. (1988). Integrated classroom versus resource model: Academic viability and effectiveness. *Exceptional Children, 54,* 339–348.

Bailey, D. B. (1989). Issues and directions in preparing professionals to work with young handicapped children and their families. In J. J. Gallagher, P. L. Trohanis, & R. M. Clifford (Eds.). *Policy implementation and PL99–457* (pp. 97–132). Baltimore: Paul H. Brookes.

Baker, M., & Zigmond, N. (1995). The meaning and practice of inclusion for students with learning disabilities: Themes and implications from the five cases. *Journal of Special Education, 29,* 163–180.

Bateman, B. (1992). Learning disabilities: The changing landscape. *Journal of Learning Disabilities, 25,* 29–36.

Bateman, B. (1996). *Better IEPs.* Longmont, CO: Sopris West.

Bateman, B., & Chard, C. J. (1995). Legal demands and constraints on placement decisions. In J. M. Kauffman, J. W. Lloyd, D. P. Hallahan, & T. A. Astuto (Eds.), *Issues in educational placement: Students with emotional and behavioral disorders* (pp. 285–316). Hillsdale, NJ: Lawrence Erlbaum Associates.

Bos, C. S., & Vaughn, S. (1994). *Strategies for teaching students with learning and behavior problems.* Boston: Allyn and Bacon.

Bruininks, R., Thurlow, M. L., & Ysseldyke, J. E. (1992). Assessing the right outcomes: Prospects for improving education for youth with disabilities. *Education and Training in Mental Retardation, 27*(2), 93–100.

Bulgren, J. A., & Carta, J. J. (1992). Examining the instructional context of students with learning disabilities. *Exceptional Children, 59,* 182–191.

Butler, R., & Marinov-Glassman, D. (1994). The effects of educational placement and grade level on the self-perceptions of low achievers and students with learning disabilities. *Journal of Learning Disabilities, 27,* 325–334.

Carlberg, C., & Kavale, K. (1980). The efficacy of special versus regular class placement for exceptional children: A meta-analysis. *Journal of Special Education, 14,* 295–309.

Carnine, D. W. (1994a). *Becoming a better consumer of educational research.* Eugene, OR: National Center to Improve the Tools of Educators.

Carnine, D. W. (1994b). *Smart schools: Beyond innovation to educational reform or looking for reform in all the wrong places.* National Center to Improve the Tools of Educators.

Carnine, D. W., & Kameenui, E. J. (1990). The general education initiative and children with special needs: A false dilemma in the face of true problems. *Journal of Learning Disabilities, 23,* 141.

Cohen, M. (1993). The politics of special ed. *The Special Educator, 8,* 266.

Cook, L. H., & Boe, E. E. (1995). Who is teaching students with disabilities? *Teaching Exceptional Children, 20,* (1), 70–72.

Deno, S., Maruyama, G., Espin, C., & Cohen, C. (1990). Educating students with mild disabilities in general education classrooms: Minnesota alternatives. *Exceptional Children, 57* (2), 150–161.

Dessent, T. (1987). *Making the ordinary school special.* London: The Falmer Press.

Ellet, L. (1993). Instructional practices in mainstreamed secondary classrooms. *Journal of Learning Disabilities, 26,* 57–64.

Elmore, R. F. (1995). Structural reform and educational practice. *Educational Researcher, 24* (9), 23–26.

Elmore, R. F., Peterson, P. L., & McCarthey, S. J. (1996). *Restructuring in the classroom: Teaching, learning, and school organization.* San Francisco: Jossey Bass.

Elrich, M. (1996). Order and learning, individuals and groups: A regular education teacher's response. In D. Speece & B. Keogh (Eds.), *Research on classroom ecologies: Implications for inclusion of children with learning disabilities* (pp. 191–202). Mahwaw, NJ: Lawrence Erlbaum Associates.

Epstein, M. H., Quinn, K. P., Cumblad, C. (1994). A scale to assess the restrictiveness of educational settings. *Journal of Child and Family Studies, 3,* (1) 107–119.

Erickson, F. (1996). Inclusion into what? Thoughts on the construction of learning, identity, and affiliation in the general education classroom. In D. Speece & B. Keogh (Eds.), *Research on classroom ecologies: Implications for inclusion of children with learning disabilities* (pp. 91–106). Mahwaw, NJ: Lawrence Erlbaum Associates.

Fuchs, D., & Fuchs, L. S. (1995a). Special education can work. In J. M. Kauffman, J. W. Lloyd, D. P. Hallahan, & T. A. Astuto (Eds.), *Issues in educational placement: Students with emotional and behavioral disorders* (pp. 363–377). Hillsdale, NJ: Lawrence Erlbaum Associates.

Fuchs, D., & Fuchs, L. S. (1995b). What's 'special' about special education? *Phi Delta Kappan, 76,* 522–530.

Fuchs, D., Fuchs, L. S., & Fernstrom, P. (1993). A conservative approach to special education reform: Mainstreaming through transenvironmental programming and curriculum-based measurement. *American Educational Research Journal, 30* (1), 149–177.

Fuchs, D., Roberts, P. H., Fuchs, L. S., & Bowers, J. (1996). Reintegrating students with learning disabilities into the mainstream: A two-year study. *Learning Disabilities Research and Practice, 11,* 214–229.

Fuchs, L. (1996). Models of classroom instruction: Implications for students with learning disabilities. In D. Speece & B. Keogh (Eds.), *Research on classroom ecologies: Implications for inclusion of children with learning disabilities* (pp. 81–88). Mahwaw, NJ: Lawrence Erlbaum Associates.

Fuchs, L. S., Fuchs, D., & Hamlett, C. L. (1989). Effects of alternative goal structures within curriculum-based measurement. *Exceptional Children, 55,* 429–438.

Fuchs, L. S., Fuchs, D., Hamlett, C. L., Phillips, N. B., & Bentz, J. (1994). Classwide curriculum-based measurement: Helping general educators meet the challenge of student diversity. *Exceptional Children, 60,* 518–537.

Gajria, M., Salend, S. J., & Hemrick, M. A. (1994). Teacher acceptability of testing modifications for mainstreamed students. *Learning Disabilities Research and Practice, 9,* 236–243.

Gallagher, J. J. (1981). Models for policy analysis: Child and family policy. In R. Haskins & J. Gallagher (Eds.), *Models for analysis of social policy: An introduction.* (pp. 37–77). Norwood, NJ: Ablex.

Garnett, K. (1996). *Thinking about inclusion and learning disabilities: A teacher's guide.* Reston, VA: Council for Exceptional Children.

Gerber, M. M. (1995). Inclusion at the high-water mark? Some thoughts on Zigmond and Baker's case studies of inclusive educational programs. *Journal of Special Education, 29,* 181–191.

Gillet, P. (1995). Commitment to quality throughout the continuum. *Teaching Exceptional Children, 27,* (2) 57.

Gottlieb, J., Alter, M., & Gottlieb, B. W. (1991). Mainstreaming academically handicapped children in urban schools. In John Wills Lloyd, Nirbhay N. Singh, & Alan C. Repp (Eds.), *The regular education initiative: alternative perspectives on concepts, issues, and models* (pp. 95–112). Sycamore, IL: Sycamore Publishing Company.

Gottlieb, J., Alter, M., & Gottlieb, B. W., & Wishner, J. (1994). Special education in urban America: It's not justifiable for many [Special issue. Theory and Practice of Special Education: Taking Stock a Quarter Century After Deno and Dunn], *Journal of Special Education, 27,* 453–465.

Greenwood, C. R. (1996). Research on the practices and behavior of effective teachers at the Juniper Gardens Children's Project: Implications for the education of diverse learners. In D. Speece & B. Keogh (Eds.), *Research on classroom ecologies: Implications for inclusion of children with learning disabilities* (pp. 39–67). Mahwaw, NJ: Lawrence Erlbaum Associates.

Hallahan, D. P., Kauffman, J. M., & Lloyd, J. W. (1996). *Introduction to learning disabilities.* Boston: Allyn and Bacon.

Hendrick Hudson District Board of Education v. Rowley, 458 U.S. 176, 102 S.Ct 3034(1982).

Houck, C. K., & Rogers, C. J. (1994). The special/general education integration initiative for students with specific learning disabilities: A "snapshot" of program change. *Journal of Learning Disabilities, 27,* 435–453.

Hoy, W. K. (1994). Foundations of educational administration: Traditional and emerging perspectives. *Educational Administration Quarterly, 30,* 178–198.

Huefner, D. S. (1994). The mainstreaming cases: Tensions and trends for school administrators. *Educational Administration Quarterly, 30,* 27–55.

Jenkins, J. R., Jewell, M., Leicester, N., Jenkins, L., & Troutner, N. M. (1991). Development of a school building model for educating students with handicaps and at-risk students in general education classrooms. *Journal of Learning Disabilities, 24,* 311–320.

Jenkins, J. R., Jewell, M., Leicester, N., O'Connor, R. E., Jenkins, L. M., & Troutner, N. M. (1994). Accommodations for individual differences without classroom ability groups: An experiment in school restructuring. *Exceptional Children, 60* (4), 344–358.

Johnson, L. J., & Pugach, M. C. (1990). Classroom teachers' views of intervention strategies for learning and behavior problems: Which are reasonable and how frequently are they used? *The Journal of Special Education, 24,* 69–84.

Kauffman, J. M. (1992). Foreword. In K. R. Howe & O. B. Miramontes, *The ethics of special education* (p. xv). New York: Teachers College Press.

Kauffman, J. M. (1993). How we might achieve the radical reform of special education. *Exceptional Children, 60,* 6–16.

Kauffman, J. M., & Trent, S. C. (1991). Issues in service delivery for students with learning disabilities. In B. Y. L. Wong (Ed.), *Learning about learning disabilities* (pp. 465–481). San Diego, CA: Academic Press.

Kavale, K. A., Fuchs, D., & Scruggs, T. E. (1994). Setting the record straight on learning disability and low achievement: Implications for policymaking. *Disabilities Research & Practice, 9,* 70–77.

Keogh, B. K. (1988). Improving services for problem learners: Rethinking and restructuring. *Journal of Learning Disabilities, 21,* 19–22.

Keogh, B. K. (1994). What the special education research agenda should look like in the year 2000. *Learning Disabilities Research and Practice, 9,* 62–69.

Keogh, B. K., & Speece, D. L. (1996). Learning disabilities within the context of schooling. In D. Speece & B. Keogh (Eds.), *Research on classroom ecologies: Implications for inclusion of children with learning disabilities* (pp. 1–14). Mahwaw, NJ: Lawrence Erlbaum Associates.

Kritsonis, M. A. (1992–93). A study of elementary school principals' knowledge about special education and special education teachers' perceptions of their principals' knowledge. *National Forum of Applied Educational Research Journal, 5* (2), 62–68.

Lieberman, L. M. (1996). Preserving special education . . . for those who need it. In W. Stainback & S. Stainback (Eds.), *Controversial issues confronting special education* (pp. 16–27). Needham Heights: Allyn & Bacon.

McLeskey, J., Lancaster, M., & Grizzle, K. L. (1995). Learning disabilities and grade retention: A review of issues with recommendations for practice. *Learning Disabilities Research and Practice, 10,* 120–128.

Marston, D. (1987/88). The effectiveness of special education: A time series analysis of reading performance in regular and special education settings. *The Journal of Special Education, 21* (4), 13–26.

Martin, E. W. (1995). Case studies on inclusion: Worst fears realized. *Journal of Special Education, 29* (2), 192–199.

Mather, N., & Roberts, R. (1994). Learning disabilities: A field in danger of extinction? *Learning Disabilities & Practice, 9* (1), 49–58.

Morsink, C. V., & Lenk, L. L. (1992). The delivery of special education programs and services. *Remedial and Special Education, 13* (6), 33–43.

Murphy, J. (1995). Insights on "the context of full inclusion" from a non-special educator. *Journal of Special Education, 29* (2), 209–211.

National Association of State Boards of Education (NASBE) (1992). *Winners all: a call for inclusive schools.* Alexandria, VA: Author.

New York State Regents Commission on Disability (1993). *Committee for Elementary, Middle, and Secondary Education Report.* Albany, NY: Author.

O'Connor, R. E., & Jenkins, J. R. (1996). Choosing individuals as the focus to study cooperative learning. *Exceptionality, 6,* (1) 65–68.

Peterson, H. (1946). *Great teachers portrayed by those who studied under them.* New York: Vintage Books.

Pugach, M. C., & Warger, C. L. (1993). Curriculum considerations. In John I. Goodlad &

Thomas C. Lovitt (Eds.), *Integrating general and special education* (pp. 125–148). New York: Macmillan.

Reyes, E. I. (1996). Constructing knowledge in inclusive classrooms: What students know and teachers need to know. In D. Speece & B. Keogh (Eds.), *Research on classroom ecologies: Implications for inclusion of children with learning disabilities* (pp. 125–134). Mahwaw, NJ: Lawrence Erlbaum Associates.

Rieth, H. J., & Polsgrove, L. (1994). Curriculum and instructional issues in teaching secondary students with learning disabilities. *Learning Disabilities Research and Practice, 9,* 118–126.

Roberts, R., & Mather, N. (1995). The return of students with learning disabilities to regular classrooms: A sellout? *Learning Disabilities Research and Practice, 10* (1), 46–58.

Sage, D. D., & Burrello, L. C. (1994). *Leadership in educational reform: An administrator's guide to changes in special education.* Baltimore: Paul H. Brookes.

Sands, D. J., Adams, L., & Stout, D. M. (1995). What is the nature and use of curriculum in special education? *Exceptional Children, 62,* 68–83.

Scanlon, D., Deshler, D. D., & Schumaker, J. B. (1996). Can a strategy be taught and learned in secondary inclusive classrooms? *Learning Disabilities and Practice, 1,* 41–57.

Schrag, J. (1994). *Organizational, instructional, and curricular strategies to support the implementation of unified, coordinated, and inclusive schools.* Reston, VA: The Council for Exceptional Children.

Schulte, A. C. (1996). Remediation and inclusion: Can we have it all? In D. Speece & B. Keogh (Eds.), *Research on classroom ecologies: Implications for inclusion of children with learning disabilities* (pp. 203–210). Mahwaw, NJ: Lawrence Erlbaum Associates.

Schulte, A. C., Osborne, S. S., & McKinney, J. D. (1990). Academic outcomes for students with learning disabilities in consultation and resource programs. *Exceptional Children, 57,* 162–171.

Schumaker, J. B., & Deshler, D. D. (1988). Implementing the regular education initiative in secondary schools: A different ball game. *Journal of Learning Disabilities, 21,* 36–42.

Schumm, J. S., & Vaughn, S. (1991). Making adaptations for mainstreamed students: Regular classroom teachers' perspectives. *Remedial and Special Education, 12*(4), 18–27.

Schumm, J. S., & Vaughn, S. (1992). Planning for mainstreamed special education students. *Exceptionality, 3,* 81–90.

Schumm, J. S., Vaughn, S., Haager, D., McDowell, J., Rothlein, L., & Saumell, L. (1995). General education teacher planning: What can students with learning disabilities expect? *Exceptional Children, 61,* 335–352.

Scruggs, T. E., & Mastropieri, M. A. (1994). Successful mainstreaming in elementary science classes: A qualitative study of three reputational cases. *American Educational Research Journal, 31,* 785–811.

Scruggs, T. E., & Mastropieri, M. A. (1995). What makes special education special? Evaluating inclusion programs with the PASS variables. *Journal of Special Education, 29,* 224–233.

Scruggs, T. E., & Mastropieri, M. A. (1996). Teacher perceptions of mainstreaming/inclusion, 1958–1995: A research synthesis. *Exceptional Children, 63,* 59–74.

Sherman, T. M. (1981). Effective management in the classroom. *Educational Technology.* August.

Skrtic, T. M. (1991). The special education paradox: Equity as the way to excellence. *Harvard Educational Review, 61,* (2) 148–182.

Society: The story rug is now full. (1995, April 3). *Newsweek, 58.*

Special educators worldwide work for common goal. (1995, August). *CEC Today, 2*(2), 10.

Speece, D., & Keogh, B. (Eds.) (1996). *Research on classroom ecologies: Implications for inclusion of children with learning disabilities.* Mahwaw, NJ: Lawrence Erlbaum Associates.

Talbott, E., Lloyd, J. W., & Tankersley, M. (1994). Effects of reading comprehension interventions for students with learning disabilities. *Learning Disabilities Quarterly, 17,* 223–232.

U.S. Department of Education. (1996). *Eighteenth annual report to Congress on the implementation of the Individuals with Disabilities Education Act.* Washington, DC: Office of Special Education Programs, U.S. Government Printing Office.

Vaughn, S., & Schumm, J. S. (1996). Classroom ecologies: Classroom interactions and implications for inclusion of students with learning disabilities. In D. Speece & B. Keogh (Eds.), *Research on classroom ecologies: Implications for inclusion of children with learning disabilities* (pp. 107–124). Mahwaw, NJ: Lawrence Erlbaum Associates.

Wagner, M. (1990). *The school programs and school performance of secondary students classified as learning disabled: Findings from the national longitudinal transition study of special education students.* Paper presented at the meetings of Division G., American Educational Research Association, Boston.

Walker, H. M., & Bullis, M. (1991). Behavior disorders and the social context of regular class integration: A conceptual dilemma? In J. W. Lloyd, N. N. Singh, & A. C. Repp (Eds.), *The regular education initiative: Alternative perspectives on concepts, issues, and models* (pp. 75–93). Sycamore, IL: Sycamore.

Wilson, D. R., & David, W. J. (1994). Academic intrinsic motivation and attitudes toward school and learning of learning disabled students. *Learning Disabilities Research and Practice, 9,* 148–156.

Zigler, E. (1996). Forward. In D. Speece & B. Keogh (Eds.), *Research on classroom ecologies: Implications for inclusion of children with learning disabilities* (pp. ix–x). Mahwaw, NJ: Lawrence Erlbaum Associates.

Zigmond, N. (1995). An exploration of the meaning and practice of special education in the context of full inclusion of students with learning disabilities. *Journal of Special Education, 29,* 109–115.

Zigmond, N., & Baker, J. M. (1995). Concluding comments: Current and future practices in inclusive schooling. *Journal of Special Education, 29,* 245–250.

Zigmond, N., Jenkins, J., Fuchs, L. S., Deno, S., Fuchs, D., Baker, J. N., Jenkins, L., & Couthino, M. (1995). Special education in restructured schools: Findings from three multi-year studies. *Phi Delta Kappan, 76,* 531–540.

A Life Span Approach to Understanding Learning Disabilities

Specific Reading and Writing Disabilities in Young Children: Assessment, Prevention, and Intervention

Virginia W. Berninger

I. DEFINITIONAL ISSUES

The term *learning disability* (LD), coined by Samuel Kirk in 1963, captured seminal insights: An individual could have difficulty learning to read or write despite normal intelligence; and not all individuals with reading and writing difficulties are mentally retarded. Today we take these insights for granted, but prior to the concept of a LD, many students with reading and writing problems were mistakenly thought to be mentally retarded.

This early definition of LD was exclusionary, that is, based on what a LD is not (Lyon, 1995). According to this definition, which is still in place in federal legislation and requires a free, appropriate education for students with educational handicaps, LD is not due to mental retardation, sensory or physical handicap, emotional problems, or cultural, socioeconomic, and linguistic difference. More recent definitions (e.g., Berninger & Abbott, 1994a; Hammill, Leigh, McNutt, & Larsen, 1981) have questioned the exclusionary criteria and recognize that children with LD can also have physical or emotional problems or cultural, socioeconomic, or linguistic difference. The absence of such comorbid conditions does not necessarily help to define who is and who is not LD.

Learning about Learning Disabilities, Second Edition   529

This early definition was inclusionary, that is based on what LD is, only to the extent that it involves a discrepancy between ability on an IQ test and achievement. However, consensus has never been reached on how the discrepancy should be measured, how large it should be, or what causes the discrepancy. Although some definitions have assumed constitutional reasons for the underachievement (e.g., Hammill et al., 1981), other definitions allow for both constitutional and experiential reasons for the underachievement (e.g., Berninger & Abbott, 1994a; Vellutino, Scanlon, Sipay, Small, Pratt, Chen, & Denckla, 1996). Such experiential reasons include the failure to individualize and provide intensive, systematic beginning reading instruction (Berninger, 1994; Vellutino et al., 1996).

A. Should IQ Be an Inclusionary Criterion?

Siegel's (1989) proposal that IQ not be used in defining LD was, therefore, revolutionary. She recommended that the definition be based only on low achievement, with no consideration of discrepancy of achievement from IQ. On the one hand, Siegel's recommendation has had the beneficial effect of causing some to question the rigidity with which LD has been defined—on the basis of IQ–achievement discrepancies that are defined in an arbitrary manner that varies widely from state to state. Learning disability may be conceptualized as any unexpected underachievement, and IQ is only one index for gauging unexpected underachievement (Lyon, 1995). Some researchers have abandoned the concept of an IQ–achievement discrepancy altogether for LD affecting word recognition (see Lyon, 1995). The rationale most often given for rejecting the discrepancy definition is that low achievers in reading, regardless of whether or not their achievement is discrepant from IQ, have been shown to have the same problems—in phonological awareness and phonological decoding (for review, see Lyon, 1995).

On the other hand, Siegel's (1989) recommendation leaves us with unresolved issues, and it may be premature to disregard IQ altogether for four reasons. First, the measures typically used to assess phonological awareness are not pure measures of the analysis of speech sounds; they also tap IQ and working memory (McBride-Chang, 1995). Likewise, measures of pseudoword decoding are correlated with IQ (Berninger, Cartwright, Yates, Swanson, & Abbott, 1994). Also, verbal intelligence predicts response to training in phonological awareness (analytical skills) (Torgesen & Davis, 1996). So, IQ may exert an indirect influence on reading via its influence on phonological skills. Thus, phonological awareness and phonological decoding may be underdeveloped for more than one reason—in one case because of low intellectual ability causing poor phonological awareness that contributes to poor reading and in the other case because of poor phonological awareness that contributes directly to poor reading in the presence of moderate to high intellectual ability. The long-term outcome in response to appropriate intervention may be different for those two cases, with the latter achieving more than the former in the long run.

Second, even if those with and without an IQ–achievement discrepancy have trouble with the same processes, eliminating IQ altogether affects *who* is identified as having LD and thus, *who* will receive special services. Berninger, Hart, Abbott, and Karovsky (1992) applied three different definitions to identify LD children in an unreferred sample: low achievement only, IQ–achievement discrepancy only, and both low achievement and IQ–achievement discrepancy. Only 44% who met the criterion for low achievement also met the criterion for IQ–achievement discrepancy. Only 36% who met the criterion for IQ–achievement discrepancy also met the criterion for low achievement. Further analysis showed that low IQ children were most likely to be identified as having LD if a criterion of low achievement was used, but that high-IQ children (gifted LD) were most likely to be identified as having LD if a criterion of IQ–achievement discrepancy was used (Berninger & Hart, 1993; Yates, Berninger, & Abbott, 1994).

Third, although findings based on group data analyses show that the IQ-discrepant and IQ-consistent achievers have problems in phonological processing, analyses based on individual subjects show that reading disabilities are a heterogeneous disorder and not all reading disabilities are due to phonological problems (Berninger, 1994; Berninger & Hart, 1993). Other contributing factors include but are not restricted to orthographic coding (Berninger & Abbott, 1994b), rapid automatized naming (Wolf, Bally, & Morris, 1986), morphological awareness (e.g., Fowler & Liberman, 1995; Henry, 1989, 1994), and working memory (Swanson & Alexander, in press). The critical issue is not whether the IQ-discrepant and IQ-consistent achievers have the same underlying processing problems, but whether IQ plays a role in response to intervention and whether it places constraints on long-term achievement.

Fourth, the United States federal definition of LD covers seven areas of impairment: receptive language (listening), expressive language (speaking), basic reading skills, reading comprehension, written expression, mathematics calculation, and mathematical reasoning. The IQ-discrepancy definition may not be the most appropriate or the only way to identify LD in basic reading skills, but it may be appropriate for identifying some or all of the other six kinds of LD (Lyon, personal communication, January 24, 1997; also see Lyon, 1995).

Our position is that multiple, flexible definitions are needed if we are to identify and serve *all* the children with learning problems (Berninger, Hart, Abbott & Karovsky, 1992). Siegel made a major contribution in mobilizing the field to question the rigidity with which the IQ–achievement discrepancy has been used to identify some children for special education services and to exclude others inappropriately for services. Yet, the IQ–achievement discrepancy is needed if we are to identify some students with some kinds of LD, particularly those with above-average IQs. Instead of eliminating IQ altogether, we need to (a) make a distinction between diagnosis and service delivery, and (b) reconsider how different kinds of LD are subtyped.

B. Distinction between Diagnosis
and Special Education Placement

The federal legislation that mandates that children with LD be identified and served and authorizes the money to support the delivery of services has spawned state-specific definitions of handicapping conditions. These definitions employ categorical criteria for deciding whether a child qualifies for special education services and, if so, under which category. Only a few states have experimented with noncategorical service delivery. The special education placement categories appear to be driven more by limited financial resources and the need to audit the spending of funds than by current research and clinical practice outside the school system.

It is very difficult to explain to a parent whose child cannot learn and perform in the classroom that the child does not qualify for special services because the discrepancy between IQ and achievement is not large enough to meet state criteria to be placed in special education. Sometimes if the child is retested the following year (after more opportunity to fail at school) the discrepancy will be large enough to qualify for services; or if the family moves to another state or school district that has fewer needy children, the child will qualify for services. Thus, we have begun to explain to parents that there is a difference between diagnosis, based on the latest research and state-of-the art clinical practice, and qualification for special education services. For example, when we see a child of average or better intelligence whose teachers report that the child has significant difficulty in the regular classroom reading program and who is underachieving to some degree in phonological processing, orthographic processing, rapid automatized naming, word identification of real words, and/or phonological decoding, we will diagnose the child as having a specific reading disability even if the IQ–achievement discrepancy is not large enough to meet our state criteria for special education services (only the 6% with the most severe discrepancy qualify for special education services). Or, when we see children whose teachers report that the child has significant difficulty in the classroom writing program and who are underachieving to some degree in orthographic, fine motor skills, spelling and/or composition, we will diagnose the child as having a specific writing disability even if the IQ–achievement discrepancy is not large enough to meet our state criteria for discrepancy. Part of the diagnosis is identifying the component reading or writing skill affected and part of the diagnosis is identifying the process(es) impairing the component reading or writing skill.

In such cases where we believe the diagnosis is warranted even though state criteria for special education placement are not met, we explain to the parents that there is a difference between diagnosis of a specific reading or writing disability and qualification for special education services in the generic category of LD. Then parents may seek private tutoring if they can afford it or modifications to the regular program under Chapter 504 in the National Rehabilitation Act, which requires that accommodations be made for students with any handicapping condition. Alternatively, parents can seek an independent evaluation to document that their child meets criteria for LD in the literature, if not the state, and possibly obtain special education services based on the professional judgment of the independent evaluator. This latter approach may necessitate the parent hiring an attorney and presenting the case at a hearing.

Unfortunately, schools often put more emphasis on special education placement decisions than on accurate diagnosis. The need for accurate diagnosis is important because it can lead to more appropriate intervention and expectations for achievement, regardless of whether or not a child qualifies for special education. Often only enough testing is done to see if a child qualifies for special education services. Comprehensive assessment based on behavioral observations, developmental history, teacher interview, and test results is needed to pinpoint the nature and cause of problems in learning written language.

Variations in diagnostic practices have led to confusion about what LD is. Parents of children with other handicapping conditions such as mental retardation, borderline IQ, and attention deficit disorder often report that their child has LD. Some professionals contribute to the confusion by using the label LD, which has less stigma, for children with mental retardation or borderline IQ. Thus, we have come full circle. The diagnostic label invented to emphasize that individuals with specific reading and writing disabilities are not retarded has been adopted by parents of children with mental retardation and other developmental disorders. The diagnostic labels of mental retardation and LD that served well in the past may not be meeting current needs in either diagnosis or placement decisions.

The classification scheme in Table 16.1 is proposed as an alternative to the current approach and assumes that multiple subtypes of LD are needed for accurate diagnosis. All of these definitions take IQ into account but only one requires an IQ–achievement discrepancy. Although we do not want to return to an era when many students with reading and writing problems were mistakenly thought to be mentally retarded or slow learners, we also want to make sure that students who are mentally retarded or slow learners are adequately diagnosed and provided with services. This classification scheme takes the "big picture" view of learning problems and acknowledges that not only children with average or better intelligence may have difficulty learning to read and write. It also assumes that we cannot ignore IQ or we may fail to differentiate between some forms of LD, namely between the second and the fourth subtypes. Although these subtypes may have basic reading or writing problems that arise from common sources, they may have different long-term learning outcomes that are reasonable to expect and achieve.

Although many children with reading and writing disabilities are not retarded, it is the case that some children with reading and writing problems are delayed in all developmental domains including cognitive and adaptive behavior; see first

Table 16.1

Subtypes of Learning Disabilities

Population	Subtype
Mentally retarded	I. Learning disability: General cognitive and developmental delays
Borderline and low average IQs (No identifiable brain damage)	II. Learning disability: slow learner
Neurologically impaired (IQ varies)	III. Learning disability: Neuropsychological disorder
Average IQ or better (No identifiable brain damage)	IV. Learning disability: discrepancy between IQ and achievement in component academic skills and identifiable processing problem(s)

subtype in Table 16.1. The learning disabilities in these children are generalized in that they occur across all domains and are not restricted to academic delays. However, such children sometimes have relative strengths and weaknesses, and some domains are relatively more affected than others. In theory, these children receive special education services under the category of mental retardation. However, there are exceptions, for example, in cases where parents do not accept the diagnosis of mental retardation and schools agree to serve their children under the category of learning disabilities or in cases where professionals are reluctant to confront parents with mental retardation as a diagnosis. Many parents of children with mental retardation prefer the term LD for their children because it has less stigma.

We have encountered cases of mental retardation that were labeled attention deficit, orthopedically impaired, emotionally disturbed, neurologically impaired, and learning disabled. If IQ is eliminated from consideration and we stop diagnosing mental retardation, then schools and parents might inappropriately expect age- and grade-appropriate achievement in reading and writing achievement for some youngsters. For example, one family was angry at the school because their 8-year-old son was not progressing in reading and had hired a Slingerland tutor to tutor him everyday after school. Careful diagnosis indicated he was moderately to mildly retarded. He had the potential for learning to read but at a much slower acquisition rate than age-mates; also, he needed more than a multisensory approach, and it was not the school's fault that he could not keep up with classmates. The point is that mental retardation may be a form of LD, but we need to distinguish between this form of LD and the form that is specific to reading and writing.

In the current categorical system for special education, the second subtype in Table 16.1 is grossly undeserved. Slow learners usually do not meet the criteria for placement in special education under either the mentally retarded or LD category and often do not get services. Their IQs are too high and often their achievement is not discrepant enough from their IQs. Yet, their achievement is usually below age- and grade-level and they struggle to keep up with the rest of the class, most of whom are achieving at higher levels. On the one hand, they would benefit from support services. On the other hand, it is important not to push them to achieve at or above grade level (at or above the 50th percentile for grade), which may result in secondary emotional problems because they cannot meet the expectations of significant adults in their lives.

Table 16.2 reports the test results for a slow learner who is achieving at expected level, but whose mother has to help her every night to keep up with schoolwork and whose extended family blames the mother for not doing enough to help the child. Support services for this child should be made available at school, but the Education of All Handicapped Children Act does not include this subtype, and therefore such services are often not provided. Many parents of slow learners have heard the term LD used in the media, and are often surprised to be told that their child does not have a LD because they see their child struggle to achieve at school. They take little comfort that their child is achieving at expected level if that level is below average. Slow learners, with low IQs, and low achievement, also need and deserve a free, appropriate education. The goal of that education should not be to remediate their reading and writing to a level above one that is reasonable given the student's cognitive limitations. Rather the goals should be to provide

Table 16.2

Examples of Slow Learner Achieving at Expected but Below Average Level

	Grade 5	Verbal IQ 83	Age-Corrected Standard Score[a]
Reading[b]			
WRMT-R Word Identification			81
WRMT-R Word Attack			86
Spelling			
WRAT-3			85
WIAT			88
Composition			
WJ-R Writing Samples			89
WJ-R Writing Fluency			78
Math			
WJ-R Calculation			87
WJ-R Applied Problems			86

[a]Standard scores have a mean of 100 and a standard deviation of 15.

[b]WRMT-R, Woodcock Reading Matery-Test—Revised; WRAT-3 Wide Range Achievement Test—3rd edition; WIAT, Wechsler Individual Achievement Test; WJ-R, Woodcock Johnson Psychoeducational Battery—Revised.

support services so that the student can maintain a reasonable rate of progress and to monitor that reasonable progress is being made. For slow learners who are achieving at expected level, like the example in Table 16.2, support services might include extra help and/or accommodation to the child's instructional level. In cases where the slow learner is underachieving relative to ability, pullout remedial services (with an individual educational plan) are needed that bring that child up to expected level.

The third subtype in Table 16.1 includes those with neurological impairment present at birth or acquired after birth. Examples of this subtype include but are not restricted to those with cerebral palsy, developmental aphasia or specific language disorder, nonverbal LD, brain tumors, head injury, or very large dissociations among mental functions (e.g., verbal intelligence in the mildly retarded range and nonverbal intelligence in the average range). Such children may or may not have significant discrepancies between overall IQ and achievement, but are very likely to need special education services. Their IQs may fall anywhere along the continuum of intellectual abilities and they are likely to show scatter or unevenness in the development of mental functions. In some states these children are served under the categories of health-impaired or neurologically impaired. Although these children are likely to get qualified for special education services, the challenge may be to convince educators and other professional that these students can learn to read and write and to figure out ways to help them to do so.

The first three subtypes may have difficulty in learning to read and/or write but only the fourth subtype in Table 16.1 has the defining feature of underachieving in reading and writing relative to an average or better IQ in the absence of brain damage. Recent research shows that individuals with specific reading and writing disabilities have structural or functional brain anomalies rather than brain damage (reviewed by Berninger, 1994a). Because IQ and reading/writing achievement occur on a continuum, the size of the discrepancy that constitutes LD is always arbitrary; and because the IQ and achievement measures are not perfectly correlated, the reliability of instruments should be taken into account in computing the size of the discrepancy. Not all children with the fourth subtype of LD qualify for special education services—either because the size of the IQ–achievement discrepancy is not quite large enough or the discrepancy is large but the achievement is at or near grade level (e.g., gifted LD).

With interventions of appropriate nature, intensity, and duration, it is reasonable to expect that reading and writing skills will be developed to a level expected based on age, grade, and IQ in the fourth subtype. The expectation of grade-level achievement is usually not reasonable for the first three subtypes. Dyslexia, which is an example of the fourth subtype of LD, is a specific reading disability at the word level. The cause of a specific disability in word recognition (subtype 4) may be the same as for the cause of a word recognition problem in a slow learner (subtype 2) (e.g., phonological processing problem), but given appropriate intervention, the achievement outcome is likely to be different in two subtypes. IQ does not cause word recognition problems but sets limits on development of word recognition skill. Specific reading disability can also occur at the text level of reading comprehension (e.g., Swanson & Alexander, in press). Specific writing disability can occur in handwriting, spelling, or composition. Students may have specific disabilities in reading only, writing only, or both reading and writing. Another specific LD not included in Table 16.1 is arithmetic disability in which underachievement occurs in arithmetic. An arithmetic disability may occur with or without specific reading and writing disability.

II. THEORY-DRIVEN RESEARCH AND THEORETICAL MODELS FOR READING AND WRITING

The theoretical models of reading and writing and the research described in this chapter can be applied to all four subtypes in Table 16.1. These models guide our theory-driven research on assessment, prevention, and intervention. (See Lyon, 1995, for the importance of theory-driven definitions of LD.) However, our long-term interventions are most relevant to the fourth subtype, while our assessment, prevention, and short-term interventions are most relevant to the second and fourth subtypes.

In this research we do not select subjects on the basis of special education placement decisions made by schools because placement decisions may be affected by referral bias (Shaywitz, Shaywitz, Fletcher, & Escobar, 1990). In the assessment and prevention research we study unreferred samples who meet a priori, investigator-defined inclusion criteria. Although children with mental retardation or borderline intelligence are excluded, children do not have to have IQ–achievement discrepancies to be included, but many do. We let IQ and achievement vary freely so that we can further investigate the role of IQ in defining and treating LD. For example, we are interested in whether IQ or an IQ–achievement discrepancy predicts response to treatment. We use only verbal IQ because that has been shown to be the best predictor of achievement in written language in referred and unreferred samples (see Berninger, 1994a).

Our *assessment studies* have included a broad spectrum of children of varying abilities on multiple measures because our initial goal was to validate theory-driven measures for the diagnosis of reading and writing problems (Berninger, 1994a). Diagnosis used in the treatment studies is based not only on a one-shot administration of an assessment battery. It is also based on a combination of pretreatment performance on an assessment battery of validated measures *and* degree of response to intervention over time. Only children who are treatment nonresponders after an appropriate intervention for a reasonable amount of time are thought to have constitutionally based LD (Berninger & Abbott, 1994a).

Our *prevention studies* are school-based and focus on first and second graders. Like Torgesen and Hecht (1996), we find first graders more responsive to intervention than kindergartners. We attribute the greater responsivity of the first and second graders to maturation of tertiary association areas in the brain at about ages 6 to 7 (Berninger, 1994a). At the same time, we think it is critical to intervene early when children first experience difficulty and not wait until they have sustained chronic difficulty. Our view of prevention is that it is not necessary to qualify a child for special education to (a) diagnose an early problem in a component reading or writing skill or in a related processing skill, and (b) initiate early intervention. Early intervention aimed at relevant skills will give children a boost to prevent more serious reading or writing problems later on and will eliminate in some, not all cases, subsequent placement in special education. In this view, there are two levels of diagnosis (Berninger, Hart et al., 1992). At the first level, diagnosis focuses on instructional interventions needed to make sure all component skills for a functional reading and writing system are being developed. This level of diagnosis precedes special education placement. At the second level, diagnosis is comprehensive and focuses on whether special education placement or other interventions are needed because a child has not responded to the first level of intervention. Berninger and Abbott (1994a) recommended that the diagnostic label of LD in reading and writing (fourth subtype in Table 16.1) be reserved for the second level of diagnosis, at which time it can be determined that the child did not respond to appropriate intervention provided at the time of the first level of diagnosis and intervention. That is, early intervention can precede the assignment of an LD diagnosis and can precede special education placement.

Prevention is not approached solely in terms of direct services for children. Teacher training is also considered important in prevention of reading and writing disabilities. Regular and special education teachers are inadequately prepared at the preservice level for dealing with the normal variation in learning to read and write (Berninger, 1994a; Nolen, McCutchen, & Berninger, 1990). They are inadequately prepared especially in the area of linguistics and the development of oral and written language (Moats, 1994; Moats & Lyon, in press). Inservice teacher training is, therefore, also a major goal of our Multidisciplinary Learning Disability Center.

Our intervention studies investigate treatment from the perspective of functional brain systems and fall into one of the following categories: design experiment, comparison of instructional components, or instructional sandwiches. Design experiments (Brown, 1992) provide comprehensive intervention in order to achieve a specified outcome. In our *design experiments* we provide intervention for all the components in Tables 16.3 or 16.4 in order to bring children up to grade or expected level in reading or writing. Teaching is a multidimensional process, unlike experimental treatments that aim to be as pure and unidimensional as possible. The aim of our experiments that make *comparisons of instructional components* is to

Table 16.3
Theoretical Model of Reading Process[a]

High-Level Comprehension Skills
    Discourse understanding (text level)
    Sentence computation (sentence level)
    Vocabulary understanding (word level)
Lexical Selection (interaction between lexical identification and textual context)
Low-level word recognition skills (word- and subword-levels for lexical-identification)
    Level 4: Coordination of multiple codes, connections, and mechanisms
    Level 3: Word-specific and rule-governed mechanisms[b,c]
    Level 2: Multiple orthographic-phonological connections
    Level 1: Orthographic awareness (coding), Phonological/Morphological awareness (coding), and
        lexical access

---

[a]Accuracy and rate must be taken into account for each component in this model.

[b]The word-specific mechanism underlies the learning of specific words that have an orthographic, phonological, and semantic representation in the internal lexicon (mental dictionary). It is a lexical-level mechanism that is also referred to as item-learning or exemplar-learning by cognitive psychologists. It underlies sight word learning, a term used by educators.

[c]The rule-governed mechanism underlies the learning of word attack skills for decoding unknown words. It is a sublexical mechanism that depends on the alphabet principle. In the past it was assumed that rules underlie the word decoding process, but recent connectionist models suggest that connections between orthographic and phonological layers in a neural network underlie the process. It may be that a combination of rules and connections drive the word decoding process.

determine which component, defined as purely as possible, is the most effective and whether a combination of components is more effective than a single component. In an *instructional sandwich experiment,* one or two sets of multiple components ("the sandwich") is kept constant across conditions and only one layer ("the filling") is systematically manipulated across conditions. By embedding the filling in the context of the constant set(s) of other needed components, comparison of growth in the reading or writing *system* can be achieved within an experimental investigation.

Our *short-term intervention* studies are clinic-based and include children at various elementary grade levels. For the most part, inclusion criteria involve low achievement, and children do not have to have an IQ–achievement discrepancy, but often do. We think that we learn useful information about the effectiveness of different instructional approaches from the prevention and short-term intervention studies that might be applied to all four subtypes above.

In contrast, the *long-term intervention studies,* which are clinic-based, are designed for children who do exhibit IQ–achievement discrepancies (the fourth subtype in Table 16.1) and have had chronic problems. Occasionally, we include a child who represents the third subtype and has a well-documented neurological

Table 16.4

Theoretical Model of Writing Process[a]

High-Level Composition Processes
    Advance and on-line planning (idea generation and goal setting)
    Text generation
        Word level
        Sentence level
        Text level
            Topic-comment units
            Text structures (genres)
    On-Line and Posttext—generation reviewing and revising
Low-Level Transcription Processes
    Spelling
        Multiple phonological-orthographic connections
        Orthographic images (representations in the mind's eye)
    Handwriting
        Letter knowledge (representing and automatically accessing and retrieving letter forms in memory)
        Fine motor planning and execution

---

[a]Accuracy and rate need to be taken into account for each component in this model.

disorder. These long-term studies are predicated upon the assumption that intense intervention over time is needed for the fourth subtype, who may have the potential of overcoming their learning problems to a greater degree than the other subtypes.

A. Theoretical Model for Reading

The theoretical model driving our research and clinical practice is designed to assess and develop all necessary components of a functional reading system, which requires an integration of low-level and high-level brain processes (Berninger, 1994a; Berninger, Abbott, Reed, et al., 1997). The component processes in Table 16.3 are organized so that they progress from the lowest (at the bottom of Table 16.3) to the highest (at the top of Table 16.3) in the functional system.

At the lowest level of word recognition are the lexical access, orthographic, and phonological processes from which the word recognition routines are constructed. Lexical access is the ability to find and retrieve name codes from memory. Orthographic awareness is the ability to attend to, code, represent in memory, and manipulate spelling units in written words. Phonological awareness is the ability to represent spoken words in memory and manipulate their component sounds. At the next level of word recognition, word-specific and rule-governed mechanisms (Carr & Pollatsek, 1985) emerge from the neural network as functionally independent mechanisms (Van Orden, Pennington, & Stone, 1990) (see footnotes b and c in Table 16.3 for further description of these mechanisms, which correspond to what educators call sight words and word attack skills). The slogan on T-shirts, "Hukt on fonics werkt fer mee" illustrates the importance of the word-specific mechanism for supplementing the phonics or rule-governed mechanism; there are alternative ways of spelling the same sound and only knowledge of the particular spelling that goes with a specific meaning (i.e., the representation of a specific word) will help decide among those alternative spellings. At the highest level of word recognition, the multiple code connections and mechanisms are coordinated by executive functions to support fluent word recognition. We know little about how to teach this coordination to create fluent reading, but Levy, Abello, and Lysynchuk (1997) have shown that practice to increase speed of reading single words transfers to more fluent text reading and comprehension. Having all the multiple connections at level 2 may also increase fluency of word recognition.

There are two lexical-level processes—one related to word recognition (lexical-identification) based on the four levels of processes within the word-recognition module) and one related to text comprehension (lexical-selection of a word that fits a particular textual context). The lexical-identification processes are not completely modular and communicate directly with the lexical-selection processes, but not with the text-level processes. The lexical-selection processes communicate with the text-level processes. For further discussion of and evidence for the two lexical-level processes proposed by Oden and his colleagues, see Berninger (1994b).

High-level comprehension processes draw upon multiple levels of language, ranging from the word-, to the sentence-, to the text-levels (Berninger, 1994a). Lexical-level processes contribute to the sentence-level and text-level processes (Berninger, Abbott, & Alsdorf, 1997), but these different levels of language may be unevenly developed within individuals (Berninger, 1994a). Likewise, word-recognition and comprehension processes may be unevenly developed within individuals (Berninger, 1994a,b).

For all the components of the functional reading system, both accuracy and rate must be considered. Disabilities can occur in rate of functioning even if a component process is accurate (Lovett, 1987).

B. Theoretical Model for Writing

The theoretical model driving our research and clinical practice related to writing is designed to assess and develop all necessary components of a functional writing system, which requires an integration of low-level and high-level brain processes (Berninger, 1994a; Berninger, Abbott, Reed et al. 1997). The component processes in Table 16.4 are organized so that they progress from the lowest (at the bottom) to the highest (at the top) in the functional writing system.

At the lowest level are the transcription processes that support the translation of language represented in memory into its written form on paper. Both handwriting and spelling contribute to the transcription process. Both orthographic (letter) knowledge and motor skills contribute to handwriting (Abbott & Berninger, 1993). Both orthographic and phonological coding contribute to spelling (Abbott & Berninger, 1993).

At the highest level are linguistic, cognitive, and metacognitive processes contributing to the composition process. Text is generated at different levels of language and intraindividual differences occur in at the word-, sentence-, and text-levels (Berninger, 1994a; Berninger, Mizokawa, Bragg, Cartwright, & Yates, 1994). Skill in generating words does not predict skill in constructing sentences or composing text; skill in constructing sentences does not predict skill in composing text. Twenty-one algorithms that children in grades 1 to 9 use to generate topic-comment units at the sentence-level and the developmental progression of emerging text structures for narrative and expository texts have been identified (Berninger, Fuller, & Whitaker, 1996). Planning occurs on-line as text is generated, but skilled writers also preplan in advance. Likewise, reviewing and revising occurs on-line as text is generated, but skilled writers also revise text after it is generated.

Again, both accuracy and rate must be considered for every component of the functional writing system. Disabilities can occur in rate of functioning even if a component process functions accurately.

C. Relationship between Functional Systems

The functional reading system and functional writing system draw upon common and unique components (Berninger, Cartwright et al., 1994). An important research question is whether training components common across the systems will transfer across the systems (Berninger, Vaughan et al., 1997).

III. BRIEF OVERVIEW OF OUR RESEARCH PROGRAM FOR READING

A. Assessment

A number of standardized psychometric instruments exist that can be used to assess the comprehension skills in the model of reading in Table 16.3. Informal reading inventories can also be used for this purpose. Here general approaches rather than specific instruments we use are discussed.

Assessment of vocabulary knowledge has been underemphasized. Vocabulary knowledge should be assessed because it contributes to morphological awareness (e.g., Fowler & Liberman, 1995; Henry, 1989, 1994). Expressive naming tasks (e.g., rapid automatized naming and word finding) are more predictive than receptive vocabulary tasks in predicting word-level and sentence-level comprehension processes (Berninger, Abbott, & Alsdorf, 1997). The cloze technique, which requires children to supply missing words, does not provide a comprehensive assessment of comprehension skills but does provide useful information on processes involved in computation of sentence meaning. Specifically, it taps sensitivity to cohesive ties and psychological coherence at the sentence level. Some children can extract propositional content at the discourse level but have difficulty with precise interpretation of individual sentences. Answering multiple-choice questions about passages should be supplemented with tasks that require summarization or retelling of passages, which are sensitive to whether and how the overall schema of text or propositions are organized in memory. In sum, a comprehensive assessment of comprehension will include measures at the word-, sentence-, and text-levels (see Table 16.3).

Standardized tests that require children to pronounce a list of real words can be used to assess word-specific mechanisms, while standardized tests that require children to pronounce a list of pseudowords can be used to assess rule-governed mechanisms. In our research we have developed or used measures of orthographic and phonological coding and rapid automatized naming to assess why children may have difficulty with word-specific or rule-governed mechanisms in word recognition (see Table 16.3). We have developed measures to assess orthographic coding of a whole word, a letter in a word, and a letter cluster in a word (Berninger, Yates, & Lester, 1991). Although many phonological tasks are described in the literature, few have been standardized on representative samples. It is important to use tasks that reflect the appropriate developmental level of the children being assessed (rhyming in preschoolers, syllable segmentation in kindergartners, and phoneme segmentation in first and second graders, etc.) and that reflect the incremental nature of the process of acquiring phonological skills (see Vandervelden & Siegel, 1995). We use several measures of phonological segmentation, including a modification of Rosner's syllable and phoneme deletion task (Berninger, Thalberg, DeBruyn, & Smith, 1987). Recently, we have begun to assess rime coding (part of syllable left when onset phoneme is deleted), rapid automatized naming (Wolf et al., 1986), and rapid automatized switching (Wolf, 1986). The latter assesses the speed of retrieval of lexical-level name codes, which should be automatized, for familiar visual stimuli. Taken together, these measures are useful for both diagnosis and generation of interventions. For example, the orthographic and phonological coding measures can be used to make inferences (see Berninger, 1994a; Berninger & Traweek, 1991) about whether the whole written word–whole spoken word connection needed for the look-say method is functional; whether the letter–phoneme or letter cluster–phoneme connection needed for phonics is functional; whether the letter cluster–rime connection needed for word families is functional; and whether the written syllable–spoken syllable connection needed for structural analysis is functional.

These measures for assessing why a child has trouble with word recognition have been given to all the participants in the family/genetics study of our Multidisciplinary Learning Disabilities Center. The results for the first 32 probands (target children in grades 1 to 6 who have specific reading and/or writing disabilities of fourth subtype in Table 16.1) cast doubt on the claim that the only cause of specific reading disability is a phonological core deficit. Not one of the 32 probands had a pure phonological deficit, that is, a deficit only in phonological coding; however, 62.5% had a phonological deficit in conjunction with an orthographic coding and/or rapid automatized naming deficit. Over half (53%) had a triple deficit in orthographic coding, phonological coding, and rapid automatized naming. Of most interest, 100% had a deficit in rapid automatized naming, indicating that inability to access name codes quickly for visual symbols is also a core problem in dyslexia. Perfetti (1992) argued that the heart of lexical access is a phonologically referenced name code. Berninger (1989) found that for familiar words this name code was accessed more quickly than was the phonemic code; and Berninger, Abbott, & Alsdorf (1997) found that tasks requiring access to a name code predicted psychometric and on-line processing measures of word recognition and comprehension. These various findings pointing to the importance of word-level name codes support the existence of the John Effect: "In the beginning was the Word, and the Word was with God, and the Word was God." (Verse 1, Chapter 1 of the Gospel According to John). Thus, lexical access is the cornerstone of the functional reading system outline in Table 16.3.

B. Prevention

Twenty second graders who qualified for Chapter 1 participated in a year-long design experiment (Berninger & Traweek, 1991). The intervention was designed to develop all the components of a functional reading system (Table 16.3). In the first phase, orthographic and phonological awareness was trained. Children played *looking games* in which a whole written word was briefly displayed for a second and then children were instructed to look closely at the word before it was covered up. After it was covered up, the children were asked to spell the whole word they saw, or to tell the letter in a designated position (e.g., first, last, third, etc.) or to tell the letters in designated positions (e.g., first, two, last two, third, and fourth). In any lesson, the looking game was played with a maximum of five to ten words. Children played *sound games* in which they deleted syllables (e.g., Say birthday; now say it again, but don't say day.) or phonemes (e.g., Say gift; now say it again, but don't say /t/a). As in all our interventions, we use phonological training that requires manipulation of phonemes. Recent research (Wise, Ring, Sessions, & Olson, 1997) has shown that phoneme manipulation is as or more effective than phonological training that provides articulatory feedback (e.g., Lindamood).

In the second phase, multiple connections between printed and spoken words were taught. Children played concentration to practice whole-word connections with the look-say method and to develop word-specific mechanisms. Children used a systematic phonics program (*Explode the Code* published by Educators Publishing Service in Cambridge, MA) to develop letter–phoneme and letter cluster–phoneme connections for the rule-governed mechanism. Children used rime units and all the consonants to generate words sharing the same word family. In addition, they read stories to practice word-specific and rule-governed mechanisms in context, they answered questions to monitor their comprehension, and they reread texts to develop fluent oral reading.

As a group, from the beginning to the end of second grade, these children improved over a standard deviation on a standardized measure of the word-specific mechanism and over a standard deviation on a standardized measure of the rule-governed mechanism. At posttest, the group was at or near the mean standard score for grade on the measures of word-specific and rule-governed mechanisms. At the individual level, 70% showed significant gains on the word-specific mechanism and 90% showed significant gains on the rule-governed mechanism. At pretest, only five children had any (and only one) functional orthographic–phonological code connection. At posttest, eighteen of the children (90%) had at least one functional orthographic–phonological code connection, and nearly half had all three code connections assessed. Early intervention appeared to give these children the boost they needed to prevent a more serious reading disability.

Recently we (Berninger, Abbott, Mostafapour et al., 1997) initiated even earlier intervention with 128 first graders, who were identified through screening in the third and fourth months of first grade. Intervention, which consisted of 24 biweekly sessions, began in the fifth month of first grade. We compared whether strategies to develop a single code connection (whole printed–whole spoken word; letter or letter cluster–phoneme; letter cluster–rime) or strategies to develop multiple code connections (combination of two strategies or all three strategies) were more effective than phonological awareness training alone in developing word-specific and rule-governed mechanisms.

C. Short-Term Intervention

Two methods of teaching word recognition to children with deficits in the word-specific mechanism were compared (Berninger, Lester, Sohlberg, & Mateer, 1991). Each child was taught each method, the order of which was counterbalanced across children. The first method was a modification of the Buschke (1973) selective reminding procedure in which all words are presented in a list on the first trial; on subsequent trials only the words missed on a preceding trial are presented (in contrast to flash cards on which all words are presented on every trial). The task was to produce the lexical-level name code in response to the printed word. The second method was a multisensory technique in which each word was presented letter by letter on a computer and the task was to write the word as well as pronounce it. Data analyses at both the group and individual levels showed that selective reminding was superior to the multisensory technique, suggesting that retrieval of the name code was more effective than writing the word in developing the word-specific mechanism.

Multiple strategies have been found to be more effective than a single strategy in developing the rule-governed mechanism (Hart, Berninger, & Abbott, 1997). In this study, twelve children with reading disability were randomly assigned to one of two treatments for 16 half-hour individual sessions. Growth in the rule-governed mechanism was faster for the group taught multiple orthographic–phonological code connections (whole printed word–whole spoken word; letter- or letter cluster–phoneme; letter cluster–rime) than for the group taught a single orthographic–phonological code connection (orthographic and phonological awareness and the letter- or letter cluster–phoneme connection). This result supports the conclusion that phonics is necessary but not sufficient for helping children with reading disabilities learn the rule-governed mechanism.

In another study, we (Berninger, Abbott, Zook, et al., 1996) compared three treatments for teaching 48 children referred at the end of first grade both the word-specific and rule-governed mechanisms. Children were randomly assigned to one of three treatments that were used to teach words that varied in letter-sound predictability (Venezky, 1995) in eight half-hour sessions. The first treatment emphasized the whole word, the second treatment emphasized the subword, and the third treatment emphasized a combination of the whole word and subword. Over the course of this short-term intervention each of the three groups improved significantly in both the word-specific and rule-governed mechanism, and there were no main effects related to treatment. However, there was one interaction between treatment and sessions for the word-specific mechanism: By posttest there was an advantage for the subword strategy in which spelling units of varying letter size were color coded. These results, along with the results of Berninger, Lester et al. (1991), suggest that the word-specific mechanism can be improved by focusing on lexical retrieval of name codes and color coding of spelling units of varying size in the printed word.

D. Long-Term Intervention

Sixteen children referred at the end of first grade for reading problems participated in a year-long tutorial that (a) included instruction aimed at all the components of the functional reading system in Table 16.3 (Abbott, Reed, Abbott, & Berninger, 1997; and Berninger, Abbott, Reed et al., 1997) and (b) was designed to bring the children up to grade level. At the group level of analysis, children improved on all component reading skills and reading-related processes taught. At the individual level of analysis, all children reached expected level for grade or verbal IQ on at least some of the measures in this design experiment. Tutoring that lasts for more than 1 year is probably needed to bring all children up to grade or expected level on all components of a functional reading or writing system. There are no quick fixes and no magic bullets. The learning process takes time.

We are currently investigating the issue of necessary duration in a long-term tutorial for children with severe word recognition problems identified when they were in first or second grade through the family/genetics study in our Multidisciplinary Learning Disability Center. As with our previous long-term tutorial, intervention focuses on comprehension as well as word recognition. We recognize the importance of explicit teaching of comprehension skills (see Pressley & Wharton-McDonald, 1997) as well as explicit teaching of word recognition skills. Over one-fourth of the children were brought up to grade level within 6 months. Others clearly have severe problems that will take longer to remediate. To date, children have not achieved at levels beyond those expected based on verbal IQ.

IV. BRIEF OVERVIEW OF OUR RESEARCH PROGRAM FOR WRITING

A. Assessment

Standardized, psychometric measures for spelling and writing can be used to assess achievement outcome. Our research program has focused, in contrast, on the assessment of processes that contribute to the achievement outcome.

We have developed and validated measures of fine motor skills (Berninger & Rutberg, 1992) and of orthographic coding (Berninger et al., 1991) that contribute to *handwriting* skill. Although there is a myth that handwriting is primarily a motor skill, structural equation modeling based on students in grades 1 to 6 ($N = 600$) showed that orthographic skills contribute directly to handwriting, and fine motor skills contribute indirectly through their influence on orthographic skills (Abbott & Berninger, 1993). Letter knowledge is as, or more, important than fine motor skills in the development of handwriting; and handwriting may facilitate letter knowledge in a way that generalizes to the reading system and the composition component of the writing system (Berninger, Vaughan et al., in press). One of the best predictors of handwriting and of composition in the primary grades (Berninger, Yates, et al., 1992), intermediate grades (Berninger, Cartwright, et al., 1994), and junior high grades (Berninger, Whitaker, Feng, Swanson, & Abbott, 1996) is a task in which children print letters in alphabetic order as quickly and accurately as possible. The score is the number of letters produced correctly in the first 15 seconds, which appears to tap the preciseness of letter representation in memory and the automaticity of retrieval and production of letter forms. The more automatic letter access and production are, the more capacity-limited working memory resources are freed for the higher-level composing processes in Table 16.4 (Berninger, Yates et al., 1992).

Orthographic and phonological coding are good predictors of not only word recognition but also spelling skill (Abbott & Berninger, 1993). Verbal IQ is also a good predictor of *spelling* skill (Berninger, Yates, et al., 1992; Berninger, Cartwright, et al., 1994). Low-level handwriting (Berninger, Vaughan, et al., 1996) and word recognition skills (Abbott & Berninger, 1993) and high-level oral language (Abbott & Berninger, 1993) and working memory (Berninger, Cartwright, et al., 1994) are good predictors of *composition* skills (fluency and/or quality). Berninger and Whitaker (1993) proposed a model of theory-based, branching diagnosis that utilizes these process measures validated in our research program for the assessment of writing disabilities.

B. Prevention

Nearly 700 first graders were screened to identify 144 children with handwriting problems, who were randomly assigned to one of five handwriting treatments or a contact control treatment (phonological awareness training) delivered to triads (Berninger, Vaughan, Abbott, Abbott, et al., 1997). All treatments were more effective than the contact control group in improving handwriting. Of the handwriting treatments (copy, motor imitation, numbered arrow cues, memory retrieval, numbered arrow cues + memory retrieval), the latter, which instructed children to look carefully at the numbered arrow cues (to develop a precise representation of the letter in memory) and to cover the letter for increasing intervals of time (to create memory retrieval routines), was the most effective in improving handwriting and compositional fluency. That is, there was transfer from a low-level transcription to a high-level composition skill in Table 16.4.

In a recent study (Berninger, Vaughan, Abbott, Reed, et al., 1997), all second graders in eight schools were screened to identify 128 children with spelling problems who were randomly assigned to one of seven treatment groups or a contact control (phonological awareness training). The seven treatments, which were delivered in 24 sessions to dyads, are three single strategies for phonological–orthographic connections (whole spoken–whole printed word; phoneme–letter to letter cluster; rime–letter cluster) and four strategies that consist of a combination of two of the single strategies or of all three of the single strategies.

C. Short-Term Intervention

In a short-term intervention experiment (Berninger, Abbott, Rogan, et al., in press), half of the 48 children referred at the end of second grade for spelling problems had spelling problems only, while half had spelling and handwriting problems. Children with each type of problem were randomly assigned to a treatment that used a pencil to practice spelling words or to a treatment that used a computer keyboard to practice spelling words. Children in all groups were taught an orthographic imaging strategy to study 48 words that differed in letter-sound predictability (Venezky, 1995). In orthographic imaging, a child is (a) encouraged to look carefully at a written word and name it; (b) then to close the eyes and visualize the word in the mind's eye and spell it naming letters in left-to-right order; (c) then to open the eyes and spell the word in writing or on keyboard; and (d) to compare the production with the original written model of the target word to be studied. To facilitate use of sound–letter connections, words were also pronounced spelling unit by spelling unit, and the spelling units were color coded. Although there were no treatment effects related to the pencil or computer and both groups improved over six sessions, the group with handwriting and spelling problems performed worse than the group with only spelling problems. Apparently the ability to retrieve and produce letter forms automatically affects one's ability to learn to spell words whether or not writing is required.

In another study (Berninger, Abbott, Whitaker, Sylvester, & Nolen, 1995), of the 39 children referred at the end of third grade for writing problems, 24 were randomly assigned to a 16-lesson individual tutorial (1 hour each) and 15 to an untreated control group. The tutorial was designed to integrate instruction aimed at the low-level and high-level skills in Table 16.4 in each lesson. The treatment group outperformed the control group on measures of handwriting, spelling, and composition; and the relative superiority was maintained on at least one measure of handwriting, spelling, and composition at 6-month follow-up.

D. Long-Term Intervention

Third and fourth graders who are underachieving in spelling were identified through the family/genetics study in our Multidisciplinary Learning Disabilities Center. These children, who also have significant problems in handwriting and composition, participate in 1-hour weekly individual tutoring sessions aimed at the low-level and high-level skills in Table 16.4 in each session. Wave 1 that began in summer 1996 will be compared with Wave 2 that began in winter 1997. Results to date for Wave 1 show that spelling problems are not remediated over the short-run (7 months), but that significant progress can be made in improving handwriting and composition skills (often several grade levels on standardized measures) within this same time frame.

V. PRACTICE ISSUES

The cases below, which have come to our attention through our research efforts, illustrate some of the challenges facing practitioners who serve children with LD. Future success in serving these children will depend on our collective wisdom in meeting these challenges.

A. Early Identification and Intervention as an Alternative to Grade Repetition

A. B. repeated kindergarten. At the end of her second year in kindergarten, her teacher informed her parents that she will still not ready for first grade. At that time they sought the advice of a school psychologist, who referred her to our Multidisciplinary Learning Disabilities Center. Level 1 diagnosis documented significant problems in orthographic and phonological coding and in handwriting. Initial early intervention focused on phonological awareness training. A. B. is now in first grade and has begun to learn to read. She is now participating in a long-term tutorial focused on all the skills in Table 16.3. A diagnosis of LD (level 2 diagnosis) will await her response to this long-term tutorial. Clearly, early diagnosis and intervention has been more effective than merely repeating the grade. See Berninger (1994a) for further discussion of alternatives to grade repetition.

B. Consequences of Delayed Identification

C. D.'s parents were told not to worry about his struggle in learning to read and write. They were told that with maturation he would outgrow the problems he was experiencing in first grade. However, C. D.'s problems did not disappear. Finally, at the end of third grade, the school agreed to honor the parents' request and to test him. Results showed that C. D. has above-average verbal intelligence (86th percentile), but that his reading skills were below average: 21st percentile in word-specific mechanism; 22nd percentile in rule-governed mechanism; 21st percentile in oral reading in context; 21st–27th percentile in spelling; and 12th percentile in written composition. Mild problems in phonological coding and severe problems in orthographic coding and rapid automatized naming were noted. Had level 1 diagnosis and intervention been begun in first grade, the results of the level 2 diagnosis in third grade might have looked very different, and C. D. would not have endured nearly 3 years of chronic failure in reading and writing. E. F., who was assessed in first grade, did not fare much better. Although E. F. was shown to have severe problems in orthographic and phonological coding and rapid automatized naming, the discrepancy between her Full Scale IQ and Basic Skills Reading Cluster on the Woodcock Johnson-Revised missed the cutoff by one point for special education services. Like C. D., E. F. had to wait until third grade and fail in reading and writing for nearly 3 years to qualify for special education services. See Berninger (1994a) for discussion of the pitfalls in thinking that (a) reading and writing problems will disappear simply with maturation without individualized intervention and (b) arbitrary cutoffs really differentiate who is and who is not LD.

C. Victims of Inclusion

G. H.'s learning problems were documented during second grade. He qualified for special education services, but his school is deeply committed to the philosophy of inclusion, that is, delivery of special services in the regular classroom. His regular classroom teacher has not had training in teaching reading and writing to children with LD. His special education teacher has time to meet with him only one half hour a week in this regular class—in a small group of other children with learning problems but not the same kind of learning problems as G. H. So, 2 years later there is still a sizable discrepancy in age-corrected standard scores between Verbal IQ (115) and Word Identification (91), Word Attack (96), Oral Reading Quotient (88), and Spelling (91). His severe processing problems in phonological coding, orthographic coding, and rapid automatized naming are untreated and persist. This case suggests that the time has come to devote less attention to philosophy and more attention to the nature, delivery, and monitoring of comprehensive interventions that results in measurable gains.

VI. REASONS FOR CAUTIOUS OPTIMISM

In a large-scale, longitudinal study, Shaywitz et al. (1995) charted the progress of children with reading problems in grade one as they progressed in school through sixth grade. Despite the frequent claim of a Matthew Effect according to which the rich (good readers) get richer (at reading) and the poor (poor readers) get worse (at reading), they did not find evidence of the Matthew effect. Poor readers did not lose relative ground over the course of schooling. Rather, those with initial problems had lower starting points but grew at a rate that paralleled those of the better readers who began at higher starting points. Those with initial problems did not reach the same end point as those who started out as better readers, but they reached reasonable end points associated with functional reading skills. Reading skill falls along a continuum. Children vary in where they start and where they finish. The important goal is to keep them moving along the continuum.

VII. CONCLUSION

The field of LD is still in its infancy with respect to diagnosis and intervention. Rigid, categorical criteria for special education placement have impeded progress in both practice and research. Theory-driven research offers promise for advancing diagnosis and intervention. However, the ultimate contribution of research to assessment, prevention, and intervention will depend on the willingness of researchers to create partnerships with the practitioners who face the day-to-day challenges of serving students with LD. Research will benefit from infusion of the experiences of practitioners who have first-hand knowledge of the real-world issues in the field of LD. Practitioners will benefit from infusion of theory-driven, research-validated approaches to diagnosis and intervention. Hopefully, in the future, policy makers, who may be removed from the daily challenges of the practitioners and researchers in this field, will also join the partnership.

Acknowledgments

Preparation for this chapter was supported by grants No. 25858-08 and 33812-01 from the National Institute of Child Health and Human Development. The author thanks Robert Abbott, Reid Lyon, and Bernice Wong for helpful comments on an earlier version of this chapter.

References

Abbott, R., & Berninger, V. (1993). Structural equation modeling of relationships among developmental skills and writing skills in primary and intermediate grade writers. *Journal of Educational Psychology, 85*(3), 478–508.

Abbott, S., Reed, L., Abbott, R., & Berninger, V. (1997). Year-long balanced reading/writing tutorial: A design experiment used for dynamic assessment. *Learning Disabilities Quarterly, 20,* 249–263.

Berninger, V. (1989). Orchestration of multiple codes in developing readers: An alternative model of lexical access. *International Journal of Neuroscience, 48,* 85–104.

Berninger, V. (1994a). *Reading and writing acquisition: A developmental neuropsychological perspective.* W. C. Brown & Benchmark: Madison, WI. Reprinted in 1996 by Westview Press, Boulder, CO.

Berninger, V. (1994b). Intraindividual differences in levels of language in comprehension of written sentences. *Learning and Individual Differences, 6,* 433–457.

Berninger, V., & Abbott, R. (1994a). Redefining learning disabilities: Moving beyond aptitude-achievement discrepancies to failure to respond to validated treatment protocols. In G. R. Lyon (Ed.), *Frames of reference for the assessment of learning disabilities: New views on measurement issues* (pp. 163–202). Baltimore: Paul H. Brookes Publishing Co.

Berninger, V., & Abbott, R. (1994b). Multiple orthographic and phonological codes in literacy acquisition: An evolving research program. In V. Berninger (Ed.), *The varieties of orthographic knowledge I: Theoretical and developmental issues* (pp. 277–317). The Netherlands: Kluwer Academic Publishers.

Berninger, V., Abbott, R., & Alsdorf, B. (1997). Lexical- and sentence-level processes in comprehension of written sentences. *Reading and Writing: An Interdisciplinary Journal, 9,* 135–162.

Berninger, V., Abbott, R., Mostafapour, E., Lemos, Z., Ogier, S., Brooksher, R., & Zook, D. (1997). Teaching the alphabet principle within a connectionist framework: Aiming instruction at all levels of language. Submitted.

Berninger, V., Abbott, S., Reed, L., Greep, K., Hooven, C., Sylvester, L., Taylor, J., Clinton, A., & Abbott, R. (1997). Directed reading and writing activities: Aiming interventions to working brain systems. In S. Dollinger & L. DiLalla (Eds.), *Prevention and intervention issues across the life span,* pp. 123–158. Hillsdale, NJ: Erlbaum.

Berninger, V., Abbott, R., Rogan, L., Abbott, S., Reed, L., Brooks, A., Vaughan, K., & Graham, S. (in press). Teaching spelling to children with specific learning disabilities: The mind's ear and eye beat the computer or the pencil. *Learning Disability Quarterly.*

Berninger, V., Abbott, R., Whitaker, D., Sylvester, L., & Nolen, S. (1995). Integrating low-level and high-level skills in treatment protocols for writing disabilities. *Learning Disabilities Quarterly, 18,* 293–309.

Berninger, V., Abbott, R., Zook, D., Ogier, S., Lemos, Z., & Brooksher, R. (1996). Early intervention for reading disabilities: Teaching the aphabet principle within a connectionist framework. Revision under review.

Berninger, V., Cartwright, A., Yates, C., Swanson, H. L., & Abbott, R. (1994). Developmental skills related to writing and reading acquisition in the intermediate grades: Shared and unique variance. *Reading and Writing: An Interdisciplinary Journal, 6,* 161–196.

Berninger, V., Fuller, F., & Whitaker, D. (1996). A process approach to writing development across the life span. *Educational Psychology Review, 8,* 193–218.

Berninger, V., & Hart, T. (1993). From research to clinical assessment of reading and writing disorders: The unit of analysis problem. In R. M. Joshi & C. K. Leong (Eds.), *Reading disabilities: Diagnosis and component processes* (pp. 33–61). The Netherlands: Kluwer Academic Publishers.

Berninger, V., Hart, T., Abbott, R., & Karovsky, P. (1992). Defining reading and writing disabilities with and without IQ: A flexible, developmental perspective. *Learning Disabilities Quarterly, 15,* 103–118.

Berninger, V., Lester, K., Sohlberg, M., & Mateer, C. (1991). Intervention based on the multiple connections model of reading for developmental dyslexia and acquired deep dyslexia. *Archives of Clinical Neuropsychology, 6,* 375–391.

Berninger, V., Mizokawa, D., Bragg, R., Cartwright, A., & Yates, C. (1994). Individual differences in levels of written language. *Reading and Writing Quarterly, 10,* 259–275.

Berninger, V., & Rutberg, J. (1992). Relationship of finger function to beginning writing: Application to diagnosis of writing disabilities. *Developmental Medicine & Child Neurology, 34,* 155–172.

Berninger, V., & Traweek, D. (1991). Effects of two-phase reading intervention on three orthographic-phonological connections. *Learning and Individual Differences, 3,* 323–338.

Berninger, V., Thalberg, S., DeBruyn, I., & Smith, R. (1987). Preventing reading disabilities by assessing and remediating phonemic skills. *School Psychology Review, 16,* 553–564.

Berninger, V., Vaughan, K., Abbott, R., Abbott, S., Brooks, A., Rogan, L., Reed, L., & Graham, S. (1997). Treatment of handwriting fluency problems in beginning writing: Transfer from handwriting to composition. *Journal of Educational Psychology, 89,* 652–666.

Berninger, V., Vaughan, K., Abbott, R., Brooks, A., Abbott, S., Reed, E., Rogan, L., & Graham, S. (1997). Early intervention for spelling problems: Teaching spelling units of varying size within a multiple connections framework. Revision under review.

Berninger, V., & Whitaker, D. (1993). Theory-based, branching diagnosis of writing disabilities. *School Psychology Review, 22,* 623–642.

Berninger, V., Whitaker, D., Feng, Y., Swanson, H. L., & Abbott, R. (1996). Assessment of planning, translating, and revising in junior high writers. *Journal of School Psychology, 34,* 23–52.

Berninger, V., Yates, C., Cartwright, A., Rutberg, J., Remy, E., & Abbott, R. (1992). Lower-level developmental skills in beginning writing. *Reading and Writing: An Interdisciplinary Journal, 4,* 257–280.

Berninger, V., Yates, C., & Lester, K. (1991). Multiple orthographic codes in acquisition of reading and writing skills. *Reading and Writing: An Interdisciplinary Journal, 3,* 115–149.

Brown, A. (1992). Design experiments: Theoretical and methodological challenges in creating complex interventions in classroom settings. *The Journal of the Learning Sciences, 2,* 141–178.

Buschke, H. (1973). Selective reminding for analysis of memory and learning, *Journal of Verbal Learning and Verbal Behavior, 12,* 543–550.

Carr, T., & Pollatsek, A. (1985). Recognizing printed words: A look at current models. In *Reading Research: Advances in Theory and Practice,* Vol. 5 (pp. 1–82). New York: Academic Press.

Fowler, A., & Liberman, I. (1995). The role of phonology and orthography in morphological awareness. In L. Feldman (Ed.), *Morphological aspects of language processing.* Hillsdale, NJ: Lawrence Erlbaum Associates.

Hammill, D., Leigh, J., McNutt, G., & Larsen, S. (1981). A new definition of learning disabilities. *Journal of Learning Disabilities, 4,* 336–342.

Hart, T., Berninger, V., & Abbott, R. (1997). Comparison of teaching single or multiple orthographic-phonological connections for word recognition and spelling: Implications for school psychology consultation. *School Psychology Review, 26,* 279–297.

Henry, M. (1989). Children's word structure knowledge: Implications for decoding and spelling instruction. *Reading and Writing: An Interdisciplinary Journal, 1,* 135–152.

Henry, M. (1994). Integrating decoding and spelling instruction for the disabled reader. *Reading & Writing Quarterly: Overcoming Learning Difficulties, 10,* 143–158.

Levy, B., Abello, B., & Lysynchuk, L. (1997). Transfer from word training to reading in context: Gains in reading fluency and comprehension. *Learning Disability Quarterly, 20,* 173–188.

Lovett, M. (1987). A developmental approach to reading disability: Accuracy and speed criteria of normal and deficient reading skill. *Child Development, 58,* 234–260.

Lyon, G. R. (1986). Learning disabilities. The future of children. *Center for the Future of Children. The David and Lucille Packard Foundation, 6*(1), 54–76.

Lyon, G. R. (1995). Toward a definition of dyslexia. *Annals of Dyslexia, 35,* 3–27.

McBride-Chang, C. (1995). What is phonological awareness? *Journal of Educational Psychology, 87,* 179–192.

Moats, L. (1994). The missing foundation in teacher education: Knowledge of the structure of spoken and written language. *Annals of Dyslexia, 44,* 81–104.

Moats, L., & Lyon, R. (in press). Wanted: Teachers with knowledge of language. *Topics in Language Disorders.*

Nolen, P., McCutchen, D., & Berninger, V. (1990). Ensuring tomorrow's literacy: A shared responsibility. *Journal of Teacher Education, 41,* 63–72.

Perfetti, C. (1992). The representation problem in reading acquisition. In P. Gough, L. Ehri, & R. Treiman (Eds.), *Reading acquisition* (pp. 145–174). Hillsdale, NJ: Erlbaum.

Pressley, M., & Wharton-McDonald, R. (in press). Skilled comprehension and its development through instruction. *School Psychology Review, 26,* 448–466.

Shaywitz, B., Holford, T., Holahan, J., Fletcher, J., Stuebing, K., Francis, D., & Shaywitz, S. (1995). A Matthew effect for IQ but not for reading: Results from a longitudinal study. *Reading Research Quarterly, 30,* 894–906.

Shaywitz, S., Shaywitz, B., Fletcher, J., & Escobar, M. (1990). Prevalence of reading disability in boys and girls: Results of the Connecticut longitudinal study. *Journal of the American Medical Association, 264,* 998–1002.

Siegel, L. (1989). IQ is irrelevant to the definition of learning disabilities. *Journal of Learning Disabilities, 22,* 469–486.

Swanson, H. L., & Alexander, J. (in press). Cognitive processes as predictors of word recognition and reading comprehension in learning-disabled and skilled readers: Revisiting the specificity hypothesis. *Journal of Educational Psychology.*

Torgesen, J., & Davis, C. (1996). Individual difference variables that predict response to training in phonological awareness. *Journal of Experimental Child Psychology, 63,* 1–21.

Torgesen, J., & Hecht, S. (1996). Preventing and remediating reading disabilities: Instructional variables that make a difference for special students. In M. Graves, B. Taylor, & P. van den Broek (Eds.), *The first R: A right of all children* (pp. 133–159). Cambridge, MA: MIT Press.

Vandervelden, M., & Siegel, L. (1995). Phonological recoding and phoneme awareness in early literacy: A developmental approach. *Reading Research Quarterly, 30,* 854–875.

Van Orden, G., Pennington, B., & Stone, G. (1990). Word definition in reading and the promise of subsymbolics. *Psychological Review, 97,* 1–35.

Vellutino, F., Scanlon, D., Sipay, E., Small, S., Pratt, A., Chen, R., & Denckla, M. (1996). Cognitive profiles of difficult-to-remediate and readily remediated poor readers: Early intervention as a vehicle for distinguishing between cognitive and experiential deficits as basic causes of specific reading disability. *Journal of Educational Psychology, 88,* 601–638.

Venezky, R. (1995). From orthography to psychology of reading. In V. W. Berninger (Ed.), *The varieties of orthographic knowledge II: Relationships to phonology, reading, and writing* (pp. 23–46). Dordrecht, The Netherlands: Kluwer Academic.

Wise, B., Ring, J., Sessions, L., & Olson, R. (1997). Phonological awareness with and without articulation: A preliminary study. *Learning Disabilities Quarterly, 20,* 211–226.

Wolf, M. (1986). Rapid alternating stimulus naming in the developmental dyslexias. *Brain and Language, 27,* 360–379.

Wolf, M., Bally, H., & Morris, R. (1986). Automaticity, retrieval processes, and reading: A longitudinal investigation. *Child Development, 57,* 98–1000.

Yates, C., Berninger, V., & Abbott, R. (1994). Writing problems in intellectually gifted children. *Journal for the Education of the Gifted, 18,* 131–155.

CHAPTER 17

Adolescents with Learning Disabilities

Martha J. Larkin and Edwin S. Ellis

I. INTRODUCTION

The ultimate goal of working with adolescents with learning disabilities (LD) is to ensure they become self-reliant, confident, competent, well-adjusted adults who are generally happy and productive citizens. The process of attaining such a quality of life is often a considerable journey, both for the individual with the LD and for those who are attempting to facilitate this success. For the individual with the LD, the journey began long before the onset of adolescence, and these individuals tend to change a great deal as they travel the path from early childhood to adolescence and eventually to adulthood. Since the condition is usually chronic, most young children with LD eventually become adults with LD. Having LD, however, does not preclude attaining self-reliance though it can certainly make the journey arduous.

To facilitate this journey, critical to understand are the characteristics of self-reliance. Since the best indicators of these are revealed in studies of successful adults with LD, this will be one of the first areas examined in this chapter. Second, it is important to fully understand the personal characteristics of LD that impede or facilitate the journey to self-reliance. Thus, the cognitive, motivational, academic, and social characteristics of adolescents with LD will be examined relative to the goal of attaining self-reliance.

II. WHAT SUCCESSFUL ADULTS WITH LEARNING DISABILITIES REVEAL ABOUT WHAT WE SHOULD TEACH ADOLESCENTS WITH LEARNING DISABILITIES

Many adults with LD are very successful and productive members of society, and examination of their characteristics may provide substantial guidance for what we should be doing to prepare adolescents with LD to attain similar success (Reiff, Ginsberg, & Gerber, 1995). Polloway, Schewel, and Patton (1992) noted that there is much to be learned from individuals "who have grown up learning to come to grips with a disability."

Research is beginning to focus upon highly successful adults with LD with particular emphasis on the characteristics that have helped them to be successful (see Gerber, Ginsberg, & Reiff, 1992; Kershner, Kirkpatrick, & McLaren, 1995; Reiff, Gerber, Ginsberg, 1996; Spekman, Goldberg, & Herman, 1992). For example, Gerber et al. (1992) interviewed 46 highly successful and 25 moderately successful adults with LD in the United States and Canada to determine how vocational success was achieved. Success, a subjective construct, was defined with regard to five variables: (a) income level, (b) job classification, (c) education level, (d) prominence in one's field, and (e) job satisfaction. Results of the study revealed a set of distinct themes that were not necessarily mutually exclusive. All of the themes transcended both the highly successful and the moderately successful adults with LD. The differences between the two groups seemed to be in the degree or level of attainment. Predictably, highly successful adults with LD were more advanced than those in the moderately successful group.

Control was the overriding theme for this sample of highly and moderately successful adults with LD. The study noted that many adults with LD experienced years of failure until they *made conscious decisions to take control of their lives* (i.e., internal decisions) and adapted and shaped themselves to move ahead (i.e., external manifestations). Moderately successful adults with LD did not acquire the level of control as did their highly successful counterparts. Many of *the moderately successful adults wanted control to hide weakness* rather than focus on moving ahead. Also, the moderate group seemed to be less certain of the direction in which they were headed or what they were doing.

The quest for adults with LD to gain control of their lives centers around two sets of themes: (a) internal decisions such as a desire to succeed, being goal-oriented (Spekman et al., 1992), and internally reframing LD into a more positive or productive experience (see Gerber, Reiff, & Ginsberg, 1996; Spekman et al., 1992; Vogel & Adelman, 1992); and (b) external manifestations or adaptability that included individual persistence (see Corcoran, 1994; Spekman et al., 1992), a set of coping mechanisms (Druck, 1994; Kershner et al., 1995; Polloway et al., 1992) or learned creativity (Lee & Jackson, 1992; Wiig, 1994), a goodness of fit between

Table 17.1

Characteristics of Highly Successful Adults with Learning Disabilities[a]

Internal decisions
1. Have the desire to excel in order to excel.
   - Desiring to excel comes early in life for some and for others develops over time.
   - The desire to excel is very conspicuous and powerful.
2. Consciously set explicit goals for themselves.
   - Setting explicit goals allows for realistic, achievable aspirations.
   - Setting explicit goals provides sharper focus for those who have experienced difficulty in learning and common activities.
   - Success from achieving minimal goals can be the basis for more challenging future goals.
   - Moderately successful adults set more short-term goals and seem to be more easily diverted from their goals than do the highly successful.
3. Reframe or reinterpret the LD experience in a more positive or productive manner.
   - Four stages in this process include (a) recognize the disability, (b) accept the disability, (c) understand the disability by accepting weaknesses and building on strengths, and (d) take specific action towards one's goals.
   - Moderately successful adults have more trouble with and may avoid complete acceptance. They may not have as complete understanding and may not take decisive action like their highly successful counterparts.

External manifestations—Adaptability
1. Persistence or working hard is a way of life.
   - Highly successful adults are driven, take more risks, and appear more resilient.
2. Try to fit to environments in which their skill and abilities can be optimized.
   - Highly successful adults with LD display a passion for their work.
   - They often select work where they have the flexibility to control their own destiny and make decisions regarding their work.
3. Display learned creativity (i.e., strategies, techniques, and mechanisms) to enhance their ability to perform.
   - Highly successful adults with LD take advantage of their strengths to excel creatively rather than just cope.
   - They are protective, especially during the formative years (e.g., use spell checkers, word processors, tape recorders, etc., for reading and writing problems).
4. Surround themselves with supportive and helpful people and upgrade skills by designing personal improvement programs.
   - Highly successful adults with LD create support networks of family, friends, spouse, and consciously select mentors.
   - Moderately successful adults may rely totally on others, whereas highly successful do not.

[a]Adapted from Gerber, Ginsberg, and Reiff (1992)

one's abilities and the environment, and a pattern of personal support (Minskoff, 1994; Polloway et al., 1992; Spekman et al., 1992; Wambsgans, 1990; Werner, 1993) and planned experiences to promote success. See Table 17.1 for a brief summary of these themes.

Examining some of the internal decisions and external manifestations of the highly successful adults with LD in the study can provide some insight for educators who have a significant role to play in ensuring that all students, including those with LD, are prepared for their places in society. Success for adults with LD is an evolutionary process that spans many years and commences with a conscious set of decisions (Gerber et al., 1992). In the beginning, decisions may regard personal matters and later involve the pursuit of career excellence.

One must keep in mind that the Gerber et al., 1992 study is only one in a new but promising line of research. Although findings point to commonalties among highly successful adults with LD, there is no guarantee that possessing all of these characteristics ultimately will result in success. Also notable is that success is not an absolute state. Individuals may achieve degrees of success that differ across areas (e.g., employment, social relationships, etc.), may be affected by a variety of internal factors and external events, or may change within time (Spekman et al., 1992).

Nonetheless, though not a prescription for success, the findings provide an important guide and clarify key goals educators should strive for when teaching adolescents with LD if these youth are eventually to share the same characteristics as their highly successful adult counterparts. In short, teachers should strive to ensure their students do the following:

1. Have a desire to excel and thus are willing to take risks, continue learning, and display persistence when the going gets tough.
2. Set goals and use effective and efficient strategies to attain these goals.
3. Fully understand themselves (e.g., their own academic, cognitive, social, motivational, and psychological strengths and weaknesses) so that they are able fit themselves into environments that offer both challenge and stimulation, but also the possibility of significant success.
4. Understand their LD and reframe it into something unique and positive about themselves.
5. Know how to seek out and recruit resources so that they have supportive and helpful people at hand when needed.

As would be expected, the ideal characteristics of successful adults with LD versus those who are still adolescents are often very different. To provide effective interventions for adolescents with LD, it is important to understand who they are and the environments in which they must function, while at the same time, keeping in mind the long-term goals for self-reliance. The following section will summarize what research has shown about the interactions of secondary setting expectations and the characteristics of adolescents with LD in the following areas: academic, social, motivation, and cognition.

III. SECONDARY SCHOOL SETTING EXPECTATIONS AND HOW THEY INTERACT WITH THE CHARACTERISTICS OF ADOLESCENTS WITH LEARNING DISABILITIES

In considering the issues of becoming an adolescent, most people typically think of the changes brought on by hormones, emotional upheaval, and psychosocial development issues. Adolescents' bodies are changing, as well as their family structures and social climate. In addition, young adolescents face a whole new scenario regarding the expectations of school and nonschool environments (Schumaker & Deshler, 1988). In elementary school, the primary emphasis is on instruction in basic skills (e.g., reading, writing, mathematics, etc.) in relatively protective environments. In secondary schools, however, teachers assume that most students have mastered basic skills, so instruction in content subject matter (e.g., science, social studies, literature, etc.) becomes the primary focus (Deshler, Ellis & Lenz, 1996; Robinson, Braxdale, & Colson, 1985), and students are expected to use their basic skills to master the content subject matter. Moreover, in the short time of a summer vacation, students move from being treated as children who require management and structure to expectations of behaving as independent young adults who effectively use self-management skills. Many students who have traditionally received the bulk of their educational experiences in self-contained settings must suddenly adjust to meting the expectations of multiple settings.

"Setting expectations" encompass the set of expectations students must meet in order to experience success in a given setting. Clearly, adolescents with LD must face many setting expectations as well as the many concomitant task demands within each. Most setting expectations in both school and nonschool environments can be categorized into four areas: (a) academic expectations, (b) social expectations, (c) motivational expectations, and (d) cognitive expectations (Lenz, Clark, Deshler, & Schumaker, 1989). An explanation of each of these areas is presented below followed by related research findings on the characteristics of adolescents with LD.

A. Academic Expectations

Because most secondary students have different teachers, textbooks, and so on for different subjects, each course they take presents unique setting expectations. Effective presentation of new information in textbooks or lectures organizes it in a way to help the learner understand and assimilate the information quickly. Cues such as whether the information is theoretical or factual and its text structure (e.g., compare-contrast, problem-solution) also may be provided (Anderson & Arm-

Table 17.2
Academic Expectations in Secondary Schools

1. Reading: students must independently gain information from textbooks.
   - Textbook content is the single largest determinant of the curriculum in a course (Clark & Peterson, 1986). As much as 44% of the information that students are expected to learn is found in textbooks (Zigmond, Levin, & Laurie, 1985) but not in class lectures.
   - The readability of many textbooks may exceed the grade level for which they are intended (Schumaker & Deshler, 1984). The manner in which texts are written are "inconsiderate" because the organization and flow of ideas is poor (Armbruster & Anderson, 1988). They also reported that textbooks too often lack features conducive to learning such as introductory statements, adjunct questions, objectives, advance organizers, summaries, pointer words (e.g., first, second, third) and textual highlighting (e.g., italicized words, boldfaced print). Most texts are illogical and present information in a list-like format that fails to convey relationships, has sudden transitions between topics, and the sequence of text information does not correspond with actual chronological occurrence (Armbruster & Anderson, 1988).
2. Listening and note-taking expectations: Students must independently gain information from lectures.
   - Students are responsible for gaining and quickly processing a significant amount of information from lectures. Seventh graders were expected to process information as quickly as high school seniors during fast-paced lectures (Moran, 1980). Moran noted: (a) teachers used few advance organizers to facilitate activation of prior knowledge, aid student listening, or make note taking more effective; (b) students infrequently were asked to paraphrase or demonstrate their understanding of information presented in lectures; and (c) teachers failed to provide students with feedback and reinforcement.
3. Writing: not a common expectation in secondary school settings, but is likely to change because of school reform movements and competency testing.
   - Teachers reported short-answer responses (e.g., fill in the blank, spell a word) were the most important writing demands, followed by note taking from lectures (Moran, 1980). Essay writing was not a significant requirement. The highest grades were given to students who wrote long and complete sentences with correct spelling (Moran & Deloche, 1982). With schools' increasing participation in reform movements, writing is likely to be a greater demand for secondary students.
4. Test taking: usually traditional paper/pencil tests requiring recall of facts and lists.
   - The traditional paper/pencil test still dominates evaluation of student learning (Putnam, 1992b). Many of the class test questions require list memorization (See Nagel, Schumaker, & Deshler, 1986) and recall of specific items of information in a rote fashion (Putnam, 1992a). The reading level of test questions is not always consistent with the grade level of the students (e.g., test questions were written at the 8.9 grade level for both 7th and 10th graders) (Putnam, 1992a).
5. Students must have a set of basic academic skills and use these skills systematically in problem-solving situations.
   - Many secondary school settings provide two types of classes: content area and skill-based classes (e.g., language arts). Often students are expected to infer relationships from skills learned in one class to the content area of another class. For example, few attempts may be made at teaching paragraph writing in conjunction with social studies or science content. Students are expected to make effective decisions when and how to use skills learned in different contexts and situations.

Continued

Table 17.2

Continued

6. Students must use effective and efficient learning and performance strategies.
   - Secondary school students must not only possess skills but organize the skills into problem-solving strategies. For example, a student may be knowledgeable about prefixes, suffixes, and content analysis but must also apply this knowledge to decipher words.
7. Students must possess sufficient content-area knowledge to readily learn new content information.
   - Content-area teachers expect students to have a working knowledge of basic concepts and vocabulary of the subject matter when entering class. For example, students in a ninth-grade health science class are expected to possess some general knowledge of basic science. As new information is presented, students will be able to understand and remember it more readily if they can relate it to an existing framework of information.
8. Students must take advantage of learning enhancers provided by the environment.
   - Effective teachers employ learning enhancers to help students understand and remember new information, such as advance organizers to facilitate motivation, help students activate prior knowledge, and help them to understand what they are expected to learn. Other learning enhancers like graphic organizers, study guides, and mnemonic devices assist students in understanding the material. In addition, teachers can make sure that effectively written textbooks (i.e., those that provide advance organizers, statements of goals, meaningful headings, as well as meaningful and clarifying graphics) are selected. Due to the breadth of information to which students are exposed, they must take full advantage of enhancers provided by teachers and instructional materials in order to focus their attention on and understand the most relevant information.

bruster, 1984). In school, new information that students are expected to master is not always presented in a manner conducive to effective information processing. Additional difficulties arise for some students when they are demanded to process new information effectively and efficiently. Table 17.2 summarizes academic expectations for secondary students.

Similar academic expectations are found in non-school environments. For example, employees are often expected to gain information independently from procedure manuals (e.g., manufacturer's instructions for replacing faulty engine valves), learn difficult concepts (understanding the role of valves in an internal combustion engine), as well as demonstrate competency (adjust valves in an efficient and effective manner so that the engine runs smoothly and complete written reports so that the owner can be billed appropriately).

Academic expectations for secondary students are great and may differ substantially from expectations found in elementary school. As students make the transition from elementary settings to secondary settings and from secondary settings to the workplace, they are expected to possess the maturity and characteristics to be successful. Unfortunately, this appears to be a difficult, if not impossible task for many adolescents with LD. Examining the academic characteristics of adolescents with LD will provide insight into the academic difficulties they experience in secondary school.

Table 17.3

Academic Characteristics of Adolescents with Learning Disabilities

1. Lack the basic academic skills necessary to meet academic demands.
   - Basic skills are considerably behind those of normal-achieving peers and do not change during secondary school. May reach an "academic plateau" (e.g., average reading level of 3rd–5th grade) (Bender, 1995; Warner, Alley, Deshler, & Schumaker, 1980).
   - Most states now require high school students to pass minimum competency tests (MCT's) before they can graduate with a diploma (Lerner, 1993). Some students with LD may be able to pass the MCT exams when provided intensive instruction on specific competencies, but they may not graduate with the skills to truly be literate (e.g., dynamic and strategic problem solving) (Ellis, 1996).
2. Possess knowledge of a variety of basic skills but fail to use them systematically in problem-solving situations.
   - No significant differences were found between 10th-grade normal-achieving students and students with LD on knowledge of decoding skills, yet normal-achieving students tended to apply what they knew about decoding to meet the reading expectations while those classified with LD did not (Warner et al., 1980).
   - Students with LD who knew basic conventions of print (e.g., rules of capitalization, punctuation, etc.) often failed to apply them when writing (Schumaker, Hazel, Sherman, & Sheldon, 1982).
   - May fail to generalize skills because they have not been taught to do so (Roehler & Duffy, 1984). Some teachers emphasize specific skills (e.g., prefixes and suffixes) and school compliance behaviors (e.g., correct responses on prefix and suffix worksheets), but do not emphasize how to use these skills in problem-solving contexts (e.g., how to use knowledge of prefixes and suffixes to decode words when reading).
3. Are not likely to use effective or efficient learning/performance strategies.
   - Some do not use effective or efficient strategies because they do not know about them (cf. Westberry, 1994). Others know and can perform these strategies, but fail to do so at opportune times (Ellis, 1989; Lenz, Clark, Deshler, & Schumaker, 1989). May fail to use the strategies because they did not analyze a problem-solving situation and reflect on the best approach for the task. In some situations, students may perceive the benefits of using the strategy as not worth the effort required (Wong, 1985b).
   - Use cognitive avoidance more frequently than nondisabled peers with regard to academic problems (Geisthardt & Munsch, 1996).
   - Are often bright and inventive persons who spend their school years learning the art of conning to avoid facing their problems instead of learning academics (see Lee & Jackson, 1992).
4. Are not likely to have sufficient knowledge in order to learn the level of new content information presented in secondary schools.
   - Do not possess enough of the prerequisite knowledge of the subject matter to readily learn by association (Wong, 1985a). Adolescents with LD had significantly less background knowledge of social studies content than normal achieving adolescents (Lenz & Alley, 1983). An interdependence exists between ability to employ effective study/performance strategies and the knowledge base upon which the strategy is to be employed (Chi, 1981; Ellis & Lenz, 1990; Voss, 1982; Wong, 1985a).
   - Are denied opportunities to acquire semantic knowledge. Many students with LD attend special education classes in elementary school during times when their normal-achieving peers are receiving content instruction (e.g., social studies, science) (Ellis & Lenz, 1990).
5. Frequently fail to take advantage of learning enhancers in the environment.
   - For example, to make difficult concepts more understandable, analogies between new concepts and familiar ones (e.g., comparing a camera to the human eye when teaching how the eye works) are often made (Schumaker, Deshler, McKnight, 1989). Many students do not necessarily benefit from such enhancers because they might not attend to them, recognize their value in facilitating the learning process, know how to use them to make learning easier. (Lenz, Alley, & Schumaker, 1987) or may not have been taught to recognize or take advantage of them (Ellis & Lenz, 1990).

B. Academic Characteristics of Adolescents with LD

Typically, persons with LD were not often identified as such until mid to late in elementary school after a history of academic failure prior to entrance in high school (Zigmond & Thornton, 1988). These students begin high school with substantially deficient basic skills, continue to have low levels of achievement in reading and math throughout high school, and tend to display poor performance in other content areas, too. Grades of adolescents with LD suggest that these students have considerable difficulty in content-area subjects such as social studies, health, and science (Donahoe & Zigmond, 1990). Overall, students with LD have difficulty completing secondary school or its equivalent (Mellard & Hazel, 1992). Table 17.3 summarizes conclusions that can be drawn from the literature with regard to characteristics of adolescents with LD in relation to meeting academic expectations in school.

Adolescents with LD often experience similar problems in non-school settings. For example, fast-food employers typically require persons who take orders and run the cash register to quickly and accurately both read the labels of food products and count change. The youth with LD may not possess some of the academic skills, or fluency in using these skills, necessary to complete the tasks quickly. As a result, the employee with LD may be less likely to be given opportunities to develop these skills with a degree of fluency, and thus are more likely to be regulated to the "flip'n and wrap'n job" (cooking hamburgers and wraping them) that requires no academic skills to be successful. In sum, many adolescents with LD are not effectively meeting the academic expectations of their environments. Many of the reasons for these difficulties are also applicable to understanding the difficulties they experience in the social domain.

C. Social Expectations

Like academic expectations, the social expectations adolescents must meet will vary among settings, and social demands are present in both school and non-school settings. Expectations focus primarily on demonstrating effective and efficient social behaviors at appropriate times. These demands can be grouped into three main areas (Hazel, Schumaker, Sherman, & Sheldon-Wildgen, 1981). The first area, conversation and friendship, concerns expectations related to day-to-day interactions with peers and adults. Expected behaviors include use of active listening, greeting others, saying good-bye, initiating conversations, interrupting of others, asking questions, etc.). The second area of social demand focuses on expectations related to getting along with others. Expected behaviors include accepting/saying thanks, giving/receiving compliments, giving/receiving criticism, apologizing, and so on. The third area of social demands concerns problem solving. Expectations include appropriate use of social behaviors related to following instructions,

Table 17.4
Social Expectations in Secondary Schools

1. Display respect for authority; follow classroom rules.
   - Students are expected to respect the teacher as an authority figure and to do what is asked of them by the teacher without questioning. They may be reluctant to act favorably toward a teacher who "demands" rather than "commands" respect. Adolescents who perceive that rules are imposed on them may be less likely to comply than adolescents who have been given the opportunity to offer input for the establishment and maintenance of classroom rules.
2. Accept criticism and assistance; recruit assistance as needed.
   - Students are expected to recruit assistance when needed. Kowalchuk and Nostbakken (1990) found that both adolescents with LD and their normal-achieving classmates sought help instrumentally more often from their peers than from the teacher.
3. Work collaboratively as a team member.
   - Cooperative learning techniques and dialectal or interactive instructional techniques (e.g. Bos & Anders, 1990; Ellis, 1993a) will become common as schools participate in educational reform movements.
4. Participate in group social activities and in discussions and conversations with peers and adults.
   - Some adolescents consider being friendly with teachers or appearing too knowledgeable in class as undesirable (i.e., "uncool," "geekish," "nerdish," etc.). Adolescents have to learn to maintain a balance between the often different social expectations of teachers and peers in order to succeed socially. Students may find confusing situations where they are expected to act differently interacting with teachers than when interacting with adults in non-school environments (e.g., on the job when interacting with the supervisor). To further complicate the situation, providing a warm, friendly greeting to one teacher may be welcomed and reinforced, whereas the same behavior might be punished by another teacher's interpretation of the behavior (i.e., "He's doing that to 'brown-nose' the teacher.").
5. Resist inappropriate peer pressure.
   - Some adolescents in an effort to be accepted by their peers and feel important will succumb to peer pressure (e.g., dress, hairstyles, language, interests, etc.) Sometimes the peer pressure is so great, adolescents lose sight of their better judgment and give in to cheating, stealing, lying, doing drugs, drinking, or having sex even if they ordinarily do not approve of such behaviors. Secondary school expectations of resisting peer pressure are very difficult for some students.
6. Generally maintain a pleasant social manner across situations.
   - The word change best describes the adolescent period of changing bodies and emotions as well as academic and social settings. More is expected of adolescents at the secondary level; yet, at the same time, adolescents are expected to maintain composure and display a pleasant demeanor in a variety of situations. This certainly is not an easy task for some students.
7. Actively participate in class discussions.
   - Currently in secondary schools, the lecture-type presentation is the most frequent instructional method used. As students progress through secondary school, Schumaker, Sheldon-Wildgen, and Sherman (1980) found that discussions occurred less frequently.
   - Active class participation is an important factor for students' learning (Riveria & Smith, 1997) and success. Such participation can result in an increased rate of academic-related responses (cf. Brophy, 1979; Brophy & Good, 1985; Stevens & Rosenshine, 1981), practice in verbal expression (Oliver, 1958), and development of critical thinking skills (Monteau, 1961). Verbal elaboration of new information can be an effective information processing strategy, too. (cf. Pressley, Johnson, & Symons, 1987).
   - Ellis (1989) concluded that teachers are likely to respond positively (e.g., eye contact, smile, cue students to elaborate, give feedback, and provide additional text structure clues). Active participation clearly helps students to meet school expectations.

getting/giving help, asking for feedback, giving rationales, solving problems, persuading others, negotiating, joining group activities, starting activities, and so on. Table 17.4 summarizes the literature on social-setting expectations of secondary schools.

These areas of social expectations are prevalent in non-school as well as school environments. For example, Mathews, Whang, and Fawcett (1980) found that several social-interactional skills were validated as highly important for attaining and maintaining employment. These included both listening and oral language social skills (e.g., accepting suggestions and criticism from an employer, telephoning to request an interview, interviewing, explaining a problem to an employer, complimenting others, etc.). The social behaviors used to meet an expectation will differ, depending on the characteristics of the setting. For example, to meet a setting expectation associated with accepting criticism, a student might use an entirely different set of social behaviors when receiving criticism from a teacher than when receiving it from a peer or a supervisor on a job. To meet social expectations, students must not only know how to perform key social skills, they must make effective decisions concerning when and where to use them. Examining the social characteristics of adolescents with LD will aid in understanding why social expectations can be problematic for these students.

D. Social Characteristics of Adolescents with LD

Much of the research on social characteristics of LD has focused on children with LD with a limited amount of research examining social dimensions in adolescents with LD. The research indicates the adolescents with LD often experience many problems in social functioning (cf. Schumaker, 1992; Swanson & Malone, 1992). Table 17.5 provides a summary of the literature on social characteristics of adolescents with LD.

In sum, students with LD often fail to meet the social expectations of school. These problems may be due to skill or strategy deficits, or they may be a function of personal needs and motivation.

E. Motivational Expectations

Like academic and social setting demands, motivational expectations and students' abilities to meet these expectations are influenced by the variables within the environment. An important dimension to motivation concerns students' beliefs about the probability of future success in attaining goals. Students' perceptions of probability of attaining short-term goals can be affected by environments created by teachers. For example, many teachers create competitive situations (e.g., academic contests, grading on a curve, challenging students to "see who can have the highest grade," etc.) in their classrooms in an attempt to motivate students to put

Table 17.5
Social Characteristics of Adolescents with Learning Disabilities

1. May lack the basic social *skills.*
   - For example, adolescents may not know how to look at someone in a pleasant manner when having a conversation; do not know how to maintain voice control in tense situations, etc. necessary to meet social expectations.
   - Many possess a knowledge of a variety of basic social skills, but fail to incorporate them into social strategies for use in specific situations. For example, students may know how to give appropriate eye contact, maintain voice control, maintain a relaxed posture, etc., but not know how to systematically integrate these and other important social skills into a social skill strategy for asking adults for permission to do something.
   - They may have a limited repertoire of social skills that are appropriate for some situations, but they may generalize the skills as being appropriate to all situations (see Cordoni, 1987). For example, patting a child on the head affectionately might be appropriate, but this would not be a suitable way for an adolescent male to greet his date.
   - Many may have knowledge of effective and efficient social skills strategies, but fail to generalize them for a variety of possible reasons: (a) may not recognize opportunities for social skill use, (b) may not recognize the advantages of using specific social strategies, and (c) may poorly monitor the degree to which specific social strategies should be used.
   - Some students may display inappropriate social behaviors to communicate what they believe to be important messages (e.g., an adolescent interacting with her parent might communicate, "I am more powerful than you. You can't *make* me behave the way you want. Therefore, I choose to behave in a manner in which you don't approve." etc.).
2. Are likely to misinterpret social situations involving nonverbal communication.
   - Adolescents with LD may have difficulty with nonverbal cues (e.g., smiles, frowns, eye contact, body posture) to form accurate inferences about others' feelings or interpret the cues that signal conversational events (e.g., desire for clarification, desire to end the conversation) (see Axelrod, 1982).
3. May have poorly developed understandings of the culture's moral principles.
   - Understanding of social morals becomes more sophisticated as students mature. Derr (1986) found that that moral judgement of 14–18-year-old adolescents with LD was commensurate with moral judgment levels of 10–14-year-old youth without LD.
4. Are apt to be poor social problems solvers.
   - They are less likely to display key problem-solving behaviors (e.g., clarifying problems, identifying alternative solutions, prioritizing possible solutions) than peers without LD (Pearl, Bryan, & Herzod, 1990). Some may be poor problem solvers because they do not know and/or do not use effective social strategies.
   - Some adolescents, in an effort to strive for independence, may choose to take credit for solving a problem, when in actuality they have relied on assistance (McLoughlin, Clark, Mauck, & Petrosko, 1987).
5. Participate in social activities less than their peers
   - Many are less socially active in school than their normally achieving counter-parts. For example, Deshler, Alley, Warner, and Schumaker (1981) found that they participate in less extracurricular activities (e.g., school clubs, choir, band, sports), and they are less likely to be invited to join groups.
   - Schumaker, Hazel, Sherman, and Sheldon (1982) found that many students with LD scored

continued

Table 17.5

Continued

about the same as adjudicated delinquents in a study that required students to role-play what they would do and say given various social scenarios (e.g., when peers are attempting to persuade the students to shoplift; when the student is asking a parent permission to use the car, etc.). Although some youth with LD participate in delinquent acts and subsequently become involved with the judicial system, little evidence supports a *causal* relationship between LD and juvenile delinquency.

• Schumaker, Warner, Deshler, and Alley (1980) reported that students with LD "hang around with friends" less often and participate in after-school activities less than their normally achieving counterparts. Adolescents with LD tend to participate in recreational and social activities as well as belong to community clubs and groups significantly less often than their normally achieving peers (White, Schumaker, Warner, Alley, & Deshler, 1980). Adolescents with LD report that they spend significantly more of their free time watching television (Vetter et al., 1983).

6. Are likely to have inappropriate stimulus control.

• Inappropriate stimulus control means that it may be more reinforcing to act in a socially incompetent manner than to act competently (Keer & Nelson, 1989). Ellis (1989) noted that some adolescents with LD appear to avoid participating in class in order to avoid the risk of being humiliated for giving an inept answer.

7. Tend not to actively participate in class.

• Ellis (1989) noted that class participation is particularly important for students with LD because the teacher's lectures and class discussions are two important sources for attaining new information. Many students with LD (a) fail to take advantage of these learning opportunities, (b), do not *look* like they are interested in the subject matter (As a result, educators tend to focus less instruction at apparently disinterested students.), and (c) do not frequently participate *verbally* in class, which gives opportunities to make associations between new and existing knowledge, personalize the new information, and check for comprehension.

8. Are not likely to draw upon support services when given the choice.

• Less than half of the students identified as LD self-reported this information when applying for college (Wilczenski & Gillespie-Silver, 1990). Although reasons for this have not been explored empirically, one may speculate that the students with LD did not want to be characterized as "disabled" and attempted to be successful on their own.

---

forth greater effort. Some studies examining the effects of using competition in the classroom suggest that competitive activities may effectively motivate those students who feel they have a high probability of winning the competition (e.g., the two or three brightest students in the classroom), but these procedures may have a reverse effect on those students who feel they have little chance of winning (see Ellis, 1986). Moreover, results of competitions tend to positively highlight the winners but negatively highlight the losers as well.

Beliefs about probability of future success also might affect students' willingness to make commitments to attain long-term goals. For example, students' perceptions of the relative probability of attaining a high school diploma can have a marked impact on their willingness to stay in school. Variables within students'

Table 17.6
Motivational Expectations In Secondary Schools

1. Expect students to independently expend effort needed for success.
   - To perform successfully, students must not only desire to succeed and put forth effort, but they must often do so independently. Motivation must be continuous and intrinsic. Students must know themselves as learners and realize that they are responsible for their own learning. (McCombs, 1984). Students must plan for timely task completions, complete assignments without reminders, and, when needed, request assistance (Schumaker, Deshler, Alley & Warner, 1983). They must demonstrate a proactive approach to life by setting short, intermediate, and long-term goals, and reinforcing themselves for attaining these goals.
2. Often value evidence of effort more than actual performance.
   - Ellis (1993c) suggested that, in many cases, teacher's value students' behaviors that reflect effort and motivation as much as they value students' learning outcomes. For example, adolescents who attempted to answer essay test questions using complete sentences written in a paragraph-like format often receive partial to full credit for their answers even when the content of their answers was not accurate (Ellis, 1993c). Similar results were found in nonschool settings. Crain (1984) reported that employers are often more concerned with motivation factors related to dependability, persistence, and proper attitudes than they are with grades and advanced basic skills of their employees.
3. Expect students to work independently and have independent work habits.
   - Working independently with little feedback is an expectation closely related to motivation. Salend and Salend (1986) identified 29 behaviors subgrouped into three areas essential for success in mainstream secondary classes: (a) appropriate work habits, (b) respecting others and their property, and (c) following school rules. Independent work habits (e.g., bringing materials to class, completing assignments and homework, budgeting time, requesting help) in addition to basic socialization, communication and study skills are essential for students' success in mainstream secondary settings (see Rivera & Smith, 1997). Ellett (1993) surveyed secondary school teachers to determine their perceptions of skills considered necessary for success in mainstreamed regular education classrooms. The four skills with the highest ratings were (a) follows directions in class, (b) comes to class prepared with materials, (c) uses class time wisely, and (d) makes up assignments and tests.
4. Expect students to independently create and execute effective and efficient work plans without assistance.
   - Some students in high schools need more guidance than others in independently planning and executing work plans. They may not have been shown how to set up an effective and efficient work plan. While they were in elementary school teachers and parents may have been creating work plans for them without showing the students how to assume responsibility for their own plans.

---

environments (e.g., requirements to pass standardized competency tests to receive high school diplomas; school officials requiring students to repeat a grade; difficulty of courses required for graduation, etc.) naturally have great influences on students' perceptions of probability for future success in attaining the long-term goal of graduating from school.

The perceptions of value that adolescents attribute to activities in which they are expected to participate naturally affects the degree to which they meet motivational expectations. In other words, if adolescents do not value factors such as the subject matter in which they are expected to learn, the assignments and instructional techniques employed by the teacher, the specific job responsibilities they are expected to perform, the feedback others provide, and so on, then motivation is affected. In an era when adolescents are saturated by media messages related to attaining immediate, salient stimulation (e.g., rock-video) and gratification (e.g., high frequency of commercials with the basic message of *"get it now or you'll miss out"*), and the desirability of being self-centered (e.g., *"I* want *my* M-TV"), school is a relatively boring environment and the curriculum often has little relevancy. Table 17.6 summarizes conclusions from the literature about motivational expectations of secondary school settings.

Independence seems to be the key word describing the motivational expectations of secondary school settings. By the time adolescents reach high school, they are expected to know how to work independently and have the intrinsic motivation to desire to work independently. Similar expectations may occur in the workplace. Unfortunately for many adolescents with LD, they do not have the necessary skills. The accumulation of failure experiences compounded with a "boring school or work environment" do not motivate these youth to set goals of acquiring the necessary skills and to strive for success. An exploration of the motivational characteristics of adolescents with LD may provide some insight into this sad commentary.

F. Motivational Characteristics of Adolescents with LD

Adolescents with LD often have difficulty meeting the motivational expectations of secondary school and non-school environments. The variables affecting motivation are many, complex, and multidimensional. The following, therefore, is merely an overview addressing some of the dimensions of this problem that occur in conjunction with academic and social experiences.

One of the reasons students with LD have difficulty meeting the motivational demands of secondary school concerns their purposes for attending school. For example, Adleman and Taylor (1983) identified several subgroups of students with varying levels of motivation for attending school: (a) students who want "to attend school and learn some, but not all" (p. 385) of what is expected, (b) students who wish to attend school and learn some or most of what is offered, but *do not expect to succeed* and may not value the techniques employed by their teachers, (c) students who are interested in attending school to socialize with peers, or they "have such major fears regarding failure that they avoid all discussion of their problem." (p. 385), and (d) students who are not interested in attending school. Negative attitudes towards subjects such as reading and social studies (cf. MacMillian, Widaman, Balow, Hemsley, & Little, 1992) are often compounded by the cumulative effect of years of frustration and failure (see Bender, 1995). This affects the self-esteem of adolescents with LD and their judgment regarding their competence

Table 17.7

Motivational Characteristics of Adolescents with Learning Disabilities

1. Are likely to experience great stress.
   * Adolescents must deal with the stress of the adolescent period as well as the stress associated with their disability. This results in a person with a lot of stress a great deal of the time (cf. Spekman, Goldberg, & Herman, 1992, Zetlin, 1993).
   * Some researchers may disagree as to whether adolescents with LD experience more stress than their peers. Geisthardt and Munsch (1996) indicated that junior high students with LD did not report experiencing a larger number of stressful school events than did nondisabled adolescents. Further research would need to be conducted as to why these students did not perceive themselves as experiencing more stress than their nondisabled peers.
2. May fail to see the relationship between appropriate effort and success (cf. Bender, 1995; Licht & Kistner, 1986; Werner, 1993; Zigmond & Thornton, 1988). *They are apt to be passive rather than strategic in their approach to academic tasks* (see Bender, 1985; 1987).
   * Countless parents of youth with LD have conveyed stories of the hours spent laboriously working with their children to help them prepare for tests only to find their students with LD subsequently fail the tests in spite of these efforts (cf. Osman, 1979).
   * The consistent academic failure that many students with LD experience results in less motivation to learn and poor self-perceptions. Students think, "I fail because I am dumb." The failures reinforce debilitating beliefs of the students. For example, adolescents often use ineffective and inefficient study strategies for tests. When they fail exams, the students jump to erroneous conclusions that expending effort ("I spent a lot of time studying for this test!") results in little payoff.
3. Are prone to difficulty in making a commitment to learn or perform.
   * The majority of adolescents have several years of experience with special education, and many have little faith in the effectiveness of such services in helping them overcome their difficulties. This may be due partially to the fact that the performance gap between students with LD and normally achieving students is continuously increasing. Although students with LD tend to demonstrate an initial growth spurt in achievement, the rate of achievement quickly and substantially diminishes (Warner et al., 1980). Special education interventions designed to enable students to learn how to learn and perform, therefore, lose credibility. Naturally, students are, thus, less willing to commit energies to something that has little credibility from their perspective. The second set of experiences that may contribute to the unwillingness of adolescents with LD to make commitments to learning and performing may be related, in part, to the nature of special education service that students have received in the past. Instead of viewing special education as a means for learning how to learn or perform to diminish the effects of a LD, many students with LD learn to view it as a means of support to help them "play-the-school-game."
   * In many special education programs, student participation in decisions regarding what they will learn or how they will be taught is rare. Many adolescents with LD have extensive histories working with teachers who have dictated these decisions for students. Historically, commitments have not been sought from students; compliance is often the modus operandi. Thus, while setting expectations often require commitments, students with LD often are not willing to provide them.
   * Students with LD are more likely to be motivated by teachers who make school an inviting place by caring and taking an interest in their learning needs (see Freeman & Hutchinson, 1994).
4. May avoid challenging tasks and give up easily after initial setbacks.
   * Spekman, Goldberg, and Herman (1992) noted that unsuccessful young adults with LD merely

continued

Table 17.7

Continued

responded to events, avoided them, or were passive and quit easily. A common source of motivation for many adolescents is avoiding failure experiences. Many normally achieving students are motivated by thinking positive, "I'm studying hard for the exam, so I can make an A." Adolescents with LD are more likely to think negatively, "I'm studying hard for the exam, so I won't be embarrassed by failing it." Avoiding challenging tasks and giving up easily denies students exposure to new problem-solving strategies and opportunities to modify and adapt known strategies for new tasks. This suggests a negative cycle of the use of ineffective learning strategies and avoiding opportunities to learn new strategies to alleviate failure resulting in failure because the students do not know effective strategies.

- Ellis (1986) found that students with LD experience less stress when they fail under circumstances in which they are in control of the experience (e.g., purposefully not putting forth the effort) than in circumstances in which they are trying to succeed but do not (e.g., using a paragraph writing strategy on an essay exam, but failing the exam anyway).

6. May depend on extrinsic sources of motivation.
   - Rather than intrinsic motivation or that which comes from within (e.g., learning more about a subject because it is interesting), adolescents with LD tend to rely on extrinsic sources (e.g., tokens or points to be "cashed in" for free time or prizes) of motivation (cf. Adelman & Taylor, 1990). Secondary school for many adolescents too often has been unengaging and boring because emphasis is placed on school compliance behaviors (e.g., answering questions at the end of the chapter, memorizing facts for tests, copying notes) rather than on meaningful, authentic instruction. Teachers frequently resort to extrinsic motivation tactics in an effort to motivate students to engage in these uninviting learning experiences.

7. Tend to experience difficulty setting goals or making future plans.
   - In a study of young adults with LD, Spekman, Goldberg, and Herman (1992) found that those in the unsuccessful group had no goals or sense of directions. The unsuccessful youths with LD who talked about goals expressed grandiose or unrealistic plans for their abilities.
   - Golumbia and Hillman (1990) noted that instead of learning goals (i.e., orientation toward developing competence), adolescents with LD think in terms of performance goals (orientation toward documenting competence). These students are not likely to set goals beyond the immediate future (e.g., passing a test, get an assignment completed) and perhaps do not see the relationship of the immediate goals to the big picture of future goals.

8. Are at risk for dropping out of school.
   - Many adolescents with LD do not perceive the benefits of staying in school as outweighing the benefits of dropping out. As a result, the dropout rate among this population has been alarmingly high. The dropout rates of the general population are about 17% (Thompson-Hoffman & Hayward, 1990) and the dropout rates of youth with LD are typically around 50% (Levin, Zigmond, & Birch, 1985; Mellard & Hazel, 1992; Zigmond & Thornton, 1985).
   - Incidences of grade repetition in high school are effective predictors of drop-out (see Zigmond and Thornton, 1985). Students with LD are more often required to repeat grades (35%) than normally achieving students. Absenteeism and grade failure were among the two strongest predictors of dropout of adolescents with LD (Newman, 1991).

in executing plans of action for situations. Table 17.7 summarizes from the literature the motivational dimension of adolescents with LD.

In summary, adolescents with LD often experience trouble meeting the motivational expectations of their environment. Some have misperceptions about the relationship between appropriate effort and success. They are often reluctant to make commitments, and many have not established long-term goals. The fourth area of expectations with which adolescents with LD experience difficulty is cognition.

G. Cognitive Expectations

In the business world, executives are those persons who are responsible for organizing information and resources, making key decisions, solving problems, and evaluating effectiveness. Meeting these responsibilities requires executives to be knowledgeable and independent and to apply their skills and knowledge across a wide variety of problems. Executives must be effective managers of information and resources. Adolescents are essentially expected to act in a similar fashion. For example, students in secondary schools are typically expected to work independently with little feedback, to organize to-be-learned information and resources for learning, solve problems, and apply their knowledge across content areas. Evaluating the effectiveness of strategies used to meet these demands is left to individual students.

The characteristics of settings in which adolescents must function can influence the extent to which they are successful in meeting executive or cognitive expectations. Since teachers are typically responsible for up to 150 students, and they are in contact with individual students for only a short time, their ability to assist individuals in becoming more effective executives is greatly limited (Robinson et al., 1985). In many instances, teachers in secondary schools are mandated to follow specific curriculum guides related to their content areas and are often under pressure "to finish the book" by the end of the semester (Schumaker & Deshler, 1988). Chronic failure of many students, including those with LD who fail to perform successfully in regular classes tends to place teachers "between a rock and a hard place." Given the current full-inclusion impetus, teachers are encountering ever-increasing numbers of low achievers in their classes while also facing escalating pressures to be accountable. Much is being demanded of content teachers in spite of limited resources. Teachers are encouraged to supplement their instruction with microcomputers, tape recordings of textbooks, study guides, etc., or to modify their expectations of what is to be learned by using alternative textbooks. Sometimes they are urged to reduce the amount of content to be learned in order for low-achieving students to experience more success. Many teachers who employ some of these recommendations experience little or no success, and their efforts to accommodate low achievers are often punished. Skepticism of special techniques and pessimism about teaching these students inevitably increases. This makes it more difficult to motivate teachers to try other alternatives that create instructional atmospheres more conducive to enabling students to meet executive expectations of school. In short, teachers are rarely afforded opportunities to teach stu-

Table 17.8

Cognitive Expectations in Secondary Schools

1. Utilize key information-processing skills by using prior knowledge and skills.
   - Research in the areas of thinking and schema theory suggest that effective learners engage in a recursive process of becoming aware of the need to focus attention on new information, set a purpose for learning, activate prior knowledge of related information and use it to form predictions or hypotheses about the new information, and test these hypotheses against additional prior knowledge and new information (cf. Brandsford & Johnson, 1972; Brandsford, Sherwood, Vye, & Rieser, 1986; Jones et al., 1987; Resnick, 1985; Wittrock, 1983). Secondary students are expected to utilize these key cognitive skills related to using their prior knowledge and skills to gain and organize new information, to solve problems, and to self-regulate thoughts and actions.
2. Know and independently use effective and efficient strategies for learning and performing.
   - Students are expected to have effective strategies or approaches for a variety of tasks. These tasks include acquiring and retaining new information (e.g., strategies for reading texts and listening to lectures), demonstrating knowledge and competence (e.g., strategies for preparing for tests, taking tests, or completing writing assignments) (Shumaker, Deshler & Ellis, 1986), and meeting organizational expectations (e.g., strategies for having supplies ready at the onset of class or organizing resources for projects.
3. Use effective metacognitive processes for regulating thinking processes.
   - Students must use effective metacognitive processes, higher order thinking skills, and problem-solving processes in order to be successful in school (cf. Schumaker & Deshler, 1984). These are used for regulating the thinking processes in deciding what strategies to use, monitoring their effectiveness, and manipulating these strategies effectively and efficiently to complete tasks.

dents strategies for cognitive functioning. Table 17.8 summarizes the cognitive expectations of adolescents with LD.

As if adolescents with LD do not have enough on their minds, they are expected to be aware of the thinking processes they are using and to make sure they have employed effective ones. Examining the cognitive characteristics of adolescents with LD will contribute to an understanding of why this can be so difficult for these students.

H. Cognitive Characteristics of Adolescents with LD

Although some adolescents with LD effectively meet cognitive expectations most of the time, and some effectively meet them some of the time, many experience a great deal of difficulty in this area almost all of the time. Disabilities related to cognitive functioning were found in over 50% of the 318 adolescents with LD studied by Warner, Schumaker, Alley, and Deshler (1980). Table 17.9 summarizes research in the area of cognition with regard to the information-processing characteristics of adolescents with LD.

Table 17.9

Cognitive Characteristics of Adolescents with Learning Disabilities

1. Are prone to cognitive problems due to language deficits (see Lee & Jackson, 1992).
   - Problems of adolescents with poorly developed language skills may be manifested in many ways (e.g., limited skills in developing relational understandings of abstract concepts, poor social problem solving due to poor pragmatic language). The relationship between language-based disabilities and academic difficulty appears to be strong (Bender, 1995; Wilczenski & Gillespie-Silver, 1990) as well the relationship between language-based disabilities and social difficulty.
2. Are prone to memory problems.
   - Memory deficiency is a persistent cognitive problem of adolescents with LD (cf. Ackerman & Dykman, 1993; Swanson, 1993, 1994; Swanson & Ramalgia, 1992). Failure in various forms of memory function may result in a loss of information. The sensory memory (i.e., takes place during the first 3 to 5 seconds while processing new information) of youth with LD is generally intact but, short-term, working, and long-term memory problems are likely (Swanson, 1991). Remembering for adolescents with LD may not be a problem of motivation. Scolding or asking the student to try harder to remember may cause only more anxiety. Some youth with LD may try to hide behind their LD label (Osman, 1979). Therefore, teachers have to use clinical judgment when determining if a student with LD really did forget or chose to forget.
3. Are apt to experience problems when using metacognition and executive processes.
   - Few adolescents with LD are able to work independently with little feedback, and they often rely on others to perform key cognitive tasks for them. For example, effective use of cognitive skills in a problem-solving situation such as studying for a test requires one to *think ahead, think during, and think back.* Many adolescents with LD, however, often rely on peers, teachers, or their parents to think ahead for them (e.g., determining what needs to be learned for the test, estimating how much time will be needed, organizing information and resources, as well as figuring out the best approach for learning material, etc.) They may rely on others to perform key "think during" cognitive tasks (monitoring what has been learned and how well, what still should be learned, how much time remains with regard to completing the task, etc.). Thinking back and reflecting about the effectiveness of strategies previously used is not a frequently used problem-solving behavior, nor is it necessarily viewed by adolescents with LD as important (Ellis, Deshler, & Schumaker, 1989).
   - Due to mediation and memory deficits of many adolescents with LD, educators need to present new information in a manner to maximize student interaction with the information to promote understanding and remembering. The more a student is limited in internally mediating learning through appropriate cognitive strategies, the greater the need will be for the teacher to provide opportunities for instructional cues, routines, and enhancement devices (Ellis & Lenz, 1990).
4. May lack knowledge of various cognitive strategies.
   - Adolescents with LD may not know various cognitive strategies that are essential learning tools. Research suggests that cognitive strategies are teachable and that students with LD tend to respond to this type of instruction, particularly within real learning contexts.
   - A number of studies (see Alley, Deshler, Clark, Schumaker, & Warner, 1983, for an in-depth review) have demonstrated that adolescents with LD often maintain their ability to perform skills at or near mastery levels for at least moderate periods of time (2–8 weeks) following instruction, and they demonstrate an ability to generalize a skill to differing tasks demands (e.g., adapt a writing strategy for descriptive paragraphs for use when writing sequential paragraphs).
   - What many students with LD often fail to do, however, is generalize the skill to different settings to solve problems encountered in that setting (see Ellis, Lenz, & Sabornie, 1987, for review). For example, a student with LD might master a strategy for writing paragraphs in a special education setting but rarely use the strategy to meet the writing demands in other classes. Implications are that simply enabling students with LD to perform a new skill at mastery levels will likely prove to have minimal impact on the future success of these students. Not only must students with LD learn to perform key skills, they must learn the executive skills necessary to generalize them.

IV. CONCLUSION

In sum, examining the setting expectations of secondary schools and the characteristics of adolescents with LD reveals three key factors. First, the expectations of secondary schools are very different from those encountered during the elementary years—the most fundamental difference is the expectations of independent functioning in students. The expectations of non-school environments have many of the same expectations as those found in school environments. Second, although students are expected to meet the demands independently, many students with LD often fail to do so because (a) they often lack basic academic, social, and motivational skills and knowledge; (b) they do not use effectively or generalize existing skills and knowledge when performing tasks; (c) they often do not know or use effective and efficient routines or strategies for learning and performing; (d) they tend to ignore various learning enhancers found in the environment; and (e) they often lack skills related to cognitive functioning. Third, the nature of the adolescents' settings often interacts with the nature of students to exacerbate the problem. Thus, when considering interventions for adolescents with LD, it is important to consider intervening with students *and* their environments.

The differences between the characteristics of successful adults with LD and those of adolescents with LD are considerable. Although some of these adolescents already may have begun to embrace the "taking control of my life/being self-reliant" mentality that characterizes successful adults, most have not and will not unless teachers, parents, and other supportive persons take specific actions to facilitate it. The following chapter highlights promising instructional practices that promote the development of self-reliance in adolescents with LD.

References

Ackerman, P. T., & Dykman, R. A. (1993). Phonological processes, confrontational naming, and immediate memory in dyslexia. *Journal of Learning Disabilities, 26,* 597–609.

Adleman, H. S., & Taylor, L. (1983). Enhancing motivation for overcoming learning and behavior problems. *Journal of Learning Disabilities, 16,* 384–392.

Adleman, H. S., & Taylor, L. (1990). Intrinsic motivation and school misbehavior: Some intervention implications. *Journal of Learning Disabilities, 23,* 541–550.

Alley, G. R., Deshler, D. D., Clark, F. L., Schumaker, J. B., & Warner, M. M. (1983). Learning disabilities in adolescent and young adult populations: Research implications (Part II). *Focus on Exceptional Children, 15*(1), pp. 1–16.

Anderson, T. H., & Armbruster, B. B. (1984). Studying. In P. D. Pearson (Ed.), *Handbook of reading research.* pp. 657–744. New York: Longman.

Armbruster, B. B., & Anderson, T. H. (1988). On selecting "considerate" content area textbooks. *Remedial and Special Education, 9,* 4–52.

Axelrod, L. (1982). Social perceptions in learning disabled adolescents. *Journal of Learning Disabilities, 15,* 610–613.

Bender, W. N. (1985). Differential diagnoses based on the task-related behavior of learning disabled and low-achieving adolescents. *Learning Disability Quarterly, 8,* 261–266.

Bender, W. N. (1987). Behavioral indicators of temperament and personality in the inactive learner. *Journal of Learning Disabilities, 20,* 301–305.

Bender, W. N. (1995). Characteristics of adolescents with learning disabilities in secondary classes. In W. N. Bender (Ed.), *Learning disabilities: Characteristics, identification, and teaching strategies* (pp. 176-197). Boston: Allyn and Bacon.

Bos, C. S., & Anders, P. L. (1990). Interactive teaching and learning: Instructional practices for teaching content and strategic knowledge. In B. Y. L. Wong & T. E. Scruggs (Eds.), *Intervention research in learning disabilities* (pp. 166-185). New York: Springer-Verlag.

Brandsford, J. D., & Johnson, M. K. (1972). Contextual prerequisites of comprehension and recall. *Journal of Verbal Learning and Verbal Behavior, 11,* 717–716.

Brandsford, J. D., Sherwood, R., Vye, N., & Rieser, J. (1986). Teaching and problem solving. *American Psychologist, 41,* 1078–1089.

Bransford, J. D., Vye, N., Kinzer, C., & Risko, V. (1990). Teaching and content knowledge: Toward an integrated approach. In B. F. Jones & L. Idol (Eds.), *Dimensions of thinking and cognitive instruction* (pp. 381–414). Hillsdale, NJ: Erlbaum.

Brophy, J. E. (1979). Teacher behavior and its effects. *Journal of Educational Psychology, 71,* 733–750.

Brophy, J. E., & Good, T. (1985). Teacher behavior and student outcomes. In M. C. Wittrock (Ed.), *Handbook on research on teaching* (3d ed.). New York: Macmillan.

Chi, M. T. H. (1981). Interactive roles of knowledge and strategies in development. In S. Chipman, J. Segal, & R. Glaser (Eds.), *Thinking and learning skills: Current research and open questions* (Vol. 2). Hillsdale, NJ: Erlbaum.

Clark, C. H., & Peterson, P. L. (1986). Teachers' thought processes. In M. C. Wittrock (Ed.), *Handbook of research on teaching,* (Third ed., pp. 255–296). New York: Macmillan.

Corcoran, J. (1994). Personal perspectives on vocational issues. In P. J. Gerber & H. B. Reiff (Eds.), *Learning disabilities in adulthood: Persisting problems and evolving issues* (pp. 214–217). Boston: Andover Medical Publishers.

Cordoni, B. (1987). *Living with a learning disability.* Carbondale, IL: Southern Illinois University Press.

Crain, R. L. (May, 1984). *The quality of American high school graduates: What personnel officers say and do about it.* (Report #354). Baltimore: The Johns Hopkins University, Center for Social Organization of Schools.

Derr, A. M. (1986). How learning disabled adolescent boys make moral judgments. *Journal of Learning Disabilities, 13,* 160-164.

Deshler, D. D., Alley, G. R., Warner, M. M., & Schumaker, J. B. (1981). Instructional practices for promoting skill acquisition and generalization in severely learning disabled adolescents. *Learning Disability Quarterly, 4,* 415–421.

Deshler, D. D., Ellis, E. S., & Lenz, B. K. (1996). *Teaching adolescents with learning disabilities: Strategies & methods.* Denver: Love Publishing, Inc.

Donahoe, K., & Zigmond, N. (1990). Academic grades of ninth-grade urban learning-disabled students and low achieving peers. *Exceptionality: A Research Journal, 1,* 17–22.

Druck, K. (1994). Personal perspectives on learning differences: Coming out of the shadow. In P. J. Gerber & H. B. Reiff (Eds.), *Learning disabilities in adulthood: Persisting problems and evolving issues* (pp. 93–96). Boston: Andover Medical Publishers.

Ellett, L. (1993). Instructional practices in mainstreamed secondary classrooms. *Journal of Learning Disabilities, 26*(1), 57–64.

Ellis, E. S. (1986). The role of motivation and pedagogy on the generalization of cognitive strategy training. *Journal of Learning Disabilities, 19*, 66-70.

Ellis, E. S. (1989). A metacognitive intervention for increasing class participation. *Learning Disabilities Focus, 5*(1), 36-46.

Ellis, E. S. (1993a). Integrative Strategy Instruction: A potential model for teaching content-area subjects to learning disabled adolescents. *Journal of Learning Disabilities, 26*, 358–383.

Ellis, E. S. (1993b). On teaching strategy sameness in integrated formats. *Journal of Learning Disabilities, 26*(7), 448–482.

Ellis, E. S. (1993c). A learning strategy for meeting the writing demands of secondary mainstream classrooms. *The Alabama Council for Exceptional Children Journal, 10*(1), 21–38.

Ellis, E. S. (1996). *Watering-up the curriculum using graphic organizers: Facilitating relational understanding of big ideas & higher order thinking skills.* Unpublished manuscript. University of Alabama at Tuscaloosa.

Ellis, E. S., Deshler, D. D. & Schumaker, J. B. (1989). Teaching learning disabled adolescents an executive strategy for generating task-specific strategies. *Journal of Learning Disabilities, 22*, 108–119.

Ellis, E. S., & Lenz, B. K. (1990). Adaptive techniques for mediating content-area learning: Issues and research. *Focus on Exceptional Children, 22*(9), 1–16.

Ellis, E. S., Lenz, B. K., & Sabornie, E. J. (1987). Generalization and adaptation of learning strategies to natural environments—Part 2: Research into practice. *Remedial and Special Education, 8*(2), 6-23.

Freeman, J. G., & Hutchinson, N. L. (1994). An adolescent with learning disabilities: Eric: The perspective of a potential dropout. *Canadian Journal of Special Education, 9*(4), 131–147.

Geisthardt, C., & Munsch, J. (1996). Coping with school stress: a comparison of adolescents with and without learning disabilities. *Journal of Learning Disabilities, 29*(3), 287–296.

Gerber, P. J., Ginsberg, R., & Reiff, H. B. (1992). Identifying alterable patterns in employment success for highly successful adults with learning disabilities. *Journal of Learning Disabilities, 25*, 475–487.

Gerber, P. J., Reiff, H. B., & Ginsberg, R. (1996). Reframing the learning disabilities experience. *Journal of Learning Disabilities, 29*, 98–101, 97.

Golumbia, L. R., & Hillman, S. B. (1990, August). *A comparison of learning disabled and nondisabled adolescent motivational processes.* Paper presented at 98th Annual Meeting of American Psychological Association, Boston.

Hazel, J. S., Schumaker, J. B., Sherman, J. A., & Sheldon-Wildgen, J. (1981). "ASSET: A Social Skills Program For Adolescents". Champaign, IL: Research Press.

Jones, B. F., Palincsar, A. S., Ogle, D. S., & Carr, E. G. (1987). *Strategic teaching and learning: Cognitive instruction in the content-areas.* Alexandria, VA: ASCD.

Kerr, M. M., & Nelson, C. M. (1989). *Strategies for managing behavior problems in the classroom.* Columbus, OH: Merrill.

Kershner, J., Kirkpatrick, T., & McLaren, D. (1995). The career success of an adult with a learning disability: A psychosocial study of amnesic-semantic aphasia. *Journal of Learning Disabilities, 28,* 121–126.

Kowalchuk, V. L., & Nostbakken, M. A. (1990). Help seeking: How successful is the learning disabled adolescent? *Canadian Journal of Special Education, 6*(2), 121–31.

Lee, C., & Jackson, R. (1992). *Faking it: A look into the mind of a creative learner.* Portsmouth, NH: Boynton/Cook.

Lenz, B. K., & Alley, G. R. (1983). *The effects of advance organizers on the learning and retention of learning disabled adolescents within the context of a cooperative planning model.* Final research report submitted to the U.S. Department of Education, Office of Special Education.

Lenz, B. K., Alley, G. R., & Schumaker, G. R. (1987). Activating the inactive learner: Advance organizers in the secondary content classroom. *Learning Disability Quarterly, 10*(1), 53–67.

Lenz, B. K., Clark, F. L., Deshler, D. D., & Schumaker, J. B. (1989). *The strategies instructional approach: A training package.* Lawrence, KS: The University of Kansas Institute for Research in Learning Disabilities.

Lerner, J. (1993). *Learning disabilities: Theories, diagnosis & teaching strategies* (6th ed.). Boston: Houghton Mifflin.

Levin, E., Zigmond, N., & Birch, J. (1985). A follow-up study of 52 learning disabled students. *Journal of Learning Disabilities, 18,* 2–7.

Licht, B. C., & Kistner, J. A. (1986). Motivational problems of learning disabled children: Individual differences and their implications for treatment. In J. K. Torgesen & B. Y. L. Wong (Eds.), *Psychological and educationally perspectives on learning disabilities* (pp. 225–255). New York: Academic Press.

MacMillian, D. L., Widaman, K. F., Balow, I. H., Hemsley, R. E., & Little, R. D. (1992). Difference in adolescent school attitudes as a function of academic level, ethnicity, and gender. *Learning Disabilities Quarterly, 15*(1), 39–50.

Mathews, R. M., Whang, P., & Fawcett, S. B. (1980). *Behavioral-assessment of job related skills: Implications for learning disabled young adults* (Research Report No. 6). Lawrence, KS: The University of Kansas Institute for Research in Learning Disabilities.

McCombs, B. L. (1984). Processes and skills underlying continuing intrinsic motivation to learn: Toward a definition of motivational skills training interventions. *Educational Psychologist, 19*(4), 199–218.

McLoughlin, J. A., Clark, F. L., Mauck, A. R., & Petrosko, J. (1987). Comparison of parent–child perceptions of student learning disabilities. *Journal of Learning Disabilities, 20*(6), 357–360.

Mellard, D. F., & Hazel, J. S. (1992). Social competence as a pathway to successful life transitions. *Learning Disability Quarterly, 15,* 251–271.

Minskoff, E. H. (1994). Post-secondary education and vocational training: Keys to success for adults with learning disabilities. In P. J. Gerber & H. B. Reiff (Eds.), *Learning disabilities in adulthood: Persisting problems and evolving issues* (pp. 111–120). Boston: Andover Medical Publishers.

Monteau, J. J. (1961). The discussion group method in science education. *Science Education, 45,* 227–230.

Moran, M. R. (1980). *An investigation of the demands on oral language skills of learning disabled students in secondary classrooms (Research Report #1)*. Lawrence, KS: University of Kansas Center for Research on Learning.

Moran, M. R., & Deloache, R. F. (1982). *Mainstream teacher's responses to formal features of writing by secondary learning disabled students (Research Report)*. Lawrence, KS: University of Kansas Center for Research on Learning.

Nagel, D. R., Schumaker, J. B., & Deshler, D. D. (1986). *The learning strategies curriculum: the FIRST-letter mnemonic strategy*. Lawrence, KS: Edge Enterprise.

Newman, L. (1991). *The relationship between social activities and school performance for secondary students with learning disabilities* (research report). Menlo Park, CA: SRI International.

Oliver, R. T. (1958). Group discussions in the English class. *English Journal, 47,* 87–89.

Osman, B. B. (1979). *Learning disabilities: A family affair.* New York: Random House.

Pearl, R., Bryan, T., & Herzod, A. (1990). Resisting or acquiescing to peer pressure to engage in misconduct: Adolescents' expectations of probable consequence. *Journal of Youth Adolescence, 19,* 43–55.

Polloway, E. A., Schewel, R., & Patton, J. R. (1992). Learning disabilities in adulthood: Personal perspectives. *Journal of Learning Disabilities, 25*(8), 520-522.

Pressley, M., Johnson, C. J., & Symons, S. (1987). Elaborating to learn and learning to elaborate. *Journal of Learning Disabilities, 20,* 76-91.

Putnam, M. L. (1992a). Characteristics of questions on tests administered by mainstream secondary classroom teachers. *Learning Disabilities Research & Practice, 7,* 129–136.

Putnam, L. (1992b). The testing practices of mainstream secondary classroom teachers. *Remedial and Special Education, 13*(5), 11–21.

Reiff, H. B., Ginsberg, R., & Gerber, P. J. (1995). New perspectives on teaching from successful adults with learning disabilities. *Remedial and Special Education, 16*(1), 29–37.

Reiff, H. B., Gerber, P. J., & Ginsberg, R. (1996). What successful adults with learning disabilities can tell us about teaching children. *Teaching Exceptional Children, 29*(2), 10-16.

Resnick, L. (1985). *Education and learning to think.* Special report prepared for Commission on Behavioral and Social Sciences and Education. National Research Council.

Rivera, D. P., & Smith, D. D. (1997). *Teaching students with learning and behavior problems.* Boston: Allyn and Bacon.

Robinson, S., Braxdale, C. T., & Colson, S. E. (1985). Preparing dysfunctional learners to enter high school: A transitional curriculum. *Focus on Exceptional Children, 18*(4), pp. 1–12.

Roehler, L. R., & Duffy, G. G. (1984). Direct explanation of comprehension processes. In G. G. Duffy, L. R. Roehler, & J. Mason (Eds.), *Comprehension instruction: Perspectives and suggestions* (pp. 265–280). New York: Longman.

Salend, S. J., & Salend, S. M. (1986). Competencies for mainstreamed secondary level learning disabled students. *Journal of Learning Disabilities, 19*(2), 91–94.

Schumaker, J. B. (1992). Social performance of individuals with learning disabilities: Through the looking glass of KU-IRLD research. *School Psychology Review, 21*(3), 387–399.

Schumaker, J. B., & Deshler, D. D. (1984). Setting demand variables: A major factor in program planning for LD adolescents. *Topics in Language Disorders, 4*(2), 22–40.

Schumaker, J. B., & Deshler, D. D. (1988). Implementing the Regular Education Initiative in secondary schools: A different ball game. *Journal of Learning Disabilities, 21*(1), 36–41.

Schumaker, J. B., Deshler, D. D., Alley, G. R., & Warner, M. M. (1983). Toward the development of an intervention model for learning disabled adolescents: The University of Kansas. *Exceptional Education Quarterly, 4,* 45–74.

Schumaker, J. B., Deshler, D. D., & Ellis, E. S. (1986). Intervention issues related to the education of learning disabled adolescents. In J. Torgesen & B. Wong (Eds.), *Psychological and educational perspectives on learning disabilities* (pp. 329–364). New York: Academic Press.

Schumaker, J. B., Deshler, D. D., & McKnight, P. (1989). *Teaching routines to enhance the mainstream performance of adolescents with learning disabilities.* Final report submitted to the U.S. Office of Education, Special Education Services.

Schumaker, J. B., Hazel, S., Sherman, J. A., & Sheldon, J. (1982). *Social skill performances of learning disabled, non-learning disabled, and delinquent adolescents* (Research Report #60). Lawrence, KS: The University of Kansas Institute for Research in Learning Disabilities.

Schumaker, J. B., Sheldon-Wildgen, I., & Sherman, J. A. (1980). An observational study of the academic and social behaviors of learning disabled adolescents in the regular classroom (Research Report No. 22). Lawrence, KS: University of Kansas Institute for Research in Learning Disabilities.

Schumaker, J. B., Warner, M. M., Deshler, D. D., & Alley, G. R. (1980). *An epidemiological study of learning disabled adolescents in secondary schools: Details of the methodology* (Research Report No. 12). Lawrence: University of Kansas Institute for Research in Learning Disabilities.

Spekman, N. J., Goldberg, R. J., & Herman, K. L. (1992). Learning disabled children grow up: A search for factors related to success in the young adult years. *Learning Disabilities Research & Practice, 7,* 161–170.

Stevens, R., & Rosenshine, B. (1981). Advances in research on teaching. *Exceptional Education Quarterly, 2,* 1–10.

Swanson, H. L. (1991). Learning disabilities and memory. In D. K. Reid, W. P. Hresko, & H. L. Swanson (Eds.), *A cognitive approach to learning disabilities* (2d ed., pp. 159–182). Austin, TX: PRO-ED.

Swanson, H. L. (1993). Executive processing in learning disabled readers. *Intelligence, 17*(2), 117–149.

Swanson, H. L. (1994). Short-term memory and working memory: Do both contribute to our understanding of academic achievement in children and adults with learning disabilities. *Journal of Learning Disabilities, 27*(1), 34–50.

Swanson, H. L., & Malone, S. (1992). Social skills and learning disabilities: A meta-analysis of the literature. *School Psychology Review, 21*(3) 427–443.

Swanson, H. L., & Ramalgia, J. M. (1992). The relationship between phonological codes on memory and spelling tasks for students with and without learning disabilities. *Journal of Learning Disabilities, 25*(6), 396-407.

Thompson-Hoffman, S., & Hayward, B. J. (1990, March). *Students with handicaps who drop out of school.* Paper presented at fourth annual conference of the National Rural and Small Schools Consortium, Tucson, AZ.

Vetter, A. A., Deshler, D. D., Alley, G. R., Schumaker, J. B., & Warner, M. M. (1983). *Post-*

secondary follow-up study of a group of learning disabled and low achieving young adults (Research Report). Lawrence, KS: The University of Kansas Institute for Research in Learning Disabilities.

Vogel, S. A., & Adelman, P. B. (1992). The success of college students with learning disabilities: Factors related to educational attainment. *Journal of Learning Disabilities, 25,* 430-441.

Voss, J. F. (1982, March). *Knowledge and social science problem solving.* Paper presented at American Educational Research Association meeting, New York City.

Wambsgans, D. T. (1990). Being successful with dyslexia. *Journal of Learning Disabilities, 23,* 9–10.

Warner, M. M., Alley, G. R., Deshler, D. D., & Schumaker, J. B. (1980). *An epidemiological study of learning disabled adolescents in secondary schools: Classification and discrimination of learning disabled and low achieving adolescents* (Research Report No. 20). Lawrence, KS: The University of Kansas Institute for Research in Learning Disabilities.

Warner, M. M., Schumaker, J. B., Alley, G. R., & Deshler, D. D. (1980). *An epidemiological study of learning disabled adolescents in secondary schools: Performance on a serial recall task and the role of executive function* (Research Report No. 55). Lawrence, KS: The University of Kansas Institute for Research in Learning Disabilities.

Werner, E. E. (1993). Risk and resilience in individuals with learning disabilities: Lessons learned from the Kauai longitudinal study. *Learning Disabilities Research & Practice, 8*(1), 28–34.

Westberry, S. J. (1994). A review of learning strategies for adults with learning disabilities preparing for the GED exam. *Journal of Learning Disabilities, 27,* 202–209.

White, W. J. (1992). The postschool adjustment of persons with learning disabilities: Current status and future projections. *Journal of Learning Disabilities, 25,* 448–456.

White, W. J., Schumaker, J. B., Warner, M. M., Alley, G. R., & Deshler, D. D. (1980). *The current status of young adults identified as learning disabled during their school career.* Research Report #21). Lawrence: The University of Kansas Institute for Research in Learning Disabilities.

Wiig, E. H. (1994). Personal perspectives on adult educational issues. In P. J. Gerber & H. J. Reiff (Eds.), *Learning disabilities in adulthood: Persisting problems and evolving issues,* (pp. 163–167). Boston: Andover Medical Publishers.

Wittrock, M. C. (1983). *Generative reading comprehension.* Boston: Ginn.

Wilczenski, F. L., & Gillespie-Silver, P. (1990, May). *Profile of university students with learning disabilities.* Paper presented at annual conference of New England Educational Research Organization, Rockport, ME.

Wong, B. Y. L. (1985a). Potential means of enhancing content skills acquisition in learning disabled adolescents. *Focus on Exceptional Children, 17,* 1–8.

Wong, B. Y. L. (1985b). Issues in cognitive-behavior interventions in academic skill areas. *Journal of Abnormal Child Psychology, 2,* 123–131.

Zetlin, A. G. (1993). Everyday stress in the lives of Anglo and Hispanic learning handicapped adolescents. *Journal of Youth and Adolescence, 22*(3), 327–335.

Zigmond, N., Levin, E., & Laurie, T. (1985). Managing the mainstream: An analysis of teacher attitudes and student performance in mainstream high school programs. *Journal of Learning Disabilities, 18,* 535–541.

Zigmond, N., & Thornton, H. (1985). Follow-up of postsecondary age learning disabled graduates and drop-outs. *Learning Disabilities Research, 1*(1), 50-55.

Zigmond, N., & Thornton, H. S. (1988). Learning disabilities in adolescents and adults. In K. Kavale (Ed.), *Learning disabilities: State of the art and practice.* San Diego: College Hill Press.

CHAPTER 18

Strategic Instruction for Adolescents with Learning Disabilities

Edwin S. Ellis and Martha J. Larkin

I. INTRODUCTION

Ultimately, the ideal educational programming for students with learning disabilities (LD) results in both competence and confidence necessary for autonomous functioning in the adult world. Competence and confidence, however, are very broad terms and can mean very different things to different individuals. Some of the difficulty in identifying effective instructional approaches for students with LD is that the condition itself covers a very broad area, thus there is no typical student with LD (Mercer, 1997; Reiff, Gerber, & Ginsberg, 1996). As a result, no one method addressing particular learning styles or needs will be appropriate for all or many of these students. Although adolescents with LD comprise a very heterogeneous group, a great deal has been learned in the last two decades about how to improve the effectiveness of interventions for these students. Although there are many unanswered questions about how to best meet the needs of this population, there is reason for considerable optimism about our ability to significantly impact adolescents with LD in substantially positive ways regardless of whether students pursue postsecondary education via college or technical training or whether they immediately enter the world of work upon completion of secondary school. In short, a number of very robust ways of teaching adolescents with LD have been developed and validated.

The discussion that follows reviews some key instructional principles, tools, and procedures that hold great promise for teaching adolescents with LD. These techniques are appropriate for teaching a wide range of subjects (e.g., science, social studies, social skills, vocational/technical skills, learning strategies, survival skills, etc.). Thus, these techniques are applicable regardless of whether the special education program is based primarily on facilitating success in traditional curriculum formats (e.g., meeting the demands of regular classes) or facilitating success in alternative curriculum formats (e.g., teaching transitional skills). Many of the interventions discussed are *powerful and appropriate for use with all students* regardless of whether they are in a general education or a special education classroom.

This chapter is organized in six main sections. Each section provides a sampling of the types of interventions that research suggests are particularly promising for use with adolescents with LD. The first discusses principles of strategic instruction. Here, critical pedagogues found most effective with adolescents with LD are identified and discussed. The second section addresses tools for independence designed to promote the idea of students taking responsibility for their lives, gaining independence, and being in control of their own destinies. The third section focuses on tools for strategic learning, and the fourth section focuses on providing strategic instruction via content enhancement techniques. The last section to review intervention techniques focuses on facilitating transition. The chapter ends with a discussion of additional research needs.

II. PRINCIPLES OF STRATEGIC INSTRUCTION

A. Providing Explicit Instruction

Although there are a number of instructional models with growing popularity that might be effective when teaching adolescents with LD (e.g., whole language or holistic instruction, discovery learning, thematic instruction, reciprocal teaching, etc.), those that focus on making instruction as explicit as possible have received the most research scrutiny and have, by far, the greatest empirical support as a means of effectively teaching adolescents with LD. Although the relative effectiveness of less explicit instructional models is unknown due to limited research in this area, the effectiveness of using explicit instruction is *well* documented. Deciding to employ less explicit instructional techniques should be a carefully deliberated and purposeful decision in light of insufficient evidence to warrant their use. Teachers who choose to provide a less explicit approach to teaching their students should carefully monitor and measure the degree to which students are actually learning what it is they need to learn. Less explicit approaches to instruction often *create an illusion that students are learning* when in fact they may not be.

Explicit instruction means that the teacher ensures that students are well informed about what is expected, what is being learned, why it is being learned, and how it can be used. Students are also informed about the instructional techniques that will be used to help them learn and why these techniques are useful to students in helping them master what is being taught. For example, if the teacher was teaching a textbook reading strategy to students, the purpose for learning the strategy, when and where the strategy can be used, the rationale and function of each strategy step, as well as the behaviors that are expected to result from performing the step are explained explicitly to students. Clear explanations of the mental actions that are to take place when performing each of the strategy steps are provided. Students are not only taught how to perform the strategy, but also how to be in control of key cognitive processes when using the strategy. To explicitly model how the strategy is used, teachers think aloud while performing the strategy so that students can witness effective use of self-regulation processes. In addition, students are informed about what they will be doing during each stage of the learning process and how these activities will help them master the strategy and use it in their regular classes to be more successful. Many of the specific instructional techniques reviewed below illustrate the concept of using explicit instruction.

B. Making Covert Processing More Explicit

In order to meet specific task demands (e.g., writing an essay, reading a textbook chapter, etc.), students must systematically apply problem-solving processes. Although the results of performing some of these processes are readily observable, the processes themselves are often covert, thus not readily observable. For example, many processes involve use of *cognitive strategies,* such as visual imagery, prioritizing, hypothesis generating, relating new information to prior knowledge, or paraphrasing; and *metacognitive strategies,* such as problem analysis, decision making, goal setting, task analysis, and self-monitoring (Ellis & Lenz, 1996). An aspect of teaching that tends to be, perhaps, the least explicit is instruction in the covert processes that take place when performing tasks. For example, teachers may model and remodel the overt processes associated with writing a short essay, and then prompt students to write their own essays. Often, students are required to *infer the mental processes that take place* when performing the task. They must infer what must be thought (a) prior to beginning the task (e.g., the thinking processes associated with analyzing the task requirements, reflecting on prior experiences with similar tasks, considering how best to approach the task, using self-motivation strategies, etc.), (b) while performing the task (monitoring the effectiveness of the strategy they are using, monitoring stress levels, etc.), as well as (c) after the task has been completed (reflecting on the effectiveness of the strategy employed, using self-reinforcement, etc.). Research has demonstrated that making covert processes more explicit for adolescents with LD greatly increases effectiveness of instruction (Ellis, Deshler, Schumaker, Lenz, & Clark, 1993). For example, when teaching a reading comprehension strategy that involves paraphrasing the main idea of a paragraph, an effective teacher will *explain and demonstrate* the cognitive processes one might use to find and state the main idea. This teacher would also coach students to enable them to perform these cognitive processes effectively and efficiently. Roehler and Duffy (1984) have called instruction that emphasizes covert processing "direct explanation" (p. 265). In short, they argue that effective teachers focus not only on the mechanical aspects of learning and performing, but also on directly teaching students to understand and use the covert processes involved in the task. A less effective teacher, on the other hand, might simply instruct the student to perform the covert behavior while providing *no* explanation or demonstration of the covert behaviors and then provide feedback with regard to whether the desired outcome was attained. In sum, adolescents with LD seem to learn best when instruction is explicit. Therefore the covert processes they are expected to master must be explicitly explained.

C. Modeling Procedures and Processes

Modeling important procedures and processes should be considered the "heart of instruction" (Schumaker, 1989). Unfortunately, teachers tend to model more overt procedures and *tell* students what they are doing (e.g., "Now I'm going to find the main idea of this paragraph. Let's see . . . the main idea is . . . traveling light—it's important to travel light when back-packing.") as opposed to "thinking aloud," during the overt procedures to model more covert processes (Brown, 1978; Duffy & Bursuck, 1994; Fulk, 1994; Palincsar & Brown, 1984). The result is that students with LD can witness how effective problem solvers think. Thus, effective teachers not only need to thoroughly explain covert processes to adolescents with LD, they need to explicitly model them as well. Schumaker (1989) identified three major phases of instructing involving modeling. In Phase I, teachers provide an organizer for the lesson that, among other things, alerts students to the fact that modeling will be provided and cues students to attend to the covert processes being modeled as they think aloud and ask students to imitate them. In Phase II, the teacher demonstrates the procedures and processes while thinking aloud and emphasizing the cognitive processes involved. The teacher demonstrates self-instruction and self-monitoring processes while performing the task. In Phase III, students are prompted to gradually perform more and more of the required thought processes and physical acts themselves; that is, they become the demonstrators. Initially, students can be prompted to name the next step of the task. Once mastered, they should be prompted to say what they would say as they (a) check their progress, (b) evaluate their performance, (c) make adjustments, and (d) problem solve. By involving students, the teacher can check their understanding of the procedures and processes involved in performing them. Ellis et al. (1993) noted that forcing students to "think aloud" before they are ready can bog instruction down and make the task difficult. Students should participate in the modeling at a level that will prompt maximum involvement but still assure success.

D. Mediating and Scaffolding Procedures and Processes

Lenz, Ellis, and Scanlon (1996) noted that mediation involves making decisions about when to use a procedure, determining how it should be used, as well as regulating the process involved in applying the various steps of the procedure (e.g., deciding what to do next) and monitoring the whole process to assure that things are going as they should. Mastering the procedure, therefore, involves both learning how to perform overt behaviors (e.g., steps to the procedure) *and* learning how to perform critical covert behaviors associated with "mediation" or regulation of the problem-solving process (what one thinks while performing the steps). Ultimately, students should be able to take full responsibility for the mediation process. When teaching a procedure, however, effective teachers of students with LD carefully structure practice activities so that the responsibility for mediating correct use of the procedure gradually shifts from the teacher to the student.

Scaffolding or mediated scaffolding can be defined as the "personal guidance, assistance, and support that a teacher, peer, materials or task provides a learner" (Baker, Simmons, & Kameenui, 1994, p. 14; also see Dickson, Chard, & Simmons, 1993; Dickson, Simmons, & Kameenui, 1995). Scaffolding may be a temporary support, particularly during initial learning or may be substantial during new and/or difficult tasks and then removed as students acquire the necessary skills to work with less assistance.

When students first begin practicing use of the procedure, others who are more familiar with the process (e.g., teachers) assist with the mediation process involved with covert behaviors so that students can focus their attention on mastering the more overt behaviors associated with the procedure. During these early practice attempts, teacher mediation is *intensive*. Students receiving intensive teacher-mediated practice tend to be very dependent on teachers for direction and feedback, and if these students attempt to perform the procedure independently, there is a high probability of incorrect responses. During intensive teacher-mediated practice, effective teachers frequently model and remodel specific behaviors associated with using the procedure, as well as provide ample prompts and cues to mediate use of the procedure and to assure there is a very low level of incorrect responses from students. As students begin to assume more responsibility for mediating use of the procedure themselves, teacher mediation should become more *intermittent*. At this point in the learning process, students are generally familiar with how to perform the more overt behaviors associated with using the procedure. Now, the emphasis subtly shifts, so that the focus is more on mastering the covert, or mediation processes associated with using the procedure independently. In other words, the prompts and cues extensively provided earlier are gradually faded until students are able to perform the procedure independently.

This mediating or scaffolding instruction in processes or strategies can be viewed as a four-stage process (see Figure 18.1). During the initial "Teacher does it," phase of the scaffolding process, the teacher models for the students how to perform a task (i.e., work through the steps of a learning strategy, how to use a graphic organizer, how to tune a small engine carburetor, etc.). For example, the teacher may have a partially completed graphic organizer on an overhead transparency; as completion of the graphic organizer is being modeled by the teacher, she "thinks aloud," describing the information and how the relationships among the information are illustrated on the graphic organizer.

The second phase, "Class does it," involves the teacher and the class coconstructing or coperforming the task. Here, the teacher may display a partially completed content organizer on an overhead transparency, and students have paper copies of the same organizer at their desks. The teacher facilitates a discussion of the information, and students are guided by the teacher. They fill in the blanks on their organizers while the teacher simultaneously completes the organizer on the transparency. To guide students' thinking and mediate connections to background knowledge, the teacher may ask many questions of the students and encourage them to become less dependent on the teacher to supply the answers. The questions promote verbal elaboration of the processes used in completing the organizer and elaboration of the content material.

The third stage, "Group does it," gives the students an opportunity to work with a partner or in small cooperative groups to complete a partially completed organizer or one that is totally blank. During this in-class activity, the teacher moves around the room monitoring students' progress and providing assistance or feedback when needed. Both the "Class does it" and the "Group does it" stages can be considered forms of guided practice, although the former would be considered teacher-mediated and the latter would be considered peer-mediated practice.

Peer-mediated practice serves a slightly different, but equally important, purpose than teacher-mediated practice. Because students with LD may learn as much from their peers as they do from teachers about how a procedure is performed, it is important to provide opportunities for students to interact among themselves when practicing the procedure as well as to use dialogue among themselves about how the procedure is perceived and used. Students participating in peer-mediated

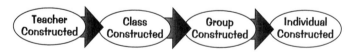

Figure 18.1   Four-stage process for scaffolding instruction. (From Ellis, in press a.)

practice activities should be less in need of teachers for mediation and feedback, but require more opportunities to practice using the procedure to build fluency. Various cooperative learning group dynamics can be used to provide peer-mediated practice. Figure 18.2 illustrates the shift in instruction from teacher-mediated to peer- or student-mediated forms of practice.

The last stage, "Individual does it" refers to the independent practice stage where students work independently on completing a partially filled or totally blank graphic organizer. *Student-mediated practice* is designed to provide students with opportunities to practice independently using the procedure to build fluency, so that both the overt and covert behaviors associated with using the procedure can be performed automatically and quickly. This may be done as an in-class activity where students can still receive assistance or feedback from the teacher if needed. Later the "Individual does it" step may be a homework assignment for a graphic organizer.

1. Providing Appropriate Situations and Contexts for Practicing Use of Procedures or Processes

When students first begin learning to use a new procedure, they often are unfamiliar with "how it feels to use it," and they are not familiar enough with the procedure to apply in a context filled with nuances that will make it difficult to apply. It is important, therefore, to select materials and design practice situations that will allow students to first become confident and competent at using a procedure in relatively trouble-free contexts. These types of practice activities are targeted at enabling students to use the procedure *accurately* and *fluently*. Once students have learned to mediate use of the procedure in these simple situations, then they will need to learn to apply it to problems more like those encountered in real life, so that students must learn to use the procedure *strategically*. In other words, they must learn to recognize situations to use the procedure, and apply it as necessary. For example, if the procedure students with LD were learning is a strategy for reading text chapters, the stimulus materials used as students initially begin practicing the strategy should be devoid of many of the demands of the regular class setting (e.g., complex vocabulary and concepts, lengthy reading selections, etc.), so that students can focus their attention on learning the technique and can build confidence and fluency in performing the strategy steps. As students become fluent in applying the strategy to these earlier materials, increasingly more complex materials for practicing the strategy should be provided. Thus, students learn to use the strategy when interacting with materials that gradually approximate the difficulty of those found in their regular educational settings. Once students are able to perform the strategy when reading these easier materials, they are asked to apply the strategy to more challenging reading selections.

Although it is important to carefully design practice activities so that students gradually learn to apply the procedure to increasingly more complex tasks, it is

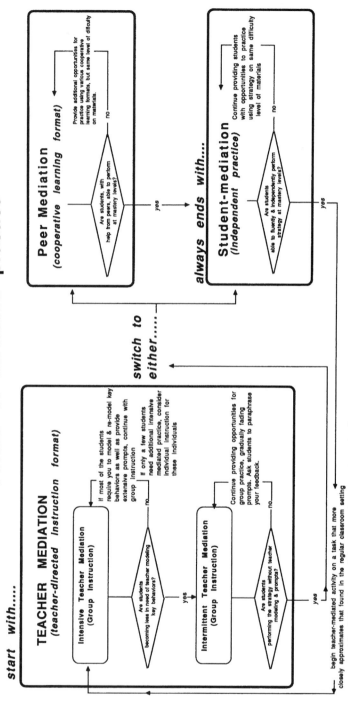

Figure 18.2 Forms of mediated practice that shifts responsibility from the teacher to the students.

equally important for students to understand why a particular type of practice activity is being provided. It is, therefore, important for teachers to orient students to the purpose of the specific practice activity and to inform them of how the activity fits into an overall plan for enabling them to apply the procedure to real-life tasks.

2. Providing Generalization Practice

If students will not likely need to use a procedure in real-life situations (e.g., one rarely, if ever, has to identify the parts of speech in real life), then investing considerable time and energy to teach students with LD to use the procedure is a highly questionable practice. If, however, students are expected to use the procedure in real-life situations, it is often necessary not only to teach them how to perform the procedure, but also to teach them how to generalize it as well. As noted by Gable, Hendrickson, and Shellady (1992), in order for learning to be relevant to a student's daily life and future, "it must endure and be accessible to that student under conditions that differ from those in which the learning occurred" (p. 35).

Unfortunately, because of the lack of teacher attention to the transition from the acquisition process to the generalization process, many students with LD fail to generalize the recently learned procedure. Teachers must adopt an instructional philosophy in which the *success of instruction is defined only by the degree to which the student uses the technique to meet demands of natural settings.* In addition, this perspective must be transferred to students. When providing generalization practice, the teacher should ensure that students are aware of the general goals of the generalization process, as well as the specific consequences related to focusing versus not focusing attention on the generalization process. Explicit commitments from students to generalize the skills should be sought.

For successful generalization to take place, Ellis et al. (1993) noted that students must also be able to recognize naturally occurring cues across settings that signal appropriate opportunities for applying the skill. Therefore, the instructional processes for promoting generalization must focus on enabling the student to (a) discriminate when to use the procedure to meet everyday demands, (b) develop methods for remembering to use the procedure, (c) experiment with how the skill can be used across circumstances, (d) receive and use feedback to develop goals and plans to improve performance, (e) adapt the procedure to meet additional problems and demands, and (f) incorporate the procedure and various adaptations of it into the student's permanent system for approaching problems across settings and time. Practice activities should be designed specifically to target these goals.

E. Promoting Verbal Elaboration of To-Be-Learned Material

Pressley, Johnson, and Symons (1987) noted that facilitating students' elaboration of to-be-learned information is an excellent way to promote learning. Elaboration promotes comprehension and new information is more effectively stored in long-term memory. Essentially, elaboration involves translating new information into one's own language structures by relating new information to that previously learned. Verbal elaboration can be promoted by teachers when teaching both processes and concepts.

1. Elaborating Processes

Ellis et al. (1993) reported that teachers of students with LD must ensure that students comprehend the process involved in applying multistep procedures and processes. To effectively use self-instructional processes while performing a procedure, students need to be able to use their own language structures to communicate with themselves about the strategic process. Thus, instruction that focuses on having students describe, in their own words, key procedures and processes used when completing a task can facilitate students' understanding of the procedure and memory of what to do while performing it. Initially, the focus of instruction is on facilitating students' ability to elaborate on the "big picture" or intent of the overall strategy (what the strategy is designed to accomplish and generally what the process involves). Then the focus of instruction shifts to facilitating student elaboration of the specific steps in the procedure. Here, students describe what each step is designed to do and *why* it is an important component to the overall strategic process. Once students can accurately describe the strategy steps, they should be asked to discuss, in their own words, how self-instruction is used with regard to performing the strategy. Ellis et al. (1993) also noted that students with LD should memorize the steps to the procedure to an automatic level so they can use self-instruction to prompt themselves on what to do next when performing the procedure.

2. Elaborating Concepts

Johnson and Johnson (1992) noted the importance of elaboration in stating that "meaning is formulated via the process of conveying it". Scruggs, Mastropieri, Sullivan, and Hesser (1993) found that students who were questioned to give an explanation about one of the nine ordered reasons for dinosaur extinction demonstrated higher recall than did students who only received direct teaching. Teachers can promote elaborative learning by prompting students to employ various cognitive processes (e.g., paraphrasing, summarizing, identifying main ideas and important details, predicting, generating questions, imagining, and relating new information to personal experiences and interests) while interacting with the to-be-learned material. An example of an activity that promotes verbal elaboration of content subjects is the "instructional pause procedure" (Rowe, 1976, 1980, 1983). To use the procedure, the teacher provides direct instruction on the content subject matter for approximately 8–10 minutes and then initiates an activity that requires students to use various cognitive learning strategies (e.g., "Talk among the other members in your group and decide on what was the main idea and the

Preparing the lesson
Step 1: Generate an outline of the relevant information students need to master.
Step 2: Divide the information into 10–15-minute instructional modules.
Step 3: Identify specific tasks that will require students to employ elaboration strategies.

Teaching the lesson
Step 1: Divide the class into small groups (approximately 4 students per group).
Step 2: Provide an advance organizer of the lesson for the entire class.
Step 3: Teach the first module of the subject matter.
Step 4: Cue each group to perform the same cognitive strategy.
    *Be explicit in what they are being asked to do.
    *Be sure to inform students of the time allotment to activity.
Step 5: Allow students approximately 3-5 minutes to perform the elaboration activity and discuss among themselves to formulate their response.
Step 6: Randomly select only one group to report their response to the entire class.
Step 7: Ask other groups to compare/critique their response to the one reported by the other group. Use as a basis for discussing the subject matter.

Examples of tasks that require students to use cognitive elaboration strategies when interacting with the subject matter

Sample tasks that cue use of summarizing and prioritizing strategies
"Decide what was the main idea of the last module."
"Decide what was the main important piece of information ... ."
"Decide which of these details we've been discussing should be remembered."
"Write a telegraph message that states what happened. Each word will cost a dollar."

Sample tasks that cue use of questioning, predicting, and monitoring strategies
"Decide what you think happened next ... ."
"Tell me when you know the answer to the following question ... ."
"Tell me three things your group would like to find out about ... ."
"During the next instructional module, decide if _____ is what really happened."
"Tell me two things about what we just talked about that are confusing or difficult to understand."

Sample tasks that cue use of mnemonic strategies
"Figure out a good way to remember this list of key information."
"Generate a mini-story about these terms that will help you remember what they mean."

Sample tasks that cue use of activity prior to knowledge strategies
"You guys have three minutes to list everything you already know about ... ."
"How can what you already know about this topic help you remember this new information?"
"Look at this section of the block. Identify all the clues the book provides that help you identify important information."

Figure 18.3 Examples of tasks used to promote elaborated learning.

two most important details of what I just taught." or "Talk among the other members in your group and make a prediction about what will happen when I add sulphur to this mixture. Then we'll see if your prediction is correct." or "Decide what would be a good way to remember"). The teacher then allows the students about 2 minutes to formulate their response and then picks one group to express their response to the entire class. The other groups compare their response to the one expressed to class. Figure 18.3 shows sample tasks teachers can assign students to promote elaborative learning during instruction.

F. Using Effective Feedback

Most teachers are aware that effective feedback is both positive and corrective. However, recent studies have demonstrated that that there are some specific things that can be done to enhance the effectiveness of feedback. The following outlines recent research concerning effective feedback for adolescents with LD.

1. Feedback Should Focus on *Types* of Correct Behavior as Well as Error Types

Teachers often provide feedback that, regrettably, is often either too global for students to clearly understand the problem, or it is too specific (e.g., focuses on specific errors). Recent research on adolescents with LD suggests feedback that focuses students' attention on the *types* of behaviors correctly performed as well as types of errors made and how to avoid these types of errors is more effective (Howell, 1986; Kea, 1987; Kline, 1989).

2. Feedback Should Focus on the Effectiveness of Strategic Behaviors, as Opposed to Qualitative Indices

Teachers often use qualitative descriptors when providing feedback (e.g., "This was a *good* use of the paraphrasing strategy," or "That was *not a good* main idea statement"). Some educators have expressed concern that feedback based on qualitative indices may be counterproductive if used injudiciously (Licht & Kistner, 1986). Its use may subtly encourage students to rely on others, thus it may reinforce external locus of control. It also encourages the student to perform the learning tasks in order to impress others, rather than to be successfully self-sufficient. It also undermines the importance of *effective* use of those strategies that enable students to attain their goals. In lieu of using qualitative descriptors, feedback should focus on the *effectiveness* of behaviors (e.g., "That was an effective use of the paragraph writing strategy because you really explained yourself clearly.").

3. Feedback on Performance Should Be Relative to an Established Mastery Criteria

Students naturally perform better when (a) clear expectations have been communicated to them, and (b) they know how well they need to perform the behaviors to be considered competent. Feedback, therefore, should be relative to a mastery criteria. In other words, students should understand both how well they need to be able to perform specific behaviors as well as how close they are to performing at this level. As an alternative to rewarding students with extrinsic reinforcers (e.g., points, prices, etc.) for effective performance, providing students with charts that allow them to record their performance scores has been found to be an effective means of promoting intrinsic motivation in students (Lenz et al., 1996). The charts should have the mastery criteria indicated on them so that students can view their progress toward mastery and ascertain how close they are performing at mastery levels.

4. Effective Feedback Involves the Students' Elaboration on the Feedback

Language deficits are a common characteristic of many students with mild LD. Since using language, or self-speech, can play an important role in the problem-solving process, providing students with opportunities to elaborate, using their own language, on the feedback can be an effective technique. For example, after explaining to students the types of errors they have been making when writing paragraphs, an effective teacher cues students to discuss the feedback. Students are asked to explain the feedback to the teacher by telling what they were doing that was less effective and what they need to do to improve the quality of their writing. The importance of encouraging students with LD to elaborate on feedback is based on the work of Vygotsky (1978) and several other educators (Adelman & Taylor, 1983; Pressley, Johnson, & Symons, 1987).

5. Effective Feedback Includes Establishing Goals for Improving Specific Behaviors in Subsequent Attempts

Many adolescents with LD tend to depend on others for direction and perform academic tasks because others (e.g., teachers) expect them to be dependent. Having students establish goals, based on feedback, regarding future performance plays an important motivational role. The practice also places more responsibility on students for self-direction and assures that students understand the desired behavior. The importance of tying goal-setting instruction to feedback is becoming increasingly more clear from recent research (see Adelman & Taylor, 1983; Bandura & Schunk, 1981; Deshler, Schumaker, & Lenz, 1984; Seabaugh & Schumaker, 1981).

6. Effective Feedback Is Also Provided Just before a Practice Attempt

Although feedback is effective when it immediately follows a behavior, research has shown that it is also important that students with LD receive feedback immediately *before* beginning the next practice attempt. By reviewing the feedback on the previous performance and establishing goals for the next attempt, the critical features of the correct behavior more likely will be incorporated into the student's upcoming practice attempt.

7. During the Initial Stages of Practicing a Skill, Feedback Should Be Directive

In other words, teachers should diagnose the type of error made by the students and provide explicit feedback regarding the error. Effective directive feedback is often composed of two components. First, the directive feedback focuses on examining the critical features of the behavior that need to be performed correctly, and second, it often involves modeling the correct behavior (Lenz, Ellis, & Scanlon, 1996).

8. When Students Are Building Fluency, Feedback Should Be Meditative

Once students have mastered the basic behaviors associated with performing the task (e.g., teacher prompts infrequently are needed), the nature of feedback provided should shift from being directive (teacher diagnoses the problem and directs the desired behaviors) to being *mediative* (Stone & Wertsch, 1984; Vygotsky, 1978). Here, the teacher *cues* students to diagnose the problem and to generate their own solutions. In mediative feedback, the responsibility for monitoring and adjusting behaviors shifts from the teacher to the student. Mediative feedback structures opportunities for students to learn how to self-evaluate the effectiveness of their behaviors.

9. Feedback Should Be Structured so That an Awareness of Where Students Have Been and Where They Are Going Is Facilitated

Sometimes the best feedback originates from students themselves. Ellis (1991) found that some effective LD teachers facilitate self-evaluation in their students by having them maintain Journey Logs that reflect an ongoing record of students' progress. Journey Logs can be used in different ways. One approach is to have students record their perceptions of their ability to perform a specific task (e.g., how well the student writes paragraphs) just before teaching the strategy, and then record brief daily comments reflecting their perceptions of where they improved that day or other pertinent information about its use (i.e., information about attempts to use the strategy in a regular classroom, what they value about the strategy, recording attainment of a personal goal related to using the strategy, completing an instructional stage, etc.). Later, teachers can have students look back over their comments to review their "journey" mastering the strategy.

G. Requiring Mastery

An important principle underlying effective instruction of adolescents with LD is to require student mastery of instructional objectives. Because concepts addressed in content area classes often build upon each other, failure to master prerequisite concepts often assures difficulty mastering future, more complex concepts. Regrettably, many content-area teachers teach a unit, test students, and then move on to the next unit with little regard for how well students mastered concepts in the previous unit. Mastery of concepts means that students can *distinguish the critical features of the concept* that are always present, from those that are never present or only sometimes present, as well as *recognize examples and non-examples* of the concept (Bulgren, Schumaker, & Deshler, 1988). In addition, the student must be able to *relate the new concept to previously learned concepts* in a meaningful way. Mastering skill-based objectives is equally important. For example, research has shown that unless students can proficiently perform the skill at the specified mastery levels (Schmidt, Deshler, Schumaker, & Alley 1989), generalization is not likely to occur. Mastery of a skill involves three types of performance: (a) *accuracy* (student correctly performs the skill), (b) *fluency* (student performs the skill quickly and smoothly), and (c) *strategically* (student must independently use the skill at appropriate times when solving problems).

There are two implications associated with maintaining an "attain mastery" orientation to teaching students with LD. The first is that the progress of students and their readiness for more complex instruction is the primary factor in instructional decisions. Conversely, school climate factors (e.g., teachers' perception that school administrators expect them to "finish the book before the end of the year") become less important or less influential factors in determining future instruction. A second implication is that effective special education programs are "focused." In other words, effective programs focus on key areas and teach these areas intensively and extensively (i.e., Pressley, Johnson, & Symons, 1987). Less effective programs, on the other hand, bend to the many needs of students with LD and often attempt to address all needs (e.g., attempt to provide tutoring services, basic skill remediation, counseling, transitional programming, social skills training, learning strategy instruction, etc.). Inevitably, the result of such practices is that too little instruction is provided in any one area, and thus, the overall intervention program has minimal effectiveness. In short, the "spray and pray" approach (spray students with a little of everything—pray something has a positive affect on the students) to teaching adolescents with LD is not effective because too little is ever mastered.

III. TOOLS FOR INDEPENDENCE

One of the highest priorities of the teacher of students with LD should be creating an atmosphere in their instructional setting that reinforces in these students the idea of taking responsibility for their lives, gaining independence, and being in control of their own destinies. Specific techniques for creating such an atmosphere include addressing the issue of who is in control and clarifying the role of a special education teacher, creating an atmosphere permeated by a student goal setting and self-reinforcement orientation, communicating and teaching confidence, and emphasizing the role of personal effort.

A. Clarifying Who Is in Control and Self-Monitoring

Many students with LD perceive themselves as passive recipients of "whatever life dishes out" and that they have little control over their own destinies. To address these debilitating beliefs, effective teachers invest considerable time counseling their students about who's in control of their lives to help them realize that they are already making adult decisions in their lives and to capitalize on this power to more actively take control. This concept of "who is in control" permeates the instructional atmosphere on a daily basis. The language used by effective teachers of students with LD consistently communicates this concept, and the manner in which instruction is delivered reinforces it.

Many students with LD become dependent on their special education teachers to mediate their success in regular classrooms. For example, many view behaviors related to finding out what assignments need to be completed in regular classes, determining how best to perform the assignments, "spoon feeding" the information, and checking to see that the assignment has been effectively performed in a timely fashion as the special education teachers' responsibility. Such beliefs are counterproductive to instructional goals related to facilitating independence in students. It is often necessary, therefore, to address counterproductive beliefs about the nature of the special education teacher's role. To change these beliefs, effective teachers frequently reiterate the role of special education in relation to facilitating independence (see Field, 1996) over the long term (e.g., teaching skills that can be widely used now and in the future), as opposed to assuring short-lived success (e.g., tutoring a student so that she passes a test), and always relate what is being learned to how it will help students with LD become more independent.

One way of helping students to become more independent is facilitating the use of self-monitoring behaviors in the classroom and encouraging students to generalize such behaviors to other settings and situations. Self-monitoring helps students to determine whether or not a particular behavior has occurred and then to record the result. This is especially useful for adolescents with LD to reinforce the idea that they are in control of their own behavior (King-Sears & Cummings, 1996) and that positive behavior can lead to positive outcomes (Rankin & Reid, 1995). King-Sears and Cummings (1996) advocated the use of self-management techniques such as self-monitoring for the following reasons: (a) to alleviate problem behaviors in general education classrooms as a prereferral intervention, (b) to precede or follow more intrusive behavior management systems, (c) to assist students in focusing attention on specific academic and social behaviors, (d) to promote student's responsibility for and control of their behavior, and (e) to provide natural consequences and opportunities for generalization of appropriate behaviors.

Self-monitoring procedures are especially appropriate for secondary students (Carter, 1993) due to increased student–teacher ratios and increased demands on student productivity (Prater, Joy, Chilman, Temple, & Miller, 1991). If students in secondary special education placements are taught to self-monitor their behavior, then their chances of being mainstreamed into the general education setting are increased. Prater et al. (1991), in five single-subject studies of adolescents with LD, concluded that these youth can successfully implement self-monitoring procedures in both special and regular education settings to improve their on-task behavior. These researchers also found that self-monitoring works well in settings where much time is spent in independent seatwork. Reinforcement was teamed with self-monitoring in some of the studies, but results indicated that both can be faded effectively and removed without affecting the students' on-task behavior.

Dunlap, Dunlap, Koegel, and Koegel (1991) outlined the following steps for self-monitoring procedures to increase student independence: (a) define target behavior so that it is clearly understood by the student, (b) identify functional reinforcers and allow the student to select them, (c) design the self-monitoring method/device, (d) teach the student to use the device (e.g., teacher modeling and/or student modeling), and (e) fade the use of the self-monitoring device. Carter (1993) suggested the following additional steps in the self-monitoring procedure once the student had been taught how to use the recording device: (a) choose a strategy for ensuring accuracy (e.g., student has opportunity to match his or her record with the teacher's), (b) teacher and student select goal and contingencies, and (c) review goal and student performance. Also, once fading the use of the self-monitoring device begins, there should be a plan in place for generalization and maintenance.

Reid (1996) reported that recent research on self-monitoring has shown positive results in three major areas: (a) on-task behavior, (b) academic productivity (i.e, the amount or rate of academic responding), and (c) accuracy. Self-monitoring can be use in a variety of ways as illustrated by the following studies. Adolescents with LD in grades 7 through 10 were taught how to use self-monitoring procedures to increase the number of daily homework assignments completed (i.e., academic productivity) (Trammel, Schloss, & Alper, 1994). The students learned how to graph their homework-completion data. The researchers concluded that the students displayed an understanding of the importance of homework completion and began to receive higher daily grades. Martin and Manno (1995), in a study of middle school boys with learning and behavior problems, found that students' story compositions were more complete (i.e., accurate) when they were taught how to use a checkoff system to ensure that essential elements were included in their narratives. Dunlap and Dunlap (1989) studied the effectiveness of self-monitoring for accuracy with three students with LD who had a track record of highly inconsistent and unsuccessful responding to subtraction problems. The self-monitoring procedures resulted in immediate gains in correct responding and more stable levels of correct performance overall. During the maintenance phase, checklists were removed and the previous incentive condition reinstated, which still resulted in continued levels of successful responding.

B. Facilitating Goal Setting and Self-Reinforcement

Luckner (1994) noted that responsible people set goals and determine steps to achieve them. Teachers can help students learn this essential life skill by talking about goals and assisting students to set and strive for achievable personal goals.

Spekman, Goldberg, and Herman (1992) recommended that interventions focus on goal setting and self-directedness along with the academic curriculum:

> We need to help individuals face their learning disability, accommodate their goals accordingly, accept responsibility for their actions, and prepare for appropriate careers. Experiences need to be meaningful and a safe environment provided to review failures and setbacks. Perseverance and proactivity can be nurtured in this context. (p. 169)

Bender (1994) noted that students can be trained to attribute their successes positively. Duchardt, Deshler, and Schumaker (1995) evaluated the BELIEF strategy, a task-specific strategy designed to teach students with LD how to understand, identify, discuss, and transform ineffective beliefs. They found that students with LD can be taught to apply the BELIEF strategy effectively. In other words, students are able to examine elements of existing beliefs and independently alter them if the beliefs are perceived to be incompatible with personal needs and goals.

Since many adolescents with LD do not use effective self-motivation strategies such as making self-coping and affirmation statements, establishing their own goals, and providing themselves with reinforcement, these motivation strategies are explicitly taught to students with LD. The overriding purpose of self-motivation training is to promote in students a perception of self-efficacy and personal control (McCombs, 1984). These perceptions underlie the ability of students to take positive self-control and change negative attitudes and orientations toward learning.

Many teachers teach goal setting both as a skill and as a philosophy. For example, they teach their students how to set annual goals for learning and how to present these goals at their Individual Education Planning (IEP) conferences in such a way that the goals are included in their formal educational plans (Van Reusen, Bos, Deshler, & Schumaker, 1987; Van Reusen & Bos, 1990). Considerable time is spent with students discussing goals and teaching how to determine long-term (i.e., post-secondary, yearly, and semester), weekly, and even daily performance goals and how these goals relate to each other. For example, potential to-be-taught strategies are presented as a "vehicle to realize personal goals" (Lenz, 1991, p. 17), and students subsequently participate in decisions regarding which strategies to learn. If students express the desire to learn a specific strategy, their subsequent commitment to the task is stronger and more enduring.

Effective teachers help students write these commitments in the form of goal statements that reflect intended real-life future applications of the to-be-learned strategy (Ellis et al., 1993). Moreover, conversations between teachers and their students with LD constantly reflect a goal-setting orientation. Students are encouraged to collaborate with teachers in the evaluation of the effectiveness of instruction as well as the effectiveness of the strategy in helping them meet specific tasks in their settings. Each week, specific time is allotted for discussing students' long-term goals, how they are being met, and progress toward meeting them. On a daily basis, students are encouraged to set performance goals and then provide time at the end of class for students to assess whether their goals were met. Lenz, Ehren, and Smiley (1991) suggested that beginning with goal-setting applications that students face daily may be more appropriate because goal attainment applied to weekly, monthly, yearly, or longer applications could be too abstract. They found that training in goal attainment increased the rate of project completion for adolescents with LD. In short, student goals permeate the atmosphere of effective LD classrooms (Lenz et al., 1996).

In addition to teaching goal-setting strategies, effective teachers also teach students with LD to make positive affirmation, and self-coping statements to motivate themselves as they work through a task, to evaluate their own performances, to use self-reinforcement and self-correction procedures, and to monitor progress toward their goals (Seabaugh & Schumaker, 1981). Thus, the instructional process in highly effective special education programs is driven by student goals, *not* teacher goals. For example, Ellis (1989) taught students, just prior to the beginning of a content lesson, to set goals for learning content by (a) writing a question about the content they hope will be answered in the upcoming lesson, and (b) noting goals for participating in class. At the end of the content lesson, Students with LD were taught to think back and determine whether their question had been answered and whether they met their participation goals. Ellis (1989) reported that, as a result, the level of student participation significantly increased during the class and that teachers perceived students with LD as more interested in the subject matter.

C. Communicating and Teaching Confidence

Many students with LD who have a history of failure experiences have little confidence in their own abilities (see Litcht & Kistner, 1986). They often attribute their successes to variables beyond their control (e.g., attribute a successful outcome to good luck—"The teacher made the test easy this time") and their failures to their own perceived ineptitudes (e.g., "I failed because I'm not good at taking tests). Many students also crucify themselves with negative self-statements (e.g., "I'm too dumb for this"). In a study examining the motivation techniques employed by expert master teachers, effective teachers of students with LD frequently communicated a confidence in their students using such statements as "I know you can do it" or "Now you're ready for a more difficult problem because you'll be able to handle it." The expert teachers also taught students to communicate their confidence to peers. For example, some expert teachers employ cooperative learning techniques for group practice activities. One person in the group is designated the "encourager." During the activity, the encourager is responsible for encouraging and reinforcing others, as well as communicating confidence in others during difficult or frustrating circumstances.

D. Emphasizing the Role of Personal Effort

Because many adolescents with LD seem to believe that their successes are due largely to factors beyond their personal control (e.g., "I did well on the test because the test was easy"), the role of personal effort as a key factor in any formula for success should be continuously emphasized when teaching adolescents with LD. Successful problem solving, in the simplest terms, is related to one's choosing a strategy that can effectively address the demand of the setting and then trying as hard as possible to use the strategy in an effective way. Ellis and Lenz (1996) noted that students with LD should be taught that the key elements in the formula for successful problem solving in an academic setting are the following:

Appropriately Chosen Learning Strategy + Personal Effort = Successful Problem Solving

By frequently referring to this formula when discussing progress and providing feedback, students' understanding that personal effort must be exerted to ensure success is enhanced as well as their understanding of the learning process. Likewise, students are taught to attribute failure experiences to use of less effective or efficient strategies, or both. Emphasis is placed on encouraging students to try harder to use the *best* strategy (i.e., the most effective and efficient strategy) for the task.

Scruggs and Mastropieri (1992) and Fulk (1994) noted the importance of "attribution training" or stressing the importance of effort combined with effective strategies to help students be successful. Although a number of studies have examined the effects of focusing students' attention on the importance of effort and attribution retraining on students with histories of failure experiences, only a few have specifically focused on students classified as LD (see Licht & Kistner, 1986; Anderson & Jennings, 1980; McNabb, 1984). Frequently encouraging students to make positive attribution and affirmation statements can also, over time, help students use more effective motivation strategies.

As noted previously, many students with LD attribute failure experienced to their own personal attributes rather than on use of less effective strategies for the task. To facilitate more positive beliefs, teachers can employ a form of attribution retraining by requiring students to acknowledge the positive attributions (e.g., "You got a B on the test. One of the reasons you got a 'B' instead of a lower grade was because you were really trying to use a good strategy for preparing for the test, right?") or to make the positive choice between negative and positive attributions (e.g., "You got a B on the test. Was it because the teacher made the test easy or because your studying hard made it easy?"), and then facilitate students' selection of the choice that reflects self-control. Because some students with LD frequently use counterproductive negative self-talk (i.e., "I can't do this, I'm too dumb"), teachers can teach students to make positive affirmation statements prior to and during difficult tasks. For example, students can be taught to write at the top of the first page of their tests a positive affirmation statement (e.g., "I'm going to smoke this test") before beginning the test (Hughes, Schumaker, Deshler, & Mercer, 1988).

IV. TOOLS FOR STRATEGIC LEARNING

Learning strategies can help students to become successful and independent learners (Day & Elksnin, 1994). In order for students to learn large amounts of content material, they need to know how to use a variety of learning strategies for thinking about, completing, and evaluating school tasks and assignments (Schumaker & Deshler, 1994–95). Strategy instruction is different from basic skill instruction. A strategy is how an individual thinks and acts when planning, executing, and evaluating performance on a task and its outcomes—in short, a strategy is an individual's approach to a task (Lenz, 1991, p. 4). Basic skills are often used when performing a strategy, but strategy instruction focuses on the problem-solving aspects of using knowledge. The Strategies Intervention Model (Schumaker, Deshler, Alley, & Warner, 1983) developed by colleagues associated with the University of Kansas Center for Research in Learning is perhaps the best example of an intervention model based on a strategies instructional approach. Specific learning strategies have been and continue to be designed and taught to students to enable them to meet academic demands related to knowledge acquisition, storage, and expression or demonstration of competence. Because some of the strategies students with LD use do not always lead to success, specific strategies are designed that will be more optimally useful to them. For example, several knowledge acquisition strategies related to increasing students' abilities to meet reading expectations have proven promising.

The *steps of effective learning strategies are designed to be memorable*. Strategy steps are often encapsulated into a remembering device, and the device is often representative of the strategic process reflected by the strategy or the type of task the strategy is designed to target. For example, Figure 18.4 illustrates a strategy for point-of-view writing. The steps of the strategy of encapsulated using a first-letter mnemonic remembering device, "DEFENDS," as in defending a point-of-view (Ellis, 1993a). Bulgren, Deshler, and Schumaker (1990) found that test performance for students with LD as well as their nondisabled peers was significantly higher when guided practice was provided with mnemonics rather than without. Hudson, Lignugaris-Kraft, and Miller (1993) noted that the results of mnemonic studies were encouraging.

Strategies that have proven to be the most beneficial to adolescents with LD share a number of critical features, although a given strategy might not contain all of these features (Ellis & Lenz, 1987). First and foremost, the strategy is designed

Decide on goals & theme

Decide who will read this & what you hope will happen when they do.
Decide what kind of information you need to communicate.
Decide what your theme will be about.
Note the theme on your planning form.

Estimate main ideas & details

Think of at least two main ideas that will explain your theme.
Make sure the main ideas are different.
Note the main ideas on your planning form.
Note at least 3 details that can be used to explain each main idea.

Figure best order of main ideas & details

Decide which main idea to write about first, second, etc., & note on the planning form.
For each main idea, note the best order for presenting the details on planning form.
Make sure the orders are logical.

Express the theme in the first sentence

The first sentence of your essay should state what the essay is about.

Note each main idea and supporting points

Note your first main idea using a complete sentence; explain this main idea using the details you ordered earlier.
Tell yourself positive statements about your writing and tell yourself to write more.
Repeat for each of the other main ideas.

Drive home the message in the last sentence

Restate what your theme was about in the last sentence.
Make sure you used wording different from the first sentence.

Search for errors and correct

Look for different kinds of errors in your essay and correct them.

Set editing goals.
Examine your essay to see if it makes sense.
Ask yourself whether your message will be clear to others.
Reveal picky errors (capitalization, punctuation, spelling, etc.)
Copy over neatly.
Have a last look for errors.

Figure 18.4 An expository writing strategy.

to be useful. It must address a setting demand that is common in settings students must face, and it should also be valuable for meeting future needs as well as being generalizable. Second, the steps of the strategy are designed to be an *efficient approach to the task for adolescents with LD*. In other words, strategy steps are not just a sequenced set of "good things to do," but rather are a sequenced set of the "best mental and physical actions" organized into the "best sequence" resulting in the "best approach" for adolescents with LD. It is important to note that what might be the best procedure for youth with LD may not be the best approach for sophisticated learners. For example, the point-of-view writing strategy DEFENDS (see Figure 18.4) is a very effective writing strategy for many youth with LD because the thinking and writing processes are very structured, but sophisticated writers would not necessarily use it because it may be *too* structured.

To maximize efficiency, some strategy steps cue students to use effective thinking processes. Effective approaches to tasks often involve use of specific cognitive strategies (e.g., paraphrasing, imaging, predicting, setting priorities, etc.). Some steps cue students to use these cognitive strategies; others cue use of thinking behaviors related to reflecting on and evaluating the way a task is being approached and accomplished. The latter type of cues prompt students to use metacognitive processes involved in analyzing the task and setting goals, monitoring the problem-solving process during its implementation, and reviewing or checking to determine whether goals were met.

A. Factors for Considering Whether to Teach Learning Strategies

Although implementing a strategies instructional approach holds great potential for increasing students' abilities to meet setting demands, there are several factors that should be considered before deciding to provide this type of service. First, is there sufficient *opportunity* to thoroughly teach the strategies? Second, is there a match between the *needs* of students and the strategies that can be offered? Third, is there a match between the *skills and knowledge of students* and the strategies offered? Fourth, does the teacher possess the *skills and knowledge* to competently provide strategy instruction?

1. Is There Sufficient Opportunity to Teach Strategies?

For strategy instruction to have a sufficient impact on students, it must be *intensive* and *extensive*. (Pressley, Goodchild, Fleet, Zajchowski, & Evans, 1987). The intensity of instruction refers to the amount of work required of both teachers and students necessary for strategy instruction to have an impact. The more strategies students master, the more strategic they become. Thus, the extensiveness of instruction refers to the fact that students must learn *many* strategies before a lasting, significant impact is made on their lives. The question is, therefore, are there sufficient opportunities for strategy instructors to do a credible job in providing strategies instruction? In many schools, services that many consumers have come to expect from special education teachers (e.g., tutoring in content areas, providing instruction in social skills, survival skills, vocational, career, and transitional skills) have to be reduced in order to provide intensive and extensive strategy instruction. In order to successfully implement a strategies-based intervention program, teachers need support from their students, parents, mainstream teachers, and administrators. Gaining this support often means that consumers (e.g., students, regular teachers, etc.) must be willing to change their fundamental philosophy of the role of special education and the nature of services offered. Implications are that special education teachers must not only master knowledge and skills associated with becoming an effective teacher of strategies, they must also master knowledge and skills associated with becoming an effective change agent.

2. Is There a Match between the Needs of Students and the Strategies That Can Be Offered?

It is not always appropriate to invest large amounts of time and energy teaching learning strategies. Some students may have discovered or developed effective or efficient strategies on their own, and if students are successfully meeting setting demands using these strategies, substitute strategies should not be taught. For those adolescents who have very low functioning skills, other types of services (i.e., interventions designed to enable students to make more successful transition into postsecondary work environments) might be of greater benefit.

3. Is There a Match between the Skills and Knowledge of Students and the Strategies Offered?

Of the many factors that could affect the ultimate success or failure of strategy training, students' knowledge of critical skills and information relate to the strategy use, as well as students' motivation to learn and use strategies, are among the most important. In addition, strategies should not be taught if there is not a real and immediate need. For example, a note-taking strategy would not be taught if note taking is not a real, as opposed to perceived, setting demand in the student's school.

4. Shouldn't Students Already Know How to ... ?

Teachers at the secondary level may assume that students already are knowledgeable about efficient strategies to help them perform tasks required of them in school (e.g., learning vocabulary, reading for comprehension, writing a paragraph or essay, preparing for tests, organizational skills for materials and information, as well as social skills). As noted earlier in the chapter, students with LD are not as likely as their general education peers to come to high school prepared with such strategic tools. Even relating prior knowledge and experiences to new to-be-learned information may appear quite difficult for some students with LD. Ellis (1993a) outlined a simple learning strategy, FLASH, that teachers could teach students to use to activate their prior knowledge (see Figure 18.5).

Instead of assuming that all secondary students, particularly those with LD, are prepared with strategic learning tools, perhaps better questions for teachers to ask are, "Which students seem to be having difficulty with . . . (e.g., activating prior knowledge, learning vocabulary, words, etc.)? Are there ways I can model for them how to do these things? Are there strategies I can teach them so they will become more proficient at doing these things independently? The learning strategies described below are only a few of the many available that can help students to become successful, independent learners.

Keep in mind that teaching students to use successfully any one of the following strategies independently requires a significant investment of time. Therefore,

Focus on a topic

Look for familiar information

Activate knowledge & ask questions

See what's connected

Hypothesize

Figure 18.5   FLASH: A 'making connections' elaboration strategy. (From Ellis, 1993b.)

teachers need to focus on a limited number of strategies to be taught thoroughly and intensively before moving on to other strategies. Learning strategies can be taught in a upward or downward fashion (Graham, 1992), which means that students are taught the basic strategy and later gain more sophisticated understanding of its use.

B. Sample Learning Strategies

1. LINCS: A Vocabulary Learning Strategy

Secondary school demands require that students know the meaning and spelling of numerous vocabulary words. In addition, students often are asked to show that they understand the meaning of the vocabulary words through essay writing, worksheet exercises, experiments, projects, and so on. This can be a most difficult task for some adolescents with LD. Students may be able to put the vocabulary meanings into short-term memory (i.e., about 20 seconds), but too often the information is quickly forgotten (Hughes, 1996), partly because many students use less efficient and effective learning strategies, such as repetition or verbal rehearsal (i.e., saying information over and over) in an attempt to remember the words. Verbal rehearsal may be appropriate for remembering briefly a telephone number to call a friend, but the approach is usually a very poor long-term memory strategy.

Many adolescents with LD greatly benefit from instruction in a more efficient and effective strategy for learning vocabulary. In other words, they need to be able to use the vocabulary information in working memory (i.e., "held in mind") and file away the information in long-term memory for retrieval later (Hughes, 1996). For many adolescents with LD, retrieving the information from long-term memory can be just as difficult as learning the information in the first place. Therefore, an appropriate vocabulary strategy will not only aid the students in learning the information, but also in retrieving it as well.

Mnemonics are remembering devices that help to make meaningful connections from seemingly unconnected information. Such connections aid in memory storage and later retrieval (Hughes, 1996). Although there are several kinds of mnemonics, keyword is one variety that is often used for learning vocabulary. Keywords are familiar concrete words that visually or acoustically resemble an obvious portion of the unfamiliar word (Bulgren & Lenz, 1996). Brigham, Scruggs, and Mastropieri (1995) found that students with LD recalled significantly more feature locations of American Revolution battles using keyword and pictorial mnemonics than students who were given only drawings of actual features pertaining to battle sites. They further noted that positive effects occur for students with LD because concreteness is enhanced. Mastropieri, Scruggs, and Whedon (1997) stated that mnemonic instruction for students with LD produced positive effects on learning information about U.S. presidents. Bulgren, Hock, Schumaker, and Deshler (1995) found that students with LD instructed in a paired associates strategy involving mnemonics made substantial improvement in the creation of study cards and in test performance. (See Greene [1994] for a discussion of how mnemonics can be applied to various content areas.) Evers and Bursuck (1995) suggested mnemonics as a way for students with LD in technical classes to remember machine parts, the steps to complete a task, or shop procedures.

LINCS (Ellis, 1995)[1] is a vocabulary strategy based on the keyword mnemonic method (Figure 18.6). Each letter of the word LINCS cues students to perform a step to aid in learning vocabulary. For example, to perform the first step, *List the parts,* students determine important words and information to record on an index card. The word is written and circled on the front of the card, and a short definition is written on the back. For example, this may be done for the vocabulary word *fief* and its definition, land given by king for fighting in his army.

For the second stem, *Imagine a picture,* students begin to use memory-enhancing devices and create a mental image of the term and its meaning. They describe that image to themselves or to someone else. For example, a student's mental image may be of a king giving a knight a piece of land in return for the knight's agreeing to serve in the king's army.

To perform the third step, *Note a familiar reminding word,* students identify from their background knowledge a common word that is similar acoustically to the new vocabulary word. In the example, life (a familiar word from the student's background knowledge) sounds like *fief.* Therefore, the rhyming word life is written on the lower half of the front of the index card.

The fourth step, *Construct a "LINCing" story,* requires that the student make an association between the vocabulary word fief and the rhyming or LINCing word life. For example, the student might think, "For life refers to the period of time someone exists." "When the knight returns from fighting, he will be in charge of his land for life."

---

[1]Information about training in the LINCS vocabulary strategy procedures and instructional resources and materials for teaching the LINCS strategy can be obtained by contacting The University of Kansas Center for Research on Learning (913-864-4780).

A CLOSE-UP OF THE LINCS STRATEGY

Step 1: List the parts
■ List the word on a study card.
■ List the most important parts of the definition on the back of the study card.

Step 2: Imagine a picture
■ Create an image in your mind of what the word is about.
■ Describe the image.

Step 3: Note a Reminding Word
■ Think of a familiar word that sounds like the new word, or part of the new word.

Step 4: Construct a LINCing Story
■ Make up a short story about the meaning of the new word that includes the Reminding Word.
■ Change your image to include your story.

Step 5: Self-test
■ Self-test "forwards":
  1. Say the new word.
  2. Say the Reminding Word.
  3. Think of the LINCing Story.
  4. Think of the image.
  5. Say the meaning of the new word.
  6. Check to see if you're correct.

■ Self-test "backwards":
  1. Say the meaning of the new word.
  2. Think of the image.
  3. Think of the LINCing Story.
  4. Think of the Reminding Word.
  5. Say the new word.
  6. Check to see if you're correct.

Figure 18.6   LINCS: a vocabulary learning strategy. (From Ellis, 1995.)

The fifth and final step in LINCS is *Self-test*, in which the student uses forward (i.e., vocabulary word to LINCing word to LINCing story to definition) and backwards (i.e., definition to LINCing story to LINCing word to vocabulary word) retrieval methods. Students are reminded of the chain analogy and encouraged to make strong LINCS. In other words, a chain is only as strong as its weakest link. Good LINCing words and stories are what make this vocabulary strategy successful.

Preview, review & predict

Preview by reading the heading and/or one or two sentences.
Review what you already know about this topic.
Predict what you think the text will be about.

Ask & answer questions

Content-focused questions
Who? What? When? Where? Why? How?
How does this relate to what
I already know?

Monitoring questions
Is my prediction correct?
How is this different from
what I thought it was going
to be about?
Does this make sense?

Problem-solving questions
Is it important that it make sense?
Do I need to reread part of it?
Can I visualize the information?
Do I need to read it more slowly?
Does it have too many unknown words?
Do I need to pay more attention?
Should I get help?

Summarize

Say what the short passage was about.

Synthesize

Say how the short passage fits in with the whole passage.

Say how what you learned fits with what you knew.

Figure 18.7 PASS: a reading comprehension strategy. (From Ellis, 1993c.)

The LINCS vocabulary strategy was used with students with LD in a 6th grade social studies class. The students with LD gained 24% after learning the strategy (Wedel, Deshler, Schumaker, & Ellis, 1992). Results indicate that students with LD are capable of learning a vocabulary memory strategy, and some are able to generalize its use to other subjects and settings. This study indicated that teacher-created mnemonics seemed to be more effective and efficient than student-generated for unknown reasons. More research needs to be conducted as to how to instruct students to consistently and proficiently generalize this technique (Hughes, 1996).

2. PASS: A Reading Comprehension Learning Strategy

PASS is a generic cognitive literacy strategy developed to facilitate students' understanding of using metacognitive and cognitive strategies (Ellis & Feldman, 1994). PASS helps students to think strategically, curb impulsiveness, encourage reflection, and develop effective information processing and problem solving "habits of mind." PASS is composed of steps corresponding to three critical thinking phases. Jones, Palinscar, Ogle, and Carr (1987) referred to these three recursive phases as (a) preparing for learning, (b) on-line processing, and (c) consolidating/extending processing. Weintraub (1990) termed these as *think-ahead, think-during,* and *think-back* processes. During the *think-ahead* phase students activate background knowledge, compare new information to this knowledge, and form hypotheses about the new information. At this time goals for engaging in the learning task are developed. *Think during* or on-line processing refers to students engaged in thinking and tasks to confirm hypotheses or predictions made earlier as well as raise additional questions and/or predictions in a search for understanding (Jones et al., 1987). During the third phase or *think-back*, students focus on consolidating what was learned about the new information with prior knowledge in memory (Jones et al., 1987). In addition, the *think-back* process may involve coming to an understanding about how the information or skill can be extended or generalized to other situations and settings. Jones and colleagues (1987) cautioned that these three phases may occur in a somewhat linear fashion, but also are recursive. Notice how a variety of cognitive strategies are cued in the PASS reading comprehension strategy illustrated in Figure 18.7.

3. DEFENDS: A Writing Learning Strategy

Wong, Wong, and Blenkinsop (1989) found that adolescents with LD performed similar to younger achieving students rather than same-age classmates with regard to essay writing. The essays of students with LD were less interesting and shorter, contained less clarity in communication of written goals, used inferior word choices, and exhibited more spelling errors. Many students with mild LD produce as little as possible to meet the demands of the task. Students whose writing demonstrates a disorganized flow of ideas and poor paragraph structure can benefit from explicit instruction in paragraph and essay writing. Writing strategy instruction enables students "to use an efficient, effective approach to expository writing and to facilitate students' use of self-regulation—self-motivation, self-reinforcement, and goal-directed self-speech—during the prewriting production process, and revising" (Ellis & Colvert, 1996, p. 173). Writing is thinking on paper, so students must use logical methods of organization in order for their writing to make sense to others.

Zipprich (1995) indicated that teaching students with LD a strategy to assist with the planning and organization of writing was beneficial. She found that students who lacked a strategy for planning produced stories that were more poorly written and often were not aware of the component parts of a story. Wong, Butler, Ficzere, and Kuperis (1997) found that adolescents with LD who were taught a writing strategy for compare-and-contrast essays improved the quality of their essays substantially after the training. Particular areas of improvement noted were clarity, appropriateness, and organization of ideas. Hallenbeck (1996) affirmed the value of a writing approach for adolescents with LD that incorporates both cognitive strategy instruction within process writing. He found that junior high and high school students with LD improved in the areas of paragraph structure, inclusion of introductions and conclusions, and development of author voice after writing strategy training and practice for a year.

Modeling of process writing to adolescents with LD helped them to be more willing to share their written work with others (Milem & Garcia, 1996), and goal setting could be combined with a strategy to improve students' writing (Voth &

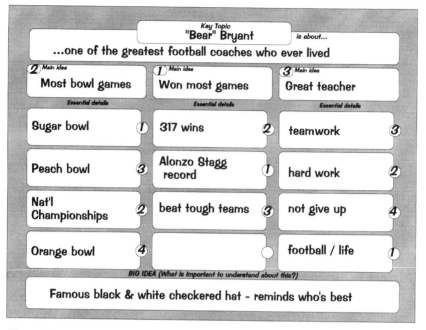

Figure 18.8 Student completed planning form and essay. (From Lenz, Ellis, & Scanlon, 1996.)

Graham, 1993). MacArthur (1994) noted that writing strategies, word processing, and peers were powerful in helping students to revise their writing. Bergen (1994) found that electronic spelling devices were particularly useful for younger students to determine the correct spelling or a word during the editing stage of writing. One writing area that seemed to be more problematic was for students with LD to develop adequate metacognition about their audience's needs. Wong, Wong, Darlington, and Jones (1991) found that interactive teaching (i.e., instructional dialogues with the teacher) improved the clarity and thematic salience of students' expository essays, but the students still had much to learn about adequate revision.

DEFENDS is a paragraph and essay writing strategy that can assist students with meeting the many common writing demands found in academic and nonacademic settings (Ellis & Colvert, 1996). Figure 18.4 illustrates the steps of the DEFENDS strategy, which can be used in conjunction with various planning forms to assist adolescents with LD with their writing. Figure 18.8 shows a student-completed hierarchical or whole-to-part planning form that is beneficial to use with DEFENDS and a student essay written after using the planning form. Both the strategy and planning form are based on the work of Schumaker (1997). The steps of the DEFENDS strategy and the planning form give students with LD a framework for examining specific situations, perceiving key elements for writing topics, and organizing major attributes. The planning form assists students in the

Prepare to succeed

Put name on test.

Allot time & order sections.

Say something positive.

Start within 2 minutes.

Inspect instructions

Read instructions carefully.

Underline how and where to respond.

Notice special requirements.

Read, remember, reduce

Read whole questions.

Remember with memory strategies.

Reduce choices.

Answer or abandon

Turn back

Estimate

Avoid absolutes.

Choose longest or most detailed answer.

Eliminate choices.

Survey to ensure all questions are answered

Figure 18.9 PIRATES: a test taking strategy. (From Hughes et al., 1993.)

thinking process by helping them to focus on "the big picture." The form is easy to use, and is readily adaptable for use when teaching content information.

4. PIRATES: A Test-Taking Learning Strategy

Students with LD may not perform well in testing situations because they do not know how to effectively take tests. Often, they may think that "studying hard" is the only thing they have to do to get a good grade. A history of poor test performance naturally leads to test anxiety and an "I don't care" coping attitude. Test-taking strategies can be taught to students to assist them in performing better on tests and reducing anxiety. Students must be cautioned that learning a test-preparation strategy does not mean that they are free from studying (Hughes, 1996). Rather it is a test-taking strategy in combination with good study habits that provide a formula for success in testing situations.

PIRATES (Hughes, Schumaker, Deshler, & Mercer, 1993)[2] is a test-taking strategy mainly designed for use with objective test formats (see Figure 18.9). Adolescents with LD and those with behavior problems have successfully used the

[2]Information about training in the PIRATES test-taking strategy procedures and instructional resources and materials for teaching the PIRATES strategy can be obtained by contacting The University of Kansas Center for Research on Learning (913-864-4780).

strategy (Hughes, Ruhl, Deshler, & Schumaker, 1993; Hughes & Schumaker, 1991a, 1991b). The first step, *Prepare to succeed* helps to establish a proactive frame of mind (Hughes, 1996). Students put their name and PIRATES on the test, determine the order in which they wish to work test items and the time that should be allotted to each, as well as say some affirmations, and begin the test within 2 minutes (Hughes, 1996). Order of items is a matter of preference. Some students choose the harder items first while others choose the easy ones.

The second step, *Inspect the instructions* cues students with LD to focus on the directions, something they otherwise may fail to do (Hughes, 1996). This step has a substep, RUN, which stands for *Read instructions carefully, Underline what to do and where to respond,* and *Notice special requirements*. Students are taught the importance of reading directions and how to read the directions. Then students are to notice whether letters are to be circled or underlined and if they are to indicate the correct answer or one that is not correct.

Step three, *Read, remember, and reduce* encourages students to read the question in its entirety before answering rather than acting like eager game show contestants who blurt out an answer before the question is finished. Students also are taught to read all possible choices before answering. Remember cues students to remember what they have learned and studied that would help them to answer the item. Then students reduce the number of possible choices by eliminating obviously incorrect ones and crossing them out.

Step four, *Answer or abandon,* reminds students to answer the question if they are relatively sure of the answer or abandon the item if they are unsure. Abandoned items should be marked in a way that they cannot be mistaken for answers, but will be easily recognized later. Steps 2, 3, and 4 are repeated for each section of the test until all sections have been attempted.

In step five, *Turn back* students return to abandoned items to see if they can remember anything that would help them to answer the questions. Relevant knowledge may have been found in another item. If they still do not know the answer and will not be penalized for guessing, then they can apply three guessing strategies as cued by the mnemonic ACE in the sixth step (*Estimate*): (a) A stands for avoid absolutes (specific determiners); (b) C means choose the longest, most detailed option; and (c) E or eliminate (cross off) similar options.

The seventh step *Survey* ensures that students have responded to all items and that they have responded to all items in the way in which they intended. Students are taught that changing answers is appropriate only if they are sure that the new choice is correct. If they are unsure, it is better to remain with the original choice (Hughes, 1996).

C. Social Skills

Approximately one-third (Sabornie, Marshall, & Ellis, 1990) to over one-half of students with LD are at risk for social problems. The number of students lacking social competence also is evidenced in teacher ratings (see Tur-Kaspa & Bryan, 1995), peer sociometric measures (see Conderman, 1995; Stone & LaGreca, 1990), and self-ratings (see Vaughn & Haager, 1994). Social perception problems were found to improve with age, but a constant proportionate difference between students with LD and their nondisabled peers remained through age 17 (Jackson, Enright, & Murdock, 1987).

Scanlon (1996) noted that poor social skills in school can be related to (a) limited opportunities to learn, (b) negative academic and social self-concept, and (c) social isolation. For example, if a student does not know how to appropriately ask for help, then the student either may not ask the question or ask the question in a manner that draws more attention to the way the question was asked rather than providing an answer to the question. Difficult interactions may place students at risk for developing a negative self-concept. If a student does not share his or her ideas for fear of being labeled "dumb" then he or she will have no reason to develop faith in them or develop skills to express ideas effectively (Scanlon, 1996; see Scarpati, Malloy, & Fleming, 1996). After a history of social failure experiences, a student with LD may be likely to withdraw from social situations as much as possible or be considered a social outcast by peers. Socialization may be confusing for adolescents who must deal with adult issues concerning their independence, responsibility, physical and sexual development, and changing societal pressures and expectations (Scanlon, 1996).

The causes of social problems, experienced by students with LD are unknown (Bryan, 1997; Kavale & Forness, 1996). Evidence of the consequences for students with LD who do not develop adequate social relationships is mounting and has been linked to the following factors: (a) loneliness (Margalit & Levin-Alyagon, 1994); (b) depression (Huntington & Bender, 1993; Maag & Behrens, 1989; Maag & Forness, 1991; Putnam, 1995; Wright-Strawderman & Watson, 1992), and (c) suicide (Hayes & Sloat, 1988; Huntington & Bender, 1993; Putnam, 1995). Therefore, educators need to be aware of students with LD experiencing depression and if students are engaging in solitary activities, is it by choice or due to coerced loneliness (Bryan, 1997).

Bryan (1997) targeted the following five goals as crucial in the social assessment of students with LD: (a) students should be relatively happy and not debilitated by negative affect (affective status); (b) students should believe they can achieve goals and overcome adversity (self-efficacy and optimism); (c) students should have at least one peer friend and adult supporter; (d) students should have attention, perceptual, cognitive, and behavioral skills to develop appropriate interpersonal relationships (social skills); and (e) students should not be aggressive toward self or others or be subjected to teasing/bullying (no destructive behavior). Negotiation, conversation, social problem solving, promotion of self and ones' own ideas were viewed as necessary skills for success in social situations (Serna & Lau-Smith, 1995). Also interesting to note is that high school students with LD and their nondisabled peers referred to similar social and school skills that are important for success in the mainstream (McLeod, Kolb, & Lister, 1994).

Mellard and Hazel (1992) noted that individuals with LD need to understand the social demands of the workplace, which may be somewhat different than those addressed in school settings. Several factors contribute to the difficulty of understanding the workplace environment: (a) rules may not be as explicit as in school settings, (b) workplace social skills vary greatly depending on one's position, and (c) little direct feedback may be available for poor social performance.

Clearly, most adolescents would benefit from some degree of social skills training. Since social skills instruction is typically not part of the traditional school program, the intervention must be added to the existing curriculum, or parts of the existing curriculum must be eliminated to make room for social skills instruction. Earlier, it was noted that for learning strategies instruction to be worthwhile, instruction had to be intensive and extensive. Essentially, the same principle holds true for social skills training. Providing only *periodic* instruction in social skills looks good on paper (e.g., Parents like the fact that the IEP reflects that their adolescent with LD is receiving social skills training), but, unfortunately, this approach will have little impact on the adolescent! For the most part, intermittent, unsystematic social skills instruction likely will be a *complete waste of time*. Elksnin (1994) advocated a "training loosely" approach "which involves teaching multiple social skills during an instructional period, introducing new skills prior to skill mastery, teaching social skills several times a day, and using instructional language resembling that of the natural setting" (p. 36). Thus, effective training in social skills for adolescents is focused, intensive, extensive, and ongoing. Because social skills training requires a considerable commitment of time and energy, its implementation should be carefully weighed against other forms of interventions that might be offered to students. Rarely is there sufficient time to address *all* the needs of students with LD by offering intensive social skills instruction, strategy instruction, tutoring in content areas, basic skill remediation, and so on.

Educators must proceed with social skills training for adolescents with LD with caution. A recent meta-analysis found limited positive effects of social skills training (Forness & Kavale, 1996). Possible reasons for limited positive effects were due to the intensity of training, measurement issues, training package components, genesis of social skill deficits, and research design issues.

Scanlon (1996) suggested that the most worthwhile social skill interventions include the promotion of strategic use of social skills. In other words, students are strategic when they know how, when, and why to use the skill and are able to monitor their performance. Some of the following activities may be helpful in assisting students acquire the necessary social skills and use them strategically: (a) promoting social awareness, (b) self-monitoring through interview, journal keeping, or record keeping, (c) contracts and posted rules, (d) role playing, and (e) praise/reinforcement (Scanlon, 1996). Cooperative learning requires the use of appropriate social skills and also may be a useful technique. Other social skills interventions such as ASSET (Hazel, Schumaker, Sherman, & Sheldon-Wildgen, 1981) are fully developed instructional routines complete with materials (see Scanlon, 1996, for a review of ASSET and other social skills programs).

Regardless of the social skills training selected for adolescents with LD, teachers need to examine the students' environment. Sometimes inappropriate social behavior may be linked primarily to environmental factors, which may or may not be changeable. For example, a student may react inappropriately when being bullied by another student. Certainly, both students need to learn appropriate social skills, but targeting social skills training for the student being bullied without examining the underlying problem of the "bullier" would be "a case of punishing the victim" (Scanlon, 1996). Elksnin (1994) pointed to other important environmental considerations for social skills training. For example, students are more likely to use social skills in real-life settings when they are reinforced by peers. As specific social skills are selected to target for training, educators should take into consideration skills that teachers, peers, and employers value and are apt to reinforce (also see Elksnin & Elksnin, 1995).

V. STRATEGIC INSTRUCTION VIA CONTENT ENHANCEMENT

The principles of strategic instruction can be used effectively with instructional routines and devices to enhance learning for all students (Bulgren & Lenz, 1996; Lenz, Bulgren, & Hudson, 1990). These devices are particularly beneficial to adolescents with LD to help them recognize organizational patterns of instruction. In addition, showing students, as precisely as possible, the organizational pattern of effective problem-solving processes, as well as organizational structures of content subject matters appears to help students with LD more readily understand and remember them. Content-area instruction can be enhanced using a variety of organizational devices. These include instructional organizers, process organizers, and content organizers.

A. Instructional Organizers

Teaching routines help to structure information in order to anticipate and address potential learning difficulties (Bulgren & Lenz, 1996). Instructional organizers are teaching routines used to help students understand what is being learned and to integrate new information with that which is previously learned. They also help students distinguish between important and unimportant information during the lesson and help them store the new information for future recall. The power of instructional organizers is significant when used with adolescents with LD. Research has demonstrated that when instructional organizers are used and *teachers specifically instruct students to take advantage of them,* students with LD are able to answer correctly more questions about important information than unimportant information following the lesson; when not used, they tend to answer more questions correctly about unimportant information (Lenz, 1984; Lenz, Alley, & Shumaker, 1987).

There are three types of instructional organizers that have been found highly beneficial when teaching adolescents with LD. These include the advance organizer, lesson organizer cues, and the postorganizer.

1. FORM as an Advance Organizer

The *advance organizer* is provided at the beginning of the lesson and provides a general description of the lesson (Ausubel & Robinson, 1969). Luten, Ames, and Ackerson (1980) found that advance organizers facilitate learning and retention in various content areas with individuals of all grade and ability levels. Lenz (1983) noted that advance organizers address some major organizational problems found in adolescents with LD. For example, information contained on an advance organizer may be used to organize notes. Lenz et al. (1987) found that when students were trained to identify and record information from an advance organizer, substantially more advance organizer information statements appeared on tests following the lesson.

When providing an advance organizer, the teacher gains students' attention and cues them that an organizer is being provided. Previous learning is reviewed, and then topic and goals of the current lesson are discussed. Next, the content of the lesson is defined for students. Here, the teacher informs students what they will be learning *about* the topic of the lesson followed by a discussion or review of key vocabulary that will be used during the lesson. Learning is then personalized by discussing "if–then" statements (e.g., IF you learn to explain each of the steps of the writing strategy in your own words, THEN you will be better able to use the strategy because you can tell yourself what to do."). Finally, expectations are clearly identified by discussing how the goals of the lesson will be achieved. For example, the teacher informs students about the *way* the lesson will be taught and *how* the activities that may follow the lesson will be *useful* in helping them master the information.

Ellis (1998) developed a simple procedure to facilitate implementation of advance organizers. Teachers use the "FORM" device (Figures 18.10 and 18.11) to introduce content-area lessons. "FORM" is a way of matching the content instructional routine for beginning the lesson with a task-specific strategy for activating learning.

2. Lesson Organizer Cues

During the lesson, effective teachers provide various *lesson organizer cues*. For example, the teacher will cue students about the organization or structure of the lesson by using organizing words such as "first," "second," "third," and so on, as they teach (e.g., "There were *four* main results of the French/Indian War. *First*, . . ."). They also provide important cues to help students distinguish critical

.........FORM the BIG PICTURE of the lesson........

Focus: *What will we be focusing on?*
Students focused on teacher
What will the focus of the lesson be about?
What are the key points that will be addressed?
What are some questions students want answered?

Organization: *How will we learn it?*
Organizational devices to be used
What learning enhancers will be used to make it easier?

Organization of lesson
What is the sequence of activities you will be using during this lesson?

Relationship: *How will it effect you?*
Relationship to **past**
What have you learned before that will help you now?

Relationship to **future**
If you master the material, then how will you benefit?

Most important goal: *What do you need to learn if you don't learn anything else?*

Figure 18.10   The FORM routine: an advance organizer teaching procedure for introducing content area lessons. (From Ellis, 1998.)

from superfluous information (e.g., "This is critical to understand; let's review it once more."). Relationships also are explicitly cued to help students integrate information by drawing students' attention to associations between new information and that which is familiar to them.

Another type of lesson organizing device is *cuing expectations*. Although the expectations should have been explicitly communicated during the advance organizer, they are also cued throughout the lesson. As new information is presented, students are cued to how it relates to the instructional goals, mastery requirements, and so on, of the lesson.

3. The CROWN Post Organizer Routine

The third type of instructional organizer is the use of a *post organizer* at the end of a lesson. During the postorganizer, students first are cued that a post organizer is being provided, (e.g., *"Now I'm giving you a post organizer to review what we learned today."*). To determine whether students have sufficiently acquired and integrated the new information, students then are evaluated (oral or written) and informed with regard to how well they are attaining the goals of the lesson. When teaching a skill, generalization is forecasted by discussing how what is being

Focus:

Focus of lesson *1920s Development of organized crime*
gangsters & gangster "families"

Focus of students' questions:

Why did gangsters shoot people from cars?
Where did they get their machine guns?
What did gangsters do?

Organization:

Organizational devices to be used: *Compare / contrast form*

Organization of lesson:

1st *discuss modern-day drug lords & cartels*

2nd *compare drug cartels with gangster families*

3rd *discuss how gangsters became so powerful*

4th *quiz*

Relationship:

Relationship to **past:**
yesterday -- why people wanted prohibition
today -- what happened as a result

Relationship to **future:**
If..... you learn why gangsters became so powerful

Then... you 'll understand why some people want to legalize
drugs today

Most important goal: *understand how gangsters get & keep power*

Figure 18.11   Illustration of an application of the FORM routine when applied to an American history lesson about the development of organized crime. (From Ellis, 1998.)

learned can be used across settings and situations. The post organizer ends with a forecast of future learning by discussing the focus of the next lesson. Figure 18.12 depicts the steps to the CROWN post organizer routine:

In addition to instructional organizers, *process* and *content* organizers can be used to help explicitly communicate to-be-learned information. Pressley, Johnson, and Symons (1987) noted that it is often necessary to restructure material into a form that is "more learnable." The characteristics of the more learnable material are that the material is presented in such a way (a) as to facilitate elaboration, and (b) that it is rich with organizational structures and cues that facilitate learning. Both process and content organizers are designed to address this need.

Communicate what you learned

Specific things you learned...
General things you learned...
How are they different from what you knew before?

Reaction

What was your reaction (surprises, connections, images, conflicts, regrets or other reactions) to the information presented in this lesson?

One sentence that sums up the *whole* lesson

Where are some *different* places you could use this?

Note how well we did today

The *best* part was...
The part I liked *least* was...
Did you meet a personal goal?

Figure 18.12 The CROWN routine: a post organizer for bringing closure to a lesson. (From Ellis, 1989.)

B. Process Organizers: The Project Planning Strategy

As school reform efforts continue to be implemented throughout the nation, teachers can expect an increase in the amount of student and group investigations that occur in general education classrooms (Sharan & Sharan, 1990, 1994). Typically, students are expected to target a topic of interest related to an area of study, and then conduct an investigation to learn more about it and subsequently make an oral and/or written presentation about it. Students often are expected to conduct multisource investigations. This means that not only are they expected to glean information from traditional print sources such as books and encyclopedias, they also are often expected to attain information from other sources such as the Internet or World Wide Web and by conducting experiments, interviews, and surveys.

An effective investigation involves three phases: (a) planning a multisource investigation and presentation, (b) conducting the multisource investigation, and (c) developing and delivering a presentation. These processes can be greatly facilitated by providing students with "process organizers." These organizers are designed to provide students with sufficient structure to enable them to engage in the tasks in a systematic and strategic manner while at the same time not overstructuring the task so that creativity and opportunities for problem solving are impaired.

PROJECT (Ellis, in press, b) is an example of a process organizer for helping students plan for a quality project (see Figure 18.13). Each step is designed to cue students to *proactively* engage in essential behaviors associated with planning an effective investigation and presentation. The first step, *Preview the task,* cues students to determine task parameters such as who the intended audience will be and what the expectations are for the project. To perform the second step, *Rough out a plan,* students identify potential topics and subtopics that will be addressed by the

PROJECT planning strategy

Preview the task
* nature of project
* audience
* expectations
  - what will be evaluated? how? rubric?
  - due date?
  - presentation expectations (format? length? graphics? etc.)
  - content expectations (theme? how detailed? topics to include?)
  - collaboration/individual accountability expectations?

Rough-out a plan
* overview of topics & subtopics
* basic plan for investigating, experimenting and/or inventing
* tentative plan for presenting

Organize tasks & resources
* brainstorm to identify specific tasks
* determine priority & order that tasks should be completed
* brainstorm to identify potential resources for each task

Jot down job assignments
* dissect each task & identify specific jobs
* match jobs with unique talents & abilities

Examine obstacles and develop strategies
* brainstorm to identify potential obstacles that might be encountered for each task
* brainstorm to identify potential solutions to each obstacle

Commit to goals
* make commitments with regard to quality of project & presentation
* make commitments regarding use of collaboration skills
* make commitments regarding use of mind habits

Target time-lines
* note due date & how long you have to complete the whole project
* determine order of tasks and indicate due dates for each
* identify team-meeting dates and record
* make a copy of the time-line for each member of team

Figure 18.13 PROJECT: A project planning strategy. (From Ellis, in press b.)

project, create a tentative plan for conducting research, as well as making the presentation. Figure 18.14 shows a completed graphic organizer students should use when performing this step. The following three steps, *Organize tasks and resources, Job assignments,* and *Expected obstacles* identified, are completed using the graphic organizer depicted in Figure 18.15. Once students have completed these steps, they make *Commitments* (step 6) to engage in quality work (see Figure 18.16). To complete the last step of the process, students construct a *Time line* depicting due dates for various tasks associated with completing the project, as well as team meeting dates.

C. Content Organizers and Instructional Routines

Effective teachers of students with LD also make the organization of the content subject matter as explicit as possible for students. Various forms of graphics that provide visual displays of the subject matter's organization or structure (e.g.,

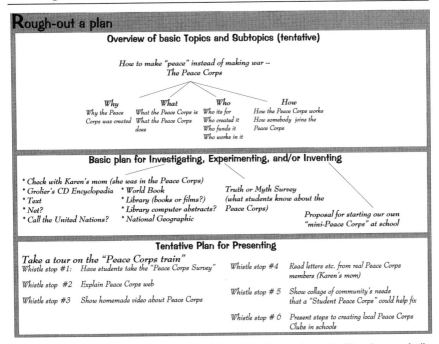

Figure 18.14 Illustration of a completed graphic organizer for completing the "Rough-out a plan" step of the PROJECT planning strategy. (From Ellis, in press, b.)

charts, diagrams, etc.) are an effective means of providing content organizers. These are known as content organizers, graphic organizers, or visual displays that provide a visual and verbal organizational structure that helps students to view information as a meaningful whole rather than a series of unrelated facts, terms, or concepts (Horton & Lovitt, 1989). Graphic organizers are fundamental to skilled thinking because they provide information and opportunities for analysis that cannot be provided by reading and/or linear outlines, which is especially beneficial for low-achieving students (Jones, Pierce, & Hunter, 1989).

Graphic organizers should not only be viewed as a means for teaching content, but also within an overall framework of providing students with LD with explicit organizer devices to facilitate success. The "organizational function of pictures" have been used in various ways, including "semantic maps" (D. D. Johnson & Pearson, 1978; Scanlon, Duran, Reyes, & Gallego, 1992), "story maps" (Idol, 1987), "networks" (Dansereau & Holley, 1982), and what Scruggs et al. (1985) referred to as "figural taxonomies," or graphics that display superordinate, coordinate, and subordinate relationships among concepts, facts, and/or details. Graphic representations can assist in making the material more learnable because

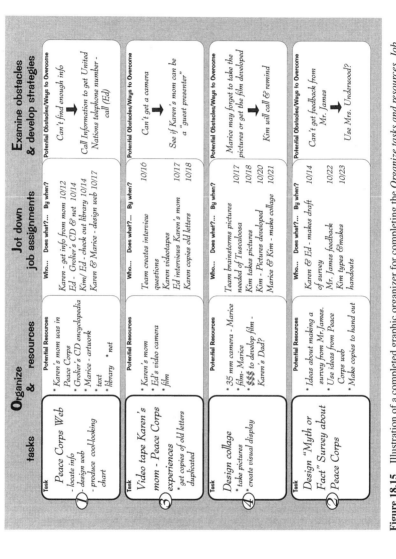

Figure 18.15 Illustration of a completed graphic organizer for completing the *Organize tasks and resources, Job assignments,* and *Expected obstacles* steps of the PROJECT planning strategy. (From Ellis, in press, b.)

Commitments to quality of project and presentation

By signing my name below, I am making a commitment to:

1. Developing a high-quality product that I will be proud of,
2. Creating a product that will make sense, and be interesting and informative to my audience.
3. Being neat and careful.
4. Doing my share on time.
5. Doing my best.

Signatures of team members

Goals for collaborating effectively

check 3 that will be *primary goals*

- ☐ Listening without interrupting
- ☐ Turn-taking & involving everyone
- ☐ Offering assistance
- ☐ Communicating about difficulties

- ☐ Respecting different opinions, skills, & abilities
- ☐ Encouraging & complimenting others
- ☐ Recognizing and celebrating others' successes
- ☐ Recognizing unique talents of others

- ☐ Giving "I" messages
- ☐ Consensus building
- ☐ Giving negative feedback
- ☐ Peacefully resolving conflicts

☐ Other_____

Goals for using effective habits of the mind

check 3 that will be *primary goals*

- ☐ Using & keeping time lines
- ☐ Resisting impulsiveness
- ☐ Engaging in challenging tasks
- ☐ Persisting during tough times

- ☐ Organizing ideas & being clear
- ☐ Being accurate
- ☐ Noticing how you & others think
- ☐ Using information resources

- ☐ Being open minded
- ☐ Being creative
- ☐ Viewing an idea in unusual ways
- ☐ Presenting an idea in usual ways

☐ Other_____

Figure 18.16   The Commitments and Goals form used when completing the Make Commitments"
step of the PROJECT planning strategy. (From Ellis, in press, b.)

students with LD often lack the basic reading skills to extract the information from texts (Torgesen & Licht, 1983), and the texts themselves are often "inconsiderate" due to poor structure and organization (Anderson & Armbruster, 1984).

Several studies demonstrated that less capable learners (i.e., those with poor reading ability, low verbal ability, and underdeveloped vocabulary) perform better when graphics were used to supplement regular content-area text chapters (Koran & Koran, 1980; Moyer, Sowder, Threadgill-Sowder, & Moyer, 1984). Recent studies provide positive evidence that the use of graphics as supplements to textbook material can be an effective instructional technique for students with LD. For instance, Bergerud, Lovitt, and Horton (1988) found that using graphics for 9th-grade basic science was most effective in helping students attain the highest test scores (60.5% of the students had scores above the minimal mastery level of 80% when graphics were used to facilitate the organization of the material as compared to 42.1% in the study guide condition, and 31.6% in the self-study condition). A study by Horton, Lovitt, and Bergerud (1990) conducted in middle and high school science and social studies found that students with LD averaged 73% correct in the teacher-directed graphic organizer condition and 30% correct with self-study. Crank (1993) found that using visual depictions rather than outlining or listing information in lecture resulted in statistically higher posttest quiz scores for secondary students with LD. Also, 18 of the 23 students in the study showed higher postinstruction test scores. In a review of eight studies using various kinds of graphic organizers, Hudson, Lignugaris-Kraft, and Miller (1993) found positive results that suggested that graphic organizers can be used to enhance content learning in different areas. They urged that the content enhancement devices and lesson objectives be matched appropriately and that effective teaching practices also be used.

Keep in mind that teaching students to successfully use any one of the following content organizers independently may require a significant investment of time (Jones, Pierce, & Hunter, 1989), particularly for students with LD. Therefore, teachers need to focus on a limited number of organizers to be taught thoroughly and intensively before moving on to other content organizers. Schmid and Telaro (1990) found that it took a minimum of 2 weeks of daily usage for all students in a high school biology class to independently generate an acceptable concept map.

1. The Clarifying Table

Students need to know the definition of a concept in order to communicate about the concept and be able to identify and interpret it (Toumasis, 1995). Teaching students how to express the definition in their own words rather than just repeating a textbook definition helps them to increase their understanding and usage of terms. Students with LD often have difficulty learning the meaning of target words associated with events, ideas, historical figures, and so on. The Clarifying Routine[3] (Ellis, 1997) was developed to help students with what seems to be an insurmountable task of completing end-of-chapter exercises or learning terms on study guides (see Figure 18.17). Students with LD tend to perform poorly on these kinds of exercises and on tests covering information they should have learned from the exercises or study guides. Students must learn new terms in a meaningful way and meaningful context if these terms are to be useful. Rote memorization does not help students with LD to remember and be able to do so effectively over a long period of time.

The Clarifying Routine is used to reveal the meaning of the term by (a) naming the new term; (b) identifying the "core idea" of the term; (c) identifying specific information related to the term; (d) having students connect the meaning of the new term to their background knowledge and experiences; (e) creating examples

---

[3]Information about training in the Clarifying Routine for Content Enhancement and instructional resources and materials can be obtained by contacting the Center for Research in Learning (913-864-4780).

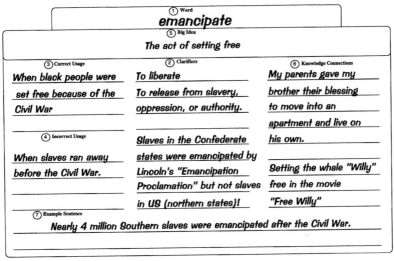

Figure 18.17   Illustration of a completed Clarifying Table. (From Ellis, 1997.)

and nonexamples for term usage; and (f) creating an example sentence using the term. Baker, Simmons, and Kameenui (1994) defined the big idea as

> concepts and principles that facilitate the most efficient and broad acquisition of knowledge across a range of examples . . . , make it possible for students to learn the most and learn it as efficiently as possible, and serve as anchoring concepts by which "small" ideas can often be understood. (p. 14)

In order for the Clarifying Routine to be successful, it should be explicitly introduced to the whole class, used regularly, and adapted to meet the unique needs of students and teacher. In addition, students need to become actively involved in the routine and become responsible for using the routine on their own to learn new terms and help other students learn new terms. Ellis, Raines, Farmer, and Tyree (1997) evaluated the effectiveness of the Clarifying Routine in low, middle, and high socioeconomic schools and found that students, regardless of their socioeconomic background, increased the percentage of correct answers on tests addressing vocabulary taught via the Clarifying Routine by an average of 22%.

The Clarifying Routine is centered around a content organizer called the Clarifying Table (Figure 18.17). This enables the teacher to display important information related to the targeted word or phrase in order to help students think and talk about the word and learn its meaning. Prior to class, the teacher completes a draft of the table to use as a private guide during instruction. During class as the meaning of the vocabulary is being explored, the students help the teacher to coconstruct the table during an interactive process.

Designate the term

* Focus on the most critical terms.

Explore the clarifiers

* Note essential details that should be remembered.
* Note 'cultural-expected trivia'.

Figure out correct usage

* Note an example of the concept.

Identify incorrect usage

* Note a parallel nonexample of the concept.

Name the big idea

* Note the main idea of what the term is about.

Evaluate knowledge connections

* List items from students' background knowledge or previous learning.

Set up an example sentence

* Use the term appropriately in the sentence.

Figure 18.18   DEFINES steps for using Clarifying Tables. (From Ellis, 1997.)

Section 1 of the Clarifying Table includes the term, word, or phrase to be learned. It may be a vocabulary word or the name of a person, place, event, process, or a time in history. Typically, the terms are nouns, but can be adjectives, verbs, or other words. Section 2 contains the clarifiers that are related details that help to clarify a term's meaning. These are recorded in the middle column of the table under the word clarifiers. Section 3, Core Idea, is either a brief definition of the targeted term or a summary of its primary importance and is located at the top of the table under the targeted term. In Section 4, Knowledge Connections are listed that reflect ideas or experiences from the learner's personal background knowledge to which the term relates. Sections 5 and 6 address examples and nonexamples of the concept. In Section 5, students list either a related concept that the term is "used to describe" or is an "example of." In Section 6, students identify similar ideas that the new term "should not be confused with" or a concept that the term is "not an example of." In Section 7, students demonstrate the correct usage of the term in a sentence written at the bottom of the table. The Clarifying Routine also contains a set of linking steps in the form of the mnemonic DEFINES (see Figure 18.18).

2. Hierarchical Frames

A hierarchical structure is a device that focuses on one major topic and is used to rank information (Crank & Bulgren, 1993).[4] Ranking is usually achieved by plac-

---

[4]Information about training in the Framing Routine for Content Enhancement and instructional resources and materials can be obtained by contacting The University of Kansas Center for Research on Learning (913-864-4780).

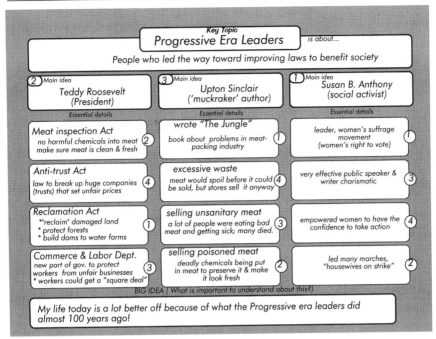

Figure 18.19   Sample completed Frame graphic organizer. (From Ellis, in press, a.)

ing a supraordinate item above other items in the depiction. Simple hierarchical depictions contain two levels in which major concept(s) are placed near the top of the graphic organizer and subsumed concepts or details are placed below the major concept. The structure itself implies a particular meaning. This provides a way of breaking down one or more "big ideas" into several component parts, or small ideas (Ellis, in press, a). Hierarchic graphics are especially helpful tools to aid students in understanding relationships between different parallel ideas as well as their relationship to a larger picture. These graphics also help to reduce confusion about which details are associated with which main idea. Figure 18.19 depicts a basic frame for organizing information into a hierarchical format. Figure 18.20 depicts the steps to the Framing Routine that can be followed when teaching content subjects using the frame. The basic hierarchic frame also can be readily adapted to show other types of information structures. For example, Figure 18.21 is an example of how the frame can be adapted to depict a cause–effect relationship.

3. Compare–Contrast

Crank and Bulgren (1993) defined a comparative structure as a graphic organizer that shows the relationship between at least two concepts that are compared or contrasted. Characteristics of items presented side by side highlight the similarities

Focus on the topic
Focus attention.
Focus on activating knowledge related to the topic.
Focus on clarifying what is to be learned about the topic.

Reveal relationships
Reveal how the information will be organized.
Reveal main ideas associated with the topic.

Analyze features
For each main idea, analyze and elaborate about essential features.
Address other features only to clarify a main idea, but do not note them on the Framing graphic.

Mediate connections
* Connections to other ideas being learned.
* Connections to background knowledge.
* Connections to real-world contexts & experiences.

Extend understanding of the BIG IDEA
* Making many and varied ways of viewing/using the BIG IDEA.
* Creating metaphors & similes.
* Forecasting, predicting, applying &/or anticipating.
* Creating generative statements.

Figure 18.20   Framing steps for using the Frame graphic organizer. (From Ellis, in press, a.)

and differences of selected concepts. Figure 18.22 is a sample compare–contrast graphic organizer using the comparison frame format.

Some newer textbooks are beginning to have more content organizers either as text illustrations or in supplementary materials (e.g., black-line masters, remedial or enrichment worksheets). In addition, there are books of blank content organizer forms that contain templates to be completed and copied. Some contain corresponding computer software for a nominal price. The point is that it may not be necessary to "reinvent the wheel" if there is an existing content organizer or blank form suitable for student needs. If an existing content organizer or blank form is not available, teachers and students can be creative and design their own organizers.

D. Uses of Content Graphic Organizers

Content or graphic organizers can be used in a variety of ways to facilitate success of students with LD. A few of these include using graphics (a) to enhance advance and post-organizers, (b) as study guides, (c) to facilitate guided note taking, and (d) as assessment tools.

1. Using Graphic Organizers to Enhance, Advance, and Post Organizers

Once teachers are experienced in using content organizers and feel comfortable in using them, they are likely to provide their students with a variety of content or-

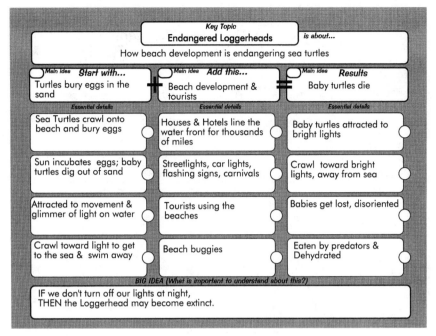

Figure 18.21   Illustration of how the Frame graphic can be adapted for use to depict cause–effect relationships. (From Ellis, in press, a.)

ganizers to assist students in recognizing and understanding the relationships in the to-be-learned material. The graphic devices can be used in a variety of ways throughout the instructional process. These include (a) before reading an instructional unit of text (advance organizer), (b) during an instructional unit of text (intermediate organizer), or after reading an instructional unit of text (post organizer) (Horton & Lovitt, 1989; Readance, Bean, & Baldwin, 1992). They may be constructed to provide a broad overview or "Big Picture" of information contained in a chapter or unit. They also may provide a more detailed sample of information contained in the same chapter or unit. Teachers may want to create a content organizer that shows the broad overview of a chapter or unit to introduce the new information and provide a "road map" for the lessons to follow. Each subsequent lesson may contain another content organizer that focuses in depth on a portion of the chapter or unit. The overview content organizer shared as an introduction may reappear at the end of the chapter or unit to provide a summary of "the journey" or what has been studied. This organizer also provides a framework that can help students to synthesize all the information they have learned in the chapter or unit and provides a bridge to the next topic of study.

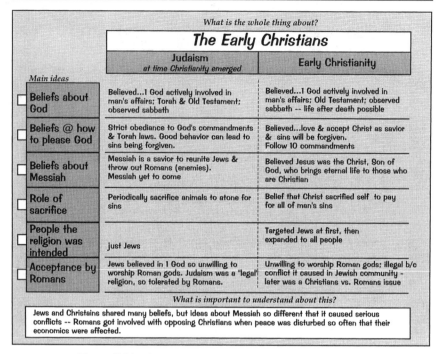

Figure 18.22 Illustration of a compare–contrast graphic organizer.

The principles of strategic instruction discussed earlier are applicable when using content organizers in the classroom. For example, scaffolding means that students who are not familiar with content organizers will need a great deal of explicit instruction from the teacher at first. Later, as students have had more practice in using the organizers and have developed the necessary skills for using them, the teacher can turn more responsibility for their use and creation over to the students. Each time a new content organizer is introduced, the teacher briefly explains the value of using the organizer and describes the procedure for its use. Next the teacher models the necessary student behaviors, provides guided practice, and provides independent practice (see Lazarus, 1996).

One of the reasons that content organizers are a powerful tool for all students is that various forms of the scaffolding process can be occurring simultaneously in the same classroom. Students with LD and lower achieving students may need more teacher support and/or peer support for a longer period of time. Therefore, they may be given partially completed content organizers more often and either work with the teacher or with peers to complete them. Average to above-average students may be successful working with blank organizers and working individually once they have received a brief explanation from the teacher and been provided with an example. Gifted and talented students may be ready to create and complete their own content organizer forms to show their understanding of relationships contained in the content information. Thus, in a classroom the topic may be the same for all students, but the content organizers may look very different based on student needs.

2. Using Graphic Organizers as Study Guides

Another way teachers can provide explicit organizational cues is through the use of structured study guides consisting of sets of statements or questions designed to accompany reading assignments or teacher's lectures. Horton and Lovitt (1989) found that the use of study guides, whether teacher-directed or student-directed, resulted in significantly higher performance than self-study for students with LD, remedial students, and general education students. Three common types of study guides are (a) multilevel guides, (b) concept guides, and (c) pattern guides (Horton & Lovitt, 1987). Multilevel guides are designed to address literal, interpretive, and applied levels of comprehension. Horton, Lovitt, and Christensen (1991) found that multilevel study guides were more effective than single-level guides in science and social studies classes on factual test questions. Concept guides are designed to make new information more memorable by facilitating conceptual links or associations between the new information and that previously learned. Pattern guides are designed to enable the learner to recognize patterns of information (e.g., enumeration, sequence, compare–contrast, cause–effect).

To determine the relative effectiveness of multilevel study guides under teacher-mediated conditions (i.e., the teacher explicitly taught the content of the lesson using the study guide to provide structure to the lesson) relative to self-study conditions, Horton and Lovitt (1987) developed multilevel study guides to accompany two science and social studies textbook chapters for middle and high school classes. Study results indicated that almost half of the students scored below minimal mastery levels (80%) in the self-study condition. However, when these same students were exposed to the teacher-mediated study guide condition, at least 90% of these students improved and 60% scored at or above the minimal mastery levels.

The researchers conducted a similar study to examine the relative effects of student-directed study guides in which the student is provided the study guide, but the teacher does not mediate the learning process by conducting a discussion of the study guide questions. In this study, the students independently completed the study guides at their desks, participated in a 5-min feedback session to check their accuracy, followed by a 5-min study session, and then took a 15-item test. Results indicated that about half the students scored below the minimal mastery level following the self-study condition. In the student-directed study guide condition, 63% to 74% of these same students scored above the minimal mastery levels.

Unfortunately, the small number of students classified as LD precluded a separate analysis of their performances, but the researchers reported that 13 out of 16 of these students improved with study guides, but only seven of these improved to levels at or above the minimal mastery levels. In other words, the study guides helped considerably, but were insufficient, in and of themselves, to facilitate mastery of the material. A possible explanation is that although the learning process may be facilitated by the teacher providing organizational cues in the form of study guides and teacher-directed use of the guides, the learning process may continue to be impaired due to memory deficits of students with LD or lack of cognitive learning strategies (e.g., students did not know *how* to use the guides to facilitate their learning). To summarize, students with LD tend to greatly benefit from instruction embodied by explicit organizers. Toumasis (1995) noted that concept diagrams not only gave the teacher an easy way to identify students' misconceptions and misunderstandings during instruction, but also provided students with an efficient tool for reviewing information for an exam.

3. Using Graphic Organizers to Facilitate Guided Note Taking

Guided notes and guided notes with in-class review are promising strategies for students with disabilities integrated into general education content classes (Lazarus, 1991, 1993). Lazarus (1996) suggested the use of guided notes as a study aid to assist students in gleaning the main ideas and related details of a lecture. She compared the chapter test scores of students in a secondary science class under three conditions: (a) baseline personal note taking), (b) guided notes, and (c) guided note taking with a 10-min supervised review period. The results of the study indicated that students with disabilities as well as their nondisabled peers received a greater percentage of correct responses on chapter tests during the guided note taking and review condition. In the guided note-taking procedure, students fill in the designated spaces of a skeleton outline during the teachers' lecture in order to have a completed set of notes to study. The amount and kind of information included in the guided notes outline may vary, depending on the students' skill levels and subject matter. Guided notes may be taken from existing lecture notes and/or text chapters. A variety of note-taking formats may be used, including a basic outline or any of the three content organizer formats illustrated in this chapter (i.e., clarifying routine, hierarchical, and compare–contrast). The teacher should choose a format that corresponds with the information to be learned. In addition, the students should be familiar with the format. Lazarus (1996) found that students like to place a check mark on a review tally each time the notes have been reviewed from beginning to end. She suggested that teachers use a reasonable number of boxes (e.g., five) to be checked in the review tally because students are likely to view the number of boxes as the number of times the notes must be reviewed.

A key to the success of guided note taking is providing opportunities for maximum student response. Lazarus (1996) offered the following suggestions: (a) the teacher has an overhead transparency of the completed guided notes which is uncovered to reveal each related phrase as it is discussed, helping students to keep their place and obtain accurate information; (b) visual cues (e.g., blanks, alphabet letters or numbers, labels, etc.) on the students' copies show the amount and type of information that should be recorded; (c) students are given a copy of the guided notes for an entire chapter to use as a guide for assigned reading; (d) a 5–10-min supervised review at the end of class gives the students review time, an opportunity to clarify confusing information, and the teacher a chance to evaluate and provide corrective feedback as needed; and (e) having all students using guided notes in a class is a strategy that helps to fully integrate students with mild disabilities in the class.

The "flip-flop" study guide is an organizer that can enable students with LD to work independently as well as prepare for exams. Chalmers (1995) suggested using "flip-flop" study guides to provide students with a means of gaining key vocabulary and concepts. Students with LD often experience difficulty with typical study guides consisting of open-ended questions. Students with LD often have problems with reading and writing, which make it difficult for them to focus on the correct information. In contrast, a "flip-flop" study guide provides a definition of a term and the student identifies the correct term to match the definition. This format eliminates the chance of error in miscopying information and eliminates difficulties with writing long definitions or explanations. The "flip-flop" format enables students to follow along more easily in a teacher-directed activity because written answers are kept short. Students are more likely to work independently using the "flip-flop" study guide, since the amount of reading and writing is reduced. Page numbers may be provided if the study guide is used as a student-directed activity. Although the "flip-flop" study guide has merit for students with LD, teachers need to ensure that students using it are not just memorizing facts without understanding big ideas and important concepts.

4. Using Graphic Organizers as Assessment Tools

The preceding discussion illustrated how content organizers can be used as tools during various phases of the instructional process and how they can be used as study guides as well as guided note-taking devices to aid students in preparing for various forms of assessment. Content organizers also can be used as viable alternatives to traditional paper-and-pencil exams. Rafferty and Fleschner (1993) advocated the use of concept maps as an alternative assessment form. The concept map involves the identification of concepts in the form a "web" to show the relationship among several concepts. Concept maps also incorporate the general to specific structure of the hierarchical content organizer that was discussed earlier in this chapter. Schmid and Telaro (1990) studied the use of concept maps in high school biology, where students produced their own maps and received feedback from the teacher prior to the next class session. When given a traditional test to measure students' achievement on conceptual relations, the lower-ability concept-mapping group outperformed the lower-ability group who did not use concept mapping. In fact, the lower-ability concept-mapping group performed as well as the higher reading ability learners. Schmid and Telaro (1990) concluded that the *process* of creating the concept map is often more important than the resulting map. Jones, Pierce, and Hunter (1988–89) noted the importance of teaching students to construct graphic representations of text that they read to better understand which text ideas are important, how they relate, and what points need to be clarified. These findings suggest that the process of constructing content or graphic organizer devices such as concept maps for assessment tools also may beneficial for students.

Rafferty and Fleschner (1993) noted that concept maps used as assessment tools could check on learning in progress or could provide a summative evaluation after completion of a unit to assess depth and breadth of understanding. They indicated that some teachers may be reluctant to use graphic representations as assessment due to the difficulty in scoring. A suggested scoring guide might include 1 point for all valid relationships, 5 points for each valid level of hierarchy, 10 points for each cross-link between two distinct segments, and $\frac{1}{2}$ to 1 point for each example given. Students should be given oral or written opportunities to further explain their maps, since maps may contain information that may not be scored easily.

VI. TOOLS FOR FACILITATING TRANSITION

Students with LD are more likely than their nondisabled peers to drop out of school and to be underemployed and unemployed, and, as adults, they are more likely to live at home with their parents relying on them for financial, psychological, and social support for many more years than their normal-achieving counterparts. Likewise, for those who enter postsecondary education settings (i.e., technical schools or college), many students with LD attempt to hide their condition as they begin postsecondary classes in the hope that it will not matter, but this behavior too often has disastrous affects. Although studies have demonstrated that successful adults with LD both are able to discuss their condition with others as well as actively seek appropriate assistance from outside resources when it is needed (Reiff, Ginsberg, & Gerber, 1995), a great many students with LD who exit high school are unable or unwilling to do either.

Clearly, successful transition from high school to the world of work or to postsecondary school is not something that, for most adolescents with LD, just simply happens. Rather, it must be carefully planned, and students should be taught essential transition skills. Rojewski (1996) suggested that adolescents with LD may benefit from transition planning that helps them to explore perceived barriers that may contribute to lowered educational and/or occupational aspirations. Gerber (1992) noted that individuals with LD need to have a clear understanding of their strengths and weaknesses to facilitate the process of formulating reasonable accommodations in employment settings. In order for students with LD to compete in the world of work, they need to be able to identify and solve problems independently, a skill that employers highly value (Elksnin & Elksnin, 1996). Also important are a high literacy level, responsible work attitudes, good communication skills, and the capacity to learn. At the core of successful transition, however, is effective self-determination and self-advocacy.

Self-determination is the ability to consider options and make appropriate choices at home, school, work, and during leisure time (Schloss, Alper, & Jayne, 1993). It is composed of a knowledge base and a motivational base and is influenced by environmental variables. Environmental factors may either facilitate or hinder attempts to exert personal control (Abery, 1994; Abery, Rudrud, Arndt, Schauben, & Eggebeen, 1995; Wehmeyer, 1995). Mithaug, Campeau, and Wolman (1994) postulated that self-determined persons self-regulate their choices and actions more successfully than others and are less influenced by others and their environments in goal setting and attainment. Field and Hoffman (1994) developed a five-component model that promotes self-determination: (a) Know Yourself, (b) Value Yourself, (c) Plan, (d) Act, and (e) Experience Outcomes and Learn (also see Hoffman & Field, 1995).

Introducing self-determination skills and concepts to parents and students should begin earlier in the educational process rather than waiting for the teen years (Ludi & Martin, 1995). A number of instructional strategies also facilitate self-determination. Modeling (discussed earlier in this chapter) has been emphasized strongly with regard to self-determination (Field, 1996). Adult role models as well as peer role models through cooperative learning provide powerful learning opportunities for students (Field, 1996; Hoffman & Field, 1995; see Ludi & Martin, 1995). Giving students opportunities for choice is a strategy that may help students acquire self-determination skills and knowledge (Field, 1996; Schloss et al., 1993; Lane, 1995; Wehmeyer, 1995). Opportunities for choice allow students to learn while experiencing the natural consequences of their decision in real-world environments. Attribution retraining is another strategy that may help students to understand the consequences of their active roles in the learning process (Field, 1996). In addition, behavioral strategies such as reinforcement that foster internal motivation, self-esteem, and creativity are recommended to promote self-determination.

Perhaps one of the most important social skills that adolescents with LD should master is self-advocacy. Self-advocacy is a term that is sometimes used interchangeably with self-determination. Some prefer to view self-advocacy as a subset of self-determination in that self-advocacy refers to taking action on one's own behalf, and acts of self-advocacy lead to self-determination (Wehmeyer & Berkobien, 1991). Traditionally, a special education teacher has been the primary advocate for students with LD who are mainstreamed (Weimer, Cappotelli, & DiCamillo, 1994). As students with LD spend more time in the general education program, it becomes essential for them to talk directly with classroom teachers about their needs and concerns. These behaviors can lead to use of self-advocacy skills in postsecondary settings. Durlak, Rose, and Bursuck (1994) suggested that students need intensive practice in describing their disabilities to be able to communicate clearly with postsecondary service providers.

Weimer et al. (1994) developed a self-advocacy program begun in middle school that helped mainstreamed sixth graders to become aware of their individual disabilities and possible helpful modifications. In seventh grade, the responsibility of self-advocacy was gradually shifted to the students and in eighth grade, students were assisted in independently applying skills learned the previous year. Instruction in a specific self-advocacy strategy for preparing and participating in educational planning conferences such as IEP meetings can also be beneficial (VanReusen et al., 1987).[5] To use the I-PLAN strategy, students Inventory strengths and weaknesses, Provide their inventory with information, Listen and respond, Ask questions, and Name goals. Students interviewed at two high schools in the Lovitt, Cushing, and Stump (1994) study may have benefited from a strategy such as I-PLAN because the students were unfamiliar with the IEP process and contributed little to it. Once students learn self-advocacy skills, they must realize that it is their responsibility to apply these skills (Brinckerhoff, 1994).

Students can become "self-determined adults through opportunities and experiences leading to success, constructive experiences with failure and opportunities to explore, take risks, and learn from consequences, and by watching adults take control and make decisions" (Wehmeyer, 1995, p. 158). As noted by Lane (1995), any instructional situation that encourages independent thinking provides an opportunity to practice self-determination. Although research on self-determination is relatively new, a number of instructional interventions aimed at promoting self-determination have emerged. These interventions include curricula and strategies that can assist students in developing beliefs, knowledge, and skills that lead to self-determination. ChoiceMaker (Martin & Huber Marshall, 1994) is a self-determination curriculum, assessment, and instructional program that focuses on seven areas: (a) self-awareness, (b) self-advocacy, (c) self-efficacy, (d) decision making, (e) independent performance, (f) self-evaluation, and (g) adjustment (Martin & Huber Marshall, 1995). ChoiceMaker teaches leadership of the IEP process through acquisition of critical self-determination skills. Students gain an

---

[5]Information about training in the I-PLAN self-advocacy strategy procedures and instructional resources and materials for teaching the I-PLAN strategy can be obtained by contacting The University of Kansas Center for Research on Learning (913-864-4780).

experiential understanding of their interests, strengths, and weaknesses. In addition, students learn to choose and express goals as well as take action. Hoffman and Field (1995) reported positive results in a field test of a Self-Determination Knowledge Scale (SDKS) associated with the Steps to Self-Determination curriculum. Adolescents and young adults who received the Steps to Self-Determination curriculum scored significantly higher on the SDKS than those who did not. In addition, the effectiveness of the curriculum was indicated by a significant increase in students' behaviors that are considered correlates of self-determination.

To promote vocational success, Elksnin and Elksnin (1996) suggested using educational planning strategies such as I-PLAN to assist students in participating in individualized education, vocational, and transition planning meetings. They also suggested using a community-based exploration guide (CBEG, Neubert & Foster, 1988) to assist students in matching their employability strengths to potential jobs and job sites. Elksnin and Elksnin (1996) suggested Job Clubs as a third strategy for promoting success in vocational settings. Job Clubs help students learn how to be successful at job-finding skills like asking for job leads and arranging interviews.

There is a great need for more research and development of interventions specifically designed to empower students to make decisions for themselves, to set goals, and to monitor progress based on their own analysis of abilities. Such strategies hold great promise for restoring self-esteem and imbuing students with a sense of control over their destinies. "The successful transition of persons with disabilities will take place only when such individuals are able to create a vision for their own future and follow that vision, making choices and exerting personal control in a manner that leads to the attainment of life goals" (Abery et al., 1995, p. 178).

VII. ISSUES FOR FUTURE RESEARCH

Although many adolescents with LD experience difficulty meeting the academic, social, motivational, and executive demands of their environments, research and development of interventions specifically designed to enable them to *independently* meet these demands has yielded some very promising results. The most promising interventions share some common characteristics. First, instructional techniques are designed to be as explicit as possible. Second, to help students with LD meet academic and social demands of their settings, basic academic and social skills are taught, not as isolated parts of the curriculum that must be mastered, but rather as integrated components of problem-solving strategies. Third, to help students with LD meet the motivational demands of their settings, students are being explicitly taught to set goals, monitor their progress toward goals, and reinforce themselves. The philosophy of student goal setting permeates the atmosphere of effective LD classrooms. Fourth, to help students meet executive demands, principles gained from basic research in cognitive psychology are becoming increasingly more integrated into practical instructional techniques for adolescents with LD. Increasingly, key thinking processes involved in effective learning and performing are targeted for instruction. Students are explicitly informed, cued, and frequently reminded why a particular instructional procedure is being used to enhance their learning.

Teaching adolescents with LD is a highly stimulating and worthwhile endeavor, and the effectiveness of interventions for enabling students with LD to become more independent holds great promise. Unfortunately, many teachers of adolescents with LD face complex decisions regarding the selection of interventions to be provided. The expectation placed on teachers of students with LD to "be all things and teach all things to all students with LD" is nothing short of impossible to meet. Teachers must be very selective with regard to the interventions they choose to implement. As a general rule, implementing fewer interventions at more in-depth, intensive, and extensive levels is far more preferable to attempting to implement a wide variety of techniques, but doing so only superficially. Time is limited, and one cannot do it all (see Cushman, 1994; Newman & Wehlage, 1993).

Given the plethora of potentially effective interventions and the complexity of the students' characteristics and needs, as well as the environmental factors such as school climate, which impact these needs, coupled with the time constraints teachers face, decision making regarding selecting interventions is a highly complex task, and few teachers are prepared to address all of the critical variables involved. As a result, decision making is often by default and largely influenced by constraints imposed by the school climate and the teachers' instructional preferences and styles and content knowledge base rather than the true needs of the student. The business community has long had access to systems analysis software for facilitating more effective decision making. Research is needed to develop and validate similar programs for the education community.

Currently, the LD field is being significantly influenced by two trends. One is the movement toward use of full-inclusion approaches to service delivery. The other is the emphasis on providing "constructivist" instruction. Full inclusion provides students with more opportunities to interact with normal-achieving peers and participate in the same kinds of instruction. All special education is provided within the context of the general education classroom. Constructivism creates opportunities for students to engage in experiential learning, discover information or strategies and construct their own understanding of them. Generally speaking, constructivist instructional paradigms are not mastery-oriented; instruction is more holistic in nature, thus the curriculum is not segmented into parts or components that are targeted for mastery-oriented, "reductionist" instruction. The teacher's role is to act as a guide by creating opportunities for students to discover knowledge as opposed to providing students with direct instruction of the to-be-learned information. Rather than memorizing someone else's understanding of something, the constructivist teacher's role is to facilitate ongoing student construction of understandings in order to promote less erroneous and increasingly more sophisticated understandings.

Both full-inclusion and constructivist instructional paradigms hold promise for students with LD. Much of the support for both full-inclusive education and constructivist approaches to teaching adolescents with LD is largely rhetorical and there is only a fledging database to support these approaches. Although both may eventually prove to be far superior to what the existing body of research indicates is "best practice," future research also may prove otherwise. Unfortunately, social policy (i.e., how special education services and instruction are to be provided) is often more heavily influenced by popular and compelling rhetoric than by empirical data. Furthermore, existing intervention research has, in many ways, contributed to the problem. A new teaching technique or intervention is often tested and compared to whatever constituted traditional practice in the classroom at the time of the study. Although most studies meticulously document the nature of new intervention, few adequately document the nature of instruction to that which the new intervention was compared. As a result, few studies actually reveal critical information, such as whether a constructivist pedagogical procedure indeed was less or more effective than a technique representing more traditional reductionist paradigm. In short, more comparative analysis research is needed, and in the absence of this type of research methodology, future trends in practice will continue to be more heavily influenced by popular rhetoric than by empirical data.

This position does not imply, however, that rhetoric, in the absence of data, is unhealthy, as the debate regarding reductionism and constructivism has caused professionals to seriously reflect on and question current practice. Unfortunately, debates often cause supporters, in an effort to more clearly define the differences in new and old ideas, to dichotomize their positions, and ideas become cast into an "either/or" or "right/wrong" perspective—that is, one cannot be both a constructivist and a reductionist (Ellis, 1993b). For example, some educators who are heavily invested in constructivist forms of teaching argue that there is no role for direct instruction in a constructivist paradigm; conversely, many direct instruction advocates scorn discovery learning approaches (see Pressley, Harris, & Marks, 1992; Moshman, 1982).

Many of the principles that best characterize constructivism apply equally well to reductionist paradigms. For example, both are based on the following assumptions: (a) that students understand new information in relation to what they already know (i.e., prior knowledge) and their own experiences (see Reid, Kurkjian, & Caruthers, 1994); (b) student understandings are not static, but rather, constantly changing as new information is gained and information is viewed from different perspectives; and (c) even understandings of facts are relative and never static (Wansart, 1995). However, these arguments are just as true and applicable to reductionist paradigms as they are to those associated with constructivism.

There is little doubt that adolescents with LD benefit greatly from many of the features of a constructivist instructional paradigm. For example, few would argue against the importance of providing "hands-on," experiential learning activities. Where these methods often fall short for adolescents with LD, however, is when teachers allow students to infer their own meanings from these experiences by not supplementing the experiences with more direct explanation and mediation to ensure students are gaining an accurate interpretation.

The most effective paradigm likely involves integrating both reductionist and constructivist techniques, strategically using features from both as the developmental needs of the student requires them. Thus, the developmental needs of the adolescent and the nature of the curriculum being taught (rather than the philosophical orientation of the teacher) are the variables that most likely dictate the kind of instruction that should be provided. Research is needed to clarify how teachers can integrate these models in an effective manner for adolescents with LD in secondary school settings.

Larkin (1998), in a study of teacher's perspectives on instructional practice for students with LD, found that teachers of students with LD seemed to fall in the middle of the continuum with regard to their beliefs about reductionist and constructivist techniques. The LD teachers studied were invested in both approaches. Results of the study also indicated, however, that the teachers did not possess an in-depth knowledge base about *when* various approaches should be ideally utilized, depending on the developmental needs of students. In short, they valued the techniques but lacked the conditional knowledge of how to employ various features of each in a strategic manner for individual or even groups of students. Rather, management considerations (i.e., when is the most convenient time to provide an experiential activity in a heterogeneous classroom) rather than learner characteristics appeared to be the significant drivers of teacher's decisions. Research is needed to clarify ways to help teachers recognize when each approach is needed and how to coordinate these various instructional paradigms in heterogeneous classrooms, such as those found in inclusive settings.

Although there are many compelling arguments in support of full inclusion, there are a number of pending issues where research is needed. The first issue is an extension of the issue concerning use of constructivist paradigms in secondary school settings. At the heart of special education philosophy is providing students with instruction appropriate to their unique needs, and when teaching adolescents with LD, this goal is best attained by providing these students with intensive and extensive instruction. This requires careful and intentional monitoring of individual student progress, and on a microlevel, monitoring student understanding of what is being learned in any given lesson. It also provides extensive, explicit positive and corrective feedback.

Intensive instruction certainly can take place using constructivist approaches to teaching via mediative feedback techniques; what is often required to do this is *opportunity* to provide it (see Scanlon, Deshler, & Schumaker, 1996). Although there are exceptions, studies involving constructivist models of instruction typically involved working with small groups of students or even one-on-one instructional paradigms where the opportunity existed for ongoing mediation between the learners and teacher and careful monitoring and provision of feedback. A critical research question is whether it is possible to provide sufficient intensive and extensive constructivist instruction to adolescents with LD in heterogeneous general education classrooms when there are not only large numbers of students in a class period (e.g., 25–35 students), but also where the teacher is also responsible for up to six different classes, and thus must monitor the understanding of approximately 150 or more students. The question is, at what point does the instructional paradigm collapse due to constraints imposed by the school climate? Of critical concern is the potential results of having teachers thoroughly invested in a constructivist approach to teaching due to the compelling rhetorical arguments supporting it, and then partially implementing the procedures by eliminating the dimension that involves careful monitoring and mediating feedback because of lack of opportunity to do it; what happens to the learning of adolescents with LD attending the inclusive classroom under these circumstances?

A second critical issue related to use of full-inclusion classrooms concerns how this model meets the curricular needs of adolescents with LD (see Schumaker & Deshler, 1988). That is, because of the nature of their disability, many, if not most, adolescents with LD need to be taught skills, processes, strategies, and concepts not normally addressed in the context of a general education classroom. For example, research clearly points to the need for effective transition programs for this population. Among the many areas addressed in an effective transition program, both self-advocacy skills and problem-solving social skills necessary for job maintenance are critical needs of many adolescents with LD, but these are not traditional curriculum areas addressed in general education classrooms. In light of the rush toward use of full inclusion, meaningfully meeting the needs of adolescents with LD in inclusive education classes, particularly those needs that do not reflect the traditional secondary school curriculum, is critical.

In order to make progress towards furthering self-determination for individuals with LD, future research needs to address a redefinition of roles (e.g., teacher, student, parent), the importance of risk taking, the role of the individual versus the role of the group, and the timing of interventions and supports (Field, 1996). Additional investigations need to focus on maintenance and generalization of self-determination skills that students are taught (Durlak et al., 1994). Clearly, more research is needed to understand the dynamics of classroom ecologies and context variables that facilitate acquisition of academic, social, and vocational skills (see Reith & Polsgrove, 1994).

A third critical issue regarding the use of full-inclusion secondary classrooms concerns use of cooperative learning procedures. Clearly, there are many advantages associated with these techniques, and one of the mainstays of implementing inclusive education is via use of cooperative learning. If not used appropriately, these procedures can be very debilitating to students with LD. These students are often ostracized by their normal-achieving counterparts because they are considered a liability to their groups, and as a result, risk taking by the adolescent can be punished. Likewise, there are numerous cooperative learning procedures, each addressing a different instructional purpose (some are most ideally suited for team-building activities, others for facilitating elaboration of a new concept or reviewing previously learned concepts or skills, etc.). Unfortunately, many general education teachers' conditional knowledge of the procedures is similar to that illustrated by Larkin (1998). That is, many are aware of specific techniques, but lack a sophisticated understanding of when, in the instructional sequence and developmental levels of students, the techniques are most appropriate to employ. What happens to the learning of adolescents with LD when they are placed in full-inclusion classes where cooperative learning is used extensively, but ineffectively?

Reith and Polsgrove (1994) suggested that additional studies need to clarify the nature of thinking skills and learning potential of students with LD. Although the attention to higher-order thinking skills and problem-solving strategies seems to be lucrative, effort needs to be continued to ensure that adolescents with LD acquire, maintain, and transfer academic and social skills. This effort should be designed to ultimately reduce the rate of failure, increase skills, and improve chances for graduation and employment.

Recent research concerning the characteristics of successful adults with LD (Gerber, Ginsberg, & Reiff, 1992; Kershner, Kirkpatrick, & McLaren, 1995; Reiff, Gerber, & Ginsberg, 1996; Spekman, Goldberg, & Herman, 1992) has provided important insights into the nature of interventions that should be provided during the secondary school years. Future research should investigate how successful adults have capitalized on their strengths and compensated for their weaknesses and why they have selected some adaptive strategies over others (see Weller, Wattyne, Herbert, & Creely, 1994). This may help educators to recognize and articulate the need for individuals with LD to make independent choices, set their own goals, and initiate actions to achieve those goals.

References

Abery, B. (1994). A conceptual framework for enhancing self-determination. In M. F. H. B. H. Abery (Ed.), *Challenges for a service system in transition,* (pp. 345–380). Baltimore: Brookes.

Abery, B., Rudrud, L., Arndt, K., Schauben, L., & Eggebeen, A. (1995). Evaluating a multicomponent program for enhancing the self-determination of youth with disabilities. *Intervention In School And Clinic, 30*(3), 170-179.

Adelman, H. S., & Taylor, L. (1983). Enhancing motivation for overcoming learning and behavior problems. *Journal of Learning Disabilities, 16,* 384–392.

Anderson, C. A., & Jennings, D. L. (1980). When experiences of failure promote expectations of success: The impact of attributing failure to ineffective strategies. *Journal of Personality, 48,* 393–407.

Anderson, T. H., & Armbruster, B. B. (1984). Studying. In P. D. Pearson (Ed.), *Handbook of reading research* (pp. 657–744). New York: Longman.

Ausubel, D. P., & Robinson, F. G. (1969). *School learning: An introduction to educational psychology.* New York: Holt, Rinehart, & Winston.

Baker, S. K., Simmons, D. C., & Kameenui, E. J. (1994). Making information more memorable for students with learning disabilities through the design of instructional tools. *LD Forum, 19*(3), 18.

Bandura, A., & Schunk, D. M. (1981). Cultivating competence, self-efficacy, and intrinsic interest through proximal self-motivation. *Journal of Personality/Social Psychology, 41,* 456–498.

Bender, W. N. (1994). Social-emotional development: The task and the challenge. *Learning Disability Quarterly, 17,* 250-252.

Bergen, R. (1994). Improving the writing performance of students with learning disabilities through the use of electronic reference devices. *LD Forum, 19*(2), 26–27.

Bergerud, D., Lovitt, T., & Horton, S. (1988). The effectiveness of textbook adaptations in life science for high school students with learning disabilities. *Journal of Learning Disabilities, 21,* 70-76.

Brigham, F. J., Scruggs, T. E., & Mastropieri, M. A. (1995). Elaborative maps for enhanced learning of historical information: Uniting spatial, verbal, and imaginal information. *The Journal of Special Education, 28*(3), 440-460.

Brinckerhoff, L. C. (1994). Developing effective self-advocacy skills in college-bound students with learning disabilities. *Intervention In School And Clinic, 29*(4), 229–237.

Brown, A. L. (1978). Knowing, when, where, and how to remember: A problem of metacognition. In R. Glaser (Ed.), *Advances in instructional psychology* (Vol. 7, pp. 55–113). Hillsdale, NJ: Erlbaum.

Bryan, T. (1997). Assessing the personal and social status of students with learning disabilities. *Learning Disabilities Research & Practice, 12*(1), 63–76.

Bulgren, J. A., Deshler, D. D., & Schumaker, J. B. (1990). Effectiveness of remembering strategies in enhancing the learning of students with and without learning disabilities in mainstream content classes. Unpublished manuscript.

Bulgren, J. A., Hock, M. F., Schumaker, J. B., & Deshler, D. D. (1995). The effects of instruction in a paired associated strategy on the information mastery performance of students with learning disabilities. *Learning Disabilities Research & Practice 10*(1), 22–27.

Bulgren, J., & Lenz, K. (1996). Strategic instruction in the content areas. In D. D. Deshler, E. S. Ellis, & B. K. Lenz (Eds.), *Teaching adolescents with learning disabilities: Strategies and methods* (2nd ed., pp. 409–473). Denver: Love.

Bulgren, J. A., Schumaker, J. B., & Deshler, D. D. (1988). Effectiveness of a concept teaching routine in enhancing the performance of students with LD in secondary level mainstream classes. *Learning Disability Quarterly, 11,* 3–17.

Carter, J. F. (1993). Self-management: Education's ultimate goal. *Teaching Exceptional Children, 25*(3), 28–32.

Chalmers, L. (1995). Mediating content area learning through the use of flip-flop study guides. *LD Forum, 20*(4), 37–38.

Conderman, G. (1995). Social status of sixth and seventh-grade students with learning disabilities. *Learning Disability Quarterly, 18,* 13–24.

Crank, J. (1993). *Validation of a visual depiction instructional routine.* Las Vegas: University of Nevada.

Crank, J. N., & Bulgren, J. A. (1993). Visual depictions as information organizers for enhancing achievement of students with learning disabilities. *Learning Disabilities Research & Practice, 8*(3), 140-147.

Cushman, K. (1994). Less is more: The secret of being essential. *Horace, 11*(2), 1–12.

Dansereau, D. F., & Holley, C. D. (1982). Development and evaluation of a text mapping strategy. In A. Flammer & W. Kintsch (Eds.), *Discourse processing* (pp. 536–554). New York: Elsevier.

Day, V. P., & Elksnin, L. K. (1994). Promoting strategic learning. *Intervention In School And Clinic, 29*(5), 262–270.

Deshler, D. D., Schumaker, J. B., & Lenz, B. K. (1984). Academic and cognitive interventions for LD adolescents: Part I. *Journal of Learning Disabilities, 17,* 108–117.

Dickson, S. V., Chard, D. J., & Simmons, D. C. (1993). An integrated reading/writing curriculum: A focus on scaffolding. *LD Forum, 18*(4), 12–16.

Dickson, S. V., Simmons, D., & Kameenui, E. J. (1995). Instruction in expository text: a focus on compare/contrast structure. *LD Forum, 20*(2), 8–15.

Duchardt, B. A., Deshler, D. D., & Schumaker, J. B. (1995). A strategic intervention for enabling students with learning disabilities to identify and change their ineffective beliefs. *Learning Disability Quarterly, 18,* 186–201.

Duffy, M. L., & Bursuck, W. D. (1994). Adapting the secondary curriculum: Considerations for teachers. *LD Forum, 19*(2), 18–21.

Dunlap, L. K., & Dunlap, G. (1989). A self-monitoring package for teaching subtraction with regrouping to students with learning disabilities. *Journal of Applied Behavior Analysis,* (22), 309–314.

Dunlap, L. K., Dunlap, G., Koegel, L. K., & Koegel, R. L. (1991). Using self-monitoring to increase independence. *Teaching Exceptional Children, 23*(3), 17–22.

Durlak, C. M., Rose, E., & Bursuck, W. D. (1994). Preparing high school students with learning disabilities for the transition to postsecondary education: Teaching the skills of self-determination. *Journal of Learning Disabilities, 27*(1), 51–59.

Elksnin, L. K. (1994). Promoting generalization of social skills. *LD Forum, 20*(1), 35–37.

Elksnin, L. K., & Elksnin, N. (1995). Teaching social skills to students with learning disabilities. *LD Forum, 20*(4), 16–19.

Elksnin, L. K., & Elksnin, N. (1996). Strategies for transition to employment settings. In D. D. Deshler, E. S. Ellis, & B. K. Lenz (Eds.), *Teaching adolescents with learning disabilities: Strategies and methods,* (2nd ed., pp. 525–578). Denver: Love.

Ellis, E. S. (in press, a). *Content enhancement series: The Framing routine.* Lawrence, KS: Edge Enterprises.

Ellis, E. S. (in press, b). *Using project-based learning to water up the curriculum.* Tuscaloosa, AL: Masterminds, LLC.

Ellis, E. S. (1998). *Using graphic organizers to water up the curriculum.* Tuscaloosa, AL: Masterminds, LLC.

Ellis, E. S. (1997). *The content enhancement series: The clarifying routine.* Lawrence, KS: Edge Enterprises.

Ellis, E. S. (1995). *LINCS: The vocabulary strategy: LINCS (2nd ed.)*. Lawrence, KS: Edge Enterprises.

Ellis, E. S. (1993a). A learning strategy for meeting the writing demands of secondary mainstream classrooms. *Alabama Council for Exceptional Children Journal, 10*(1), 21–38.

Ellis, E. S. (1993b). Integrative strategy instruction: A potential model for teaching content area subjects to adolescents with learning disabilities. *Journal of Learning Disabilities, 26*, 358–383, 398.

Ellis, E. S. (1993c). Teaching strategy sameness using integrated formats. *Journal of Learning Disabilities, 26*, 448–481.

Ellis, E. S. (1991). *Perspectives from expert strategy teachers: What they do to motivate students to learn and use strategies*. Columbia, SC: The University of South Carolina.

Ellis, E. S. (1989). A metacognitive intervention for increasing class participation. *Learning Disabilities Focus, 5*(1), 36–46.

Ellis, E. S., & Colvert, G. (1996). Writing strategy instruction. In D. D. Deshler, E. S. Ellis, & B. K. Lenz (Eds.), *Teaching adolescents with learning disabilities: Strategies and methods* (2nd ed., pp. 127–207). Denver: Love.

Ellis, E. S., Deshler, D. D., Schumaker, J. B., Lenz, B. K., & Clark, F. L. (1993). An instructional model for teaching learning strategies. In E. Meyen, G. A. Vergason, & R. Whelan (Eds.), *Educating students with mild disabilities* (pp. 151–187). Denver: Love Publishing Co.

Ellis, E. S., & Feldman, R. K. (1994). Creating "thought-full" classrooms: Fostering cognitive literacy via cooperative learning and integrated strategies instruction. In S. Sharan (Ed.), *Handbook of cooperative learning methods* (pp. 157–176). New York: Preager.

Ellis, E. S., & Lenz, B. K. (1996). Perspectives on instruction in learning strategies. In D. D. Deshler, E. S. Ellis, & B. K. Lenz (Eds.), *Teaching adolescents with learning disabilities: Strategies and methods,* (2nd ed., pp. 9–60). Denver: Love.

Ellis, E. S., & Lenz, B. K. (1987). A component analysis of effective learning strategies for LD students. *Focus on Learning Disabilities, 2*(2), 94–107.

Ellis, E. S., Raines, C., Farmer, T., Tyree, A. (1997). Effectiveness of a concept clarifying routine in upper-elementary and middle school mainstream classes. Unpublished manuscript, The University of Alabama Multiple Abilities Program, Tuscaloosa, Al.

Evers, R. B., & Bursuck, W. D. (1995). Helping students succeed in technical classes: Using learning strategies and study skills. *Teaching Exceptional Children, 28*(3), 22–27.

Field, S. (1996). Self-determination instructional strategies for youth with learning disabilities. *Journal of Learning Disabilities, 29*(1), 40-52.

Field, S., & Hoffman, A. (1994). Development of a model for self-determination. *Career Development For Exceptional Individuals, 17*(2), 159–169.

Forness, S. R., & Kavale, K. A. (1996). Treating social skill deficits in children with learning disabilities: A meta-analysis of the research. *Learning Disability Quarterly, 19,* 2–13.

Fulk, B. M. (1994). Mnemonic keyword strategy training for students with learning disabilities. *Learning Disabilities Research & Practice, 9*(3), 179–185.

Gable, R. A., Hendrickson, J. M., & Shellady, S. (1992). Strategies for improving maintenance and generalization of academic skills—So students "Don't leave class without it." *Preventing School Failure, 37*(1), 35–40.

Gerber, P. J., Ginsberg, R., & Reiff, H. B. (1992). Identifying alterable patterns in employment success for highly successful adults with learning disabilities. *Journal of Learning Disabilities, 25*(8), 475–487.

Graham, S. (1992, October). *Issues in strategy instruction.* Paper presented at the International Conference on Learning Disabilities, Kansas City, MO.

Greene, G. (1994). The magic of mnemonics. *LD Forum, 19*(3), 34-37.

Hallenbeck, M. J. (1996). The cognitive strategy in writing: Welcome relief for adolescents with learning disabilities. *Learning Disabilities Research & Practice, 11*(2), 107–119.

Hayes, M. L., & Sloat, R. S. (1988). Preventing suicide in learning disabled children and adolescents. *Academic Therapy, 24*(2), 221–230.

Hazel, J. S., Schumaker, J. B., Sherman, J. A., & Sheldon-Wildgen, J. (1981). *ASSET: A social skills program for adolescents.* Champaign, IL: Research Press.

Hoffman, A., & Field, S. (1995). Promoting self-determination through effective curriculum development. *Intervention in School and Clinic, 30*(3), 134-141.

Horton, S. V., & Lovitt, T. (1987). *Information organization for secondary students: Study guides.* Unpublished manuscript, University of Washington, Seattle.

Horton, S. V., & Lovitt, T. C. (1989). Construction and implementation of graphic organizers for academically handicapped and regular secondary students. *Academic Therapy, 24,* 625–640.

Horton, S. V., Lovitt, T. C., & Bergerud, D. (1990). The effectiveness of graphic organizers for three classifications of secondary students in content area classes. *Journal of Learning Disabilities, 23,* 12–22.

Horton, S. V., Lovitt, T. C., & Christensen, C. C. (1991). Matching three classifications of secondary students to differential levels of study guides. *Journal of Learning Disabilities, 24,* 518–529.

Howell, S. B. (1986). *A study of the effectiveness of TOWER: The theme writing strategy.* Unpublished master's thesis, University of Kansas, Lawrence.

Hudson, P., Lignugaris-Kraft, B., & Miller, T. (1993). Using content enhancements to improve the performance of adolescents with learning disabilities in content classes. *Learning Disabilities Research & Practice, 8*(2), 106-126.

Hughes, C. A. (1996). Memory and test-taking strategies. In D. D. Deshler, E. S. Ellis, & B. K. Lenz (Eds.), *Teaching adolescents with learning disabilities: Strategies and methods,* (2nd ed., pp. 209–266). Denver: Love.

Hughes, C. A., Ruhl, K. L., Deshler, D. D., & Schumaker, J. B. (1993). Test-taking strategy instruction for adolescents with emotional and behavior disorders. *Journal of Emotional and Behavioral Disorders, 1,* 189–198.

Hughes, C. A., & Schumaker, J. B. (1991a). Reflections on test-taking strategy instruction for adolescents with learning disabilities. *Exceptionality, 2,* 237–242.

Hughes, C. A., & Schumaker, J. B. (1991b). Test-taking strategy instruction for adolescents with learning disabilities. *Exceptionality, 2,* 205–221.

Hughes, C. A., Schumaker, J. B., Deshler, D. D., & Mercer, C. (1993). *The test-taking strategy.* Lawrence, KS: Edge Enterprises, Inc.

Huntington, D. D., & Bender, W. N. (1993). Adolescents with learning disabilities at risk? Emotional well-being, depression, suicide. *Journal of Learning Disabilities, 26,* 159–166.

Idol, L. (1987). Group story mapping: A comprehension strategy for both skilled and unskilled readers. *Journal of Learning Disabilities, 20,* 196–205.

Jackson, S. C., Enright, R. D., & Murdock, J. Y. (1987). Social perception problems in learning disabled youth: Developmental lag versus perceptual deficit. *Journal of Learning Disabilities, 20*, 361–364.

Johnson, D. W., & Johnson, R. (1992). Encouraging thinking through constructive controversy. In N. Davidson & T. Worsham (Eds.), *Enhancing thinking through cooperative learning,* (pp. 120–137). New York: Teachers College Press.

Johnson, D. D., & Pearson, P. D. (1978). *Teaching reading vocabulary.* New York: Holt & Co.

Jones, B. F., Palincsar, A. S., Ogle, D. S., & Carr, E. G. (1987). *Strategic teaching and learning: Cognitive instruction in the content-areas.* Alexandria, VA: ASCD.

Jones, B. F., Pierce, J., & Hunter, B. (1988–89). Teaching students to construct graphic representation. *Educational Leadership, 46*(4), 20–25.

Kavale, K. A., & Forness, S. (1996). Social skill deficits and learning disabilities: A meta-analysis. *Journal of Learning Disabilities, 29*(3), 226–237.

Kea, C. D. (1987). *An analysis of critical teaching behaviors employed by teachers of students with learning disabilities.* Unpublished doctoral dissertation, The University of Kansas, Lawrence.

Kershner, J., Kirkpatrick, T., & McLaren, D. (1995). The career success of an adult with a learning disability: A psychosocial study of amnesic-semantic aphasia. *Journal of Learning Disabilities, 28*, 121–126.

King-Sears, M. E., & Cummings, C. S. (1996). Inclusive practices of classroom teachers. *Remedial and Special Education, 17*, 217–225.

Kline, F. M. (1989). *The development and validation of feedback routines for use in special education settings.* Unpublished doctoral dissertation, University of Kansas, Lawrence.

Koran, M. L., & Koran, J. (1980). Interaction of learner characteristics with pictorial adjuncts in learning from science text. *Journal of Research in Science Teaching, 1*, 4–483.

Lane, G. (1995). Empowerment in transition planning: Guidelines for special educators. *LD Forum, 21*(1), 34–38.

Larkin, M. J. (1998). *Teachers' perspectives of learning disabilities pedagogy.* Unpublished manuscript.

Lazarus, B. D. (1991). Guided notes, review, and achievement of secondary students with learning disabilities in mainstream content courses. *Education and Treatment of Children, 14*(2), 112–127.

Lazarus, B. D. (1993). Guided notes: Effects with secondary and post-secondary students with mild disabilities. *Education and Treatment of Children, 16*(3), 272–289.

Lazarus, B. D. (1996). Flexible skeletons: Guided notes for adolescents. *Teaching Exceptional Children, 28*(3), 36–40.

Lenz, B. K. (1991). In the spirit of strategies instruction: Cognitive and metacognitive aspects of the Strategies Intervention Model. In S. Vogel (Ed.), *In proceedings of the Second Annual Conference of the National Institute of Dyslexia.* White Plains, NY: Longman.

Lenz, B. K. (1983). Using advance organizers. *The Pointer, 27*(2), 11–14.

Lenz, B. K. (1984). *The effect of advance organizers on the learning and retention of learning disabled adolescents within the context of a cooperative planning model.* Final research report submitted to the U.S. Department of Education, Special Education Services.

Lenz, B. K., Alley, G. R., & Schumaker, G. R. (1987). Activating the inactive learner: Advance organizers in the secondary content classroom. *Learning Disability Quarterly, 10*(1), 53–67.

Lenz, B. K., Bulgren, J., & Hudson, P. (1990). Content enhancement: A model for promoting the acquisition of content by individuals with learning disabilities. In T. E. Scruggs & B. Y. L. Wong (Eds.), *Intervention research in learning disabilities* (pp. 122–165). New York: Springer-Verlag.

Lenz, B. K., Ehren, B. J., & Smiley, L. R. (1991). A goal attainment approach to improve completion of project-type assignments by adolescents with learning disabilities. *Learning Disabilities Research & Practice, 6,* 166–176.

Lenz, B. K., Ellis, E. S., & Scanlon, D. (1996). *Teaching learning strategies to adolescents and adults with learning disabilities.* Austin, TX: Pro-Ed.

Lictht, B. C., & Kistner, J. A. (1986). Motivational problems of learning disabled children: Individual differences and their implications for treatment. In J. K. Torgesen & B. Y. L. Wong (Eds.), *Psychological and educationally perspectives on learning disabilities* (pp. 225–255). New York: Academic Press.

Lovitt, T. C., Cushing, S. S., & Stump, C. S. (1994). High school students rate their IEPs: Low opinions and lack of ownership. *Intervention In School and Clinic, 30*(1), 34–37.

Luckner, J. (1994). Developing independent and responsible behaviors in students who are deaf or hard of hearing. *Teaching Exceptional Children, 26*(2), 13–17.

Ludi, D. C., & Martin, L. (1995). The road to personal freedom: Self-determination. *Intervention In School And Clinic, 30*(3), 164–169.

Luten, J., Ames, W., & Ackerson, G. (1980). A meta-analysis of the effects of advance organizers on learning and retention. *American Educational Research Journal, 17,* 211–218.

MacArthur, C. (1994). Peers + word processing + strategies = A powerful combination for revising student writing. *Teaching Exceptional Children, 27*(1), 24–29.

Maag, J. W., & Behrens, J. T. (1989). Depression and cognitive self-statements of learning disabled and seriously emotionally disturbed adolescents. *The Journal of Special Education, 23*(1), 17–27.

Maag, J. W., & Forness, S. R. (1991). Depression in children and adolescents: Identification, assessment, and treatment. *Focus on Exceptional Children, 24*(1), 1–19.

Margalit, M., & Levin-Alyagon, M. (1994). Learning disability subtyping, loneliness, and classroom adjustment. *Learning Disability Quarterly, 17,* 297–310.

Martin, J. E., & Huber Marshall, L. (1994). *ChoiceMaker self-determination transition curriculum matrix.* Colorado Springs: Colorado Springs Center for Educational Research.

Martin, J. E., & Huber Marshall, L. (1995). ChoiceMaker: A comprehensive self-determination transition program. *Intervention In School And Clinic, 30*(3), 147–156.

Martin, K. F., & Manno, C. (1995). Use of a check-off system to improve middle school students' story compositions. *Journal of Learning Disabilities, 28,* 137–149.

Mastropieri, M. A., Scruggs, T. E., & Whedon, C. (1997). Using mnemonic strategies to teach information about U.S. presidents: A classroom-based investigation. *Learning Disability Quarterly, 20,* 13–21.

McCombs, B. L. (1984). Processes and skills underlying continuing intrinsic motivation to learn: Toward a definition of motivational skills training interventions. *Educational Psychologist, 19*(4), 199–218.

McLeod, T. M., Kolb, T. L., & Lister, M. O. (1994). Social skills, school skills, and success in the high school: A comparison of teachers' and students' perceptions. *Learning Disabilities Research & Practice, 9*(3), 142–147.

Mellard, D., & Hazel, J. S. (1992). Social competencies as a pathway to successful life transitions. *Learning Disability Quarterly, 15,* 251–271.

Mercer, C. D. (1997). *Students with learning disabilities.* Upper Saddle River, NJ: Merrill.

Milem, M., & Garcia, M. (1996). Student critics, teacher models: Introducing process writing to high school students with learning disabilities. *Teaching Exceptional Children, 28*(3), 47–48.

Mithaug, D., Campeau, P., & Wolman, J. (1992). *Self-determination assessment.* Unpublished manuscript.

Moshman, D. (1982). Exogenous, endogenous, and dialectical constructivism. *Developmental Review, 2,* 371–384.

Moyer, J. C., Sowder, L., Threadgill-Sowder, J., & Moyer, M. B. (1984). Story problem formats: Drawn versus telegraphic. *Journal for Research in Mathematics Education, 15,* 342–351.

Neubert, D. A., & Foster, J. (1988). *Community-based exploration guide.* Washington, DC: George Washington University Department of Teacher Preparation and Special Education.

Newman, F. M., & Wehlage, G. G. (1993). Five standards of authentic instruction. *Educational Leadership, 50*(7), 8–12.

Palincsar, A. M., & Brown, A. L. (1984). Reciprocal teaching of comprehension fostering and monitoring activities. *Cognition and Instruction, 1,* 117–175.

Prater, M. A., Joy, R., Chilman, B., Temple, J., & Miller, S. R. (1991). Self-monitoring of on-task behavior by adolescents with learning disabilities. *Learning Disability Quarterly, 14,* 164–167.

Pressley, M., Goodchild, F., Fleet, J., Zajchowski, R., & Evans, E. D. (1987). *What is good strategy use and why is it hard to teach? An optimistic appraisal of the challenges associated with strategy instruction* (unpublished manuscript). Department of Psychology, University of Western Ontario, London, Ontario.

Pressley, M., Harris, K., & Marks, M. B. (1992). But good strategy instructors are constructivists!! *Educational Psychology Review, 4,* 3–31.

Pressley, M., Johnson, C. J., & Symons, S. (1987). Elaborating to learn and learning to elaborate. *Journal of Learning Disabilities, 20,* 76–91.

Putnam, M. L. (1995). Crisis intervention with adolescents with learning disabilities. *Focus on Exceptional Children, 28*(2), 1–24.

Rafferty, C. D., & Fleschner, L. K. (1993). Concept mapping: A viable alternative to objective and essay exams. *Reading Research and Instruction, 32*(3), 25–34.

Rankin, J. L., & Reid, R. (1995). The SM rap—Or, here's the rap on self-monitoring. *Intervention In School and Clinic, 30*(3), 181–188.

Readance, J. E., Bean, T. W., & Baldwin, R. S. (1992). *Content area reading.* (4th ed.). Dubuque, IA: Kendall Hunt.

Reid, D. K., Kurjian, C., & Caruthers, S. S. (1994). Special education teachers interpret constructivist teaching. *Remedial & Special Education, 15*(5), 267–280.

Reid, R. (1996). Research in self-monitoring with students with learning disabilities: The present, the prospects, the pitfalls. *Journal of Learning Disabilities, 29,* 317–331.

Reiff, H. B., Gerber, P. J., & Ginsberg, R. (1996). What successful adults with learning disabilities can tell us about teaching children. *Teaching Exceptional Children, 29*(2), 10–16.

Reiff, H. B., Ginsberg, R., & Gerber, P. J. (1995). New perspectives on teaching from successful adults with learning disabilities. *Remedial and Special Education, 16*(1), 29–37.

Reith, H. J., & Polsgrove, L. (1994). Curriculum and instructional issues in teaching secondary students with learning disabilities. *Learning Disabilities Research & Practice,* 9(2), 118–126.

Roehler, L. R., & Duffy, G. G. (1984). Direct explanation of comprehension processes. In G. G. Duffy, L. R. Roehler, & J. Mason (Eds.), *Comprehension instruction: Perspectives and suggestions* (pp. 265–280). New York: Longman.

Rojewski, J. W. (1996). Educational and occupational aspirations of high school seniors with learning disabilities. *Exceptional Children, 62*(5), 463–476.

Rowe, M. B. (1976). The pausing principle: Two invitations to inquiry. *Research on College Science Teaching, 5,* 258–259.

Rowe, M. B. (1980). Pausing principles and their effects on reasoning in science. *New Directions in Community Colleges, 31,* 27–34.

Rowe, M. B. (1983). Getting chemistry off the killer-course list. *Journal of Chemical Education, 60,* 954–956.

Sabornie, E. J., Marshall, K. J., & Ellis, E. S. (1990). Restructuring of mainstream sociometry with learning disabled and nonhandicapped students. *Exceptional Children, 56,* 314–323.

Scanlon, D. (1996). Social skills strategy instruction. In D. D. Deshler, E. S. Ellis, & B. K. Lenz (Eds.), *Teaching adolescents with learning disabilities: Strategies and methods* (2nd ed., pp. 369–408). Denver: Love.

Scanlon, D., Deshler, D. D., & Schumaker, J. B. (1996). Can a strategy be taught and learned in secondary inclusive classrooms? *Learning Disabilities Research & Practice, 111*(1), 41–57.

Scanlon, D. J., Duran, G. Z., Reyes, E. I., & Gallego, M. A. (1992). Interactive semantic mapping: An interactive approach to enhancing LD students' content area comprehension. *Learning Disabilities Research & Practice, 7,* 142–146.

Scarpati, S., Malloy, T. E., & Fleming, R. (1996). Interpersonal perception of skill efficacy and behavioral control of adolescents with learning disabilities: A social relations approach. *Learning Disability Quarterly, 19,* 15–22.

Schloss, P. J., Alper, S., & Jayne, D. (1993). Self-determination for persons with disabilities: Choice, risk, and dignity. *Exceptional Children, 60*(3), 215–225.

Schmid, R. F., & Telaro, G. (1990). Concept mapping as an instructional strategy for high school biology. *Journal of Educational Research, 84*(2), 78–85.

Schmidt, J. L., Deshler, D. D., Schumaker, J. B., & Alley, G. R. (1989). Effects of generalization instruction on the written language performance of adolescents with learning disabilities in the mainstream classroom. *Journal of Reading, Writing, and Learning Disabilities, 4*(4), 291–311.

Schumaker, J. B. (1997). *TOWER: The essay writing strategy.* Unpublished manuscript, The University of Kansas, Lawrence, KS.

Schumaker, J. B. (1989). The heart of strategies instruction: Effective modeling. *Strategram 1*(4), 1–5.

Schumaker, J. B., & Deshler, D. D. (1988). Implementing the Regular Education Initiative in secondary schools: A different ball game. *Journal of Learning Disabilities, 21*(1), 36–41.

Schumaker, J. B., & Deshler, D. D. (1994–95). Secondary classes can be inclusive, too. *Educational Leadership, 52*(4), 50–51.

Schumaker, J. B., Deshler, D. D., Alley, G. R., & Warner, M. M. (1983). Toward the development of an intervention model for learning disabled adolescents: The University of Kansas. *Exceptional Education Quarterly, 4,* 45–74.

Scruggs, T. E., & Mastropieri, M. A. (1992). Classroom applications of mnemonic instruction: Acquisition, maintenance, and generalization. *Exceptional Children, 58*(3), 219–229.

Scruggs, T. E., Mastropieri, M. A., Levin, J. R., McLoone, B., Gaffney, J. S., & Prater, M. A. (1985). Increasing content-area learning: A comparison of mnemonic and visual-spatial direct instruction. *Learning Disabilities Research, 1,* 18–31.

Scruggs, T. E., Mastropieri, M. A., Sullivan, G. W., & Hesser, L. S. (1993). Improving reasoning and recall: The differential effects of elaborative interrogation and mnemonic elaboration. *Learning Disability Quarterly, 16,* 233–240.

Seabaugh, G. O., & Schumaker, J. B. (1981). *The effects of self-regulation training on the academic productivity of LD and non-LD adolescents* (Research Report #37). Lawrence, KS: The University of Kansas Institute for Research in Learning Disabilities.

Serna, L. A., & Lau-Smith, J.-A. (1995). Learning with purpose: Self determination skills for students who are at risk for school and community failure. *Intervention In School and Clinic, 30*(3), 142–146.

Sharan, Y., & Sharan, S. (1990). Group investigation expands cooperative learning. *Educational Leadership, 47*(4), 17–21.

Sharan, Y., & Sharan, S. (1994). Group investigation in the cooperative classroom. In S. Sharan (Ed.). *Handbook of cooperative learning methods.* Westport, CT: Greenwood.

Spekman, N. J., Goldberg, R. J., & Herman, K. L. (1992). Learning disabled children grow up: A search for factors related to success in the young adult years. *Learning Disabilities Research & Practice, 7,* 161–170.

Stone, C. A., & Wertsch, J. V. (1984). A social interactional analysis of learning disabilities remediation. *Journal of Learning Disabilities, 17,* 194–199.

Stone, W. L., & La Greca, A. M. (1990). The social status of children with learning disabilities: A reexamination. *Journal of Learning Disabilities, 23,* 32–37.

Toumasis, C. (1995). Concept worksheet: An important tool for learning. *The Mathematics Teacher, 88*(2), 98–100.

Torgesen, J., & Licht, B. (1983). The learning disabled child as an inactive learner: Retrospect and prespects. In J. D. McKinny & L. Feagans (Eds.), *Topics in Learning Disabilities,* Vol. 1 (pp. 3–31). Rockville, MO: Aspen Press.

Trammel, D. L., Schloss, P. J., & Alper, S. (1994). Using self-recording, evaluation and graphing to increase completion of homework assignments. *Journal of Learning Disabilities, 27,* 75–81.

Tur-Kaspa, H., & Bryan, T. (1995). Teachers' ratings of the social competence and school adjustment of students with LD in elementary and junior high school. *Journal of Learning Disabilities, 28,* 44–52.

VanReusen, A., Bos, C., Deshler, D., & Schumaker, J. (1987). *The educational planning strategy (I-PLAN).* Lawrence, KS: Edge Enterprises.

VanReusen, A. K., & Bos, C. S. (1990). I PLAN: Helping students communicate in planning conferences. *Teaching Exceptional Children, 22,* 30–32.

Vaughn, S., & Haager, D. (1994). Social competence as a multifaceted construct: How do students with learning disabilities fare? *Learning Disability Quarterly, 17,* 253–267.

Voth, V. P., & Graham, S. (1993). The application of goal setting to writing. *LD Forum, 18*(3), 14–17.

Vygotsky, L. S. (1978). *Mind in society: The development of higher psychological processes.* Cambridge, MA: Harvard University Press.

Wansart, W. L. (1995). Teaching as a way of knowing: Observing and responding to students' abilities. *Remedial & Special Education, 16*(3), 166–177.

Wedel, M., Deshler, D. D., Schumaker, J. B., & Ellis, E. S. (1992). *Effects of instruction of a vocabulary strategy in a mainstream class.* Lawrence, KS: Institute For Research In Learning Disabilities.

Wehmeyer, M. L. (1995). A career education approach: Self-determination for youth with mild cognitive disabilities. *Intervention In School And Clinic, 30*(3), 157–163.

Wehmeyer, M. L., & Berkobien, R. (1991). Self-determination and self-advocacy: A case of mistaken identity. *The Association for Persons with Severe Handicaps Newsletter, 17*(7), 4.

Weimer, B. B., Cappotelli, M., & DiCamille, J. (1994). Self-advocacy: A working proposal for adolescents with special needs. *Intervention in School and Clinic, 30*(1), 47–52.

Weintraub, P. (1990, October). *Metacognition and reading.* Paper presented at the Strategic Learners Conference, University of South Carolina-Aiken, Aiken, SC.

Weller, C., Watteyne, L., Herbert, M., & Crelly, C. (1994). Adaptive behavior of adults and young adults with learning disabilities. *Learning Disability Quarterly, 17,* 282–295.

Wong, B. Y. L., Butler, D. L., Ficzere, S. A., & Kuperis, S. (1997). Teaching adolescents with learning disabilities and low achievers to plan, write, and review compare-and-contrast essays. *Learning Disabilities Research & Practice, 12*(1), 2–15.

Wong, B. Y. L., Wong, R., & Blenkinsop, J. (1989). Cognitive and metacognitive aspects of learning disabled adolescents' composing problems. *Learning Disability Quarterly, 12*(300–322).

Wong, B. Y. L., Wong, R., Darlington, D., & Jones, W. (1991). Interactive teaching: An effective way to teach revision skills to adolescents with learning disabilities. *Learning Disabilities Research & Practice, 6,* 117–127.

Wright-Strawderman, C., & Watson, B. L. (1992). The prevalence of depressive symptoms in children with learning disabilities. *Journal of Learning Disabilities, 25*(4), 258–264.

Zipprich, M. A. (1995). Teaching web making as a guided planning tool to improve student narrative writing. *Remedial and Special Education, 16*(1), 3–15.

CHAPTER 19

Adults with Learning Disabilities

Pamela B. Adelman and Susan A. Vogel

I. INTRODUCTION

Currently, greater attention is directed to the characteristics and needs of adults with learning disabilities (LD). Recent follow-up studies have reported less than favorable outcomes for adults with LD; however, conflicting results exist. Some studies report positive outcomes in educational and occupational attainments and emotional and social/interpersonal adjustment, but other studies describe higher high school drop-out rates, unemployment, underemployment, and significant social and emotional problems. The first section of this chapter focuses on the characteristics of adults with LD in the following seven areas: (a) academic achievement, (b) cognitive abilities, (c) personality and behavior traits, (d) psychological/ emotional adjustment, (e) social and interpersonal abilities, (f) educational achievement, and (g) independent living skills. The second section is an in-depth view of adults with LD in the workplace and addresses the effect of education and vocational training on occupational attainment. We present research that compares adults with LD to nondisabled workers.

II. CHARACTERISTICS OF ADULTS WITH LEARNING DISABILITIES

A. Academic Achievement

In the research literature concerning academic achievement of adults with LD the most consistent finding is continued difficulty in reading performance (Adelman

& Vogel, 1990; Balow & Blomquist, 1965; Blalock, 1982; Frauenheim, 1978; Johnson, 1987a; Rogan & Hartman, 1990; Vogel & Reder, in press, a). Johnson (1987a) reported on the varied reading problems of a group of 83 adults evaluated at the Learning Disabilities Center of Northwestern University who were classified as poor readers. Poor decoding and oral reading were noted, including problems with phoneme segmentation and structural analysis, retrieval, and pronunciation. Johnson attributed these problems to difficulties with auditory analysis, linguistic awareness, and decoding. With respect to reading comprehension abilities, Johnson identified three patterns: (a) approximately 50% of the deficient readers' scores were at the same level on vocabulary and passage comprehension tests, indicating problems with decoding and word meanings; (b) approximately 25% scored higher on passage comprehension than on vocabulary, indicating good use of background information and context to aid comprehension, but also indicating inadequate and vague understanding of word meanings; and (c) the remaining 25% performed better on vocabulary than passage comprehension, indicating significant problems with comprehension, including the ability to read critically, reason, and infer information. A pervasive problem was reading rate, which affected all of the adults tested. This problem was attributed to several causes, including lack of automaticity, decoding problems, underlying language deficits, and anxiety.

In contrast to the studies described above, The National Adult Literacy Survey (NALS) has provided a national perspective regarding overall literacy functioning among adults with self-reported LD (SRLD) as compared to the general population (Vogel & Reder, in press, a). The primary purpose of the NALS was to identify the skills needed to function in a literate society and to measure the functional English literacy skills of adults in the United States using tasks from everyday life situations and written materials. The participants responded to open-ended questions (rather than multiple-choice items) divided into three scales: the prose, document, and quantitative scales. Because the three scales were so highly intercorrelated as to be effectively unidimensional, the three scores were averaged for each individual for a composite literacy score (Reder, 1995).

1. The Target Population

The target population for the analyses reported here is defined as a subpopulation of individuals living in the United States who met four conditions: (a) native born; (b) spoke English before entering school; (c) did not report any mental retardation; (d) not students at the time of the survey; and (e) between the ages of 25 and 64. The target population is restricted to native-born individuals who spoke English before entering school because of the concern that individuals who first attended foreign schools would not have spoken English at the time they started school in the United States and their literacy proficiency may have been adversely affected. Finally, individuals who were students at the time of participation were excluded because their educational attainment would have still been in a state of flux. Of the 24,944 individuals in the household sample (drawn from a population of 191 million adults in the nation aged 16 and above), 14,519 satisfied the four selection criteria (referred to as the non-SRLD population) and consisted of 8,232 females and 6,242 males between 25 and 64 years of age. This target sample represents 100.6 million individuals. There were 48.2 million males (48%) and 52.2 million females (52%). Within the target sample, 392 individuals (representing 2.8 million adults) indicated that they had an LD. Among those with SRLD, there were more men than women (56% as compared to 44%). There was no significant difference in the incidence of SRLD between the African-American and non-African-American populations.

Not surprisingly, Vogel and Reder (in press, a) reported that adults with SRLD scored significantly lower on the NALS than those in the non-SRLD population. More than half of the adults with SRLD (57%) scored at Level 1 (the lowest among five levels) as compared to only 10% in the non-SRLD group. However, 21% scored at levels 3 or above and 2% had even performed at the highest level, confirming that LDs exist on a continuum from mild to severe and/or can also be overcome. These results confirm that LDs can have a significant impact on literacy skills throughout life. Moreover, the lower the literacy proficiency, the higher the prevalence rate of SRLD. Thirteen percent of the adults who scored at Level 1 had SRLD as compared to the overall prevalence rate of 2.9%. In contrast, there was no contribution of gender to literacy acquisition. Gender ratios of those who scored within levels 2, 3, and 4 were approximately one-to-one, with slightly more females than males at each level other than at the lowest one, where there were about 50% more males than females (1.5:1). This difference was thought to relate to the finding that males more often than females experience more severe LD.

There is also evidence of poor progress in mathematics literacy even among college students with LD (Adelman & Vogel, 1990; Blalock, 1982, 1987a; Bruck, 1985; Cordoni, 1979; Cowen, 1988; Dalke, 1988; Frauenheim, 1978; Johnson, 1987; Hoffmann, et al., 1987; Rogan & Hartman, 1990; Vogel & Moran, 1982; Vogel, 1985; Vogel & Konrad, 1988). In several studies, math was the lowest or among the lowest scores in academic achievement (Adelman & Vogel, 1990; Bruck, 1985; Rogan & Hartman, 1990). Rogan & Hartman (1990) noted that individuals who were deficient in math avoided taking courses in math; this avoidance of the subject matter may have contributed to the lower scores. Frauenheim (1978) tested 40 men who were diagnosed dyslexic in childhood and found problems remembering multiplication tables, understanding place value, and accurately recalling the procedures of basic operations. Mathematical problems affected daily living, which were evident from difficulties with checking change received, balancing checkbooks, and estimating or taking measurements (Blalock, 1987a; Bruck, 1985).

A major residual effect of having an LD, even for highly accomplished adults with LD, is poor spelling. After reviewing 18 follow-up studies, Schonhaut and Satz (1983) concluded that even successful adults who were diagnosed as having a reading disability during childhood have life-long problems with using language, particularly evident from their difficulty with spelling. Underlying language deficits were often evident from analysis of spelling errors, which revealed problems with sound discrimination, memory, and understanding of linguistic patterns. Table 19.1 presents several studies that assessed reading, mathematics, and spelling achievement of adults with LD. Included in the table are size of the sample, IQ, the time between initial evaluation and the age at follow-up (if applicable), the age at initial evaluation or at follow-up, the dependent measures, and a summary of the results.

There are other important aspects of written language in addition to spelling, and although less easily quantified, these deficits are often significant. An LD may also affect development of basic writing skills, and these difficulties often persist even in students with LD who enter postsecondary educational environments.

Vogel and Moran (1982) examined written language abilities of college students with LDs. They compared writing samples of students with LDs to those of their nondisabled peers. Their essays were compared on frequency, type, and accuracy of punctuation and capitalization marks, spelling accuracy, and usage. Not only did the writers with LD use significantly fewer punctuation marks, but they used only 69% correctly, whereas their nondisabled peers used 85% correctly. In regard to spelling accuracy, the students with LD made significantly more spelling errors than their nondisabled peers ($p < .008$). This difference occurred despite the fact that when writing essays, writers may avoid words that they do not know how to spell. Cordoni (1979) also reported that the lowest subtest score on the Peabody Individual Achievement Test (PIAT) for a group of college students with LD was the spelling subtest (see Table 19.1).

Correct usage, another aspect of basic writing skills, was also found to discriminate between students with and without LD (Vogel & Konrad, 1988). Characteristic usage and sentence construction errors in college students with LD included sentence fragments, run-on sentences or comma splice errors, lack of subject/predicate agreement, and inappropriate coordination and/or subordination (Vogel & Konrad, 1998).

Dalke (1988) also studied written language abilities in college students with LD, comparing the performance of college freshman with and without LDs on the Woodcock-Johnson (W-J) Psycho-Educational Battery (Woodcock & Johnson, 1977). Although significant differences existed between the two groups on all of the cognitive and achievement tests, the lowest mean standard score for the group with LD was on the Written Language cluster, which is composed of measures of basic writing skills.

Research findings also suggest that written expression of students with LD is

Table 19.1

Results of Studies Assessing Reading, Mathematics, and Spelling Achievement of Adults with Learning Disabilities[a,b]

Study	Sample size	IQ M (SD)	Time between initial evaluation and follow-up	Age at initial evaluation or at follow-up	Dependent measures	Results (approximate grade equivalent percentile [or standard scores])
Adelman and Vogel (1990)	36	WAIS Full Scale IQ 103.97 (9.81)	NA$_p$	M = 22; 18–44 years	Reading Comprehension:	
					SDRT	9.7
					PIAT	10.7
					W-J Passage	
					Comprehension	11.0
					Spelling:	
					TOWL	8.4
					WRAT	8.3
					PIAT	10.4
					Math:	
					PIAT	9.6
					WRAT	6.9
					W-J	
					Quantitative concepts	10.0
					Calculation	9.0
					Applied problems	9.0
Bruck (1985)	101	WAIS Full Scale IQ 103 (11.22)	M = 13 years	M = 21.1 years	Reading comprehension:	
					SDRT	10.2
					Spelling:	
					WRAT	8.7
					Math:	
					WRAT	6.5
Blalock (1987c)	80		Na$_p$	NA	Math:	
					WRAT	6.68

continued

Table 19.1

(Continued)

Study	Sample size	IQ M (SD)	Time between initial evaluation and follow-up	Age at initial evaluation or at follow-up	Dependent measures	Results (approximate grade equivalent percentile [or standard scores])
Balow and Blomquist (1965)	32	WAIS FS IQ range 91–100; M = 100	10–15 years	20–26 years	Gates Reading Survey given to nine subjects: Comprehension Vocabulary Speed Spelling PIAT: Reading recognition Arithmetic WRAT Reading Arithmetic	10.2 10.9 9.6 10.5 9.8 12.0 8.4 7.2
Cordoni (1979)	NA	NA	NA_p	NA		
Cordoni and Snyder (1981)	16	NA	NA_p	19 years, 4 mos.		
Cowen (1988)	25	W-J: Tests of cognitive ability 101.24	NA_p	NA	W-J Clusters: Reading achievement Math	94.76 102.8
Dalke (1988)	36	W-J: Tests of cognitive ability 89.69	NA_p	NA	W-J Clusters: Reading achievement Math	88.06 89.81
Frauenhein (1978)	40	WAIS Full Scale IQ range 80–112; M = 94	10–15 years	M = 21 years 10 months; 18–31 years	Gate-McKillop Reading Diagnostic Test, oral reading; Gates Reading Test, vocabulary and comprehension Group Diagnostic Reading Aptitude	M = 3.6 on oral reading, vocabulary, and comprehension; range 1.5–8.4

Study	N	IQ / Measure[b]	Age range		Tests and Achievement	
					Spelling	M = 2.9, range 1.3–6.6
					Math	M = 4.6, range 3.0–7.6
Gerber et al. (1990)	222	Self-reporting Likert Scale	23–71 years	NA	Self-reporting Likert Scale:	Problems in these areas worsened when comparing school age to adult years
					Listening	
					Speaking	
					Reading	
					Writing	
					Spelling	
					Math	
Rogan and Hartman (1990)	23	WAIS Full Scale IQ 113(12)	20–30 years	30–40 years	WRAT:	
					Reading	12.3
					Spelling	10.3
					Math	9.6
					Nelson-Denny:	
					Vocabulary	14.4
					Comprehension	12.7
	28	98 (10)			WRAT:	
					Reading	10.9
					Spelling	8.6
					Math	5.6
					Nelson-Denny	(n = 19)
					Vocabulary	13.0
					Comprehension	10.1
	17	79 (8)			WRAT	
					Reading	7.2
					Spelling	5.5
					Math	4.3
					Monroe-Sherman paragraph comprehension	5.7

[a]NA, not available; NA$_p$, not appropriate; SD, standard deviation.
[b]Wechsler Adult Intelligence Scale (WAIS); Woodcock-Johnson (W-J); Stanford Diagnostic Reading Test (SDRT); Peabody Individual Achievement Test (PIAT); Test of Written Language (TOWL); Wide Range Achievement Test (WRAT).

poorer than their peers even among college-able students with LD. When Vogel and Moran (1982) compared holistically scored essays written in the compare–contrast mode of 226 nondisabled college students to those of college students with LD, they found the LD writers' essays were significantly poorer in overall quality. When the essays were scored analytically on organization, development, style, and mechanics, Vogel and Moran found that LD writers' essays were most discrepant from their nondisabled peers on development of ideas and writing style. Writing style is especially significant in mature writers and refers to variety, complexity, and accuracy of sentence structure. On visual examination, Vogel and Moran found that approximately 50% of the sentences written by students with LD were simple sentence patterns, as compared to only 34% of the sentences written by their nondisabled peers. For each of the complex sentence types, the frequency counts were higher for the nondisabled writers. They concluded that students with LD have less variety and complexity in sentence construction. This finding was confirmed and extended in another study by Vogel (1985b), which demonstrated that college students with LD used fewer syntactically complex structures than nondisabled writers as indicated by the number of subordinate clauses and main clause word length.

Given the considerable underachievement among college students with LD, it is not surprising that these deficits exist in secondary school students as well. Wagner and Shaver (1989) found that achievement in secondary school varies widely. Their research project, the National Longitudinal Transition Study (NLTS), identified a nationally representative sample of more than 8,000 youth between the ages of 13 and 23 who were in special education during the 1985–86 school year. In their study, Wagner and Shaver assessed academic achievement by looking at failing grades, promotion, and performance on competency tests. Of the 812 students with LD in the sample, who were in specific grade levels or who were in ungraded programs but received a grade for at least one class in which they were enrolled, 34.8% received a failing grade in one or more courses in their most recent year in secondary school. These data were based on information taken from the students' records and/or from parents' reports. Wagner and Shaver also measured successful completion of the school year and whether the subjects were promoted to the next grade level by examining the most recent school year posted on school records. For this measure of performance, students in 12th grade and students who were in ungraded programs were not included. From a sample of 503 students with LD, they found that 76.9% were promoted. Meeting minimum competency requirements was the third measure of achievement assessed in the NLTS. With respect to performance on competency tests, 25% of 314 respondents who were in schools that required competency tests were exempted from taking the tests. Of those required to take the tests, 47.9% passed all of the tests, 31.7% passed some of the tests, and 23.6% did not pass any of the tests.

B. Cognitive Abilities

Several research studies attempted to determine characteristic cognitive abilities and profiles of adults with LD by administration of the Wechsler Adult Intelligence Scale-Revised (WAIS-R) (Adelman & Vogel, 1990; Blalock, 1987b; Buchanan & Wolf, 1986; Cordoni, O'Donnell, Ramaniah, Kurtz, & Rosenshein, 1981; Salvia, Gajar, Gajria, & Sylvia, 1988; Vogel, 1986). For example, Adelman and Vogel (1990) reported on the cognitive abilities of 36 college graduates with LD and found that the mean Verbal, Performance, and Full Scale IQs were average and quite even (X = approximately 103) with Similarities and Comprehension the two highest mean scaled scores (11.23 and 12.45, respectively), and the Arithmetic, Information, Digit Span, Comprehension (ACID) subtests were the four lowest. The pattern of grouped subtests according to the Bannatyne categories was similar to other samples of LD and non-LD college students in the average IQ range with Verbal Conceptualization the highest or next to highest, and ACID the next to lowest (Cordoni et al., 1981; Vogel, 1986).

1. Profiles of Adults with LD

After reviewing several studies that assessed intellectual functioning by administering the Wechsler Scales of intelligence in adults and children and the revised versions (WISC, WISC-R, WAIS, WAIS-R), Salvia et al. (1988) concluded that, "like children with learning disabilities, adults with learning disabilities may show VIQ-PIQ [Verbal IQ and Performance] differences, considerable scatter on subtests, Bannatyne's hierarchy of category scores, and lower performance on the ACID cluster" (p. 633). Although no characteristic cognitive profile (i.e., VIQ-PIQ discrepancy) that diagnoses LD has emerged from these studies, significant variability in the subtest scores has been a pervasive finding (Blalock, 1987b; Buchanan & Wolf, 1986; Salvia et al., 1988; Vogel, 1986). Salvia et al. (1988) individually tested 74 LD and 74 non-LD college students. Results of the WAIS-R indicated that no one profile characterized the LD sample, but the students with LD had more variable profiles than the non-LD students as measured by the range of WAIS-R verbal subtests, performance subtests, or among all subtests.

2. Intraindividual Discrepancies

Further evidence of the range of cognitive abilities among adults with LD was noted by Cowen (1988) and Stone (1987). Cowen (1988) administered the W-J Psychoeducational Battery to 25 college students previously identified as having an LD. She found that 22 of the 25 students had one of three profiles associated with LDs: six subjects had low verbal ability and high reasoning ability; five subjects had high verbal ability and low reasoning ability; and 11 subjects had high verbal ability and reasoning and low perceptual speed and memory. Stone (1987) also found considerable variability on a problem-solving strategy that assessed abstract reasoning ability.

Although there is considerable evidence that VIQ-PIQ discrepancy should not be used for diagnosing LDs, this information has significance in understanding the manifestations of the LD and in planning remedial and support services (Vogel, 1986). When VIQ is lower than PIQ, verbal deficits may be present, indicating underlying problems in oral language (Blalock, 1981, 1982, 1987c; Vogel, 1986) and may require long-term support in order to improve basic skills. Blalock (1987c) reported on the evaluation of 93 adults who were diagnosed as having an LD at the Learning Disabilities Center of Northwestern University. Seventy-eight percent were diagnosed as having some oral language, auditory processing, or metalinguistic problems. Deficits in all areas of language processing were noted, including problems with auditory perception, comprehension, and memory.

When PIQ is lower than VIQ, nonverbal deficits have a significant impact upon social maturity and independence and these individuals may require extensive psychotherapy (Blalock, 1981, 1982; Johnson, 1987b; Vogel, 1986). Johnson (1987b) reported that 18 of the 93 adults evaluated at the Learning Disabilities Center of Northwestern University had primary nonverbal disorders that significantly affected their daily functioning. Minor repairs and tasks such as changing license plates requiring visual-motor skills were extremely difficult for them. In addition to problems with visual-motor integration, these adults also had significant deficits in visual analysis and synthesis. Blalock (1981, 1982) reported the effects of nonverbal LD on interpersonal relationships. Problems with social perception prevented individuals from accurately assessing situations, facial expressions, and/or body language.

C. Personality and Behavior Traits

Little research exists on the personality and behavior traits of adults with LDs. Schonhaut and Satz (1983) concluded that the association between early learning problems and later antisocial behavior and emotional problems was unclear, and they noted the need for research to explore conduct disorders and emotional adjustment. Horn, O'Donnell, and Vitulano (1983) identified self-concept as a neglected variable in determining adult outcomes. They suggested that gaining a better understanding of the importance of this variable may explain why some individuals are successful in employment even though their basic skills are low, and why others, who have good educational and vocational attainment, have poor emotional and behavioral adjustments.

Buchanan and Wolf (1986) analyzed the personal and educational histories of

33 adults with LD. In their study, subjects were asked to check behavioral characteristics that they perceived as strengths and those perceived as problem areas. The most common problems identified were shyness, self-consciousness, insecurity, passivity, and withdrawal.

Evidence of personal and emotional problems was also found by Hoffmann et al. (1987) who conducted a needs assessment of 381 persons with LD who were eligible for vocational rehabilitation by surveying these adults, providers of services to persons with LD, and advocates for persons with LD. All three groups identified impulsive social behavior as the major deficit. The findings from this study also point to personal problems ranging from frustration and low self-confidence to depression.

D. Psychological and Emotional Problems

Cohen (1985) compared 15 high school and college students with LD who ranged in age from 16 to 21 years old with a similar group of 15 non-LD students, who were struggling with comparable types of issues related to work, school, and social activities. He concluded that the students with LD were at risk for emotional problems even when they were diagnosed and received appropriate help. Cohen identified a high propensity for distress and anxiety among the LD group, particularly in response to other people finding out about their weaknesses. They suffered from low levels of chronic depression, which was largely due to feeling "painfully damaged, inadequate, dumb, and vulnerable" (p. 183).

From his evaluations, Cohen also suggested that LDs contribute to an individual's belief that frustration and failure are unpredictable and uncontrollable. He explains that "these repeated moments of frustration, failure, and helplessness seem to be accompanied by a painful lowering of self-esteem and negative self-representations. Gradually, these repeated moments (and the anxious anticipation of them) seem to result in trauma" (p. 186).

The students seen by Cohen responded to their feelings of helplessness and inadequacy by developing compensatory strategies and rigid types of behavior that often also had a negative psychological impact. For example, a student who compensated by working slowly on schoolwork generalized this behavior to being "slow" in all areas of functioning. Colon also found "that the adolescents' defensive and coping strategies were employed in a relatively rigid fashion" (p. 190). Like the compensatory strategies, rigidity was also generalized and became part of the students' character. Cohen noted the negative impact rigidity has on therapy; it is often a major obstacle to making therapeutic gains because it undermines integration and educational and psychological development.

Cohen also found that the way others respond to individuals with LDs is extremely important in their psychological development. He found a strong relationship between feelings of how they think they are treated as adolescents and how they were treated as children.

Spekman, Oi, Goldberg, and Herman (1989) interviewed 50 young adults who had attended the Marianne Frostig Center of Educational Therapy for at least one academic year. After developing the criteria for identifying a subject as successful, former students were placed in either the successful or the unsuccessful group. Success was defined as achievement of certain accomplishments that are age appropriate and socially acceptable, personal satisfaction with activities, accomplishments, and relationships, and effective coping strategies. Major factors differentiating the successful and unsuccessful subjects were psychological and emotional traits, including self-awareness and acceptance of their LD, the ability to plan and set realistic goals, participation in and enjoyment of social interactions, perseverance, and the ability to cope with stress and frustration.

An important longitudinal study that investigated the psychological and emotional status of 22 adults with LD (32 years old at last data collection) as compared to their non-LD peers matched on gender, socioeconomic status, and ethnic background was conducted by Werner and Smith (1992). This study, the Kauai Longitudinal Study, periodically assessed this multiracial cohort of 698 infants born on the island of Kauai in 1955. The twenty-two individuals from the total cohort who were identified at age 10 as having an LD and their matched controls have been studied closely to identify the risk and resiliency factors that have contributed to the reported outcomes, one of the researchers' areas of special interest. In addition, these researchers have made a unique contribution to our understanding of LDs, as they have followed these individuals into the fourth decade of life.

One of the surprising findings of this study is that the outcomes have changed over time. If the last data collection had been when the cohort was 17–18 years old, we would have been left with a very discouraging prognosis. Namely, we would have learned that 27% of the individuals with LDs had some contact with the police as compared to only 5% of the non-LD teenagers. Some of the offenses were larceny, burglary, repeated truancy, or car theft. It isn't any wonder that 27% had a delinquency record and 95% were having trouble in school (as compared to 0% among the non-LD matched controls), and 32% had mental health problems.

On formal testing, these individuals scored significantly lower than their peers on self-assurance, internal locus of control, socialization and responsibility, and interpersonal adequacy.

But the story doesn't end there. In 1987 Werner was able to locate 18 of the 22 young adults with LD and 20 of the 22 matched controls. At age 32, the LD and non-LD young adults appear very similar in that there was no significant difference in the percent who had a record with criminal, civil, or family court, had significant mental health problems, in divorce, welfare, or unemployment rates and, moreover, by the fourth decade they seem to have turned their lives around (Werner, 1993). The percent who had a criminal record or persistent mental health problems went from 27% and 32% respectively to less than 10%.

E. Social and Interpersonal Skills

Several studies report problems with making and keeping friends (Blalock, 1981; Bruck, 1985; Fafard & Haubrich, 1981). In addition, the range of leisure activities in which some adults with LD participate is limited, and many are dependent on family support for social activities (Blalock, 1981; Fafard & Haubrich, 1981; Haring, Lovett, & Smith, 1990; Hoffmann, et al., 1987). The ability of some adults with LD to participate in specific social and recreational activities is affected by social perception problems, which manifest themselves in poor eye contact, saying the wrong thing, or interrupting behaviors. Some adults with LD could not participate in activities such as word games, card games, or dances and sports because of problems with language and motor coordination (Blalock, 1981; Fafard & Haubrich, 1981).

The findings of Scuccimarra and Speece (1990) were more positive. Employment outcomes and social adjustment were examined in a study of 70 mildly handicapped students who participated in special education, 60 of whom were diagnosed as LD. Scuccimara and Speece (1990) reported that the majority of participants were active and engaged in a variety of leisure activities with peers. However, they also found that a consistent number of respondents (24–29%) reported participating in only two or fewer activities, had no close friendships, and were generally dissatisfied with their social lives. The respondents who expressed the most satisfaction with their social lives were employed and active socially.

F. Educational Attainments

1. High School

The literature on educational attainment is inconsistent. Some studies found that there is a higher dropout rate among adolescents with LD (Levin, Zigmond, Birch, 1985; Wagner, 1989a). From the results of the NLTS, Wagner (1989a) found that 61% of 533 students with LD graduated, whereas the U.S. Department of Education (1995) estimated the graduation rate for the students with LD to be approximately 50% as compared to the general population (71%). The high school dropout rate was 12%, but that is felt to be an underestimation since there were another 18% whose status is unknown who were also probably high school dropouts bringing the total to a 30% dropout rate. According to Wagner (1989), the most commonly cited reasons for youth with LD to drop out of school were that students did not like school (30%) and/or they were not doing well in school (28%).

Vogel and Reder (in press, b) reported almost identical findings to those of the

NLTS based on the NALS national database. They reported that the high school graduation/GED completion rate for adults with SRLD ages 25–64 was 48% as compared to 84% in the general population. Moreover, while in the general population there was virtually no difference in high school graduation rate for males and females, in the SRLD population, 55% of the graduates were women as compared to 42% males. As might be expected, the reverse trend was seen in high school or earlier dropout rate in which more males with SRLD (58%) than females (45%) dropped out of school (Vogel & Reder, in press, b).

However, it is important to mention that there are a few other studies that reported more positive outcomes, indicating that students with LD can graduate at the same rate as their non-LD peers and also go on to postsecondary education (Bruck, 1985; Preston & Yarington, 1967). Studies that reported the same high school graduation rate for students with and without LD pointed out that students with LD often repeated grades and/or attended summer school to prevent failure and subsequent high school dropout (Edgington, 1975; Preston & Yarrington, 1967). The most common reason cited for these inconsistent results is differences in socio-economic status (SES) of the samples studied (O'Connor & Spreen, 1988; Schonhaut & Satz, 1983; Wagner, 1989a). O'Connor & Spreen (1988) found a significant correlation between the parents' SES, particularly the father's SES, and the educational achievement of the students with LD. Wagner (1989b) also identified lower socio-economic status as a significant contributing factor to handicapped youth's dropping out of school.

2. Postsecondary

A few studies reported the percent of students with LD who attended postsecondary institutions (Scuccimarra & Speece, 1990; Wagner & Shaver, 1989). Wagner and Shaver (1989) found that among an LD sample of 245 students, 10% attended vocational or trade schools, 7% attended 2-year colleges, and 1.8% attended 4-year colleges. They pointed out that these figures are significantly below the participation rate for nondisabled students in postsecondary education. Among the nondisabled students, 28% attended 4-year colleges and 28% attended 2-year colleges. For vocational or trade schools, the rate of participation was the same for disabled and nondisabled students (10%). These findings are similar to those of Werner (1993) regarding schooling beyond high school. She reported that 60% of those with LD as compared to 21% without LD had no additional education beyond high school. Fewer adults with LD attended technical school or a junior college (10% for the LD group and 21% for the non-LD), whereas only a fraction of the adults with LD in the Kauai cohort attended 4-year institution (10% as compared 50%).

Similar percentages, though slightly lower than those reported for the NLTS follow-up data, were reported by Fairweather and Shaver (1991). They found that the overall enrollment in postsecondary school was 17%. The largest proportion were enrolled in vocational programs (8.5%), while almost 7% attended 2-year colleges, and less than 2% were enrolled in 4-year colleges or universities.

Butler-Nalin and Wagner (1991) reported on the NLTS findings with respect to postsecondary enrollment immediately after graduation from high school. They found that significantly fewer students with LD (23%) enrolled in postsecondary education as compared to the general population (56%). However, whereas only 12.5% of students with LD surveyed enrolled in 2- or 4-year college program, approximately 12% enrolled in vocational or trade schools, which was higher than students in the general population (8%). Factors influencing whether students with LD attended college were graduating from high school and participation in mainstreamed classes. Butler-Nalin and Wagner also found that enrollment in postsecondary schools increased over time. Whereas 16.4% of students with LD in their study were enrolled 1 year after high school, 29.1% were enrolled a postsecondary school 3 to 4 years out of high school.

Blackorby and Wagner (1996) reported on a subsample of 1,990 students in the NTLS. Results from this subsample corroborated findings of the Butler-Nalin and Wagner (1991) study. Approximately 14% of students with LD were enrolled in postsecondary education less than 2 years out of high school, but 30.5% were enrolled 3–5 years out of school. Although this is a significant increase, youth in the general population are enrolling in postsecondary education at a much higher rate (47% vs. 30.5%).

A few contradictory studies provided evidence that some adults with LD have not only attended, but graduated from college, and some completed graduate degrees (Rawson, 1968; Rogan & Hartman, 1976; Silver & Hagin, 1985). Within the last 15 years, the number of students with LD attending college has increased dramatically, attributable in large part to the passage of the Rehabilitation Act of 1973 and its implementing regulations (Mangrum & Strichart, 1988; Scheiber & Talpers, 1987; Vogel, 1993). In view of how recently the number of students with LD on college campuses has increased, limited national statistics are as yet available regarding graduation and attrition rate of students with LD. Statistics are not even available from colleges where support services specifically for students with LD have been available since the early 1980s and that offered an environment of greater awareness and understanding of this disability. Bursuck, Rose, Cowen, and Yahaya (1989) reported on the results of 197 surveys received from community colleges and 4-year colleges. Only 20 schools (10%) provided data for the number of students graduating or completing a course of study. Schools that responded reported a completion rate of approximately 30%, but it is unclear if this represents program completion or graduation rate.

To address this question, Vogel and Adelman's (1990) began to report on the 4-year college degree completion and academic failure rate of 110 students with LD. The students with LD were compared to a random stratified sample of 153 peers attending the same college for at least one semester. They reported that students with LD graduated at the same rate (approximately 37%) and within the same time frame as their nondisabled peers. Moreover, their academic failure rate was no higher than that of the nondisabled students. Vogel and Adelman identified three factors that contributed to these positive outcomes: (a) the students with LD self-referred at admissions; (b) they were screened for intellectual abilities, type and severity of LD, and motivation and attitude toward the teaching–learning process; and (c) they required and used comprehensive, highly coordinated support services, and special academic advisors.

But can one generalize from a sample from one specific 4-year college any more than from one college preparatory school or special school for students with LD? Obviously not. To date there are two national databases that have provided data regarding postsecondary completion rate, namely, the NLTS and NALS databases. Of the NLTS participants, 3–5 years after exiting high school, Blackorby and Wagner (1996) reported that 3% had completed a 2-year degree and 0.4% had completed a 4-year degree. These degree completion rates were very discouraging, indeed, yet we have since learned that 3–5 years after exiting high school is an insufficient period of time to allow for completion of a higher education degree. This problem was overcome by Vogel and Reder (in press, b) by using the NALS database, which includes adults across the life span. Vogel and Reder reported that although only 12% of the adults with SRLD who participated in the NALS were enrolled in a postsecondary setting as compared 22% of the non-LD, almost 9% graduated from an undergraduate, graduate, or professional school. Moreover, when the data were analyzed by gender, there were no differences in the non-LD population; however, in the LD population, there were more females than males (12.5% vs. 5.70%) among the college graduates. These differences can be best understood in light of the differences between school-identified and research-identified samples in which females with LD tend to be lower in cognitive abilities and have more severe deficits than males.

G. Independent Living Skills

A consistent finding in the research literature is that most adults with LD live with their parents longer than their non-LD peers (Fafard & Haubrich, 1981; Haring, Lovett & Smith 1990; Menkes, Rowe & Menkes, 1967; Scuccimarra & Speece, 1990; Spekman, Oi, Goldberg, & Herman, 1989; Wagner, 1989b). Scuccimarra and Speece (1990) surveyed students 2 years after graduating from high school and found that over 80% resided with their parents, which they attributed primarily to the cost of living independently. These findings were consistent with Wagner's (1989b) data in which only 22% of youth with LD lived independently 1–2 years after graduation, and with a study conducted by Haring, Lovett, and Smith (1990), who found that wages earned were insufficient for self-support. Blackorby and Wagner (1996) found that significantly more youth with LD were living independently 3–5 years out of secondary school (14.7% vs. 44.1%). Despite the increase, they still lagged behind youth in the general population (44.1% vs. 60%).

Scuccimarra and Speece (1990) concluded that given the low number of individuals who received additional training after high school, significant income increases that would enhance independence are unlikely unless there are opportunities for on the job training. Even among the college-educated participants in the Greenbaum et al. (1996) study, 43% lived with their parents; the remaining 57% lived in with roommates or were married and lived with their spouses.

Although some individuals with LD either did not apply or were not eligible for a driver's license and had orientation problems that inhibited their mobility (Blalock, 1981; Fafard & Haubrich, 1981), there is also evidence that adults with LD have no problems with accessing the communities in which they live (Haring et al., 1990). In a study by Haring et al. (1990), 64 students with LD who had attended self-contained special education classes were sent questionnaires to assess vocational and community adjustment. Thirty-one percent did not have drivers' licenses, but they used city buses, asked friends or family to transport them, or rode their bicycles as their main methods of transportation.

III. EMPLOYMENT ATTAINMENTS

A. Transition

In 1990 the Education for All Handicapped Children Act of 1975 (P.L. 94-142) was reauthorized and renamed the Individuals with Disabilities Education Act (IDEA; P.L. 101-476). New mandates were included that required individual transition planning for all students served in special education.

Within the last several years, there has been a proliferation of studies focusing on transition services and programs. A consistent theme is the importance of a coordinated approach that involves the students, teachers, parents, and representatives of community services (Blalock, 1996; DeFur & Reiff, 1994; Halldefur & Taymans, 1995; Halpern, 1992; Morningstar, Turnball, & Turnball, 1996, Repetto & Correa, 1996). DeFur and Taymans (1996) surveyed transition specialist practitioners from across the United States in the fields of vocational special education, special education, and vocational rehabilitation. These specialists were asked to identify competencies they considered most important to effectively provide transition services. The results pointed out that although it may be important for transition specialists to be skilled in direct service provision, the ability to work with others and coordinate services is of paramount importance. A study by Morningstar et al. (1996) provides further support for DeFur's and Tayman's results. The Morningstar et al. study had focus groups meet with students with disabilities to determine the student's perspectives on family involvement in the transition from school to adult life. The results showed the importance of family input and support to these students, which documents the need for transition specialists to involve parents in the transition process.

B. Effect of High School Educational and Vocational Training

There is considerable evidence that high school vocational training has either been ineffective or nonexistent for individuals with LD (Fafard & Haubrich, 1981; Haring et al., 1990; Hoffmann et al., 1987; Scuccimarra & Speece, 1990; Weisenstein, Stowitschek, & Affleck, 1991). Haring et al. (1990) found that those who received training were less likely to be employed, and they suggested that this training "did not greatly enhance employability." After surveying service providers and LD advocates, Hoffmann et al. (1987) found that most adults with LD received limited vocational or career training in high school. Schwarz and Taymans (1991) surveyed former students with LDs who had completed mainstream vocational/technical programs between 1986 and 1988. Individuals reported difficulty with finding employment. "Sixty-one percent stated they were not qualified for jobs in the vocational area in which they were trained" (p. 18). Approximately 40% received career guidance. Vocational courses were selected by 22% of the students as a result of the special education teacher's or the counselor's recommendation. The rest selected courses for personal reasons (e.g., proximity, friends in the same program, or parent recommendation). Schwarz and Taymans also found that respondents neither received services from adult service provider agencies nor were they referred to these agencies. In addition, respondents were not aware of such services. Weisenstein et al. (1991) found that although students with disabilities constitute approximately 10% of school enrollment, they only make up approximately 3.3% of students in vocational training.

Further evidence of the inadequacy of vocational training was found by Shapiro and Lentz (1991), who conducted a 2-year follow-up study of students with LD who had attended vocational-technical programs. Students were surveyed at graduation and at 6, 12, and 24 months after graduation. The study included matched groups of students without LD who attended the vocational-technical programs and randomly selected students without disabilities from regular high schools. A major finding was that at graduation, 50% of the students did not feel they received training in academic and job-related skills that they desired. Consistent with the findings of Schwarz and Taymans (1991), Shapiro and Lentz also found that almost 50% or more of both LD and non-LD students who attended vocational training programs were not in a job for which they were trained.

In contrast to the Shapiro and Lentz findings, the results of Scuccimarra and Speece's (1990) study were more positive. Approximately an equal number of employed and unemployed respondents reported a high degree of satisfaction with their high school training. Scuccimarra and Speece also found a relationship between finding summer jobs in high school and obtaining employment after high school.

D'Amico (1991) also noted the positive impact of both work experience and vocational education on future employment. His findings, part of the comprehensive NLTS research project, were that approximately 63% of secondary school students with LD had paid jobs; 62% of disabled students who worked during high school had jobs out-of-school compared to 45.2% of disabled students who did not work during high school. A study by Sitlington & Frank (1989) also found a significant relationship between holding a paid job in high school and adult employment. With respect to vocational training, 63% of students with LD who took at least one vocational course during high school were employed compared to 48% of students with LD who took no vocational courses.

C. Effect of Vocational Training

Of the students surveyed in the study by Hoffmann et al. (1987), 29% reported that they had enrolled in technical, vocational, or trade schools after high school. These experiences included the Job Corps, military training programs, CETA, on-the-job training, and apprenticeships. Sixty-two percent of the participants reported that the experiences were valuable.

D. Effect of High School Graduation

D'Amico (1991) found that 64% of students with LD who graduated from high school were employed compared to 47.7% who had either dropped out or were expelled. Geographic location appears to have an impact on dropout rate and upon later employment. Whereas deBettencourt, Zigmond, and Thornton (1989) found that in rural areas, dropping out of school did not affect employment, Zigmond and Thornton (1989) reported that students with LD who did not finish high school in urban areas experienced greater difficulty with finding employment than those who graduated. In a study by Karpinski, Neubert, and Graham (1992), graduates and dropouts were interviewed twice, 7 months apart. They found that the majority of graduates and dropouts were employed during both interviews. However, at the second interview, graduates had worked more time since high school and were employed in their current job for a longer period of time.

E. Effect of College Graduation

Adelman and Vogel (1990) reported employment patterns for LD 4-year college graduates who participated in a highly coordinated, comprehensive support program for college students with LD at a small, competitive (defined by Barron, 1986, as a college with a median Freshman ACT composite score between 19 and

22), private college. Data were also gathered from nongraduates who withdrew from the college due to academic failure (defined as below 2.0 on a 4.0 scale).

Adelman and Vogel (1990) found that graduates often applied the same compensatory strategies to work assignments that they used while completing school work (i.e., spending additional time completing assignments and taking tests, and/or asking for help to clarify lecture notes and assignments). Adelman and Vogel concluded that self-understanding may be a significant, long-term benefit of having received services in college since it assisted these individuals in understanding their LD and in developing compensatory strategies as they entered and progressed in their work. Unlike the graduates, many nongraduates did not extend the insight they may have acquired regarding the nature of their learning disabilities from the academic to the job setting.

F. Obtaining Employment

In a study by Fafard and Haubrich (1981), 21 young adults were interviewed regarding their adjustment as adults. With respect to obtaining employment, they found that these individuals were motivated to work but experienced considerable difficulty with finding employment. Subjects in the study conducted by Haring et al. (1990) reported that they were most successful finding employment when they had personal contacts. In the study conducted by Schwarz and Taymans (1991), 84% of the respondents found jobs through self-family-friend networks. In a follow-up study conducted by Roessler, Brolin, and Johnson (1990), these findings were confirmed with 79% of the respondents with LD finding jobs through personal contacts. For all groups in the Shapiro and Lentz (1991) study, the family–friend network was the primary means of finding jobs.

G. Type of Employment

Students who were employed in high school and students who completed vocational training programs worked in entry-level positions in clerical, craft, laborer, and service positions (D'Amico, 1991; Schwarz & Taymans, 1991). D'Amico noted that major differences between individuals with LD and the general population were in sales and clerical positions. Whereas 12% of both males and females in the general population were in sales, only 3% of LD individuals held that type of job. Considerably more females in the general population held clerical jobs as compared to both males and females with LD (23% vs. 11.8%).

Among students who graduated from college, Adelman and Vogel (1990) found that the greatest number of graduates (42%) went into some area of business. Adelman and Vogel surveyed 36 students who received LD services in college. In addition to management and business, these graduates majored in computer programming, education, and social sciences. Although some graduates were not employed in their specific areas of preparation, a number reported holding highly responsible positions in business. For example, one education major was the manager of a travel agency, and a social science major was an outside sales representative for a large district. Greenbaum et al. (1996) surveyed 49 students with LD who had attended the University of Maryland between 1980 and 1992 and had received assistance from the office of Disability Support Services. Using the classification system in the Dictionary of Occupational Titles (U.S. Department of Labor, 1991), they found that 25 (71%) of the employed participants were in professional, technical, or managerial positions; 8 (23%) were in clerical and sales occupations; and 2 (6%) were in service occupations.

H. Rate of Employment

There is evidence of considerable unemployment among individuals with LD (Blalock, 1981, 1982; Haring et al., 1990; Scuccimarra & Speece, 1990). However, when compared to nondisabled individuals, some studies found that the unemployment rate is not significantly greater for individuals with LD (Bruck, 1985; Preston & Yarington, 1967). Bruck (1985) found the unemployment rate for the students with LD was the same as their non-LD siblings in the control group. She reported that the individuals with LD were employed in a wide range of occupations and only a few were employed in unskilled jobs. Wagner and Shaver (1989) confirmed Bruck's findings and reported that the employment rate for the individuals with LD 1 year after graduation was 58%, which approached the rate of 62% for nondisabled individuals. D'Amico (1991) also confirmed Bruck's findings and reported that the employment rate for the individuals with LD 1 to 2 years after graduation was approximately 58%, which approached the rate of 61% for nondisabled individuals. He also noted that over a 2-year period, the employment rate for individuals with LD steadily increased from 62.7% during the summer of 1987 to 75.8%.

Data on labor force participation revealed that there were no differences in employment rate when the LD group was compared to the general population. For a subgroup of the NLTS participants ages 15–20 who were not enrolled in school in the preceding year, Marder and D'Amico (1992) reported only a slight difference in employment rates in the LD and general populations: 56.9% of the LD group was employed compared to 60.2% of the general population (based on the adjusted rate). Three to five years after secondary school students with LD continued to be employed at approximately the same rate (70%) as youth in general.

In fall, 1989, Schwarz and Taymans (1991) reported that all respondents in their study held at least one job since graduating from high school. However, an important finding was that 77% only worked up to 6 months.

I. Demographics

Although D'Amico (1991) did not differentiate between disability groups, he found that demographic factors affected employment of individuals with disabilities. Minorities, youths from households that had lower socioeconomic status, and youths in urban areas were less likely to be employed. Blackorby and Wagner (1996) found that African-American youth with disabilities were employed at a much higher rate in 1990 vs. 1987. However, employment of African-American students 3–5 years after secondary school was still significantly lower than white students with disabilities (47% vs. 61%). They also found that wages did not increase for African-American students at the same rate as for white students.

J. Gender Differences

Considerable evidence indicates that disabled women are unemployed at a significantly higher rate than disabled men (Buchanan & Wolf, 1988; Haring & Lovitt, 1990; Haring, Lovitt, & Smith, 1990; Kranstover, Thurlow, & Bruininks, 1989; Scuccimarra & Speece, 1990). In a study of 70 mildly handicapped students who participated in special education, 60 of whom were diagnosed as having an LD, Scuccimarra and Speece (1990) reported the unemployment rate for women with disabilities was 23.8% as compared to 6.8% for men. When students work while they are still attending high school, gender differences also exist. In the NLTS study (1991), 66.5% of the men and 53.1% of the females had paid employment when they were enrolled in secondary school. D'Amico found that the gap widens once students leave school, with 63.5% of males employed compared with 39.6% of the females. Whereas employment for men with LD approaches the same percentage as for the general population, the employment of females with LD is considerably lower (39.6% vs. 53.7%).

Nisbet and Lichtenstein (1992) corroborated the findings regarding the NLTS gender differences in full-time and part-time employment rate in a follow-up study conducted in the state of New Hampshire among a group of 100 high school graduates with LD. They reported that more than twice as many males with LD were employed full-time (38% vs. 16%), whereas the reverse pattern was found in part-time employment rate with half as many males as females employed part-time (18% vs. 40%). In addition to reporting that women worked fewer hours, they found that women earned lower wages and had fewer opportunities for job training.

Blackorby and Wagner (1996) found that the trend for men with disabilities to be employed at a higher rate 3–5 years out of school continued. Whereas employment increased 12% for men and was statistically significant, it increased 9% for women and was not significant. This finding was in contrast to employment rates for the general population, where employment for men increased 9 percentage points, and for women, the increase was 12 percentage points.

The underidentification of females with LD may account for their significantly lower employment than LD males. In an extensive review of the literature, Vogel (1990) found that in order for females with LD to be identified in school, they have to be (a) significantly lower in intelligence, (b) more severely impaired in their language abilities and/or academic achievement, and (c) have a greater aptitude–achievement discrepancy than their male counterparts. The evidence suggests that females with LD with the same level of intelligence and type and severity of LD as males will not be as frequently identified. Thus, Vogel's findings may explain in part why fewer females are employed; those that have been identified have significantly lower intelligence and more severe LD than males identified as LD.

Reasons for the underidentification of females with LD include teacher referral bias, lack of understanding of the nature of LD in females, differences in psychometric profiles of females and males (Vogel & Walsh, 1987), and the differential incidence of attention deficit and hyperactivity in males and females (Vogel, 1990). Vogel concluded that gender differences found in longitudinal and follow-up studies on samples of school-identified males and females with LD may be the result of bias of ascertainment and must be interpreted cautiously.

In addition to underidentification of females, there is evidence that females with LD are at particularly high risk of setting limits on their occupational futures. Rojewski (1996) used the database of the National Education Longitudinal Study of 1988 (NELS,88) to study the influence of gender and LD on the occupational aspiration adolescents at grades 8 and 10. Student aspirations were assessed by asking them what job or occupation they hoped to have at 30 years of age. Rojewski found that females with LD set lower aspirations than both males with and without LDs and nondisabled females.

K. Underemployment

There is a common perception that many individuals with LD are underemployed. Their specific deficit areas prevent them from obtaining certain jobs, accepting promotions, or succeeding when promoted (Blalock, 1981). Scuccimarra and Speece (1990) found low levels of employment, with respondents in primarily unskilled and semiskilled positions such as clerical, sales, and service positions. Data from the NLTS study corroborate Scuccimarra's and Speece's findings (Wagner, D'Amico, Newman, & Blackorby, 1992). Although 3–5 years after leaving school, 71% of the young adults were employed, about 70% of the adults with LD were employed in clerical jobs, such as postal clerks; 14.2% were employed as craft workers such as auto mechanics; 19.9% were employed in operative jobs, such as service station attendants; and 38.7% were laborers or service workers such as gardeners, maids, or janitors. In contrast, Bruck (1985) reported no underemployment. Respondents in her study held a wide range of occupations and only a few subjects were employed in unskilled jobs.

L. Wages

Consistent with research that adults with LD often remain in entry-level positions, a pervasive finding is the low pay that individuals with LD receive (Herzog & Falk, 1991; Roessler, Brolin & Johnson, 1990; Siegel, Matt, Waxman, Gaylord-Ross, 1992; Shapiro & Lentz, 1991; Wagner, et al., 1992). Herzog and Falk conducted a vocational follow-up study of 113 young adults with LD who graduated from a 2-year paraprofessional training program in human services careers between 1969 and 1987. Although 76% of the graduates were employed, 60% earned salaries of $10,000 or less. The individuals with LD in the follow-up study of Roessler et al. (1990) earned an average of $5.06 an hour. Shapiro and Lentz (1991) also found among all groups surveyed that most students, even 2 years after graduation, held near minimum-wage-level jobs. However, Blackorby and Wagner (1996) found that wages increased significantly for students with LD 3–5 years out of secondary school versus less than 2 years out of school (45.2% vs. 9.0%).

M. Results from the NALS Database

In an in-depth analysis of the results regarding employment and economic outcomes for individuals with SRLD who responded to the NALS, Reder and Vogel (1997) reported that adults with SRLD were less likely to be employed full-time (37.9% for SRLD vs. 51.9% for non-SRLD), more likely to be unemployed (15.6% for SRLD vs. 6.4% non-SRLD), worked substantially fewer weeks per year, and worked for lower wages and in lower status jobs than their nondisabled peers. They also earned substantially less over the course of a year than members of the general adult population. The mean annual earnings (among those who worked at least at some point in the year) of adults with SRLD, for example, was $14,958, which represented 64.7% of that earned by their nondisabled peers ($23,131). These differences, of course, go well beyond mere statistical significance; they signal the serious impact that LD have on adults' lives. Consider, for example, that when family size and income were used to determine whether families were living below or near the federally defined poverty level, 42.2% of the families of adults with SRLD were found to be living in or near poverty, compared to only 16.2% of the families of their nondisabled peers (Reder, 1995). These findings, based on a nationally representative sample of adults, partially confirm previous findings from studies of the experiences of high school students during the first few years of transition from school. Like those studies, the NALS results indicated that adults with self-identified LD tended to work in lower status occupations at lower wages than their nondisabled peers. In contrast to the earlier studies, however, the present findings indicated that adults with SRLD worked fewer hours and weeks than did their peers in the general population. The decrease in quantity of work combined with the lower rate of pay translates of course into greatly reduced earnings and substantially increased risk of living in poverty.

Reder and Vogel also found persistent effects of gender in these data, with women tending to participate less in the workforce, to work more in part-time and less in full-time jobs (when they were employed), and to work in lower paying and lower status jobs than their male peers. Just as SRLD had a significant negative effect on each measure of adult employment and economic outcomes examined, so too did gender affect each measure.

N. Job Success

Studies on LD adults' success in the workplace have also produced conflicting results (Horn, O'Donnell, & Vitulano, 1983; O'Connor & Spreen, 1988). Whereas some studies on adults with LD found significant problems with obtaining and maintaining jobs (Blalock, 1981, 1982; Hoffmann et al., 1987), other studies reported successful employment of adults with LD (Felton, 1986; Gerber, 1988; Gerber, Finsberg, & Reif, 1992; Preston & Yarington, 1967; Rawson, 1968; Silver & Hagin, 1985).

From research with successful and moderately successful adults, Gerber et al. (1992) developed a model of vocational success for adults with LD that has both internal and external elements. The model suggests a dynamic interaction between internal decisions and external manifestations—adaptability that ultimately leads to high levels of control over one's life. Gerber et al. consider control the key to success for adults with LD.

In recent research on adults with LD who were not successfully employed, lack of self-understanding was cited as a pervasive characteristic (Blalock, 1981, 1982; Buchanan & Wolf, 1986; Hoffmann et al., 1987). Although they knew they were having problems, these adults with LD did not understand how their specific deficits impacted on their difficulties. Consequently, they did not apply for jobs that capitalized upon their strengths, and they could not anticipate problems nor develop compensatory strategies when they were having trouble with meeting the demands of accurate and timely completion of their work responsibilities.

In contrast, the successful employment of individuals with LD has been attributed to their choosing careers in their areas of strength. For example, those with strengths in the visual perceptual and quantitative areas chose fields such as engineering, filmmaking, art history, medical illustration, accounting, and finance (Rogan & Hartman, 1976; Silver & Hagin, 1985). Those with reading disorders accepted jobs with relatively low dependence on reading, sometimes found in business, management, and administration (Felton, 1986). Silver and Hagin (1985) concluded that it is particularly important for individuals with LD to receive career counseling and guidance during transition from school to employment and from one job to another in order to help them carefully select careers that will utilize strengths and deemphasize weaknesses. Those individuals who failed to find the right match between career and personal strengths continued to experience frustration and disappointment.

Another factor in predicting success on the job relates to specific verbal strengths. In a recent study by Faas and D'Alonzo (1990), 86 adults, 18 to 59 years old with LD, were evaluated clinically. They found that the comprehension cluster of the WAIS-R consisting of the Comprehension, Information, Vocabulary, and Similarities subtests was predictive of successful employment. Faas and D'Alonzo concluded that the verbal abilities of adults with LD are very important as determinants of success in the workplace.

O. Job Satisfaction

There are very little data on job satisfaction of LD adults. Some of the individuals evaluated by Blalock (1982) considered their jobs temporary until they could improve their skills. Others were satisfied with their jobs, but feared failure and were afraid to accept promotions. Greenbaum et al. (1996) found that although 94% of the participants reported that they like their jobs, 60% stated that they would like a different one. Schonhaut and Satz (1983), Scuccimarra and Speece (1990), and Rogan and Hartman (1990) reported high levels of job satisfaction. However, Schonhaut and Satz noted the need for further studies to assess occupational status.

P. Effect of Learning Disabilities on Work

Little data exist on how specific LDs affect individuals on the job and how they compensate. Blalock (1981) described several ways LDs were manifested in the workplace. For example, individuals with auditory processing deficits reported problems with telephone work and/or communicating in noisy environments. Some individuals turned in unfinished projects or forgot to complete tasks because of memory deficits and problems with organization.

Blalock (1981) and Brown (1984) described several ways LDs were manifested in the workplace. For example, individuals with auditory-processing deficits reported problems with telephone work and/or communicating in noisy environments. Some individuals turned in unfinished projects or forgot to complete tasks because of memory deficits and problems with organization.

For many adults with LD, poor social skills account for problems on the job (Brown, 1984; Clement-Heist, Siegel, & Gaylord-Ross, 1992; Mathews, Whang, & Fawcett, 1982). Brown described problems getting along with others because of difficulty with accurately perceiving nonverbal language (i.e., interpreting body language and intonation correctly). Mathews, Whang, and Fawcett (1982) compared 25 LD and non-LD high school students on 13 job-related skills; 10 social interaction skills and 3 nonsocial interaction skills. They found that non-LD students performed significantly better on four social interaction skills (participating in a job interview, accepting criticism from an employer, providing constructive criticism to a co-worker, and explaining a problem to a supervisor). The non-LD students were also significantly better on all the nonsocial interaction skills, which included writing letters and completing a federal income tax form.

In a study conducted with four high school seniors with LD, Clement-Heist, Siegel, and Gaylord-Ross (1992) simulated specific vocational social skills first in a classroom situation, and then in the student's workplace for those who could not generalize the skills after only classroom instruction. Pre- and postassessment of social skills were conducted at the students' work site. Clement-Heist et al. found considerable improvement in the three behaviors studied: ordering job duties, conversational skills, and giving instructions. They recommended further use of on-site training as an adjunct to simulated training for individuals with deficient social/vocational skills.

Gerber et al. (1990) sent a questionnaire to 133 adults with LD and asked them to rate themselves on 13 common characteristics associated with LD (e.g., listening, reading, visual perception, distractibility, and attention span). The results indicated that for both moderately successful and successful adults, in employment, there was general deterioration of abilities and behaviors. Although the authors did not cite specific ways abilities affected work performance, it is reasonable to assume that deterioration of skills must have had some impact on work.

Adelman and Vogel (1990) reported employment patterns for 4 -year college graduates with LD who participated in a highly coordinated, comprehensive support program for college students with LD at a small, moderately selective, private college. Most graduates responded that their LDs do affect their work. Processing difficulties, including their ability to retain information, the amount of time to complete work, and perception (particularly number and letter reversals), were the most common difficulties.

Greenbaum et al. (1996) found that 80% of participants reported that their LDs continue to affect them, either at their job or in other facets of their lives. Difficulties with reading, writing, mathematics and memory persisted.

Q. Compensatory Strategies

Even though the college graduates in the Adelman and Vogel (1990) study indicated that their LDs affected their work, an important finding was that the college graduates developed compensatory strategies. The most commonly used compensatory strategies included spending additional time to finish work, asking for additional help, and carefully monitoring work for errors. Adelman and Vogel suggests that these graduates' insight into how their LDs affected them on the job helped them to determine ways to compensate. This is consistent with the findings of other studies on adults who were successfully employed (Gerber, 1988; Rawson, 1968). For example, Rawson (1968) described a lawyer who compensated for his inability to remember large amounts of reading material by applying his analytical skills first to reason through a legal problem. As a result, his reading was more focused, and he could more effectively remember the information.

Although there is evidence of the creative ways adults with LD have compensated for their LDs, Blalock (1981) pointed out that they devote a great deal of effort to hiding their LD from employers and co-workers. For example, some describe taking reports home for spouses to write and calling upon friends for help with spelling.

Greenbaum et al. (1996) documented LD individuals' reluctance to self-disclose their LD because of their fear of discrimination. In the study, less than half of the participants disclosed their LD. For those that did, the major accommodations were auxiliary aids (i.e., dictaphone, word processor, spell checker). Other accommodations reported were a lighter workload, sensitivity on the part of the employer, and writing assistance from another employee to proofread written work.

R. Employer Perceptions

There is evidence that employer awareness of LD is increasing. For example, Blalock (1981) noted an increase in the number of referrals from the employers of individuals who were evaluated. Minskoff, Sautter, Hoffmann, and Hawks (1987) surveyed 326 employers. Seventy-two percent of the employers responded that they would make special allowances for workers with disabilities that they would not make for nondisabled workers. Special allowances identified included providing additional support and encouragement, providing extra time for training, providing more detailed directions, and helping workers with disabilities find the right job. Employers reported that they would not reduce work demands or become involved in the worker's personal life. The pervasive attitude was one of support as long as the individual accomplished his or her responsibilities.

However, a discouraging finding of this study was that employers appeared to be more willing to make allowances for individuals with disabilities in general than for workers with LD in particular. Minskoff et al. (1987) suggested that employers may have a more positive attitude toward individuals with physical disabilities than cognitive disabilities, which may indicate a lack of understanding of LDs.

From September 1991 to May 1992, Gerber (1992) provided technical assistance on employability and employment issues for persons with LDs to 25 companies in the greater Richmond community. He observed that companies are sympathetic to persons with all disabilities and interested in modifying training procedures so they are consistent with the best practices for those with LDs. How-ever, Gerber cautioned that businesses are still looking for employees who have mastered basic skills and have good social skills.

IV. CRITIQUE OF RESEARCH

As can be seen from the above review, the results of studies on adults with LD have been inconsistent. Several reasons have been cited for these inconsistencies, including differences in intellectual ability and socioeconomic status of the spe-cific population sampled, the amount of family support, and the degree and qual-ity of educational intervention (O'Connor & Spreen, 1988; Silver & Hagin, 1985; Vogel, 1996a, 1996b). Considerable evidence exists regarding the methodological factors that account for the conflicting results including, (a) choice of outcomes, (b) selection criteria, (c) severity of LD, (d) sample size and subject attrition, (e) IQ level, (f) demographics, (g) educational opportunity and remediation or inter-vention, (h) comparison groups, and (i) instrumentation (Herjanic & Penick, 1972; Horn et al., 1983; O'Connor & Spreen, 1988; Schonhaut & Satz, 1983).

A. Choice of Outcomes

After reviewing 24 follow-up studies of persons with learning disabilities, Horn, et al. (1983) identified the choice of outcome measures as the most important methodological consideration in designing follow-up studies. They found that the dependent variables selected will generally determine the overall prognosis. When educational and vocational outcomes are the dependent variables, the outcomes are usually favorable. However, measurement of basic skills generally yields poor prognosis for adults with LD.

The number of dependent variables in a study also has a significant effect on the outcomes. In past research studies, areas of investigation were mainly limited to aca-demic and occupational achievement, and, therefore, little is known about adjust-ment in social and emotional domains (Herjanic & Penick, 1972; Horn et al., 1983; Schonhaut & Satz, 1983). Herjanic and Penick (1972) pointed out that "studies have generally ignored other kinds of intervening situational events, behavioral and per-sonality characteristics, or personal experiences which could possibly augment or mitigate the effect of a childhood reading disorder upon adult functioning" (p. 407). Thus, both the type and number of outcome measures may determine not only the favorable or unfavorable prognosis but also the scope of the study,

Regardless of the choice of outcomes and prognosis, quantitative data analysis from grouped data should not be the only method for measuring outcomes (Horn et al., 1983). Because there are often significant differences between subjects, Horn, et al. suggested assessing individual achievements that may yield valuable information on the educational intervention or compensatory strategies that contributed to the success of some of the individuals.

B. Selection Criteria

Studies often do not clearly describe the criteria used in selecting subjects (Horn, et al., 1983). Some studies do specify the selection criteria, but there is considerable variation among them, which precludes comparing results across studies. For example, in their review of follow-up studies. Horn et al., (1983) found that some studies define LDs as a discrepancy between reading level and grade placement or between reading level and chronological age and do not indicate whether a discrepancy exists between reading level and IQ. Furthermore, they also noted the importance of describing whether the LD sample was clinically referred or school-referred, because clinically referred subjects are more likely to have more severe LDs and confounding behavioral problems. Another important variable is the age of the participants and how much time has elapsed since exit from high school. As was noted, the contradictory results form the NLTS and NALS databases regarding postsecondary attainment may be due in no small part to the fact that the last NLTS data collection was only 3–5 years after exiting from high school. Since it takes adults with LD longer to complete their postsecondary education, at the very least 6 years have to elapse when examining postsecondary completion. Lastly, inconsistent results can be due to differences in definition, in operationalizing the identification criteria (i.e., use of a regression model versus a discrepancy model versus a diagnostic/clinical model), and sample ascertainment (i.e., school, clinic, research, or self-identified participants).

C. Severity of Learning Disabilities

The severity of the LD is not always addressed in designing studies, and yet, a commonly held perception is that the more severe the LD, the greater possibility of a poor prognosis with respect to educational and employment attainments (Bruck, 1985; Herjanic & Penick, 1972; Horn et al., 1983; Vogel et al., 1993). Silver and Hagin (1985), for example, identified a subgroup of children whose performance on neurological exams indicated structural defects of the central nervous system. They noted the importance of identifying this subgroup, which they termed "organic," because educational outcomes were less favorable and indicated the persistent effect of neuropsychological problems of adults.

Bruck (1985) believes her sample is well defined because she only examined children with primary LD and included in her sample students whose disabilities ranged in severity. Bruck suggested that her results are better able to be generalized to other samples because of the variability of the LD sample examined.

D. Sample Size and Subject Attrition

A consistent problem cited in the critiques of studies on adults with LD is inadequate sample size (Bruck, 1985; Haring, Lovitt, & Smith, 1990; Herjanic & Penick, 1972). For example, samples cited in Table 19.1 range from 9 subjects to 101 subjects. Subject attrition is another critical methodological variable. If attrition alters the sample size, the characteristics and the outcome results may also be altered. The outcome results may be specific to the follow-up sample and not to the original LD sample (Haring et al., 1990; Horn et al., 1983). Not only is it often questionable as to whether the sample in the follow-up study is representative, but the reduced sample itself may also bias the results. It is important to determine why individuals did not participate and whether their reasons for not participating will bias the outcomes. Whereas the omission of subjects who cannot be located may have neither a positive nor negative impact on the results, the lack of participation of reluctant subjects may decrease the number of negative outcomes and therefore bias the results.

E. IQ Level

Intelligence, like severity of the LD, is a very important variable in research studies of adults with LD. A reasonable expectation is that the higher the IQ, the better the prognosis. Rawson's (1968) study on the educational and occupational achievement of 20 dyslexic men is often cited as an example of a study with extremely favorable outcomes. The mean childhood IQ of this sample was 130.

The effect of IQ upon outcomes is particularly evident from a follow-up study conducted by Rogan and Hartman (1990). They presented data on 68 young adults who attended a private school. The sample of 68 participants was divided into three subgroups: college graduates, high school graduates, and students who were placed in self-contained special education classes. The mean full scale IQ scores differed significantly: college graduates ($X = 113$), high school graduates ($X = 98$), and those in self-contained special education classrooms ($X = 79$).

Although participants in all groups continued to experience residual academic deficiencies, levels of academic achievement were also significantly disparate. However, Rogan and Hartman concluded that overall outcomes for most of the college and high school graduates and for several in the self-contained special education classrooms were favorable, which indicates that although intelligence is a significant factor, several other variables contribute to outcomes for adults with LD as well. These variables include effective intervention during elementary and middle school years, appropriate course support in mainstreamed classes, supportive parents, counseling and therapy when necessary, and the absence of severe emotional and neurological problems.

F. Demographics

The demographic variables of the LD sample can also affect outcomes. These demographic factors include socioeconomic status, age of onset, gender, and regional differences.

1. Socioeconomic Status

Several reviews of follow-up studies emphasize the significance of socioeconomic status of the LD sample (Horn et al., 1983; O'Connor & Spreen, 1988; Schonhaut & Satz, 1983; Silver & Hagin, 1985) After reviewing 18 follow-up studies, Schonhaut and Satz (1983) concluded that SES is a powerful variable that is related to the probability of developing learning problems and to academic prognosis. The socioeconomic status of the dyslexic men in Rawson's (1968) study is also cited as a major reason for their excellent educational and occupational attainment (Herjanic & Penick, 1972; Schonhaut & Satz, 1983).

2. Age

Another demographic variable that affects outcomes is age. (Horn et al., 1983). Age of diagnosis may be an indication of severity of the LD (Horn et al., 1983; Schonhaut & Satz, 1983). Since school districts do not typically screen for LD, but rely on teacher referrals, it is reasonable to expect youngsters with more severe LD to be identified earlier.

Since age of identification is often an indication of severity, it is also an indication of a poorer prognosis for educational and occupational attainments. However, Schonhaut and Satz (1983) also noted that SES can "attenuate this prediction." Youngsters from higher socioeconomic backgrounds often benefit from considerable family support and appropriate early identification and educational intervention. In addition, parental and teacher understanding is better because these students are not perceived as stupid, lazy, and/or emotionally disturbed. This information suggests the importance of describing age of onset, socioeconomic status, and educational and family background. Age at follow-up is also important, particularly because adults with LD may continue to improve in academic achievement skills after completion of formal education as a result of greater motivation and access to remediation. Outcomes regarding the level of basic skill attainment and educational attainment are generally less favorable than occupational attainment in follow-up studies, which may be due to the subjects' age at follow-up (Horn et al., 1983). Based on their review of follow-up studies, Horn et al. (1983) suggest looking at outcomes at middle age and older.

3. Gender

Other important demographic information (not always provided) is the gender of the subjects and proportion of males and females in the sample. Because the ratio of males to females in the school-identified population is approximately four to one (Finucci & Childs, 1981), many research samples have been all male. Moreover, some have assumed that findings on male research samples generalize to all individuals with LD, when in actuality we have very scant information regarding the nature of LD in females.

When females with LD are included in research samples, very few studies have reported data separately for males and females (Horn et al., 1983). Moreover, even when this analysis has been conducted, there are significant methodological problems. In an extensive review of the literature, Vogel (1990) found that in order for females with LD to be identified, they have to be (a) significantly lower in intelligence, (b) more severely impaired in their language abilities and/or academic achievement, and (c) have a greater aptitude–achievement discrepancy than their male counterparts. The evidence suggests that females with LD with the same level of intelligence and type, and severity of LD as males, will not be as frequently identified.

Reasons for the underidentification of females with LD include teacher referral bias, lack of understanding of the nature of LD in females, differences in psychometric profiles of females and males (Vogel & Walsh, 1987), and the differential incidence of attention deficit and hyperactivity in males and females (Vogel, 1990). As a result, gender differences found in longitudinal and follow-up studies on samples of school-identified males and females with LD may be the result of bias of ascertainment and must be interpreted cautiously.

4. Regional Differences

Another important demographic factor is regional differences (deBettencourt et al., 1989; Herjanic & Penick, 1972). In a study of youngsters with LD who lived in a rural area, dropping out of high school did not affect employment opportunities (deBettencourt et al., 1989), whereas in a study of students with LD in an urban area, dropping out of high school affected successful employment. From this research, deBettencourt et al., (1989) emphasized the importance of noting regional differences as an important variable in determining outcomes.

G. Educational Opportunity and Remediation/Intervention

There is evidence that the length and quality of educational support and remedial contribute to occupational and academic success (Blalock, 1981; Silver & Hagin, 1985) Yet, several reviews of follow-up studies found that in virtually none of the studies did the researchers focus on the quality of treatment as it affected outcomes (Schonhaut & Satz, 1983; Herjanic & Penick, 1972; Horn et al., 1983). However, when samples have shared a common educational experience, for example, in Rawson (1968), Rogan and Hartman (1990), and Vogel and Adelman's (1990) studies, this experience provides an indirect measure of intervention effectiveness.

H. Comparison Groups

A major criticism of studies on adults with LD is the absence of an appropriate control group (Bruck, 1985; Herjanic & Penick, 1972; Horn et al., 1983). Without control or comparison groups, it is impossible to determine the effect of LD upon adult adjustment and attainments. In addition, the absence of control groups also renders an inaccurate assessment of the long-term effects of remedial programs.

I. Instrumentation

Another limitation of studies on adults with LD is the lack of valid and reliable measures for assessment (Herjanic & Penick, 1972; Vogel 1982). Only recently, diagnostic instruments such as the Psychoeducational Battery—Revised, have been developed and standardized on representative samples of the adult population (Cuenin, 1990). These new or revised instruments will not only enable more accurate and complete assessment immediately after high school, but they will also provide the means for ongoing evaluation through middle age and beyond.

V. FUTURE RESEARCH RECOMMENDATIONS

Results of research on adults with LD should be interpreted in light of the above critique. Overgeneralizing should be avoided when studies are flawed by use of nonrepresentative samples, bias of ascertainment, small sample size, lack of a comparison group, or attrition, to mention only a few. Moreover, the following recommendations are made for those planning descriptive, longitudinal, and/or follow-up studies of adults with LD:

1. The definition, criteria for determining the presence of an LD, and the selection criteria for the sample should be carefully delineated.
2. The subject pool from which the sample was drawn should be specified (e.g., a school-identified, clinic-identified, research-identified, or self-identified sample), as well as the influence this may have on the results.
3. Demographic information should be delineated and used in interpretation of findings in light of the previous studies regarding the importance of age at first evaluation, retesting, or follow-up, and gender and socioeconomic status.
4. Aptitude–achievement discrepancy as it reflects the severity of the LD of the sample studied should also be described at initial evaluation and at follow-up. Severity has been found to be one of several important variables influencing educational and occupational attainments and academic achievement levels in adulthood. The methods of quantification of severity should also be described as well as the rationale for selection of the specific model.

5. Etiology of the LD can have a significant impact on later achievement. Individuals whose LD is the result of known trauma to the brain comprise a distinct subgroup within the LD population and should be studied as a comparison group.

6. In conducting longitudinal and follow-up studies, researchers should determine whether or not the resultant sample has the same characteristic as the original sample, as well as the reasons for nonparticipation. In the discussion of findings, researchers can then provide documentation as to whether the reasons for subject withdrawal have biased the results of the study.

7. Results have to be interpreted in light of the sample studied. Descriptive data should be provided in all research studies on adults with LD including:
   a. Cognitive abilities
   b. Academic achievement
   c. Age at first identification
   d. Educational history

8. Selection of reliable and valid instrumentation appropriate to the age level of subjects is an important factor in designing research on adults with LD. Recently, several measures have been revised that include adults in the standardization sample at various educational attainment levels. However, use of informal measures will still be required to supplement the available diagnostic tests. The importance of a control and/or comparison group will remain central in understanding and interpreting findings.

VI. CONCLUSIONS

As a result of methodological differences and weakness in the research studies to date, findings on adults with LD are inconsistent. Nevertheless, there are some themes that emerge. For example, there is considerable evidence of underachievement in the areas of reading, written language, and mathematics. With respect to cognitive abilities, the most consistent finding is that significant variability exists among subtest scores of both the WAIS-R and the W-J Psychoeducational Battery. Processing deficits are still present in adults with LD as they continue to demonstrate problems with auditory perception, comprehension, and memory. Although not as prevalent as verbal deficits, particularly in the area of oral language, nonverbal abilities are also deficient in many adults with LD, including problems with visual analysis and synthesis, visual-motor integration, orientation, and social perception. The persistent processing difficulties and resulting underachievement have affected academic progress; there is considerable evidence of grade repetition, higher incidence of high school dropout rate, and failure to go on to postsecondary programs.

The problems caused by LD have also interfered with the psychological well-being of adults with LD and have placed their emotional health at risk. Although there is much diversity with respect to the severity of personality and behavior traits, low self-esteem was repeatedly identified as a characteristic of individuals with LD. Even as adults, they continued to struggle with feelings of helplessness, inadequacy, and stupidity.

Adults with LDs are often dependent upon their families for financial and social support. Many continue to live with their parents well past the traditional age of independence and their social lives tend to revolve around family functions well beyond the norm. Problems with making friends and participating in social activities with peers continue into adulthood.

Although it cannot be said that some adults with LD achieved success in the workplace, they still experience disproportionate unemployment and underemployment. Self-understanding of one's LD helps in selecting a career in which the individual's area of strength predominates and is the major factor differentiating individuals who are successfully and unsuccessfully employed. Vocational training has essentially been either nonexistent or ineffective for individuals with LD. Despite the fact that employers are becoming increasingly aware of how certain modifications in the workplace could enable greater success for workers with LD, it appears that employers are less understanding of individuals with cognitive disabilities and are focused on accommodating those with physical disabilities.

A. Implications

1. Educational Needs

Early identification of the disability is of primary importance to the future success of individuals with LDs. Although many schools have screening programs prior to kindergarten, screening after kindergarten is generally terminated; post-kindergarten, schools rely almost exclusively on teacher referral. The benefits of early diagnosis (appropriate intervention, parent and teacher support, counseling and psychotherapy when necessary) have been documented and support the need to extend screening beyond kindergarten. Teacher referral bias that has contributed to the underidentification of females with LD also supports the need for extended screening.

A lack of understanding of LDs in general and the specific differences between males and females with LD is pervasive. It is important to disseminate this information through the schools, medical professionals, and parent support groups. Parents must not just be aware of LDs; the opportunity to obtain a more thorough understanding must be made more accessible. Inferentially, the parents' lack of understanding has contributed to the limited and vague understanding that individuals with LD have of their own strengths and weaknesses, even as adults. More extensive preservice and inservice training is important: (a) to ensure that teachers are properly prepared to accurately identify and refer students experiencing difficulties that may be due to an LD; (b) to enable teachers to more effectively help LD students who are mainstreamed; and (c) to provide teachers with a framework for understanding the psychological concomitants of an LD.

Because the manifestations of LDs change with age, updated diagnostic information should be obtained prior to and during transitional periods (e.g., entering kindergarten, middle school, junior high, high school, postsecondary, and employment). There is a need to continually design and update intervention that addresses areas affected by processing deficits using individually prescribed strategies and remediation that target affected areas. Diagnostic reports should identify individual strengths and weaknesses, and then provide remedial techniques and compensatory strategies that will specifically address problems caused by LDs in academic, social, and employment situations.

Whether or not students with LD go on to postsecondary programs, there is a need for ongoing assistance with developing skills in reading, written language, and mathematics. Since there is evidence that many students with LD take longer to "catch up" academically and socially, some students might benefit from a fifth year of high school or a precollege program. This is particularly important for students who were in self-contained special education classes and/or in lower-track courses where they never had the opportunity to take college-preparatory classes. Many of these students may be capable of attending 2- or 4-year colleges if they are first given the opportunity to take more challenging classes, particularly in English and mathematics in precollege programs.

Students who are qualified to attend college need to be aware of the range of available services for college students with LD and how to access information not only about the programs, but also their individual rights to reasonable accommodations in the application process, program planning, and specific course work.

For those students who have either graduated from a postsecondary institution or for whom postsecondary education was not appropriate, there is need for ongoing assistance with improving reading, written language, math abilities, enhancing self-understanding, and developing and using compensatory strategies and interpersonal skills. Such assistance is vital for them to obtain appropriate jobs, maintain jobs, receive promotions, and improve the quality of their personal lives. Adult education centers that provide training in basic skills, personal and career counseling, job placement, and support groups should address these continuing needs of adults with LD.

Of paramount importance is the need to educate employers about LD. If employers do not understand the nature of LD and how they may affect job performance, employees with LD will be prevented from demonstrating their ability to successfully complete job responsibilities. Employers must also understand the rights and responsibilities of the employee and the employer with respect to reasonable accommodations; without tandem knowledge and cooperation, frustration and not progress is the likely result.

2. Psychosocial Needs

The debilitating psychosocial effects of an LD certainly highlight the need for addressing emotional, behavioral, and social problems. There needs to be greater awareness of the importance of psychotherapy for individuals with LD throughout their lives. During various transitions and/or periods of extreme stress, individual therapy might be necessary; at other times, it may be helpful for the individuals with LD to participate in therapy with peers, family members, and spouses. During transitional times, support groups can be beneficial in addressing issues of adjustment and overcoming the feelings of fear and inadequacy that new situations tend to generate.

Some individuals with LD need to acquire daily living skills that would enhance their ability to live independently and to have more active and fulfilling personal lives. A range of independent living facilities may address these issues. Some of these facilities might only provide support groups and the opportunity to participate in social activities, whereas other facilities might be designed to help individuals learn to cook, care for their apartments, and manage their finances.

3. Employment Needs

There is a need for vocational education and career counseling for individuals with LD who must be assisted with identifying appropriate jobs, in the job search process, and in understanding their rights under federal and state civil rights law that entitle them to reasonable accommodations in connection with all aspects of employment. Even highly educated individuals with LDs express need for assistance with all aspects of employment. In a survey conducted by the Adult Issues Committee of the Learnings Disabilities Association of America, 31% of the respondents indicated that they had difficulty finding a job, 28% had difficulty keeping a job, and 40% experienced difficulty in career or job advancement. In addition, 47% reported having problems on the job, while almost half (49%) were seeking better employment (Griffin, 1996).

During enrollment in high school and in postsecondary educational programs, prework experiences should provide internships, job shadowing, and mentoring that would enhance future employability. Students with LD need to experience first-hand how their LD may affect job performance and the compensatory skills required to accomplish job tasks. Some individuals with LD would also benefit from ongoing mentoring to assist with solving problems that arise on the job and to help with working toward advancement. Services are needed that offer retraining and remediation to enhance basic skills, which will in turn lead to better wages, greater independence, and the likelihood of achieving a more satisfying life.

Acknowledgments

We gratefully acknowledge the Thorn River Foundation for its generous support of our research.

References

Adelman, P. B., & Vogel, S. A. (1990). College graduates with learning disabilities; Employment attainment and career patterns. *Learning Disabilities Quarterly, 13*(3), 154–166.

Balow, B., & Blomquist, M. (1965). Young adults ten to fifteen years after severe reading disability. *Elementary School Journal, 66*, 44–48.

Blackorby, J., & Wagner, M. (1996). Longitudinal postschool outcomes of youth with disabilities: Findings from the National Longitudinal Transition Study. *Exceptional Children, 62*(5), 399–414.

Blalock, G. (1996). Community transition teams as the foundation for transition services for youth with learning disabilities. *Journal of Learning Disabilities, 29*(2), 148–160.

Blalock, J. W. (1981). Persistent problems and concerns of young adults with learning disabilities. In W. Cruickshank, & A. Silver (Eds.), *Bridges to tomorrow* (Vol. 2, The Best of ACLD, pp. 35–55). Syracuse: Syracuse University Press.

Blalock, J. W. (1982). Residual learning disabilities in young adults: Implications for rehabilitation. *Journal of Applied Rehabilitation Counseling, 13*(2), 9–13.

Blalock, J. W. (1987a). Problems in mathematics. In D. Johnson & J. Blalock (Eds.), *Young adults with learning disabilities: Clinical studies* (pp. 205–217). Orlando, FL: Grune & Stratton.

Blalock, J. W. (1987b). Intellectual levels and patterns. In D. Johnson & J. Blalock (Eds.), *Young adults with learning disabilities: Clinical studies* (pp. 47–65). Orlando, FL: Grune & Stratton.

Blalock, J. W. (1987c). Auditory language disorders. In D. Johnson & J. Blalock (Eds.), *Young adults with learning disabilities: Clinical studies* (pp. 81–105). Orlando, FL: Grune & Stratton.

Brown, D. (1984). Employment considerations for learning disabled adults. *Journal of Rehabilitation, 74*, 77–88.

Bruck, M. (1985). The adult functioning of children with specific learning disabilities: A follow-up study. In I. E. Sigel (Ed.), *Advances in Applied Developmental Psychology* (Vol. 1, pp. 91–129). Ablex Publishing Corporation: Norwood, NJ.

Buchanan, M., & Wolf, J. (1986). A comprehensive study of learning disabled adults. *Journal of Learning Disabilities, 19*(1), 34–38.

Bursuck, W. D., Rose, E., Cowen, S., & Yahaya, M. A. (1989). Nationwide Survey of postsecondary education services for students with learning disabilities. *Exceptional Children, 56*(3), 236–245.

Butler-Nalin, P., & Wagner, M. (1991). Enrollment in postsecondary schools. In M. Wagner, L. Newman, R. D'Amico, E. D. Jay, P. Butler-Nalin, C. Marder, & R. Cox, *Youth with Disabilities: How Are They Doing? The First Comprehensive Report from the National Longitudinal Transition Study of Special Education Students* (Chapter 9). Menlo Park, CA: SRI International.

Clement-Heist, K., Siegel, S., & Gaylord-Ross, R. (1992). Simulated and *in situ* vocational social skills training for youths with learning disabilities. *Exceptional Children, 58*(4), 336–345.

Cohen, J. (1985). Learning disabilities and adolescence: Developmental considerations. In M. Sugar, A. Esman, J. Looney, A. Schwartzberg & A. Sorosky (Eds.), *Adolescent psychiatry: Developmental and clinical studies* (Vol. 12, pp. 177–196), Chicago: The University of Chicago.

Cordono, B. (1979). Assisting dyslexic college students: An experimental program design at a university. *Bulletin of the Orton Society, 29,* 263–268.

Cordoni, B., O'Donnell, J., Ramaniah, N., Kurtz, J., & Rosenshein, K. (1981). Wechsler Adult Intelligence score patterns for learning disabled young adults. *Journal of Learning Disabilities, 14*(7), 404–407.

Cordoni, B. K., & Snyder, M. K. (1981). A comparison of learning disabled college students' achievement from WRAT and PIAT grade, standard, and subtest scores. *Psychology in the Schools, 18,* 28–34.

Cowen, S. E. (1988). Coping strategies of university students with learning disabilities. *Journal of Learning Disabilities, 21*(3), 161–164.

Cuenin, L. (1990). Use of the Woodcock-Johnson Psycho-Educational Battery with learning disabled adults. *Learning Disabilities Focus, 5*(2), 119–123.

Dalke, C. (1988). Woodcock-Johnson Psycho-Educational Test Battery profiles: A Comparative study of college freshmen with and without learning disabilities. *Journal of Learning Disabilities, 21*(9), 567–570.

D'Amico, R. (1991). The working world awaits: Employment experiences during and shortly after secondary school. In M. Wagner, L. Newman, R. D'Amico, E. D. Jay, P. Butler-Nalin, C. Marder, & R. Cox (Eds.), *Youth with disabilities: How are they doing? The first comprehensive report from the National Longitudinal Transition Study of Special Education Students* (Chapter 8). Menlo Park, CA: SRI International.

deBettencourt, L. U., Zigmond, N., & Thornton, H. (1989). Follow-up of postsecondary-age rural learning disabled graduates and dropouts. *Exceptional Children, 56*(1), 40–49.

Dunn, L., & Markwardt, F. (1970). *Peabody Individual Achievement Test.* Circle Pines, MN: American Guidance Service.

Edgington, R. E. (1975). SLD children: A ten-year follow-up. *Academic Therapy, 11,* 53–64.

Educational Testing Service. (1977). *Sentence structure test, college broad descriptive tests of language skills.* Princeton, NJ: Author.

Faas, L. A., & D'Alonzo, B. J. (1990). WAIS-R scores as predictors of employment success and failure among adults with learning disabilities. *Journal of Learning Disabilities, 23*(5), 311–316.

Fairweather, J. S., & Shaver, D. M. (1991). Making the transition to postsecondary education and training. *Exceptional Children, 57*(3), 264–270.

Fafard, M.-B., & Haubrich, P. A. (1981). Vocational and social adjustment of learning disabled young adults: A follow-up study. *Learning Disability Quarterly, 4,* 122–130.

Felton, R. (1986, November). Bowman-Gray follow-up study. Paper presented at the Orton Dyslexia National Conference, Philadelphia, Pennsylvania.

Finucci, J. M., & Childs, B. (1981). Are there really more dyslexic boys than girls? In A. Ansara, N. Geschwind, A. Galaburda, M. Albert, & N. Gartrell (Eds.), *Sex differences in dyslexia* (pp. 1–10). Baltimore: Orton Dyslexia Society.

Frauenheim, J. G. (1978). Academic achievement characteristics of adult males who were diagnosed as dyslexic in childhood. *Journal of Learning Disabilities, 11,* 476–483.

Gerber, P. (1988, July). *Highly successful learning disabled adults: Insights from case interviews.* Paper presented at the Annual AHSSPPE Conference, New Orleans.

Gerber, P. (1992). At first glance: Employment for people with learning disabilities at the beginning of the Americans-with-disabilities-act ERA. *Learning Disabilities Quarterly, 15,* 330–332.

Gerber, P. J., Finsberg, R., & Reiff, H. B. (1992). Identifying alterable patterns in employment success for highly successful adults with learning disabilities. *Journal of Learning Disabilities, 25*(8), 475–487.

Gerber, P. J., Schneiders, C. A., Paradise, L. V., Reiff, H. B., Ginsberg, R., & Popp, P. A. (1990). Persisting problems of adults with learning disabilities: Self-reported comparisons from their school-age and adult years. *Journal of Learning Disabilities, 23*(9), 570–573.

Greenbaum, B., Graham, S., & Scales, W. (1996). Adults with learning disabilities: Occupational and social status after college. *Journal of Learning Disabilities, 29*(2), 167–173.

Griffin, M. (1996). Some years later: Present life status of adults with learning disabilities. In *They Speak for Themselves: A survey of adults with learning disabilities* (pp. 33–44). Adult Issues Committee, Pittsburgh, PA: LDA of America.

Hall deFur, S., & Taymans, J. M. (1995). Competencies needed for transition specialists in vocational rehabilitation, vocational education, and special education. *Exceptional Children, 62*(1), 31–52.

Halpern, A. (1992). Transition: Old wine in new bottles. *Exceptional Children, 8,* 202–211.

Haring, K. A., Lovett, D. L., & Smith, D. D. (1990). A follow-up study of recent special education graduates of learning disabilities programs. *Journal of Learning Disabilities, 23,* 108–113.

Herjanic, B. M., & Penick, E. C. (1972). Adult outcomes of disabled child readers. *Journal of Special Education, 6,* 397–410.

Herzog, J. E., & Falk, B. (1991). A follow-up study of vocational outcomes of young adults with learning disabilities. *Journal of Postsecondary Education and Disability, 9*(1&2), 219–226.

Hoffmann, F. J., Sheldon, K. L., Minskoff, E. H., Sautter, S. W., Steidle, E. F. Baker, D. P., Bailey, M. B., & Echols, L. D. (1987). Needs of learning disabled adults. *Journal of Learning Disabilities, 20*(1), 43–52.

Horn, W. F., O'Donnell, J. P., & Vitulano, L. A. (1983). Long-term follow-up studies of learning-disabled persons. *Journal of Learning Disabilities, 16*(9), 542–555.

Jastak, J., & Jastak, S. (1978). *The Wide Range Achievement Test.* Wilmington, DE: Jastak Associates, Inc.

Johnson, D. (1987a). Reading disabilities. In D. Johnson & J. Blalock (Eds.), *Young adults with learning disabilities: Clinical studies* (pp. 145–172). Orlando, FL: Grune & Stratton.

Johnson, D. (1987b). Nonverbal disorders and related learning. In D. Johnson & J. Blalock (Eds.), *Young adults with learning disabilities: Clinical studies* (pp. 219–232). Orlando, FL: Grune & Stratton.

Karpinski, M. J., Neubert, D. A., & Graham, S. (1992). A follow-along study of postsecondary outcomes for graduates and dropouts with mild disabilities in a rural setting. *Journal of Learning Disabilities, 25*(6), 376–385.

Kranstover, L. L., Thurlow, M. L., & Bruininks, R. H. (1989). Special education graduates: A longitudinal study of outcomes. *Career Development for Exceptional Individuals, 12*(2), 153–156.

Levin, E., Zigmond, N., Birch, J. (1985). A follow-up study of 52 learning disabled students. *Journal of Learning Disabilities, 13,* 542–547.

Mangrum, C. T. II, & Strichart, S. S. (1988). *Petersen's guide to colleges with programs for learning disabled students.* Princeton, NJ: Peterson's Guides, Inc.

Marder, C., & D'Amico, R. (1992). *How are youth with disabilities really doing: A comparison of youth with disabilities and youth in general.* Menlo Park, CA: SRI International.

Mathews, R. M., Whang, R. L., & Fawcett, S. B. (1982). Behavioral assessment of occupational skills of learning disabled adolescents. *Journal of Learning Disabilities, 15*(1), 38–41.

Menkes, M. M., Rowe, J. S., & Menkes, J. H. (1967). A twenty-five year follow-up on the hyperactive child with MED. *Pediatrics, 39,* 393–399.

Minskoff, E. H., Sautter, S. W., Hoffmann, F. J., & Hawks, R. (1987). Employer attitudes toward hiring the learning disabled. *Journal of Learning Disabilities, 20*(1), 53–57.

Morningstar, M. E., Turnball, A. P., & Turnball, H. R. (1996). What do students with disabilities tell us about the importance of family involvement in the transition from school to adult life? *Exceptional Children, 62*(3), 249–260.

Nisbet, J. & Lichtenstein, S. (1992). *Gender differences in the postschool status of young adults with mild disabilities. Fact Sheet: Following the lives of young adults.* (Institute on Disability at the University of New Hampshire) *4*(1), 1–5.

O'Connor, S. C., & Spreen, O. (1988). The relationship between parents' socioeconomic status and education level, and adult occupational and educational achievement of children with learning disabilities. *Journal of Learning Disabilities. 21*(3), 148–153.

Preston, R. C., & Yarington, D. J. (1967). Status of fifty retarded readers eight years after reading clinic diagnosis. *Journal of Reading, 11,* 122–129.

Rawson, M. R. (1968). *Developmental language disability: Adult accomplishments of dyslexic boys.* Baltimore: The Johns Hopkins Press.

Reder, S. (1995). *Literacy, education, and learning disabilities.* Portland, OR: Northwest Regional Educational Laboratory.

Reder, S., & Vogel, S. A. (1979). Life-span employment and economic outcomes for adults with self-reported learning disabilities. In P. Gerber & D. Brown (Eds.), *Learning disabilities and employment* (pp. 371–394). Austin, TX: Pro-ed.

Repetto, J. B., & Correa, B. I. (1996). Expanding views on transition. *Exceptional Children, 62*(6), 551–563.

Roessler, R. T., Brolin, D. E., & Johnson, J. M. (1990). Factors affecting employment success and quality of life: A one year follow-up of students in special education. *Career Development for Exceptional Individuals, 13*(2), 95–107.

Rogan, L., & Hartman, L. (1976). *A follow-up study of learning disabled children as adults. Final Report.* Evanston, IL: Cove School. (ERIC Document Reproduction Service No. ED 163–728).

Rogan, L. L., & Hartman, L. D. (1990). Adult outcome of learning disabled students ten years after initial follow-up. *Learning Disabilities Focus, 5*(2), 91–102.

Rojewski, J. W. (1996). Educational and occupational aspirations of high school seniors with learning disabilities. *Exceptional Children, 62*(5), 463–476.

Salvia, J., Gajar, A., Gajria, M., & Salvia, S. (1988). A comparison of WAIS-R profiles of nondisabled college freshmen and college students with learning disabilities. *Journal of Learning Disabilities, 21*(10), 632–641.

Scheiber, B., & Talpers, J. (1987). *Unlocking potential: College and other choices for learning disabled people—A step-by-step guide.* Bethesda, MD: Adler & Adler.

Schonhaut, S., & Satz, P. (1983). Prognosis for children with learning disabilities: A review of follow-up studies. In M. Rutter (Ed.), *Developmental neuropsychiatry* (pp. 542–563). New York: Guilford Press.

Schwarz, S. L., & Taymans, J. M. (1991). Urban vocational/technical program completers with learning disabilities: A follow-up study. *The Journal for Vocational Special Needs Education, 13*(3), 15–20.

Scuccimarra, D. J., & Speece, D. L. (1990). Employment outcomes and social integration of students with mild handicaps: The quality of life two years after high school. *Journal of Learning Disabilities, 23*(4), 213–218.

Shapiro, E. S., & Lentz, Jr., F. (1991). Vocational-technical programs: Follow-up of students with learning disabilities. *Exceptional Children, 58*(1), 47–60.

Siegel, S., Matt, R., Waxman, M., & Gaylord-Ross, R. (1992). A follow-along study of participants in a longitudinal transition program for youths with mild disabilities. *Exceptional Children, 58*(4), 346-356.

Silver, A. A., & Hagin, R. A. (1985). Outcomes of learning disabilities in adolescence. In M. Sugar, A. Esman, J. Looney, A. Schwartzberg & A. Sorosky (Eds.) *Adolescent psychiatry: Developmental and clinical studies* (Vol. 12, pp. 197–211), Chicago: The University of Chicago.

Sitlington, P. L., & Frank, A. R. (1990). Are adolescents with learning disabilities successfully crossing the bridge into adult life? *Learning Disabilities Quarterly, 13*(2), 97–111.

Spekman, N. J., Oi, M. T., Goldberg, R. J., & Herman, K. (1989). LD Children grow up: What can we expect for education, employment, and adjustment? Presented at the 40th Annual Conference of The Orton Dyslexia Society, Dallas, TX.

Stone, C. A. (1987). Abstract reasoning and problem solving. In D. Johnson & J. Blalock (Eds.), *Young adults with learning disabilities: Clinical studies* (pp. 67–79). Orlando, FL: Grune & Stratton.

U.S. Department of Education (1987). *State education statistics wallchart.* Washington, DC: U.S. Government Printing Office.

U.S. Department of Education (1995). *Eighteenth annual report to Congress on the implementation of the Individuals with Disabilities Act.* Washington, DC: Office of Special Education Programs.

U.S. Department of Labor. (1991). *Dictionary of occupational titles* (4th ed.). Indianapolis: IN: JIST Works.

Vogel, S. A. (1982). On developing LD college programs. *Journal of Learning Disabilities, 15,* 518–528.

Vogel, S. A. (1985a). *The college student with a learning disability: A handbook for college LD students, admissions officers, faculty, and administrators.* Lake Forest, IL: Author.

Vogel, S. A. (1985b). Syntactic complexity in written expression of college writers. *Annals of Dyslexia, 35,* 137–157.

Vogel, S. A. (1986). Levels and patterns of intellectual functioning among LD college students: Clinical and educational implications. *Journal of Learning Disabilities, 19*(2), 71–79.

Vogel, S. A. (1990). Gender differences in intelligence, language, visual-motor abilities, and academic achievement in students with learning disabilities: A review of the literature. *Journal of Learning Disabilities, 23,* 44–52.

Vogel, S. A. (1996a). Employment: A research review and agenda. In S. C. Cramer & W.

Ellis (Eds.), *Learning disabilities—Lifelong issues* (pp. 151–163). Baltimore, MD: Paul H. Brookes.

Vogel, S. A. (1996b). Adults with learning disabilities: Research questions and methodological issues in planning a research agenda for 2000 and beyond. *The Canadian Journal of Special Education, 11*(2), 33–54.

Vogel, S. A. (1993). A retrospective and prospective view of postsecondary education for adults with learning disabilities. In S. A. Vogel & P. B. Adelman (Eds.), *Success for college students with learning disabilities* (pp. 3–20). New York: Springer-Verlag.

Vogel, S. A. & Adelman, P. B. (1990). Extrinsic and intrinsic factors in graduation and academic failure among LD college students, *Annals of Dyslexia, 40,* 119–137.

Vogel, S. A., & Konrad, D. (1988). Characteristic written expressive language deficits of the learning disabled: From general and specific intervention strategies. *Journal of Reading, Writing, & Learning Disabilities International, 4,* 88–99.

Vogel, S., & Moran, M. (1982). Written language disorders in learning disabled college students; A preliminary report. In W. Cruickshank & J. Lerner (Eds.), *Coming of age: The best of ACLD 1982* (Vol. 3, pp. 211–225). Syracuse, NY: Syracuse University Press.

Vogel, S. A., & Reder, S. (in press a). Literacy proficiency of adults with self-reported learning disabilities. In M. C. Smith (Ed.), *Literacy for the 21st century: Research policy, practices, and the National Adult Literacy Survey.* Westport, CN: Greenwood Press.

Vogel, S. A. & Reder, S. (in press, b). Educational attainment in adults with self-reported learning disabilities. In S. A. Vogel & S. Reder (Eds.), *Learning disabilities, adult education, and literacy.* Baltimore, MD: Paul H. Brookes.

Vogel, S. A., & Walsh, P. (1987). Gender differences in cognitive abilities in learning disabled females and males. *Annals of Dyslexia, 37,* 142–165.

Wagner, M. (1989a). The transition experiences of youth with disabilities: A report form The National Longitudinal Transition Study. Presented to the Division of Research, Council for Exceptional Children annual meetings, San Francisco.

Wagner, M. (1989b). Youth with disabilities during transition: An overview of descriptive findings from The National Longitudinal Transition Study. SRI International: Menlo Park, CA.

Wagner, M., D'Amico, R., Marder, C., Newman, L., & Blackorby, J. (1992). *What happens next: Trends in postschool outcomes of youth with disabilities.* Menlo Park, CA: SRI International.

Wagner, M., & Shaver, D. M. (1989). Educational programs and achievements of secondary special education students: Findings from The National Longitudinal Transition Study. Presented to the Special Education Special Interest Groups at the meetings of the American Educational Research Association, San Francisco.

Weisenstein, G. R., Stowitschek, J. J., & Affleck, J. Q. (1991). Integrating students enrolled in special education into vocational education. *Integrating Special Education Students, 14*(2), 131–144.

Werner, E. E. (1993). Risk and resilience in individuals with learning disabilities: *Learning Disabilities Research and Practice, 8*(1), 28–34.

Werner, E. E., & Smith, R. S. (1992). *Overcoming the odds: High risk children from birth to adulthood.* Ithaca, NY: Cornell University Press.

Woodcock, R., & Johnson, M. B. (1977). *The Woodcock-Johnson Psycho-Educational Battery.* Allen, TX: DLM Teaching Resources.

Woodcock, R., & Johnson, M. B. (1989). *The Woodcock-Johnson Psycho-Educational Battery-Revised.* Allen, TX: DLM Teaching Resources.

Zigmond, N., & Thornton, H. (1989). Follow-up of postsecondary age learning disabled graduates and dropouts. *Learning Disabilities Research, 1*(1), 50–55.

Author Index

Spivack, G., 260, *272, 273,* 459, *485*
Sprafkin, R. P., 473, *483, 484*
Sprague, R. L., 85, 86, *103*
Spratt, J. E., 344, *365*
Spreen, O., 670, 685, 688, *698*
Stabb, S. D., 476, *482*
Stahl, S., 345, 349, *361, 364*
Stanley, G., 215, 216, 217, 218, 221, *233, 234*
Stanovich, K. E., 10, 15, 20, 21, 23, 24, *32, 33,* 109, 122, 136, *159,* 171, 172, 175, 176, 179, 180, 181, 185, 187, 190, 191, 192, *195, 199, 200,* 209, 212, *235,* 294, 295, *306,* 317, 331, 335, *340,* 368, 370, 371, 374, 378, *388, 389*
Stark, C., 459, *482*
Stecker, P. M., 47, 48, *63, 64*
Steger, B. M., 17, *34*
Steger, J. A., 225, 226, *235*
Steidle, E. F., 659, 667, 669, 674, 675, 682, *697*
Stein, J. F., 121, *155*
Stein, M., 439, *451*
Sternberg, R. J., 345, *364*
Steubing, K. K., 186, 191, *195*
Steven, D., 394, 400, *418*
Stevens, D., 18, *32*
Stevens, D. D., 296, *303*
Stevens, R., 566, *582*
Stevenson, H. W., 169, 174, *200,* 321, *340*
Stevenson, J., 23, *33*
Stewart, I., 311, *340*
Stewart, S. R., 290, *304,* 408, *418*
Stiegler, J. W., 169, 174, *200*
Stiliadis, K., 256, *273*
Stipek, D. J., 249, *273*
Stoddard, B., 410, *423*
Stokes, T. F., 460, *485*
Stone, C. A., 598, *655,* 665, *699*
Stone, G., 540, *555*
Stone, P., 78, 80, *103*
Stone, W. L., 237, 252, 255, 257, *270, 274,* 454, 461, *485,* 616, *655*
Stout, D. M., 504, *524*

Stowitschek, J. J., 674, *700*
Strain, P. S., 469, 470, *484, 485*
Strauss, A. A., 11, *31, 33*
Streisguth, A. P., 81, *104*
Streitfeld, D., 392, *423*
Strichart, S. S., 669, *697*
Strosnider, R., 426, *450*
Studdert-Kennedy, M., 174, 175, 184, *196, 198, 200*
Stuebing, K. K., 15, 22, 23, 24, *29, 30,* 191, *199,* 551, *554*
Sullivan, G. W., 594, *655*
Sullivan, K., 241, *267*
Sulzby, E., 313, 314, 316, *340*
Sulzer-Azeroff, R., 406, *419*
Sumbler, K., 221, *235, 236*
Sutlin, L., 392, *423*
Swanson, H. L., 107, 113–116, 115, 116, 121, 123, 124, 130, 132, 133, 134, 135, 137, 138, 139, 142, 144, 145, 147–149, 148, 150, *158, 160, 161,* 284, 290, 297, *306,* 344, 345, 346, 347, 353, *364,* 455, *485,* 530, 531, 537, 542, 547, 548, *553, 555,* 567, 576, *582*
Swanson, J., 86, *102*
Swanson, J. M., 80, 81, *101*
Swanson, J. W., 86, *104*
Swanson, L., 172, *200,* 212, 226, *235*
Swinney, D., 183, *196*
Sykes, D., 86, *104*
Sykes, R., 124, *156*
Sylvester, L., 394, *417,* 540, 541, 546, 549, *552*
Symons, S., 348, *363,* 566, *581,* 593, 597, 599, 621, *653*
Syrdal-Lasky, A. K., 175, *195*
Szatmari, P., 78, 79, 81, *104*

Talbott, E., 348, *364,* 510, *525*
Tallal, P., 184, *198, 200,* 218, *235*
Talpers, J., 671, *698*
Tamaoka, K., 174, *196*
Tangel, D. M., 188, 189, *193*

Subject Index